SKILLS for Success
Premium Media Site

D0026496

Improve your grade with hands-on tools and resources!

- Master *Key Terms* to expand your vocabulary.
- Prepare for exams by taking practice quizzes in the *Online Chapter Review*.
- Download *Student Data Files* for the application projects in each chapter.

And for even more tools, you can access the following Premium Resources using your Access Code. Register now to get the most out of *Skills for Success!*

- *Student Training Videos* are instructor-led videos that walk through each skill in a chapter.*
- *BizSkills Videos* cover the important business skills students need to be successful—Interviewing, Communication, Dressing for Success, and more.*

*Access code required for these premium resources

Your Access Code is:

Note: If there is no silver foil covering the access code, it may already have been redeemed, and therefore may no longer be valid. In that case, you can purchase online access using a major credit card or PayPal account. To do so, go to **www.pearsonhighered.com/skills**, select your book cover, click on "Buy Access" and follow the on-screen instructions.

To Register:
- To start you will need a valid email address and this access code.
- Go to **www.pearsonhighered.com/skills** and scroll to find your text book.
- Once you've selected your text, on the Home Page for the book, click the link to access the Student Premium Content.
- Click the Register button and follow the on-screen instructions.
- After you register, you can sign in any time via the log-in area on the same screen.

System Requirements

Windows 7 Ultimate Edition; IE 8
Windows Vista Ultimate Edition SP1; IE 8
Windows XP Professional SP3; IE 7
Windows XP Professional SP3; Firefox 3.6.4
Mac OS 10.5.7; Firefox 3.6.4
Mac OS 10.6; Safari 5

Technical Support

http://247pearsoned.custhelp.com

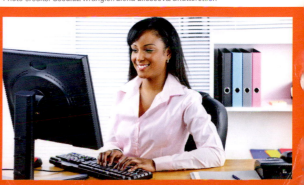

SKILLS For SUCCESS

with Microsoft® Word 2013

TOWNSEND | JAHN HOVEY

PEARSON

Boston   Columbus   Indianapolis   New York   San Francisco   Upper Saddle River
Amsterdam   Cape Town   Dubai   London   Madrid   Milan   Munich   Paris   Montréal   Toronto
Delhi   Mexico City   São Paulo   Sydney   Hong Kong   Seoul   Singapore   Taipei   Tokyo

Library of Congress Cataloging-in-Publication Data

Townsend, Kris.
   Skills for success with Microsoft Word 2013 comprehensive / Kris Townsend and Christie Hovey.
      pages cm
   Includes index.
   ISBN-13: 978-0-13-314785-8
   ISBN-10: 0-13-314785-1
   1. Microsoft Word.   2. Word processing.   I. Hovey, Christie.   II. Title.
   Z52.5.M52T693 2013
   005.52—dc23

                                        2013015914

Editor in Chief: *Michael Payne*
Executive Editor: *Jenifer Niles*
Product Development Manager: *Laura Burgess*
Editorial Assistant: *Andra Skaalrud*
Development Editor: *Jennifer Lynn*
Director of Business & Technology Marketing: *Maggie Leen*
Marketing Manager: *Brad Forrester*
Marketing Coordinator: *Susan Osterlitz*
Managing Editor: *Camille Trentacoste*
Senior Operation Manager/Site Lead: *Nick Sklitsis*
Operations Specialist: *Maura Zaldivar-Garcia*

Senior Art Director: *Jonathan Boylan*
Text and Cover Designer: *Jonathan Boylan*
Director of Media Development: *Taylor Ragan*
Media Project Manager, Production: *John Cassar*
Full-Service Project Management: *Jouve North America*
Full-Service Project Manager: *Kevin Bradley*
Composition: *Jouve*
Printer/Binder: *RR Donnelley*
Cover Printer: *Lehigh-Phoenix Color/Hagerstown*
Typeface: *Palatino LT Std Roman 10/12*

Credits and acknowledgments borrowed from other sources and reproduced, with permission, in this textbook appear on appropriate page within text.

Many of the designations by manufacturers and seller to distinguish their products are claimed as trademarks. Where those designations appear in this book, and the publisher was aware of a trademark claim, the designations have been printed in initial caps or all caps.

10 9 8 7 6 5 4 3
ISBN 10: 0-13-314785-1
ISBN 13: 978-0-13-314785-8

Contents in Brief

Table of Contents

Contributors

We'd like to thank the following people for their work on Skills for Success:

Focus Group Participants

Rose Volynskiy	*Howard Community College*
Fernando Paniagua	*The Community College of Baltimore County*
Jeff Roth	*Heald College*
William Bodine	*Mesa Community College*
Lex Mulder	*College of Western Idaho*
Kristy McAuliffe	*San Jacinto College South*
Jan Hime	*University of Nebraska, Lincoln*
Deb Fells	*Mesa Community College*

Reviewers

Barbara Anderson	*Lake Washington Institute of Technology*
Janet Anderson	*Lake Washington Institute of Technology*
Ralph Argiento	*Guilford Technical Community College*
Tanisha Arnett	*Pima County Community College*
Greg Ballinger	*Miami Dade College*
Autumn Becker	*Allegany College of Maryland*
Bob Benavides	*Collin College*
Howard Blauser	*North GA Technical College*
William Bodine	*Mesa Community College*
Nancy Bogage	*The Community College of Baltimore County*
Maria Bright	*San Jacinto College*
Adell Brooks	*Hinds Community College*
Judy Brown	*Western Illinois University*
Maria Brownlow	*Chaminade*
Jennifer Buchholz	*UW Washington County*
Kathea Buck	*Gateway Technical College*
LeAnn Cady	*Minnesota State College—Southeast Technical*
John Cameron	*Rio Hondo College*
Tammy Campbell	*Eastern Arizona College*
Patricia Christian	*Southwest Georgia Technical College*
Tina Cipriano	*Gateway Technical College*
Paulette Comet	*The Community College of Baltimore County*
Jean Condon	*Mid-Plains Community College*
Joy DePover	*Minneapolis. Com. & Tech College*
Gina Donovan	*County College of Morris*
Alina Dragne	*Flagler College*
Russ Dulaney	*Rasmussen College*
Mimi Duncan	*University of Missouri St. Louis*
Paula Jo Elson	*Sierra College*
Bernice Eng	*Brookdale Community College*
Jill Fall	*Gateway Technical College*
Deb Fells	*Mesa Community College*
Tushnelda C Fernandez	*Miami Dade College*
Jean Finley	*Asheville-Buncombe Technical Community College*
Jim Flannery	*Central Carolina Community College*
Alyssa Foskey	*Wiregrass Georgia Technical College*
David Freer	*Miami Dade College*
Marvin Ganote	*University of Dayton*
David Grant	*Paradise Valley Community College*
Clara Groeper	*Illinois Central College*
Carol Heeter	*Ivy Tech Community College*
Jan Hime	*University of Nebraska*
Marilyn Holden	*Gateway Technical College*
Ralph Hunsberger	*Bucks County Community College*
Juan Iglesias	*University of Texas at Brownsville*
Carl Eric Johnson	*Great Bay Community College*
Joan Johnson	*Lake Sumter Community College*
Mech Johnson	*UW Washington County*
Deborah Jones	*Southwest Georgia Technical College*
Hazel Kates	*Miami-Dade College, Kendall Campus*
Jane Klotzle	*Lake Sumter Community College*
Kurt Kominek	*Northeast State Community College*
Vivian Krenzke	*Gateway Technical College*
Renuka Kumar	*Community College of Baltimore County*
Lisa LaCaria	*Central Piedmont Community College*
Sue Lannen	*Brazosport College*
Freda Leonard	*Delgado Community College*
Susan Mahon	*Collin College*
Nicki Maines	*Mesa Community College*
Pam Manning	*Gateway Technical College*
Juan Marquez	*Mesa Community College*

Alysia Martinez	*Gateway Technical College*	Jeff Roth	*Heald College*
Kristy McAuliffe	*San Jacinto College*	Diane Ruscito	*Brazosport College*
Robert McCloud	*Sacred Heart University*	June Scott	*County College of Morris*
Susan Miner	*Lehigh Carbon Community College*	Vicky Seehusen	*MSU Denver*
Namdar Mogharreban	*Southern Illinois University*	Emily Shepard	*Central Carolina Community College*
Daniel Moix	*College of the Ouachitas*	Pamela Silvers	*A-B Tech*
Lindsey Moore	*Wiregrass Georgia Technical College*	Martha Soderholm	*York College*
Lex Mulder	*College of Western Idaho*	Yaacov Sragovich	*Queensborough Community College*
Patricia Newman	*Cuyamaca College*	Jody Sterr	*Blackhawk Technical College*
Melinda Norris	*Coker College*	Julia Sweitzer	*Lake-Sumter Community College*
Karen Nunan	*Northeast State Community College*	Laree Thomas	*Okefenokee Technical College*
Fernando Paniagua	*The Community College of Baltimore County*	Joyce Thompson	*Lehigh Carbon Community College*
Christine Parrish	*Southwest Georgia Technical College*	Barbara Tietsort	*University of Cincinnati, Blue Ash College*
Linda Pennachio	*Mount Saint Mary College*	Rose Volynskiy	*Howard Community College*
Amy Pezzimenti	*Ocean County College*	Sandra Weber	*Gateway Technical College*
Leah Ramalingam	*Riversity City College*	Steven Weitz	*Lehigh Carbon Community College*
Mary Rasley	*Lehigh Carbon Community College*	Berthenia Williams	*Savannah Technical College*
Cheryl Reuss	*Estrella Mountain Community College*	David Wilson	*Parkland College*
Wendy Revolinski	*Gateway Technical College*	Allan Wood	*Great Bay Community College*
Kenneth Rogers	*Cecil College*	Roger Yaeger	*Estrella Mountain Community College*

What's New for Word 2013

With Office 2013, Microsoft is taking the office to the cloud. The Skills for Success series shows students how to get the most out of Office 2013 no matter what device they are using—a traditional desktop or tablet.

Whether you are tapping and sliding with your finger or clicking and dragging with the mouse, Skills for Success shows you the way with the hallmark visual, two-page, easy-to-follow design. It covers the essential skills students need to know to get up and running with Office quickly, and it addresses Web Apps, touch screens, and the collaborative approach of Office 365. Once students complete the Instructional Skills, they put their knowledge to work with a progression of review, problem-solving, and challenging, end-of-chapter projects.

What's New for Office 2013

Coverage of new features of Office 2013 in an approach that is easy and effective for teaching students the skills they need to get started with Microsoft Office.

Skills Summary—new summary chart of all the Skills and Procedures covered in the chapter makes remembering what was covered easier!

Application Introductions—provide a brief overview of each application and put the chapters in context for students.

Student Training Videos—new, author-created training videos for each Skill in the chapters!

Application Capstone Projects— Chapter 4 and Chapter 10 conclude with a capstone project. These will also be grader projects in MyITLab.

Web Apps Projects (formerly Collaboration Project)—use a variety of the web apps available at the end of Chapter 4 and Chapter 10. Also includes an online "On Your Own" project to let students try an additional project.

Additional Grader Projects—two new grader projects based on the Skills Review provide a broader variety of homework and assessment options; written by the book authors.

New Training and Assessment Simulations—written by the book authors to provide enhanced one-to-one content match in MyITlab.

SkyDrive Coverage—included in the Common Features chapter.

MOS mapping—located on the Instructor Resource Site and provides a guide to where the MOS Core exam objectives are covered in the book, on the Companion Website, and in MyITLab to help students prepare to ace the exam!

Skills for Success

with Microsoft® Word 2013 Volume 1

- **10 × 8.5 Format**—Easy for students to read and type at the same time by simply propping the book up on the desk in front of their monitor

- **Clearly Outlined Skills**—Each skill is presented in a single two-page spread so that students can easily follow along

- **Numbered Steps and Bulleted Text**—Students don't read long paragraphs of text; instead they get a step-by-step, concise presentation

- **Broad Coverage of Skills**—Gives students the knowledge needed to get up and running quickly

Two Page Chapter Introduction—Briefs students on what is important and sets the stage for the project they will create

File Summary—A quick summary of the files the students need to open and the names of the files they will turn in

Outcome—Shows students up front what their completed project will look like

Clock—Tells how much time students need to complete the chapter

Student Training Videos for each Skill in the chapter provide a personal, instructor-led walk through

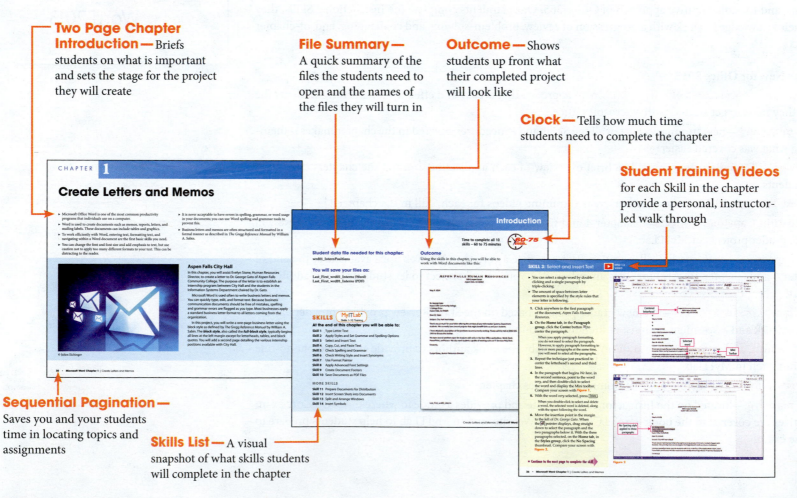

Sequential Pagination—Saves you and your students time in locating topics and assignments

Skills List—A visual snapshot of what skills students will complete in the chapter

Skills for Success

Written for Today's Students — Skills are taught with numbered steps and bulleted text so students are less likely to skip valuable information

Two-Page Spreads — Each skill is presented in a concise, two-page spread to give students the visual illustration right with the steps—no flipping pages

Colored Text — Clearly shows what a student types

Larger Screen Images — Provide a view of the full ribbon and include concise callouts for easy reference

Done! — Students always know when they've completed a skill

New BizSkills Videos — Covering the important business skills students need to succeed: *Communication, Dress for Success, Interview Prep,* and more. Available for Chapters 1-4 only.

Hands-On — Students start working on their skills from Step 1

More Skills — Additional skills included online

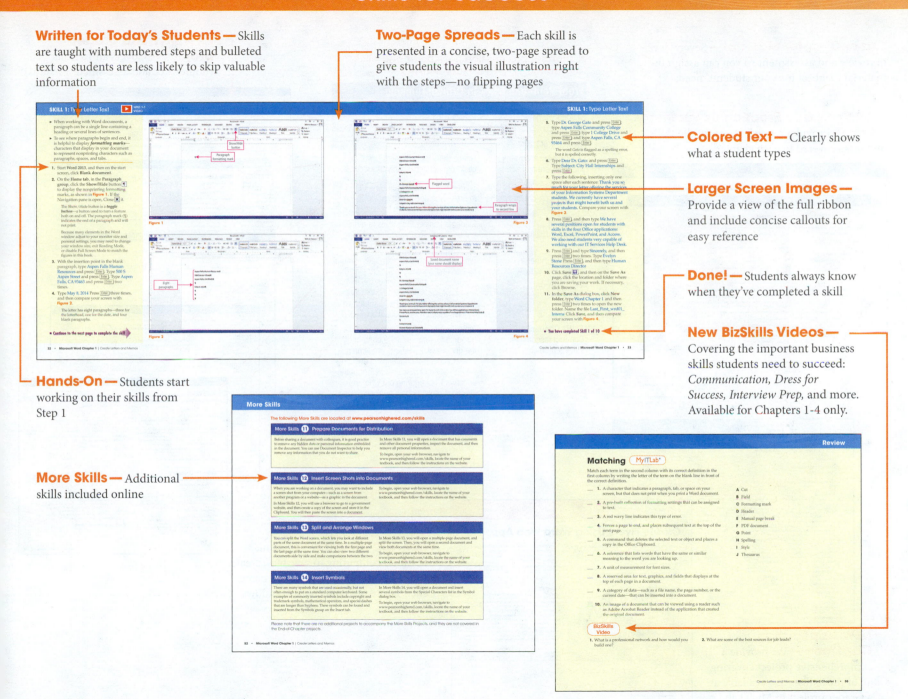

Skills for Success

End-of-Chapter Material— Several levels of review and assessment so you can assign the material that best fits your students' needs

NEW Skills and Procedures Summary Chart— Provides a quick review of the skills and tasks covered in each chapter

A stronger progression from point and click to practice, and to critical thinking.

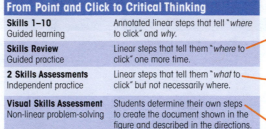

From Point and Click to Critical Thinking

Skills 1–10 Guided learning	Annotated linear steps that tell "*where* to click" and *why*.
Skills Review Guided practice	Linear steps that tell them "*where* to click" one more time.
2 Skills Assessments Independent practice	Linear steps that tell them "*what* to click" but not necessarily where.
Visual Skills Assessment Non-linear problem-solving	Students determine their own steps to create the document shown in the figure and described in the directions.
My Skills Transfer of skills	Students transfer their skills to a different scenario—a personal document, instead of business document.
Skills Challenge 1 Apply skills to fix problems	Typically a document that needs "fixed" by applying the skills in the chapter. The problems are described in a way that the *challenge* is deciding how to fix the problems, not figuring out what the directions mean or how it will be graded.
Skills Challenge 2 Conduct research to solve a problem	Typically a project that requires some research to determine the content of the document. Directions are written in a way that the *challenge* is deciding what to say and how best to format the document, not figuring out what the directions mean or how it will be graded.

NEW MyITLab grader project— Covers all 10 skills (homework and assessment versions)

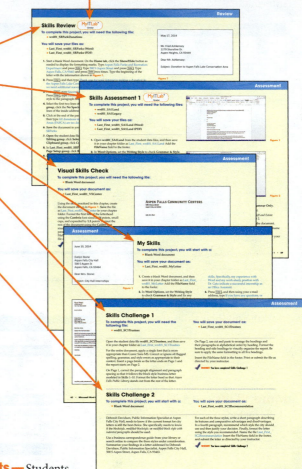

NEW Application Capstone— We provide a comprehensive project covering all of the Skills. Also available as a Grader project in MyITLab.

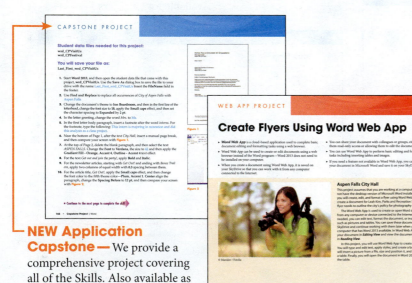

Web App Projects— Students use Cloud computing to save files; create, edit, and share Office documents using Office Web Apps; and create Windows Live groups.

MyITLab [MyITLab®]

Skills for Success combined with MyITLab gives you a completely integrated solution:

- Instruction, Training, & Assessment
- eText
- Training & Assessment Simulations
- Grader Projects

Student Videos!

Student Training Videos — Each skill within a chapter comes with an instructor-led video that walks students through each skill.

(BizSkills Video) Cover the important business skills students need to be successful—*Interviewing, Communication, Dressing for Success,* and more. **Available for Chapters 1-4 only**.

Student Data — Files are all available on the Companion Website using the access code included with your book. Pearsonhighered.com/skills

Instructor Materials

NEW Application Capstone Projects — Two projects cover Skills from Chapters 1-4 and Skills from Chapters 5-10. Also available as MyITLab grader projects

NEW MOS map — Guides you and your students to coverage of the MOS Exam objectives for each application

Instructor's Manual — Teaching tips and additional resources for each chapter

Student Assignment Tracker — Lists all the assignments for the chapter; you just add in the course information, due dates, and points. Providing these to students ensures they will know what is due and when

Scripted Lectures — Classroom lectures prepared for you

Annotated Solution Files — Coupled with the scoring rubrics, these create a grading and scoring system that makes grading so much easier for you

PowerPoint Lectures — PowerPoint presentations for each chapter

Audio PPTs — Provide an audio version of the PowerPoint presentations for each chapter

Prepared Exams — Exams for each chapter and for each application

NEW Detailed Scoring Rubrics — Can be used either by students to check their work or by you as a quick check-off for the items that need to be corrected

Syllabus Templates — For 8-week, 12-week, and 16-week courses

Test Bank — Includes a variety of test questions for each chapter

Companion Website — Online content such as the More Skills Projects, Online Chapter Review, Glossary, and Student Data Files are all at www.pearsonhighered.com/skills

All Student and Instructor Materials available at our Companion Websites ... pearsonhighered.com/skills

About the Authors

Kris Townsend is an Information Systems instructor at Spokane Falls Community College in Spokane, Washington. Kris earned a bachelor's degree in both Education and Business, and a master's degree in Education. He has also worked as a public school teacher and as a systems analyst. Kris enjoys working with wood, geocaching, and photography. He commutes to work by bike and also is a Lewis and Clark historical reenactor.

Christie Jahn Hovey is a Professor of Business & Technologies at Lincoln Land Community College in Springfield, Illinois. Christie has a bachelor's degree in Education from Illinois State University, a master's degree in Education/Human Resource Development from the University of Illinois at Urbana-Champaign, and is A.B.D. in Community College Leadership, at the University of Illinois at Urbana-Champaign. She has taught high school and was a corporate training consultant for Fortune 500 companies, as well as for state government and numerous small businesses.

A Special Thank You

Pearson Prentice Hall gratefully acknowledges the contribution made by Shelley Gaskin to the first edition publication of this series—*Skills for Success with Office 2007*. The series has truly benefited from her dedication toward developing a textbook that aims to help students and instructors. We thank her for her continued support of this series.

Dedication

I dedicate this book to the visionaries who saw the possibilities in moving from manual to electric typewriters that served as some of the first word processors. I recall using the first word processing applications, such as WordStar, Professional Write, Scripsit, WordPerfect, AmiPro, and early versions of Microsoft Word, which ultimately defined word processing. I hope you enjoy working with Word 2013!

Christie Hovey

Acknowledgments

When taking on an authoring project such as this one, many people deserve special mention. To my husband, Robyn, thank you for taking on more responsibilities with our son, Will, such as taking him to and from school and to all of his many after-school practices while I stayed home to write. To Will, thank you for reading or playing quietly while I worked in the office for countless hours. To Kris Townsend and to Jennifer Lynn, thank you for offering your ideas and suggestions. To Laura Burgess, thank you for always finding answers to my questions and for keeping me on target with due dates! To all the reviewers of the text and MyITLab content, thank you for your technical and grammatical expertise. And, to my current and former students at Lincoln Land Community College, thank you for all you have taught me over the years!

Christie Hovey

SKILLS For SUCCESS

with Microsoft®

Word 2013

Common Features of Office 2013

- ▶ Microsoft Office is a suite of several programs—Word, PowerPoint, Excel, Access, and others.

- ▶ Each Office program is used to create different types of personal and business documents.

- ▶ The programs in Office 2013 share common tools that you use in a consistent, easy-to-learn manner.

- ▶ Common tasks include opening and saving files, entering and formatting text, and printing your work.

- ▶ Because of the consistent design and layout of the Office applications, when you learn to use one Microsoft Office application, you can apply many of the same techniques when working in the other Microsoft Office applications.

© spaxiax / Fotolia

Aspen Falls City Hall

In this project, you will create documents for the Aspen Falls City Hall, which provides essential services for the citizens and visitors of Aspen Falls, California. You will assist Janet Neal, Finance Director, to prepare a presentation for the City Council. The presentation will explain retail sales trends in the city. The information will help the council to predict revenue from local sales taxes.

Microsoft Office is a suite of tools designed for specific tasks. In this project, the data was originally stored in an Access database. You will use Excel to create a chart from that data and then use PowerPoint to display the chart to an audience. Next, you will use Word to write a memo to update your supervisor about the project's status. In this way, each application performs a different function and creates a different type of document.

In this project, you will create a new Word document from an online template and open existing files in Excel and PowerPoint. You will write a memo, format an Excel worksheet and update chart data, and then place a copy of the chart into a PowerPoint presentation. You will also format a database report in Access. In all four applications, you will apply the same formatting to provide a consistent look and feel.

Time to complete all 10 skills – 60 to 90 minutes

Student data files needed for this chapter:

cf01_RetailChart (Excel)   cf01_RetailData (Access)
cf01_RetailSlides (PowerPoint)

You will save your files as:

Last_First_cf01_RetailMemo (Word)
Last_First_cf01_RetailChart (Excel)
Last_First_cf01_RetailSlides (PowerPoint)
Last_First_cf01_RetailData (Access)

Outcome

Using the skills in this chapter, you will be able to work with Office documents like this:

Aspen Falls City Hall

Memo

To:	Janet Neal
From:	Your Name
cc:	Maria Martinez
Date:	July 1, 2014
Re:	Sales Revenue

As per your request, the *Retail Sales* slides will be ready by the end of today. I will send them to you so you can insert them into your presentation. Let me know if you have any questions.

SKILLS

At the end of this chapter you will be able to:

Skill 1   Start Office Applications
Skill 2   Create Documents from Templates
Skill 3   Type and Edit Text
Skill 4   Save Files and Create Folders
Skill 5   Apply Themes and Format Text
Skill 6   Preview and Print Documents
Skill 7   Open and Save Student Data Files
Skill 8   Format Worksheets
Skill 9   Copy and Paste Objects and Format Slides
Skill 10 Format Access Reports

MORE SKILLS

Skill 11 Store Office Files on SkyDrive
Skill 12 Use Office Help
Skill 13 Send Files as E-mail Attachments
Skill 14 Optimize Office 2013 RT

CF 1-1
VIDEO

▶ The way that you start an Office application depends on what operating system you are using and how your computer is configured.

▶ Each application's Start screen displays links to recently viewed documents and thumbnails of sample documents that you can open.

1. If necessary, turn on the computer, sign in, and navigate to the desktop. Take a few moments to familiarize yourself with the various methods for starting Office applications as summarized in **Figure 1**.

   One method that works in both Windows 7 and Windows 8 is to press [⊞]—the Windows key located between [Ctrl] and [Alt]—to display the Start menu or screen. With Start displayed, type the application name, and then press [Enter].

2. Use one of the methods described in the previous step to start **Word 2013**, and then take a few moments to familiarize yourself with the Word Start screen as shown in **Figure 2**.

   Your list of recent documents will vary depending on what Word documents you have worked with previously. Below the list of recent documents, the *Open Other Documents* link is used to open Word files that are not listed.

Common Methods to Start Office 2013 Applications	
Location	**Description**
Start screen tile	Click the application's tile.
Desktop	Double-click the application's desktop icon.
Taskbar	Click the application's taskbar button.
Windows 7 Start menu	Click Start, and look in the pinned or recently used programs. Or click All Programs, and locate the Office application or the Microsoft Office 2013 folder.
All locations	Press [⊞], type the application's name, and then press [Enter].

Figure 1

Figure 2

■ **Continue to the next page to complete the skill** ➤

Figure 3

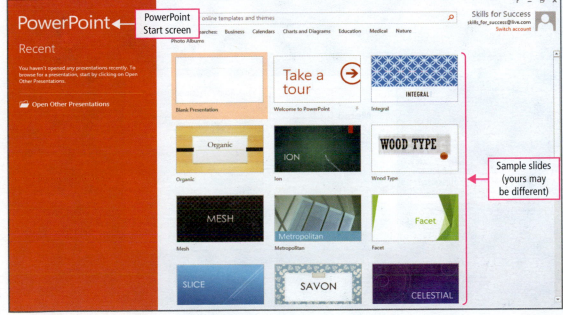

Figure 4

3. If desired, click **Sign in to get the most out of Office**, and then follow the onscreen directions to sign in using your Microsoft account.

   Logging in enables you to access Microsoft Cloud services such as opening and saving files stored on your SkyDrive. Unless otherwise directed, signing in to your Microsoft account is always optional in this book. To protect your privacy, you should sign in only if you are already signed in to Windows using a unique username, not a shared account. For example, many public computers share an account for guests.

4. Using the technique just practiced, start **Excel 2013**, and then compare your screen with **Figure 3**.

   Worksheets are divided into *cells*—boxes formed by the intersection of a row and column into which text, objects, and data can be inserted. In Excel, cells can contain text, formulas, and functions. Worksheets can also display charts based on the values in the cells.

   When you are logged in to your Microsoft account, your name and picture will display in the upper right corner of the window.

5. Start **PowerPoint 2013**, and then compare your screen with **Figure 4**.

   PowerPoint presentations consist of *slides*—individual pages in a presentation that can contain text, pictures, or other objects. PowerPoint slides are designed to be projected as you talk in front of a group of people. The PowerPoint Start screen has thumbnails of several slides formatted in different ways.

■ **You have completed Skill 1 of 10**

▶ Office provides access to hundreds of *templates*—pre-built documents into which you insert text using the layout and formatting provided in the documents.

▶ Templates for Word documents, Excel workbooks, PowerPoint presentations, and Access databases can be opened from the start screen or the New page on each application's File tab.

1. On the taskbar, click the **Word** button [W] to make it the active window.

2. If the Word Start screen no longer displays, on the File tab, click New.

3. Click in the **Search for online templates** box, and then type memo Click the **Start searching** button [🔍], and then compare your screen with **Figure 1**.

    The New page displays templates that are available online. These online templates are provided by Microsoft and others who submit them to microsoft.com. These online templates must be downloaded before you can work with them. Because the template list is dynamic, your search results may be different.

    On the New page, the right pane can be used to filter your search by category. You can also pin a template so that it always displays on the start screen and New page.

4. Scroll down the list of memos, and then click the **Memo (Professional design)** thumbnail. Compare your screen with **Figure 2**.

    The preview screen provides information about the template so that you can evaluate it before deciding to download it to your computer. You should download templates only from sources that you trust.

■ **Continue to the next page to complete the skill** ➤

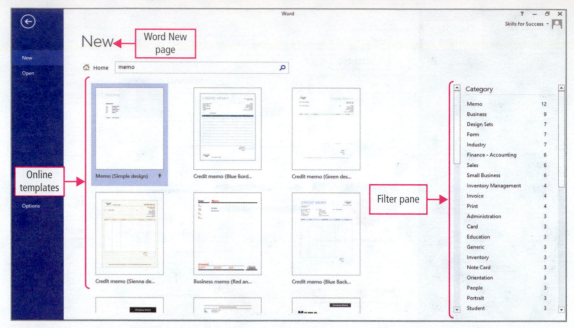

Figure 1

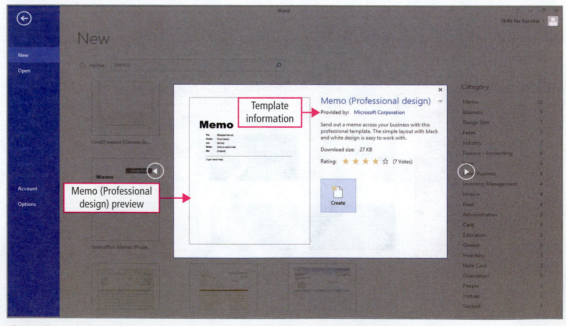

Figure 2

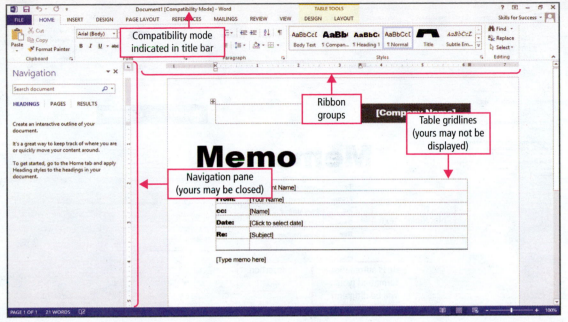

Compatibility mode indicated in title bar

Ribbon groups

Table gridlines (yours may not be displayed)

Navigation pane (yours may be closed)

Figure 3

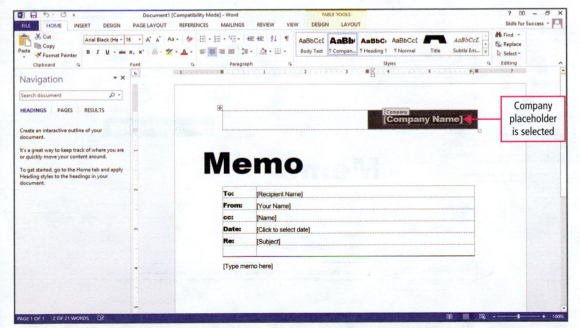

Company placeholder is selected

Figure 4

5. In the **Memo (Professional design)** preview, click the **Create** button. Wait a few moments for the memo to download and open. Compare your screen with **Figure 3**.

   Templates create new, unsaved documents. Here, the title bar displays the text *Document1* and **Compatibility Mode**—a mode that limits formatting and features to ones that are supported in earlier versions of Office.

   Above the memo, the Quick Access Toolbar and Ribbon display. The Office Ribbon organizes commands into groups. Because the Ribbon adapts to the size of the document window, you may need to adjust the size of your window if you want your Ribbon to display exactly as shown in the figures in this book.

   To the left of the document, the Navigation pane is used to move through the document. Below the word *Memo*, the table gridlines may or may not display depending on your settings. These gridlines do not print, and you can work with documents with them displayed or turned off.

6. In the upper-right corner of the memo, click—or tap—the **Company** placeholder—*[Company Name]*—to select it, and then compare your screen with **Figure 4**.

   Templates often contain **placeholders**— reserved, formatted spaces into which you enter your own text or objects. If no text is entered, the placeholder text will not print.

7. With the **Company** placeholder selected, type Aspen Falls City Hall

8. Leave the memo open for the next skill.

■ **You have completed Skill 2 of 10**

CF 1-3
VIDEO

▶ To **edit** is to insert, delete, or replace text in an Office document, workbook, or presentation.

▶ To edit text, you need to position the **insertion point**—a flashing vertical line that indicates where text will be inserted—at the desired location, or select the text you want to replace.

1. Click the first **Name** placeholder—*[Recipient Name]*—and then type Janet Neal

2. Click the second **Name** placeholder—*[Your Name]*—and then type your own first and last name.

3. In the third **Name** placeholder—*[Name]*—type Maria Martinez

4. Click the **Date** placeholder—*[Click to select date]*— and then type the current date.

5. In the **Subject** placeholder, type Sales Tax Revenue Compare your screen with **Figure 1**.

6. Click *[Type memo here]*, and then type the following: As per your request, the Retail Sales slides will be ready by the end of today. I will send them to you so you can insert them into your presentation. Let me know if you have any questions. Compare your screen with **Figure 2**.

As you type, the insertion point moves to the right. To improve clarity, the figures in this book typically will not display the insertion point.

At the right margin, Word determines whether the word you are typing will fit within the established margin. If it does not fit, Word moves the entire word to the beginning of the next line. This feature is called **word wrap**. Within a paragraph, you do not need to press ⌈Enter⌋ to create new lines.

■ **Continue to the next page to complete the skill** ▶

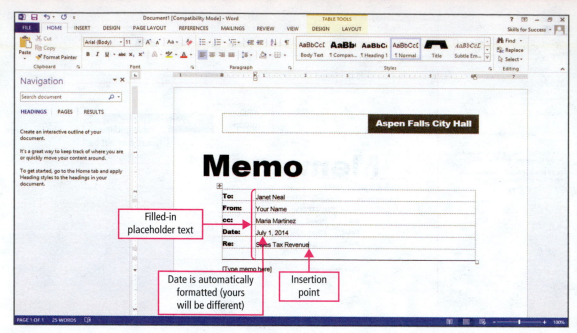

Figure 1

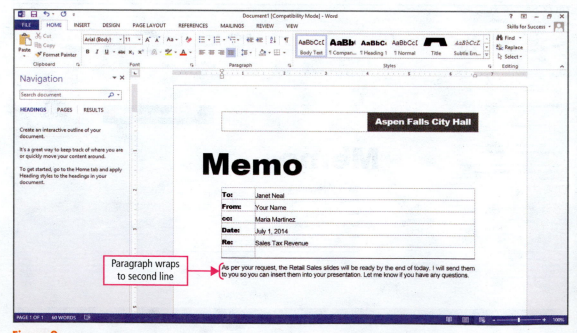

Figure 2

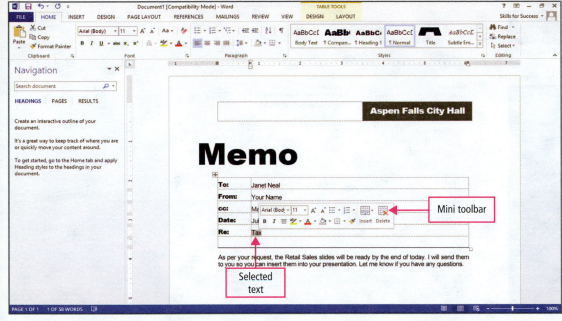

Figure 3

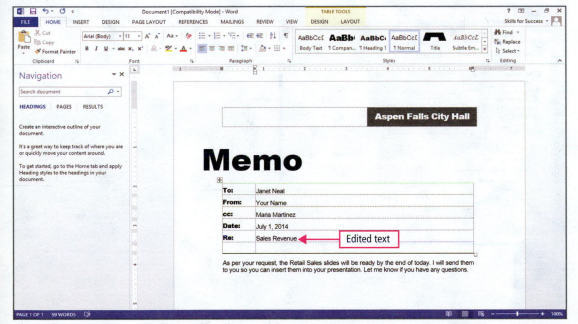

Figure 4

7. In the **Re:** line, click to the left of *Sales* to place the insertion point at the beginning of the word. Press `Delete` six times to delete the word *Sales* and the space that follows it.

   The Delete key deletes one letter at a time moving from left to right. The name on your keyboard may vary—for example, DEL, Del, or Delete.

8. In the **Re:** line, click to the right of *Revenue* to place the insertion point at the end of the word.

9. Press `Backspace` eight times to delete the word *Revenue* and the space that precedes it.

   The Backspace key deletes one letter at a time moving from right to left. The name on your keyboard may vary—for example, BACK, Backspace, or simply a left-facing arrow.

10. In the **Re:** line, double-click—or double-tap—the word *Tax* to select it, and then compare your screen with **Figure 3**.

    To **double-click** is to click the left mouse button two times quickly without moving the mouse. To **double-tap**, tap the screen in the same place two times quickly.

    After selecting text, the **Mini toolbar**—a toolbar with common formatting commands—displays near the selection.

11. Type Sales Revenue to replace the selected word, and then compare your screen with **Figure 4**.

    When a word or paragraph is selected, it is replaced by whatever you type next, and the Mini toolbar no longer displays.

■ **You have completed Skill 3 of 10**

► New documents are stored in **RAM**—the computer's temporary memory—until you save them to more permanent storage such as your hard drive, USB flash drive, or online storage.

1. If you are saving your work on a USB flash drive, insert the drive into the computer. If a notice to choose what happens with removable drives displays, ignore it.

   This book assumes that your work will be saved to SkyDrive or a USB flash drive. If you are saving your work to a different location, you will need to adapt these steps as necessary.

2. On the Word **Quick Access Toolbar**, click the **Save** button 🖫, and then compare your screen with **Figure 1**.

   The Save As page is used to select the location where you want to save your work. You can choose to save to your SkyDrive or other locations on your computer. If you have favorite folders in which you like to save your files, you can add them to the Save As page so that you can then select them with a single click.

3. Under **Recent Folders**, click the location where you are saving your work. If your location is not displayed, click the **Browse** button, and then in the Save As dialog box, navigate to your location.

4. On the **Save As** dialog box toolbar, click the **New folder** button, and then type Common Features Chapter 1 Compare your screen with **Figure 2**.

■ **Continue to the next page to complete the skill**

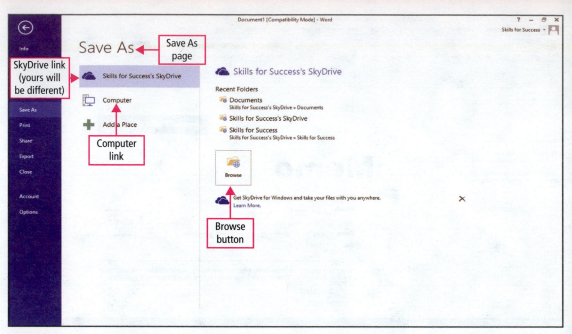

Figure 1

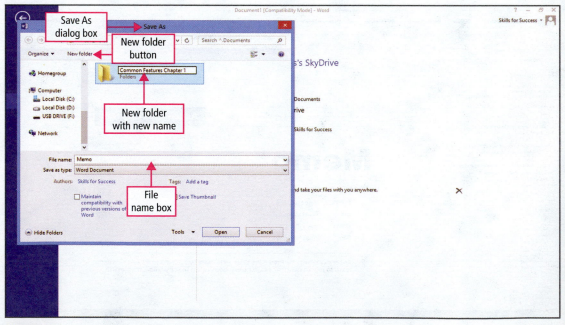

Figure 2

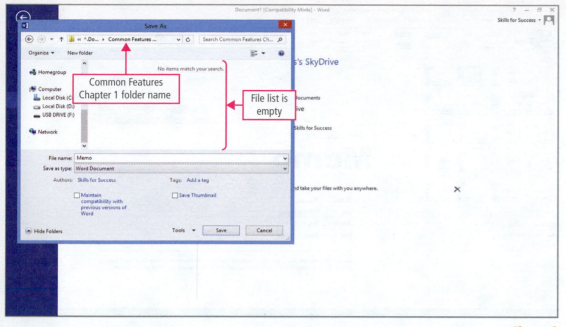

Common Features
Chapter 1 folder name

File list is
empty

Figure 3

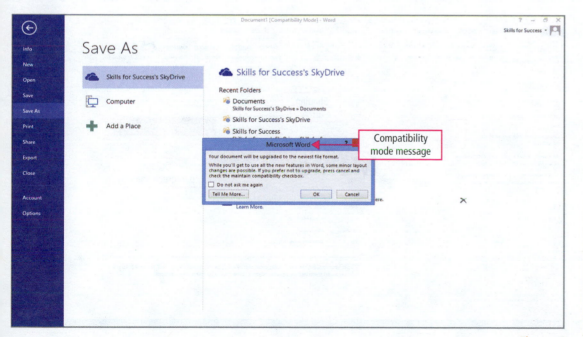

Compatibility
mode message

Figure 4

5. Press [Enter] to accept the folder name, and then press [Enter] again to open the new folder as shown in **Figure 3**.

> Before saving a new file, you should open the folder in which you want to store the file.

6. In the **Save As** dialog box, click in the **File name** box one time to highlight all of the existing text.

7. With the text in the **File name** box still highlighted, using your own name, type Last_First_cf01_RetailMemo

> In this book, you should substitute your first and last name whenever you see the text *Last_First* or *Your Name*.

8. Click **Save**, and then compare your screen with **Figure 4**.

> A message may display to inform you that the document will convert to the latest file format for Word documents.

9. Read the displayed message, and then click **OK**.

> After the document is saved, the name of the file displays on the title bar at the top of the window and the text *[Compatibility Mode]* no longer displays.

10. Leave the memo open for the next skill.

■ **You have completed Skill 4 of 10**

▶ To **format** is to change the appearance of the text—for example, changing the text color to red.

▶ Before formatting an Office document, it is a good idea to pick a **theme**—a pre-built set of unified formatting choices including colors and fonts.

1. Click the **Design tab**. In the **Themes group**, click the **Themes** button, and then compare your screen with **Figure 1**.

> Each theme displays as a thumbnail in a **gallery**—a visual display of selections from which you can choose.

2. In the **Themes** gallery, point to—but do not click—each thumbnail to preview its formatting with **Live Preview**—a feature that displays what the results of a formatting change will be if you select it.

3. In the **Themes** gallery, click the third theme in the second row—**Retrospect**.

> A **font** is a set of characters with the same design and shape. Each theme has two font categories—one for headings and one for body text.

4. Click anywhere in the text *Aspen Falls City Hall* to make it the active paragraph. With the insertion point in the paragraph, click the **Home tab**.

5. In the **Paragraph group**, click the **Shading arrow**. In the first row of the gallery under **Theme Colors**, click the sixth choice—**Orange, Accent 2**. Compare your screen with **Figure 2**.

> In all themes, the Accent 2 color is the sixth choice in the color gallery, but the color varies depending on the theme. Here, the Retrospect theme Accent 2 color is a shade of orange.

■ **Continue to the next page to complete the skill** ➤

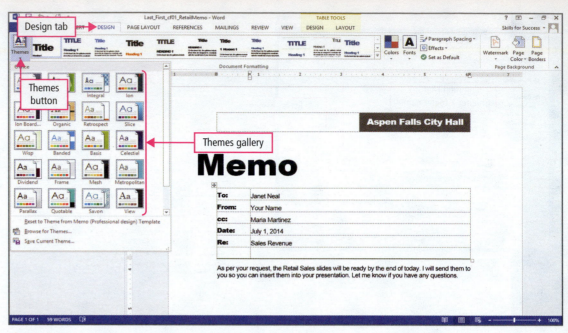

Figure 1

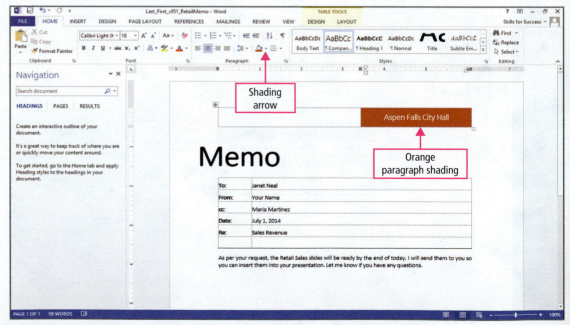

Figure 2

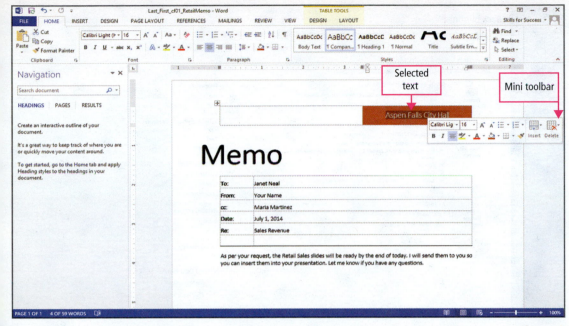

Figure 3

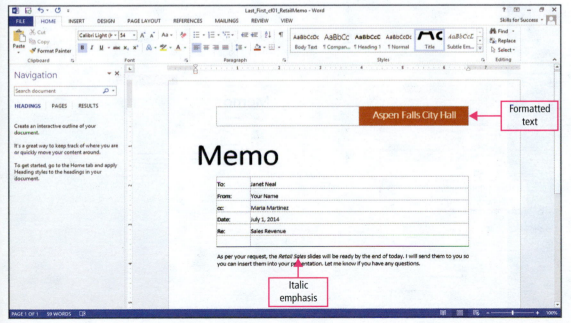

Figure 4

6. In the upper-right corner, **drag**—press and hold the left mouse button while moving the mouse—to select the text *Aspen Falls City Hall*, and then compare your screen with **Figure 3**. To select by dragging with a touch display, tap in the text, and then drag the selection handle.

   Before formatting text, the text must be selected. If the Mini toolbar does not display, you can right-click or tap the selected text.

7. On the Mini toolbar, click the **Font Size arrow** 11 ▾ , and then from the list, click **20** to increase the size of the selected text. On the Mini toolbar, click the **Bold** button B .

8. On the Mini toolbar, click the **Font Color arrow** A ▾ , and then under **Theme colors**, click the fifth color in the second row—**Orange**, **Accent 1**, **Lighter 80%**. Alternately, on the Home tab, in the Font group, click the **Font Color arrow** A ▾ .

9. In the paragraph that begins *As per your*, drag to select the text *Retail Sales*. From the Mini toolbar, click the **Italic** button I .

   Alternately, you can use a **keyboard shortcut**—a combination of keys that performs a command. Here, you could press Ctrl + I .

10. Click a blank area of the document, and then compare your screen with **Figure 4**. Carefully check the memo for spelling errors. If spelling errors are found, use the techniques practiced previously to correct them.

11. Click the **Save** button 🖫 .

■ **You have completed Skill 5 of 10**

CF 1-6
VIDEO

▶ Before printing, it is a good idea to preview the document on the Print page.

▶ On the Print page, you can check that blank pages won't be printed by accident.

1. Click the **File tab**, and then compare your screen with **Figure 1**.

    Backstage view is a collection of pages on the File tab used to open, save, print, and perform other file management tasks. In Backstage view, you can return to the open document by clicking the Back button.

2. On the **File tab**, click **Print** to display the Print page. Click the **Printer** menu, and then compare your screen with **Figure 2**.

    The Printer list displays available printers for your computer along with their status. For example, a printer may be offline because it is not turned on. The ***default printer*** is indicated by a check mark, and is automatically selected when you do not choose a different printer.

    In a school lab or office, it is a good idea to check the list of available printers and verify that the correct printer is selected. It is also important that you know where the printer is located so that you can retrieve your printout.

3. Press Esc —located in the upper-left corner of most keyboards—to close the Printer menu without selecting a different printer.

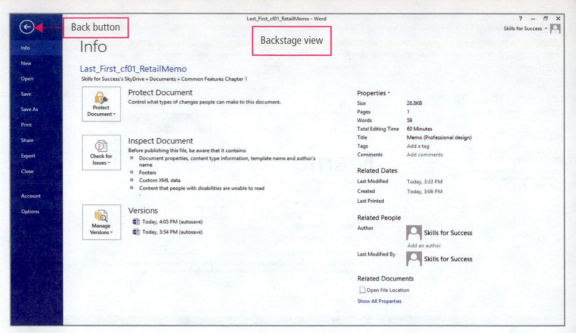

Figure 1

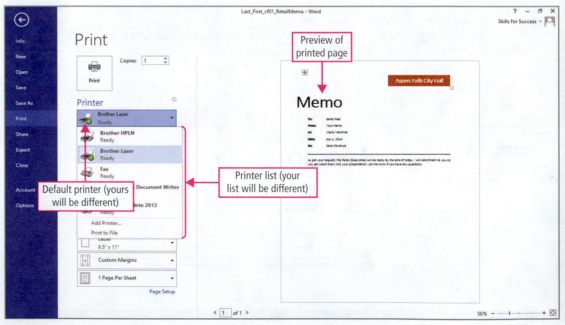

Figure 2

■ **Continue to the next page to complete the skill** ➤

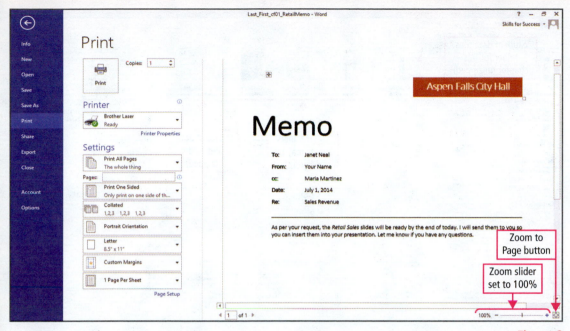

Figure 3

Common Touch Screen Gestures	
Gesture	**Description**
Tap	Touch one time with the finger.
Slide	Touch an object and then move the finger across the screen.
Swipe	Slide in from a screen edge to display app commands, charms, or other temporary areas.
Pinch	Slide two fingers closer together to shrink or zoom in.
Stretch	Slide two fingers apart to enlarge or zoom out.

Figure 4

4. In the lower-right corner of the **Print** page, click the **Zoom In** button until the zoom level displays **100%**. Compare your screen with **Figure 3**.

> The size of the print preview depends on the size of your monitor. When previewed on smaller monitors, some documents may not display accurately. If this happens, you can zoom in to see a more accurate view.

5. To the right of the **Zoom** slider, click the **Zoom to Page** button [⊡] to return to your original zoom level.

> If you are working at a touch display, you can zoom in and out using gestures. The gestures are summarized in the table in **Figure 4**.

6. If you are printing your work for this project, note the location of the selected printer, click the **Print** button, and then retrieve your printouts from the printer.

> You should print your work only if your instructor has asked you to do so. Many instructors prefer to grade electronic versions that have been sent as e-mail attachments, copied to a network drive, or uploaded to a learning management system such as Blackboard.

7. In the upper-right corner of the window, click the **Close** button [x].

> If you have made changes to a document without saving them, you will be prompted to save those changes when you close the document.

■ **You have completed Skill 6 of 10**

CF 1-7
VIDEO

▶ In this book, you will frequently open student data files.

1. Before beginning this skill, the student files folder for this chapter should be downloaded and unzipped or copied similar to the one described in **Figure 1**. Follow the instructions in the book or provided by your instructor.

2. On the taskbar, click the **Excel** button to return to the Excel 2013 Start screen. If necessary, start Excel.

3. On the **Excel 2013** Start screen, click **Open Other Workbooks** to display the Open page. If you already had a blank workbook open, click the File tab instead.

4. On the **Open** page, click **Computer**, and then click the **Browse** button.

5. In the **Open** dialog box Navigation pane, navigate to the student files for this chapter, and then compare your screen with **Figure 2**.

6. In the **Open** dialog box, select **cf01_RetailChart**, and then click the **Open** button.

7. If the Protected View message displays, click the **Enable Editing** button.

   Documents downloaded from a website typically open in *Protected View*—a view applied to documents downloaded from the Internet that allows you to decide if the content is safe before working with the document.

8. Click the **File tab**, and then click **Save As**. On the **Save As** page, click the location where you created your chapter folder, and then navigate as needed to open the **Common Features Chapter 1**. If necessary, click Browse and then navigate in the Save As dialog box.

■ **Continue to the next page to complete the skill** ➤

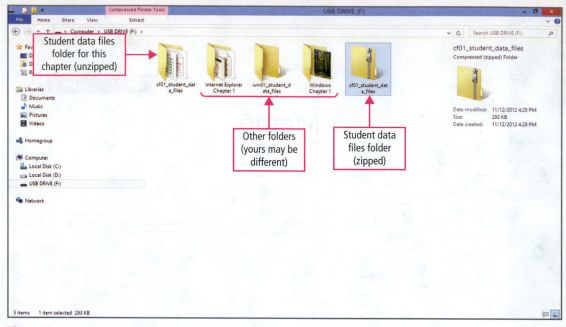

Figure 1

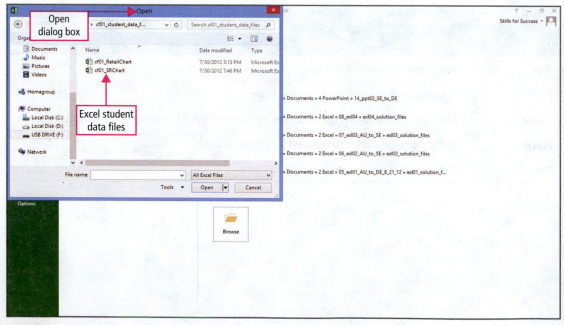

Figure 2

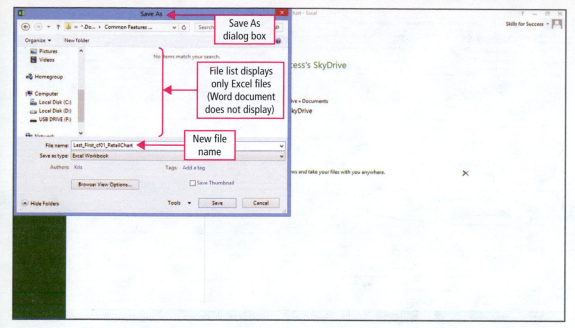

Figure 3

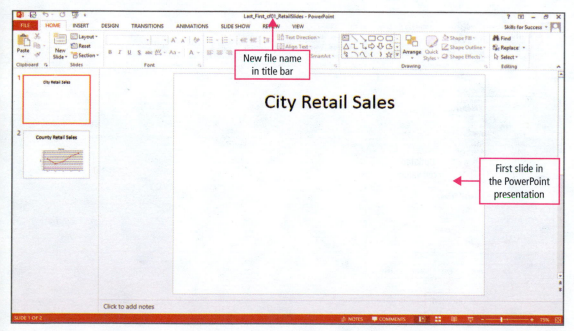

Figure 4

9. In the **File Name** box, change the existing text to Last_First_cf01_RetailChart using your own name.

10. Compare your screen with **Figure 3**, and then click the **Save** button.

    In this manner, you can use the Save As command to create a copy of a file with a new name. The original student data file will remain unchanged.

    By default, the Save As dialog box displays only those files saved in the current application file format. Here, the Excel file is listed, but the Word file you saved previously may not display.

11. On the taskbar, click the **PowerPoint** button 📧 to return to the PowerPoint Start screen. If necessary, start PowerPoint.

12. On the **PowerPoint 2013** Start screen, click **Open Other Presentations** to display the Open page. If you already had a blank presentation open, click the File tab instead.

13. On the **Open** page, click **Computer**, and then click the **Browse** button. In the **Open** dialog box, navigate to the student files for this chapter, and then open **cf01_RetailSlides**. If necessary, enable the content.

14. On the **File tab**, click **Save As**, and then use the Save As page to navigate as needed to open your **Common Features Chapter 1** folder in the Save As dialog box.

    On most computers, your Word and Excel files will not display because the PowerPoint Save As dialog box is set to display only presentation files.

15. Name the file Last_First_cf01_RetailSlides and then click **Save**. Compare your screen with **Figure 4**.

■ **You have completed Skill 7 of 10**

▶ To keep formatting consistent across all of your Office documents, the same themes are available in Word, Excel, PowerPoint, and Access.

▶ To format text in Excel, you typically select the cell that holds the text and then click the desired formatting command.

1. On the taskbar, click the **Excel** button to return to the workbook.

2. Click cell **B9**—the intersection of column **B** and row **9**—to select the cell. Compare your screen with **Figure 1**.

    A selected cell is indicated by a thick, dark-green border.

3. With cell **B9** selected, type 4.37 and then press Enter to accept the change and update the chart.

    The chart is based on the data in columns A and B. When the data is changed, the chart changes to reflect the new values.

4. On the **Page Layout tab**, in the **Themes group**, click the **Themes** button, and then click the **Restrospect** thumbnail. Compare your screen with **Figure 2**.

    The Retrospect theme applies the same colors, fonts, and effects as the Retrospect theme in other Office applications. Here, the font was changed to Calibri.

5. At the top of the worksheet, right-click the title *Aspen Falls* to display the Mini toolbar. Click the **Font Size arrow**, and then click **14** to increase the font size.

■ **Continue to the next page to complete the skill**

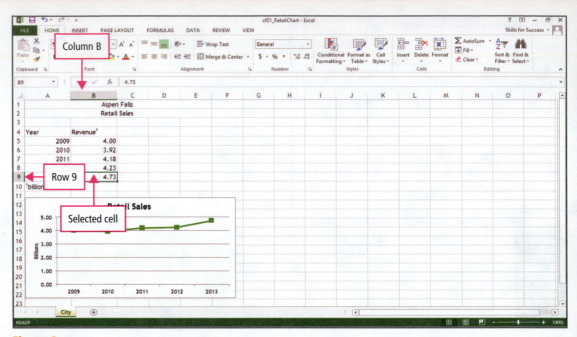

Figure 1

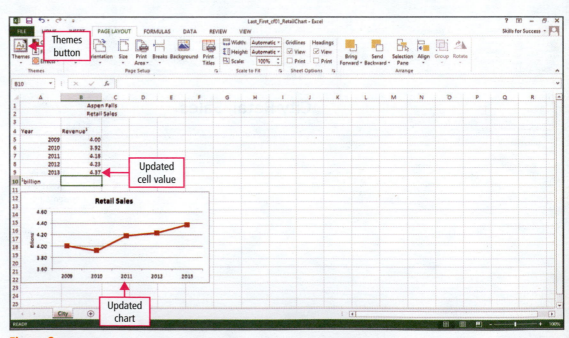

Figure 2

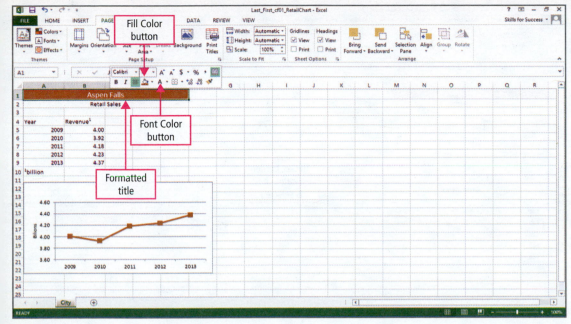

Figure 3

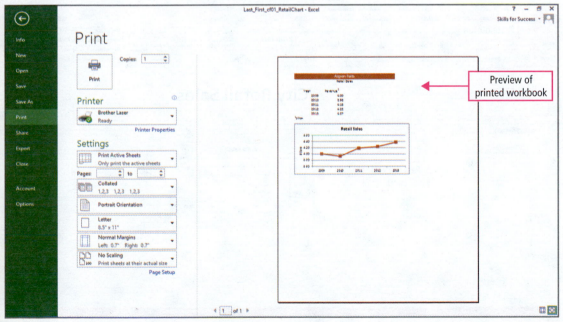

Figure 4

6. With the title cell still selected, on the Mini toolbar, click the **Fill Color arrow**, and then under **Theme Colors**, click the sixth choice—**Orange, Accent 2**.

7. In the **Font group**, click the **Font Color arrow** , and then under **Theme Colors**, click the first choice—**White, Background 1**. Compare your screen with **Figure 3**.

8. Click cell **A4**. On the **Home tab**, in the **Alignment group**, click the **Center** button to center the text. Repeat to center the text in cell **B4**.

9. Click cell **A10**, and then in the **Font group**, change the **Font Size** to **9**.

10. On the **File tab**, click **Print**, and then compare your screen with **Figure 4**.

 The Excel Print page is used in the same manner as the Word Print page. Here, you can preview the document, select your printer, and verify that the worksheet will print on a single page. By default, the gridlines do not print.

11. If you are printing your work for this project, print the worksheet. Otherwise, click the **Back** button to return to Normal view.

12. On the **Quick Access Toolbar**, click **Save** .

■ **You have completed Skill 8 of 10**

▶ In Office, the *copy* command places a copy of the selected text or object in the *Office Clipboard*—a temporary storage area that holds text or an object that has been cut or copied.

▶ The *paste* command inserts a copy of the text or object from the Office Clipboard.

1. In the Excel window, click the chart's border to select the chart, and compare your screen with **Figure 1**.

   In Office, certain graphics such as charts and SmartArt display a thick border when they are selected.

2. On the **Home tab**, in the **Clipboard group**, click the **Copy** button 🗐 to place a copy of the chart into the Office Clipboard.

3. On the taskbar, click the **PowerPoint** button 📘 to return to **Last_First_ cf01_RetailSlides**, which you saved previously.

4. With **Slide 1** as the active slide, on the **Home tab**, in the **Clipboard group**, click the **Paste** button to insert the copied Excel chart. If you accidentally clicked the Paste arrow to display the Paste Options, click the Paste button that is above it. Compare your screen with **Figure 2**.

5. Click the **Design tab**, and then in the **Themes group**, click the **More** button ⬇. Point to several thumbnails to preview their formatting, and then under **Office**, click the seventh choice—**Retrospect**.

   In PowerPoint, themes are sets of colors, fonts, and effects optimized for viewing in a large room with the presentation projected onto a screen in front of the audience.

■ **Continue to the next page to complete the skill** ➤

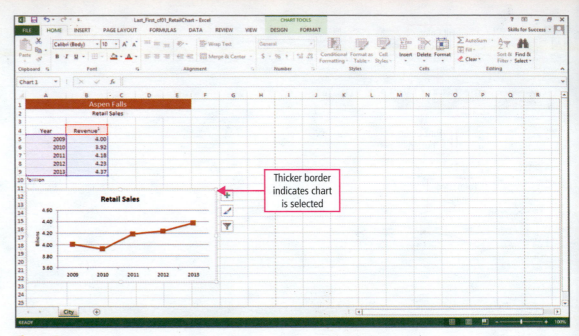

Thicker border indicates chart is selected

Figure 1

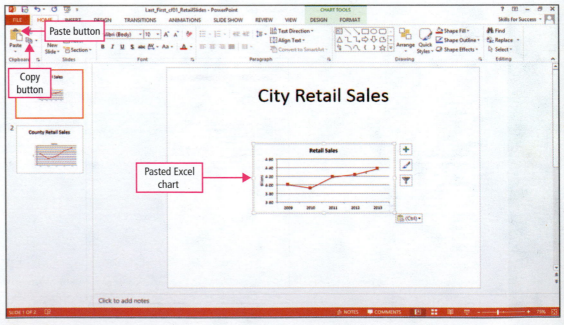

Paste button

Copy button

Pasted Excel chart

Figure 2

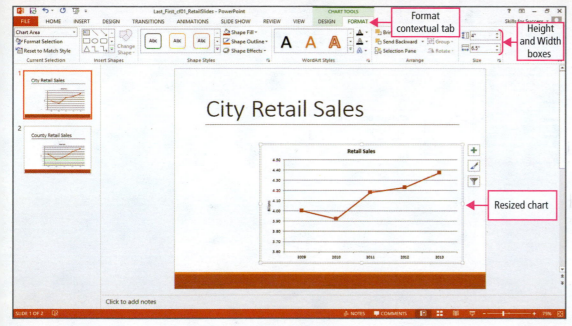

6. Drag through the slide title text *City Retail Sales* to select it. On the **Home tab**, in the **Font group**, click the **Font Size arrow**, and then click **60**. Alternately, right-click the selected text, and then use the Mini toolbar to change the font size.

7. Click any area in the chart, and then click the chart's border so that only the chart is selected.

8. Click the **Format tab**, and then in the **Size group**, click the **Height** spin box up arrow until the value is **4"**. Repeat this technique to change the **Width** value to **6.5"**, and then compare your screen with **Figure 3**.

   The Format tab is a *contextual tab*—a tab that displays on the Ribbon only when a related object such as a graphic or chart is selected.

9. On the **File tab**, click **Print**. On the **Print** page, under **Settings**, click the button with the text *Full Page Slides*. In the gallery that displays, under **Handouts**, click **2 Slides**. Compare your screen with **Figure 4**.

10. If you are printing your work, click **Print** to print the handout. Otherwise, click the **Back** button to return to Normal view.

11. Click **Save**, and then **Close** the presentation window.

12. On the taskbar, click the **Excel** button to make it the active window, and then **Close** the window. If a message displays asking you to save changes, click Save.

- **You have completed Skill 9 of 10**

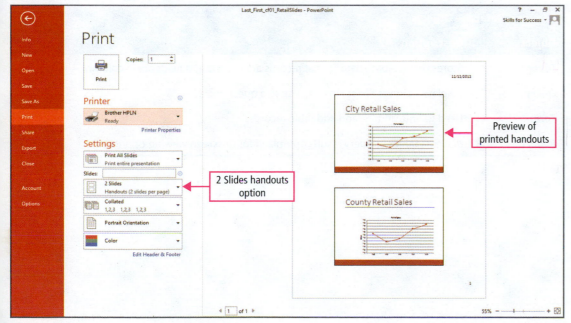

Figure 4

▶ Access reports present data in a way that is optimized for printing.

1. Start **Access 2013**, and then on the Start screen, click **Open Other Files**. On the **Open** page, click **Computer**, and then click **Browse**.

2. In the **Open** dialog box, navigate to the location where you are storing your student data files for this chapter. In the **Open** dialog box, select **cf01_RetailData**, and then click the **Open** button.

3. Take a few moments to familiarize yourself with the Access Window objects as described in **Figure 1**.

    Database files contain several different types of objects such as tables, queries, forms, and reports. Each object has a special purpose summarized in the table in **Figure 2**.

4. On the **File tab**, click **Save As**. With **Save Database As** selected, click the **Save As** button.

5. In the **Save As** dialog box, navigate to your **Common Features Chapter 1** folder. In the **File name** box, name the file Last_First_cf01_RetailData and then click **Save**. If a security message displays, click the Enable Content button.

    Malicious persons sometimes place objects in database files that could harm your computer. For this reason, the security message may display when you open a database that you did not create. You should click the Enable Content button only when you know the file is from a trusted source.

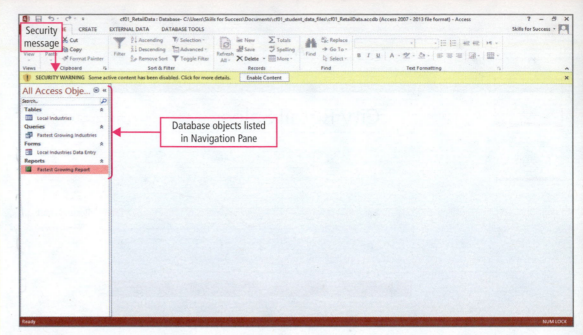

Figure 1

Common Database Objects	
Object	**Description**
Table	Stores the database data so that records are in rows and fields are in columns.
Query	Displays a subset of data in response to a question.
Form	Used to find, update, and add table records.
Report	Presents tables or query results optimized for onscreen viewing or printing.

Figure 2

■ Continue to the next page to complete the skill ▶

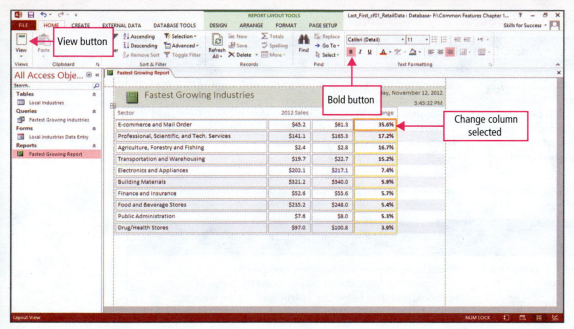

View button

Bold button

Change column selected

Figure 3

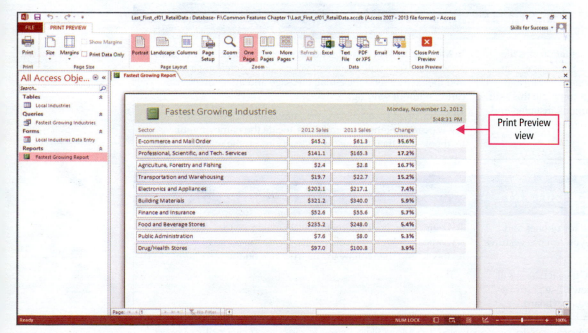

Print Preview view

Figure 4

6. In the **Navigation pane**, under **Reports**, double-click **Fastest Growing Report**.

7. On the **Home tab**, in the **Views group**, click the **View** button one time to switch to Layout view.

8. On the **Design tab**, in the **Themes group**, click **Themes**, and then click the seventh thumbnail—**Retrospect**.

9. Near the top of the **Change** column, click the first value—*35.6%*—to select all the values in the column.

10. Click the **Home tab**, and then in the **Text Formatting group**, click the **Bold** button
    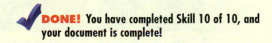. Compare your screen with **Figure 3**.

11. On the **Home tab**, click the **View arrow**, and then click **Print Preview**. Compare your screen with **Figure 4**. If necessary, in the Zoom group, click the One Page button to zoom to 100%.

12. If your instructor asked you to print your work, click the Print button and then print the report.

13. Click **Save** 🖫 to save the formatting changes, and then **Close** ☒ the report.

    Objects such as reports are opened and closed without closing the Access application itself.

14. **Close** ☒ the Access window, and then submit your printouts or files for this chapter as directed by your instructor.

✔ **DONE!** You have completed Skill 10 of 10, and your document is complete!

The following More Skills are located at **www.pearsonhighered.com/skills**

More Skills Store Office Files on SkyDrive

You can sign in to your Microsoft account from Word, Excel, or PowerPoint, and then open and save files from online storage services such as SkyDrive. Storing files on SkyDrive enables you to access your files from any computer connected to the Internet. After signing in to your account, you can open and save files stored on SkyDrive using the same techniques used for files stored on local computer drives.

In More Skills 11, you will create a Microsoft account if you don't already have one. You will sign in to that account, connect your Office program to SkyDrive, and then save a Word, Excel, and PowerPoint file to SkyDrive. You will document your work by creating a snip of your SkyDrive folder.

To begin, open your web browser, navigate to www.pearsonhighered.com/skills, locate the name of your textbook, and then follow the instructions on the website.

More Skills Use Office Help

Microsoft Office 2013 has a Help system in which you can search for articles that show you how to accomplish tasks.

In More Skills 12, you will use the Office 2013 Help system to learn how to find out which version of Office you are using. You will then paste a snip of that screen into a Word document.

To begin, open your web browser, navigate to www.pearsonhighered.com/skills, locate the name of your textbook, and then follow the instructions on the website.

More Skills Send Files as E-mail Attachments

You can send a document, workbook, or presentation as a file attached to an e-mail message. On the Save & Send page, you can attach the file in its native format or change it to a format that can be opened in a different program. To complete this skill, you need to have a mail program such as Outlook installed and configured to send mail using your e-mail account.

In More Skills 13, you will send a Word document as an e-mail attachment. You will document your work by creating a snip, and then either send the e-mail message and attachment or cancel without sending.

To begin, open your web browser, navigate to www.pearsonhighered.com/skills, locate the name of your textbook, and then follow the instructions on the website.

More Skills Optimize Office 2013 RT

Office 2013 RT is a version of Office designed for phones and tablets. Instead of the mouse and keyboard, you can use gestures and the Touch Keyboard to perform tasks.

In More Skills 14, you will work with Excel Office RT. You will switch between Full Screen and Standard views, use gestures instead of the mouse, and type via an onscreen keyboard.

To begin, open your Internet browser, navigate to www.pearsonhighered.com/skills, locate the name of your textbook, and then follow the instructions on the website.

Please note that there are no additional projects to accompany the More Skills Projects, and they are not covered in the End-of-Chapter projects.

The following table summarizes the **SKILLS AND PROCEDURES** covered in this chapter.

Skills Number	Task	Step	Icon	Keyboard Shortcut
1	Start Office applications	Display Start menu or screen, and then type application name	⊞	
2	Open a template	Start the application; or if already started: File tab → New		
4	Create a new folder while saving	Save As dialog box toolbar → New folder		
4	Save	Quick Access toolbar → Save	💾	Ctrl + S
5	Change a font	Home tab → Font group → Font arrow	Calibri (Body) ▾	Ctrl + Shift + F
5	Apply italic	Home tab → Font group → Italic	*I*	Ctrl + I
5, 8	Change font color	Home tab → Font group → Font Color arrow	A ▾	
5, 8	Change background color	Home tab → Font group → Fill Color arrow	▾	
5, 8, 9, 10	Apply a theme	Design tab → Themes		
5, 8, 9, 10	Change font size	Home tab → Font group → Font Size arrow	11 ▾	Ctrl + Ctrl + >
5, 10	Apply bold	Home tab → Font group → Bold	**B**	Ctrl + B
6, 7, 9, 10	Preview the printed page	File tab → Print		Alt + Ctrl + I
7	Open a file	File tab → Open		Ctrl + O
7, 9, 10	Save a file with new name and location	File tab → Save As		F12
8	Center align text	Home tab → Paragraph group → Center	☰	Ctrl + E
9	Copy	Select text or object → Home tab → Clipboard group → Copy	▤	Ctrl + C
9	Paste	Home tab → Clipboard group → Paste	▥	Ctrl + V

Key Terms

Matching

Match each term in the second column with its correct definition in the first column by writing the letter of the term on the blank line in front of the correct definition.

H 1. An individual page in a presentation that can contain text, pictures, or other objects.

I 2. A pre-built document into which you insert text using the layout and formatting provided in that document.

A 3. A mode applied to documents that limits formatting and features to ones that are supported in earlier versions of Office.

C 4. To insert, delete, or replace text in an Office document, workbook, or presentation.

J 5. A pre-built set of unified formatting choices including colors, fonts, and effects.

E 6. To change the appearance of text.

D 7. A set of characters with the same design and shape.

F 8. A feature that displays the result of a formatting change if you select it.

G 9. A view applied to documents downloaded from the Internet that allows you to decide if the content is safe before working with the document.

B 10. A command that moves a copy of the selected text or object to the Office clipboard.

A Compatibility
B Copy
C Edit
D Font
E Format
F Live Preview
G Protected
H Slide
I Template
J Theme

Multiple Choice

Choose the correct answer.

1. The flashing vertical line that indicates where text will be inserted when you start typing.
   A. Cell reference
   B. Insertion point
   C. KeyTip

2. A reserved, formatted space into which you enter your own text or object.
   A. Gallery
   B. Placeholder
   C. Title

3. Until you save a document, the document is stored here.
   A. Office Clipboard
   B. Live Preview
   C. RAM

4. A collection of pages on the File tab used to open, save, print, and perform other file management tasks.
   A. Backstage view
   B. Page Layout view
   C. File gallery

5. A temporary storage area that holds text or an object that has been cut or copied.
   A. Office Clipboard
   B. Dialog box
   C. Live Preview

6. A toolbar with common formatting buttons that displays after you select text.
   A. Gallery toolbar
   B. Mini toolbar
   C. Taskbar toolbar

7. A command that inserts a copy of the text or object from the Office Clipboard.
   A. Copy
   B. Insert
   C. Paste

8. A visual display of choices—typically thumbnails—from which you can choose.
   A. Gallery
   B. Options menu
   C. Shortcut menu

9. A tab that displays on the Ribbon only when a related object such as a graphic or chart is selected.
   A. Contextual tab
   B. File tab
   C. Page Layout tab

10. A database object that presents tables or query results in a way that is optimized for onscreen viewing or printing.
    A. Form
    B. Report
    C. Table

Topics for Discussion

1. You have briefly worked with four Microsoft Office programs: Word, Excel, PowerPoint, and Access. Based on your experience, describe the overall purpose of each program.

2. Many believe that computers enable offices to go paperless—that is, to share files electronically instead of printing and then distributing them. What are the advantages of sharing files electronically, and in what situations is it best to print documents?

Skills Review

To complete this project, you will need the following files:

- cf01_SRData (Access)
- cf01_SRChart (Excel)
- cf01_SRSlide (PowerPoint)

You will save your files as:

- **Last_First_cf01_SRData (Access)**
- **Last_First_cf01_SRChart (Excel)**
- **Last_First_cf01_SRSlide (PowerPoint)**
- **Last_First_cf01_SRMemo (Word)**

1. Start **Access 2013**, and then click **Open Other Files**. Click **Computer**, and then click **Browse**. In the **Open** dialog box, navigate to the student data files for this chapter, click **cf01_SRData**, and then click **Open**.

2. On the **File tab**, click **Save As**, and then click the **Save As** button. In the **Save As** dialog box, navigate to your chapter folder. Name the file Last_First_cf01_SRData, and then click **Save**. If necessary, enable the content.

3. In the **Navigation** pane, double-click **Budget Report**, and then click the **View** button to switch to Layout view. On the **Design tab**, click **Themes**, and then click **Retrospect**.

4. Click the **View arrow**, click **Print Preview**, and then compare your screen with **Figure 1**. If you are printing this project, print the report.

5. Click **Save**, **Close** the report, and then **Close** Access.

6. Start **Excel 2013**, and then click **Open Other Workbooks**. Use the **Open** page to locate and open the student data file **cf01_SRChart**.

7. On the **File tab**, click **Save As**. Click **Browse**, and then navigate to your chapter folder. Name the file Last_First_cf01_SRChart and then click **Save**.

8. With the worksheet title selected, on the **Home tab**, in the **Font group**, click the **Font Size arrow**, and then click **24**.

9. Click cell **B7**, type 84.3 Press ⌅Enter, and then click **Save**.

10. Click the border of the chart, and then compare your screen with **Figure 2**.

Figure 1

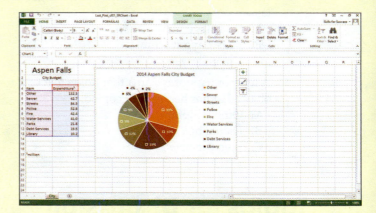

Figure 2

■ Continue to the next page to complete this Skills Review ➤

11. On the **Home tab**, in the **Clipboard group**, click the **Copy** button.

12. Close the **Excel** window, and then start **PowerPoint 2013**. Click **Open Other Presentations**, and then open the student data file **cf01_SRSlide**.

13. On the **File tab**, click **Save As**. Click **Browse**, and then navigate to your chapter folder. Name the file Last_First_cf01_SRSlide and then click **Save**.

14. On the **Home tab**, in the **Clipboard group**, click **Paste** to insert the chart.

15. On the **Design tab**, in the **Themes group**, click the seventh choice—**Retrospect**. Compare your screen with **Figure 3**.

16. If you are printing this project, on the File tab, click Print, change the Settings to Handouts, 1 Slide, and then print the handout.

17. Click **Save**, and then **Close** PowerPoint.

18. Start **Word 2013**. On the Start screen, in the **Search for online templates** box, type memo and then click the **Start searching** button. Locate the **Memo (Elegant design)**, click its thumbnail, and then click the **Create** button to open it.

19. Click *[RECIPIENT NAME]*, and then type Janet Neal

20. Change *[YOUR NAME]* to your own name, and then change *[SUBJECT]* to City Budget

21. Change *[CLICK TO SELECT DATE]* to the current date, and then change *[NAME]* to Maria Martinez

22. Change *[Type your memo text here]* to the following: I am pleased to tell you that the city budget items that you requested are ready. I will send you the Access report and PowerPoint slide today.

23. Click to the left of *INTEROFFICE* and then press Delete several times to delete the word and the space following it.

24. On the **Design tab**, click the **Themes** button, and then click **Retrospect**.

25. Double-click the word *MEMORANDUM* to select it. On the Mini toolbar, click the **Font Color arrow**, and then click the fifth color—**Orange, Accent 1**.

26. With *MEMORANDUM* still selected, on the Mini toolbar, click the **Bold** button one time to remove the bold formatting from the selection, and then change the **Font Size** to **24**.

27. Click **Save**, click **Browse**, and then navigate to your chapter folder. Name the file Last_First_cf01_SRMemo and then click **Save**. In the compatibility message, click **OK**. Click a blank area of the document, and then compare your screen with **Figure 4**.

28. If you are printing your work, print the memo.

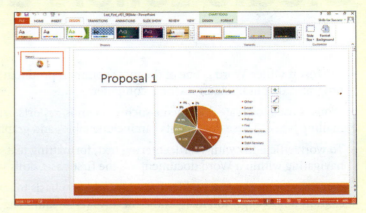

Figure 3

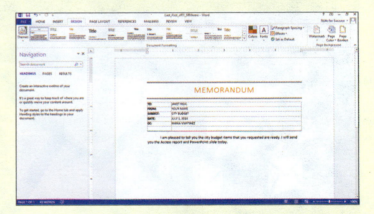

Figure 4

29. Click **Save**, and then **Close** the memo. Submit your printouts or files as directed by your instructor.

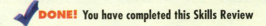 **DONE! You have completed this Skills Review**

Create Letters and Memos

- ► Microsoft Office Word is one of the most common productivity programs that individuals use on a computer.

- ► Word is used to create documents such as memos, reports, letters, and mailing labels. These documents can include tables and graphics.

- ► To work efficiently with Word, entering text, formatting text, and navigating within a Word document are the first basic skills you need.

- ► You can change the font and font size and add emphasis to text, but use caution not to apply too many different formats to your text. This can be distracting to the reader.

- ► It is never acceptable to have errors in spelling, grammar, or word usage in your documents; you can use Word spelling and grammar tools to prevent this.

- ► Business letters and memos are often structured and formatted in a formal manner as described in *The Gregg Reference Manual* by William A. Sabin.

© Julien Eichinger

Aspen Falls City Hall

In this chapter, you will assist Evelyn Stone, Human Resources Director, to create a letter to Dr. George Gato of Aspen Falls Community College. The purpose of the letter is to establish an internship program between City Hall and the students in the Information Systems Department chaired by Dr. Gato.

Microsoft Word is used often to write business letters and memos. You can quickly type, edit, and format text. Because business communication documents should be free of mistakes, spelling and grammar errors are flagged as you type. Most businesses apply a standard business letter format to all letters coming from the organization.

In this project, you will write a one-page business letter using the block style as defined by *The Gregg Reference Manual* by William A. Sabin. The **block style**, also called the **full-block style**, typically begins all lines at the left margin except for letterheads, tables, and block quotes. You will add a second page detailing the various internship positions available with City Hall.

Time to complete all 10
skills – 60 to 75 minutes

Student data file needed for this chapter:

wrd01_InternPositions

You will save your files as:

Last_First_wrd01_Interns (Word)
Last_First_wrd01_Interns (PDF)

Outcome

Using the skills in this chapter, you will be able to
work with Word documents like this:

> **ASPEN FALLS HUMAN RESOURCES**
> *500 S Aspen Street*
> *Aspen Falls, CA 93463*
>
> May 8, 2014
>
> Dr. George Gato
> Aspen Falls Community College
> 1 College Drive
> Aspen Falls, CA 93464
>
> Dear Dr. Gato
>
> Subject: City Hall Internships
>
> Thank you so much for your letter offering the services of your Information Systems Department
> students. We currently have several projects that might benefit both us and your students.
>
> I have attached a description of the positions we are currently seeking. Please call City Hall at (805) 555-
> 1016 to discuss this further.
>
> We have several positions open for students with skills in the four Office applications: Word, Excel,
> PowerPoint, and Access. We also need students capable of working with our IT Services Help Desk.
>
> Sincerely,
>
> Evelyn Stone, Human Resources Director
>
> Last_First_wrd01_Interns

SKILLS

Skills 1-10 Training

At the end of this chapter you will be able to:

Skill 1 Type Letter Text
Skill 2 Apply Styles and Set Grammar and Spelling Options
Skill 3 Select and Insert Text
Skill 4 Copy, Cut, and Paste Text
Skill 5 Check Spelling and Grammar
Skill 6 Check Writing Style and Insert Synonyms
Skill 7 Use Format Painter
Skill 8 Apply Advanced Font Settings
Skill 9 Create Document Footers
Skill 10 Save Documents as PDF Files

MORE SKILLS

Skill 11 Prepare Documents for Distribution
Skill 12 Insert Screen Shots into Documents
Skill 13 Split and Arrange Windows
Skill 14 Insert Symbols

▶ When working with Word documents, a paragraph can be a single line containing a heading or several lines of sentences.

▶ To see where paragraphs begin and end, it is helpful to display *formatting marks*—characters that display in your document to represent nonprinting characters such as paragraphs, spaces, and tabs.

1. Start **Word 2013**, and then on the start screen, click **Blank document**.

2. On the **Home tab**, in the **Paragraph group**, click the **Show/Hide** button ¶ to display the nonprinting formatting marks, as shown in **Figure 1**. If the Navigation pane is open, Close ☒ it.

   The Show/Hide button is a *toggle button*—a button used to turn a feature both on and off. The paragraph mark (¶) indicates the end of a paragraph and will not print.

   Because many elements in the Word window adjust to your monitor size and personal settings, you may need to change your window size, exit Reading Mode, or disable Full Screen Mode to match the figures in this book.

3. With the insertion point in the blank paragraph, type Aspen Falls Human Resources and press Enter. Type 500 S Aspen Street and press Enter. Type Aspen Falls, CA 93463 and press Enter two times.

4. Type May 8, 2014 Press Enter three times, and then compare your screen with **Figure 2**.

   The letter has eight paragraphs—three for the letterhead, one for the date, and four blank paragraphs.

■ **Continue to the next page to complete the skill**

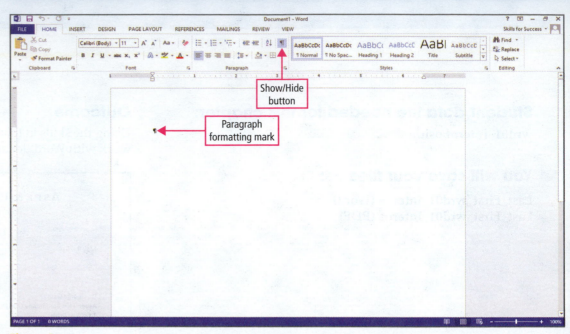

Figure 1

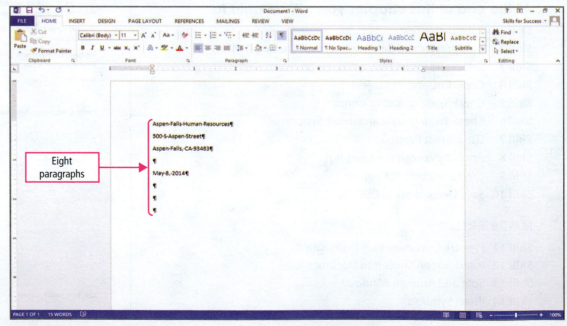

Figure 2

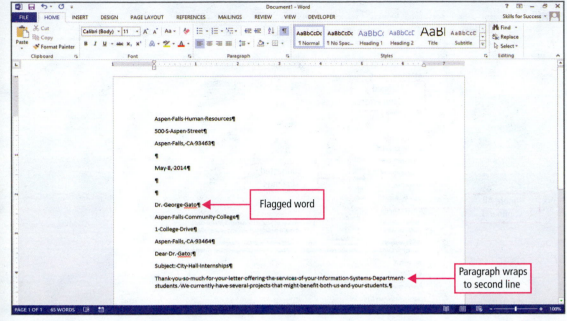

Flagged word

Paragraph wraps to second line

Figure 3

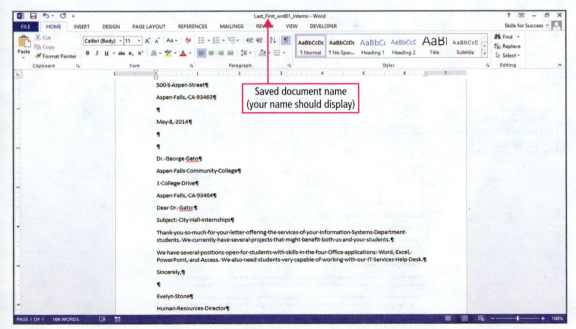

Saved document name (your name should display)

Figure 4

5. Type Dr. George Gato and press [Enter]; type Aspen Falls Community College and press [Enter]; type 1 College Drive and press [Enter]; and type Aspen Falls, CA 93464 and press [Enter].

   The word *Gato* is flagged as a spelling error, but it is spelled correctly.

6. Type Dear Dr. Gato: and press [Enter]. Type Subject: City Hall Internships and press [Enter].

7. Type the following, inserting only one space after each sentence: Thank you so much for your letter offering the services of your Information Systems Department students. We currently have several projects that might benefit both us and your students. Compare your screen with **Figure 3**.

8. Press [Enter], and then type We have several positions open for students with skills in the four Office applications: Word, Excel, PowerPoint, and Access. We also need students very capable of working with our IT Services Help Desk.

9. Press [Enter] and type Sincerely, and then press [Enter] two times. Type Evelyn Stone Press [Enter], and then type Human Resources Director

10. Click **Save** [💾], and then on the **Save As** page, click the location and folder where you are saving your work. If necessary, click Browse.

11. In the **Save As** dialog box, click **New folder**, type Word Chapter 1 and then press [Enter] two times to open the new folder. Name the file Last_First_wrd01_Interns Click **Save**, and then compare your screen with **Figure 4**.

- **You have completed Skill 1 of 10**

▶ You can format text quickly by applying *styles*—pre-built collections of formatting settings that can be assigned to text.

▶ During the writing process, it is a good idea to look for *flagged errors*—wavy lines indicating spelling or grammar errors. You can right-click these flagged errors to see a list of suggestions for fixing them.

1. In the inside address, right-click the word *Gato*, and then compare your screen with **Figure 1**.

   Red wavy lines indicate words that have been flagged as possible spelling errors, and the shortcut menu provides suggested spellings.

2. From the shortcut menu, click **Ignore All**, and verify that both instances of the word *Gato* are no longer flagged as spelling errors.

3. Hold down [Ctrl], and then press [Home], to move the insertion point to the beginning of the document.

4. Move the pointer to the left of the first line of the document to display the [↗] pointer. Drag down to select the first two lines of the document. On the **Home tab**, in the **Styles group**, click the **No Spacing** thumbnail. Compare your screen with **Figure 2**.

   The Normal style has extra space after each paragraph. The No Spacing style does not apply this extra space after each paragraph, and the extra space between the lines of the letterhead have been removed.

■ Continue to the next page to complete the skill ▶

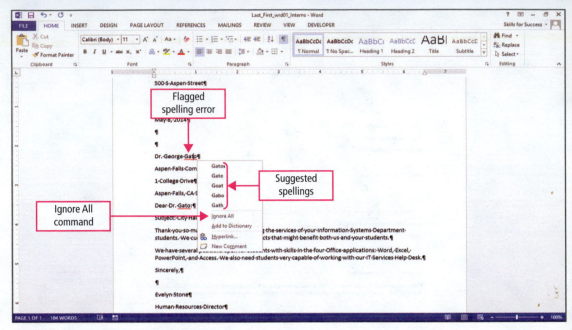

Figure 1

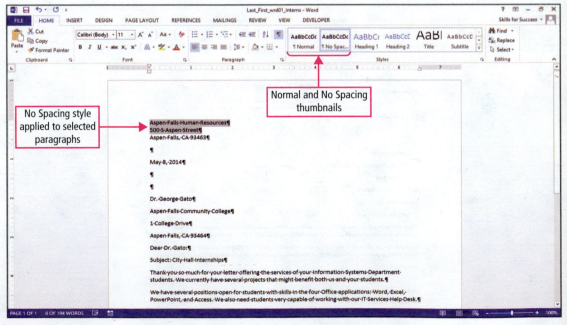

Figure 2

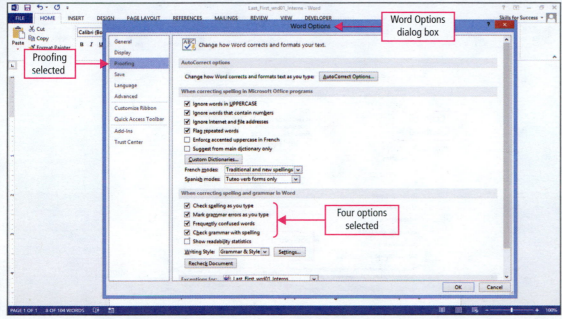

Figure 3

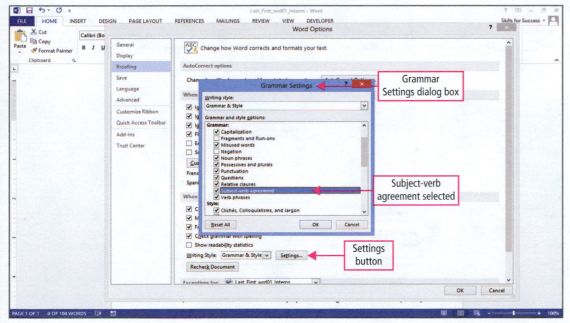

Figure 4

5. Click the **File tab**, and then click **Options**. On the left pane of the **Word Options** dialog box, click **Proofing**.

6. Under **When correcting spelling and grammar in Word**, verify that the first four check boxes are selected as shown in **Figure 3**.

7. To the right of **Writing Style**, click the **Settings** button. In the **Grammar Settings** dialog box, under **Writing style**, be sure that **Grammar Only** is selected.

8. In the **Grammar Settings** dialog box, scroll down to display all the **Grammar** options. Select the **Subject-verb agreement** check box. Compare your screen with **Figure 4**, and then click **OK**.

   In this manner you can customize the types of errors that should be flagged as you work with a document. At the end of this project, you will return the grammar and spelling options back to their original settings.

9. Click **OK** to close the **Word Options** dialog box.

10. Click the **Save** button 🖫. Alternately, press Ctrl + S.

■ **You have completed Skill 2 of 10**

▶ WRD 1-3
VIDEO

► You can select a single word by double-clicking and a single paragraph by triple-clicking.

► The amount of space between letter elements is specified by the style rules that your letter is following.

1. Click anywhere in the first paragraph of the document, *Aspen Falls Human Resources*.

2. On the **Home tab**, in the **Paragraph group**, click the **Center** button to center the paragraph.

   When you apply paragraph formatting, you do not need to select the paragraph. However, to apply paragraph formatting to two or more paragraphs at the same time, you will need to select all the paragraphs.

3. Repeat the technique just practiced to center the letterhead's second and third lines.

4. In the paragraph that begins *We have*, in the second sentence, point to the word *very*, and then double-click to select the word and display the Mini toolbar. Compare your screen with **Figure 1**.

5. With the word *very* selected, press Delete.

   When you double-click to select and delete a word, the selected word is deleted, along with the space following the word.

6. Move the insertion point in the margin to the left of *Dr. George Gato*. When the pointer displays, drag straight down to select the paragraph and the two paragraphs below it. With the three paragraphs selected, on the **Home tab**, in the **Styles group**, click the **No Spacing** thumbnail. Compare your screen with **Figure 2**.

■ **Continue to the next page to complete the skill** ➤

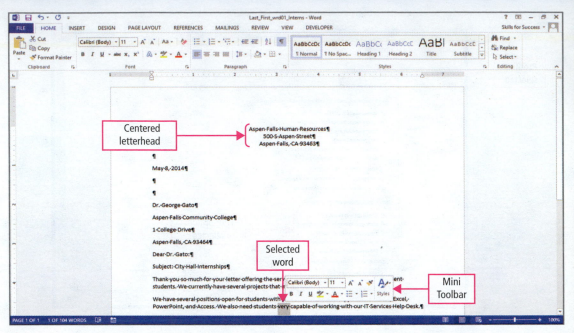

Figure 1

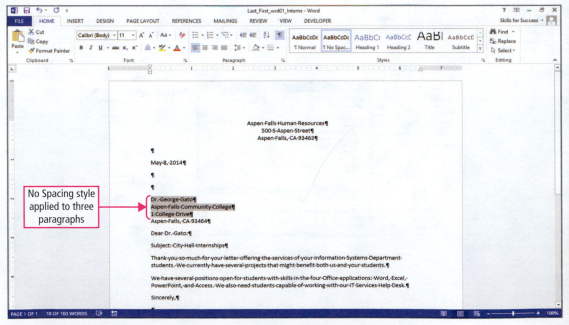

Figure 2

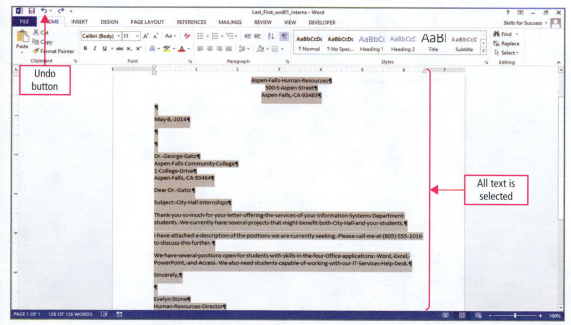

Figure 3

Undo button

All text is selected

Figure 4

7. Triple-click the signature, *Evelyn Stone,* to select the paragraph, and then apply the **No Spacing** style.

8. In the paragraph that begins *Thank you,* double-click the word *us* to select it, and then type City Hall

9. In the paragraph that begins *Thank you,* click to position the insertion point at the end of the paragraph—following the period after *students.*

10. Press Enter one time, and then type I have attached a description of the positions we are currently seeking. Please call me at (805) 555-1016 to discuss this further. Compare your screen with **Figure 3**.

11. On the **Home tab**, in the **Editing group**, click **Select**, and then click **Select All** to select all of the text in the document. Alternately, press Ctrl + A.

12. On the **Home tab**, in the **Font group**, click the **Font arrow**. Scroll down the list of fonts, and then click **Cambria**.

13. Press Ctrl + Home, and then on the Quick Access Toolbar, click the **Undo** button one time to change the font back to Calibri. Compare your screen with **Figure 4**.

As you work with a document, you need to be aware when text is selected. For example, if you start typing when the entire document is selected, all the text will be replaced with whatever new text you type. You can use the Undo button to fix this type of mistake.

14. Click anywhere in the document to deselect the text, and then **Save** the changes.

■ **You have completed Skill 3 of 10**

WRD 1-4
VIDEO

▶ The copy command places a copy of the selected text or object in the *clipboard*—a temporary storage area that holds text or an object that has been cut or copied.

1. Press [Ctrl] + [End] to move the insertion point to the end of the document.

2. Click the **Page Layout tab**. In the **Page Setup group**, click **Breaks**, and then click **Page**. Alternately, press [Ctrl] + [Enter]. Compare your screen with **Figure 1**.

 A *manual page break*—forcing a page to end at a location you specify—is added at the end of Page 1.

3. On the **File tab**, click **Open**. On the **Open** page, click **Computer**, and then click the **Browse** button.

4. In the **Open** dialog box, navigate to the student files for this chapter. Click **wrd01_InternPositions**, and then click **Open**.

5. On the **Home tab**, in the **Editing group**, click **Select**, and then click **Select All**.

6. With the text selected, on the **Home tab**, in the **Clipboard group**, click the **Copy** button. Alternately, press [Ctrl] + [C].

7. On the taskbar, point to the **Word** button [W]. Click the **Last_First_wrd01_Interns** thumbnail to make it the active window.

8. With the insertion point still at the end of the document, click the **Home tab**. In the **Clipboard group**, click the **Paste arrow**, and then compare your screen with **Figure 2**.

 The Paste button has two parts—the Paste button and the Paste arrow that displays paste options.

■ **Continue to the next page to complete the skill** ➤

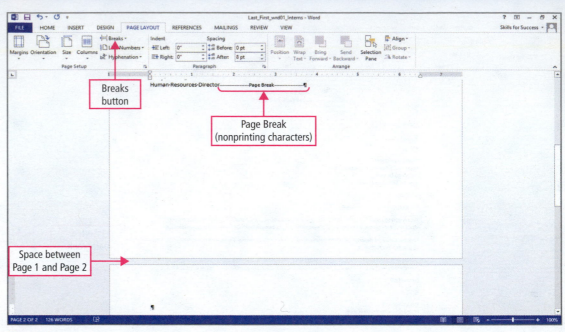

Figure 1

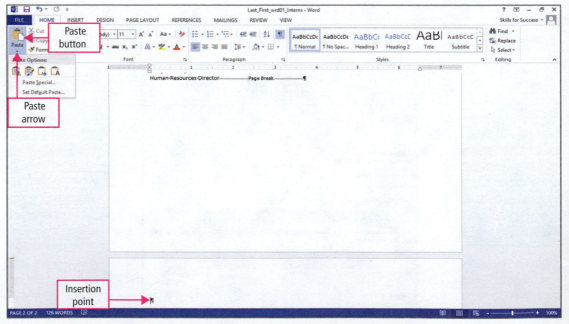

Figure 2

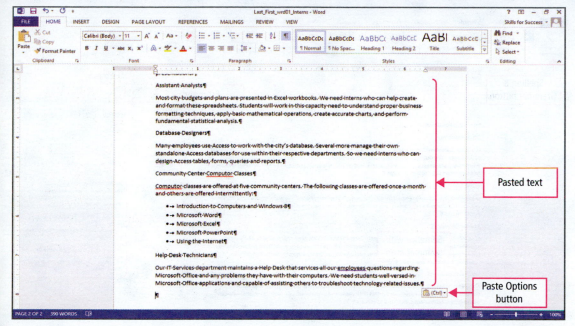

Figure 3

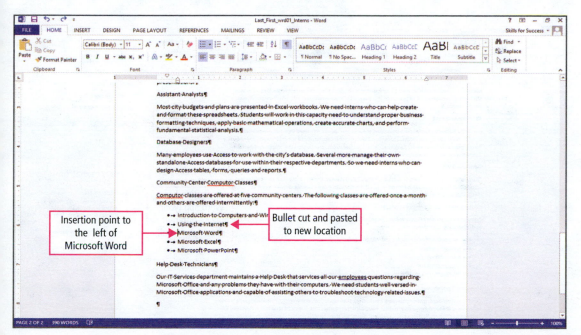

Figure 4

9. Click the **Paste** button, and then compare your screen with **Figure 3**.

   When you paste, you insert a copy of the text or object stored in the clipboard and the Paste Options button displays near the pasted text. The spelling and grammar errors in the pasted text will be corrected in the next skill.

10. Press ⎋Esc to hide the Paste Options button. In the bulleted text, select the paragraph *Using the Internet* including the paragraph mark.

11. On the **Home tab**, in the **Clipboard group**, click the **Cut** button. Alternately, press ⎈Ctrl + X.

    The *cut* command deletes the selected text or object and places a copy in the Office clipboard.

12. In the bulleted list, click to place the insertion point to the left of the text *Microsoft Word* and to the right of the bullet and tab formatting mark. In the **Clipboard group**, click the **Paste** button. Alternately, press ⎈Ctrl + V. Compare your screen with **Figure 4**.

    In this manner, you can move text by cutting it and then pasting it somewhere else.

13. On the taskbar, point to the **Word** button 📘, point to the **wrd01_InternPositions** thumbnail, and then click the thumbnail's **Close** button ❎.

14. Click in the letter document to make it the active window, and then **Save** 💾 the changes.

■ **You have completed Skill 4 of 10**

WRD 1-5 VIDEO

▶ When you are done typing the text of a document, it is a good idea to run the Spelling and Grammar checker to check for potential errors.

1. Press [Ctrl] + [Home] to place the insertion point at the beginning of the document.

2. Click the **Review tab**, and then in the **Proofing group**, click **Spelling & Grammar**. Alternately, press [F7]. Compare your screen with **Figure 1**.

Spelling and grammar errors display in a task pane on the right side of the window. The first error is a grammar error indicating the verb *has* is not in the correct form. The checker suggests that the verb be changed to *have*.

3. In the **Grammar** pane, click the **Change** button to accept the suggested verb form change and move to the next error.

4. In the **Spelling** pane, click the **Delete** button to remove the repeated word *the*, and then compare your screen with **Figure 2**.

When a misspelled word is encountered, you can replace it with one of the suggested spellings or add it to the custom dictionary. Words added to the custom dictionary will not be flagged as spelling errors. If you accidentally add a misspelled word to the dictionary, you can open the dictionary from the Options dialog box and delete the word.

The Spelling task pane often displays definitions to help you decide if the suggested spelling is the correct choice. By signing in to your Microsoft account, you can access additional online dictionaries.

■ **Continue to the next page to complete the skill** ▶

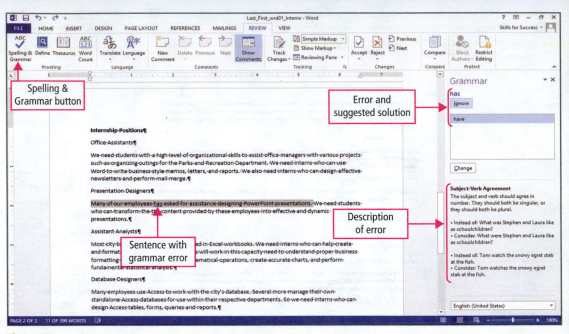

Figure 1

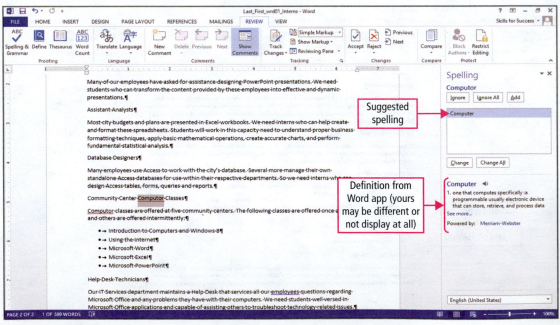

Figure 2

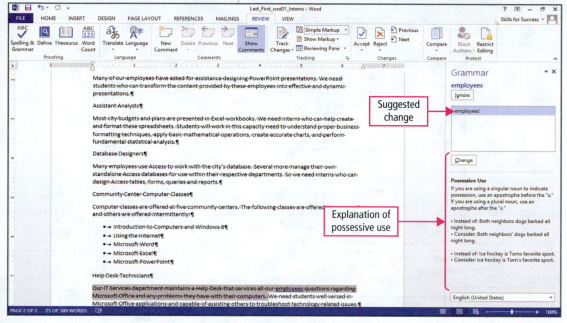

Suggested change

Explanation of possessive use

Figure 3

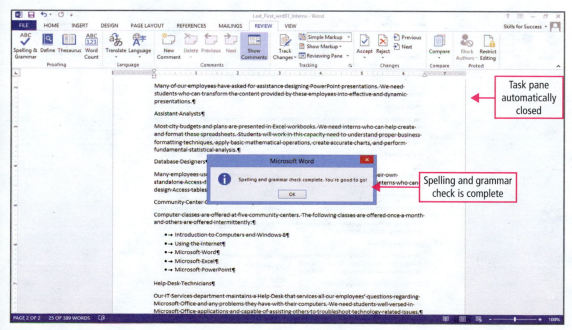

Task pane automatically closed

Spelling and grammar check is complete

Figure 4

5. In the **Spelling** pane, click the **Change All** button to change both instances of the misspelled word, and then compare your screen with **Figure 3**.

Many grammar errors are explained in the Grammar pane so that you can make an informed decision to ignore or accept the suggested change. Here, the word *employees* should have an apostrophe to indicate possessive use.

6. In the **Grammar** pane, click the **Change** button to add the apostrophe, and then compare your screen with **Figure 4**.

When all flagged errors have been changed or ignored, a message displays indicating that the check is complete. If you did not receive this message after completing this step, you may have typing errors, and you should fix them before continuing.

7. In the message indicating that the spelling and grammar check is complete, click **OK**, and then **Save** ⊟ the document.

■ **You have completed Skill 5 of 10**

WRD 1-6
VIDEO

▶ To help improve your writing style, you use the Style Checker to find weaknesses in your writing style. You can also insert synonyms.

1. On the **File tab**, click **Options**. In the **Word Options** dialog box, click **Proofing** to display the spelling and grammar options.

2. Click the **Writing Style arrow**, and then click **Grammar & Style**. Compare your screen with **Figure 1**.

3. In the **Word Options** dialog box, click the **Recheck Document** button. Read the message that displays, click **Yes**, and then click **OK**.

4. Press Ctrl + Home, and then notice that *Gato* is again flagged as a potential spelling error.

   By clicking the Recheck Document button, you can run the Spelling & Grammar checker again and previously ignored errors will again be flagged.

5. Scroll as needed to display the heading *Assistant Analysts* on Page 2. Right-click the flagged words *are presented*, and then from the shortcut menu, click **Ignore Once**.

   Although passive voice is not a grammar error, too much use of passive voice weakens your writing. Some instances can be ignored.

6. Under the heading *Database Designers*, right-click the word *So*, and then compare your screen with **Figure 2**.

7. From the shortcut menu, click **Therefore**, to correct the style error.

8. Under the heading *Community Center Computer Classes*, right-click to read the first error message, and then press Esc to close the shortcut menu.

■ Continue to the next page to complete the skill

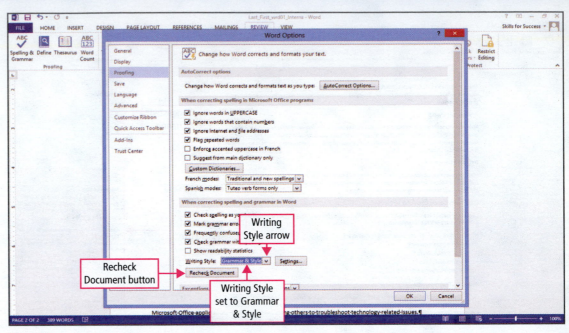

Figure 1

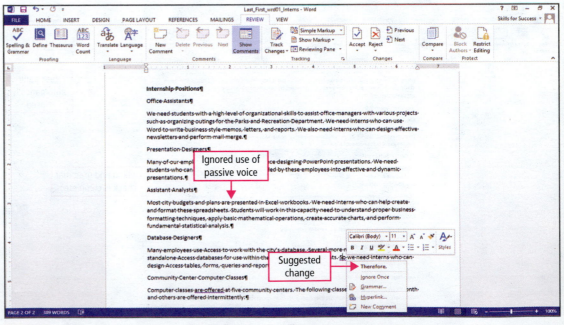

Figure 2

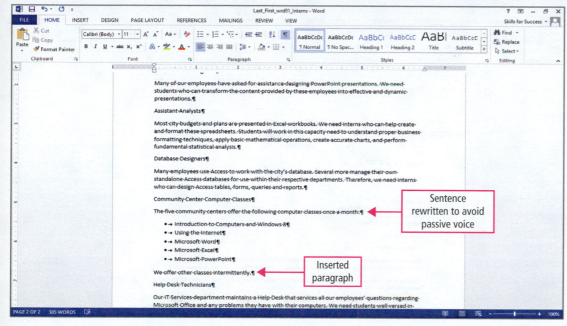

Sentence rewritten to avoid passive voice

Inserted paragraph

Figure 3

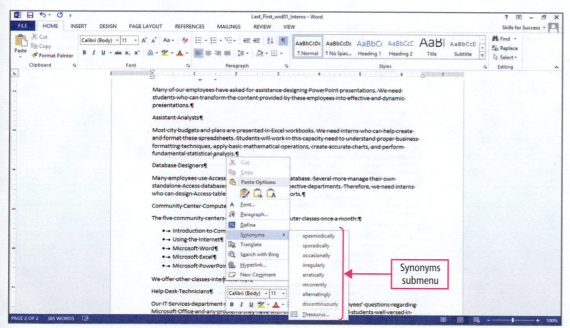

Synonyms submenu

Figure 4

9. Point to the left of the paragraph starting *Computer classes are offered,* and then when the pointer displays, double-click to select the entire paragraph.

10. With the entire paragraph selected, type the following: The five community centers offer the following computer classes once a month: to remove the two instances of passive voice.

11. In the bulleted list, click to the right of *PowerPoint,* and then press Enter. On the **Home tab,** in the **Styles group,** click **Normal** to apply the default document formatting. Type We offer other classes intermittently. and then compare your screen with **Figure 3.**

12. Right-click the word *intermittently,* and then from the shortcut menu, point to **Synonyms.** Compare your screen with **Figure 4.**

    The Synonyms command displays a submenu with alternate word choices. In this manner, Word Thesaurus can be accessed quickly. A ***thesaurus*** lists words that have the same or similar meaning to the word you are looking up.

13. From the **Synonyms** submenu, click **occasionally** to replace the word *intermittently.*

14. Open the **Word Options** dialog box, display the **Proofing** options, and then change the **Writing Style** to **Grammar Only.**

15. Click the **Settings** button, and then in the **Grammar Settings** dialog box, click **Reset All.** Click **OK** two times to close all open dialog boxes.

16. **Save** your work.

■ **You have completed Skill 6 of 10**

▶ Formatting document text should help organize the document visually without detracting from its message.

▶ A set of formatting choices can be applied with Format Painter quickly and consistently.

1. Select the first paragraph of the letterhead, *Aspen Falls Human Resources*. On the **Home tab**, in the **Font group**, click the **Font Size arrow**, and then click **16**.

2. With the first paragraph still selected, click the **Font arrow**, click **Cambria**, and then apply **Bold** [B].

3. In the letterhead, drag to select the two paragraphs beginning with *500* and ending with *93463*. In the **Font group**, click the **Italic** button [I], and then compare your screen with **Figure 1**.

4. In the letterhead, click in the text *Aspen Falls Human Resources*. On the **Home tab**, in the **Clipboard group**, click the **Format Painter** button [icon].

5. Press [PageDown] as needed to display the top of Page 2. With the [icon] icon, drag through the heading *Internship Positions*. Compare your screen with **Figure 2**, and then release the left mouse button.

   In this manner you can copy a collection of formatting settings to other text in the document. When you release the left mouse button, Format Painter will no longer be active.

■ **Continue to the next page to complete the skill**

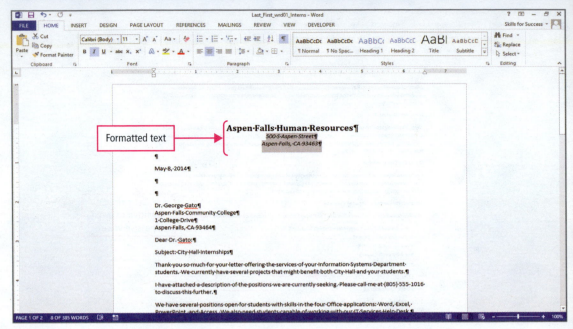

Formatted text

Figure 1

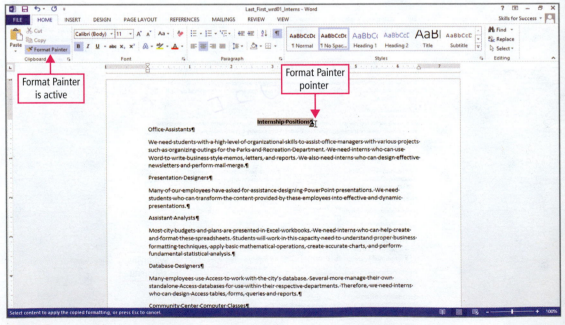

Format Painter is active

Format Painter pointer

Figure 2

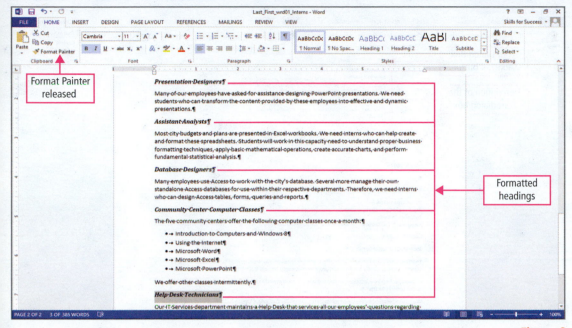

> Format Painter released

> Formatted headings

Figure 3

6. Near the top of Page 2, select the heading *Office Assistants,* and then apply the **Cambria** font, **Bold** B , and **Italic** I .

7. With the heading *Office Assistants* still selected, in the **Clipboard group**, double-click the **Format Painter** button . Drag through the *Presentation Designers* heading, and then notice that Format Painter remains active.

8. Drag through the *Assistant Analysts* heading to apply the formatting, and then repeat this technique to apply the formatting to the three remaining headings on Page 2.

9. In the **Clipboard group**, click the **Format Painter** button to release it, and then compare your screen with **Figure 3**.

    In this manner you can use Format Painter multiple times to format headings and other document elements. You can also release Format Painter by pressing Esc , clicking Undo, or pressing Ctrl + Z .

10. **Save** the document, and then take a moment to review the common formatting options as described in the table in **Figure 4**.

■ **You have completed Skill 7 of 10**

Common Formatting Options

Format	Description
Font	A set of characters with a common design.
Font size	The size of the characters typically measured in points.
Bold	Extra thickness applied to characters to emphasize text.
Italic	A slant applied to characters to emphasize text.
Underline	A line under characters used to emphasize text.
Text effects	A set of decorative formatting applied to characters.
Highlight color	Shading applied to the background of characters.
Font color	The color applied to the characters.

Figure 4

▶ Dialog boxes often contain commands that are not on the Ribbon. Many of these dialog boxes can by launched from their Ribbon group. For example, the Font dialog box can be opened by clicking the Dialog Box Launcher button in the Font group.

1. At the beginning of the letter, select the first paragraph, *Aspen Falls Human Resources*.

2. On the **Home tab**, in the **Font group**, point to—do not click—the **Font Dialog Box Launcher** , and then compare your screen with **Figure 1**.

> When you point to a Dialog Box Launcher button, the name of the dialog box and the name of the keyboard shortcut that opens it display. A thumbnail of the dialog box displays next to its description.

3. Click the **Font Dialog Box Launcher** button to open the Font dialog box.

4. In the **Font dialog** box, under **Font style**, click **Regular** to remove the Bold font style.

5. Under **Effects**, select the **Small caps** check box, and then compare your screen with **Figure 2**.

> The *small caps* effect displays all characters in uppercase while making any character originally typed as an uppercase letter taller than the ones typed as lowercase characters. Small caps is an alternate to using bold or italic to emphasize text. A preview of the effect displays at the bottom of the Font dialog box.

■ **Continue to the next page to complete the skill**

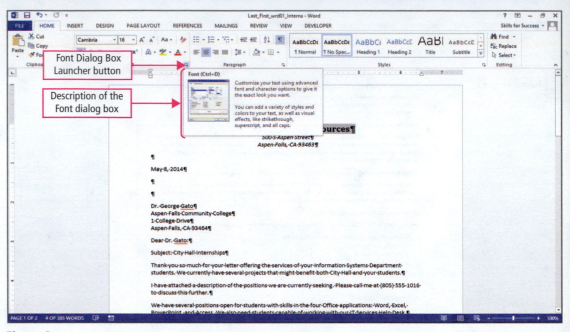

Figure 1

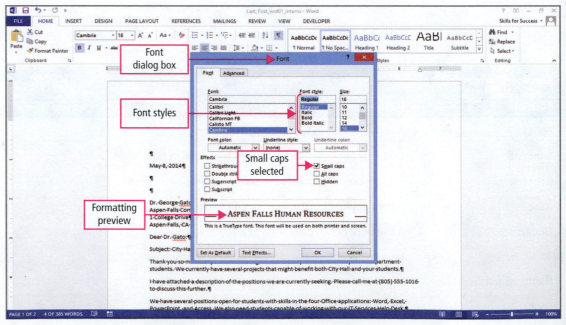

Figure 2

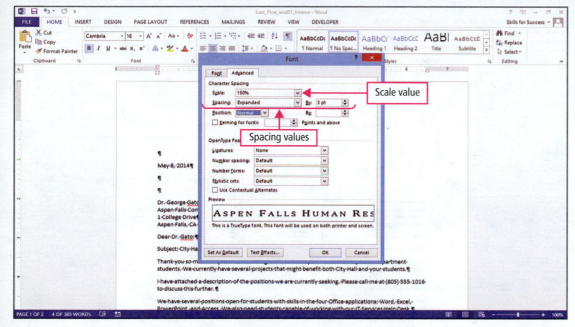

Figure 3

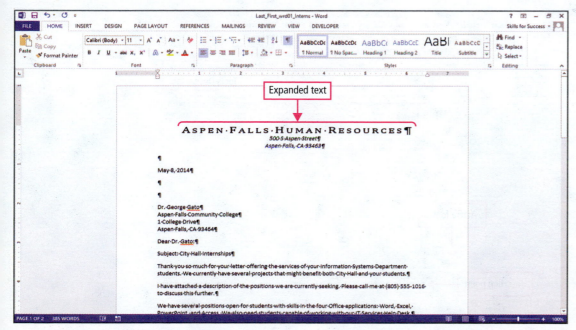

Figure 4

6. In the **Font** dialog box, click the **Advanced tab**.

7. On the **Advanced tab** of the **Font** dialog box, under **Character Spacing**, click the **Scale arrow**, and then click **150%**.

8. Under **Character Spacing**, click the **Spacing arrow**, and then click **Expanded**.

9. To the right of **Spacing**, in the **By** box, replace the value *1 pt* with *3 pt*.

10. Press Tab, and then compare your screen with **Figure 3**.

   Font sizes and the spacing between characters are measured in *points*—a unit of measure with 72 points per inch. Here, the characters will have an additional 3 points of space between them.

11. Click **OK** to accept the changes and close the dialog box.

12. Click anywhere in the document to deselect the text, and then compare your screen with **Figure 4**.

   An organization's letterhead is typically formatted differently than the rest of the letter to make it stand out. Here, the text is centered and the department's name has been expanded and stretched.

13. **Save** 💾 the document.

■ **You have completed Skill 8 of 10**

WRD 1-9
VIDEO

▶ A *header* and *footer* are reserved areas for text, graphics, and fields that display at the top (header) or bottom (footer) of each page in a document.

▶ You can insert a built-in header or footer, or you can create your own custom header or footer.

▶ Throughout this book, you will insert the document file name in the footer of each document.

1. Press ⟨Ctrl⟩ + ⟨Home⟩ to move to the beginning of the document. On the **Insert tab**, in the **Header & Footer group**, click the **Footer** button.

2. In the **Footer** gallery, scroll down the gallery of built-in footers, and then compare your screen with **Figure 1**.

   You can quickly insert a footer by selecting a built-in from the Footer gallery.

3. Below the **Footer** gallery, click **Edit Footer**. Notice that at the bottom of Page 1, below **Footer**, the insertion point is blinking in the footer, and the **Design** contextual tab displays on the Ribbon, as shown in **Figure 2**.

   When you want to create or edit your own custom footer, you need to make the footer area active. You can do this using the Edit Footer command or by double-clicking in the footer area.

4. On the **Header & Footer Tools Design tab**, in the **Insert group**, click the **Quick Parts** button. From the displayed list, click **Field**.

   A *field* is a category of data—such as a file name, a page number, or the current date—that can be inserted into a document.

■ **Continue to the next page to complete the skill** ▶

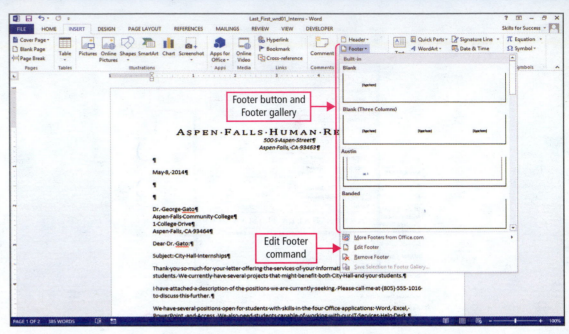

Figure 1

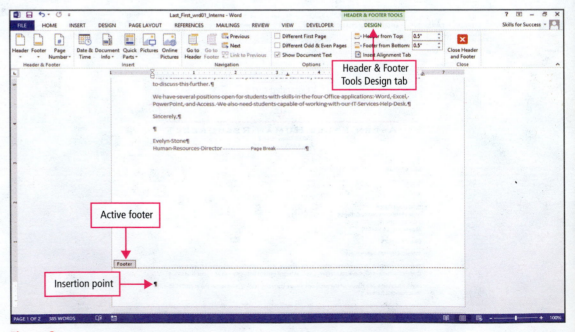

Figure 2

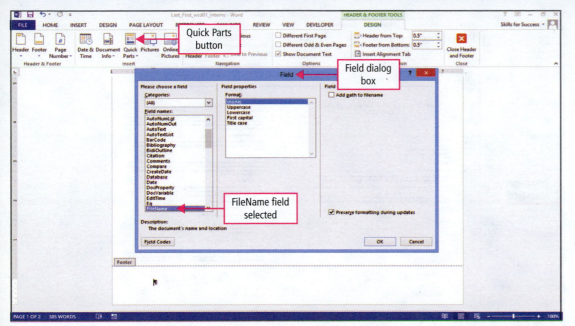

Figure 3

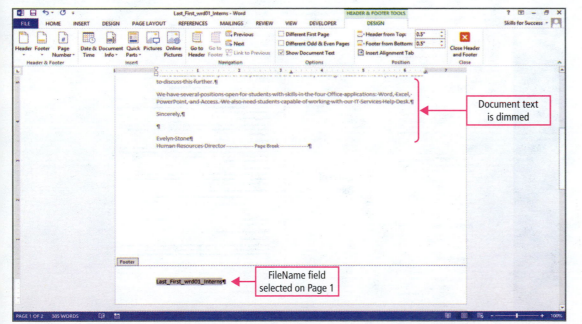

Figure 4

5. Under **Field names**, scroll down to see what types of fields are available, and then click the **FileName** field. Compare your screen with **Figure 3**.

   Spaces between multiple words in field names are removed to create a single word.

6. Under **Format**, be sure that **(none)** is selected, and then at the bottom of the **Field** dialog box, click **OK** to insert the file name in the footer.

7. Scroll to display the bottom of Page 1, click the **FileName** field one time to select it, and then compare your screen with **Figure 4**.

   By default, footers are inserted on each page of the document. When you select a field, it is shaded in gray.

8. On the **Design tab**, click the **Close Header and Footer** button. Scroll to display the bottom of Page 1 and the top of Page 2, and then notice that the header and footer areas are inactive as indicated by the dimmed file name.

   While the document text is active, the footer text cannot be edited. When the footer area is active, the footer text is black, and the document text is dimmed and cannot be edited.

9. Save ⊟ the document.

■ **You have completed Skill 9 of 10**

▶ Before printing, it is a good idea to set the zoom level to view one or more pages without scrolling.

▶ You can save documents in different formats so that people who do not have Word can read them.

1. Press [Ctrl] + [Home] to move to the beginning of the document. On the **Home tab**, in the **Paragraph group**, click the **Show/Hide** button ¶ so that the formatting marks do not display.

   Because formatting marks do not print, hiding them gives you a better idea of how the printed page will look.

2. On the **View tab**, in the **Zoom group**, click **Multiple Pages**, and then compare your screen with **Figure 1**.

   When you zoom to display multiple pages, a best fit is calculated based on your monitor size. Here, two pages are displayed with a zoom level of 52 percent. If you have a different-sized monitor, your zoom percentage may be different.

3. In the **Zoom group**, click the **100%** button to return to your original zoom level.

4. On the **File tab**, click **Print**. On the **Print** page, click the **Next Page** button ▶ to preview Page 2, and then compare your screen with **Figure 2**.

5. If you are printing your work for this project, print the letter. Otherwise, click the **Back** button ⬅.

6. Click **Save** 🖫. Click the **File tab**, and then click **Export**. On the **Export** page, click the **Create PDF/XPS** button.

■ Continue to the next page to complete the skill ➤

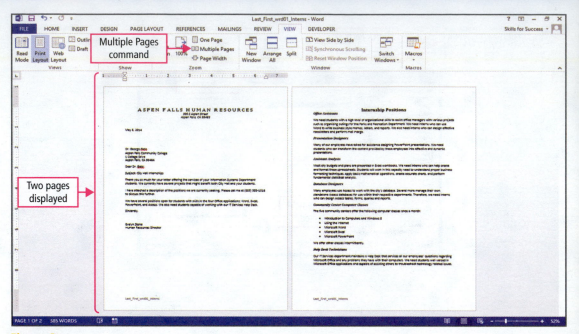

Figure 1

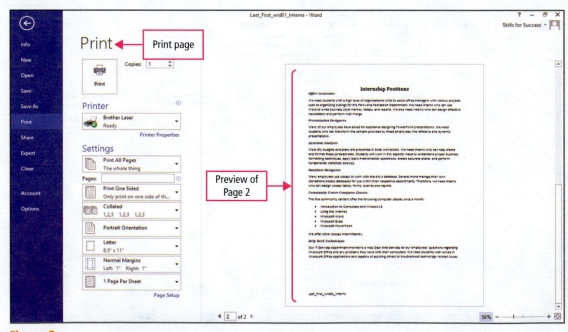

Figure 2

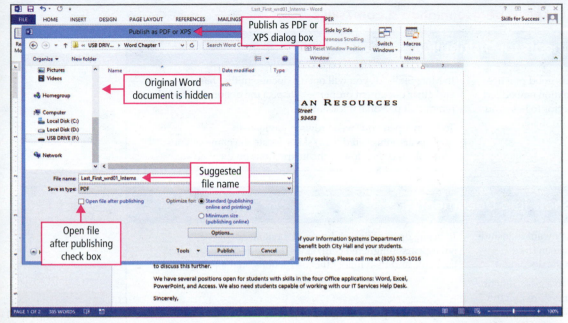

Publish as PDF or XPS dialog box

Original Word document is hidden

Suggested file name

Open file after publishing check box

Figure 3

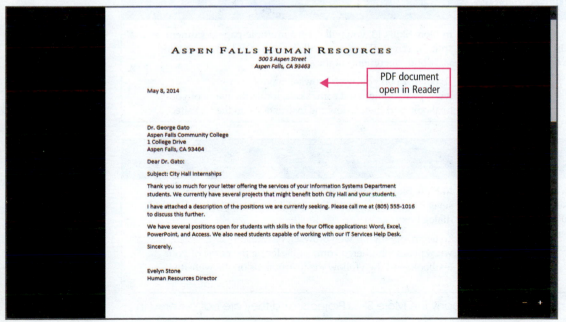

PDF document open in Reader

Figure 4

7. In the **Publish as PDF or XPS** dialog box, navigate to your **Word Chapter 1** folder. Notice that the Word document is not listed and the suggested file name is identical to the Word memo as shown in **Figure 3**.

   A *PDF document* is an image of a document that can be viewed using a PDF reader such as Adobe Acrobat Reader or Windows 8 Reader instead of the application that created the original document.

   Here, you can use the same file name as the Word document because a PDF document file extension will be *.pdf* instead of *.docx*—the file extension assigned to Word documents.

   The Word file is not listed in the dialog box because only files with the extensions .pdf and .xps will be listed. The original Word file is in the folder and will not be altered.

8. Select the **Open file after publishing** check box, and then click **Publish**.

9. Wait a few moments for the document to publish and then open in your default PDF viewer. Compare your screen with **Figure 4**.

10. If your file opened in Reader, press ⊞, and then click the Desktop tile, and then on the taskbar, click the Word button 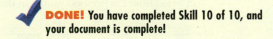 to return to Word. Otherwise, Close your PDF viewer application window.

11. **Close** ☒ the Word letter. If you are prompted to save changes, click Save. Submit your printout or files as directed by your instructor.

✔ **DONE!** You have completed Skill 10 of 10, and your document is complete!

More Skills

The following More Skills are located at **www.pearsonhighered.com/skills**

More Skills Prepare Documents for Distribution

Before sharing a document with colleagues, it is good practice to remove any hidden data or personal information embedded in the document. You can use Document Inspector to help you remove any information that you do not want to share.

In More Skills 11, you will open a document that has comments and other document properties, inspect the document, and then remove all personal information.

To begin, open your web browser, navigate to www.pearsonhighered.com/skills, locate the name of your textbook, and then follow the instructions on the website.

More Skills Insert Screen Shots into Documents

When you are working on a document, you may want to include a screen shot from your computer—such as a screen from another program or a website—as a graphic in the document.

In More Skills 12, you will use a browser to go to a government website, and then create a copy of the screen and store it in the Clipboard. You will then paste the screen into a document.

To begin, open your web browser, navigate to www.pearsonhighered.com/skills, locate the name of your textbook, and then follow the instructions on the website.

More Skills Split and Arrange Windows

You can split the Word screen, which lets you look at different parts of the same document at the same time. In a multiple-page document, this is convenient for viewing both the first page and the last page at the same time. You can also view two different documents side by side and make comparisons between the two.

In More Skills 13, you will open a multiple-page document, and split the screen. Then, you will open a second document and view both documents at the same time.

To begin, open your web browser, navigate to www.pearsonhighered.com/skills, locate the name of your textbook, and then follow the instructions on the website.

More Skills Insert Symbols

There are many symbols that are used occasionally, but not often enough to put on a standard computer keyboard. Some examples of commonly inserted symbols include copyright and trademark symbols, mathematical operators, and special dashes that are longer than hyphens. These symbols can be found and inserted from the Symbols group on the Insert tab.

In More Skills 14, you will open a document and insert several symbols from the Special Characters list in the Symbol dialog box.

To begin, open your web browser, navigate to www.pearsonhighered.com/skills, locate the name of your textbook, and then follow the instructions on the website.

Please note that there are no additional projects to accompany the More Skills Projects, and they are not covered in the End-of-Chapter projects.

The following table summarizes the **SKILLS AND PROCEDURES** covered in this chapter.

Skills Number	Task	Step	Icon	Keyboard Shortcut
1	Display formatting marks	Home tab → Paragraph group → Show/Hide	¶	Ctrl + *
2	Apply styles	Home tab → Styles group → click desired style		
2	Ignore flagged words	Right-click the word, and click Ignore All		
2	Change spelling and grammar options	File tab → Word Options → Proofing page → Settings button		
3	Select paragraphs	Triple-click the paragraph, or with the ⬧ pointer, double-click		
3	Undo an action	Quick Access Toolbar → Undo (repeat as needed)	↺	Ctrl + Z
3	Select all	Home tab → Editing group → Select → Select All		Ctrl + A
3	Move to beginning of document			Ctrl + Home
4	Move to end of document			Ctrl + End
4	Copy text	Select text, then Home tab → Clipboard group → Copy	📋	Ctrl + C
4	Cut text	Select text, the Home tab → Clipboard group → Cut	✂	Ctrl + X
4	Paste text	Position insertion point, then Home tab → Clipboard group → Paste		Ctrl + V
5	Check spelling and grammar	Review tab → Proofing group → Spelling & Grammar		F7
6	Check writing style	On Proofing page, set Writing Style to Spelling & Grammar		
7	Use Format Painter	Select formatted text, then Home → Clipboard group → Format Painter Click once for one time, double-click for multiple times		
8	Open the Font dialog box	Home tab → Font group → Dialog Box Launcher	⬑	Ctrl + D
8	Apply small caps	In Font dialog box, select Small caps check box		
8	Expand or stretch text	Font dialog box → Advanced tab		
9	Make footers active	Insert tab → Header & Footer group → Footer → Edit Footer		
9	Insert file names in footers	With footer active → Design tab → Insert group → Quick Parts		
10	View two pages	View tab → Zoom group → Multiple Pages		
10	Save as PDF documents	File tab → Export → Create PDF/XPS		

Key Terms

Online Help Skills

1. Start **Word 2013**, and then in the upper-right corner of the Word Start screen, click the **Help** button ? .

2. In the **Word Help** window **Search help** box, type screentips and then press Enter .

3. In the search result list, click **Show or hide ScreenTips**. Read the article, and then scroll to the video at the end of the article. Compare your screen with **Figure 1**.

Figure 1

4. Turn on your speakers or put on headphones, and then watch the video to answer the following questions: What are the three options for viewing ScreenTips? Which option do you think you prefer, and why?

Matching

Match each term in the second column with its correct definition in the first column by writing the letter of the term on the blank line in front of the correct definition.

 1. A character that indicates a paragraph, tab, or space on your screen, but that does not print when you print a Word document.

 2. A pre-built collection of formatting settings that can be assigned to text.

 3. A red wavy line indicates this type of error.

 4. Forces a page to end, and places subsequent text at the top of the next page.

 5. A command that deletes the selected text or object and places a copy in the Office Clipboard.

 6. A reference that lists words that have the same or similar meaning to the word you are looking up.

 7. A unit of measurement for font sizes.

 8. A reserved area for text, graphics, and fields that displays at the top of each page in a document.

 9. A category of data—such as a file name, the page number, or the current date—that can be inserted into a document.

 10. An image of a document that can be viewed using a reader such as Adobe Acrobat Reader instead of the application that created the original document.

A Cut

B Field

C Formatting mark

D Header

E Manual page break

F PDF document

G Point

H Spelling

I Style

J Thesaurus

BizSkills Video

1. What is a professional network and how would you build one?

2. What are some of the best sources for job leads?

Multiple Choice MyITLab®

Choose the correct answer.

1. A button used to turn a feature both on and off.
   A. Dialog Launcher button
   B. Spin button
   C. Toggle button

2. To change Proofing settings, first display the:
   A. File tab
   B. Home tab
   C. Reference tab

3. In the Grammar Options dialog box, which is a category that can be enabled or disabled?
   A. Check spelling as you type
   B. Small caps
   C. Subject-verb agreement

4. A wavy line indicating a possible spelling, grammar, or style error.
   A. AutoComplete error
   B. Flagged error
   C. ScreenTip

5. This keyboard shortcut places the insertion point at the beginning of the document.
   A. Ctrl + A
   B. Ctrl + PageUp
   C. Ctrl + Home

6. The Spelling & Grammar group is located on this Ribbon tab.
   A. Home
   B. References
   C. Review

7. The Undo button is located here.
   A. Quick Access Toolbar
   B. Ribbon Home tab
   C. Ribbon Review tab

8. A font effect that displays all characters in uppercase while making any character originally typed as an uppercase letter taller than the ones typed as lowercase characters.
   A. CamelCase
   B. Small caps
   C. Uppercase

9. To view two pages at the same time, on the View tab, in the Zoom group, click this command.
   A. Fit Two
   B. Multiple Pages
   C. Two Pages

10. The typical file extension assigned to a Word document.
    A. .docx
    B. .pdf
    C. .xps

Topics for Discussion

1. Many organizations have professionally designed letterhead printed on sheets of paper. When writing a letter such as the one in this chapter, what would you need to do differently to accommodate stationery that already has your organization's name and address printed at the top? What might you need to do differently to print the letter?

2. When you check the spelling in a document, one of the options is to add unrecognized words to the dictionary. If you were working for a large company, what types of words do you think you would add to your dictionary?

Skills Review

To complete this project, you will need the following file:

- wrd01_SRParkDonations

You will save your files as:

- Last_First_wrd01_SRParks (Word)
- Last_First_wrd01_SRParks (PDF)

1. Start a blank Word document. On the **Home tab**, click the **Show/Hide** button as needed to display the formatting marks. Type Aspen Falls Parks and Recreation Department and press [Enter]. Type 500 S Aspen Street and press [Enter]. Type Aspen Falls, CA 93463 and press [Enter] two times. Type the beginning of the letter with the information shown in **Figure 1**.

2. Press [Enter], and then type Thank you for your interest in making a donation to the Aspen Falls Lake Conservation Area. You asked about projects for which we need additional resources, so I have attached a list of possible projects.

3. Press [Enter], type Sincerely, and then press [Enter] two times. Type Leah Kim Press [Enter], type Parks and Recreation Director and then apply the No Spacing style to the paragraph *Leah Kim*.

4. Select the first two lines of the letterhead. On the **Home tab**, in the **Styles group**, click the **No Spacing** button. Repeat this procedure with the first two lines of the inside address.

5. Click at the end of the paragraph that ends *possible projects*. Press [Enter], and then type All donations made to the Friends of the Aspen Falls Conservation Areas (FAFCA) are tax deductible. Compare your screen with **Figure 2**.

6. **Save** the document in your **Word Chapter 1** folder as Last_First_wrd01_SRParks

7. **Open** the student data file, **wrd01_SRParkDonations**. On the **Home tab**, in the **Editing group**, click **Select**, and then click **Select All**. On the **Home tab**, in the **Clipboard group**, click **Copy**. **Close** the document.

8. In **Last_First_wrd01_SRParks**, press [Ctrl] + [End]. On the **Page Layout tab**, in the **Page Setup group**, click **Breaks**, and then click **Page**.

9. On the **Home tab**, in the **Clipboard group**, click **Paste**.

May 17, 2014

Mr. Fred Ashkenazy
2279 Shoreline Dr.
Aspen Heights, CA 93449

Dear Mr. Ashkenazy:

Subject: Donation to Aspen Falls Lake Conservation Area

Figure 1

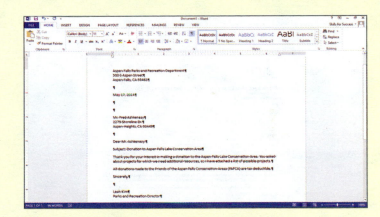

Figure 2

■ **Continue to the next page to complete this Skills Review** ➤

Figure 3

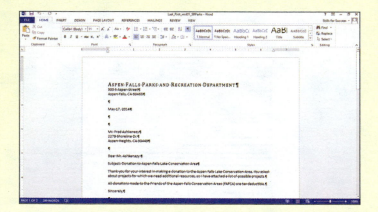

Figure 4

10. Select the heading *Land Acquisitions Trust Fund* and the paragraph that follows it. On the **Home tab**, in the **Clipboard group**, click **Cut** to remove the two paragraphs.

11. Click to the left of the heading *Invasive Species Abatement*, and then in the **Clipboard group**, click **Paste**.

12. On the **File tab**, click **Options**, and display the **Proofing** page. Change the **Writing Style** setting to **Grammar & Style**, and then click **OK**.

13. In the paragraph starting *The Land Acquisitions*, select the text *is used to expand*, and then type expands In the same sentence, change *purchase* to purchases

14. On the **File tab**, click **Options**, and display the **Proofing** page. Change the **Writing Style** setting to **Grammar Only**, and then click **OK**.

15. On the **Review tab**, in the **Proofing group**, click the **Spelling & Grammar** button. Use the **Spelling** and **Grammar** task panes to fix all spelling and grammar errors in the document.

16. In the paragraph below the *Wildlife Viewing Blinds* heading, right-click *inhabitants*, and then use the **Synonyms** submenu to change the word to **populations**.

17. Using the **Format Painter**, apply the formatting in the *Land Acquisitions Trust Fund* heading to the five other headings on the page. Compare your screen with **Figure 3**.

18. In the letterhead, select the paragraph starting *Aspen Falls Parks*. On the **Home tab**, in the **Font group**, click the **Font Dialog Box Launcher**.

19. In the **Font** dialog box, select **Small caps**, and then click the **Advanced tab**. Change the **Spacing** to **Expanded**, leave the **By** value at **1 pt**, and then click **OK**. Apply the **Cambria** font and font size **16**.

20. On the **Insert tab**, in the **Header & Footer group**, click the **Footer** button, and then click **Edit Footer**.

21. On the **Design tab**, in the **Insert group**, click the **Quick Parts** button, and then click **Field**. Under **Field names**, scroll down and click **FileName**. Click **OK**, and then click **Close Header and Footer**. Compare your screen with **Figure 4**.

22. On the **File tab**, click **Export**. On the **Export** page, click the **Create PDF/XPS** button.

23. In the **Publish as PDF or XPS** dialog box, navigate to your **Word Chapter 1** folder. Be sure the **Open file after publishing** check box is selected, and then click **Publish**.

24. View the document in a PDF viewer, and then **Close** the window.

25. Click **Save**, and then **Close** ⊠ Word. Submit the files as directed by your instructor.

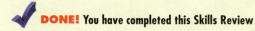 **DONE!** You have completed this Skills Review

Skills Assessment 1

To complete this project, you will need the following files:

- wrd01_SA1Land
- wrd01_SA1Legacy

You will save your files as:

- Last_First_wrd01_SA1Land (Word)
- Last_First_wrd01_SA1Land (PDF)

1. Open **wrd01_SA1Land** from the student data files, and then save it in your chapter folder as Last_First_wrd01_SA1Land Add the **FileName** field to the footer.

2. In **Word Options**, set the **Writing Style** to check **Grammar & Style**.

3. After the date, insert two blank lines and the following inside address: Ms. Shawn McCready; 1414 Barbary Dr.; Aspen Falls, CA 93464

4. For the first three lines of the letterhead, apply the **No Spacing** style. Repeat this procedure with the first two lines of the inside address.

5. For the letterhead's first line, apply the **Cambria** font, font size **16**, and then set the **Character Spacing** to **Expanded** by **1.3 pt**.

6. Below the inside address, add the salutation Dear Ms. McCready:

7. After the salutation, insert a new paragraph with the text Subject: McCready Farm Property Ignore all flagged errors for McCready, and then compare your screen with **Figure 1**.

8. Open the student data file **wrd01_SA1Legacy**. **Copy** all of the text, and then **Close** the document.

9. At the end of **Last_First_wrd01_SA1Land**, insert a manual page break, and then at the top of Page 2, paste the contents of the clipboard.

10. On Page 2, below *Gift and Estate Planning,* replace the word *various* with the suggested synonym **several**.

11. In the last bullet under *Life Estate Gift Annuity,* fix the style error using the suggestion in the flagged error's shortcut menu.

12. Use **Cut** and **Paste** to move the *Outright Gift* heading and its two bullets so that the section comes before the *Life Estate Gift Annuity* heading.

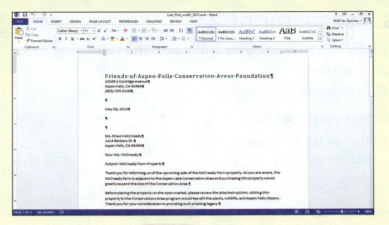

Figure 1

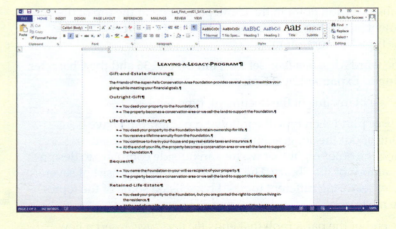

Figure 2

13. In **Word Options**, set the **Writing Style** to check **Grammar Only**.

14. Fix all spelling and grammar errors in the document.

15. Use **Format Painter** to apply the formatting in the *Gift and Estate Planning* heading to the five other headings on Page 2.

16. Compare your screen with **Figure 2**, and then **Save** the document.

17. Save the file as a PDF document in your chapter folder with the name Last_First_wrd01_SA1Land

18. **Close** all open windows, and then submit the files as directed by your instructor.

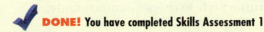

DONE! You have completed Skills Assessment 1

Skills Assessment 2

To complete this project, you will need the following files:

- wrd01_SA2Memo
- wrd01_SA2Topics

You will save your files as:

- Last_First_wrd01_SA2Memo
- Last_First_wrd01_SA2PDF

Figure 1

1. Open **wrd01_SA2Memo** from the student data files, and then save it in your chapter folder as Last_First_wrd01_SA2Memo Add the **FileName** field to the footer.

2. With the insertion point in the blank paragraph at the top of the document, apply the **No Spacing** style, and then press Enter five times. Type Memorandum

3. For the word *Memorandum*, set the **Font Size** to **36** and the **Character Spacing** to **Expanded** by **2.5 pt**.

4. In the last blank line of the document, type Jamie:

5. Press Enter, and then type the following paragraph: I have been thinking about the suggestion made at the Board of Trustees meeting the other night that we hire an outside company to design a virtual tour of the library. The virtual tour might consist of several modules featuring different topics. I have listed some of the topics on the next page.

6. At the end of the paragraph that ends *the next page*, insert a new paragraph with the text Let me know what you think. Press Enter two times, type Doug and then compare your screen with **Figure 1**.

7. At the end of the document, insert a manual page break, and then on Page 2, copy and paste all of the text from the student data file, **wrd01_SA2Topics**.

8. Cut the heading *Building Interior* and the paragraph that follows it, and then paste it before the *Building Exterior* heading.

9. In **Word Options**, set the **Writing Style** to check **Grammar & Style**. Use the **Spelling & Grammar** checker to fix all spelling, grammar, and style errors in the document.

10. In **Word Options**, set the **Writing Style** to check **Grammar Only**.

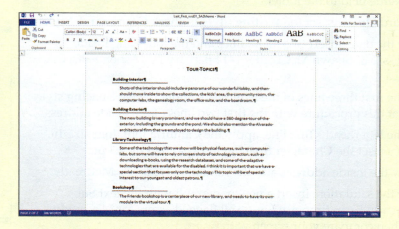

Figure 2

11. In the paragraph below *Building Exterior*, replace the word *striking* with the suggested synonym **prominent**.

12. Use **Format Painter** to apply the formatting in the *Building Interior* heading to the other four headings on Page 2.

13. Compare your screen with **Figure 2**, and then **Save** the document.

14. Save the file as a PDF document in your chapter folder with the name Last_First_wrd01_SA2PDF

15. **Close** all open windows, and then submit the files as directed by your instructor.

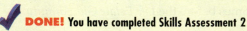

DONE! You have completed Skills Assessment 2

Visual Skills Check

To complete this project, you will need the following file:

- Blank Word document

You will save your document as:

- Last_First_wrd01_VSCenter

Using the skills practiced in this chapter, create the document shown in **Figure 1**. **Save** the file as Last_First_wrd01_VSCenter in your chapter folder. Format the first line of the letterhead using the **Cambria** font sized at **24** points, small caps, and expanded by **1.5** points. Format the rest of the document using the **Calibri** font sized at **11** points. Maintain the space between paragraphs as shown in **Figure 1**. Insert the FileName field in the footer. Print or submit the file as directed by your instructor.

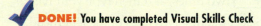

DONE! You have completed Visual Skills Check

ASPEN FALLS COMMUNITY CENTERS
500 S Aspen Street
Aspen Falls, CA 93463

July 14, 2014

Mrs. Natalie Lee
3947 Strong Rd
Aspen Heights, CA 93464

Dear Mrs. Lee:

Subject: Community Center Closings for the 2015 Calendar Year

Thank you for your inquiry about next year's community center closings. Please refer to the following:

Holidays: We will be closed on New Year's Day, Easter, Memorial Day, the Fourth of July, Labor Day, Thanksgiving, and Christmas.

In-Service Days: We will be closed on April 15th for a session on library security, and on November 7th for a session that will focus on streamlining the material handling process.

Close Early: We will close early on New Year's Eve, the day before Easter, the day before Thanksgiving, and Christmas Eve.

If you have any question, feel free to contact me again.

Sincerely,

Lorrine Deely
Community Center Supervisor

wrd01_VSCenter_solution

Figure 1

June 10, 2014

Evelyn Stone
Aspen Falls City Hall
500 S Aspen St
Aspen Falls, CA 93464

Dear Mrs. Stone:

Subject: City Hall Internships

Figure 1

Your Name
1234 N Your St
Your City, State 99999

June 10, 2014

Evelyn Stone
Aspen Falls City Hall
500 S Aspen St
Aspen Falls, CA 93464

Dear Mrs. Stone:

Subject: City Hall Internships

One of my instructors at Aspen Falls Community College, Dr. Gato, suggested that I contact you regarding internships at Aspen Falls City Hall. My studies at the college qualify me for such a position starting as early as next term.

As you review the enclosed resume, please notice my training in Microsoft Office and my organizational skills. Specifically, my experience with Word and my work-study position with Dr. Gato indicate a successful internship as an Office Assistant.

If you have any questions, or if you want to schedule an interview, please contact me at (805) 555-3355 or e-mail me at youremail@address.

Sincerely,

Your Name

Last_First_wrd01_MyLetter.docx

Figure 2

My Skills

To complete this project, you will start with a:
- Blank Word document

You will save your document as:
- Last_First_wrd01_MyLetter

1. Create a blank Word document, and then save it in your chapter folder as Last_First_wrd01_MyLetter Add the **FileName** field to the footer.

2. In **Word Options**, set the **Writing Style** to check **Grammar & Style** and fix any flagged errors as you compose the letter in the next steps.

3. Type your first and last name, and then press Enter . On the next two lines of the letterhead, type your own address information. Complete the beginning of the letter as follows with the information shown in **Figure 1**.

4. Press Enter and type One of my instructors at Aspen Falls Community College, Dr. Gato, suggested that I contact you regarding internships at Aspen Falls City Hall. My studies at the college qualify me for such a position starting as early as next term.

5. Press Enter and type As you review the enclosed resume, please notice my training in Microsoft Office and my organizational skills. Specifically, my experience with Word and my work-study position with Dr. Gato indicate a successful internship as an Office Assistant.

6. Press Enter , and then using your e-mail address, type If you have any questions, or if you want to schedule an interview, please contact me at (805) 555-3355 or e-mail me at youremail@address.

7. Press Enter , and then type Sincerely, Press Enter two times, and then type your name.

8. Select the first two lines of the letterhead, and then apply the **No Spacing** style. Repeat this procedure with the first three lines of the inside address.

9. Using the techniques practiced in this chapter, format the letterhead to make it stand out slightly from the rest of the letter, and then compare your screen with **Figure 2**.

10. Print or submit the files as directed by your instructor.

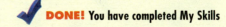 **DONE!** You have completed My Skills

Skills Challenge 1

To complete this project, you will need the following file:

- **wrd01_SC1Trustees**

You will save your document as:

- **Last_First_wrd01_SC1Trustees**

Open the student data file **wrd01_SC1Trustees**, and then save it in your chapter folder as Last_First_wrd01_SC1Trustees

For the entire document, apply a single font that is more appropriate than Comic Sans MS. Correct or ignore all flagged spelling, grammar, and style errors as appropriate to their context. Insert a page break so the letter ends on Page 1 and the report starts on Page 2.

On Page 1, correct the paragraph alignment and paragraph spacing so that it follows the block style business letter modeled in Skills 1–10. Format the letter head so that *Aspen Falls Public Library* stands out from the rest of the letter.

On Page 2, use cut and paste to arrange the headings and their paragraphs in alphabetical order by heading. Format the heading and side headings to visually organize the report. Be sure to apply the same formatting to all five headings.

Insert the FileName field in the footer. Print or submit the file as directed by your instructor.

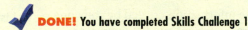 **DONE!** You have completed Skills Challenge 1

Skills Challenge 2

To complete this project, you will start with a:

- **Blank Word document**

You will save your document as:

- **Last_First_wrd01_SC2Recommendation**

Deborah Davidson, Public Information Specialist at Aspen Falls City Hall, needs to know if the current format for city letters is still the best choice. She specifically needs to know if the *blockstyle, modified-blockstyle,* or *modified-block style with indented paragraphs* should be used.

Use a business correspondence guide from your library or search online to compare the three styles under consideration. Summarize your findings in a letter addressed to Deborah Davidson, Public Information Specialist, Aspen Falls City Hall, 500 S Aspen Street, Aspen Falls, CA 93463.

For each of the three styles, write a short paragraph describing its features and comparative advantages and disadvantages. In a fourth paragraph, recommend which style the city should use and then justify your decision. Finally, format the letter using the style you recommended. Name the file Last_First_SC2Recommendation Insert the FileName field in the footer, and submit the letter as directed by your instructor.

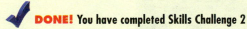 **DONE!** You have completed Skills Challenge 2

CHAPTER 2

Create Business Reports

- Informal business reports are often formatted using guidelines in *The Gregg Reference Manual* by William A. Sabin. These guidelines specify the way the text is formatted, the way notes display, and the types of citations used.

- A footnote or endnote can be inserted when you have supplemental information that does not fit well in the document.

- When you use quotations or paraphrase information created by someone else, you need to cite your sources in the document and list them at the end of the document.

- Report style guidelines specify how headings and side headings should be formatted. Your guidelines should also specify how much space should be above and below paragraphs, how the first line should be indented, and how much space should be between each line.

- Document margins are the spaces that display on the outer edges of a printed page. All four page margins can be adjusted independently.

- Lists make information easier to understand. Use numbered lists when information is displayed in a sequence and use bulleted lists when information can appear in any order.

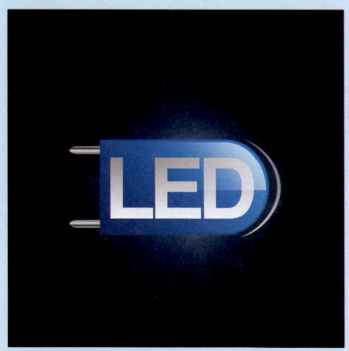

Led vectoriel © gam16

Aspen Falls City Hall

In this chapter, you will finish a report for Richard Mack, Aspen Falls Assistant City Manager. The report provides a cost-benefit analysis regarding LED lights and makes recommendations based on that analysis. The study was conducted at the request of the city in cooperation with the Durango County Museum of History located in Aspen Falls.

If someone has requested that you write a report for them, you should ask them for guidelines regarding length, style, and format. Academic reports typically follow a set of guidelines such as MLA or Chicago, while the guidelines for business reports vary. Reports are either formal or informal. Formal reports include front matter such as a separate title page and a table of contents and back matter such as bibliographies and appendixes. Informal reports do not contain front matter, are short in length, and may have an optional bibliography.

In this project, you will edit and format an informal business report using the guidelines from *The Gregg Reference Manual* by William A. Sabin. You will edit text and then insert comments in footnotes. Following *The Chicago Manual of Style,* you will add sources to the document, cite those sources, and then insert a bibliography. Finally, you will format the document following standard guidelines for informal business reports.

Time to complete all 10
skills – 60 to 75 minutes

60-75 min.

Student data file needed for this chapter:

wrd02_LEDs

You will save your document as:

Last_First_wrd02_LEDs

Outcome

Using the skills in this chapter, you will be able to work with Word documents like this:

SKILLS  Skills 1-10 Training

At the end of this chapter, you will be able to:

Skill 1 Find and Replace Text
Skill 2 Insert and Modify Footnotes
Skill 3 Add Sources
Skill 4 Insert Citations and Bibliographies
Skill 5 Format Bulleted and Numbered Lists
Skill 6 Set Paragraph Indents
Skill 7 Modify Line and Paragraph Spacing
Skill 8 Set Line and Page Break Options and Modify Styles
Skill 9 View Multiple Pages and Set Margins
Skill 10 Create Custom Headers and Footers

MORE SKILLS

Skill 11 Record AutoCorrect Entries
Skill 12 Use AutoFormat to Create Numbered Lists
Skill 13 Format and Customize Lists
Skill 14 Create Standard Outlines

LED LIGHTS

A Museum Exhibit Case Study

By Your Name

July 21, 2014

In April 2014, the Durango County Museum of History installed a small exhibit titled *Our heritage: Pictures from the past.* The collection consists of five daguerreotypes and several silver albumen prints. A study was made to measure the benefits and costs of using LED lights instead of traditional halogen lamps.

RISKS OF LIGHTING HISTORIC PHOTOGRAPHS

All lighting harms photographs. (Lavedrine 2003) It is the task of the conservator to minimize this harm so that the photographs can be viewed for a significant span of time, typically 50 to 100 years. For these reasons, historical photographs are displayed only periodically in rooms with significantly reduced lighting. These practices minimize the visitor experience and according to Hunt, reducing light levels diminishes color saturation and contrast. (Hunt 1952, 190-199)

In all lighting systems, ultraviolet light (UV) must be eliminated as that spectrum harms photographs the most. Halogen lights must have UV filters installed which adds to their cost and effectiveness. LED lamps do not emit UV light and do not need extra filters. According to a study by the Getty Conservation Institute, fading from LED lamps does not result in any more damage than conventional halogen lamps with ultraviolet filtering. They found that it is likely using LED lamps results in less fading of photographic materials. (Druzik and Miller 2011)

METHODOLOGY

In the new exhibit, 12 watt PAR38 20° lamps were utilized. The temperature rating for these lamps was 2700 Kelvin. Although the LED light output was significantly less than traditional halogen lamps, some screening was still needed. UV filters were not installed because LED lights do not emit any significant levels of ultra-violet light. This simplified the installation process.

▶ The Navigation pane can be used to find text quickly.

▶ When you need to find and then replace several instances of the same words or phrases, you can use the Find and Replace dialog box.

1. Start **Word 2013**, and then from the student files, open **wrd02_LEDs**. If necessary, display the formatting marks.

2. On the **File tab**, click **Save As**, and then click **Browse**. In the **Save As** dialog box, navigate to the location where you are saving your files. Create a folder named Word Chapter 2 and then save the document as Last_First_wrd02_LEDs

3. On the **View tab**, in the **Show group**, verify that the **Navigation Pane** check box is selected, and then compare your screen with **Figure 1**.

4. With the insertion point at the top of the document, press Enter five times. On the **Home tab**, in the **Styles group**, click the **Heading 1** thumbnail. Type LED LIGHTS and then press Enter. Type A Museum Exhibit Case Study and then press Enter.

5. Using your own name, type By Your Name and then press Enter. Type the current date, and then press Enter.

6. Click to place the insertion point to the left of the title. Press and hold Shift while clicking to the right of the date to select the four lines.

7. In the **Paragraph group**, click the **Center** button, and then compare your screen with **Figure 2**.

In an informal report, there should be 2 inches of space above the title, and the title, subtitle, writer's name, and date should be centered.

■ **Continue to the next page to complete the skill** ➤

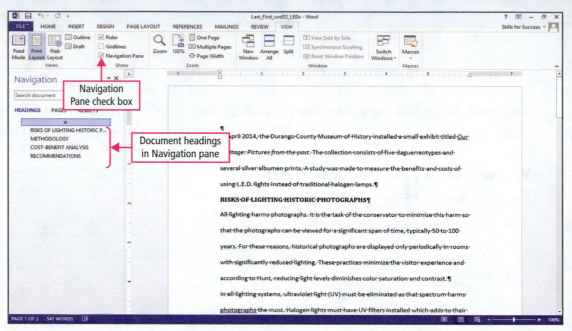

Figure 1

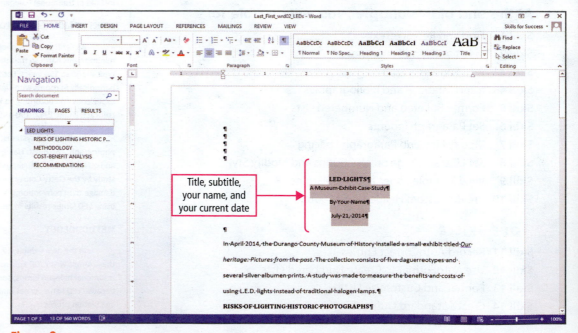

Figure 2

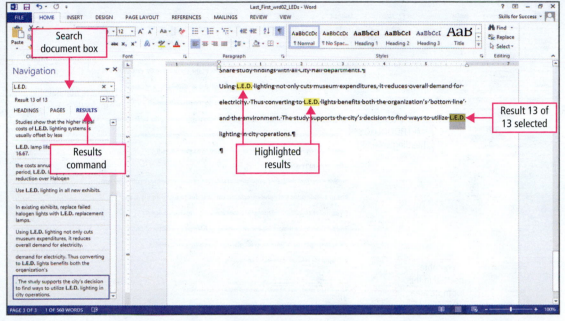

Search document box

Results command

Highlighted results

Result 13 of 13 selected

Figure 3

8. In the **Navigation** pane **Search document** box, type L.E.D. and then click **Results** to display the results.

9. Scroll to the bottom of the **Results** list, click the last search result, and then compare your screen with **Figure 3**.

   In this manner, you can quickly find and navigate to a word or phrase in a document. In the document, each instance of the searched text is highlighted.

10. Click in the document, and then press `Ctrl` + `Home` to move the insertion point to the beginning of the document. In the **Navigation** pane, click the **Search for more things arrow**, and then click **Replace** to open the Find and Replace dialog box.

11. Verify that the **Find what** box has the text *L.E.D.*, and then in the **Replace with** box, type LED Compare your screen with **Figure 4**.

   When you open the Find and Replace dialog box from the Navigation pane, the word or phrase you want to find is automatically entered into the *Find what* box.

12. Click the **Find Next** button to select the next occurrence of *L.E.D.* Click the **Replace** button to replace the initials and move to the next occurrence. Click **Replace** to replace another occurrence of *L.E.D.* with *LED*.

   In this manner, you can replace each instance one at a time.

13. Click the **Replace All** button to replace the 11 remaining occurrences. Read the message that displays, click **OK**, and then **Close** the Find and Replace dialog box. **Save** 💾 the document.

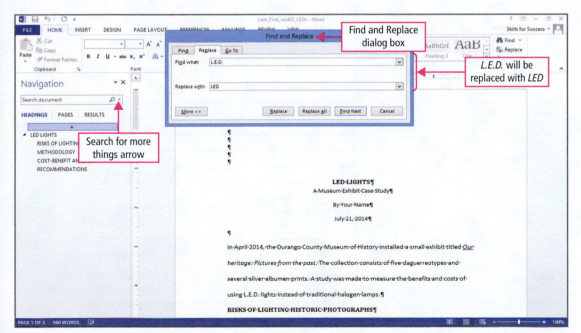

Find and Replace dialog box

L.E.D. will be replaced with *LED*

Search for more things arrow

Figure 4

- You have completed Skill 1 of 10

▶ A **footnote** is a note or comment placed at the bottom of the page. An **endnote** is a note or comment placed at the end of a section or a document.

1. In the **Navigation** pane, click the **Headings** command, and then click the **METHODOLOGY** heading to display that section of the report.

2. Click to the right of the period in the paragraph ending *output to the desired level*. Click the **References tab**, and then in the **Footnotes group**, click the **Insert Footnote** button.

> A footnote displays at the bottom of the page with a number *1* before the insertion point. A line is also inserted above the footnote area to separate it from the document text.

3. Type Screening is the process of installing layers of metal window screen. Compare your screen with **Figure 1**.

4. Navigate to the **COST-BENEFIT ANALYSIS** section, and then click to the right of the sentence ending *LED lamp life is longer by a factor of 16.67*.

5. Repeat the technique just practiced to insert a second footnote with the text Derived from industry standards. Compare your screen with **Figure 2**.

> Footnote numbers are inserted and formatted as **superscript**—text that is positioned higher and smaller than the other text.

■ **Continue to the next page to complete the skill** ➡

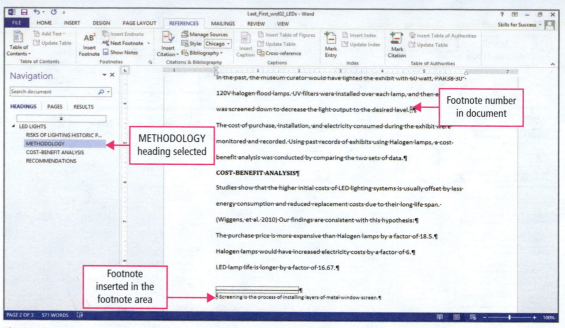

Figure 1

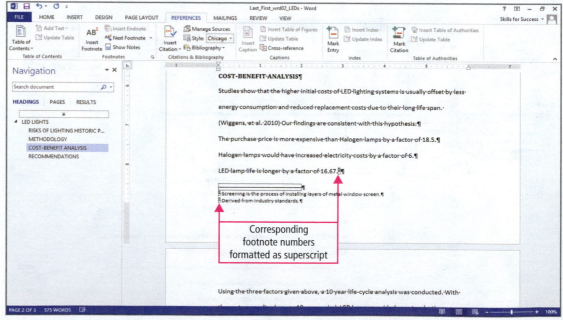

Figure 2

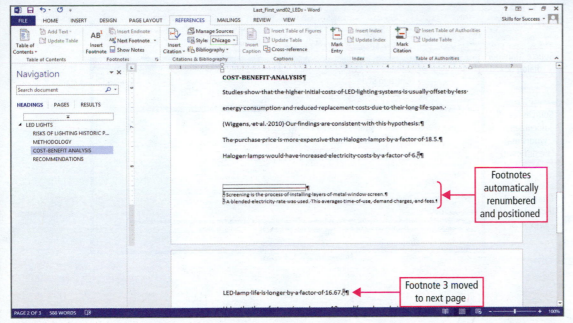

Figure 3

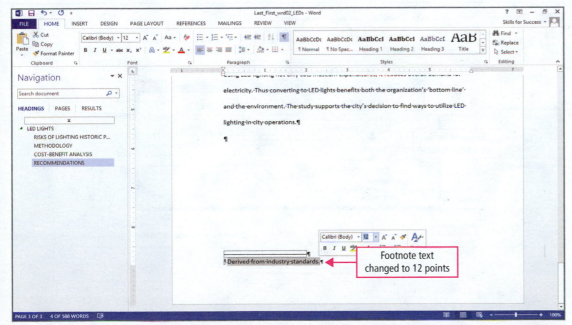

Figure 4

6. Above the footnotes, click to the right of the sentence ending *increased electricity costs by a factor of 6.* Insert another footnote with the text **A blended electricity rate was used. This averages time-of-use, demand charges, and fees.** Compare your screen with **Figure 3**.

   Footnotes automatically position themselves at the bottom of the correct page and adjust so that they are renumbered sequentially.

7. At the bottom of Page 2, select the text of the first footnote without selecting the footnote number. Change the font size to **12**.

   Most style manuals call for the footer text to be the same size as the document text. Footnote numbers are typically smaller than the report text.

8. Repeat the technique just practiced to change the text of footnote two to **12** points. Take care to format just the text and not the footnote number.

9. Scroll to the bottom of Page 3 to display the third footnote, and then change the footnote text to **12** points.

10. Compare your screen with **Figure 4**, and then **Save** 🖫 the document.

■ **You have completed Skill 2 of 10**

WRD 2-3
VIDEO

▶ A **source** is the reference used to find information or data.

1. On the **References tab**, in the **Citations & Bibliography group**, click the **Style arrow**, and then click **Chicago Sixteenth Edition**.

2. In the **Citations & Bibliography group**, click **Manage Sources**, and then under **Current List**, click the source starting *Wiggins*. Compare your screen with **Figure 1**.

   The Master List sources are available for all your documents, and the Current List sources are available only for a single document. The Preview pane displays citations and bibliography entries in the format for the selected style—here, Chicago Fifteenth Edition. The check mark indicates that the source has been cited in the document.

3. Click the **New** button, and then verify the **Type of Source** is **Book**.

4. In the **Author** box, type Bertrand Lavedrine and then in the **Title** box, type A Guide to the Preventive Conservation of Photograph Collections

5. For the **Year**, type 2003 and for the **City**, type Los Angeles For the **Publisher**, type Getty Conservation Institute and then compare your screen with **Figure 2**.

   The Create Source dialog box displays the fields required by the Chicago style for the selected source type.

6. Click **OK**, and then in **Source Manager**, preview the new source's citation and bibliography entry.

   The author's last name followed by a comma was placed before the first name when you closed the dialog box.

7. Click the **New** button, and then change the **Type of Source** to **Journal Article**.

■ **Continue to the next page to complete the skill** ➡

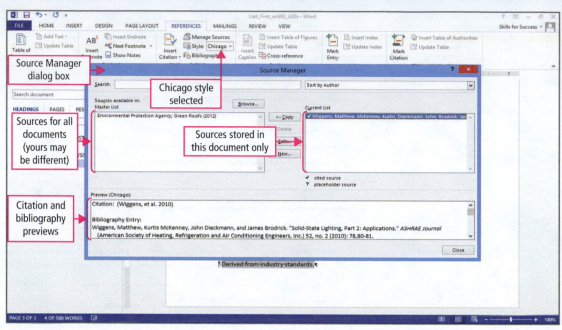

Figure 1

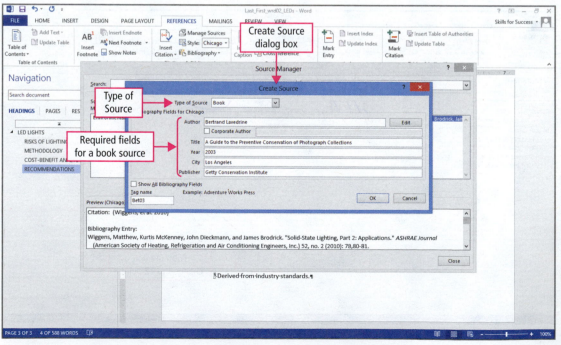

Figure 2

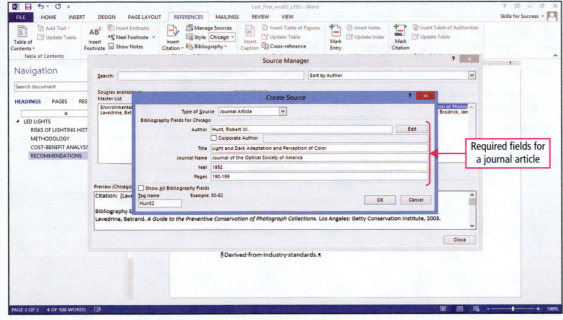

Required fields for a journal article

Figure 3

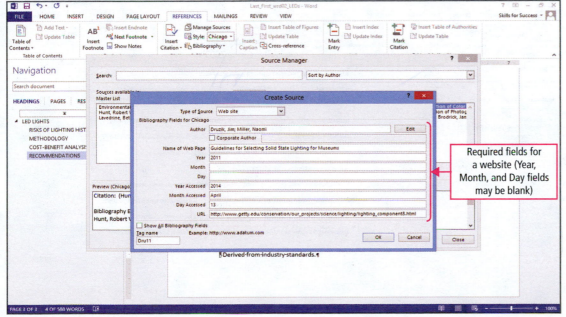

Required fields for a website (Year, Month, and Day fields may be blank)

Figure 4

8. In the **Author** box, type Hunt, Robert W and then in the **Title** box, type Light and Dark Adaptation and Perception of Color

9. For the **Journal Name**, type Journal of the Optical Society of America and in the **Year** box, type 1952 In the **Pages** box, type 190-199 Compare your screen with **Figure 3**, and then click **OK**.

10. Click the **New** button, and then change the **Type of Source** to **Web site**.

11. In the **Author** box, type Druzik, Jim; Miller, Naomi and in the **Name of Web Page** box, type Guidelines for Selecting Solid State Lighting for Museums

12. In the **Year** box, type 2011 In the **Year Accessed** box, type 2014 The **Month Accessed** is April and the **Day Accessed** is 13

13. In the **URL** box, type http://www.getty.edu/conservation/our_projects/science/lighting/lighting_component8.html Compare your screen with **Figure 4**, and then click **OK**.

14. In the **Source Manager** dialog box **Master List**, select the first source created in this skill. Verify you selected the title in the **Master List**—*not* the one in the Current List—and then click the **Delete** button. Repeat to delete the other two sources created in this skill from the **Master List**, and then click the **Close** button.

> When you add a new source, it is placed in both the Master and Current Lists. If you do not plan to use a source in other documents, it can be deleted from the Master List. However, take care to leave the sources in the Current List.

■ **You have completed Skill 3 of 10**

▶ When you quote or refer to information from another source, you need to credit that source.

▶ A **bibliography** is a compilation of sources referenced in a report and listed on a separate page.

▶ A **citation** is a note in the document that refers the reader to a source in the bibliography.

1. Navigate to the **RISKS OF LIGHTING HISTORIC PHOTOGRAPHS** section.

2. Click to the right of the period ending the first sentence *All lighting harms photographs*. On the **References tab**, in the **Citations & Bibliography group**, click **Insert Citation**, and then compare your screen with **Figure 1**.

   When you insert a citation field, the sources stored in Source Manager display in the gallery.

3. In the **Citation** gallery, click the **Lavedrine, Bertand** source to insert the citation.

4. In the same paragraph, click to the right of the period of the sentence ending *saturation and contrast*. Repeat the technique just practiced to insert the citation for **Hunt, Robert W**.

5. Click the citation just inserted, click the field's **Citation Options arrow**, and then click **Edit Citation**. In the **Pages** box, type 192 click **OK**, and then compare your screen with **Figure 2**.

   Many business reports use the **author-date citation**, which contains the author's last name, the publication year, and the specific page number(s) if one is available.

■ **Continue to the next page to complete the skill** ▶

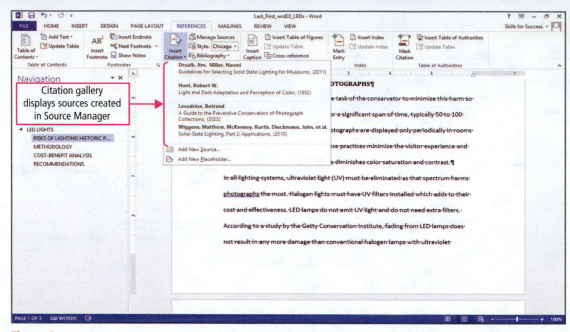

Figure 1

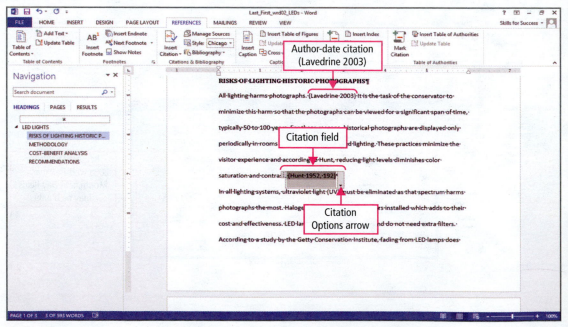

Figure 2

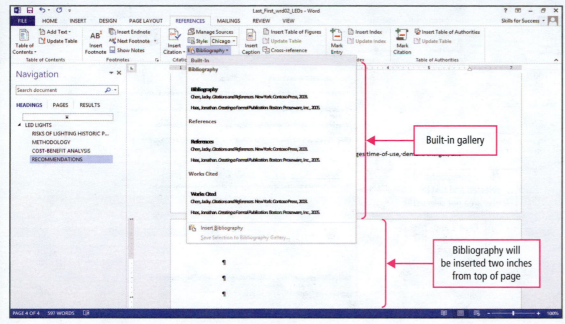

Built-in gallery

Bibliography will be inserted two inches from top of page

Figure 3

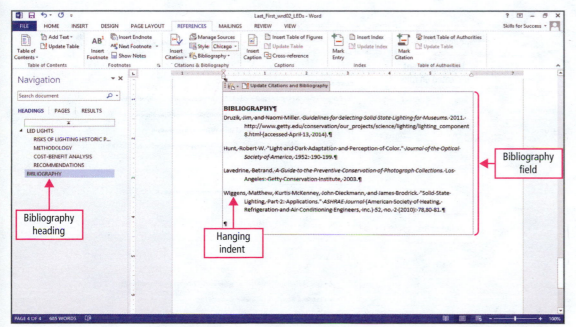

Bibliography field

Bibliography heading

Hanging indent

Figure 4

6. At the top of Page 2, click to the right of the period of the sentence ending *fading of photographic materials,* and then insert the citation for **Druzik**, **Jim R**, **Miller**, **Naomi**.

7. Press Ctrl + End, and then press Ctrl + Enter to insert a manual page break and start a new page. Press Enter two times to create about 2 inches of space from the top of the page.

8. On the **References tab**, in the **Citations & Bibliography group**, click the **Bibliography** button, and then compare with **Figure 3**.

9. From the gallery, click the **Bibliography** thumbnail to insert a bibliography field. If necessary, scroll up to display the inserted bibliography field.

> In the Chicago style, the Bibliography field displays each source using hanging indents. In a ***hanging indent***, the first line extends to the left of the rest of the paragraph.

10. Double-click the *Bibliography* title, and then type BIBLIOGRAPHY In the **Navigation** pane, verify that the *BIBLIOGRAPHY* title has been added as a level 1 heading. Compare your screen with **Figure 4**.

> In an informal report, the first-level headings should be uppercase and centered. You will center this title in a later skill.

11. **Save** the document.

> If you change the reference style or report sources, you can update the citation and bibliography fields by clicking the field, and then selecting its update command.

■ **You have completed Skill 4 of 10**

▶ A **bulleted list** is a list of items with each item introduced by a symbol—such as a small circle or check mark—in which the list items can be presented in any order.

1. Navigate to the **COST-BENEFIT ANALYSIS** section.

2. If necessary, scroll down to display the bottom of Page 2 and the top of Page 3.

3. Point to the left of the paragraph that starts *The purchase price is more* to display the 🔺 pointer, and then drag straight down to select the three paragraphs starting *The Purchase price* and ending with *factor of 16.67* including the footnote number and paragraph marks. Compare your screen with **Figure 1**.

   When you select text with footnotes, the text in the footnotes area will not be selected.

4. If your ruler does not display, on the View tab, in the Show group, select the Ruler check box.

5. On the **Home tab**, in the **Paragraph group**, click the **Bullets arrow** 🔲▾, and then in the **Bullets** gallery, click the solid circle bullet.

   The Bullets gallery displays commonly used bullet characters, and the most recently used bullet displays at the top.

6. In the **Paragraph group**, click the **Increase Indent** button 🔳 one time, and then compare your screen with **Figure 2**.

   In reports, lists are typically indented 0.5 inches on the left with a hanging indent set to 0.25 inches for the first line.

■ **Continue to the next page to complete the skill** ▶

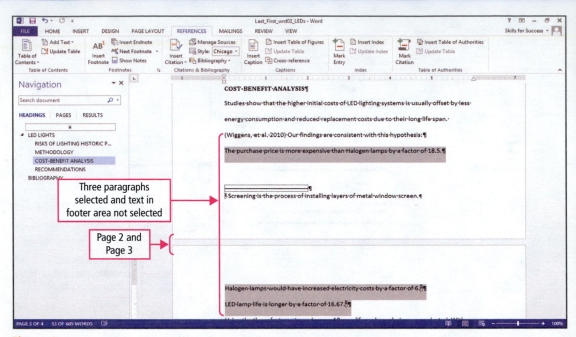

Figure 1

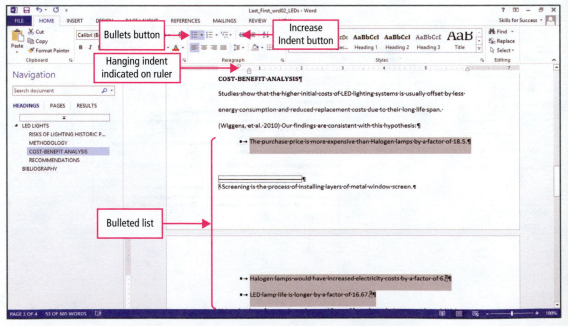

Figure 2

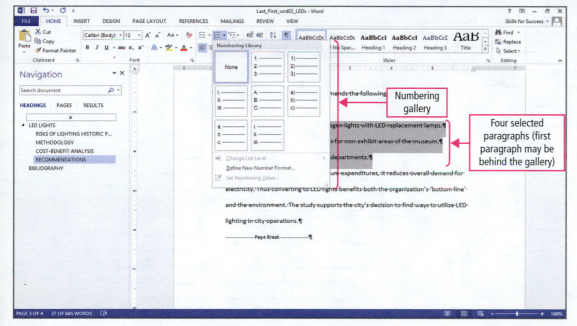

Numbering gallery

Four selected paragraphs (first paragraph may be behind the gallery)

Figure 3

7. Navigate to the **RECOMMENDATIONS** section, and then select the four paragraphs beginning *Use LED lighting in all new* and ending with *City Hall departments*.

8. On the **Home tab**, in the **Paragraph group**, click the **Numbering arrow**, and then compare your screen with **Figure 3**.

    A **numbered list** is a list of items with each item introduced by a consecutive number or letter to indicate definite steps, a sequence of actions, or chronological order.

    The Numbering gallery displays common formats that can be used to enumerate lists. For all lists, you should refer to the style guidelines specified for your report. Certain bullet characters may be specified or a different numbering system may need to be applied.

9. In the **Numbering** gallery, click the thumbnail with the *1. 2. 3.* formatting.

10. In the **Paragraph group**, click the **Increase Indent** button one time, and then compare your screen with **Figure 4**.

11. **Save** the document.

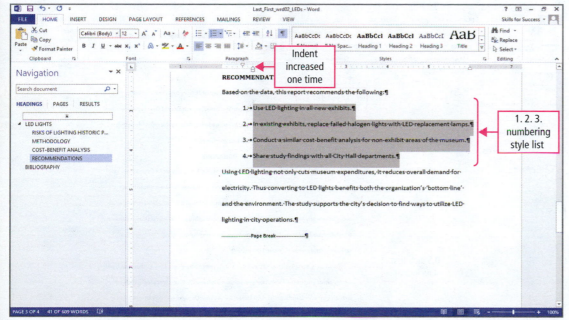

Indent increased one time

1. 2. 3. numbering style list

Figure 4

■ **You have completed Skill 5 of 10**

▶ An ***indent*** is the position of paragraph lines in relation to a page margin.

1. Navigate to the **LED LIGHTS** heading, and then click in the body paragraph that starts *In April 2014*.

2. On the **Home tab**, in the **Paragraph group**, click the **Paragraph Dialog Box Launcher** 🔲.

    The Paragraph dialog box has commands and settings that are not available in the Paragraph group.

3. Under **Indentation**, click the **Special arrow**, and then click **First line**. Compare your screen with **Figure 1**.

    The ***first line indent*** is the location of the beginning of the first line of a paragraph in relation to the left edge of the remainder of the paragraph. In this case, the *By* box displays *0.5"*, which will indent the first line of the current paragraph one-half inch.

4. Click **OK** to indent the first line of the paragraph. On the ruler, verify that the **First Line Indent** marker is now at the **0.5 inch** mark.

5. Click in the paragraph starting *All lighting harms photographs*. Press F4 to repeat the previous task.

    The F4 keyboard shortcut repeats the last command. If you performed an additional task after setting the previous indent, you will need to set the indent using the Paragraph dialog box.

6. Click in the next paragraph starting *In all lighting systems*, press F4, and then compare your screen with **Figure 2**.

■ **Continue to the next page to complete the skill** ➡

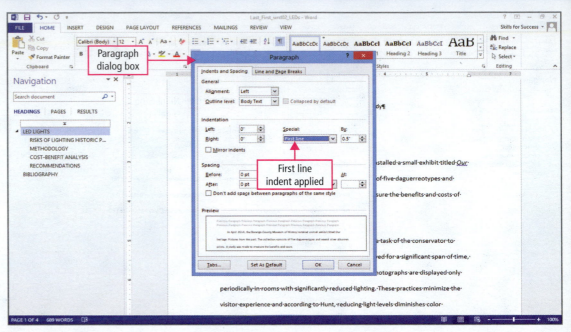

Figure 1

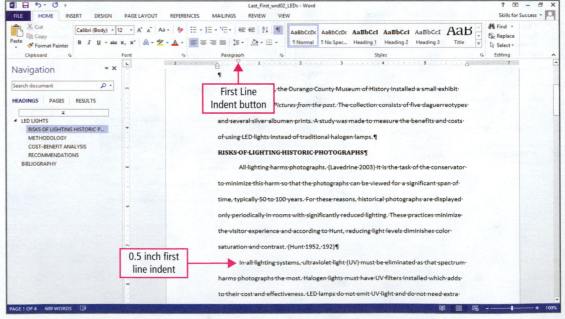

Figure 2

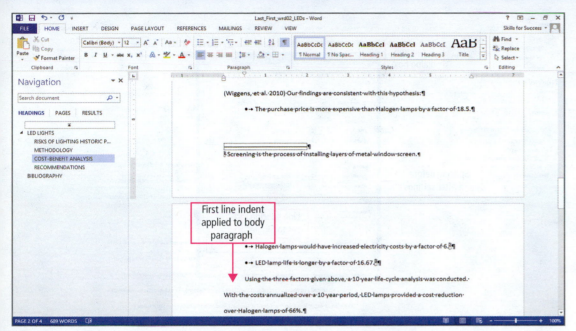

First line indent applied to body paragraph

Figure 3

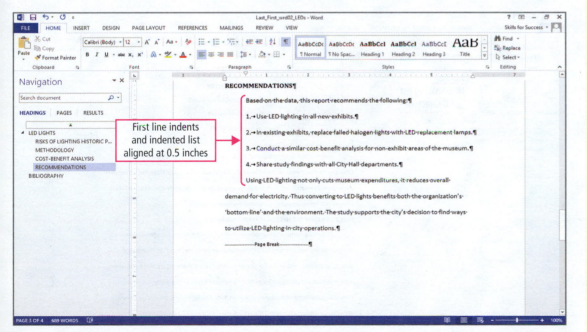

First line indents and indented list aligned at 0.5 inches

Figure 4

7. In the **METHODOLOGY** section, click in the first paragraph beginning *In the new exhibit*. On the ruler, drag the **First Line Indent** button to the **0.5 inch** mark on the ruler.

   In this manner, you can set the first line indent in the Paragraph dialog box or on the ruler.

8. Select the two paragraphs beginning *In the past* and *The cost of purchase*, and then repeat one of the techniques practiced in this skill to set a **0.5 inch** first line indent to both paragraphs.

9. Navigate to the **COST-BENEFIT ANALYSIS** section, and then apply a **0.5 inch** first line indent to the two paragraphs starting *Studies show that* and *Using the three factors*. Compare your screen with **Figure 3**.

   Recall that the bulleted list was indented to 0.5 inches in the previous skill and already has a hanging indent.

10. Navigate to the **RECOMMENDATIONS** section, and then apply a 0.5 inch first line indent to the two paragraphs starting *Based on the data* and *Using LED lighting not only cuts*. Compare your screen with **Figure 4**.

    In a report, the paragraph first line indents and the bullets or numbers in a list should all align at the 0.5 inch mark.

11. **Save** 🖫 the document.

■ **You have completed Skill 6 of 10**

► **Line spacing** is the vertical distance between lines of text in a paragraph, and **paragraph spacing** is the vertical distance above and below each paragraph. Both may need to be adjusted to match your report's style guide.

1. In the **Navigation** pane, click the **LED LIGHTS** heading. Select the title and the three paragraphs after it. On the **Home tab**, in the **Paragraph group**, click the **Paragraph Dialog Box Launcher** .

2. In the **Paragraph** dialog box, under **Spacing**, click the **Before up spin arrow** one time to change the value to **0 pt**, and then change the **After** value to **12 pt**.

3. Click the **Line Spacing arrow**, and then click **Single**. Compare your screen with **Figure 1**, and then click **OK**.

   Reports should have a blank line between each element. The style guide you follow should specify if this should be done by inserting a blank paragraph or by adjusting the paragraph spacing.

4. Click in the body paragraph that begins *In April 2014*. In the **Paragraph group**, click the **Line and Paragraph Spacing** button , and then compare your screen with **Figure 2**.

   To increase readability in longer reports, the default line spacing should be 2.0, which is **double-spacing**—the equivalent of a blank line of text displays between each line of text.

■ **Continue to the next page to complete the skill**

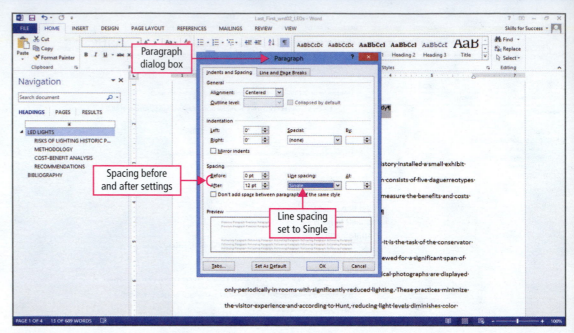

Figure 1

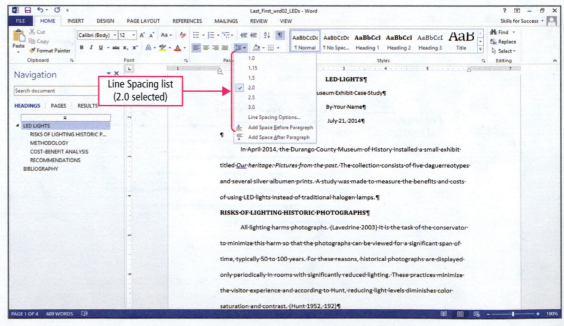

Figure 2

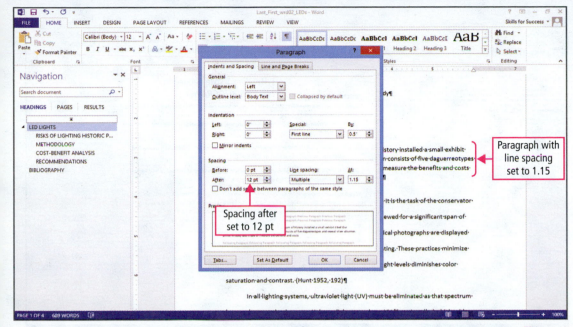

Paragraph with line spacing set to 1.15

Spacing after set to 12 pt

Figure 3

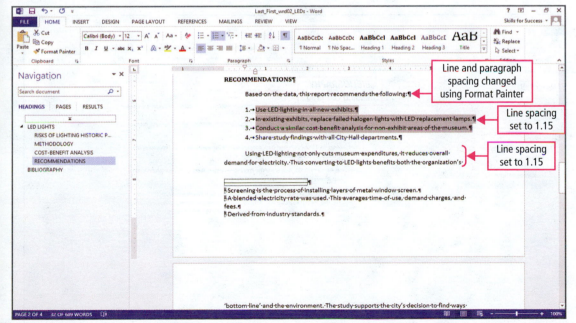

Line and paragraph spacing changed using Format Painter

Line spacing set to 1.15

Line spacing set to 1.15

Figure 4

5. In the **Line Spacing** list, point to **1.15** to preview the setting, and then click **1.15**.

   In shorter, informal reports such as this report, you can reduce the amount of line spacing so that the report fits on fewer pages. Text with a line spacing of 1.15 has been found to be easier to read than single-spaced text.

6. Open the **Paragraph** dialog box, and then change the **After** setting to **12 pt**. Compare your screen with **Figure 3**, and then click **OK**.

7. With the insertion point still in the paragraph, double-click the **Format Painter** button. With the Format Painter pointer, click one time in the nine remaining body paragraphs—do not drag—to apply the line and paragraph spacing formatting. Do not apply the formatting to the headings, bulleted list items, numbered list items, or bibliography items. When you are done, click the **Format Painter** button so it is no longer active.

8. Navigate to the **COST-BENEFIT ANALYSIS** section, and then select the first two bulleted list items. In the **Paragraph group**, click the **Line Spacing** button, and then click **1.15**.

9. In the RECOMMENDATIONS section, select the first three numbered list items, and then set the **Line Spacing** to **1.15**. Compare your screen with **Figure 4**.

10. **Save** the document.

- **You have completed Skill 7 of 10**

▶ You may need to adjust line and page break options to avoid problems when headings and paragraphs split across two pages.

▶ You can format elements quickly by modifying the styles assigned to them.

1. In the **Navigation** pane, click the **BIBLIOGRAPHY** header, and then compare your screen with **Figure 1**.

   The Bibliography header was assigned the Heading 1 style, but it does not have the same alignment and paragraph spacing as the document title.

2. Navigate to the document title, **LED LIGHTS**. With the insertion point in the title paragraph, on the **Home tab**, in the **Styles group**, right-click the **Heading 1** thumbnail. From the shortcut menu, click **Update Heading 1 to Match Selection**.

   Recall that for paragraph formatting, the paragraph does not actually need to be selected. Here, the Heading 1 style was updated based on the formatting of the paragraph the insertion point was in.

3. Navigate to the **BIBLIOGRAPHY** heading, and then compare your screen with **Figure 2**.

   The heading is now center aligned with 12 points of space below the paragraph. In this manner, you can format a document quickly by modifying its styles.

4. Navigate to the **METHODOLOGY** section. Click in the paragraph that begins *In the new exhibit,* and then open the **Paragraph** dialog box.

■ **Continue to the next page to complete the skill** ➤

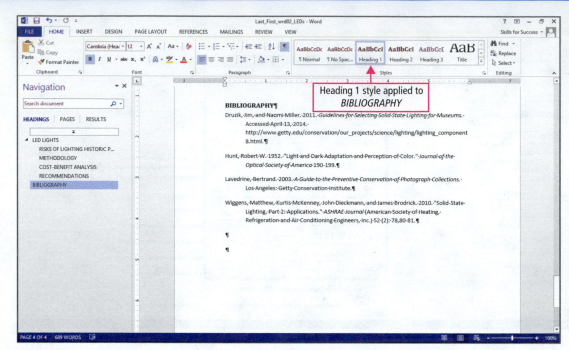

Figure 1

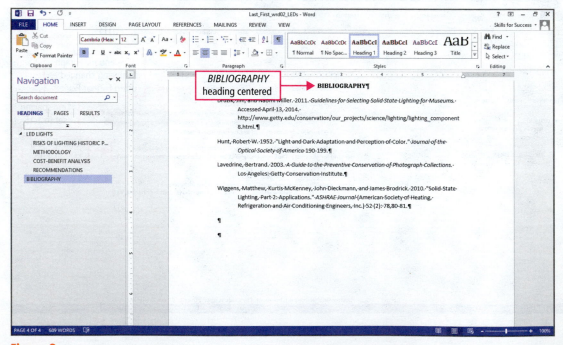

Figure 2

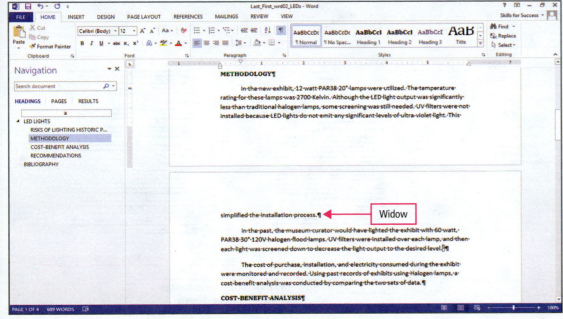

Figure 3

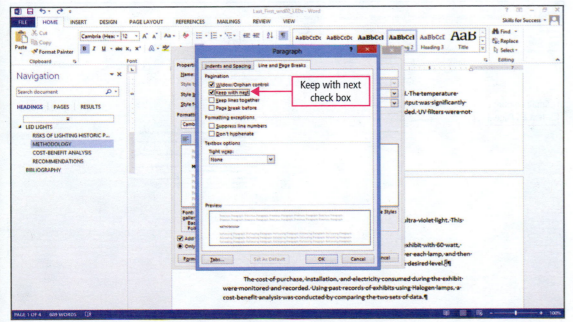

Figure 4

5. In the **Paragraph** dialog box, click the **Line and Page Breaks tab**, clear the **Widow/Orphan control** check box, and then click **OK**. Compare your screen with **Figure 3**.

   The top of Page 3 displays a *widow*—the last line of a paragraph displays as the first line of a page. An *orphan* is the first line of a paragraph that displays as the last line of a page. Both widows and orphans should be avoided.

6. On the **Quick Access Toolbar**, click the **Undo** button to enable widow and orphan control. Alternately, press Ctrl + Z.

7. Click to place the insertion point in the *METHODOLOGY* header. In the **Styles group**, right-click the **Heading 2** thumbnail, and then from the shortcut menu, click **Modify**.

8. In the lower corner of the **Modify Style** dialog box, click the **Format** button, and then click **Paragraph**.

9. On the **Line and Page Breaks tab** of the **Paragraph** dialog box, select the **Keep with next** check box, and then compare your screen with **Figure 4**.

10. Click **OK** two times to close the dialog boxes and update the Heading 2 style.

    Headings should have the *Keep with next* option selected so that at least two lines of the paragraph that follows them always display on the same page as the heading. Here, the setting has been applied to all the document's side headings—Heading 2.

11. **Save** the document.

■ **You have completed Skill 8 of 10**

▶ *Margins* are the spaces between the text and the top, bottom, left, and right edges of the paper.

▶ Viewing multiple pages on a single screen is useful when you need to evaluate the overall layout of a document.

1. Navigate to the **LED LIGHTS** heading. On the **View tab**, in the **Zoom group**, click **Multiple Pages**. Compare your screen with **Figure 1**.

   The number of pages that display when you view multiple pages depends on the dimensions of your monitor or window. On large monitors, your window may be large enough to display three pages and the text may be large enough to edit and format.

2. In the **Navigation** pane, click the **BIBLIOGRAPHY** heading. **Close ☒** the Navigation pane, and then compare your screen with **Figure 2**.

   Depending on the audience, you may want to reduce the length of a report to as few pages as possible. Here, the end of the report body uses a small portion of Page 3. Reducing the size of the side margins may fit the report on three pages instead of four.

■ Continue to the next page to complete the skill ▶

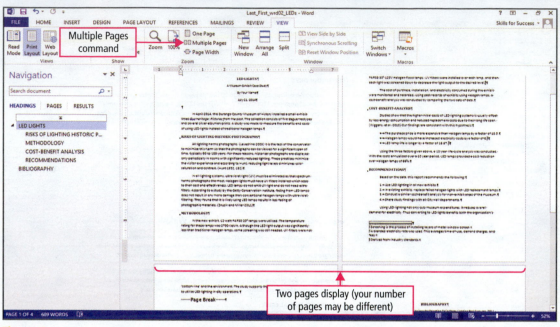

Figure 1

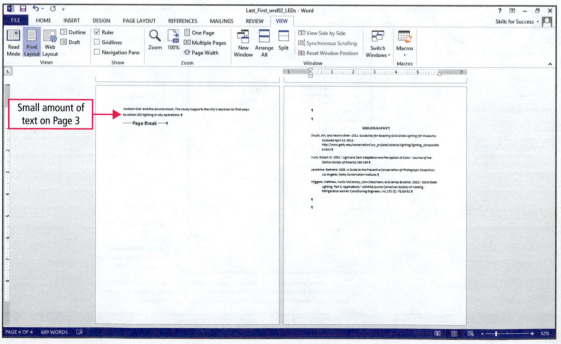

Figure 2

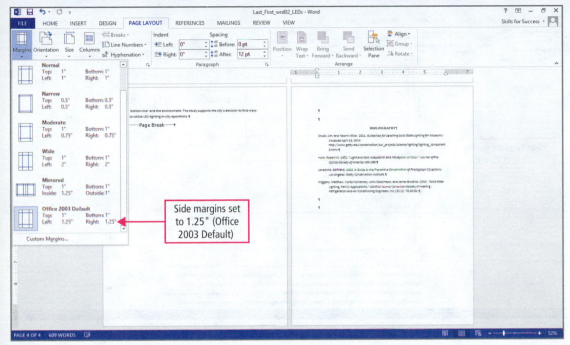

Side margins set to 1.25" (Office 2003 Default)

Figure 3

3. On the **Page Layout tab**, in the **Page Setup group**, click **Margins**, and then compare your screen with **Figure 3**.

   The Margins gallery displays thumbnails and descriptions of common margin settings. Here, the report is set to the default margin sizes used in an older version of Word—Word 2003.

   In a report, the top and bottom margins are typically 1.0 inch each, and the side margins are 1.25 inches each. In a short informal report, you can change the side margins to 1 inch each if needed.

4. In the **Margins** gallery, click the **Normal** thumbnail to set the margins to 1 inch on all four sides. Compare your screen with **Figure 4**.

   With the smaller margins, the report title and body now fit on two pages, and the Bibliography is on the third page. Before setting the margins on a report, you should check the assigned style guidelines for the dimensions that you should use.

5. Scroll up to view Page 1 and Page 2, and then on the **View tab**, in the **Zoom group**, click **100%** to return to the default view.

   If you are working on a large monitor, you may still see two pages displayed with the 100% zoom level. If so, you can snap the window to either half of the screen to see only one page at a time.

6. **Save** 🖫 the document.

■ **You have completed Skill 9 of 10**

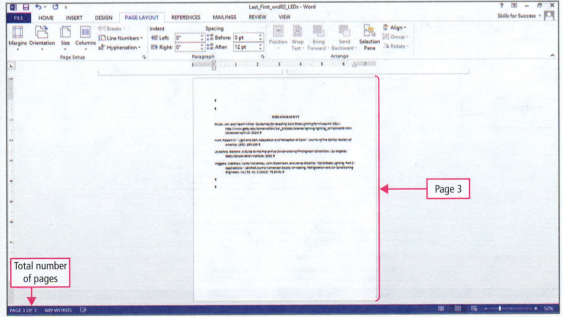

Page 3

Total number of pages

Figure 4

▶ Headers and footers can include text you type, fields, and graphics.

▶ On the first page of a document, you can set the headers and footers so that they do not display.

1. Press Ctrl + Home to move the insertion point to the beginning of the document. On the **Insert tab**, in the **Header & Footer group**, click **Page Number**. In the **Page Number** list, point to **Top of Page**, and then compare your screen with **Figure 1**.

2. In the **Page Number** gallery, use the vertical scroll bar to scroll through the page number options. When you are through, scroll to the top of the list. Under **Simple**, click **Plain Number 3** to insert the page number at the top and right margins.

   When you insert a pre-built page number in this manner, the header and footer areas are activated so that you can continue working with them.

3. Under **Header & Footer Tools**, on the **Design tab**, in the **Options group**, select the **Different First Page** check box, and notice the page number on Page 1 is removed.

4. Scroll to the top of Page 2, and verify that the page number displays, as shown in **Figure 2**.

   In reports where the body starts on the same page as the title, the page number is not included on the first page.

■ Continue to the next page to complete the skill ►

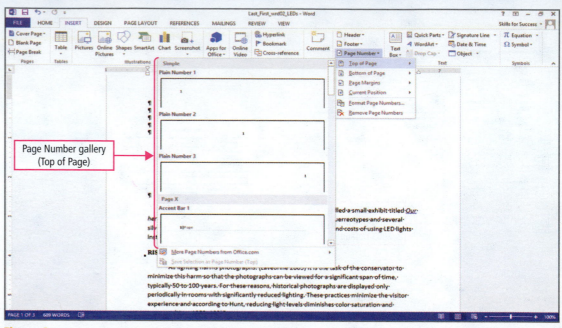

Page Number gallery (Top of Page)

Figure 1

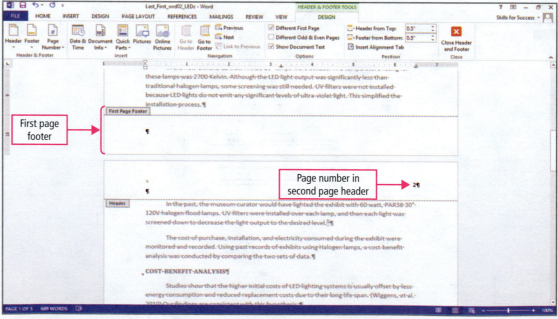

First page footer

Page number in second page header

Figure 2

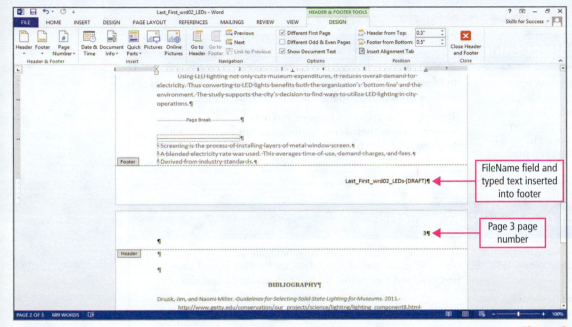

FileName field and typed text inserted into footer

Page 3 page number

Figure 3

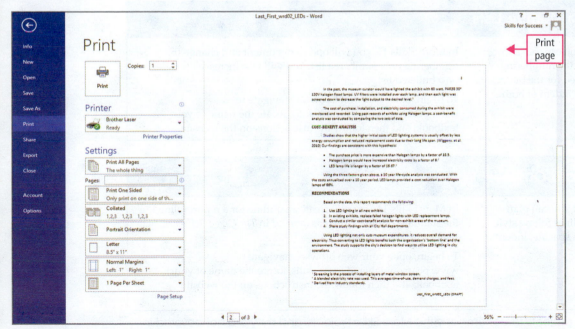

Print page

Figure 4

5. Scroll to the bottom of Page 2, and then click in the footer area. If you accidentally deactivated the header and footer areas, double-click the footer area.

6. In the **Insert group**, click the **Quick Parts** button, and then click **Field**. Under **Field names**, scroll down, click **FileName**, and then click **OK**.

7. Add a space, and then type (DRAFT) Be sure to include the parentheses.

   In this manner, headers and footers can contain both fields such as page numbers and file names and text that you type.

8. On the **Home tab**, in the **Paragraph group**, click the **Align Right** button, and then compare your screen with **Figure 3**.

   In a business setting, this footer would be removed before the report is published.

9. Double-click in the report body to deactivate the footer area. On the **File tab**, click **Print**, and then compare your screen with **Figure 4**.

10. If you are printing your work, print the report. Otherwise, click the **Back** button .

11. **Save** 🖫 the document, **Close** ✖ Word, and then submit the document as directed by your instructor.

✔ **DONE!** You have completed Skill 10 of 10, and your document is complete!

More Skills

The following More Skills are located at **www.pearsonhighered.com/skills**

More Skills Record AutoCorrect Entries

If you enable the AutoCorrect feature in Word, when you misspell a word that is contained in the AutoCorrect list, the misspelling is corrected automatically. You can add words that you commonly misspell as you type, or you can open a dialog box and add words or phrases that you want to have automatically corrected. This feature can also be used to create shortcuts for phrases that you type regularly.

In More Skills 11, you will open a short document and use two methods to add items to the AutoCorrect Options list.

To begin, open your web browser, navigate to www.pearsonhighered.com/skills, locate the name of your textbook, and then follow the instructions on the website.

More Skills Use AutoFormat to Create Numbered Lists

If you create numbered lists frequently, you can use AutoFormat to start typing the list, and the program will automatically add numbers and formatting to the list as you type.

In More Skills 12, you will open a document, set the AutoFormat options, and then create a numbered list that is formatted automatically.

To begin, open your web browser, navigate to www.pearsonhighered.com/skills, locate the name of your textbook, and then follow the instructions on the website.

More Skills Format and Customize Lists

There are several other formatting changes you can make to numbered and bulleted lists. You can change the numbering scheme, and you can change the character used for the bullet symbol. You can also increase or decrease the indent of both types of lists.

In More Skills 13, you will open a document and change the numbering on a numbered list. You will also increase the indent on a bulleted list.

To begin, open your web browser, navigate to www.pearsonhighered.com/skills, locate the name of your textbook, and then follow the instructions on the website.

More Skills Create Standard Outlines

Longer reports may require an outline so that you can plan and organize the report. Typically, report outlines follow style guidelines that specify formatting, paragraph spacing, indents, and numbering style.

In More Skills 14, you will create an outline for a report following the standard outline format as defined in *The Gregg Reference Manual* by William A. Sabin.

To begin, open your web browser, navigate to www.pearsonhighered.com/skills, locate the name of your textbook, and then follow the instructions on the website.

Please note that there are no additional projects to accompany the More Skills Projects, and they are not covered in the End-of-Chapter projects.

The following table summarizes the **SKILLS AND PROCEDURES** covered in this chapter.

Skill Number	Task	Step	Icon	Keyboard Shortcut
1	Find text	In the Navigation pane, use the search box and click Results		Ctrl + F
1	Find and replace text	In the Navigation pane, click the Search for more things arrow		Ctrl + H
1	Navigate by headings	In the Navigation pane, click Headings		
2	Insert footnotes	References tab → Footnotes group → Insert Footnote		
3	Add or edit sources	References tab → Citations & Bibliography group → Manage Sources		
3	Set reference styles	References tab → Citations & Bibliography group → Style		
4	Insert citations	References tab → Citations & Bibliography group → Insert Citation		
4	Insert a bibliography	References tab → Citations & Bibliography group → Bibliography	⬚	
5	Apply bullet lists	Home tab → Paragraph group → Bullets arrow	⬚	
5	Apply numbered lists	Home tab → Paragraph group → Numbering arrow	⬚	
5	Indent lists	Home tab → Paragraph group → Increase Indent	⬚	
6	Set first line indents	Paragraph group → Paragraph Dialog Box Launcher → Special → First Line		
7	Modify line and paragraph spacing	Paragraph group → Paragraph Dialog Box Launcher		
7	Repeat the last command			F4
8	Enable widow and orphan control	Paragraph group → Paragraph Dialog Box Launcher → Line and Page Breaks tab		
8	Set keep with next control	Paragraph group → Paragraph Dialog Box Launcher → Line and Page Breaks tab		
8	Modify styles	Right-click style thumbnail in Styles group, and then click Modify. Click the Format button and open desired dialog box.		
9	Update styles	Click or select text with desired style formatting. Right-click the style's thumbnail in Styles group, and then click Update command.		
9	Change margins	Page Layout tab → Margins		
10	Add page numbers	Insert tab → Header & Footer group → Page Number		
10	Apply different first page headers and footers	Header & Footer Tools → Design tab → Different first page		

Key Terms

Online Help Skills

1. Start **Word 2013**, and then in the upper right corner of the start page, click the **Help** button [?].

2. In the **Word Help** window **Search help** box, type word count and then press [Enter].

3. In the search result list, click **Find the word count**. Compare your screen with **Figure 1**.

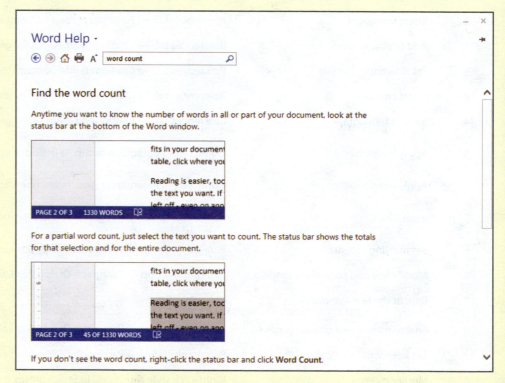

Figure 1

4. Read the article to answer to the following question: How can you find out how many words are in the document without counting the words in the footnotes?

Matching

Match each term in the second column with its correct definition in the first column by writing the letter of the term on the blank line in front of the correct definition.

G **1.** The pane used to find document text.

D **2.** A comment or notation added to the end of a section or document.

J **3.** The reference used to find information or data when writing a report.

A **4.** The citation type used for the Chicago style.

B **5.** A list of sources displayed on a separate page at the end of a report.

H **6.** The type of list used for items that are in chronological or sequential order.

C **7.** The equivalent of a blank line of text displayed between each line of text in a paragraph.

I **8.** The vertical distance above and below each paragraph in a document.

E **9.** The position of the first line of a paragraph relative to the text in the rest of the paragraph.

F **10.** The space between the text and the top, bottom, left, and right edges of the paper when you print the document.

A Author-date

B Bibliography

C Double-spacing

D Endnote

E First line indent

F Margin

G Navigation

H Numbered

I Paragraph spacing

J Source

BizSkills Video

1. What are some actions that you should take when attending a job fair?

2. What actions should be avoided when attending a job fair?

Multiple Choice

Choose the correct answer.

1. To place a note on the same page as the comment or notation, use which of these?
   - **A.** Footnote
   - **B.** Endnote
   - **C.** Citation

2. This is placed in body paragraphs and points to an entry in the bibliography.
   - **A.** Footnote
   - **B.** Citation
   - **C.** Endnote

3. The number of inches from the top edge of the paper to the beginning of the bibliography.
   - **A.** 0.5 inches
   - **B.** 1 inch
   - **C.** 2 inches

4. In a Chicago style bibliography, this type of indent is used for each reference.
   - **A.** Hanging indent
   - **B.** First line indent
   - **C.** Left alignment

5. Items that can be listed in any order are best presented using which of the following?
   - **A.** Bulleted list
   - **B.** Numbered list
   - **C.** Outline list

6. The default line spacing in a long report.
   - **A.** Custom
   - **B.** Single
   - **C.** Double

7. The vertical distance between lines in a paragraph.
   - **A.** Spacing after
   - **B.** Line spacing
   - **C.** Text wrapping

8. The last line of a paragraph that displays as the first line of a page.
   - **A.** Single
   - **B.** Stray
   - **C.** Widow

9. The pre-built setting that places all four margins at 1.0 inches.
   - **A.** Narrow
   - **B.** Normal
   - **C.** Office 2003 Default

10. This type of alignment positions the text so that it is aligned with the right margin.
    - **A.** Right
    - **B.** Center
    - **C.** Left

Topics for Discussion

1. You can build and save a list of master sources you have used in research papers and reports and display them using Manage Sources. What are the advantages of storing sources over time?

2. Paragraph text can be left aligned, centered, right aligned, or justified. Left alignment is the most commonly used. In what situations would you use centered text? Justified text? Can you think of any situations where you might want to use right alignment?

Skills Review

To complete this project, you will need the following file:

- wrd02_SRWeb

You will save your file as:

- Last_First_wrd02_Web

1. Start **Word 2013**. Open **wrd02_SRWeb**. Save the document in your chapter folder as Last_First_wrd02_SRWeb

2. Click to the right of *By,* add a space, and then type your name.

3. Click in the first body paragraph beginning *The city of Aspen Falls*. Click the **Paragraph Dialog Box Launcher**, and then in the **Paragraph** dialog box, under **Special**, select **First line**. Under **Spacing**, change the **After** value to **12 pt**, and then click **OK**. Click in the paragraph beginning *Color blindness varies,* and then press F4 to repeat the formatting.

4. Click in the side heading beginning *DESIGN FOR.* In the **Styles group**, right-click **Heading 2**, and then click **Modify**. In the **Modify Style** dialog box, click the **Format** button, and then click **Paragraph**. In the **Paragraph** dialog box, click the **Line and Page Breaks tab**, and then select the **Keep with next** check box. Click **OK** two times. Compare your screen with **Figure 1**.

5. On the **References tab**, in the **Citation & Bibliography group**, verify that **Chicago** is selected, and then click **Manage Sources**.

6. Select the source for **Bennett, Jean**, and then click the **Edit** button. Change the **Type of Source** to **Journal Article**. Add the **Journal Name** The New England Journal of Medicine and the **Pages** 2483-2484

7. Click **OK**, and then **Close** Source Manager. In the *DESIGN FOR COLOR BLINDNESS* section, click to the right of the sentence ending *degree of color blindness*. In the **Citation & Bibliography group**, click **Insert Citation**, and then click the **Bennett, Jean** source.

8. Right-click the citation just inserted, and then click **Edit Citation**. In the **Edit Citation** dialog box, type 2483 and then click **OK**. Deselect the citation, and then compare your screen with **Figure 2**.

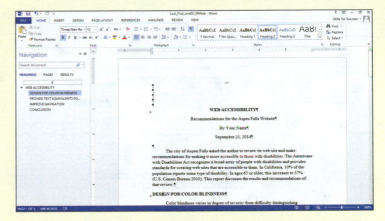

Figure 1

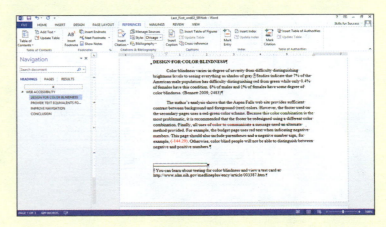

Figure 2

■ Continue to the next page to complete this Skills Review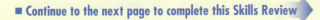

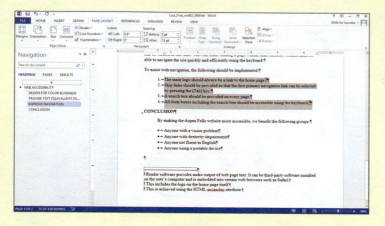

Figure 3

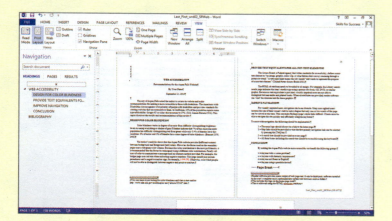

Figure 4

9. If necessary, display the Navigation pane. In the **Navigation** pane search box, type web site and then click **Results**.

10. In the **Navigation** pane, click the **Search for more things arrow**, and then click **Replace**. In the **Replace with** box, type website Click **Replace All**. Click **OK**, and then **Close** the dialog box.

11. Navigate to the *IMPROVE NAVIGATION* section, and then click to the right of the sentence ending *link to the home page*. In the **Footnotes group**, click **Insert Footnote**, and then type This includes the logo on the home page itself.

12. In the footnote just inserted, select the text but not the footnote number, and then change the font size to **12** points.

13. Select the four paragraphs beginning *The main logo* and ending with *using the keyboard*. Apply a numbered list with the *1. 2. 3.* format. In the **Paragraph group**, click the **Increase Indent** button one time.

14. In the *CONCLUSION* section, select the four paragraphs beginning *Anyone with a vision* and ending with *a portable device*. Apply a bulleted list with the solid round circle. On the **Home tab**, in the **Paragraph group**, click the **Increase Indent** button one time.

15. With the bulleted list still selected, in the **Paragraph group**, click the **Line and Spacing** button, and then click **1.15**. Repeat this formatting for the paragraphs in the numbered list.

16. On the **Page Layout tab**, in the **Page Setup group**, click the **Margins** button, and then click **Normal**. Compare your screen with **Figure 3**.

17. Move to the end of the document, and then press Ctrl + Enter to insert a page break. At the top of Page 3, press Enter two times.

18. On the **References tab**, in the **Citations & Bibliography group**, click **Bibliography**, and then click the **Bibliography** thumbnail. Change the *Bibliography* heading to BIBLIOGRAPHY

19. On the **Insert tab**, in the **Header & Footer group**, click **Page Number**, point to **Top of Page**, and then click **Plain Number 3**. In the **Options group**, select the **Different First Page** check box.

20. Navigate to the Page 2 footer, and then click in the footer. Insert the **FileName** field, add a space, and then type (DRAFT) In the **Paragraph group**, click the **Align Right** button, and then double-click in the document.

21. On the **View tab**, in the **Zoom group**, click **Multiple Pages**, and then compare your screen with **Figure 4**.

22. **Save** the document, and then submit it as directed by your instructor.

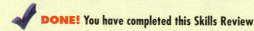

DONE! You have completed this Skills Review

Skills Assessment 1

To complete this project, you will need the following file:

- wrd02_SA1Tourism

You will save your document as:

- Last_First_wrd02_SA1Tourism

---

1. Start **Word 2013**, and then open the student data file **wrd02_SA1Tourism**. Save the document in your chapter folder as Last_First_wrd02_SA1Tourism

2. Click to the right of *By*, add a space, and then type your name.

3. Replace all occurrences of the phrase *City of Aspen Falls* with Aspen Falls

4. In the first body paragraph beginning *The Aspen Falls Tourism,* set a **0.5 inch** first line indent and the spacing after to **12 pt**. Repeat the same formatting to the paragraph beginning *The number of people visiting.*

5. Modify the **Heading 2** style so that **Keep with next** is enabled.

6. In the *DEMOGRAPHICS* section, apply a solid circle bullet to the four paragraphs beginning *Stay longer than* and ending with *drive to Aspen Falls*. Increase the list's indent to **0.5 inches** and set the line spacing to **1.15**.

7. Use **Source Manager** to edit the source for **Law, Christopher M.** Change the source type to **Journal Article**, and then add the **Journal Name** Urban Studies and the **Pages** 599-618

8. In the *DEVELOPMENT AREAS* section, after the sentence ending *is a recent practice,* insert a citation using **Law, Christopher M.** as the reference. Edit the citation field to include the pages 599-618

9. Apply a list with the *1. 2. 3.* format to the three paragraphs beginning *Agritourism* and ending with *Sports Tourism.* Increase the indent of the numbered list to **0.5 inches** and set the line spacing to **1.15**.

10. Insert a footnote after the list item *Agritourism* with the text Agritourism caters to those interested in visiting farms, ranches, and wineries. Change the footnote's text to **12** points.

11. In the blank paragraph below the *SUMMARY* section, insert a manual page break. Press ⌐Enter⌐ two times, and then insert the **Bibliography** built-in field. Change the bibliography's heading to BIBLIOGRAPHY

12. In the header, insert the **Plain Number 3** page number so that it displays on all pages except for Page 1.

13. In the **Page 2** footer, insert the **FileName** field, add a space, and then type (DRAFT) Align the footer paragraph with the right margin, and then close the footer.

14. Change the page margins to **Normal** (1 inch on all sides).

15. Compare your document with **Figure 1**. **Save** the document, and then submit it as directed by your instructor.

✔ **DONE!** You have completed Skills Assessment 1

TRAVEL AND TOURISM

Trends for the Aspen Falls Metro Area

By Your Name

September 21, 2014

The Aspen Falls Tourism Department in cooperation with the Aspen Falls Chamber of Commerce surveyed random tourists[1] about their visit to Aspen Falls. Other key indicators were assembled from public records. These include airport arrivals and departures and room tax revenues. From this analysis trends, demographics, and recommendations are provided in this report.

TRENDS

The number of people visiting Aspen Falls grew about 10% last year, and for the first time topped the 1 million mark. Over the past 10 years, spending by convention and event attendees has risen consistently. However, this past year saw a decrease in business tourist spending of 4%. This decline was offset by an increase in spending from leisure visitors. Overall, spending by business and leisure tourists increased by over 9%.

DEMOGRAPHICS

The study shows that 60% of Aspen Falls tourists are from California—resident visitors. Further, non-resident tourists:

- Stay longer than resident visitors.
- Are slightly older than resident visitors.
- Have a higher average household income than resident visitors.
- Fly in instead of drive to Aspen Falls.

Other studies have shown that on average, leisure visitors travel with larger parties and stay longer than business visitors. (Tribe 2011) These demographics suggest that marketing to

---

[1] A tourist is any person staying for one or more nights in the Aspen Falls metro area outside of their regular residence. A tourist can be classified as either a business visitor or a leisure visitor.

wrd02_SA1Tourism_solution (DRAFT)

Figure 1

---

non-resident leisure visitors would have the gre
area.

DEVELOPMENT AREAS

Treating tourism as a growth industry is
in recent years that the classifications of tourism
field. Currently, specialty tourism is seeing the
seeing robust potential.

Given its location and economy, the Asp
three specialty areas:

1. Agritourism[2]
2. Wildlife Tourism
3. Sports Tourism

According to the World Tourism Organ
of international tourism growth. (World Touris
leisure visitors from China is not mutually excl

SUMMARY

The economic benefits from promoting
would have a significant impact on the local eco
local organizations enhance the visitor experien
conservation areas attract more visitors while p
improving venues for playing sports and organi
resident and non-resident visitors.

---

[2] Agritourism caters to those interested in visiting farms, ranches, and wineries.

Skills Assessment 2

To complete this project, you will need the following file:

- wrd02_SA2Wildlife

You will save the document as:

- Last_First_wrd02_SA2Wildlife

---

1. Start **Word 2013**, and then open the student data file **wrd02_SA2Wildlife**. Save the document in your chapter folder as Last_First_wrd02_SA2Wildlife

2. Click to the right of *By*, add a space, and then type your name.

3. Replace all occurrences of the word *fisherman* with angler and then all occurrences of the word *fishermen* with anglers

4. In the first body paragraph beginning *This report summarizes,* set a **0.5 inch** first line indent and the spacing after to **12 pt**. Repeat the same formatting to the paragraph beginning *The 2013 survey was provided*.

5. Modify the **Heading 2** style so that **Widow/Orphan control** and **Keep with next** are enabled.

6. Use **Source Manager** to edit the source for **U.S. Fish & Wildlife Service**. Change the source type to **Document from a Web site**, and then add the **URL** http://www.census.gov/prod/www/abs/fishing.html

7. In the *FINDINGS* section, after the sentence ending *with the state trend,* insert a citation using **U.S. Fish_Wildlife Service** as the reference.

8. In the same section, apply a solid circle bullet to the two paragraphs beginning *Each angler spent* and ending with *equipment and trip expense.* Increase the list's indent to **0.5 inches** and set the line spacing to **1.15**.

9. At the end of the second bulleted list item, insert a footnote with the text Equipment includes binoculars, clothing, tents, and backpacking equipment. Change the footnote's text to **12** points.

10. In the *RECOMMENDATIONS* section, apply a list with the *1. 2. 3.* format to the six paragraphs beginning *Maintain existing natural areas* and ending with *wildlife recreation areas.* Increase the indent of the numbered list to **0.5 inches** and set the line spacing to **1.15**.

11. In the blank paragraph below the numbered list, insert a manual page break. Press Enter two times, and then insert the

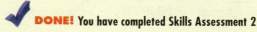

Figure 1

The study found the following economic data:

- Each angler spent an average of $1852 annually
- Each wildlife watcher spent an average of $933 [2] expenses.[2]

RECOMMENDATIONS

Based on the survey results, city planners should c... recreation opportunities. Improving and expanding the upl... provide the greatest increase in wildlife recreation. Studies ... between natural upriver habitat and healthy fish stocks. (L... The natural upriver habitat will also increase native planti... manner both populations of wildlife recreationists will be ...

To improve upland river habitat, we recommend si...

1. Maintain existing natural areas and promote co... natural areas. A natural area is defined as ¼ acr... as wood lots or open fields for the primary pur...
2. Maintain and introduce native plantings. Nativ... of food and cover plants for the primary purpos...
3. Educate the populace on how to observe and id... invasive species, and protect natural areas by st... dogs on a leash.
4. Provide wildlife photography workshops as a r... fund-raising tool.
5. Sponsor volunteer based events to remove litte... remove invasive species, and plant native plant...
6. Improve field guides and maps to wildlife recre...

[1] Trip expenses include food, fuel, and lodging. Angling equipment includes tents, clothing, and fishing gear.
[2] Equipment includes binoculars, clothing, tents, and backpacking equipment.

wrd02_SA2Wildlife_solution (DO NOT RELEASE YET)

ASPEN FALLS WILDLIFE RECREATION

An Analysis of the 2013 Visitor and Citizen Surveys

By Your Name

Oct 5, 2014

This report summarizes the findings of the annual survey of Durango County residents about their wildlife recreation. In the Aspen Falls area, wildlife recreation opportunities are limited to fishing and wildlife observation. The two activities are not mutually exclusive. Wildlife observation includes watching, photographing, or painting wildlife. Based on the annual survey, recommendations have been provided to assist Aspen Falls Parks and Recreation managers formulate policies and procedures.

METHODOLOGY

The 2013 survey was provided online and via a scripted interview process. The citizenry were invited via several media including mailings, Parks and Recreation catalogs and flyers, and public service announcements on radio and TV. A random selection of citizens were called and invited to complete the survey over the phone. Non-residents were also surveyed in the field using the interview process.

FINDINGS

An overall increase in wildlife recreation indicates that it is a significant source of enjoyment for residents and non-residents alike. However, only 23% of anglers are from out of the area and 11% are from out of state. A far higher percentage of wildlife viewers were from out of the area—nearly 45%. This indicates that the Aspen Falls area wildlife viewing opportunities attract a significant number of visitors to the area.

Over the past 10 year period, angling has decreased by 36% while wildlife viewing has increased by nearly 83%. Currently, anglers still outnumber wildlife observers nearly 2 to 1. If current trends continue, it will be several years before the number of days spent wildlife viewing will be on par with angling. This trend is consistent with the state trend. (U.S. Fish & Wildlife Service 2011)

Bibliography built-in field. Change the bibliography's heading to BIBLIOGRAPHY

12. In the header, insert the **Plain Number 3** page number so that it displays on all pages except for Page 1.

13. In the **Page 2** footer, insert the **FileName** field, add a space, and then type (DO NOT RELEASE YET) Align the footer paragraph with the right margin, and then close the footer.

14. Change the page margins to **Office 2003 Default** (1.25 inches on the sides).

15. Compare your document with **Figure 1**. **Save** the document, and then submit it as directed by your instructor.

DONE! You have completed Skills Assessment 2

Visual Skills Check

To complete this project, you will need the following file:

- wrd02_VSSecurity

You will save your document as:

- Last_First_wrd02_VSSecurity

Open the student data file **wrd02_VSSecurity**, and then save it in your chapter folder as Last_First_wrd02_VSSecurity

To complete this document, set the margins to Office 2003 Default. Format the three lists as shown in **Figure 1**. The lists have been indented to 0.5 inches, line spacing is 1.15, and the spacing after is 12 points.

The front matter is center aligned, the *By* line should display your own name, and the date should display your current date. The date paragraph's spacing after is set to 12 points.

The body paragraph has a first line indent of 0.5 inches, spacing after of 12 points, and line spacing of 1.15. At the end of the paragraph, a footnote has been inserted with the text Federal Trade Commission. Protecting Personal Information: A Guide for Business. Washington, November 2011. The footnote text is size 12, and the source title is italic.

Submit the file as directed by your instructor.

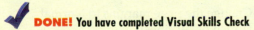 **DONE! You have completed Visual Skills Check**

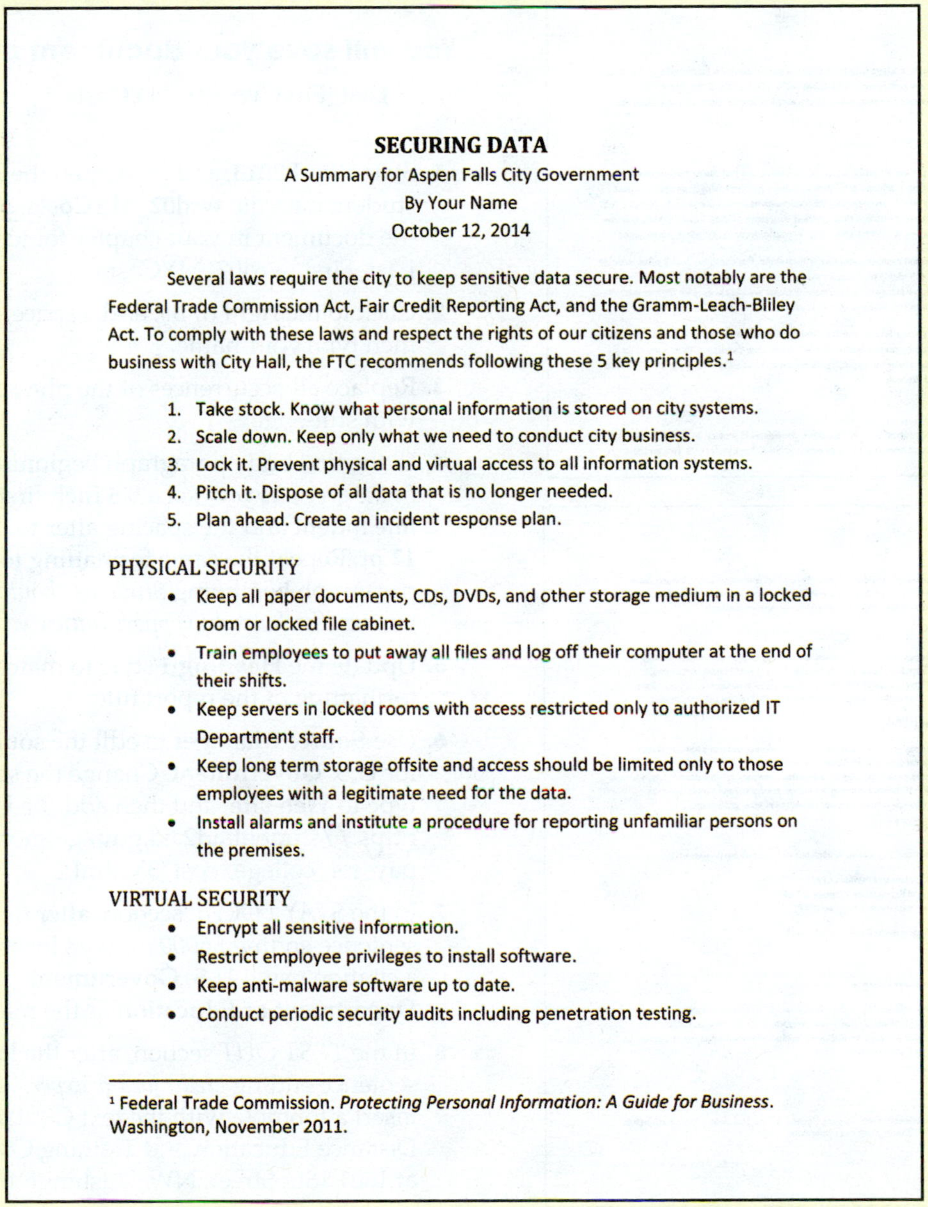

SECURING DATA

A Summary for Aspen Falls City Government

By Your Name

October 12, 2014

Several laws require the city to keep sensitive data secure. Most notably are the Federal Trade Commission Act, Fair Credit Reporting Act, and the Gramm-Leach-Bliley Act. To comply with these laws and respect the rights of our citizens and those who do business with City Hall, the FTC recommends following these 5 key principles.[1]

1. Take stock. Know what personal information is stored on city systems.
2. Scale down. Keep only what we need to conduct city business.
3. Lock it. Prevent physical and virtual access to all information systems.
4. Pitch it. Dispose of all data that is no longer needed.
5. Plan ahead. Create an incident response plan.

PHYSICAL SECURITY

- Keep all paper documents, CDs, DVDs, and other storage medium in a locked room or locked file cabinet.
- Train employees to put away all files and log off their computer at the end of their shifts.
- Keep servers in locked rooms with access restricted only to authorized IT Department staff.
- Keep long term storage offsite and access should be limited only to those employees with a legitimate need for the data.
- Install alarms and institute a procedure for reporting unfamiliar persons on the premises.

VIRTUAL SECURITY

- Encrypt all sensitive information.
- Restrict employee privileges to install software.
- Keep anti-malware software up to date.
- Conduct periodic security audits including penetration testing.

---
[1] Federal Trade Commission. *Protecting Personal Information: A Guide for Business*. Washington, November 2011.

Figure 1

PAYING FOR COLLEGE

Techniques for Saving Money

By Your Name

March 14, 2012

In the previous year, college tuition and fees at public colleges increased by over 8%. Students at private colleges saw increases of 3.2 to 4.5%. (Education & the Workforce Committee 2011). To counter this rise, students can employ several strategies to reduce the cost of attending college.

PURSUE SCHOLARSHIPS

Students should pursue all scholarship opportunities, not just those that are based on need. Scholarships based on academic achievement have been increasingly awarded in past years. (Silverstein 2002) Nearly all colleges provided merit-based scholarships to prospective students. Most states offer scholarships through their education offices. Finally, many schools offer grants and scholarships in special areas such as music, technology, math, and science.

Many companies and associations offer scholarships. For example, banks often provide scholarships or grants for students planning to work in the finance industry. Alumni organizations typically have scholarship programs. Parents should check with their employers to see if they provide assistance to children of employees.

Students should pursue all avenues for funding. For example, many schools have special scholarships for students who do not qualify for federal or state funding. Others may offer discounted tuition to older students. Typically, financial aid counselors can help students find scholarships, grants, and discounts.

STAY LOCAL

Students who attend local colleges can save considerable money on both housing and tuition. Students who live at home can save as much as $6000 per year (U.S. Government

---

2

Department of Education n.d.). Living at home also enables students to attend a community college for the first 1 or 2 years, which substantially lowers tuition costs. Tuition at local public colleges avoids the extra tuition typically charged to out-of-state residents.

WORK AND STUDY

Many students can leverage their income by working at a job coordinated through the college that they are attending. Some schools provide free room and board to students in exchange for the work they perform. Others provide discounts to student government leaders. Students should find their institution's placement office to find on and off campus jobs.

SERVE IN AN ARMED FORCE

Two programs pay for tuition and fees for those planning to be in a military service—Service Academy Scholarships and the Reserve Officers Training Corps (ROTC) Scholarship Program. Service Academy Scholarships are competitive scholarships that provide free tuition at a military academy. ROTC scholarships pay for tuition, textbooks, and a monthly living allowance. Both scholarships require a service commitment upon graduation.

TEST OUT

Receive college credit by testing through one of these test-out programs:

- Advanced Placement Program (APP)
- College-Level Examination Program (CLEP)
- Provenience Examination Program (PEP)

Some colleges give credit for life experiences.¹

OTHER OPTIONS

Several other options include:

- Take transferable summer college courses at less expensive schools.
- Take advantage of accelerated 3-year programs when they are available
- Take the maximum number of allowed credits to reduce the number of quarters or semesters needed to graduate.

---

¹ Contact the Distance Education and Training Council at 1601 18th Street, NW, Washington, DC 20009, or call (202) 234-5100 for more information.

wrd02_MYCosts_solution.docx

Figure 1

My Skills

To complete this project, you will need the following file:

- wrd02_MYCosts

You will save your document as:

- Last_First_wrd02_MYCosts

1. Start **Word 2013**, and then open the student data file **wrd02_MYCosts**. Save the document in your chapter folder as Last_First_wrd02_MYCosts

2. Click to the right of *By*, add a space, and then type your name.

3. Replace all occurrences of the phrase *you* with students

4. In the first body paragraph beginning *In the previous year*, set a **0.5 inch** first line indent and the spacing after to **12 pt**. Repeat the same formatting to the paragraph beginning *Students should pursue all scholarship opportunities*.

5. Update the **Heading 1** style to match the formatting of the report title.

6. Use **Source Manager** to edit the source for **U.S. Government**. Change the source type to **Web site**, and then add the **URL** https://studentaid2.ed.gov/getmoney/pay_for_college/cost_35.html

7. In the *STAY LOCAL* section, after the sentence ending *$6000 per year*, insert a citation using **U.S. Government Department of Education** as the reference.

8. In the *TEST OUT* section, after the last sentence ending *credit for life experiences*, insert a footnote with the text Contact the Distance Education and Training Council at 1601 18th Street, NW, Washington, DC 20009, or call (202) 234-5100 for more information.

9. In the footnote just inserted, change the footnote text font size to **12** points.

10. At the end of the document, apply a solid circle bullet to the three paragraphs beginning *Take transferable summer* and ending with *semesters needed to graduate*. Increase the indent of the list items to **0.5 inches** and set the line spacing to **1.15**.

11. In the blank paragraph below the last bulleted list, insert a manual page break. Press [Enter] two times, and then insert the **Bibliography** built-in field. Change the bibliography's heading to BIBLIOGRAPHY

12. In the header, insert the **Plain Number 3** page number so that it displays on all pages except for Page 1.

13. In the **Page 2** footer, insert the **FileName** field, align the footer paragraph with the right margin, and then close the footer.

14. Change the page margins to **Normal** (1 inch on all sides).

15. Compare your document with **Figure 1**. **Save** the document, and then submit your work as directed by your instructor.

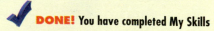 **DONE!** You have completed My Skills

Skills Challenge 1

To complete this project, you will need the following file:

- wrd02_SC1Aging

You will save your document as:

- Last_First_wrd02_SC1Aging

Open the student data file **wrd02_SC1Aging**, and then save it in your chapter folder as Last_First_wrd02_SC1Aging

Format the report following informal business report rules modeled in Skills 1–10. Take care to apply the appropriate paragraph spacing, paragraph line spacing, paragraph alignment, and indents for front matter, headings, body paragraphs, and lists. Adjust the font sizes and font colors of headings and footnotes to those used in an informal business

report. Apply one of the prebuilt margins accepted in an informal business report, making sure that the report fits within a total of three pages.

Insert your name in the By line and the FileName field in the footer. Adjust the page numbers to the correct format and placement. Submit the report as directed by your instructor.

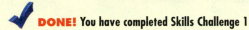 **DONE!** You have completed Skills Challenge 1

Skills Challenge 2

To complete this project, you will need the following file:

- **New blank Word document**

You will save your document as:

- Last_First_w02_SC2Parks

The Aspen Falls Planning Department is working with the Travel and Tourism Bureau to explore ways to use the city as the base of operation for tourists who want to visit important sites within a day's drive. Using the skills you practiced in this chapter, create a report on the nearby major nature attractions. These could include Yosemite National Park (250 miles), Death Valley National Park (200 miles), Sequoia National Forest (180 miles), and the Channel Islands National Park (40 miles). Research three of these sites, and write a report about the highlights of what a visitor might find at each. Include

an introduction, a section for each of the three attractions, and a conclusion. Add your sources to Source Manager, and insert them in citations and a bibliography. Format the report as an informal business report.

Save the document as Last_First_wrd02_SC2Parks Insert the FileName field and the current date in the footer, and check the entire document for grammar and spelling. Submit the report as directed by your instructor.

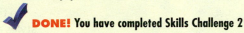 **DONE!** You have completed Skills Challenge 2

CHAPTER 3

Create Flyers

- You can enhance the effectiveness of your message and make your document more attractive by adding graphics.
- Digital images—such as those you have scanned or taken with a digital camera or a cell phone—can be added to a document and formatted using distinctive borders and other interesting and attractive effects.
- You can organize lists in rows and columns by using tabs.

- Word tables are used to organize lists and data in columns and rows without needing to create tab settings.
- You can use tables to summarize and emphasize information in an organized arrangement of rows and columns that make complex information easy to understand at a glance.
- You can format tables manually or apply a number of different formats quickly using built-in styles.

Alexey Klementiev / Fotolia

Aspen Falls City Hall

In this chapter, you will create a flyer for Carter Horikoshi, the Parks and Recreation Art Center Supervisor. The flyer will promote the art gallery and art classes provided at the Art Center. The flyer needs to describe the gallery hours, art classes, and the class fees.

An effective flyer organizes the content visually. For example, a prominent title and a graphic need to pull the reader's attention to the flyer. Subheadings should be smaller than the title, and the least prominent text should be used for the paragraphs, lists, or tables. The overall formatting and layout need to help the reader flow through the flyer's message, typically in a top to bottom direction. Wrapping text around graphics is an important technique to provide this flow.

Before formatting, you should select a theme, and then select choices from that theme's colors and fonts. In this manner, you can select formatting that works well together and does not detract from the flyer's desired look and feel. Placing content in tables or tabbed lists helps organize the flyer's message, and it is also a good idea to provide ample white space between flyer elements.

In this project, you will insert, resize, and move pictures, and apply picture styles and artistic effects. You will set tab stops and use tabs to enter data. You will also work with tables, add rows and columns, format the tables' contents, and modify their layout and design.

Time to complete all 10
skills – 45 to 60 minutes

45-60 min.

Student data files needed for this chapter:

wrd03_Art   wrd03_ArtPhoto2

wrd03_ArtPhoto1   wrd03_ArtClasses

You will save your file as:

Last_First_wrd03_Art

Outcome

Using the skills in this chapter, you will be able to
work with Word documents like this:

SKILLS

MyITLab®
Skills 1-10 Training

At the end of this chapter, you will be able to:

Skill 1   Insert Text and Pictures from Files

Skill 2   Resize and Align Pictures

Skill 3   Apply Picture Styles and Artistic Effects

Skill 4   Set Tab Stops

Skill 5   Type Tabbed Lists

Skill 6   Apply Table Styles

Skill 7   Create Tables

Skill 8   Delete and Add Table Rows and Columns

Skill 9   Format Text in Table Cells

Skill 10 Format Tables

MORE SKILLS

Skill 11 Insert Text Boxes

Skill 12 Format with WordArt

Skill 13 Convert Text into Tables

Skill 14 Insert Drop Caps

Corbett Art Center

The Art Center gallery, located in the historic Corbett
mansion, is open to the general. The gallery features
local artists and the work of students taking classes at
the center. The hours of operation are:

Day	Hours
Monday – Wednesday	noon to 5
Thursday – Friday	noon to 8
Saturday	11 to 5
Sunday	Closed

The Art Center offers art classes throughout the year. Each class has a beginning,
intermediate, and advanced section. Each section lasts two months. Art classes include
the following:

Class	Starting Months	Description
Art History	January and July	Survey of medieval to modern art.
Drawing	February and August	Freehand drawing, light and shadow, composition, and perspective, and portrait
Watercolors	March and September	Washes, wet-in-wet, and dry brush
Painting	April and October	Acrylics, oils, and watercolors.
Sculpture	May and November	Medium, modeling, busts, and abstraction
Photography	June and December	Point and Shoot, DSLRs, Photoshop, Portraits, Landscapes, and Sports

Class fees are as follows:

Class Fees		
Group	Ages	Cost
Students	12 to 17	$ 64.00
Young Adults	18 to 24	78.00
Adults	25 to 59	125.00
Seniors	60+	38.00

wrd03_Art_soluton.docx

▶ You can insert text and pictures from other files into the document you are working on.

▶ By inserting pictures from files, you can include pictures taken with digital cameras, tablets, or cell phones. You can also include files created by scanners or downloaded from the Web.

1. Start **Word 2013**, and then from the student files, open **wrd03_Art**. If your rulers do not display, on the View tab, in the Show group, select the Ruler check box.

2. On the **File tab**, click **Save As**, and then click **Browse**. In the **Save As** dialog box, navigate to the location where you are saving your files, create and open a folder named Word Chapter 3 and then **Save** the document as Last_First_wrd03_Art

3. On the **Design tab**, in the **Document Formatting group**, click the **Themes** button, and then click the **Wisp** thumbnail.

4. Select the document title *Corbett Art Center*, change the **Font Size** to **26**, and then **Center** the title. Compare your screen with **Figure 1**.

5. Position the insertion point to the left of *The Art Center gallery*. On the **Insert tab**, in the **Illustrations group**, click the **Pictures** button.

6. In the **Insert Picture** dialog box, navigate to your student files, select **wrd03_ArtPhoto1**, and then click **Insert**. Compare your screen with **Figure 2**.

   When you insert a picture, it is inserted as part of the paragraph the insertion point was in, and the Layout Options button displays to the right of the picture.

■ **Continue to the next page to complete the skill**

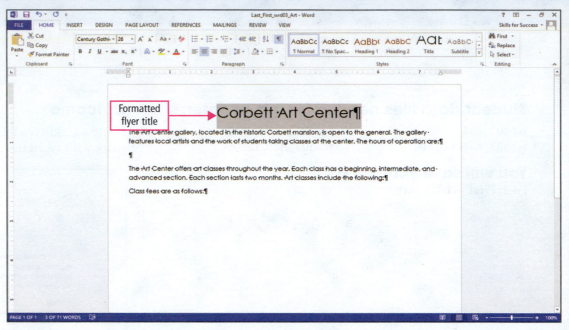

Figure 1

Figure 2

Boyan Dimitrov / Fotolia

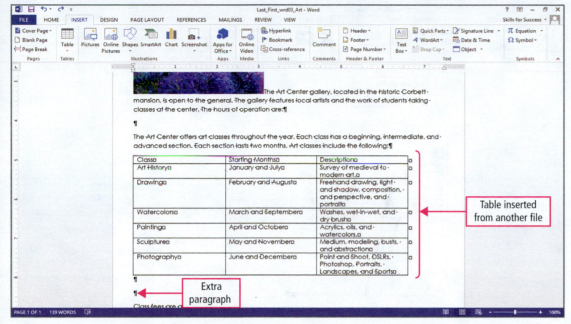

Table inserted from another file

Extra paragraph

Figure 3

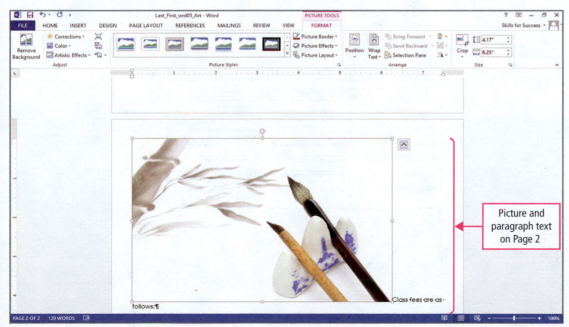

Picture and paragraph text on Page 2

Julián Rovagnati / Fotolia

Figure 4

7. At the end of the paragraph that begins *The Art Center offers art classes*, click to position the insertion point to the right of the colon, and then press Enter.

8. On the **Insert tab**, in the **Text group**, click the **Object arrow**, and then click **Text from File**.

9. In the **Insert File** dialog box, navigate to your student files, select **wrd03_ArtClasses**, and then click **Insert** to insert the table. Compare your screen with **Figure 3**.

10. With the insertion point in the second blank paragraph below the inserted table, press Backspace to remove the extra blank paragraph that is created when you insert text from a file.

11. Position the insertion point to the left of *Class fees are as follows* and then use the technique practiced previously to insert the **wrd03_ArtPhoto2** picture from the student data files for this chapter. Compare your screen with **Figure 4**.

Because the picture is too large to fit in the available space at the bottom of the first page, a new page was added containing just the picture and the paragraph. You will move the figure in the next skill.

12. **Save** the document.

■ **You have completed Skill 1 of 10**

▶ When you select a graphic, **sizing handles**—small squares or circles on an object's border—display and the Format contextual tab is added to the Ribbon.

▶ You can move graphics precisely using **Alignment Guides**—lines that display when an object is aligned with document objects such as margins and headings.

1. On Page 2, be sure the **wrd03_ArtPhoto2** paint brushes picture is selected.

2. On the right border of the picture, locate the middle—square—sizing handle. Point to the sizing handle to display the ↔ pointer, and then drag to the left to approximately **2 inches** on the horizontal ruler, as shown in **Figure 1**, and then release the left mouse button.

   When you size an image using the middle sizing handles, the picture does not resize proportionally.

3. On the **Format tab**, in the **Adjust group**, click the **Reset Picture arrow** 🖼, and then click **Reset Picture & Size**.

4. Point to the sizing handle in the lower right corner of the picture. When the ⤢ pointer displays, drag up and to the left until the right border of the picture aligns at approximately **2 inches** on the horizontal ruler. Release the left mouse button, and then compare your screen with **Figure 2**.

   When you size an image using the corner sizing handles, the picture resizes proportionally.

■ **Continue to the next page to complete the skill** ➡

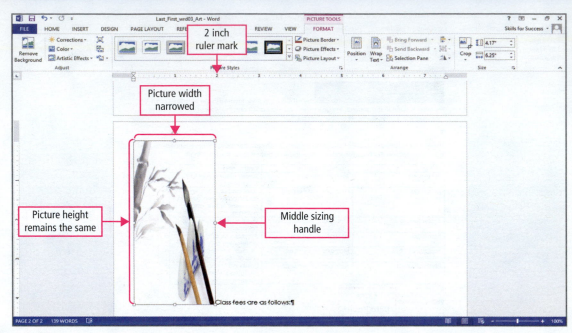

Figure 1

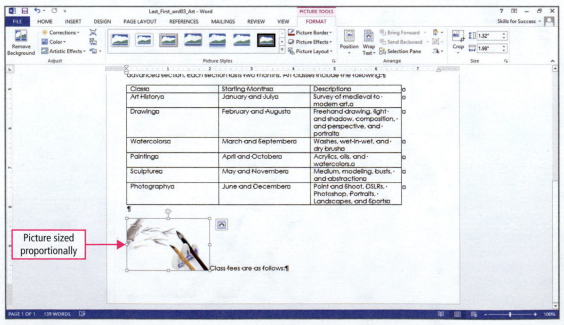

Figure 2

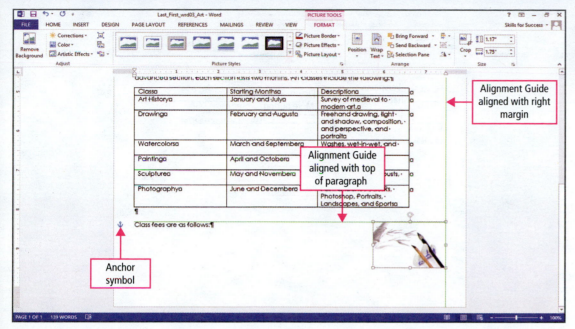

Alignment Guide aligned with right margin

Alignment Guide aligned with top of paragraph

Anchor symbol

Figure 3

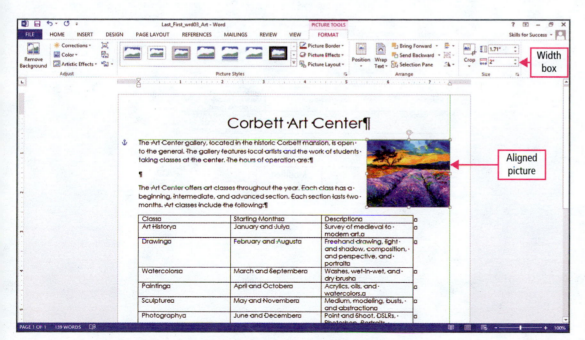

Width box

Aligned picture

Figure 4

5. With the second picture still selected, on the **Format tab**, in the **Size group**, select the value in the **Width** box. Type 1.75 and then press Enter to change the size of the picture to 1.75 inches wide and approximately 1.17 inches in height.

6. With the second picture still selected, click its **Layout Options** button, and then under **With Text Wrapping**, click the first thumbnail—**Square**.

    The Square text wrapping option changes the picture to a *floating object*, which you can move independently of the surrounding text. An *anchor* symbol displays to the left of a paragraph to indicate which paragraph is associated with the picture.

7. Point to the picture to display the pointer. Drag the picture so that the Alignment Guides align with the right margin and the top of the paragraph that begins *Class fees*. Compare your screen with **Figure 3**, and then release the left mouse button.

    If your Alignment Guides do not display, on the Page Layout group, in the Arrange group, click Align, and then click Use Alignment Guides.

8. Press Ctrl + Home , and then select the flower field picture. On the **Format tab**, in the **Size group**, change the **Width** to 2"

9. Repeat the technique practiced previously to change the picture's layout to **Square**.

10. Repeat the technique just practiced to position the picture as shown in **Figure 4**.

11. **Save** the document.

■ **You have completed Skill 2 of 10**

▶ You can add special effects to graphics to make them look like drawings or paintings.

▶ You can also apply built-in picture styles and then format that style's borders, effects, or layouts.

1. Press Ctrl + End, and then click the picture with the paint brushes.

2. On the **Format tab**, in the **Picture Styles group**, click the **More** button ⤵, and then point to several thumbnails to view them using Live Preview.

3. In the gallery, use ScreenTips text to locate and click the eighteenth thumbnail—**Perspective Shadow, White**—and then compare your screen with **Figure 1**.

4. In the **Picture Styles group**, click the **Picture Effects** button, point to **Bevel**, and then click the first effect in the second row—**Angle**.

In this manner you can adjust the Picture Style settings applied in the Quick Style gallery. Here, the bevel setting assigned by the picture style was changed from Round to Angle.

5. Click the **Picture Effects** button, point to **3-D Rotation**, and then under **Perspective**, click the first effect in the third row—**Perspective Contrasting Right**. Click in a paragraph to deselect the picture, and then compare your screen with **Figure 2**.

■ **Continue to the next page to complete the skill** ➤

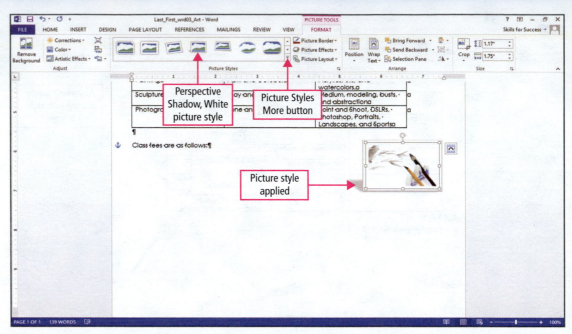

Figure 1

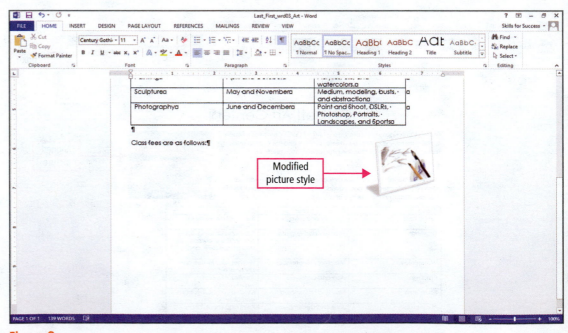

Figure 2

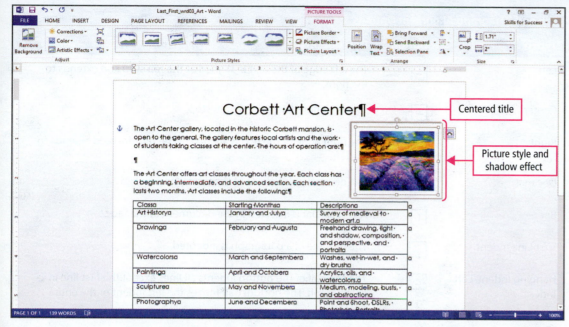

Centered title

Picture style and shadow effect

Figure 3

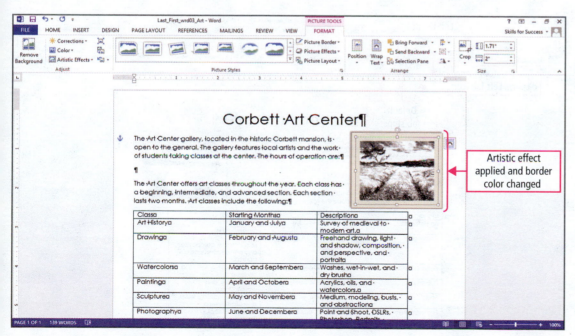

Artistic effect applied and border color changed

Figure 4

6. Press `Ctrl` + `Home` to move to the top of the document, select the flower field picture, and then apply the sixteenth picture style—**Moderate Frame, White**.

7. Click the **Picture Effects** button, point to **Shadow**, and then click the last thumbnail under **Outer—Offset Diagonal Top Left**.

   When applying shadow effects, all the shadows should be on the same side(s) of each graphic. Because the new style increased the size of the picture, the title has wrapped to the left and is no longer centered.

8. With the picture still selected, press `↓` approximately two times until the document title is centered. Compare your screen with **Figure 3**.

   To move objects in small precise increments, you can **nudge** them in this manner by selecting the object and then pressing one of the arrow keys.

9. In the **Adjust group**, click the **Artistic Effects** button. Point to several thumbnails in the gallery to preview available effects, and then click the fourth effect—**Pencil Sketch**.

10. With the picture still selected, in the **Picture Styles group**, click the **Picture Border** button. In the second row under **Theme Colors**, click the seventh color—**Brown, Accent 3, Lighter 80%**. Compare your screen with **Figure 4**.

11. Save 🖫 the document.

■ **You have completed Skill 3 of 10**

▶ A ***tab stop*** is a specific location on a line of text and marked on the Word ruler to which you can move the insertion point by pressing Tab. Tabs are used to align and indent text.

▶ Tab stops can be set and modified using the ruler or in the Tabs dialog box.

1. Click in the blank paragraph below the paragraph starting *The Art Center gallery*.

2. On the left end of the horizontal ruler, notice the **Tab Selector** button ⌊L⌋—the icon displayed in your button area may be different.

3. Click the button several times to view the various tab styles and paragraph alignment options available. Pause at each tab stop type, and then view the information in the table in **Figure 1** to see how each of the tab types is used.

4. With the insertion point still in the blank paragraph, click the **Tab Selector** button until the **Left Tab** icon ⌊L⌋ displays.

5. On the horizontal ruler, point to the mark that indicates **0.25 inches**, and then click one time to insert a left tab stop. Compare your screen with **Figure 2**.

The default tab stops are every half inch. When you add your own tab stop, it replaces the default tab stops up to that place on the ruler. To the right of that tab, the next half inch mark will be the next default tab stop.

■ **Continue to the next page to complete the skill** ➡

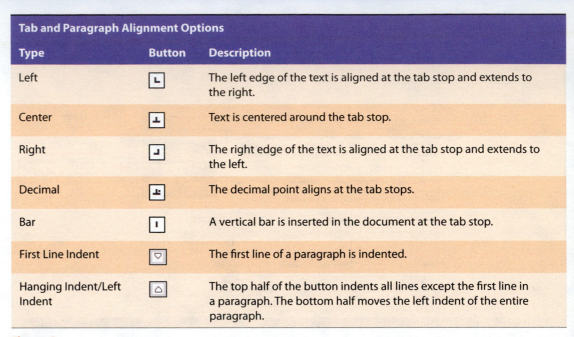

Tab and Paragraph Alignment Options		
Type	**Button**	**Description**
Left	⌊L⌋	The left edge of the text is aligned at the tab stop and extends to the right.
Center	⊥	Text is centered around the tab stop.
Right	⌐⌡	The right edge of the text is aligned at the tab stop and extends to the left.
Decimal	⊥•	The decimal point aligns at the tab stops.
Bar	I	A vertical bar is inserted in the document at the tab stop.
First Line Indent	▽	The first line of a paragraph is indented.
Hanging Indent/Left Indent	△	The top half of the button indents all lines except the first line in a paragraph. The bottom half moves the left indent of the entire paragraph.

Figure 1

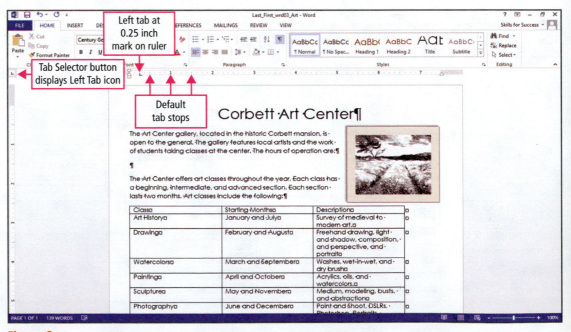

Figure 2

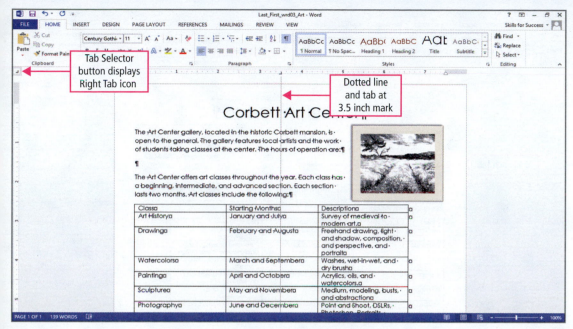

Figure 3

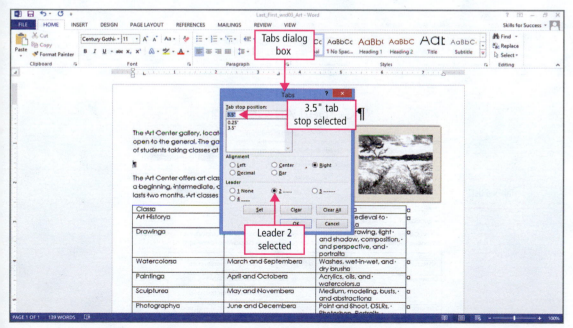

Figure 4

6. Click the **Tab Selector** button two times to display the **Right Tab** icon ⌐.

7. On the ruler, point to the mark that indicates **3.5 inches**. Click and hold down the mouse button. Notice that a dotted line indicates the tab location in the document, as shown in **Figure 3**. In this manner, you can determine whether the tab stop is exactly where you want it.

8. Release the mouse button to insert the right tab stop.

9. On the **Home tab**, click the **Paragraph Dialog Box Launcher** ⌐. At the bottom of the **Paragraph** dialog box, click the **Tabs** button. Alternately, double-click a tab stop on the ruler.

10. In the **Tabs** dialog box, under **Tab stop position**, select the tab stop at **3.5"**. Under **Leader**, select the **2** option button to add a dot leader to the selected tab stop. Near the bottom of the dialog box, click the **Set** button, and then compare your screen with **Figure 4**.

   A *leader* is a series of characters that form a solid, dashed, or dotted line to fill the space preceding a tab stop; a *leader character* is the symbol used to fill the space. A *dot leader* is a series of evenly spaced dots that precede a tab stop.

11. In the **Tabs** dialog box, click **OK**, and then **Save** ⊟ the document.

■ **You have completed Skill 4 of 10**

▶ The Tab key is used to move to the next tab stop in a line of text.

▶ When you want to relocate a tab stop, you can drag the tab stop marker to a new location on the ruler.

1. Be sure your insertion point is still in the blank paragraph and the tab stops you entered display on the horizontal ruler.

2. Press Tab to move the insertion point to the first tab stop you placed on the ruler. Type Day and then press Tab to move to the right tab with the dot leader that you created.

3. Type Hours and then press Enter. Compare your screen with **Figure 1**.

   When your insertion point is positioned at a right tab stop and you begin to type, the text moves to the left. When you press Enter, the new paragraph displays the same tab stop markers on the ruler as the previous paragraph.

4. Press Tab, type Monday - Wednesday and then press Tab. Type noon to 5 and then press Enter.

5. Press Tab, type Thursday - Friday and then press Tab. Type noon to 8 and then press Enter.

6. Press Tab, type Saturday and then press Tab. Type 11 to 5 and then press Enter.

7. Press Tab, type Sunday and then press Tab. Type Closed and compare your screen with **Figure 2**.

■ **Continue to the next page to complete the skill**

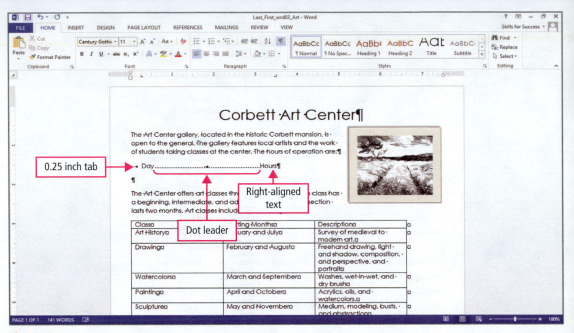

Figure 1

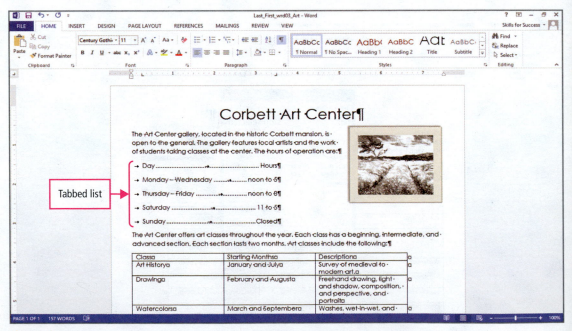

Figure 2

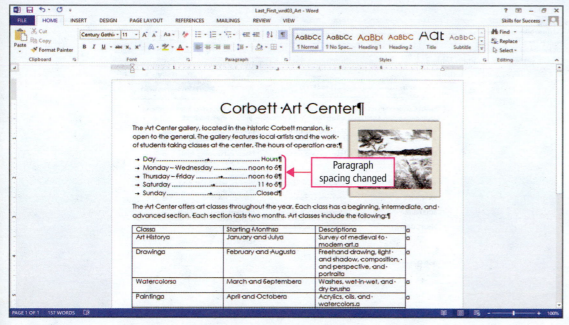

Figure 3

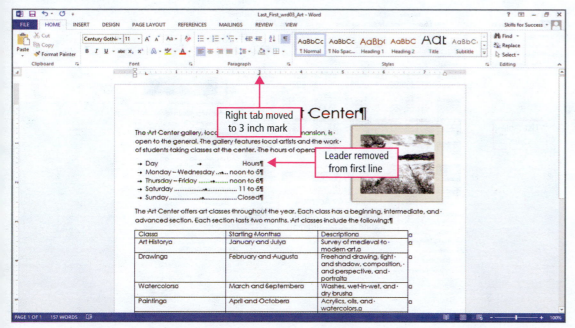

Figure 4

8. Select the first four lines of the tabbed list starting with *Day* and ending with *11 to 5*. Do not select the paragraph that begins *Sunday*.

9. On the **Home tab**, in the **Paragraph group**, click the **Line Spacing** button, and then click **Remove Space After Paragraph**. Click anywhere in the document to deselect the text, and then compare your screen with **Figure 3**.

10. Select all five lines in the tabbed list. On the horizontal ruler, place the tip of the pointer over the right tab mark at **3.5 inches** on the horizontal ruler. When the ScreenTip *Right Tab* displays, drag left to move the tab mark to **3 inches**.

11. Click in the first line of the tabbed list. On the horizontal ruler, point to the right tab mark again. When the ScreenTip *Right Tab* displays, double-click to open the **Tabs** dialog box.

12. In the **Tabs** dialog box, select the **3"** tab stop, and then under **Leader**, click the **None** option button. Click **OK**, and then compare your screen with **Figure 4**.

Tabs are added or changed only for the selected paragraphs. Here, the leader is removed only from the first line in the tabbed list.

13. **Save** the document.

■ **You have completed Skill 5 of 10**

▶ Because tables can hold text, numbers, or graphics, they are often used to lay out and summarize data.

▶ You can format each table element individually, or you can apply table styles to the entire table.

1. Scroll as needed to display the entire table.

   A table consists of cells arranged in rows and columns. Here, the table contains seven rows and three columns.

2. Click in any cell in the table to display the Table Tools contextual tabs—Design and Layout. Below Table Tools, click the **Design tab**, and then in the **Table Styles group**, notice that a number of predesigned table styles are available.

3. Point to the fourth style—**Plain Table 3**—to preview style, as shown in **Figure 1**.

4. In the **Table Styles group**, click the **More** button 🔽.

5. In the **Table Styles** gallery, use the vertical scroll bar to scroll to the bottom of the gallery. Under **List Tables**, locate the **List Table 4 - Accent 4** thumbnail, and then point to it, as shown in **Figure 2**.

   Because the width of the Table Styles gallery changes depending on the size of your window, the position of your thumbnails may be different than in the figure.

6. Click one time to apply the **List Table 4 - Accent 4** table style.

   You need only to click in a table to apply a table style. You do not need to select the table first.

■ **Continue to the next page to complete the skill**

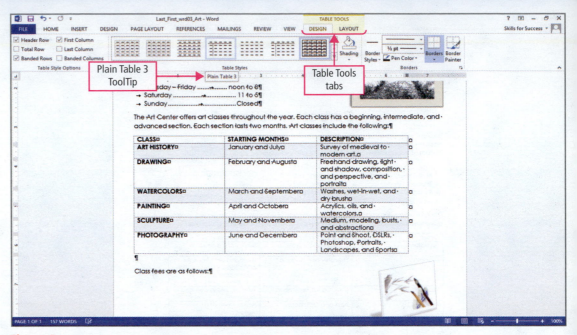

Figure 1

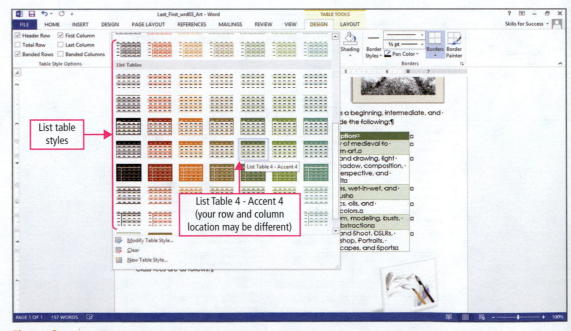

Figure 2

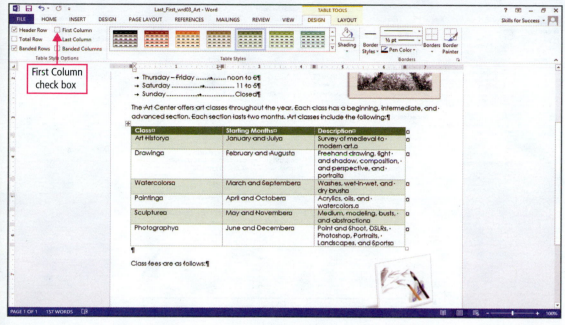

First Column check box

Figure 3

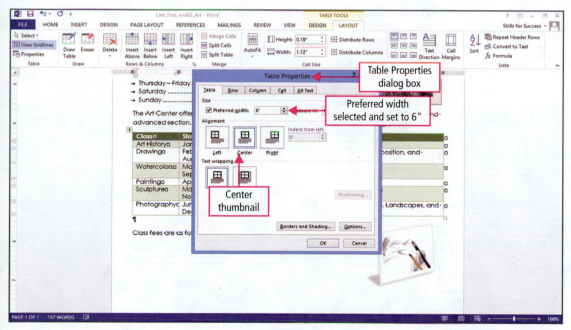

Table Properties dialog box

Preferred width selected and set to 6"

Center thumbnail

Figure 4

7. In the **Table Style Options group**, clear the **First Column** check box to remove the bold from the first column, as shown in **Figure 3**.

In this manner you can customize how a pre-built table style is applied to a table. Here, the formatting assigned to the first column was disabled.

8. Click the **Layout tab**. In the **Cell Size group**, click the **AutoFit** button, and then click **AutoFit Contents**.

The columns, which were all the same width, adjust to the best fit based on the content in the cells.

9. In the **Table group**, click the **Properties** button. In the **Table Properties** dialog box, be sure the **Table tab** is selected. Under **Size**, select the **Preferred width** check box. In the **Preferred width** box, change the existing value to **6"**.

10. In the **Table Properties** dialog box, under **Alignment**, click **Center**. Compare your screen with **Figure 4**, and then click **OK** to set the table width and to center the table between the left and right margins.

11. Save 🖫 the document.

■ **You have completed Skill 6 of 10**

▶ To create a table using the Insert Table command, you need to specify the number of rows and columns you want to start with.

▶ A table created with the Insert Table command retains the formatting of the paragraph above the table and the columns are of equal width.

1. Press `Ctrl` + `End`, and then press `Enter` to create a new blank paragraph at the bottom of the document.

2. Click the **Insert tab**, and then in the **Tables group**, click the **Table** button. In the fifth row, point to the second box, and then compare your screen with **Figure 1**.

   The top of the Table gallery displays the dimensions of the table, with the number of columns first, followed by the number of rows—in this instance, you are creating a 2x5 table.

3. Click one time to insert a **2x5 Table**. Scroll as needed to view the table just inserted, and then compare your screen with **Figure 2**.

   Like a graphic, a table is associated with a paragraph. Here, the table's paragraph formatting mark displays below the table.

   When no objects are in the way, an inserted table will extend from the left margin to the right margin. Here, the table wraps below the floating image that is attached to the paragraph above the table.

■ **Continue to the next page to complete the skill** ➤

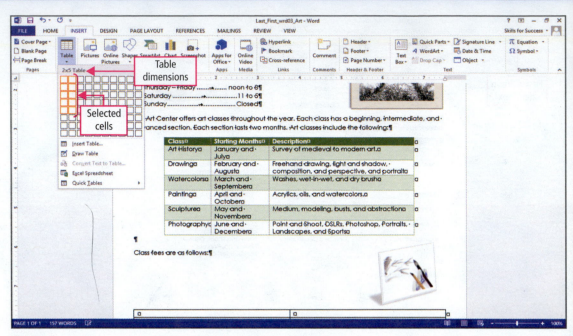

Figure 1

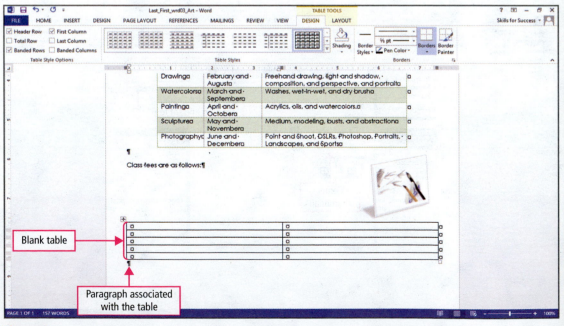

Figure 2

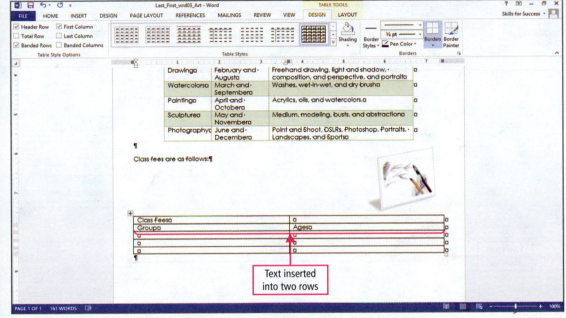

Text inserted into two rows

Figure 3

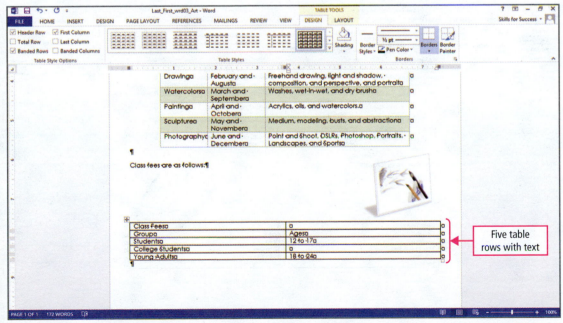

Five table rows with text

Figure 4

4. Be sure the insertion point is located in the upper left cell of the new table. Type Class Fees and then press Tab.

You can use Tab or the arrow keys to move among cells in a table. When you press Enter, a second line in the same cell is created. If this happens, you can press Backspace to remove the inserted paragraph.

5. Press Tab again to move to the first cell in the second row. Type Group and then press Tab.

6. Type Ages and then press Tab. Compare your screen with **Figure 3**.

7. With the insertion point in the first cell of the third row, type Students and then press Tab. Type 12 to 17 and then press Tab.

8. In the first cell of the fourth row, type College Students and then press ↓.

9. In the first cell of the last row, type Young Adults and then press Tab. Type 18 to 24 and then compare your screen with **Figure 4**.

10. **Save** 🖫 the document.

■ **You have completed Skill 7 of 10**

► You can add rows to the beginning, middle, or end of a table, and you can delete one or more rows, if necessary.

► You can add columns to the left or right of the column that contains the insertion point.

1. In the fourth row of the table, click anywhere in the *College Students* cell.

   To delete a row, you need only position the insertion point anywhere in the row.

2. On the **Layout tab**, in the **Rows & Columns group**, click the **Delete** button, and then click **Delete Rows**. If you accidentally click Delete Columns, on the Quick Access Toolbar, click the Undo button ↺ and try again.

3. Right-click the *Young Adults* cell. On the Mini toolbar, click the **Insert** button, and then click **Insert Below** to add a row.

4. Type Adults and then notice that although the entire row was selected when you started typing, the text was entered into the row's first cell. Press Tab, and then type 25 to 59 Press Tab to add a new row, and then compare your screen with **Figure 1**.

   When the insertion point is in the last cell, you can add another row by pressing Tab.

5. In the first cell of the new row, type Seniors and then press Tab. Type 60+ and then compare your screen with **Figure 2**.

■ **Continue to the next page to complete the skill** ➡

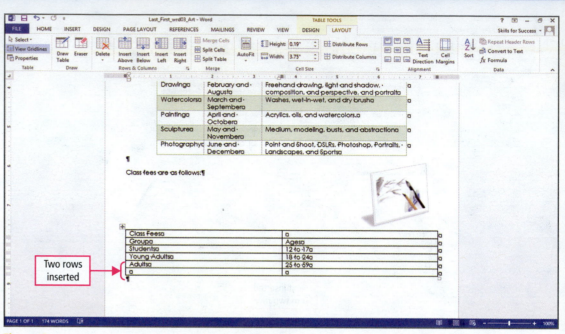

Figure 1

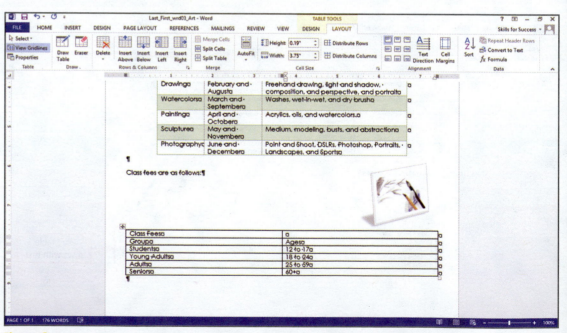

Figure 2

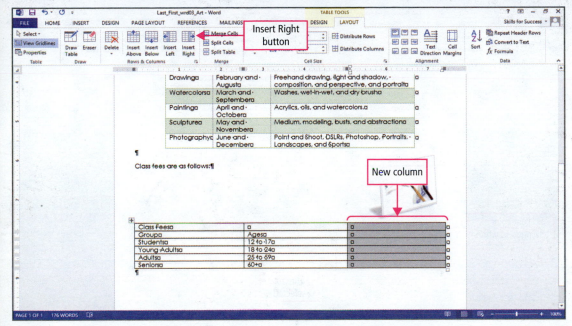

Figure 3

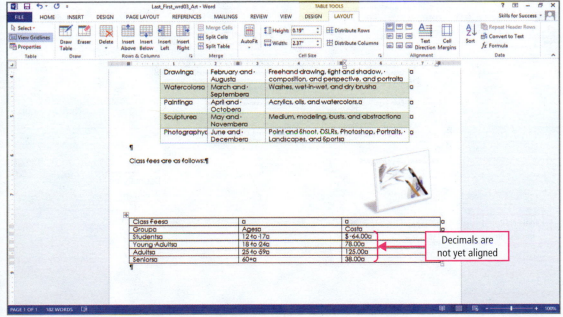

Figure 4

6. Be sure the insertion point is positioned in a cell in the second column of the table.

7. On the **Layout tab**, in the **Rows & Columns group**, click the **Insert Right** button to insert a new column to the right of the column that contained the insertion point, as shown in **Figure 3**.

   An alternate method to insert rows and columns is to point to a table border, and then click the Insert button that displays at the top of the column or beginning of the row. When you insert a new column, the existing columns are resized to fit within the width of the table.

8. In the new column, click in the second row, and then type Cost

9. Press ↓ to move to the next cell in the column, and then type 64.00

10. Press ↓, and then type 78.00 In the next cell down, type 125.00 and in the last cell of the table, type 38.00

11. In the third row, click to position the insertion point to the left of *64.00*. If the entire cell is selected, point closer to the *64.00* and click again. Type $ and then press [SpaceBar] two times. Compare your screen with **Figure 4**.

   A dollar sign is typically added only to the first row in a column of numbers and to the *Totals* row, if there is one. You will align the decimal points in this column in the next skill.

12. Save 🖫 the document.

■ **You have completed Skill 8 of 10**

► Text in a table is formatted using the same techniques as text in paragraphs.

► When you apply paragraph formatting to text in a table, it is applied only to the cell the text is in.

1. Position the pointer in the left margin to the left of the first row of the lower table to display the ⇗ pointer, and then click one time to select the row.

2. Under **Table Tools**, on the **Design tab**, in the **Table Styles group**, click the **Shading arrow** ⬛▾, and then in the first row, click the seventh color—**Brown**, **Accent 3**.

3. With the entire row still selected, change the font size to **12**, and then change the font color to the first color in the first row—**White**, **Background 1**. Compare your screen with **Figure 1**.

4. Repeat the technique just practiced to select the second row of the table, and then apply the **Center** ▤ paragraph alignment.

5. With the second row still selected, change the font color to the eighth choice in the first row—**Olive Green**, **Accent 4**.

6. Click in the third cell in the third row—*$ 64.00*. Drag down to select the remaining cells in the column, and then apply the **Align Right** ▤ paragraph alignment. Compare your screen with **Figure 2**.

Numbers are typically aligned to the right in table cells.

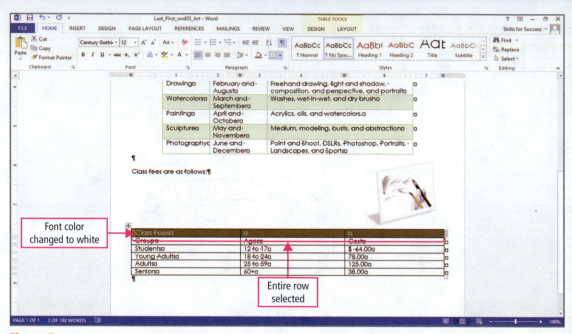

Font color changed to white

Entire row selected

Figure 1

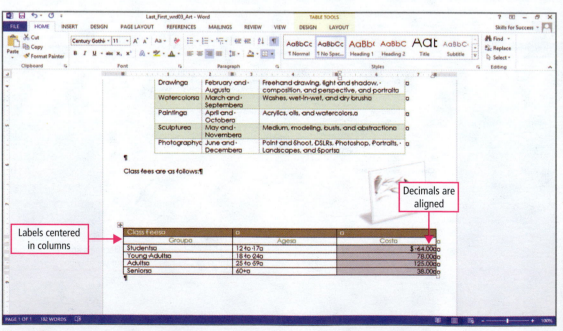

Decimals are aligned

Labels centered in columns

Figure 2

■ Continue to the next page to complete the skill ▶

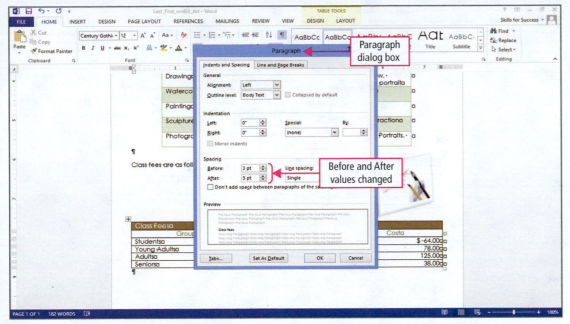

Figure 3

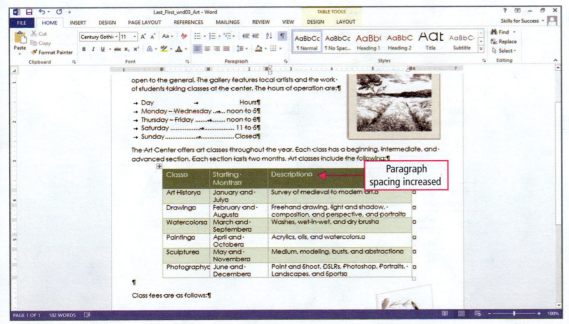

Figure 4

7. Click in the first cell—*Class Fees*. Click the **Paragraph Dialog Box Launcher** button. In the **Paragraph** dialog box, under **Spacing**, select the text in the **Before** box, and then type 3 pt Change the **After** value to 3 pt and then compare your screen with **Figure 3**.

  When you type numbers into the Before and After boxes without providing a unit of measure, the points unit will automatically be applied.

8. Click **OK** to accept the change and close the dialog box.

9. Scroll up to view the first table, select the first row, and then change the font size to **12**. Click the **Bold** button to remove the bold, and then set the paragraph spacing **Before** and **After** to 3 pt

10. Click in another cell to deselect the row, and then compare your screen with **Figure 4**.

11. **Save** the document.

■ **You have completed Skill 9 of 10**

▶ To improve a table's readability, you can merge cells, change column widths, remove borders, and align text vertically.

▶ In a table, **vertical alignment** determines the space above and below a text or object in relation to the top and bottom of the cell.

1. In the upper table, click in any cell in the middle column. On the **Layout tab**, in the **Cell Size group**, click the **Width up spin arrow** as needed to widen the middle column to **1.6"**.

2. In the lower table, repeat the technique just practiced to change the first column's width to **1.5"**, the second column's width to **1.2"**, and the third column's width to **0.8"**.

3. In the lower table, select the first row. On the **Layout tab**, in the **Merge group**, click the **Merge Cells** button.

4. On the **Layout tab**, in the **Alignment group**, click the **Align Top Center** button 🔲. Click to deselect the row, and then compare your screen with **Figure 1**.

5. In the lower table, point to the second row, and then with the 🡒 pointer, drag down to select rows two through six. In the **Cell Size group**, change the **Height** value to **0.3"**.

6. Select the second row, and then in the **Alignment group**, click the **Align Center** button 🔲. Compare your screen with **Figure 2**.

7. In the first column of the lower table, select the four cells starting with *Students* and ending with *Seniors*. In the **Alignment group**, click the **Align Center Left** button 🔲.

■ **Continue to the next page to complete the skill** ➡

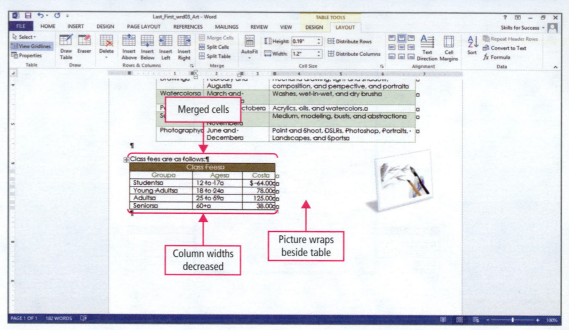

Figure 1

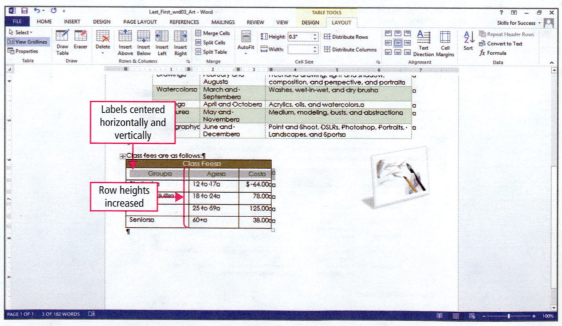

Figure 2

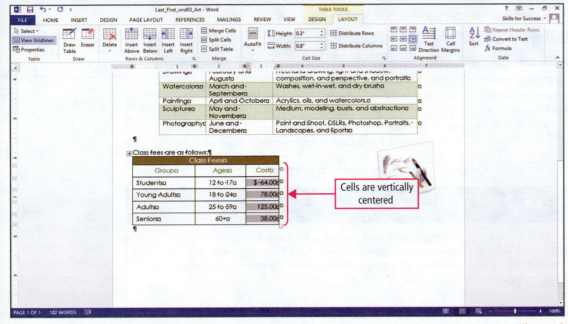

Figure 3

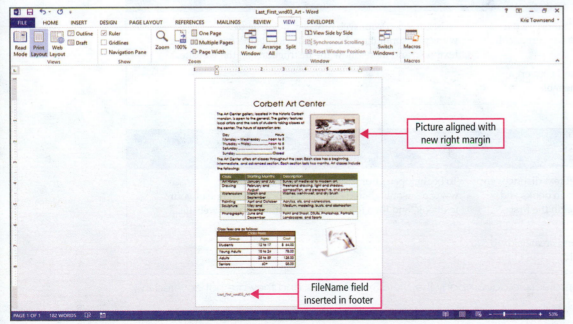

Figure 4

8. In the second column, select the cells starting with *12 to 17* and ending with *60+*. In the **Alignment group**, click the **Align Center** button.

9. In the third column, select the cells starting with *$ 64.00* and ending with *38.00*. In the **Alignment group**, click the **Align Center Right** button. Compare your screen with **Figure 3**.

10. Above and to the left of the lower table, click the **Table Selector** button to select the table.

11. On the **Table Tools Design tab**, in the **Borders group**, click the **Borders arrow**, and then notice that several types of borders are selected in the gallery.

12. In the **Border** gallery, click **Inside Vertical Border** to remove the border from the table. Click a cell to deselect the table, and then click the **Show/Hide** button to hide the formatting marks.

13. On the **View tab**, in the **Zoom group**, click **One Page**.

14. On the **Page Layout tab**, in the **Page Setup group**, click **Margins**, and then click **Normal** to increase the margin widths. Using the Alignment Guides, align the first picture with the right margin and the top of the first body paragraph.

15. Add the **FileName** field to the footer, deactivate the footer area, and then compare your screen with **Figure 4**.

16. **Save** the document, **Close** Word, and then submit your work as directed by your instructor.

DONE! You have completed Skill 10 of 10, and your document is complete!

More Skills

The following More Skills are located at **www.pearsonhighered.com/skills**

More Skills Insert Text Boxes

Text boxes are floating objects that can be placed anywhere in a document. They are useful when you want to present text in a different orientation from other text. Text boxes function as a document within a document, and they can be resized or moved. Text in a text box wraps in the same manner it wraps in any document.

In More Skills 11, you will open a document and create a text box. You will also resize and format the text box.

To begin, open your web browser, navigate to www.pearsonhighered.com/skills, locate the name of your textbook, and then follow the instructions on the website.

More Skills Format with WordArt

When you create a flyer or a newsletter, you might want to use a distinctive and decorative title. Word provides a feature called WordArt that you can use to change text into a decorative title.

In More Skills 12, you will open a document and create a title that uses WordArt.

To begin, open your web browser, navigate to www.pearsonhighered.com/skills, locate the name of your textbook, and then follow the instructions on the website.

More Skills Convert Text into Tables

You can create a new table by using the Table button on the Insert tab. You can also use the Table button to convert a tabbed list into a table.

In More Skills 13, you will open a document and convert a tabbed list into a table. You will also format the table.

To begin, open your web browser, navigate to www.pearsonhighered.com/skills, locate the name of your textbook, and then follow the instructions on the website.

More Skills Insert Drop Caps

Word provides a number of methods to format text distinctively. To give text the professional look you often see in books and magazines, you can use a large first letter to begin the first paragraph of the document.

In More Skills 14, you will open a document and create a drop cap for the first character of the first paragraph.

To begin, open your web browser, navigate to www.pearsonhighered.com/skills, locate the name of your textbook, and then follow the instructions on the website.

Please note that there are no additional projects to accompany the More Skills Projects, and they are not covered in the End-of-Chapter projects.

The following table summarizes the **SKILLS AND PROCEDURES** covered in this chapter.

Skills Number	Task	Step	Icon
1	Insert pictures	Insert tab → Illustrations group → Pictures	
1	Insert text from files	Insert tab → Text group → Object arrow, and click Text from File	
2	Resize pictures	Drag the corner resizing handles, or Format tab → Size group commands	
2	Reset pictures	Format tab → Adjust group → Reset Picture	
2	Float pictures	Select picture → Layout options button → Square	
3	Set Picture Styles	Format tab → Picture Styles group commands	
3	Set Artistic Effects	Format tab → Adjust group → Artistic Effects	
4	Set tab stops	Click the Tab Selector to pick the desired tab, and then click the ruler at the desired location.	
4	Add leaders	Home → Paragraph → Paragraph Dialog Box Launcher → Tab button In the Tabs dialog box, select the desired tab, and then select the desired leader option	
6	Apply table styles	Design tab → Table Styles group commands	
6	Modify table style options	Design tab → select or clear Table Style Options group check boxes	
6	AutoFit cells	Layout tab → Cell Size group → AutoFit	
7	Insert tables	Insert tab → Tables group → Table button → Select the desired dimensions	
8	Add or delete rows and columns	Click in the desired cell → Mini Toolbar Insert button	
9	Apply cell shading	Design tab → Table Styles group → Shading	
9	Adjust row and column sizes	Layout tab → Cell Size group commands	
10	Merge cells	Select the cells to be merged, and then Layout tab → Merge Cells	
10	Align cells vertically	Layout tab → Alignment group commands	
10	Edit table borders	Home tab → Paragraph group → Borders	

Key Terms

Online Help Skills

1. Start **Word 2013**, and then in the upper right corner of the start page, click the **Help** button ⍰.

2. In the **Word Help** window **Search help** box, type banded rows and then press Enter.

3. In the search result list, click **"Banded Rows" is under "Table Tools/Table Style Options"**. Compare your screen with **Figure 1**.

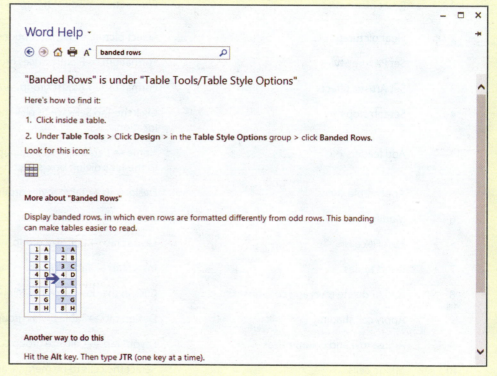

Figure 1

4. Read the article to answer the following questions: What are banded rows and how can you insert or remove them from tables? How might they be useful?

Matching

Match each term in the second column with its correct definition in the first column by writing the letter of the term on the blank line in front of the correct definition.

C **1.** When you select a picture, this button displays next to the image so that you can change text wrapping settings quickly.

G **2.** A layout option that sets a picture to "float" so that it can be moved independently of the paragraph.

B **3.** The type of sizing handle used to resize a picture proportionally.

A **4.** A line that displays when an object is aligned with a document object such as a margin or heading.

F **5.** A prebuilt set of formatting options that can be applied to a graphic with a single click.

H **6.** A specific location in the document, marked on the Word ruler, to which you can move using the Tab key.

E **7.** A series of characters that form a solid, dashed, or dotted line that fills the space preceding a tab stop.

I **8.** Information presented in rows and columns to summarize and present data effectively and efficiently.

J **9.** A pre-built set of formatting options that can be applied to a table with a single click.

D **10.** The command used to make the size of the table columns reflect the data in the columns.

A Alignment Guide

B AutoFit Contents

C Corner

D Layout Options

E Leader

F Picture Style

G Square

H Tab Stop

I Table

J Table Style

BizSkills Video

1. What types of questions should you have prepared for the interviewer?

2. What is the most important thing you can convey during an interview?

Multiple Choice MyITLab®

Choose the correct answer.

1. When you select a picture, you can use these to change the picture's size.
   A. Arrow keys
   B. Sizing handles
   C. Layout Options

2. The symbol that indicates which paragraph a picture is associated with.
   A. Anchor
   B. Paragraph mark
   C. Em dash

3. To move a selected picture small distances using an arrow key.
   A. Drag
   B. Bump
   C. Nudge

4. A series of evenly spaced dots that precede a tab.
   A. Ellipsis
   B. Tab stop position
   C. Dot leader

5. When you make a change to a tab stop in the Tabs dialog box, click this button to apply the changes.
   A. Set
   B. Clear
   C. Apply

6. The intersection of a row and column in a table.
   A. Banded row
   B. Cell
   C. Banded column

7. This command can be used to make a picture look more like a drawing or a painting.
   A. Artistic Effects
   B. Change Picture
   C. Compress Pictures

8. Use this key to move from one part of a table to another.
   A. Alt
   B. Tab
   C. Ctrl

9. How many columns are in a 3x7 table?
   A. 3
   B. 7
   C. 21

10. Numbers in a table are typically aligned this way.
    A. Left
    B. Center
    C. Right

Topics for Discussion

1. Tables have largely taken the place of tabs in most documents. Can you think of any situations where you might want to use tabs instead of tables? What would you have to do to a table to make it look like a tabbed list?

2. Pictures add interest to your documents when used in moderation. What guidelines would you recommend for using pictures—or any other type of graphics—in a document?

Skills Review

To complete this project, you will need the following files:

- wrd03_SRAdventures
- wrd03_SRGeo
- wrd03_SRHikes

You will save your file as:

- Last_First_wrd03_SRAdventures

1. Start **Word 2013**, and then open the student data file **wrd03_SRAdventures**. **Save** the file in your chapter folder as Last_First_wrd03_SRAdventures

2. Click to position the insertion point in the blank paragraph below *year's line-up includes:*. On the **Insert tab**, in the **Text group**, click the **Object button arrow**, and then click **Text from File**. Locate and insert **wrd03_SRHikes**, and then press Backspace one time to remove the extra paragraph.

3. Right-click in the first row of the table. On the Mini toolbar, click the **Insert** button, and then click **Insert Above**.

4. In the first cell of the new row, type Hike and then press Tab . In the second cell, type Length and then press Tab . In the third cell, type Difficulty and then press Tab . In the last cell, type Description

5. With the insertion point in the table, click the **Design tab**. In the **Table Styles group**, click the **More** button, and then under **Grid Tables**, click **Grid Table 7 Colorful - Accent 6**.

6. On the **Layout tab**, in the **Cell Size group**, click the **AutoFit** button, and then click **AutoFit Contents**.

7. Click the **Table Selector** button to select the entire table. On the **Layout tab**, in the **Alignment group**, click the **Align Center Left** button.

8. Click in a cell in the second column, and then in the **Cell Size group**, click the **Width up spin arrow** to set the width to column **0.9"**. Compare your screen with **Figure 1**.

9. Click in the blank paragraph below the paragraph that ends *Climbing Center*. On the **Insert tab**, in the **Tables group**, click the **Table** button, and then insert a **2x4** table.

10. In the table just inserted, add the text as shown in **Figure 2**.

Figure 1

Class	Date
Intro to Rock Climbing	March 22
Fitness through Climbing	March 29
Family Vertical Climbing	April 5

Figure 2

■ **Continue to the next page to complete this Skills Review**

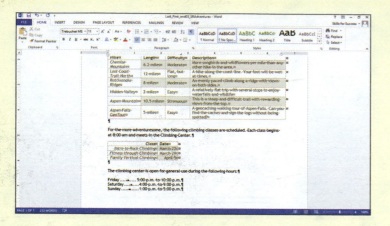

Figure 3

Figure 4

Henner Danke / Fotolia

11. On the **Design tab**, apply the same table style you applied to the upper table—**Grid Table 7 Colorful - Accent 6**. On the **Layout tab**, in the **Cell Size group**, click the **AutoFit** button, and then click **AutoFit Contents**.

12. Select the three cells that contain dates. On the **Home tab**, in the **Paragraph group**, click the **Align Right** button.

13. Press Ctrl + End to position the insertion point at the end of the document. On the left side of the horizontal ruler, click the **Tab Selector** button to display the Right Tab icon. Insert a right tab at **2.75 inches** on the horizontal ruler.

14. Double-click the tab mark. In the **Tabs** dialog box, under **Leader**, select **2**, click **Set**, and then click **OK**. Type the following tabbed list, pressing Tab before typing the text in the second column:

Friday	5:00 p.m. to 10:00 p.m.
Saturday	4:00 p.m. to 9:00 p.m.
Sunday	1:00 p.m. to 5:00 p.m.

15. Compare your screen with **Figure 3**.

16. Click to the left of the paragraph that begins *For the more adventuresome*. On the **Insert tab**, in the **Illustrations group**, click the **Pictures** button, and then locate and insert **wrd03_SRGeo**.

17. On the **Format tab**, in the **Size group**, select the number in the **Width** box, type **2.5** and then press Enter.

18. Scroll up to display the bottom of Page 1. Click the picture's **Layout Options** button, and then under **With Text Wrapping**, click **Square**.

19. Drag the picture to the right and slightly up. When the Alignment Guides display and align with the top of the paragraph beginning *For the more adventuresome* and the right page margin, release the left mouse button.

20. On the **Format tab**, in the **Picture Styles group**, click the sixth thumbnail—**Soft Edge Rectangle**.

21. In the **Picture Styles group**, click the **Picture Effects** button, point to **3-D Rotation**, and then under **Perspective**, click the second to last choice—**Perspective Heroic Extreme Left**.

22. Add the **FileName** field to the footer, and then deactivate the footer. Hide the formatting marks, set the zoom level to **One Page**, and then compare your document with **Figure 4**.

23. **Save** the document, **Close** Word, and then submit the file as directed by your instructor.

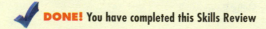

DONE! You have completed this Skills Review

Skills Assessment 1

MyITLab®
Grader

To complete this document, you will need the following files:

- wrd03_SA1Festival
- wrd03_SA1Photo
- wrd03_SA1Bands

You will save your document as:

- Last_First_wrd03_SA1Festival

1. Start **Word 2013**, and then open the student data file **wrd03_SA1Festival**. Save the file in your chapter folder as Last_First_wrd03_SA1Festival

2. With the insertion point to the left of the flyer title, insert the picture from the student file **wrd03_SA1Photo**. Apply the **Square** layout, change the **Width** to 3.5", and then align the picture with the top of the title paragraph and the document's right margin. Apply the **Bevel Rectangle** picture style (the twenty-first choice), and then apply the **Preset** picture effect—**Preset 5**.

3. In the blank paragraph below *line-up includes the following:*, insert the text from the student file **wrd03_SA1Bands**. Add a fourth column, and then in cells two to seven, add the following times:

   4:00 p.m.

   7:00 p.m.

   12:00 p.m.

   4:00 p.m.

   7:00 p.m.

   2:00 p.m.

4. Add a new row below the table's last row, and then enter the following: Obia, Afro-Latin Groove, Sunday, 5:00 p.m.

5. Select the table, and then apply the **Grid Table 1 Light - Accent 2** table style. Change the font size to **14** points and the row height to **0.3"**. Set the first row to **Align Center**, and rows two to eight to **Align Center Left**.

6. In the first row, merge cells three and four, and then **AutoFit** the columns to their contents. Change the table's **Alignment** property to **Center** the table between the side margins.

A Taste of Aspen Falls

A Taste of Aspen Falls is an annual food and music event held in Aspen Falls City Park.
This year features more than 50 food vendors and over 75 free concerts on 4 different stages. All concerts are free and no food item is over $7.95.

This year's artist line-up includes the following:

Band	Genre	Day and Time	
Noseeums	Eclectic Mix	Friday	4:00 p.m.
Fork in the Road	Electric Blues	Friday	7:00 p.m.
Hungary Creek	Folk-Americana	Saturday	12:00 p.m.
Green Sword	Mexi-Cali	Saturday	4:00 p.m.
Pete's Fork	Rock	Saturday	7:00 p.m.
Wendover	Acoustic Rock	Sunday	2:00 p.m.
Obia	Afro-Latin Groove	Sunday	5:00 p.m.

Plan your good times now!

Friday.....................4:00 to 10:00
Saturday ....10:00 to 10:00
Sunday...................10:00 to 8:00

Last_First_wrd03_SA1Festival.docx

Luchshen / Fotolia

Figure 1

7. In the blank paragraph at the end of the document, set a left tab stop at **0.25 inches** and a right tab stop at **2.5 inches**. Add a dot leader to the right tab stop, and then enter the following text to create a tabbed list:

Friday	4:00 to 10:00
Saturday	10:00 to 10:00
Sunday	10:00 to 8:00

8. Add the file name to the footer. **Save** the document, and then print or submit the file as directed by your instructor. Compare your completed document with **Figure 1**.

 DONE! You have completed Skills Assessment 1

Skills Assessment 2

To complete this document, you will need the following files:

- wrd03_SA2College
- wrd03_SA2Photo
- wrd03_SA2Prices

You will save your document as:

- Last_First_wrd03_SA2College

1. Start **Word 2013**, and then open the student data file **wrd03_SA2College**. Save the file in your chapter folder as Last_First_wrd03_SA2College

2. In the blank paragraph below *Several health care providers*, insert a 2x6 table, and then add the following text:

Provider	Plan(s)
Ultra Shield	PPO
Sunshine Health Cooperative	PPO, HMO
HealthWise Choice	PPO
United Southwest Health	HMO
Morgan Association Health Plan of CA	PPO

3. In the blank paragraph after *prices are as follows:*, insert the text from the student file **wrd03_SA2Prices**, and then remove the second blank paragraph below the table.

4. In the second table, add a new first row, and then enter the following column headings: Unit Type, Average Rate, and Vacancy Rate

5. For both document tables, apply the **Grid Table 4 - Accent 5** table style. **AutoFit** the columns to their contents, and then change the table's **Alignment** property to **Center** the table between the side margins.

6. In the second table, change the currency and percent values in the cells below *Average Rate* and *Vacancy Rate* to the **Align Right** paragraph alignment.

7. In the blank paragraph at the end of the document, click the **Tab Selector** to display the **Decimal Tab** icon, and then click the

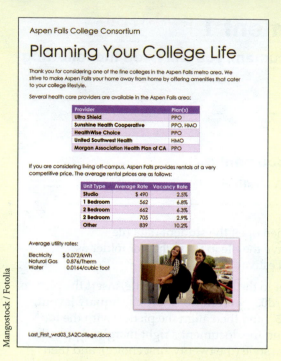

Figure 1

1.25 inch mark on the ruler. Enter the following text using the tab to align the decimal points in the second column:

Electricity	$ 0.072/kWh
Natural Gas	0.876/Therm
Water	0.0164/cubic foot

8. With the insertion point to the left of the paragraph *Average utility rates*, insert the picture from the student file **wrd03_SA2Photo**. Apply the **Square** layout, change the **Width** to **3"**, and then align the picture with the top of the *Average utility rates* paragraph and the document's right margin.

9. Apply the **Beveled Matte**, **White** picture style (the second choice), and then change the **Picture Border** color to the ninth choice in the second row—**Lavender**, **Accent 5**, **Lighter 80%**.

10. Add the file name to the footer. **Save** the document, and then print or submit the file as directed by your instructor. Compare your completed document with **Figure 1**.

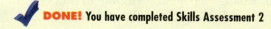

DONE! You have completed Skills Assessment 2

Visual Skills Check

To complete this document, you will need the following files:

- wrd03_VSConservation
- wrd03_VSPhoto
- wrd03_VSWildlife

You will save your document as:

- Last_First_wrd03_VSConservation

Open the student file **wrd03_VSConservation**, and then save it in your chapter folder as Last_First_wrd03_VSConservation Create the document shown in **Figure 1**.

The picture is the student data file **wrd03_VSPhoto**, has the **Soft Edge Rectangle** picture style, and is 3 inches wide. The table can be inserted from the student data file **wrd03_VSWildlife**, but you will need to add the last row and its text. The table is formatted with the **Grid Table 4 - Accent 5** table style, and the table style options have been changed. The cell sizes have been changed to AutoFit Contents, and the row headings are vertically centered in each cell. Insert the FileName field in the footer, and then print or submit the file as directed by your instructor.

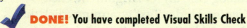 **DONE! You have completed Visual Skills Check**

Durango County
Conservation Futures Program

Aspen Falls Conservation Area

In 1994, the Durango County Commissioners created the Conservation Futures Program to preserve county natural areas in perpetuity. The program expands existing natural areas and creates new areas by acquiring properties nominated by county citizens. The Aspen Falls Conservation Area has returned the Aspen River to its natural meandering course benefiting wildlife, natural vegetation, and citizens alike.

The Aspen Falls Conservation Area features the following wildlife and plants:

Songbirds	Spring is an especially good time to observe songbirds during the breeding season. Over 100 species of birds have been spotted in the area.
Raptors	Attracted by the abundant forage fish found in the restored river, two nesting Bald eagle pairs live here year-round and several more nest each winter. Other raptors include osprey, red-tailed hawk, kestrel, and the long-eared owl.
Tule Elk	Approximately 25 elk visit the area to feed and can often be seen from the area's wildlife viewing blinds.
Beaver	Beaver are returning to the area. Their dams, diversions, and ponds attract birds, fish, and native plants which attract a wide array of wildlife to the area.
Sensitive Plants	Rare or endangered plants include Snow Mountain buckwheat, Drymaria-like western flax, Adobe lily, and Hall's madia.

Last_First_wrd03_VSConservation.docx

VL@D / Fotolia

Figure 1

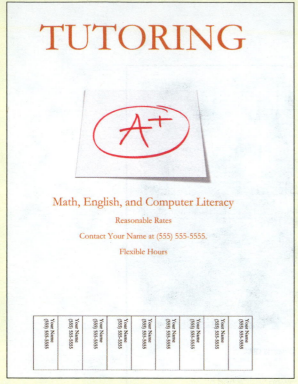

Matthew Benoit / Fotolia

Figure 1

My Skills

To complete this document, you will need the following files:

- wrd03_MYFlyer
- wrd03_MYPhoto

You will save your document as:

- **Last_First_wrd03_MYFlyer**

1. Start **Word 2013**, and then open the student data file **wrd03_MYFlyer**. Save the file in your chapter folder as Last_First_wrd03_MYFlyer

2. Apply the **Organic** theme. Select all of the document text, and then change the font color to the ninth choice in the first row— **Orange, Accent 5**.

3. Select the flyer title, *Tutoring*, and then in the **Font Size** box, replace the existing value with 84 and then press [Enter].

4. In the blank paragraph after the title, insert the picture from the student file **wrd03_MYPhoto**. Resize the picture proportionally by changing the width to **3.5"**.

5. For the picture, apply the nineteenth picture style—**Relaxed Perspective, White**.

6. In the first paragraph below the picture, change the font size to **26**. For the last three document paragraphs, change the font size to **18**.

7. Click the **Insert tab**. In the **Header & Footer group**, click the **Footer** button, and then click **Edit Footer**.

8. In the footer, insert a **9x1** table. In the first cell, type your first and last name. Press [Enter], and then type the phone number (555) 555-5555

9. Drag through the text taking care not to select the entire cell, and then on the

Home tab, click the **Copy** button. Paste the text into the table's eight remaining cells. If you accidentally copied the cell, undo and select just the text before clicking Copy.

10. Select the entire table, and then click the **Layout tab**. In the **Alignment group**, click the **Text Direction** button one time to rotate the text from top to bottom as indicated by the arrows in the Text Direction button.

11. Set the **Table Row Height** to **1.6"**, and then with the entire table selected, change the alignment to **Align Center** so that the text is centered both vertically and horizontally in the cells.

12. On the **Layout tab**, in the **Table group**, click **Properties**. In the **Table Properties** dialog box, under **Alignment**, click **Center**. Under **Text wrapping**, click the **Around** button, and then click **OK**.

13. Double-click in the body to deactivate the footer area, and then click the **Page Layout tab**. In the **Page Setup group**, click the **Margins** button, and then click **Narrow**.

14. **Save** the document, and then compare your completed document with **Figure 1**. Submit the file as directed by your instructor.

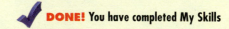 **DONE! You have completed My Skills**

Skills Challenge 1

To complete this document, you will need the following file:

- wrd03_SC1Softball

You will save your document as:

- Last_First_wrd03_SC1Softball

The Aspen Falls Parks and Recreation Department has a Spring Softball flyer that needs updating. To update the flyer, open the student data file **wrd03_SC1Softball**, and then save it in your chapter folder as Last_First_wrd03_SC1Softball Add the FileName field to the footer.

Improve the flyer by applying the skills practiced in this chapter. Assign a suitable theme, and then use the theme's fonts and colors to format the title in a manner demonstrated in this chapter's project. Create and format headings for each section. Use Online Pictures to insert a picture that complements the flyer's message. Size, position, and format

the picture using picture styles or artistic effects so that the picture attracts the reader's eye to the flyer.

Organize the content using at least one table, a tabbed list, and a bulleted list. Format the table(s) in a manner that is consistent with the title formatting. In the tabbed list(s), assign a leader and alignment as appropriate to the content. Assign paragraph spacing to provide white space between flyer elements and adjust the margins if needed so that the flyer displays on a single page. Submit your flyer as directed by your instructor.

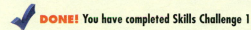 **DONE!** You have completed Skills Challenge 1

Skills Challenge 2

To complete this document, you will need the following file:

- New blank Word document

You will save your document as:

- Last_First_wrd03_SC2Resume

On the Word start page or Open page, search for and select the Basic Resume template provided by Microsoft Corporation. If that template is no longer available, pick a different résumé template. Download the template, and then save it in your chapter folder as Last_First_wrd03_SC2Resume Insert the FileName field into the footer.

Create your own résumé by filling in the template. Using the skills you have practiced in this chapter, add or remove

sections as appropriate and position the section featuring your strongest area (for example, experience, education, or skills) immediately below the objective. Be sure the résumé fits on a single page, and reformat table cells and text as needed.

Check the entire document for grammar and spelling, and then submit the file as directed by your instructor.

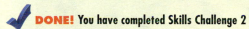 **DONE!** You have completed Skills Challenge 2

CHAPTER 4

Create Newsletters and Mail Merge Documents

- ▶ Newsletters often display articles in two or three columns and have a title that spans across the columns. Text is typically easier to read when it is in columns.

- ▶ Online images can be downloaded from Office.com and then inserted and formatted in much the same way as a picture.

- ▶ SmartArt graphics display information visually and can add a professional look to a document.

- ▶ To draw attention to a small amount of text, you can add a border and shading to the paragraph.

- ▶ You can use the mail merge feature in Word to create mailing labels to distribute flyers or brochures.

- ▶ In a mail merge, you can take an existing list of names and addresses from other Office applications and insert them into a mailing labels document.

© Kratuanoiy / Fotolia

Aspen Falls City Hall

In this chapter, you will assist Todd Austin, the Aspen Falls Tourism Director, to create a newsletter about the Aspen Falls Farmers' Market. The newsletter will be mailed to local farmers promoting their participation in the market. The newsletter will be mailed, so you will also create mailing labels with the addresses of local farms.

An effective newsletter uses large, attractive text and graphics to invite readers to read the articles. Subtitles, graphics, and other formatting can help those who only scan the newsletter to gain the information they desire. Word's library of SmartArt graphics can help you create graphics that communicate a message with very little text. You can save time by formatting as desired and then creating your own Quick Style based on that formatting. After the style is created, you apply that formatting with a single click.

In this project, you will create a one-page flyer with an artistic title and a two-column format. You will add text effects to the newsletter title, and add page and paragraph borders and shading. You will insert an online image and create a SmartArt graphic. Finally, you will create mailing labels by merging data from one file to a label template.

Time to complete all 10 skills – 60 to 90 minutes

Student data files needed for this chapter:

wrd04_Farmers
wrd04_FarmerAddresses

You will save your files as:

Last_First_wrd04_Farmers
Last_First_wrd04_FarmerAddresses (not submitted)
Last_First_wrd04_FarmerLabels (not submitted)
Last_First_wrd04_FarmerMerged

Outcome

Using the skills in this chapter, you will be able to create a Word document like this:

SKILLS

Skills 1-10 Training

At the end of this chapter you will be able to:

Skill 1 Modify Themes and Create Columns

Skill 2 Modify Margins and Columns

Skill 3 Apply Text Effects

Skill 4 Create Styles

Skill 5 Add Borders and Shading to Paragraphs and Pages

Skill 6 Insert and Adjust Online Pictures

Skill 7 Insert SmartArt

Skill 8 Format SmartArt

Skill 9 Create Labels Using Mail Merge

Skill 10 Preview and Print Mail Merge Documents

MORE SKILLS

Skill 11 Optimize Documents for Read Mode

Skill 12 Work in Outline View

Skill 13 Manage Document Properties

Skill 14 Save Documents as Web Pages

▶ You can modify a theme by selecting a different set of colors, fonts, or effects.

▶ In a newsletter, multiple columns make text easier to read.

1. Start **Word 2013**, and then open the student data file **wrd04_Farmers**. Use **Save As** to create a folder named Word Chapter 4 and then **Save** the document as Last_First_wrd04_Farmers.

2. Display the formatting marks, and then add the **FileName** field to the footer.

3. Click the **View tab**, and then in the **Zoom group**, click **One Page**. Compare your screen with **Figure 1**.

   Because you are not editing text, it is typically best to view the entire page when working with the overall look and feel of a page.

4. On the **Design tab**, in the **Document Formatting group**, click **Themes**, and then click **Wisp**.

5. In the **Document Formatting group**, click the **Fonts** button. Scroll down the list of font sets, and then click **Century Gothic-Palatino Linotype**. Compare your screen with **Figure 2**.

   To improve readability in printed newsletters, body text is often given a **serif font**—a font where the letters have extra details or hooks at the end of each stroke. Article titles are often given a **sans serif font**—a font where the letters do not have **serifs**—the extra details or hooks at the end of each stroke.

   Here, the colors and effects of the Wisp theme have been applied, but the default fonts have been changed to Century Gothic for headings and Palatino Linotype for body text.

■ **Continue to the next page to complete the skill**

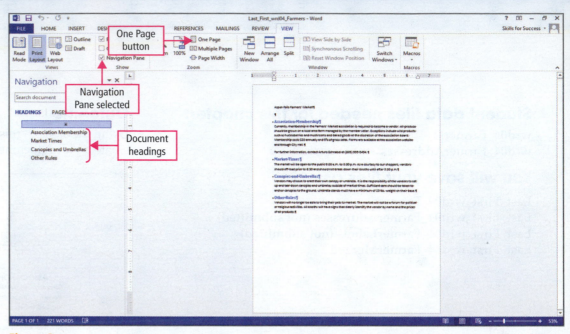

Figure 1

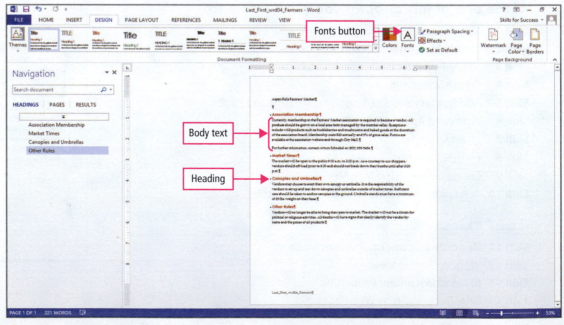

Figure 2

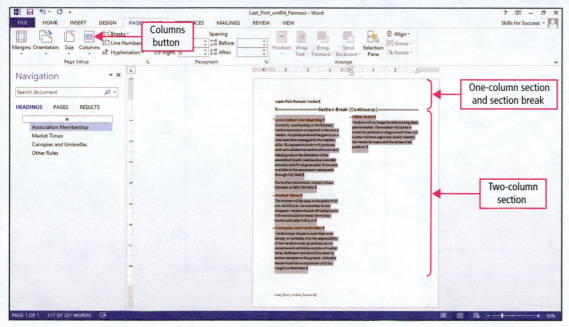

One-column section and section break

Two-column section

Figure 3

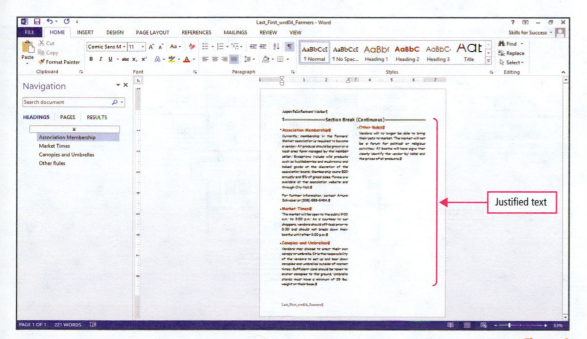

Justified text

Figure 4

6. Locate the subtitle *Association Membership*, and then position the pointer to the left of the first word in the paragraph. Drag down to the end of the document—including the paragraph mark in the last paragraph.

7. Click the **Page Layout tab**. In the **Page Setup group**, click the **Columns** button, click **Two**, and then compare your screen with **Figure 3**.

   A section break displays above the two-column text. A *section* is a portion of a document that can be formatted differently from the rest of the document. A *section break* marks the end of one section and the beginning of another section.

8. With the two columns of text still selected, change the font to **Comic Sans MS**.

   Because this newsletter is only one page long, a serif font is not needed for the body text. The new font has wider characters than the previous selection, so some of the text moved from the first column into the second column.

9. With the text still selected, on the **Home tab**, in the **Paragraph group**, click the **Justify** button.

10. Click anywhere in the two-column text to deselect the text, and then compare your screen with **Figure 4**.

    Justified text aligns the text with both the left and right margins. Justified text is often used in documents with multiple columns, although some wide gaps can occur in the text.

11. **Save** the document.

■ **You have completed Skill 1 of 10**

WRD 4-2
VIDEO

▶ You can increase or decrease the space between the columns and apply custom margins to adjust the document layout.

▶ A *column break* forces the text following the break to flow into the next column.

1. On the **Page Layout tab**, in the **Page Setup group**, click **Margins**, and then below the **Margins gallery**, click **Custom Margins** to open the Page Setup dialog box.

2. In the **Page Setup** dialog box, under **Margins**, use the **down spin arrows** to change the **Top** and **Bottom** margins to **0.8"**.

3. Under **Preview**, click the **Apply to arrow**, and then click **Whole document**. Compare your screen with **Figure 1**, and then click **OK** to close the dialog box.

   Unless you specify otherwise, when documents have multiple sections, the Page Setup dialog box applies the changes only to the current section.

4. With the insertion point in the two columns of text, on the **Page Layout tab**, in the **Page Setup group**, click the **Columns** button. Below the **Columns gallery**, click **More Columns** to display the Columns dialog box. Compare your screen with **Figure 2**.

   When you set column options, you only need to place the insertion point in the section that the columns are applied to.

   The Columns dialog box can be used to set the number of columns and the distance between them. By default, the columns are of equal width with 0.5 inches of space between them.

■ **Continue to the next page to complete the skill**

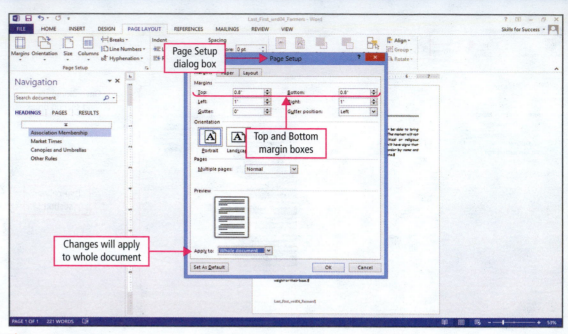

Page Setup dialog box

Top and Bottom margin boxes

Changes will apply to whole document

Figure 1

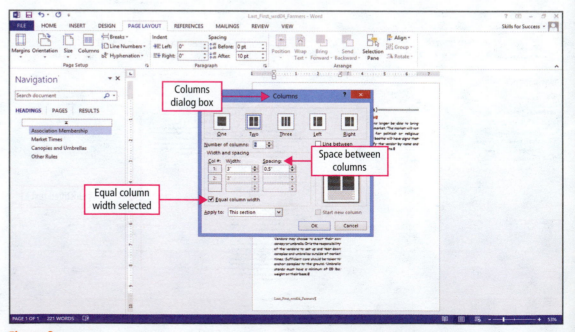

Columns dialog box

Space between columns

Equal column width selected

Figure 2

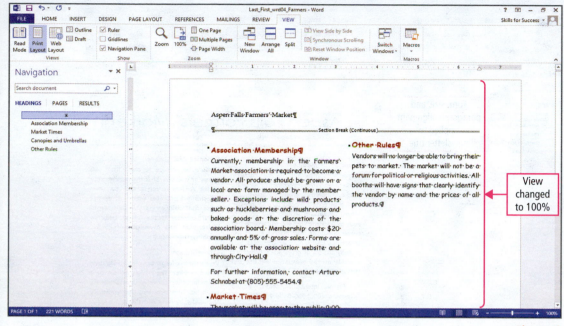

Figure 3

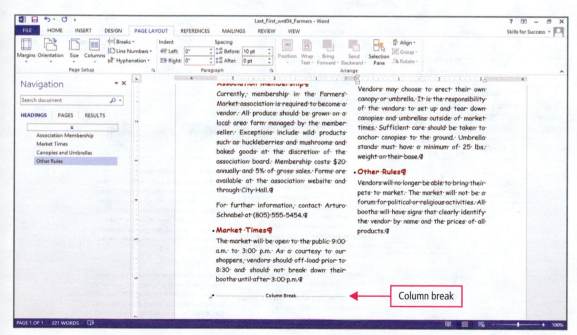

Column break

Figure 4

5. In the **Columns** dialog box, under **Width and spacing**, click the first **Spacing down spin arrow** two times to change the spacing between the columns to **0.3"**. Click **OK** to accept the changes and close the dialog box.

> Both columns will remain of equal width because the *Equal column width* check box is selected. When you decrease the spacing between columns, the width of each column is increased, in this case from 3.0 to 3.1 inches.

6. On the **View tab**, in the **Zoom group**, click **100%**. Press Ctrl + Home, and then compare your screen with **Figure 3**.

> If you are working with a larger monitor, you may prefer to work with the document in One Page view instead of at 100%.

7. In the left column, click to position the insertion point to the left of the subtitle *Canopies and Umbrellas*.

8. On the **Page Layout tab**, in the **Page Setup group**, click the **Breaks** button. In the **Breaks gallery**, under **Page Breaks**, click **Column**.

9. Scroll to display the column break at the bottom of column 1, and then compare your screen with **Figure 4**.

> Column breaks display as nonprinting characters, and after the break, the remaining text flows into the second column.

10. Save 🖫 the document.

■ **You have completed Skill 2 of 10**

▶ *Text effects* are decorative formats, such as outlines, shadows, text glow, and colors, that make text stand out in a document.

▶ You should use text effects sparingly, at most just for titles or subtitles.

1. At the top of the document, select the title *Aspen Falls Farmers' Market* including the paragraph mark.

2. With the title text still selected, on the **Home tab**, in the **Font group**, click the **Font arrow** Calibri (Body) ▾, and then under **Theme Fonts**, click **Century Gothic**.

3. In the **Font group**, click in the **Font Size** box 11 ▾ to select the existing value. Type 30 and then press Enter.

   By typing the desired size, you can assign a font size that is not included in the Font Size list.

4. On the **Home tab**, in the **Paragraph group**, click the **Center** button ≡, and then compare your screen with **Figure 1**.

5. On the **Home tab**, in the **Font group**, click the **Text Effects and Typography** button A▾. Compare your screen with **Figure 2**.

   The Text Effects gallery displays thumbnails of pre-built text effects and commands for applying individual text effects settings.

■ Continue to the next page to complete the skill ➤

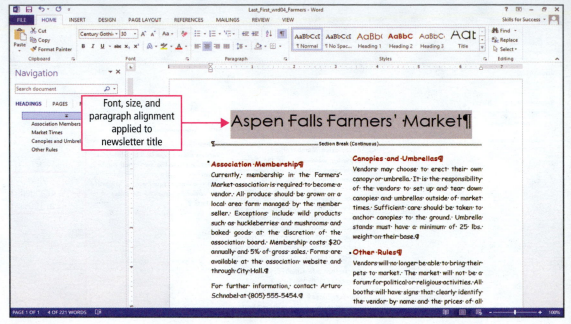

Font, size, and paragraph alignment applied to newsletter title

Figure 1

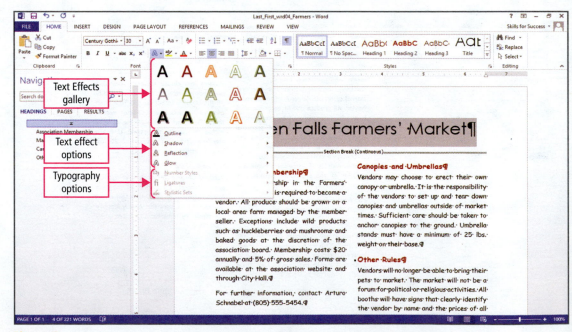

Text Effects gallery

Text effect options

Typography options

Figure 2

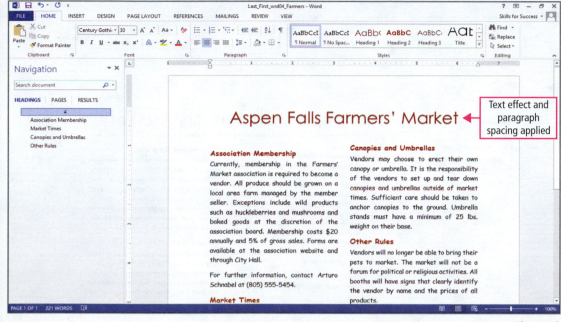

Text effect and paragraph spacing applied

Figure 3

Shadow effect modified

Figure 4

6. In the **Text Effects gallery**, in the first row, click the second thumbnail—**Fill - Dark Red**, **Accent 1**, **Shadow**.

7. On the **Home tab**, in the **Paragraph group**, click the **Show/Hide** button so that it is no longer selected.

   At times, it is helpful to format text with the nonprinting formatting marks hidden.

8. Click the **Home tab**, and then click the **Paragraph Dialog Box Launcher**. In the **Paragraph** dialog box, change the **Spacing After** to **0 pt**, change the **Line spacing** to **Single**, and then click **OK**. Click to deselect the text, and then compare your screen with **Figure 3**.

9. Select the newsletter title paragraph. In the **Fonts group**, click the **Text Effects and Typography** button. In the **Text Effects gallery**, point to **Outline**, and then point to several colors to preview the outline effects.

10. Repeat the technique just practiced to preview the shadow, reflection, and glow effects.

11. In the **Text Effects gallery**, point to **Shadow**, and then under **Outer**, click the last thumbnail—**Offset Diagonal Top Left**. Deselect the text, and then compare your screen with **Figure 4**.

    In this manner, you can modify the text effect settings. Here, the shadow's position and distance from the text were changed.

12. **Save** the document.

■ **You have completed Skill 3 of 10**

WRD 4-4
VIDEO

► A **Quick Style** is a style that can be accessed from a Ribbon gallery of thumbnails.

► You can create and name your own styles, and then add them to the Style gallery so that you can apply them with a single click.

1. Display the formatting marks, and then at the top of the left column, click to place the insertion point in the subtitle *Association Membership*. Compare your screen with **Figure 1**.

   The subtitles in this newsletter have been assigned the Heading 2 style. The black square to the left of the subtitle indicates that it will always stay with the next paragraph. Recall that text assigned a Heading style can also be collapsed and expanded.

2. Select the subtitle *Association Membership* including the paragraph mark. On the **Home tab**, in the **Font group**, click the **Font Dialog Box Launcher** .

3. In the **Font** dialog box, change the font to **Century Gothic** and the **Size** to **16**.

4. Click the **Font color arrow**, and then under **Theme Colors**, click the last color in the last row—**Green**, **Accent 6**, **Darker 50%**.

5. Under **Effects**, select the **Small caps** check box. Compare your screen with **Figure 2**, and then click **OK**.

6. With the text still selected, open the **Paragraph** dialog box. Under **General**, change the **Alignment** to **Centered**. Change the **Spacing Before** to **0 pt**, and the **Spacing After** to **6 pt**. Change the **Line spacing** to **Single**, and then click **OK**.

■ **Continue to the next page to complete the skill** ➤

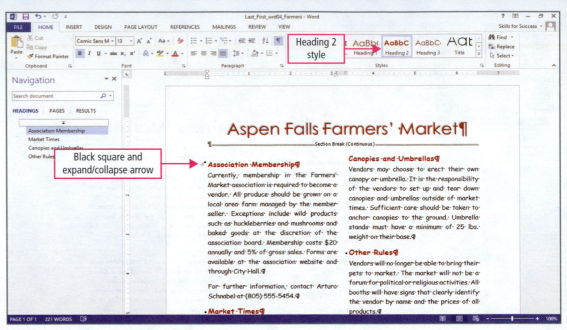

Figure 1

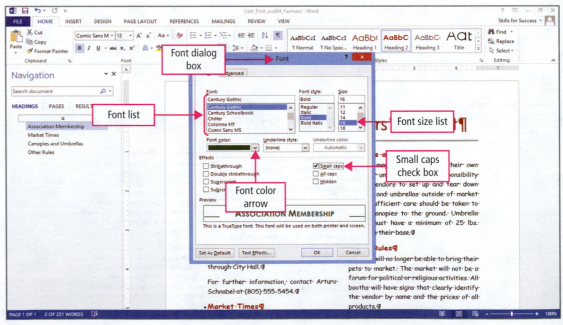

Figure 2

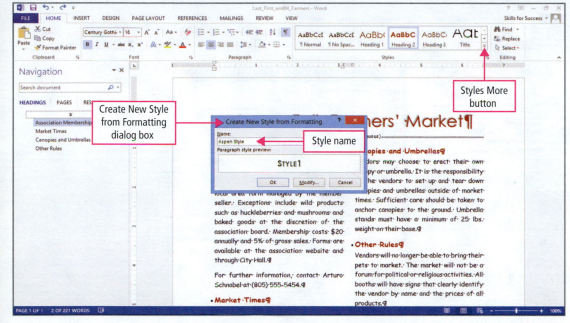

Figure 3

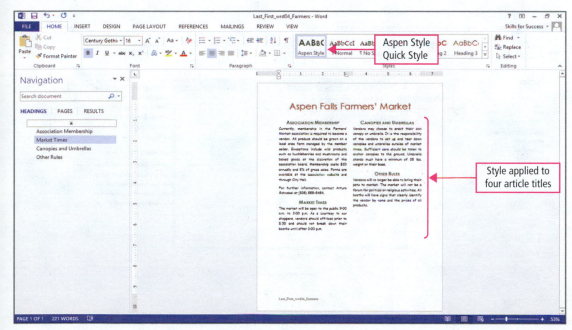

Figure 4

7. With the subtitle text still selected, on the **Home tab**, in the **Styles group**, click the **More arrow** ▼, and then below the **Styles gallery**, click **Create a Style**.

8. In the **Create New Style from Formatting** dialog box, under **Name**, type Aspen Style Compare your screen with **Figure 3**, and then click **OK** to add the style to the Styles gallery.

   When you create a style in this manner, the style is available only in the same document. In other documents, the style will not display in the Styles gallery.

9. Click to place the insertion point in the subtitle *Canopies and Umbrellas*. On the **Home tab**, in the **Styles group**, click the **Aspen Style** thumbnail to apply the style.

10. Repeat the technique just practiced to apply the **Aspen Style** style to the *Market Times* and *Other Rules* subtitles.

11. On the **View tab**, in the **Zoom group**, click **One Page**. Hide the formatting marks, and then compare your screen with **Figure 4**.

   The styles that you create can be modified and updated in the same manner that pre-built styles are updated.

12. Save 💾 the document.

■ **You have completed Skill 4 of 10**

▶ To make a paragraph stand out in a document, you can add a paragraph border or paragraph shading.

▶ You can use page borders to frame flyers or posters, giving the document a more professional look.

1. On the **Design tab**, in the **Page Background group**, click the **Page Borders** button.

2. On the **Page Border tab** of the **Borders and Shading** dialog box, under **Setting**, click **Box**.

3. Click the **Color arrow**, and then in the first row under **Theme Colors**, click the last color—**Green**, **Accent 6**. Click the **Width arrow**, and then click **1½ pt**. Compare your screen with **Figure 1**, and then click **OK** to add the page border.

4. Change the **Zoom** to **100%**, and then display the formatting marks.

5. At the end of the first article, click in the paragraph starting *For further information*.

6. On the **Home tab**, in the **Paragraph group**, click the **Borders arrow** 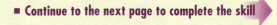, and then at the bottom of the gallery, click **Borders and Shading**.

7. In the **Borders and Shading** dialog box, click the **Shading tab**. Click the **Fill arrow**, and then under **Theme Colors**, click the last color in the third row—**Green**, **Accent 6**, **Lighter 60%**. Compare your screen with **Figure 2**.

■ **Continue to the next page to complete the skill** ➤

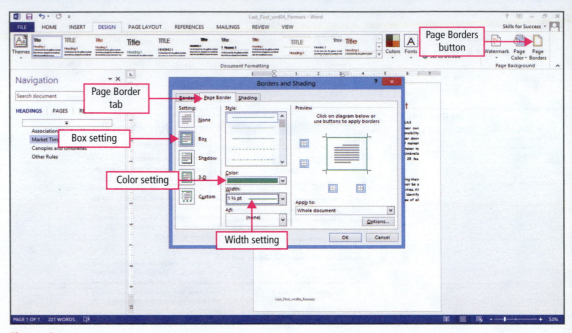

Figure 1

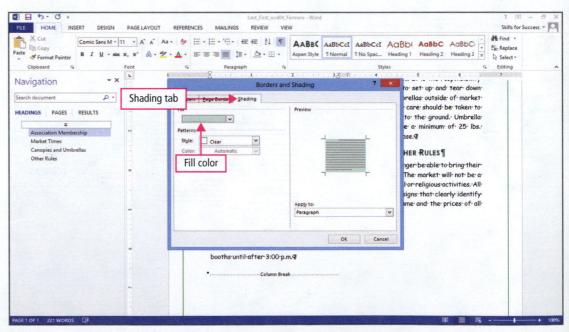

Figure 2

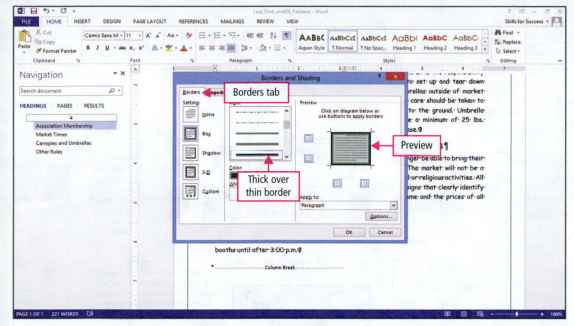

Figure 3

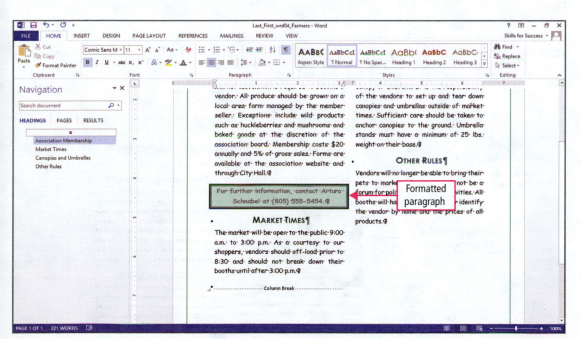

Figure 4

8. In the **Borders and Shading** dialog box, click the **Borders tab**.

9. On the **Borders tab**, under **Setting**, click **Box**. Under **Style**, scroll down and select the first line style with a thick upper line and a thin bottom line.

10. Click the **Color arrow**, and then under **Theme Colors**, click the last color in the last row—**Green, Accent 6, Darker 50%**. Notice that a preview of the box displays in the Preview area, as shown in **Figure 3**.

11. Click **OK** to apply the changes and close the dialog box. **Center** ≡ the paragraph, select the text, and then apply **Bold** B.

12. In the **Font group**, click the **Font Color arrow** A ▾, and then under **Theme Colors**, in the last row, click the first color—**White, Background 1, Darker 50%**. Deselect the text, and then compare your screen with **Figure 4**.

13. **Save** 🖫 the document.

■ **You have completed Skill 5 of 10**

▶ An *online image* is a graphic, drawing, or photograph accessed from Bing Image Search, SkyDrive, or other online providers.

▶ You search for and select graphics in the Insert Pictures dialog box.

1. In the first article, click to position the insertion point to the left of *Currently, membership in*.

2. On the **Insert tab**, in the **Illustrations group**, click the **Online Pictures** button to display the Insert Pictures dialog box.

   The Insert Pictures dialog box is used to connect with online services such as Bing Image Search and your SkyDrive. You may have additional providers listed, and if you are not signed in, your SkyDrive may not display.

3. In the **Insert Pictures** dialog box, in the **Bing Image Search** box, type grapes and then click the **Search** button. If a message displays, close it.

4. Browse the search results and click an image suitable for use in a newsletter about a Farmer's Market. Compare your screen with **Figure 1**.

   Because the online images available at Bing Image Search change frequently, your search results will likely be different than shown. If the image in Figure 1 is no longer available, choose a different image and adjust its size as necessary.

5. Click the online image to select it, and then click the **Insert** button to insert it into the document. Compare your screen with **Figure 2**.

■ Continue to the next page to complete the skill ▶

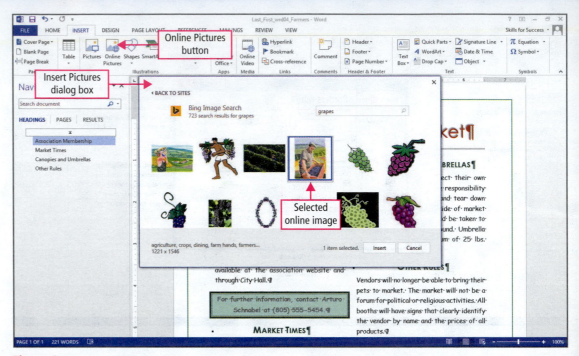
Figure 1

Figure 2

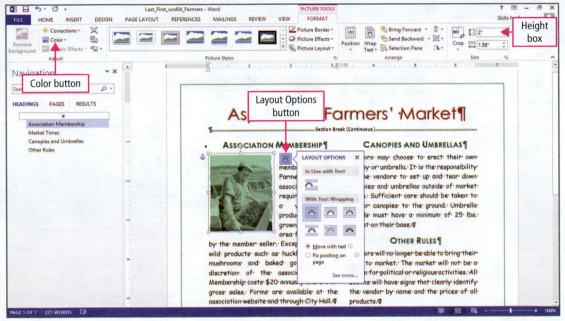

Figure 3

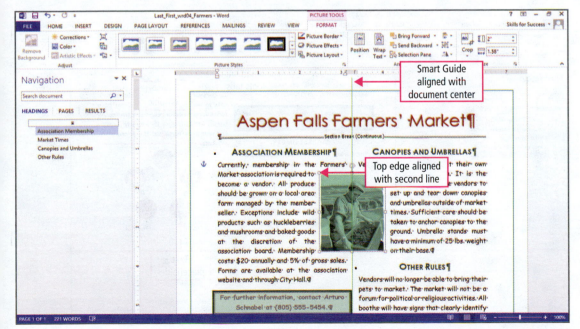

Figure 4

6. With the image selected, on the **Format tab**, in the **Adjust group**, click **Color**, and then point to several thumbnails to preview their effects.

7. In the **Recolor gallery**, in the second row, click the last choice—**Green, Accent color 6 Dark**.

   You can change picture adjustments and styles to online images in the same manner you modify photographs. Here, the look and feel of the image has been changed from a painting to a historic photograph using the same color tones as in the titles and subtitles.

8. With the image selected, click the **Layout Options** button [icon], and then under **With Text Wrapping**, click the first thumbnail—**Square**.

9. On the **Format tab**, in the **Size group**, change the **Height** value to **2"**. Compare your screen with **Figure 3**.

10. Point to the image to display the [icon] pointer. Drag the image to position it as shown in **Figure 4**.

11. Save [icon] the document.

■ **You have completed Skill 6 of 10**

▶ A **SmartArt graphic** is a pre-built visual representation of information.

▶ You can choose from many different SmartArt layouts to communicate your message or ideas.

1. Press Ctrl + End to move the insertion point to the end of the document. On the **Insert tab**, in the **Illustrations group**, click the **SmartArt** button.

2. In the **Choose a SmartArt Graphic** dialog box, scroll down and look at the various types of layouts that are available.

3. On the left side of the dialog box, click **Cycle**. Click the first layout—**Basic Cycle**, and then compare your screen with **Figure 1**.

4. In the **Choose a SmartArt Graphic** dialog box, read the description of the selected layout, and then click **OK**. Compare your screen with **Figure 2**. If the Text pane displays to the left of the graphic, click the Text Pane button on the left border to close it.

    When SmartArt is selected, two SmartArt Tools contextual tabs display—Design and Format. Inside the graphic, each shape has a text placeholder.

■ **Continue to the next page to complete the skill** ➡

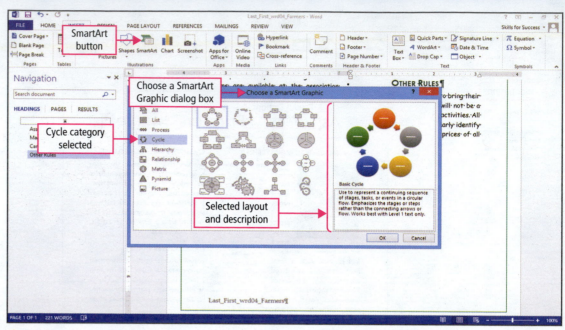

Figure 1

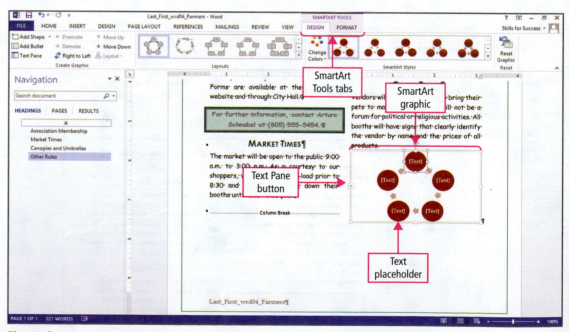

Figure 2

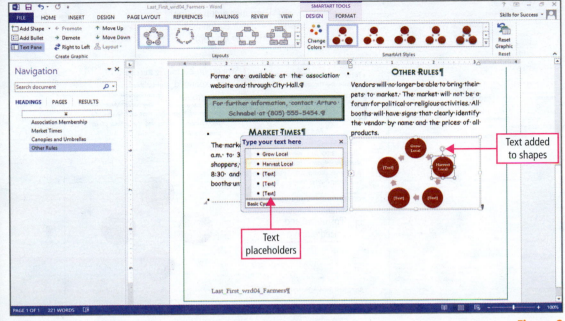

Figure 3

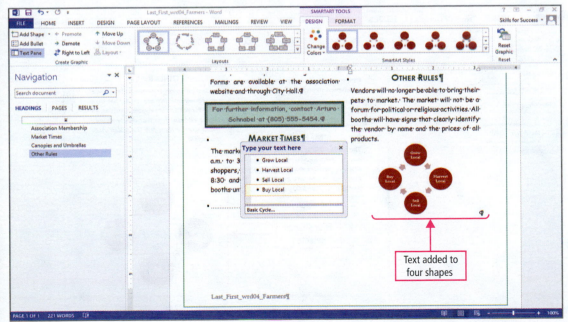

Text added to four shapes

Figure 4

5. In the upper shape, click the **[Text]** placeholder, and then type Grow Local

6. In the middle-right shape, click the **[Text]** placeholder, and then type Harvest Local

   As you work with SmartArt, the shape and font sizes automatically adjust to the contents.

7. On the left border, click the **Text Pane** button, and then compare your screen with **Figure 3**.

   The Text pane displays text as bullets and provides an alternate method of entering text. In the pane, you can remove or add shapes by removing or adding bullets, and you can insert subordinate shapes by indenting bullets.

8. In the **Text** pane, click the first **[Text]** placeholder—the third bullet, and then type Sell Local Notice that while you type in the bulleted list, the text also displays in the third SmartArt shape.

   To move to the next [Text] shape in the Text pane, you can also press ⎡Enter⎤.

9. Press ⬇ to move to the next bullet, and then type Buy Local

10. With the insertion point to the right of the text *Buy Local*, press ⎡Delete⎤ to remove the fifth shape, and then compare your screen with **Figure 4**.

11. **Close** ✖ the Text pane, and then **Save** 🖫 the document.

■ **You have completed Skill 7 of 10**

▶ You can resize an entire SmartArt graphic, or you can resize its individual shapes.

1. Click the border of the SmartArt graphic to select the graphic without selecting any of its shapes.

2. Click the **Format tab**, and then click the **Arrange group** button. Click **Position**, and then under **With Text Wrapping**, click the last thumbnail—**Position in Bottom Right with Square Text Wrapping**.

   On smaller monitors, some groups collapse and are accessed only by clicking a button. If you are working with a larger monitor, your Arrange and Size groups may not be collapsed.

3. Scroll to display the SmartArt graphic. On the **Format tab**, click the **Size group** button, change **Height** value to **2.7"**, and then compare your screen with **Figure 1**.

   When you change the height or width of a SmartArt graphic, the graphic width is not resized proportionally.

4. In the SmartArt graphic, click the first shape, and then click its border so that the border is a solid line. Press and hold Ctrl while clicking the other three shapes. Compare your screen with **Figure 2**.

■ **Continue to the next page to complete the skill** ▶

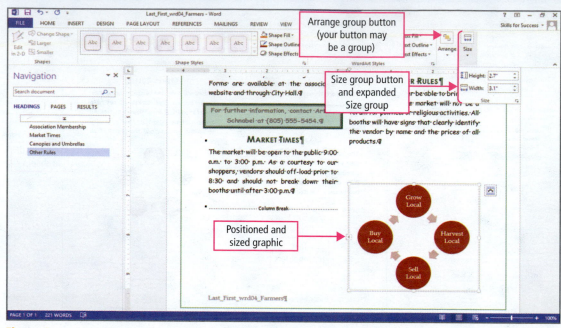

Figure 1

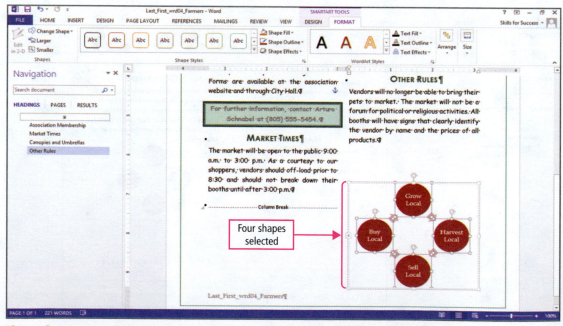

Figure 2

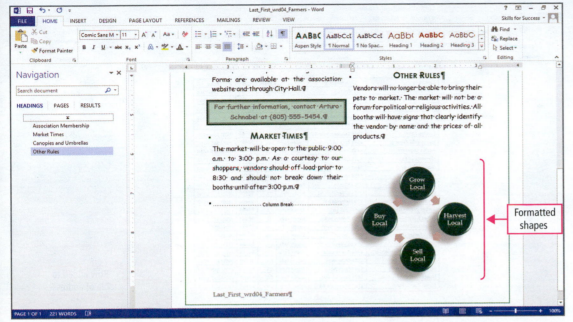

Figure 3

Figure 4

5. With all four shapes selected, on the **Format tab**, in the **Shape Styles group**, click the **Shape Fill** button. Under **Theme Colors**, click the last color in the last row—**Green, Accent 6, Darker 50%**.

6. In the **Shape Styles group**, click the **Shape Effects** button. Point to **Preset**, and then under **Presets**, click the first effect in the second row—**Preset 5**.

7. With all four shapes still selected, in the **WordArt Styles group**, click the **Text Effects** button. Point to **Reflection**, and then under **Reflection Variations**, click the first effect—**Tight Reflection, touching**.

8. Click in the text to deselect the SmartArt graphic, and then compare your screen with **Figure 3**.

9. On the **View tab**, in the **Zoom group**, click the **One Page** button. Hide the formatting marks, and then compare your screen with **Figure 4**.

10. In the **Zoom group**, click the **100%** button, and then **Save** 💾 the document.

11. **Close** ✖ the document window.

■ **You have completed Skill 8 of 10**

▶ The *mail merge* feature is used to customize letters or labels by combining a main document with a data source.

▶ The *main document* contains the text that remains constant; the *data source* contains the information—such as names and addresses—that changes with each letter or label.

1. Start **Word 2013**, and then open the student data file **wrd04_FarmerAddresses**. Save the document in your **Word Chapter 4** folder as Last_First_wrd04_FarmerAddresses Add the **FileName** field to the footer.

2. Take a moment to examine the table of names and addresses.

    This table will be the data source for the mailing labels you will create to mail the farmers' market newsletter.

3. Point to the table's lower left corner, and then click the **Insert** button ⊕ to add a new row.

4. In the new row, enter the information for Sweet Honey Farm, 173 Valley View Rd, Aspen Falls, CA, 93464, (805) 555-1821 and then compare your screen with **Figure 1**.

5. **Save** 🖫, and then **Close** ✖ the document.

6. Start **Word 2013**, and then on the start page, click **Blank document**. Save the file in your chapter folder as Last_First_wrd04_FarmerLabels

7. Click the **Mailings tab**. In the **Start Mail Merge group**, click the **Start Mail Merge** button, and then click **Labels** to open the Label Options dialog box, as shown in **Figure 2**.

■ **Continue to the next page to complete the skill** ➡

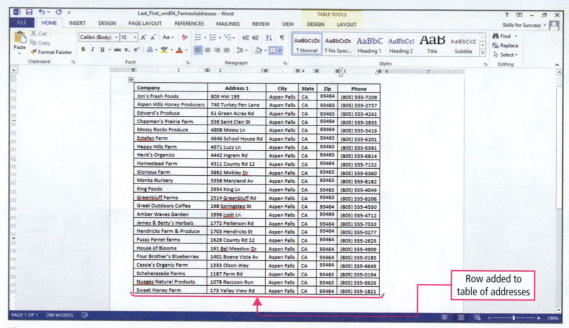

Row added to table of addresses

Figure 1

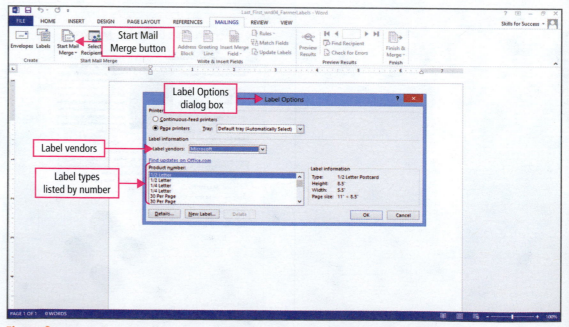

Start Mail Merge button

Label Options dialog box

Label vendors

Label types listed by number

Figure 2

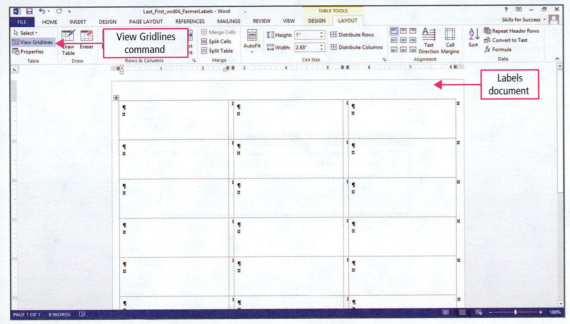

Figure 3

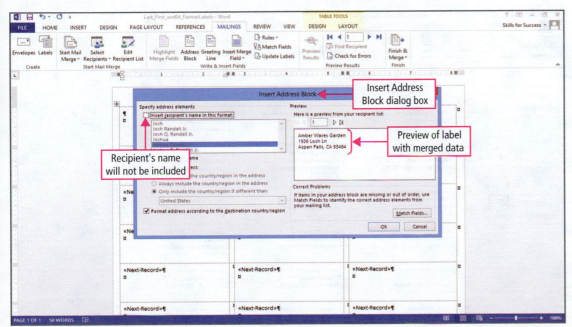

Figure 4

8. Under **Label information**, click the **Label vendors arrow**, scroll down, and then click **Avery US Letter**. Under **Product number**, click a label, and then press 5. Scroll down and click **5160 Easy Peel Address Labels**, and then click **OK**.

9. Compare your screen with **Figure 3**. If necessary, on the Layout tab, in the Table group, select View Gridlines and display the formatting marks.

   The Avery 5160 address label has precut sheets with three columns of 10 labels each.

10. On the **Mailings tab**, in the **Start Mail Merge group**, click the **Select Recipients** button, and then click **Use an Existing List**.

11. In the **Select Data Source** dialog box, navigate to your **Word Chapter 4** folder, click **Last_First_wrd04_ FarmerAddresses**, and then click **Open**.

12. In the **Start Mail Merge group**, click the **Edit Recipient List** button. In the row of column headings, click the **Company** heading one time to sort the list by company names, and then click **OK**.

13. In the **Write & Insert Fields group**, click the **Address Block** button. In the **Insert Address Block** dialog box, under **Specify address elements**, clear the **Insert recipient's name in this format** check box. Compare your screen with **Figure 4**, and then click **OK**.

   Merge fields merge and display data from specific columns in the data source. They are surrounded by nonprinting characters—for example, «AddressBlock» and «Next Record».

14. Save 🖫, and then **Close** ✕ the document.

■ **You have completed Skill 9 of 10**

 WRD 4-10 VIDEO

► When you open a merge document, you need to confirm that you want to open the document. Confirmation runs an *SQL Select Query*—a command that selects data from a data source based on the criteria you specify.

1. Start **Word 2013**, and then open **Last_ First_wrd04FarmerLabels**. Compare your screen with **Figure 1**.

   The message informs you that data from the data source will be placed in the document. If you have moved to a different computer or are saving to a network drive, you may also be asked to locate the data source file—*Last_First_wrd04_FarmersAddresses*.

2. Read the message, and then click **Yes** to open the labels document.

   If you encounter a similar message when opening a document that you did not expect to contain merged data, you should click No to protect your privacy.

3. On the **Mailings tab**, in the **Preview Results group**, click the **Preview Results** button. In the **Write & Insert Fields group**, click **Update Labels**.

   The Update Labels command is used to fill in the data for the remaining rows in the data source.

4. Click the **Table Selector** button to select all the labels. Open the **Paragraph** dialog box, change the **Spacing Before** to **0 pt**, and then click **OK**.

5. With the text still selected, click the **Layout tab**, and then in the **Alignment group**, click the **Align Center Left** button to vertically center the label text. Deselect the table, and then compare your screen with **Figure 2**.

■ **Continue to the next page to complete the skill**

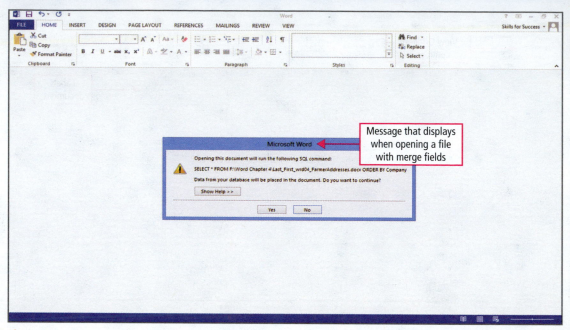

Message that displays when opening a file with merge fields

Figure 1

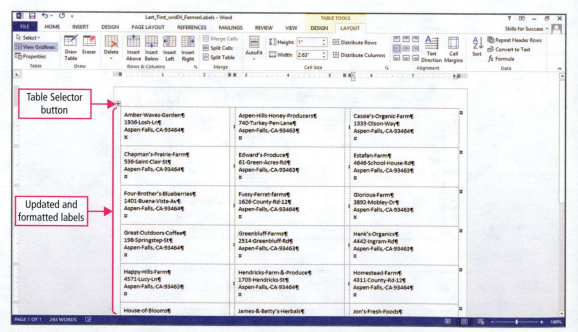

Table Selector button

Updated and formatted labels

Figure 2

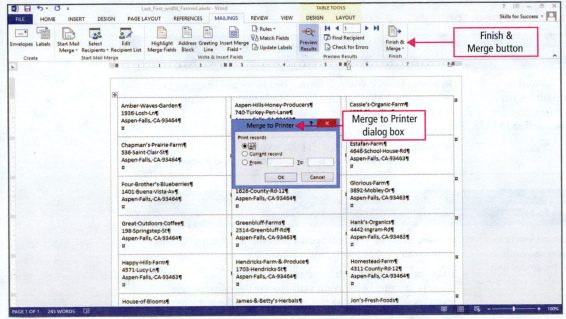

Finish & Merge button

Merge to Printer dialog box

Figure 3

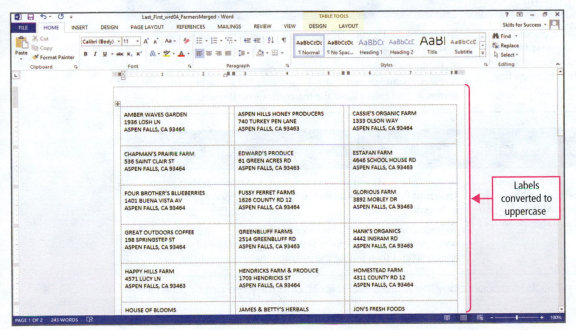

Labels converted to uppercase

Figure 4

6. Click the **Mailings tab**. In the **Finish group**, click the **Finish & Merge** button, and then click **Print Documents**. Compare your screen with **Figure 3**.

Typically a merge is complete by sending the document with its merged data to a printer with the label sheet(s) inserted into the appropriate printer tray.

7. In the **Merge to Printer** dialog box, click **Cancel**. In the **Finish group**, click the **Finish & Merge** button, and then click **Edit Individual Documents**. In the **Merge to New Document** dialog box, click **OK** to create a new document named *Labels1*.

When you merge to a new document, the merge fields are replaced with the corresponding data from each row in the data source and the new document does not contain any merge fields.

8. Save 🖫 the document in your **Word Chapter 4** folder as Last_First_wrd04_FarmersMerged Add the **FileName** field to the footer.

9. Select the table, and then click the **Home tab**. In the **Font group**, click the **Change Case arrow** Aa ⋅ , and then click **UPPERCASE**.

10. Click to deselect the table, and then hide the formatting marks. Press Ctrl + Home , and then compare your screen with **Figure 4**.

11. Save 🖫 , and then **Close** ✕ all open documents. Submit the files as directed by your instructor.

✔ **DONE!** You have completed Skill 10 of 10, and your document is complete!

More Skills

The following More Skills are located at **www.pearsonhighered.com/skills**

More Skills Optimize Documents for Read Mode

Read Mode is a view used to view, but not edit, a Word document. If you plan to share a document with others using Read Mode, you can optimize the headings and graphics for Read Mode and set the document to always open in Read Mode.

In More Skills 11, you will format headings and graphics to work in Read Mode, adjust Read Mode options, and protect a document so that it always opens in Read Mode.

To begin, open your web browser, navigate to www.pearsonhighered.com/skills, locate the name of your textbook, and then follow the instructions on the website.

More Skills Work in Outline View

When you work with a document, assigning outline levels to various parts of the text can be helpful. When you use outline levels, you can move blocks of text around in a document just by moving an outline item—all associated text moves with the outline item.

In More Skills 12, you will open a document, switch to Outline view, create outline levels, and move outline text.

To begin, open your web browser, navigate to www.pearsonhighered.com/skills, locate the name of your textbook, and then follow the instructions on the website.

More Skills Manage Document Properties

Document properties are the detailed information about your document that can help you identify or organize your files, including the name of the author, the title, and keywords. Some document properties are added to a document when you first create it. You can add others as necessary.

In More Skills 13, you will open a document, view its properties, and add additional properties.

To begin, open your web browser, navigate to www.pearsonhighered.com/skills, locate the name of your textbook, and then follow the instructions on the website.

More Skills Save Documents as Web Pages

When you plan to save a Word document as a web page, you can work in Web Layout view to preview the document as a web page. When you have the document formatted the way you want, you can save the document in a format as a web page, and then view in a web browser.

In More Skills 14, you will work with a document in Web Layout view and then save it as a web page. You will then open the file in Internet Explorer.

To begin, open your web browser, navigate to www.pearsonhighered.com/skills, locate the name of your textbook, and then follow the instructions on the website.

Please note that there are no additional projects to accompany the More Skills Projects, and they are not covered in the End-of-Chapter projects.

The following table summarizes the **SKILLS AND PROCEDURES** covered in this chapter.

Skills Number	Task	Step	Icon
1	Change the Fonts theme	Design tab → Document Formatting group → Fonts	
1	Justify text	Home tab → Paragraph group → Justify	▤
1	Create columns	Page Layout tab → Page Setup group → Columns	
2	Modify margins	Page Layout tab → Page Setup group → Margins → Custom Margins	
2	Modify columns	Layout tab → Page Setup group → Columns → More Columns	
2	Insert column breaks	Page Layout tab → Page Setup group → Breaks → Column Break	
3	Apply text effects	Home tab → Font group → Text Effects	Ⓐ▾
4	Create styles	Home tab → Styles group → More → Create a Style	
5	Add page borders	Design tab → Page Background group → Page Border	
5	Apply paragraph borders and shading	Home tab → Paragraph group → Border → Borders and Shading	▦▾
6	Insert Online Pictures	Insert tab → Illustrations group → Online Pictures	
6	Color graphics	Format tab → Adjust group → Color	
7	Create SmartArt	Insert tab → Illustrations group → SmartArt	
7	Edit SmartArt text	Type directly in each shape or type in the Text pane	
8	Format SmartArt	Use the commands in the Design and Format contextual tabs	
9	Create mail merge labels	Mailings tab → Start Mail Merge → Labels	
9	Connect to a data source	Mailings tab → Start Mail Merge group → Select Recipients	
9	Insert merge fields	Mailings tab → use the commands in the Write & Insert Fields group	
10	Preview mail merge	Mailings tab → Preview Results	
10	Fill in all labels	Mailings tab → Write & Insert Fields → Update Labels	
10	Finish mail merges	Mailings tab → Finish group → Finish & Merge → Print documents or Edit Individual Documents	

Key Terms

Online Help Skills

1. Start **Word 2013**, and then in the upper right corner of the start page, click the **Help** button ⟦?⟧.

2. In the **Word Help** window **Search help** box, type mail merge list and then press ⟦Enter⟧.

3. In the search result list, click **Set up a mail merge list with Word or Outlook**. Compare your screen with **Figure 1**.

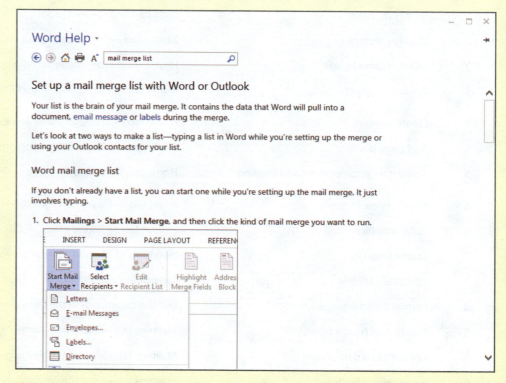

Figure 1

4. Read the article to answer the following questions: How do mail merge lists differ from external data sources? How are they the same? When might you want to use a mail merge list instead of an external data source?

Matching

Match each term in the second column with its correct definition in the first column by writing the letter of the term on the blank line in front of the correct definition.

___ **1.** You can change the font set that a theme uses by clicking the Fonts button on this tab.

___ **2.** A portion of a document that can be formatted differently from the rest of the document.

___ **3.** In the Columns gallery, the command that displays the Columns dialog box.

___ **4.** Any style that displays in a Ribbon gallery.

___ **5.** A pre-built set of decorative formats that make text stand out in a document.

___ **6.** An image, drawing, or photograph accessed from Bing Image Search and other online providers.

___ **7.** An extra detail or hook at the end of a character stroke.

___ **8.** A field that reserves space in a SmartArt shape but does not print until you insert your own text.

___ **9.** A feature that combines a main document and a data source to create customized letters or tables.

___ **10.** In mail merge, the command used to modify all labels based on changes made to the original label.

A Design

B Mail merge

C More Columns

D Online image

E Placeholder

F Quick Style

G Section

H Serif

I Text effects

J Update Labels

BizSkills Video

1. What is the purpose of a cover letter and what steps can you take to make them more effective?

2. Consider the various ways to organize resume information. Which layout do you think would be best for your particular education, skills, and experience?

Multiple Choice

Choose the correct answer.

1. A font where the letters do not have serifs.
   A. Non serif
   B. Plain print
   C. Sans serif

2. The default width assigned to columns.
   A. Proportional
   B. Equal
   C. Unbalanced

3. A paragraph alignment that aligns the text with both the left and right margins.
   A. Center
   B. Justified
   C. Left/Right

4. This moves the text that follows it to the top of the next column.
   A. Page break
   B. Column break
   C. Continuous break

5. A type of break that is used to create a new section that can be formatted differently from the rest of the document.
   A. Page
   B. Column
   C. Section

6. To change the color of the background in a paragraph, add this to the text background.
   A. Shading
   B. A border
   C. Text emphasis

7. A pre-built visual representation of information in which you can enter your own text.
   A. Mail merge
   B. Online picture
   C. SmartArt

8. Used by a mail merge document, this file contains information such as names and addresses.
   A. Data source
   B. Main document
   C. Merge document

9. In a mail merge document, this document contains the text that remains constant.
   A. Data source
   B. Main document
   C. Merge document

10. When you open a mail merge document, a message displays informing that this will be run.
    A. Insert records query
    B. SQL Select Query
    C. Update fields query

Topics for Discussion

1. In this chapter, you practiced inserting an online image in a document. When do you think online images are most appropriate, and in what kind of documents might online images be inappropriate? If you had to create a set of rules for using online images in a document, what would the top three rules be?

2. In this chapter, you used the mail merge feature in Word to create mailing labels. With mail merge, you can also insert one field at a time—and the fields do not have to be just names and addresses. Can you think of any situations where you might want to insert fields in a letter or another document?

Skills Review

To complete this project, you will need the following files:

- wrd04_SRUtilities
- wrd04_SRAddresses

You will save your files as:

- Last_First_wrd04_SRUtilities
- Last_First_wrd04_SRLabels

1. Start **Word 2013**, and then open the student data file **wrd04_SRUtilities**. Save the file in your chapter folder as Last_First_wrd04_SRUtilities Add the **FileName** field to the footer.

2. Locate the subtitle *Take the Lead with LEDs*, and then select the document text from that point to the end of the document. On the **Page Layout tab**, in the **Page Setup group**, click the **Columns** button, and then click **Two**.

3. Position the insertion point at the beginning of the subtitle *Free Energy Audits*. On the **Page Layout tab**, in the **Page Setup group**, click the **Breaks** button, and then click **Column**. Compare your screen with **Figure 1**.

4. Select the title *Utility News*. On the **Home tab**, in the **Font group**, click the **Text Effects and Typography** button. Point to **Shadow**, and then click the first choice under **Outer—Offset Diagonal Bottom Right**.

5. Select the subtitle *Take the Lead with LEDs*, and then click the **Font Dialog Box Launcher**. Under **Effects**, select the **Small caps** check box, and then click **OK**. In the **Paragraph group**, click the **Center** button.

6. With the subtitle still selected, in the **Styles group**, click the **More** button, and then click **Create a Style**. In the **Create New Style from Formatting** dialog box, name the style Utility Subtitle and then press Enter.

7. Click in the second subtitle—*Free Energy Audits*. On the **Home tab**, in the **Styles group**, click the **Utility Subtitle** thumbnail. Compare your screen with **Figure 2**.

8. On the **Insert tab**, in the **Illustrations group**, click the **Online Pictures** button. In the **Insert Pictures** dialog box, in the **Bing Image Search** box, type female architects and then click **Search**.

9. Click the image shown in **Figure 3** (or a similar image if this one is not available), and then click the **Insert** button.

■ **Continue to the next page to complete this Skills Review** ➤

Figure 1

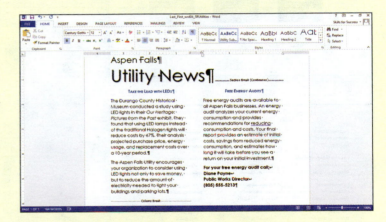

Figure 2

Figure 3

Figure 4

10. Click the picture's **Layout Options** button, and then click **Square**. On the **Format tab**, in the **Size group**, change the **Width** to **1.5"**. Use the alignment guides to center the image between the side margins and align the top with the paragraph that begins, *The Durango County*.

11. With the graphic still selected, click the **Format tab**, and then apply the first picture style—**Simple Frame**, **White**.

12. Click in the last paragraph in the document. In the **Paragraph group**, click the **Borders arrow**, and then click **Borders and Shading**. In the **Borders and Shading** dialog box, click **Box**, and then click the **Shading tab**. Click the **Fill arrow**, and then click the ninth color in the second row—**Orange, Accent 5, Lighter 80%**. Click **OK**, and then apply the **Center** paragraph alignment.

13. On the **Insert tab**, in the **Illustrations group**, click the **SmartArt** button. Click **Process**, click the first layout—**Basic Process**, and then click **OK**.

14. Click the SmartArt's border, and then click the **Format tab**. Click the **Arrange group** button, click **Position**, and then click the **Position in Bottom Center with Square Text Wrapping** thumbnail. Set the **Height** to **1.75"** and **Width** to **6.2"**.

15. On the **Design tab**, in the **SmartArt Styles group**, click the **More** button, and then click the first style under **3-D—Polished**.

16. For the three bullets, type Audit, Invest, and Save Compare your document with **Figure 3**, and then **Save** and **Close** the document.

17. Start **Word 2013**, and then create a blank document. On the **Mailings tab**, click the **Start Mail Merge** button, and then click **Labels**. In the **Label Options** dialog box, verify that **Avery US Letter** is selected. Under **Product number**, click **5160**, and then click **OK**. In the **Start Mail Merge group**, click **Select Recipients**, click **Use an Existing List**, and then locate and open **wrd04_SRAddresses**.

18. In the **Write & Insert Fields group**, click the **Address Block** button, clear the **Insert recipient's name in this format** check box, and then click **OK**. In the **Write & Insert Fields group**, click the **Update Labels** button.

19. In the **Finish group**, click the **Finish & Merge** button, click **Edit Individual Documents**, and then click **OK**. **Save** the document in your chapter folder as Last_First_wrd04_SRLabels and then add the **FileName** field to the footer. Compare your document with **Figure 4**.

20. Click **Save**, and then **Close** all other Word documents without saving changes.

✔ **DONE! You have completed this Skills Review**

Skills Assessment 1

To complete this document, you will need the following files:

- wrd04_SA1Racers
- wrd04_SA1Addresses

You will save your documents as:

- Last_First_wrd04_SA1Racers
- Last_First_wrd04_SA1Merged

1. Start **Word 2013**, and then open the student data file **wrd04_SA1Racers**. Save the file to your chapter folder as Last_First_wrd04_SA1Racers and then add the **FileName** field to the footer.

2. Apply the **Slice** theme, and then change the fonts theme to **Candara**. For the title *Aspen Falls Triathlon*, apply the last text effect—**Fill - Light Turquoise, Background 2, Inner Shadow**.

3. Search Online Pictures using the search phrase triathlon and then insert an appropriate image from the results. Compare your screen with **Figure 1**. Set the graphic's height to **1.6"**, and its position to **Position in Top Left with Square Text Wrapping**. Color the picture to **Light Turquoise, Background color 2 Light** (first column, third row).

4. Starting with the subtitle *This Year's Race* and ending with the phone number, apply the two-column layout and change column spacing to **0.3"**. Insert a column break at the beginning of the *This Year's Sponsors* subtitle.

5. Create a new Quick Style named Racers Subtitle based on the *This Year's Race* subtitle, and then apply the style to the other subtitle— *This Year's Sponsors*.

6. For the paragraph starting *Consider becoming a sponsor*, apply a box border with a **1½ pt** wide line, and a border color of **Orange, Accent 5** (ninth column, first row). For the same paragraph, set the shading to **Orange, Accent 5, Lighter 80%** (ninth column, second row).

7. Insert a SmartArt graphic with the **Basic Timeline** layout (second column, fourth row under **Process**). Set the SmartArt's position to **Position in Bottom Center with Square Text Wrapping**. Change the height to **2"** and width to **5.6"**.

8. Change the SmartArt text to Swim, Bike, and then Run as shown in **Figure 1**. **Save**, and then **Close** the document.

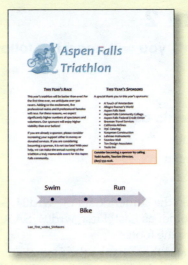

Figure 1

Figure 2

9. Create a blank document, and then start a **Labels** mail merge using **Avery US Letter** label **5160**. Use **wrd04_SA1Addresses** as the data source. Insert an **Address Block** clearing the option to include the recipient names, and then update the labels.

10. Merge the labels to a new document, and then edit that document by converting all the text to uppercase. Save the document in your chapter folder as Last_First_wrd04_SA1Merged and then insert the **FileName** field into the footer. Compare with **Figure 2**, and then **Save** and **Close** the document. **Close** the original mail merge document without saving changes.

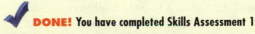

DONE! You have completed Skills Assessment 1

Skills Assessment 2

To complete this document, you will need the following files:

- wrd04_SA2Center
- wrd04_SA2Addresses

You will save your documents as:

- Last_First_wrd04_SA2Center
- Last_First_wrd04_SA2Merged

Figure 1

Figure 2

1. Start **Word 2013**, and then open the student data file **wrd04_SA2Center**. Save the file in your chapter folder as Last_First_wrd04_SA2Center and then add the **FileName** field to the footer.

2. Apply the **Retrospect** theme, and then change the fonts theme to **Corbel**. For the title *Community Center News,* apply the **Fill - White Outline**, **Accent 1**, **Shadow** text effect (fourth column, first row).

3. Search Online Pictures using the search phrase computer class and then insert an appropriate image from the results. Compare your screen with **Figure 1**. If that clip art image is not available, find a similar image. Set the graphic's height to **1.2"**, and its position to **Position in Top Right with Square Text Wrapping**. Color the picture to **Green**, **Accent color 6 Light** (last column, last row).

4. Starting with the subtitle *Computer Labs* and ending with the last paragraph, apply the two-column layout and change column spacing to **0.7"**. Insert a column break at the beginning of the *Computer Classes* subtitle.

5. Create a new **Quick Style** named Center Subtitle based on the *Computer Labs* subtitle, and then apply the style to the other two subtitles—*Computer Classes* and *Room Rentals*.

6. For the paragraph starting *To enroll in a class,* apply a box border with a **1½ pt** wide line, and a border color of **Brown**, **Accent 3** (seventh column, first row). For the same paragraph, set the shading to **Green**, **Accent 6**, **Lighter 80%** (last column, second row).

7. Insert a SmartArt graphic with the **Staggered Process** layout (third column, sixth row under **Process**). Set the SmartArt's position to **Position in Bottom Left with Square Text Wrapping**, and then change the shape's width and height to **3.0"**.

8. In the SmartArt shapes, change the text to Understand Computers, Browse and Send E-mail, and then Use Office as shown in **Figure 1**. **Save**, and then **Close** the document.

9. Create a blank document, and then start a **Labels** mail merge using **Avery US Letter** label 5160. Use **wrd04_SA2Addresses** as the data source. Insert an **Address Block** accepting the default settings, and then update the labels.

10. Merge the labels to a new document and then edit that document by converting all the text to uppercase. Save the document in your chapter folder as Last_First_wrd04_SA2Merged and then add the **FileName** field to the footer. Compare with **Figure 2**, and then **Save** and **Close** the document. **Close** the original mail merge document without saving changes.

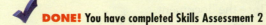

DONE! You have completed Skills Assessment 2

Visual Skills Check

To complete this document, you will need the following file:

- wrd04_VSRecycle

You will save your document as:

- Last_First_wrd04_VSRecycle

Start **Word 2013**, and then open the student data file **wrd04_VSRecycle**. Save the file in your chapter folder as Last_First_w04_VSRecycle Add the **FileName** field in the footer.

To complete this project, format the file as shown in **Figure 1**. The theme is **Ion Boardroom** with the **Tw Cen MT** fonts theme. The title is **48** points, the text effect is **Gradient Fill - Lavender**, **Accent 1**, **Reflection**, and the font color has been changed to **Dark Purple**, **Text 2**, **Lighter 40%**. Search Online Pictures for a graphic related to recycling, and then insert an appropriate image from the results. The image height has been set to **1"**.

Apply the two-column layout with **0.7"** between columns, and then add a column break as shown in **Figure 1**. Use the formatting in the first subtitle to create a Quick Style named Recycle Subtitle and then apply that style to the second subtitle. The shaded paragraph uses the default **Shadow** border, and the fill color is **Lavender**, **Accent 5**, **Lighter 80%**.

Insert and format the SmartArt as shown in **Figure 1**. The layout is **Text Cycle**, the height is **4"**, and the width is **6.5"**. The SmartArt style has been changed to **Powder**. Submit the project as directed by your instructor.

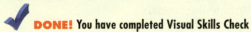 **DONE! You have completed Visual Skills Check**

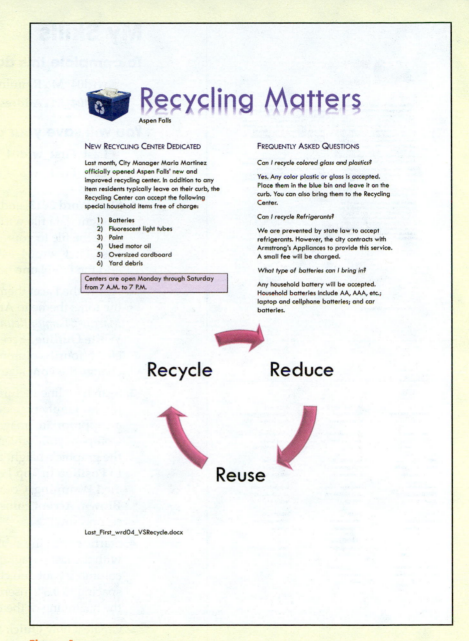

Figure 1

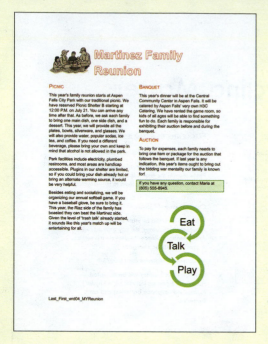

Figure 1

Figure 2

My Skills

To complete this document, you will need the following files:

- wrd04_MYReunion
- wrd04_MYAddresses

You will save your documents as:

- Last_First_wrd04_MYReunion
- Last_First_wrd04_MYLabels

1. Start **Word 2013**, and then open the student data file **wrd04_MYReunion**. Save the file to your chapter folder as Last_First_wrd04_MYReunion and then add the **FileName** field to the footer.

2. Apply the **Facet** theme, and then change the fonts theme to **Arial**. For the title *Martinez Family Reunion*, apply the **Fill - White Outline**, **Accent 1**, **Shadow** text effect (fourth column, first row), and then change the **Font size** to **32**.

3. Search Online Pictures using the search phrase family picnic and then insert an appropriate image from the results. Compare your screen with **Figure 1**. Set the graphic's height to **1"**, and its position to **Position in Top Left with Square Text Wrapping**. Color the picture to **Brown**, **Accent color 6 Dark** (last column, second row).

4. Starting with the subtitle *Picnic* and ending with the last paragraph, apply the two-column layout and change the column spacing to **0.3"**. Insert a column break at the beginning of the *Banquet* subtitle.

5. Create a new **Quick Style** named Reunion Subtitle based on the *Picnic* subtitle, and then apply the style to the other two subtitles—*Banquet* and *Auction*.

6. For the paragraph starting *If you have any questions*, apply a box border with a **1½ pt** wide line, and a border color of **Dark Green**, **Accent 2** (sixth column, first row). For the same paragraph, set the shading to **Dark Green**, **Accent 2**, **Lighter 80%** (sixth column, second row).

7. Insert a SmartArt graphic with the **Circle Arrow Process** layout. Set the SmartArt's position to **Position in Bottom Right with Square Text Wrapping**, and then change the graphic's height to **3.2"** and width to **3"**.

8. In the SmartArt shapes, change the text to Eat, Talk, and then Play as shown in **Figure 1**. **Save**, and then **Close** the document.

9. Create a blank document, and then start a **Labels** mail merge using **Avery US Letter** label **5160**. Use **wrd04_MYAddresses** as the data source. Insert an **Address Block** accepting the default settings, and then update the labels.

10. Merge the labels to a new document, and then edit that document by converting all the text to uppercase. Save the document in your chapter folder as Last_First_ wrd04_MYLabels and then add the **FileName** field to the footer. Compare with **Figure 2**, and then **Save** and **Close** the document. **Close** the original mail merge document without saving changes.

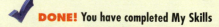

DONE! You have completed My Skills

Skills Challenge 1

To complete this document, you will need the following file:

- wrd04_SC1Fire

You will save your document as:

- Last_First_wrd04_SC1Fire

Open the student data file, **wrd04_SC1Fire**, and then save it in your chapter folder as Last_First_wrd04_SC1Fire Add the **FileName** field to the footer.

Using the techniques practiced in this chapter, format and layout the document as a two-column newsletter. Apply text effects to the title so that it stands out from the rest of the text. Locate and insert an online image that works well with the newsletter theme of fire protection. Size, format, and position the image to pull the reader's eye from the title to the newsletter text. Format the subtitles so they stand out from the articles, and then create a style for that format. Apply the style to both subtitles. Replace the text *Air → Fuel → Heat* with a SmartArt graphic that illustrates this relationship as a triangle. Format, size, and position the graphic to fill the bottom of the newsletter.

Submit the completed newsletter as directed by your instructor.

 DONE! You have completed Skills Challenge 1

Skills Challenge 2

To complete this document, you will need the following file:

- wrd04_SC2Addresses

You will save your document as:

- Last_First_wrd04_SC2Merged

Create a blank Word document, and then start the merge process to create Avery 5160 mailing labels. For the recipient's list, use **wrd04_SC2Addresses**. To complete the labels document, you will need to click the **Match Fields** button in the **Insert Address Block** dialog box and then use the **Match Fields** dialog box to match the columns in the data source. When you have inserted the Address Block with all the fields matched, update all the labels, and then merge the labels to a new document. Save the merged document as Last_First_wrd04_SC2Merged Close the merged document, and then close the original document without saving it. Submit the merged document as directed by your instructor.

 DONE! You have completed Skills Challenge 2

Student data files needed for this project:

wrd_CPVisitUs
wrd_CPFestival

You will save your file as:

Last_First_wrd_CPVisitUs

1. Start **Word 2013**, and then open the student data file that came with this project, **wrd_CPVisitUs**. Use the **Save As** dialog box to save the file to your drive with the name Last_First_wrd_CPVisitUs Insert the **FileName** field in the footer.

2. Use **Find and Replace** to replace all occurrences of *City of Aspen Falls* with Aspen Falls

3. Change the document's theme to **Ion Boardroom**, and then in the first line of the letterhead, change the font size to **18**, apply the **Small caps** effect, and then set the character spacing to **Expanded** by **2 pt**.

4. In the letter greeting, change the word *Mrs.* to Ms.

5. In the first letter body paragraph, insert a footnote after the word *interns*. For the footnote, type the following: This intern is majoring in recreation and did this analysis as a class project.

6. Near the bottom of Page 1, after the text *City Hall*, insert a manual page break, and then compare your screen with **Figure 1**.

7. At the top of Page 2, delete the blank paragraph, and then select the text *ASPEN FALLS*. Change the **Font** to **Verdana**, the size to 42 and then apply the **Gradient Fill - Orange**, **Accent 4**, **Outline - Accent 4** text effect.

8. For the text *Get out and join the party!*, apply **Bold** and **Italic**.

9. For the newsletter articles, starting with *Get Out!* and ending with *Borax Trail era*, apply two columns of equal width with **0.3** spacing between them.

10. For the article title, *Get Out!*, apply the **Small caps** effect, and then change the font color to the fifth theme color—**Plum**, **Accent 1**. **Center** align the paragraph, change the **Spacing Before** to **12 pt**, and then compare your screen with **Figure 2**.

Figure 1

Figure 2

■ **Continue to the next page to complete the skill** ➡

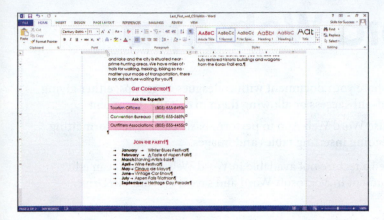

Figure 3

Figure 4

11. Create a new style named Article Title based on the formatting applied to the *Get Out!* title in the previous step. Apply the **Article Title** style to the other three article titles.

12. In the first article, apply a first line indent of 0.25 inches to the paragraph beginning *Aspen Falls is your gateway*. In the same paragraph, set the line spacing to **Single** (1.0), and the **Spacing Before** and **Spacing After** the paragraph to **6 pt** each. Set the paragraph's alignment to **Justified**.

13. Use **Format Painter** to apply the formatting of the paragraph formatted in the previous step to the article paragraphs beginning *Aspen Falls features, Improve your literacy,* and *If history is your bent.*

14. In the *Get Connected!* article, delete the text *Phone numbers* but not the paragraph mark, and then in the blank paragraph, insert a **2x3** table. In the table, add the following:

Tourism Office   (805) 555-8493

Convention Bureau   (805) 555-5689

Outfitters Association   (805) 555-4455

15. Add a new row above the table, and then merge the new row's cells into one cell. In the new row, type Ask the Experts

16. For the table, apply the **List Table 2 - Accent 1** table style, and then clear the **First Column** table style option. Set the cell sizes to **AutoFit to Contents**.

17. Select the table, and then on the **Layout tab**, in the **Cell Size group**, set the **Height** to 0.3". Set the alignment of the first row to **Center** and the alignment of the cells in rows 2 to 4 to **Center Left**. Compare your screen with **Figure 3**.

18. On Page 2, insert the picture from the student data file **wrd_CSFestival**. Set the picture's position to **Top Right with Square Text Wrapping**, and then set the **Width** to **3.0"**. Apply the **Rotated, White** picture style.

19. Insert a column break before the *Join the Party!* article title.

20. In the *Join the Party!* article, select the tabbed list, and use the **Tab** dialog box to add a **Right** tab at 1" and a **Left** tab at **1.15"**.

21. After the last item in the tabbed list, add the following event:

December   Festival of Lights

22. In the tabbed list, **Bold** the word *December*, and then compare your screen with **Figure 4**.

23. **Save**  and then **Close** Word. Submit the project as directed by your instructor.

DONE! You have completed Word Capstone Project

Create Flyers Using Word Web App

▶ **Word Web App** is a cloud-based application used to complete basic document editing and formatting tasks using a web browser.

▶ Word Web App can be used to create or edit documents using a web browser instead of the Word program—Word 2013 does not need to be installed on your computer.

▶ When you create a document using Word Web App, it is saved on your SkyDrive so that you can work with it from any computer connected to the Internet.

▶ You can share your document with colleagues or groups, either giving them read-only access or allowing them to edit the document.

▶ You can use Word Web App to perform basic editing and formatting tasks including inserting tables and images.

▶ If you need a feature not available in Word Web App, you can edit your document in Microsoft Word and save it on your SkyDrive.

© Maridav / Fotolia

Aspen Falls City Hall

This project assumes that you are working at a computer that does not have the desktop version of Microsoft Word installed. Instead, you will create, edit, and format a flyer using Word Web App. You will create a document for Leah Kim, Parks and Recreation Supervisor. The flyer needs to outline the city's policy for photography in city parks.

The Word Web App is used to create or open Word documents from any computer or device connected to the Internet. When needed, you can edit text, format the document, or insert objects such as pictures and tables. You can save these documents on your SkyDrive and continue working with them later when you are at a computer that has Word 2013 available. In Word Web App, you edit your document in **Editing View** and view the document as it will print in **Reading View**.

In this project, you will use Word Web App to create a short flyer. You will type and edit text, apply styles, and create a bulleted list. You will insert a picture from a file, size and position it, and then insert a table. Finally, you will open the document in Word 2013 to format the table.

Time to complete this project – 30 to 60 minutes

Student data file needed for this project:

wrd_WAPark

Outcome

Using the skills in this project, you will be able to create and edit a Word Web App document like this:

You will save your file as:

Last_First_wrd_WAPhotos

SKILLS MyITLab®

At the end of this project you will be able to use Word Web App to:

▶ Create new Word documents from SkyDrive

▶ Type text in Editing View

▶ Apply styles

▶ Add emphasis to text

▶ Change text alignment

▶ Insert pictures from files

▶ Create tables

▶ Switch to desktop Word to complete editing

▶ View documents in Reading View

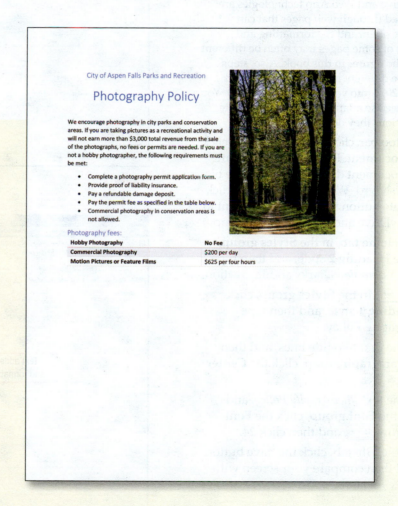

City of Aspen Falls Parks and Recreation

Photography Policy

We encourage photography in city parks and conservation areas. If you are taking pictures as a recreational activity and will not earn more than $3,000 total revenue from the sale of the photographs, no fees or permits are needed. If you are not a hobby photographer, the following requirements must be met:

- Complete a photography permit application form.
- Provide proof of liability insurance.
- Pay a refundable damage deposit.
- Pay the permit fee as specified in the table below.
- Commercial photography in conservation areas is not allowed.

Photography fees:

Hobby Photography	No Fee
Commercial Photography	$200 per day
Motion Pictures or Feature Films	$625 per four hours

1. Start **Internet Explorer** , navigate to live.com and log on to your Microsoft account. If you do not have an account, follow the links and directions on the page to create one.

2. After logging in, navigate as needed to display your **SkyDrive** page, and then compare your screen with **Figure 1**.

   SkyDrive and Web App technologies are accessed through web pages that can change often, and the formatting and layout of some pages may often be different than the figures in this book. Also, steps may be different if you have not signed Word 2013 into your Microsoft account. You may need to adapt the steps to complete the actions they describe.

3. On the toolbar, click **Create**, and then click **Word document**. In the **New Microsoft Word document** dialog box, name the file Last_First_wrd_WAPhotos and then click the **Create** button to save the document to your SkyDrive and start Word Web App.

4. On the **Home tab**, in the **Styles group**, click the **Heading 2** style, and then type City of Aspen Falls Parks and Recreation

5. Press Enter . In the **Styles group**, click the **Heading 1** style, and then type Photography Policy

6. Select the first two title lines, and then in the **Paragraph group**, click the **Center** button .

7. Select the text *Photography Policy,* and then in the **Font group**, click the **Font Size arrow** , and then click **24**.

8. Above the **File tab**, click the **Save** button , and then compare your screen with **Figure 2**.

■ Continue to the next page to complete the skill

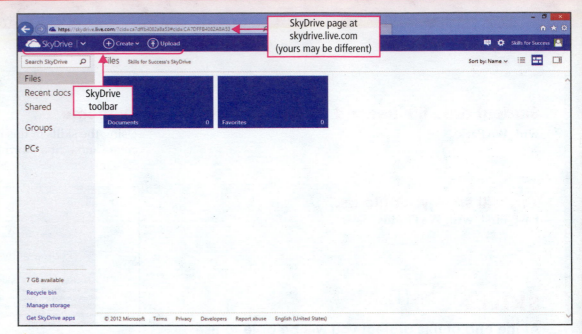

Figure 1

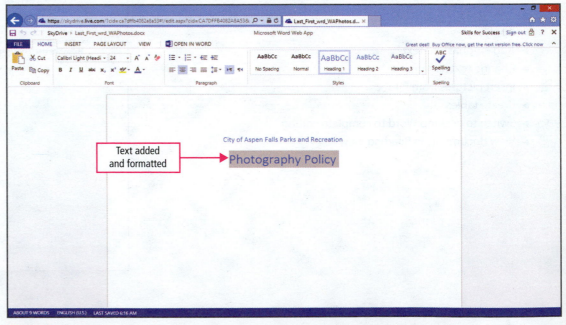

Figure 2

- Complete a photography permit application form.
- Provide proof of liability insurance.
- Pay a refundable damage deposit.
- Pay the permit fee as specified in the table below.
- Commercial photography in conservation areas is not allowed.

Figure 3

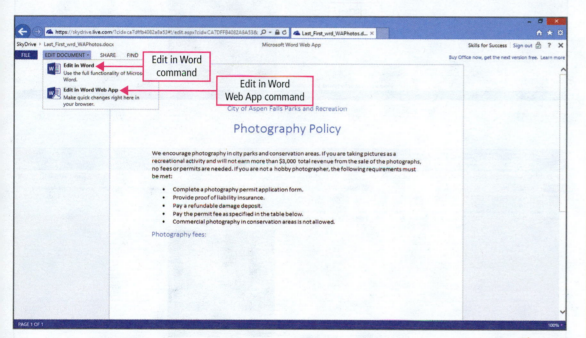

Figure 4

9. Position the insertion point to the right of *Policy*, and then press Enter two times. In the **Styles group**, click the **Normal** style to reapply the style's formatting to the blank paragraph.

10. Type the following text: We encourage photography in city parks and conservation areas. If you are taking pictures as a recreational activity and will not earn more than $3,000 total revenue from the sale of the photographs, no fees or permits are needed. If you are not a hobby photographer, the following requirements must be met:

11. Press Enter, and then in the **Paragraph group**, click the **Bullets** button. Create a bulleted list using the text found in the table in **Figure 3**.

12. After typing the list, press Enter two times, and then type Photography fees:

13. With the insertion point in the *Photography fees* paragraph, apply the **Heading 2** style.

14. Save the document. Click the **View tab**. In the **Document Views group**, click the **Reading View** button.

    Reading View displays the document as it will print, but you cannot edit in this view. You must save the document before switching to Reading View.

15. Click **Edit Document**, compare your screen with **Figure 4**, and then click **Edit in Word Web App**.

■ **Continue to the next page to complete the skill**

16. In the first bullet, position the insertion point to the right of the line that ends *permit application form*. Click the **Insert tab**, and then in the **Pictures group**, click the **Picture** button. In the **Choose File to Upload** dialog box, navigate to the student files for this project, and then open **wrd_WAPark**.

17. If necessary, click the picture to select it, and then click the **Format tab**. In the **Image Size group**, click in the **Scale** box, and then type 75 and press Enter to change the size of the picture to 75 percent of its original size. Compare your screen with **Figure 5**.

> When a picture is selected, the Format tab displays and the picture has a washed-out effect.

18. Click in the document, and then click Ctrl + End to move to the end of the document. Press Enter, and then click the **Normal** style to reapply the style's formatting.

19. Click the **Insert tab**, and then in the **Tables group**, click the **Table** button. In the third row, click the second square to create a **2x3** table.

20. In the first table cell, type Hobby Photography and then press Tab. Type No Fee and then press Tab.

21. Type Commercial Photography and then press Tab. Type $200 per day and then press Tab.

22. Type Motion Pictures or Feature Films and then press Tab. Type $625 per four hours and then compare your screen with **Figure 6**.

■ **Continue to the next page to complete the skill**

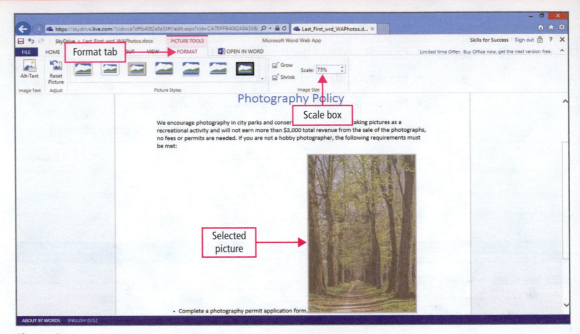

Figure 5

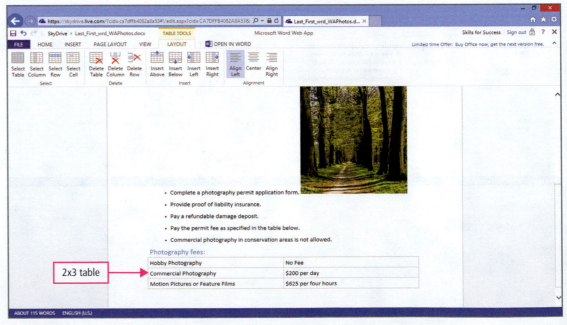

Figure 6

City of Aspen Falls Parks and Recreation

Photography Policy

We encourage photography in city parks and conservation areas. If you are taking pictures as a recreational activity and will not earn more than $3,000 total revenue from the sale of the photographs, no fees or permits are needed. If you are not a hobby photographer, the following requirements must be met:

- Complete a photography permit application form.
- Provide proof of liability insurance.
- Pay a refundable damage deposit.
- Pay the permit fee as specified in the table below.
- Commercial photography in conservation areas is not allowed.

Photography fees:

Hobby Photography	No Fee
Commercial Photography	$200 per day
Motion Pictures or Feature Films	$625 per four hours

Picture formatting displays in Reading View

Table formatting displays in Reading View

Figure 7

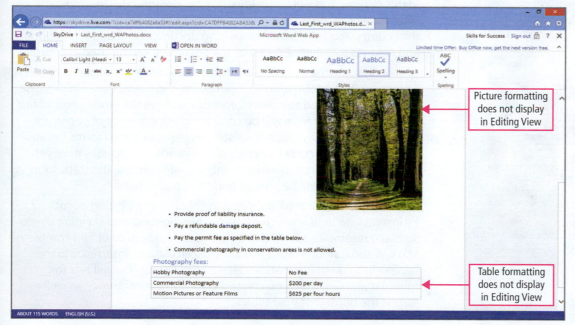

- Provide proof of liability insurance.
- Pay a refundable damage deposit.
- Pay the permit fee as specified in the table below.
- Commercial photography in conservation areas is not allowed.

Photography fees:

Hobby Photography	No Fee
Commercial Photography	$200 per day
Motion Pictures or Feature Films	$625 per four hours

Picture formatting does not display in Editing View

Table formatting does not display in Editing View

Figure 8

23. **Save** 🖫 the document. To the right of the **Layout tab**, click **Open in Word**. Read all messages that display, and then click **Allow** or **Yes** as needed to open the document in Word 2013.

24. If necessary, switch to Print Layout view. Click the picture to select it, and then click the **Format tab**. In the **Arrange group**, click the **Position** button, and then click the third thumbnail—**Position in Top Right with Square Text Wrapping**.

25. Click in the table, and then click the **Design tab**. Click the **Table Styles More** button ⤵, and then under **Grid Tables**, click the fourth style in the second row— **Grid Table 2 - Accent 3**.

26. **Save** 🖫 the document, and then **Close** ✕ Word 2013.

27. In the message that displays, click **Edit in Word Web App**. On the **View tab**, click **Reading View**, and then compare your screen with **Figure 7**.

28. Click **Edit Document**, and then click **Edit in Word Web App**. Compare your screen with **Figure 8**.

    Features not supported by Word Web App will not be available in Edit View. Here, the picture layout and table formatting do not display. These features however, do display in Reading View and when opened in Word 2013.

29. Click the **View tab**, and then click **Reading View**. **Print**, **Download** and submit, or **Share** the document as directed by your instructor.

30. In the top left corner of the **Internet Explorer** window, click the **Sign out** link, and then **Close** ✕ the browser window.

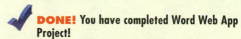 **DONE! You have completed Word Web App Project!**

CHAPTER 5

Create Static Forms

- ▶ You can improve document layouts by inserting symbol characters, continuous section breaks, custom margins, or highlighting.
- ▶ Pictures can be enhanced by changing the picture background and by wrapping text around the image.
- ▶ Tables can include formulas, and the results can be updated as the numbers change.

- ▶ You can format borders in your tables.
- ▶ You can save any text or document object so that it can be inserted with a single click.
- ▶ A static form is a document that you or others can print and then fill out.

© Pixsooz/Fotolia

Aspen Falls City Hall

In this chapter, you will assist Julia Wagner, Community Development Director, whose job is to promote the city both in Aspen Falls and around the country. You will update an existing document and add Word formats and features to enhance it so that the document can be used as a form.

Having someone complete a printed form created in Microsoft Word is a way to collect information that can be used in businesses—in this case, the form will be used to collect information about the employee and his/her shirt order. This form will be completed using a piece of paper, not filled in electronically. Businesses still create paper-based forms because not everyone has access to a computer and not all processes have yet been automated. For this assignment, you will enhance the static form document, which will be printed and filled out by hand.

In this project, you will use Word to enhance the existing document by inserting tabbed lines, check boxes, highlighting, and building blocks so that it resembles a form that employees could print out and complete. You will also format a table. You will use calculations inserted into the table cells to do mathematical calculations. Finally, you will test the formulas and functions you created in the table for accuracy, as well as format the borders of your tables.

Time to complete all 10 skills – 60 to 90 minutes

Student data file needed for this chapter:

wrd05_Order

You will save your files as:

Last_First_wrd05_Order (Word document)
Last_First_wrd05_OrderSnip (Image file)

Outcome

Using the skills in this chapter, you will be able to create static forms such as this:

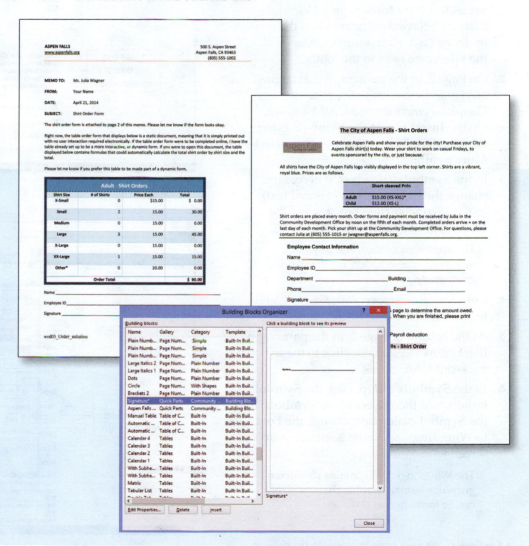

SKILLS MyITLab®
Skills 1-10 Training

At the end of this chapter, you will be able to:

Skill 1 Insert Symbols and Characters
Skill 2 Apply Margins to Sections
Skill 3 Use Paste Options and Highlight Text
Skill 4 Modify Tab Settings Using the Ruler
Skill 5 Modify Picture Backgrounds and Text-Wrap Points
Skill 6 Create and Save Building Blocks
Skill 7 Modify and Insert Building Blocks
Skill 8 Insert Formulas and Functions into Tables
Skill 9 Update Table Formulas and Functions
Skill 10 Format Tables with Border Painter

MORE SKILLS

Skill 11 Draw Tables and Convert Tables to Text
Skill 12 Merge Data from Excel
Skill 13 Edit PDF Documents
Skill 14 Insert Online Videos

▶ A *symbol* is a character such as the copyright symbol © or a bullet character that is not found on common keyboards.

▶ Most fonts include commonly used symbols, whereas some fonts include only symbols.

1. Start **Word 2013** and then open **wrd05_Order**. Use the **Save As** dialog box to create a **New folder** named Word Chapter 5 **Save** the document in the new folder as Last_First_wrd05_Order Add the **FileName** field to the footer.

2. On Page 2, in the paragraph that begins *Shirt orders are*, click to the right of *Completed orders arrive on*. Add a space. On the **Insert tab**, in the **Symbols group**, click the **Symbol** button, and then select **More Symbols**.

3. In the **Symbol** dialog box, if necessary, change the **Font arrow** to **(normal text)**. In the **Character code** box, replace the value with 2248 and then press Enter.

   The approximate sign, ≈, is a symbol, or visual representation, for the word *approximately*.

4. Compare your screen with **Figure 1**, and then click **Close**.

5. At the bottom of Page 2, in the paragraph that begins *Please select*, click to the left of the word *Cash*.

6. In the **Symbols** group, click the **Symbol** button, and then select **More Symbols**. In the **Symbol** dialog box, change the **Font** to **Wingdings**, and then compare your screen with **Figure 2**.

   The Wingdings font contains *character graphics*—small graphic characters that can be formatted as text.

■ **Continue to the next page to complete the skill** ▶

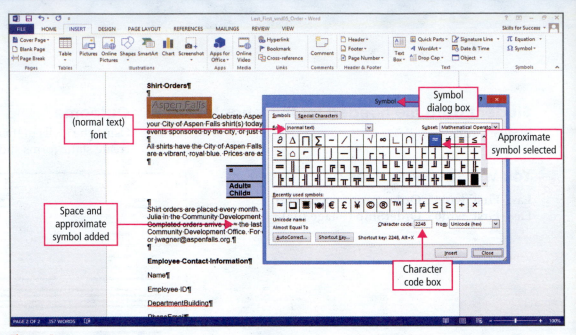

Figure 1

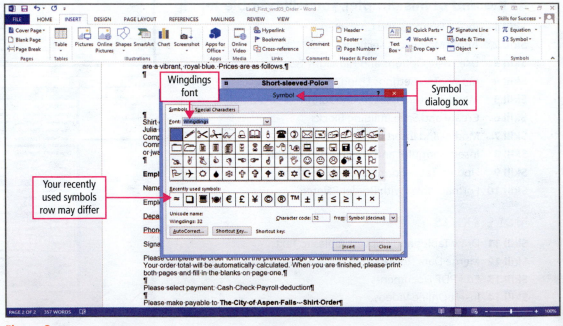

Figure 2

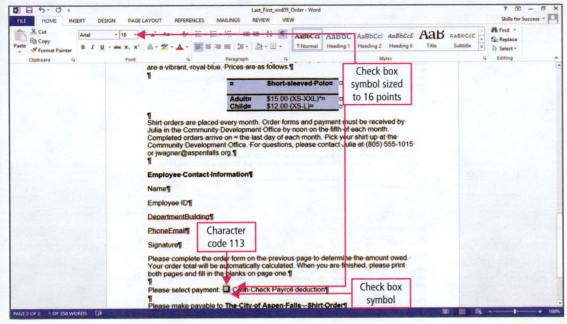

Figure 3

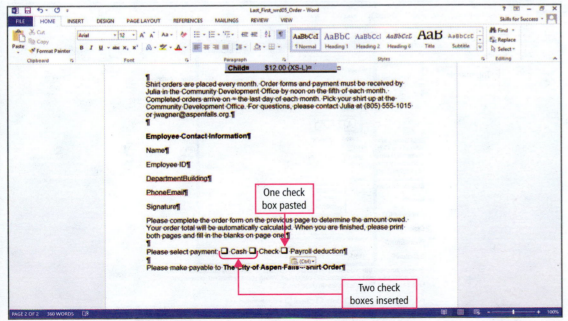

Figure 4

7. In the **Character code** box, replace the value with 113 and then press Enter to select the ☐ symbol.

You can leave the Symbol dialog box open while working in the document so that you can insert symbols in different locations without opening and closing the Symbol dialog box.

8. In the document, add a space after the symbol. Select the symbol, and then change the **Font Size** to **16**. Compare your screen with **Figure 3**.

Character graphics are formatted with the same techniques as font characters.

9. Click to the left of the word *Check*.

10. In the **Symbol** dialog box, with character code *113* still selected, click **Insert**, and then click **Close**. After the symbol, add a space. Select the symbol, and then change the **Font Size** to **16**.

11. If necessary, select the check box symbol, and then press Shift + → one time to select the space to the right of the symbol. On the **Home tab**, in the **Clipboard group**, click the **Copy** button.

12. Click to the left of *Payroll*, and then click **Paste**. Compare your screen with **Figure 4**.

13. On Page 1, in the paragraph that begins *FROM:*, update *Your Name* to reflect your name.

14. Save 🖫 the document.

■ **You have completed Skill 1 of 10**

▶ *Continuous section breaks* are inserted into a document when you want to format each section differently.

▶ Margin settings can be customized when you need margins that are different from the choices in the Margins gallery.

1. On Page 2, locate the heading that begins *Employee Contact*, and then click to the left of the word *Employee*. If necessary, display the formatting marks.

2. On the **Page Layout tab**, in the **Page Setup group**, click the **Breaks** button. Under **Section Breaks**, click **Continuous**, and then compare your screen with **Figure 1**.

   The screen displays a section break, which separates the document into two sections that can be formatted separately.

3. On Page 2, click in the paragraph above the section break notation.

4. In the **Page Setup group**, click the **Margins** button, and then select **Custom Margins**.

   Alternately, in the Page Setup group, click the Page Setup Dialog Box Launcher 🔲.

5. In the **Page Setup** dialog box, under **Margins**, replace the existing **Top** box value with .75 Compare your screen with **Figure 2**.

■ Continue to the next page to complete the skill ➡

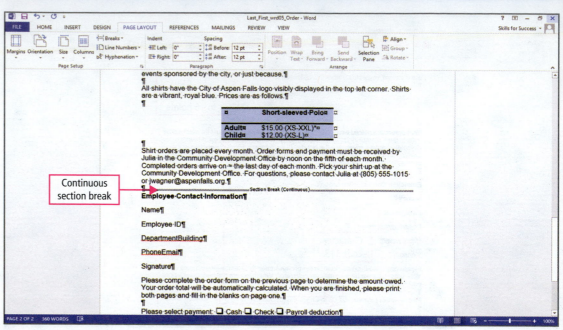

Continuous section break

Figure 1

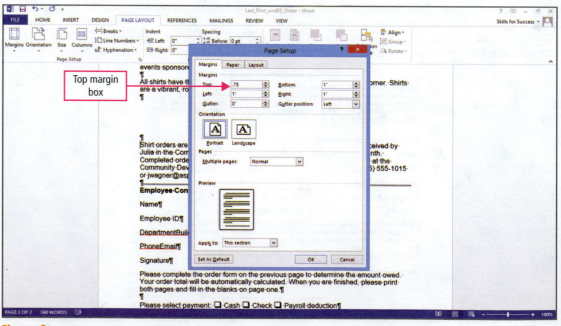

Top margin box

Figure 2

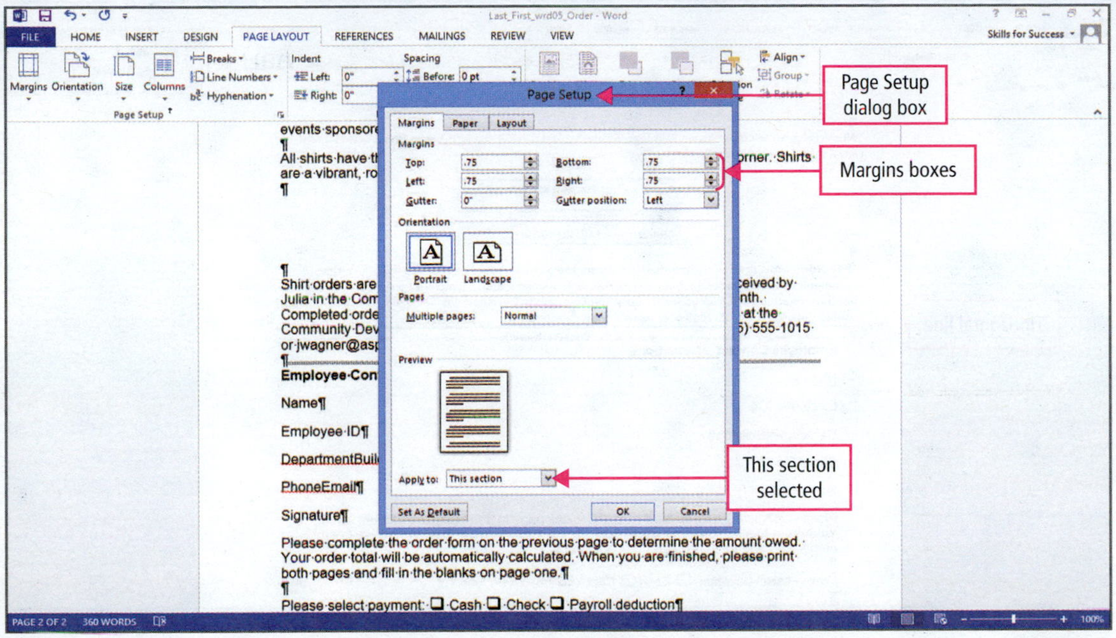

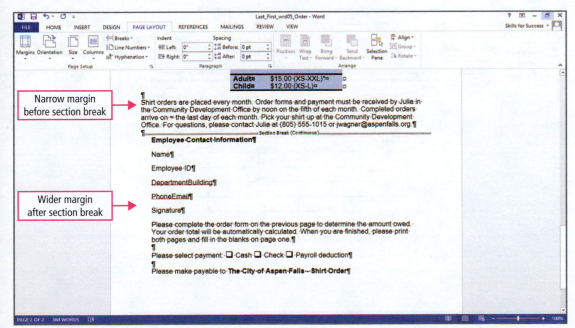

Figure 3

6. In the **Bottom** box, replace the existing text with .75 Repeat this technique to change the **Left** and **Right** margins to .75

7. Verify that the **Apply to** box displays *This section*. Compare your screen with **Figure 3**, and then click **OK**.

8. If necessary, scroll down to display the section break and verify that the margins are different in the section before the break. Compare your screen with **Figure 4**.

9. On Page 2, select all the text above the section break. On the **Home tab**, in the **Font group**, click the **Font arrow**, and then click **Calibri**.

10. Click anywhere in the *Shirt Orders* title. On the **Home tab**, in the **Paragraph group**, click the **Center** button.

11. **Save** the document.

■ **You have completed Skill 2 of 10**

Figure 4

▶ *Paste Options* provide formatting choices when pasting text into the current document.

▶ Text can be highlighted to make it stand out in the document.

1. On Page 2, click to the left of the *Section Break (Continuous)* text. Press and hold [Shift] while pressing [-] five times. Press [Enter]. Compare your screen with **Figure 1**.

   When you press and hold [Shift] while pressing [-] five times, five underlines display in the document. Pressing [Enter] converts the underlines to a ***horizontal line***—a line that separates document text so that it is easier to read—above the blank paragraph.

2. On Page 2, in the title, select the text *Shirt Orders* but not the paragraph mark that follows it. On the **Home tab**, in the **Clipboard group**, click the **Copy** button.

3. On Page 1, in the first row of the table, click to the right of the space after the word *Adult*. Type a hyphen (-), and then add another space. Click the **Paste arrow**. Compare your screen with **Figure 2**, and then click the **Keep Text Only** button.

   Paste Options include ***Keep Source Formatting***—pastes text with the formatting from the original location— ***Merge Formatting***—pastes text and applies the formatting in use in the new location—and ***Keep Text Only***—pastes text with all formatting removed.

■ **Continue to the next page to complete the skill** ▶

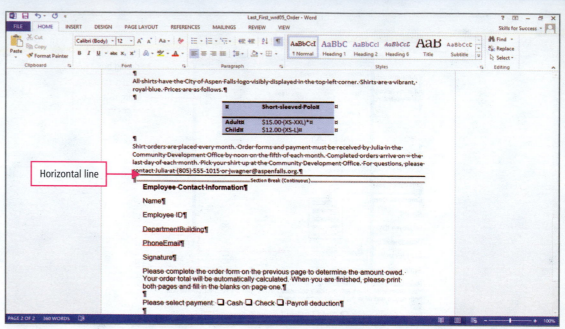

Figure 1

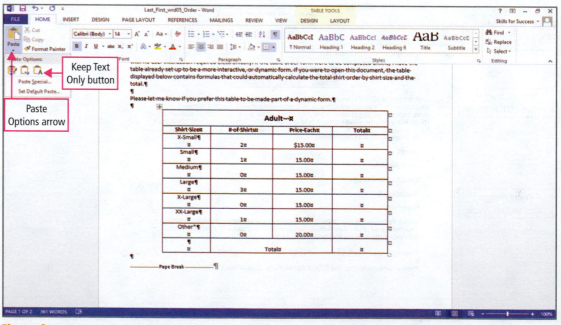

Figure 2

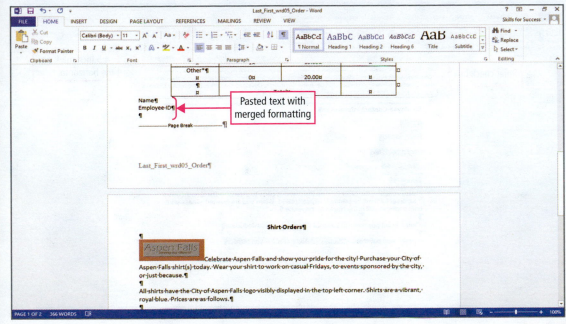

Figure 3

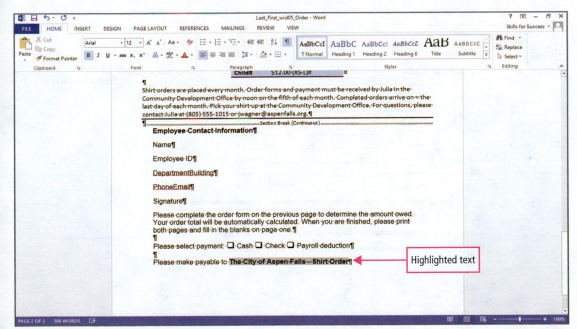

Figure 4

4. On the Page 2 form, select the paragraphs beginning *Name* and ending *Employee ID*, and then click the **Copy** button.

5. At the bottom of Page 1, click in the blank paragraph below the table. Click the **Paste arrow**, and then click **Merge Formatting** . Compare your screen with **Figure 3**.

6. At the bottom of Page 1, select the two paragraphs that you pasted. On the **Home tab**, in the **Paragraph group**, click the **Paragraph Dialog Box Launcher** .

7. In the **Paragraph** dialog box, under **Spacing**, click the **Before up spin arrow** two times to change the spacing before each paragraph to *12 pt*, and then click **OK**.

8. At the bottom of Page 2, select the text *The City of Aspen Falls – Shirt Order*. In the **Font group**, click the **Text Highlight Color arrow**, and then click **Gray-25%**— the fourth choice in the third row of the gallery. Compare your screen with **Figure 4**.

9. **Save** the document.

■ **You have completed Skill 3 of 10**

▶ Tab settings can be used to align text for ease of reading.

▶ Tab settings may be changed in the Tabs dialog box or on the ruler.

1. With the [pointer] pointer, on Page 2, select the five paragraphs beginning with *Name* and ending with *Signature*.

2. On the **View tab**, in the **Show group**, select the **Ruler** check box as shown in **Figure 1**.

   Alternately, click the View Ruler button in the vertical scroll bar.

3. On the ruler, point with the tip of the pointer and double-click the **4.5 inch** mark to open the **Tabs** dialog box. In the large **Tab stop position** box, click *4.5"*. Under **Alignment**, select the **Right** option button.

4. Under **Leader**, select the **4** option button, and then click **OK** to set up a line leader that ends at the **4.5 inch** tab.

5. Click to the right of the word *Name*. Press [Tab].

6. Repeat the technique to insert the [Tab] character after *Employee ID*, *Department*, *Phone*, and *Signature*. Compare your screen with **Figure 2**.

7. With the pointer [pointer], select the two paragraphs beginning with *Department* and *Phone*. On the horizontal ruler, double-click the **6 inch** mark.

8. In the **Tabs** dialog box, under **Tab stop position**, click **6"**. Under **Alignment**, select the **Right** option button. Under **Leader**, select the **4** option button. Click **OK**.

■ **Continue to the next page to complete the skill** ➤

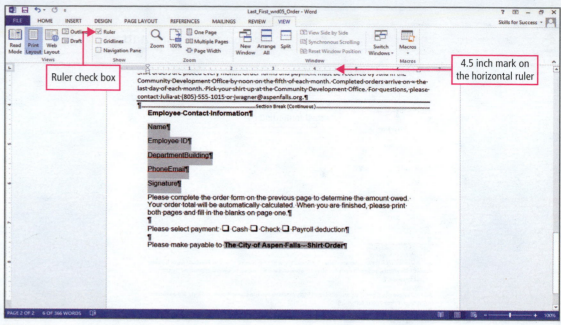

Figure 1

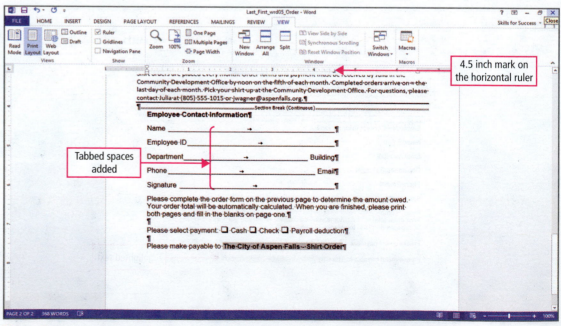

Figure 2

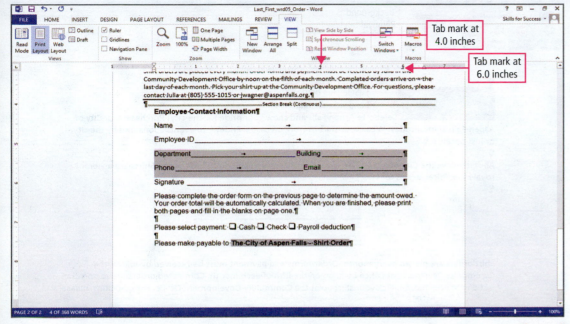

Figure 3

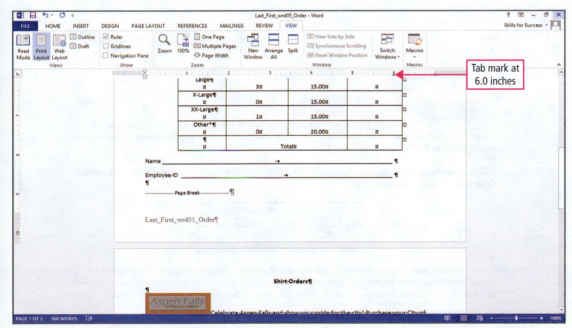

Figure 4

9. Click to the right of the word *Building* and then press [Tab]. Repeat this technique to add a [Tab] after *Email*.

10. With the pointer, select the paragraphs beginning with *Name* and *Employee ID*. Press and hold [Ctrl] and select the paragraph that begins *Signature* to select the nonconsecutive paragraphs.

11. On the ruler, point to the tab marker at **4.5 inches**, drag to the right, over to **6.0 inches**, and then release the mouse.

12. Select the two paragraphs beginning *Department* and *Phone*. Using the technique just practiced, drag the tab marker at **4.5 inches** to **4.0 inches**, and then compare your screen with **Figure 3**.

13. At the bottom of Page 1, select the paragraphs beginning *Name* and ending *Employee ID*.

14. On the ruler, double-click the tab marker at **6.0 inches** to open the **Tabs** dialog box. Under **Tab stop position**, click **6"**. Under **Alignment**, select the **Right** option button. Under **Leader**, select the **4** option button, and then click **OK**.

15. Click to the right of *Name,* and then press [Tab]. Repeat this technique to add a [Tab] after *Employee ID*. Compare your screen with **Figure 4**.

16. **Save** the document.

▪ **You have completed Skill 4 of 10**

▶ Parts of a picture, such as the background, can be adjusted to improve the appearance of the picture.

▶ When text wraps around objects, you can adjust the wrap points to move text closer to or farther away from the image.

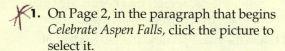

1. On Page 2, in the paragraph that begins *Celebrate Aspen Falls,* click the picture to select it.

2. On the **View tab**, in the **Zoom group**, click the **Zoom** button. In the **Zoom** dialog box, in the **Percent** box, replace the percent with 150 and then press Enter.

3. On the **Format tab**, in the **Adjust group**, click the **Remove Background** button.

> When you select the Remove Background button, the Background Removal tab displays. The selected object's selection border and sizing handles display so that you can make adjustments before removing the background.

4. On the **Background Removal tab**, in the **Refine group**, click the **Mark Areas to Remove** button.

5. Select the middle left sizing handle on the picture. Click and drag to the left edge of the inside box to resize the picture.

6. Select the right middle sizing handle on the picture. Click and drag to the right edge of the inside box. Compare your screen with **Figure 1**.

7. On the **Background Removal tab**, in the **Refine group**, click the **Delete Mark** button.

8. Click anywhere in the document to deselect the picture. Verify the brown background no longer displays around the picture and then compare your screen with **Figure 2**.

■ **Continue to the next page to complete the skill** ➤

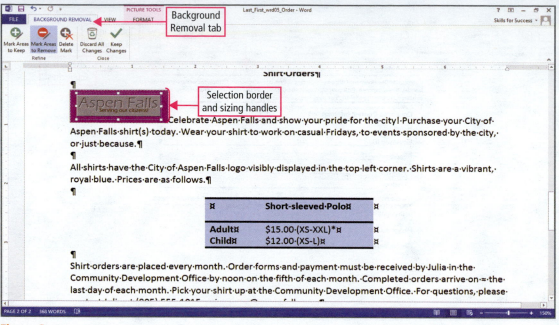

Figure 1

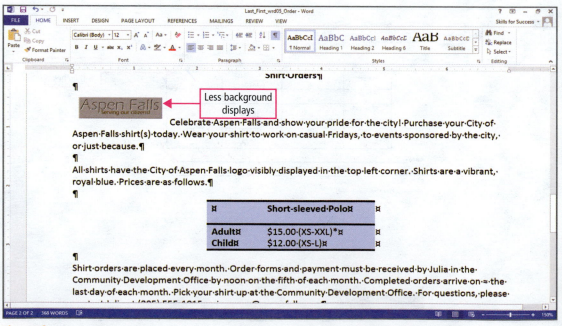

Figure 2

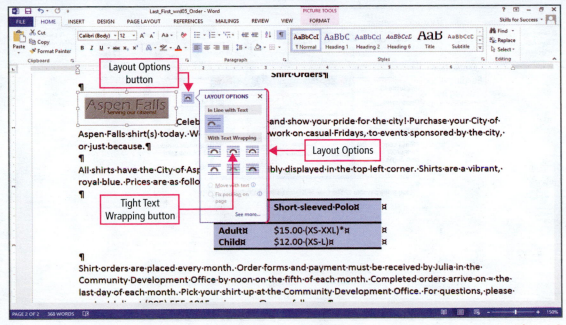

Figure 3

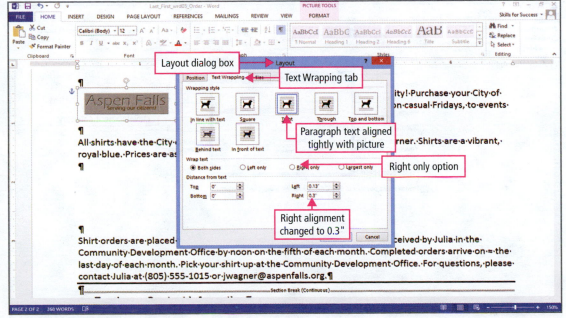

Figure 4

9. Click the picture to select it. To the right of the picture, click the **Layout Options** button, as shown in **Figure 3**.

10. Under **With Text Wrapping**, click **Tight**—the second choice in the first row—and then click in the document.

    The Tight option places the text closer to the picture. In this case, the text on each of the three lines of the paragraph moves closer in line with the picture.

11. Click the picture to select it. To the right of the picture, click the **Layout Options** button, and then click **See more**.

12. In the **Layout** dialog box, on the **Text Wrapping tab**, under **Wrap text**, select the **Right only** option button.

13. In the dialog box, under **Distance from text**, click the **Right up spin arrow** two times to change the value to **0.3"**, and then compare your screen with **Figure 4**.

14. Click **OK** and then click in the document to deselect the picture.

15. On the **View tab**, in the **Zoom group**, click the **100%** button.

16. **Save** the document.

■ **You have completed Skill 5 of 10**

► ***Building blocks*** are saved text and objects that can be retrieved and inserted into documents quickly.

► Building blocks help ensure accuracy and consistency of items shared by multiple users.

1. At the bottom of Page 2, in the paragraph that begins *Please make payable,* select the text *The City of Aspen Falls.* Be careful not to select the spaces before or after.

2. On the **Insert tab**, in the **Text group**, click the **Quick Parts** button, and then select **Save Selection to Quick Part Gallery**.

3. In the **Create New Building Block** dialog box, in the **Name** box, type Aspen Falls and then compare your screen with **Figure 1**.

   Before you can add a building block to the Quick Part gallery, you must create and save it.

4. Click the **Category arrow**, and then click **Create New Category**.

5. In the **Create New Category** dialog box, type Community Development and then click **OK**. Compare your screen with **Figure 2**.

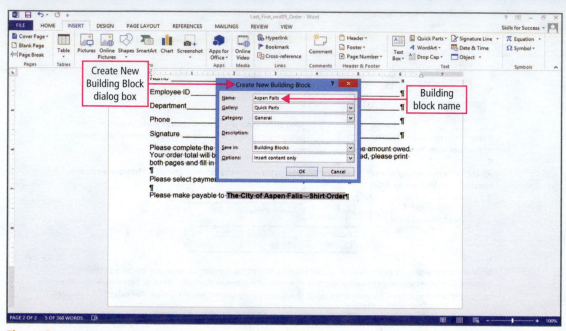

Figure 1

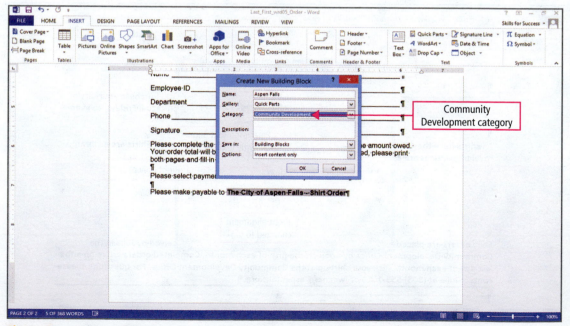

Figure 2

■ **Continue to the next page to complete the skill**

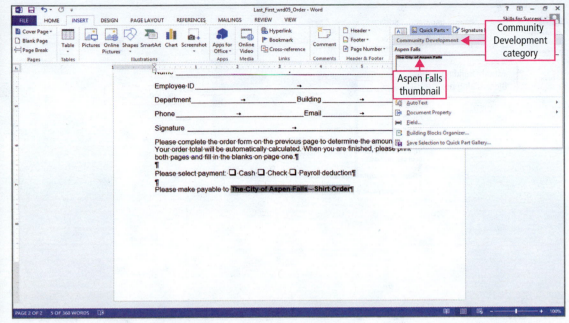

Figure 3

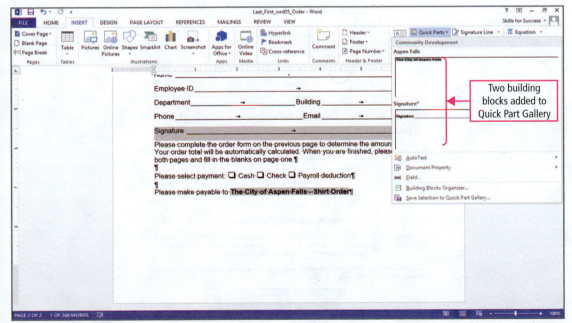

Figure 4

6. In the **Create New Building Block** dialog box, click **OK**.

7. In the **Text group**, click the **Quick Parts** button, and then compare your screen with **Figure 3**.

   The Aspen Falls building block displays in the Quick Part Gallery as a thumbnail under the Community Development category. In this manner, you can create building blocks and add them to the gallery.

8. Click anywhere in the document to close the Quick Part Gallery.

9. On Page 2, select the paragraph with the single word *Signature*.

10. In the **Text group**, click the **Quick Parts** button, and then select **Save Selection to Quick Part Gallery**.

11. In the **Create New Building Block** dialog box, in the **Name** box, verify **Signature*** displays. Click the **Category arrow** and then select **Community Development**.

    Notice that the Name displays Signature*. The * represents the tab character that was typed in the paragraph, in this case the right leader tab.

12. Click **OK**. In the **Text group**, click the **Quick Parts** button, and then verify that the two thumbnails display as shown in **Figure 4**.

13. Click anywhere in the document to close the **Quick Part Gallery**, and then click in the document to deselect the text.

14. **Save** 💾 the document.

■ **You have completed Skill 6 of 10**

► You can insert building blocks placed in the Quick Part Gallery with a single click.

► Building blocks can be renamed, modified, or deleted.

1. On the **Insert tab**, in the **Text group**, click the **Quick Parts** button.

2. Right-click the **Aspen Falls** thumbnail, and then in the displayed shortcut menu, click **Edit Properties**.

3. In the **Modify Building Block** dialog box, in the **Name** box, replace the text with Aspen Falls Employee Compare your screen with **Figure 1**.

4. Click **OK**, read the displayed message, and then click **Yes**.

5. At the top of Page 2, click to the left of the title *Shirt Orders*.

6. In the **Text group**, click the **Quick Parts** button, and then click the **Aspen Falls Employee** thumbnail. Compare your screen with **Figure 2**.

7. To the right of the word *Falls*, add a space. Add a hyphen (-), and then add another space.

8. On Page 2, select the title, and change the **Font** to **Calibri** and the **Font Size** to **14**.

9. At the bottom of Page 1, click before the paragraph mark below *Employee ID*.

10. On the **Insert tab**, in the **Text group**, click **Quick Parts**, and then click the **Signature*** thumbnail.

11. On Page 1, select the *Signature* line, and change the **Font** to **Calibri** and the **Font Size** to **11**.

■ **Continue to the next page to complete the skill**

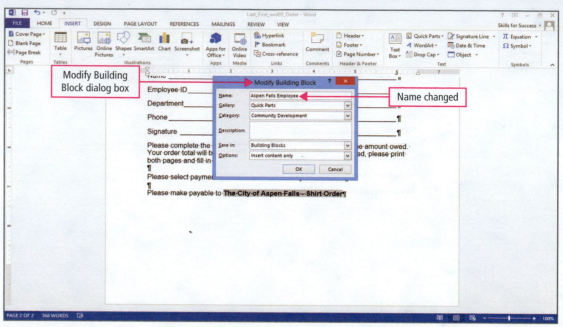

Figure 1

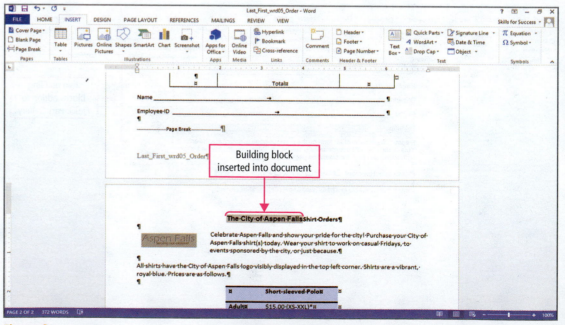

Figure 2

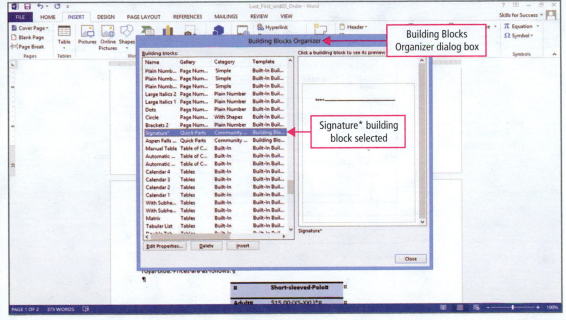

Figure 3

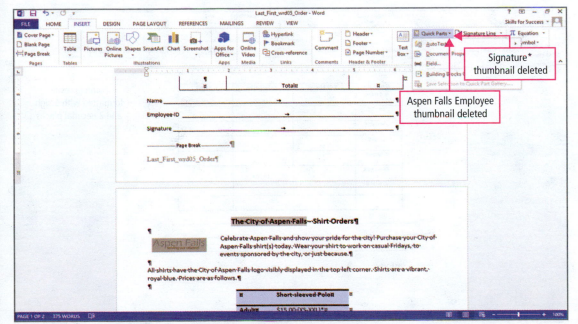

Figure 4

12. At the bottom of Page 1, in the blank line below the *Signature* line, click before the paragraph mark, and then press Delete.

13. On the **Insert tab**, in the **Text group**, click the **Quick Parts** button. Right-click the **Signature*** thumbnail, and then in the displayed shortcut menu, select **Organize and Delete**. Compare your screen with **Figure 3**.

14. **Start** the **Snipping Tool**, click the **New arrow**, and then click **Full-screen Snip**.

15. Click the **Save Snip** button 🖫. In the **Save As** dialog box, navigate to your **Word Chapter 5** folder, **Save** the file as Last_First_wrd05_OrderSnip and then **Close** ✖ the Snipping Tool window.

16. In the **Building Blocks Organizer** dialog box, click the **Delete** button. Read the displayed message, and then click **Yes**.

17. Repeat the technique just practiced to delete the *Aspen Falls Employee* building block. **Close** the dialog box.

18. On the **Insert tab**, in the **Text group**, click the **Quick Parts** button, and verify the two thumbnails are deleted. Compare your document with **Figure 4**.

19. **Save** 🖫 the document. If a message displays about saving building blocks, click **Don't Save**.

■ **You have completed Skill 7 of 10**

▶ Tables visually enhance documents and make data easier to read.

▶ Formulas and functions can be inserted into tables to provide totals, count rows, or perform other calculations.

1. On Page 1, in the third row of the table, click in the first blank cell below the word *Total*.

2. On the **Layout tab**, in the **Data group**, click the **Formula** button. In the **Formula** dialog box, under **Formula**, replace the existing formula with =B3*C3 Compare your screen with **Figure 1**.

   Table formulas refer to table cells by their position in the table. For example, in cell A1, the *A* represents the first column, and the *1* represents the first row. Here, the formula will multiply the value for shirts in cell B3 by the price of the shirts in C3.

3. In the **Formula** dialog box, click the **Number format arrow**, and then click the third choice—**$#,##0.00;($#,##0.00)**. Click **OK** and then compare your screen with **Figure 2**.

   Verify the cell displays *$ 30.00*. If your cell displays *!Undefined Bookmark*, repeat the previous step and carefully check your typing.

■ Continue to the next page to complete the skill ▶

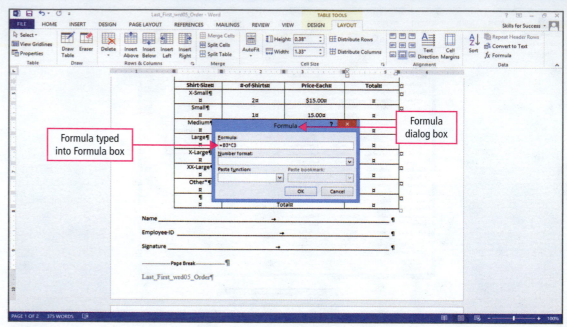

Figure 1

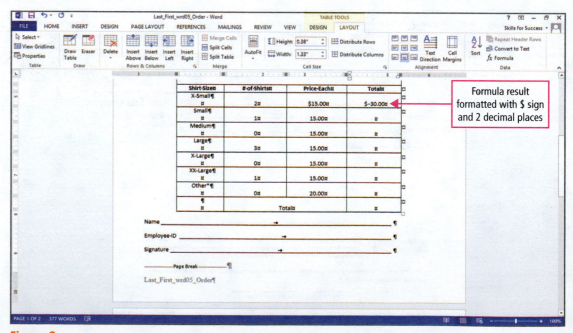

Figure 2

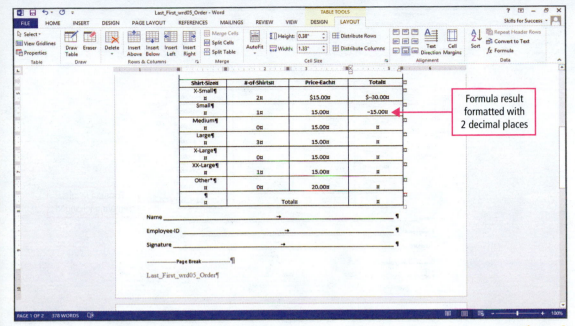

Formula result formatted with 2 decimal places

Figure 3

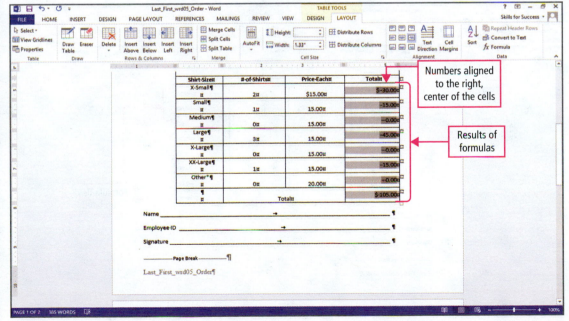

Numbers aligned to the right, center of the cells

Results of formulas

Figure 4

4. Click in the first blank cell in the *Total* column. Click the **Formula** button, and then replace the existing formula with =B4*C4 Apply the #,##0.00 number format, and then click **OK**. Compare your screen with **Figure 3**.

   In the Formula box, the cells in the formula include a 4. The 4 represents the fourth row of the table.

5. In rows 5 through 9 of the *Total* column, insert a formula that multiplies that row's B and C columns. In each cell, apply the #,##0.00 number format.

6. In the last row, click in the last cell, and then click the **Formula** button.

7. Verify that the formula box displays =*SUM(ABOVE)*. Click the **Number format arrow**, click $#,##0.00;($#,##0.00), and then click **OK**.

   In a column of dollar amounts, the dollar sign is included only in the first and last rows.

8. In the **Total** column, select the eight cells displaying the formula results, and then on the **Layout tab**, in the **Alignment group**, click the **Align Center Right** button. Compare your screen with **Figure 4**.

9. **Save** the document.

■ **You have completed Skill 8 of 10**

▸ Table cell formulas and functions are fields that need to be updated whenever changes are made to the underlying table data.

▸ Fields containing formulas or functions are updated using the Update Field command or by pressing F9 .

1. In the column for *# of Shirts*, change the *X-Small* cell value to 0

2. In the column for *# of Shirts*, change the *Small* cell value to 2 Compare your screen with **Figure 1**.

   When you make changes to cells referred to in formulas, the results do not automatically update. There, the first two totals should be *$ 0.000* and *30.00*.

3. In the *X-Small* row of the *Total* column, right-click the formula field. In the shortcut menu, select **Update Field**. Alternately, select the field and then press F9 . Using either method, update the total for the *Small* row.

   Whenever table cell data is changed, you need to remember to update any formula fields that reference those cells. In this case, the ending Total that displays $ 105.00 must also be changed.

4. Select the last cell of the table and update the total. Verify the result is *$90.00*, as shown in **Figure 2**.

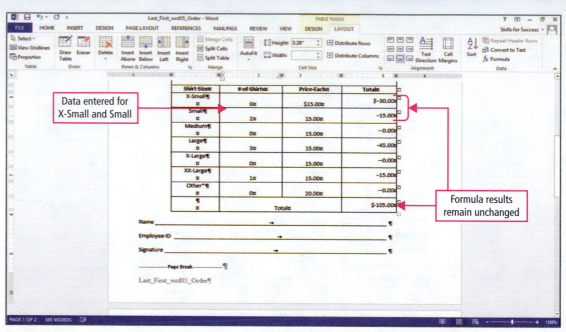

Figure 1

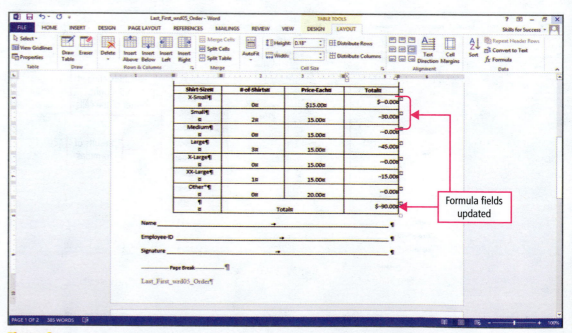

Figure 2

■ **Continue to the next page to complete the skill** ➡

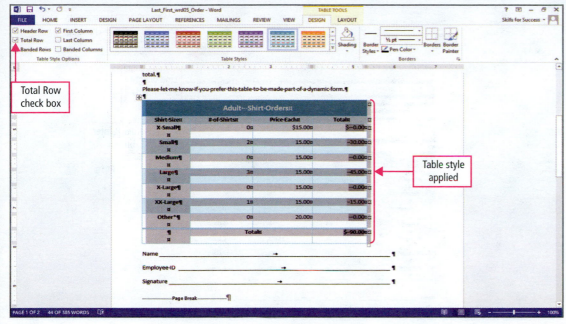

Total Row check box

Table style applied

Figure 3

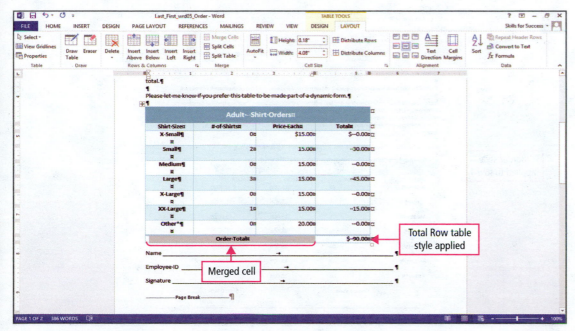

Total Row table style applied

Merged cell

Figure 4

5. In the *# of Shirts* and the *Price Each* column, select the 14 cells containing numbers. On the **Layout tab**, in the **Alignment group**, click the **Align Center Right** button.

6. Click the **Table Selector** button to select the entire table.

7. On the **Table Tools Design tab**, in the **Table Styles group**, click the **More arrow**. Locate and then click **Grid Table 4 – Accent 5**.

8. On the **Table Tools Design tab**, in the **Table Style Options** group, select the **Total Row** check box. Compare your screen with **Figure 3**.

   When the Total Row option is selected, the last row is automatically formatted.

9. In the last row, select the first two cells—end-of-cell markers will be highlighted—and then on the **Layout tab**, in the **Merge group**, click the **Merge Cells** button.

10. In the merged cell, click before *Total*, press [Backspace] two times, type Order and then press [SpaceBar].

11. In the *Order Total* cell, in the **Alignment group**, click the **Align Center** button. Compare your screen with **Figure 4**.

12. On the **View tab**, in the **Show group**, deselect the ruler, and then **Save** the document.

■ **You have completed Skill 9 of 10**

WRD 5-10
VIDEO

▶ **Border Painter** is a table feature used to apply formatted borders to table cells with a single click.

▶ Using this feature, you can change the pen color, adjust line styles and weights, and apply border styles.

1. If necessary, on Page 1, click anywhere in the table.

2. On the **Table Tools Design tab**, in the **Borders group**, click the **Pen Color arrow**, and then select **Aqua, Accent 5, Darker 50%**—the ninth button in the sixth row.

3. In the **Borders group**, click the **Line Style** arrow [____], and then select the fourth option [____].

4. In the **Borders group**, click the **Line Weight** arrow [½ pt ___], and then select **1 ½ pt**. Compare your screen with **Figure 1**.

    The Border Painter button is selected, and the pointer display changes.

5. To the left of row 1 of the table, click to apply the border style.

6. Repeat this technique to apply the border style to the top, bottom, and right of the first row. Compare your screen with **Figure 2**.

    The border style for row 1 displays a dashed line with a weight of 1 ½ points and the designated color.

7. In the **Borders group**, click the **Line Style** arrow [____], and then select the second option, a solid line.

8. In the **Borders group**, click the **Line Weight** arrow [½ pt ___], and then select **6 pt**.

■ **Continue to the next page to complete the skill** ➤

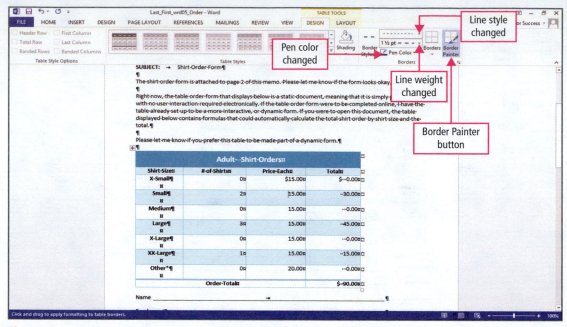

Figure 1

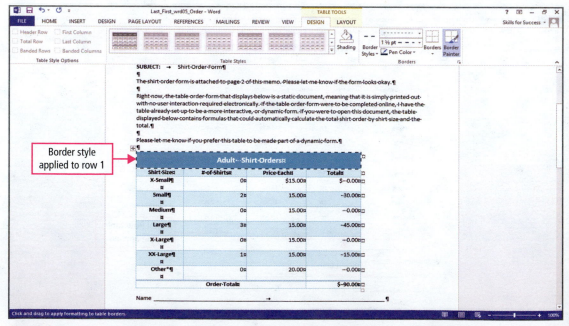

Figure 2

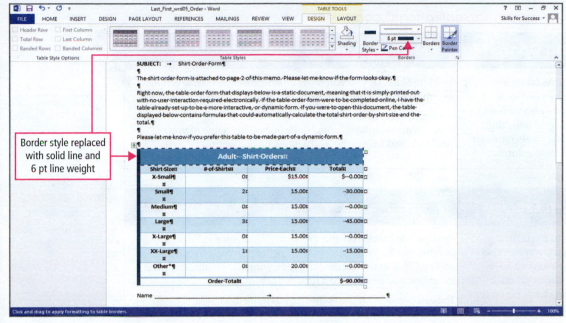

Border style replaced with solid line and 6 pt line weight

Figure 3

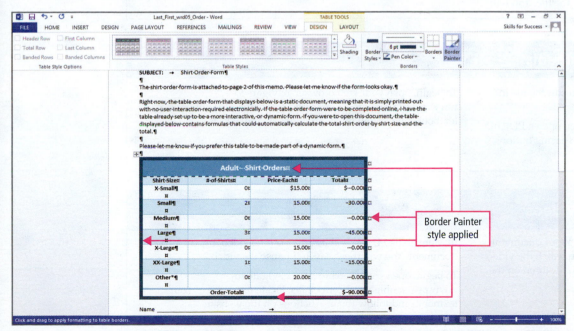

Border Painter style applied

Figure 4

9. Point to the left of row 2, and then click.

10. Display the 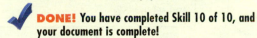 pointer to the left of row 1, and then using the **Border Painter**, drag down through the last row of the table that begins *Order Total*. Compare your screen with **Figure 3**.

   In this manner, border styles can be replaced and added to multiple cell borders.

11. Display the pointer to the right of the cell in the first row of the table, and then drag down through the last row of the table that ends *$ 90.00*.

12. Point to the top border of the table, and then using the **Border Painter**, repeat the technique to apply the border style to the top of the table.

13. Point to the bottom border of the table, and then using the **Border Painter**, repeat the technique to apply the border style to the bottom of the table. Compare your screen with **Figure 4**.

14. On the **Table Tools Design tab**, in the **Borders group**, click the **Border Painter** button to turn off the feature.

15. **Save** the document.

16. **Close** the Word window. If a message displays, click **Don't Save**. Submit your work as directed by your instructor.

   ✔ **DONE!** You have completed Skill 10 of 10, and your document is complete!

More Skills

The following More Skills are located at **www.pearsonhighered.com/skills**

More Skills Draw Tables and Convert Tables to Text

Tables can be drawn or inserted into documents. As tables are created and modified, the size of the columns may need to be adjusted to accommodate the new data. Word provides tools that distribute data evenly across rows and columns, split cells, align cell data, and change the overall table layout. You can also convert a table into text that uses tabs to arrange the data into columns.

In More Skills 11, you will draw a table, distribute table cell data evenly, split table cells, and convert table data into a text format.

To begin, open your web browser, navigate to www.pearsonhighered.com/skills, locate the name of your textbook, and follow the instructions on the website.

More Skills Merge Data from Excel

You can use data from other data sources, such as Excel, in a Word mail merge. When selecting the data source, you can also filter the fields to use only the desired records. Fields can be placed anywhere in the Word document. Once the fields are in the document, you can preview your results and check for errors. Both the original document with the merged fields and the final merged documents can be saved.

In More Skills 12, you will use an Excel 2013 worksheet and add your first and last names to the cells and save the file. You will

then use the Excel worksheet as your data source in Word to perform the mail merge steps that include filtering by a field, adding fields to the document, previewing the results, checking for errors, and merging to a new document.

To begin, open your web browser, navigate to www.pearsonhighered.com/skills, locate the name of your textbook, and follow the instructions on the website.

More Skills Edit PDF Documents

You can open a PDF file in Word. You can also edit the file in Word and then save it as a Word document.

In More Skills 13, you will open Word and then open a PDF file. You will remove any extra spaces, adjust line spacing options, and set tabs.

To begin, open your web browser, navigate to www.pearsonhighered.com/skills, locate the name of your textbook, and follow the instructions on the website.

More Skills Insert Online Videos

You can insert videos from the web into your Word document so that when you open the document, you can watch the video from within Word. In this manner, the videos are stored on the web, but viewed in the Word document.

In More Skills 14, you will insert an online video into a Word document. You will then play and pause the video.

To begin, open your web browser, navigate to www.pearsonhighered.com/skills, locate the name of your textbook, and follow the instructions on the website.

Please note that there are no additional projects to accompany the More Skills Projects, and they are not covered in End-of-Chapter projects.

The following table summarizes the **SKILLS AND PROCEDURES** covered in this chapter.

Skills Number	Task	Step	Icon	Keyboard Shortcut
2	Insert continuous section break	Page Layout tab → Page Setup group → Breaks → Continuous		
2	Create custom margins	Page Layout tab → Page Setup group → Margins → Custom Margins	Custom Margins...	
3	Apply paste options	Home tab → Clipboard group → Paste arrow		Ctrl + V
4	Open the Tab dialog box from the ruler	Double-click the desired location or tab on the Ruler bar		
5	Remove picture backgrounds	Select picture → Format tab → Adjust group → Remove Background button		
5	Change text wrap setting	Select object → Layout Options button		
5	Modify text wrap	Select object → Layout Options button → Text Wrapping tab	Text Wrapping	
6	Create a building block as a Quick Part	Select text → Insert tab → Text group → Quick Parts button → Save Selection to Quick Part Gallery		
7	Modify a building block in the Quick Part Gallery	Insert tab → Text group → Quick Parts button → Right-click desired building block → Edit Properties	Edit Properties...	
7	Insert a building block from the Quick Part Gallery	Move to desired location and click → Insert tab → Text group → Quick Parts button → Select desired building block		
7	Delete a building block	Insert tab → Text group → Quick Parts button → Right-click desired building block → Organize and Delete		
8	Insert a formula in a table	Layout tab → Data group → Formula button	fx Formula	
9	Update a table formula field	Right-click desired table cell → Update Field		F9
10	Use Border Painter	Table Tools → Design tab → Borders group → Border Painter button		

Key Terms

Online Help Skills

1. Start **Word 2013**, and then in the upper-right corner of the start page, click the **Help** button [?].

2. In the **Word Help** window **Search online help** box, type pdf and then press [Enter].

3. In the search result list, click **Edit or make changes to a PDF file**, and then below **More Information**, click **Save as PDF**. Compare your screen with **Figure 1**.

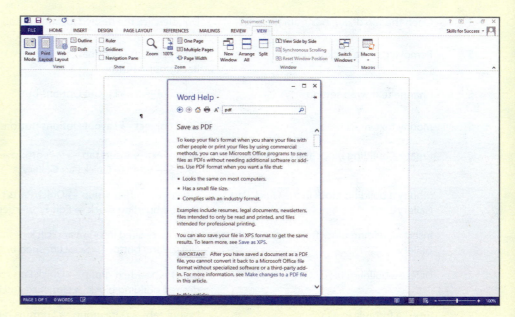

Figure 1

4. Read the article to answer the following question: Why are Word documents sometimes saved with the PDF format?

Matching  MyITLab®

Match each term in the second column with its correct definition in the first column by writing the letter of the term on the blank line in front of the correct definition.

 1. The name of a font that features character graphics. J

 2. Used to divide a document into multiple parts that can have different page layout settings, such as margins.

 3. A button that displays formatting choices when pasting text into the current document.

 4. A paste option that copies text and applies the formatting in use in the new location.

 5. A paste option that pastes text with the formatting from the original location.

 6. A line that extends from the beginning of a tab to its tab stop.

 7. A building block that can be retrieved from a gallery on the Ribbon.

 8. The dialog box that allows users to select, modify, and delete building blocks.

 9. The keyboard shortcut that updates a selected formula field.

 10. Used to apply styles to table cells with a single click.

A Border Painter

B Building Blocks Organizer

C F9

D Keep Source Formatting

E Leader

F Merge Formatting

G Paste Options

H Quick Part

I Section Break

J Wingdings

Multiple Choice MyITLab®

Choose the correct answer.

1. The character code 113, a Wingding character graphic, is an example of a
   - A. Building Block
   - B. Special Character
   - C. Symbol

2. The type of section break that divides the same page.
   - A. Continuous
   - B. Even Page
   - C. Odd Page

3. The type of line that displays when five underscore characters are typed followed by the Enter key.
   - A. Diagonal
   - B. Horizontal
   - C. Vertical

4. The Paste Option that removes all formatting from the text.
   - A. Keep Source Formatting
   - B. Keep Text Only
   - C. Merge Formatting

5. The feature used to format a background color behind the text.
   - A. Background
   - B. Bold
   - C. Highlight

6. The feature that will take away parts of the selected picture.
   - A. Background Removal
   - B. SmartArt
   - C. Wrap Text

7. This text wrapping setting moves the text the closest to the picture.
   - A. In line with text
   - B. Square
   - C. Tight

8. In cell A1, the A represents the
   - A. Column
   - B. Row
   - C. Table

9. The function that will add all the cells in the previous rows in a table column.
   - A. =SUM
   - B. =TOTAL(ROWS)
   - C. =SUM(ABOVE)

10. The table feature that combines two cells.
    - A. Distribute Columns
    - B. Merge Cells
    - C. Split Cells

Topics for Discussion

1. What are three advantages of using a static form within Word?

2. Building blocks help ensure accuracy and consistency of items shared by multiple users. How could a business use building blocks? What are some examples of the building blocks that they might use?

Skills Review

To complete this project, you will need the following file:

- wrd05_SRLunch

You will save your document as:

- Last_First_wrd05_SRLunch

1. Start **Word 2013** and then open **wrd05_SRLunch**. **Save** the file in your **Word Chapter 5** folder as Last_First_wrd05_SRLunch Add the **FileName** field to the footer. In the *FROM:* line, replace *Your Name* with your first and last name.

2. Select the picture. On the **Format tab**, in the **Adjust group**, click the **Remove Background** button. On the **Background Removal tab**, in the **Refine group**, click the **Mark Areas to Remove** button, and then click the **Delete Mark** button. Click in the document.

3. Select the picture. Click the **Layout Options** button, and then under **With Text Wrapping**, click **Square**. Click **See more**, and then on the **Text Wrapping tab**, under **Wrap text**, select the **Right only** option button. Under **Distance from text**, click the **Right up arrow** two times. Compare your screen with **Figure 1** and then click **OK**.

4. In the subject, select *Lunch Reimbursement*. On the **Insert tab**, in the **Text group**, click the **Quick Parts** button, and then select **Save Selection to Quick Part Gallery**. Click **OK**.

5. Click the **Quick Parts** button and then right-click the **Lunch Reimbursement** thumbnail. Click **Edit Properties**, click the **Category arrow**, and then click **Create New Category**. In the **Name** box, type Community Click **OK** two times. Read the message and then click **Yes**.

6. Locate and select *"The Most Responsive City Office"*. On the **Home tab**, in the **Font group**, click the **Text Highlight Color arrow**, and then click **Turquoise**.

7. Click the blank paragraph above *Name*. On the **Page Layout tab**, in the **Page Setup group**, click the **Breaks** button, and then click **Continuous**.

8. Click anywhere in the top section. In the **Page Setup group**, click the **Margins** button, and then click **Custom Margins**. Change the left and right margins in the top section only to *.8"* and then click **OK**. Compare your screen with **Figure 2**.

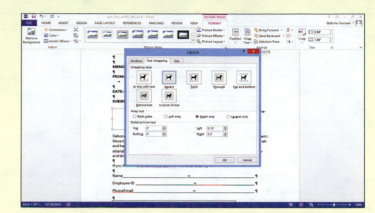

Figure 1

Figure 2

■ **Continue to the next page to complete this Skills Review**

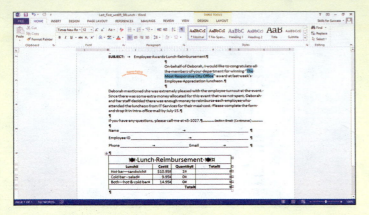

Figure 3

Figure 4

9. Click in the paragraph that begins *PhoneEmail*. Turn on the ruler. On the ruler, point with the tip of the pointer, and then double-click on the **3.5 inch** mark.

10. In the large **Tab stop position** box, click *3.5"*, under **Alignment**, select the **Right** option button. Under **Leader**, select the **4** option button, and then click **OK**. Click after *Phone* and then press [Tab].

11. Click in row 1 of the table. On the **Insert tab**, in the **Symbols group**, click the **Symbol** button, and then click **More Symbols**. Click the **Font arrow**, and then click **Webdings**. Insert the 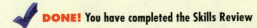 symbol (character code 228) and then click **Close**. Select the symbol. Change the **Font Size** to **20**. After the symbol, add a space.

12. On the **Insert tab**, in the **Text group**, click the **Quick Parts** button, and then click the **Lunch Reimbursement** thumbnail. Add a space.

13. In the **Text group**, click the **Quick Parts** button. Right-click *Lunch Reimbursement*, and then select **Organize and Delete**. **Delete** the *Lunch Reimbursement* building block and then click **Close**.

14. Copy the symbol. Position the pointer after the space after *Reimbursement*. On the **Home tab**, in the **Clipboard group**, click the **Paste arrow**, and then click **Keep Source Formatting**. Compare your screen with **Figure 3**.

15. Click the table's first blank cell in the *Total* column. On the **Layout tab**, in the **Data group**, click the **Formula** button. In the **Formula** box, replace the existing formula with =B3*C3 to multiply the *Cost* by the *Quantity*. Click the **Number format arrow**, and then click **$#,##0.00;($#,##0.00)**. Click **OK**.

16. In the table's fourth and fifth row *Total* columns, repeat the technique to insert a similar formula with the **#,##0.00** format.

17. Click in the last cell of the table. Click the **Formula** button and verify that the formula box displays *=SUM(ABOVE)*. Apply the **$#,##0.00;($#,##0.00)** format. Click **OK**.

18. In the table, select the Quantity *1*. Replace it with 2 In the *Hot bar* row of the *Total* column, right-click the formula field. In the shortcut menu, select **Update Field**. Update the formula field for the final *Total*. Compare your screen with **Figure 4**.

19. On the **Table Tools Design tab**, click the **Pen Color arrow**, and then click **Dark Blue, Text 2**—the fourth color in the first row. Click the **Line Style arrow**, and then select the third style from the bottom. Click the **Line Weight arrow**, and then click **2 ¼ pt**.

20. Point to the left of row 1, and then click and hold the mouse to drag it down the left border of the table. Repeat the technique just practiced to apply the **Border Painter** to the top, bottom, and right border of the table. Click the **Border Painter** button to turn off Border Painter.

21. **Save** the document and **Close** Word. Submit your work as directed by your instructor.

DONE! You have completed the Skills Review

Skills Assessment 1

To complete this project, you will need the following file:

- wrd05_SA1Computers

You will save your document as:

- Last_First_wrd05_SA1Computers

---

1. Start **Word 2013** and then open **wrd05_SA1Computers**. **Save** the file in your **Word Chapter 5** folder as Last_First_wrd05_SA1Computers Add the **FileName** field to the footer.

2. For the picture at the top of the document, remove the background using the default removal settings.

3. For the picture, change the layout options to **Square** with the **Right only** Wrap text option and a distance of **0.1"** from the text at the right.

4. Save the *Computer Training Registration* text, without the paragraph symbol, as a building block in the Quick Part Gallery with the name Register Modify the building block to include the Community category.

5. At the end of the paragraph that begins *Register*, insert a **Continuous** section break. Delete the first blank line below the section break.

6. In the lower section of the document, change the left and right margins to .75"

7. In the *Signature* line, move the tab marker at **4.5 inches** to **3.5 inches**.

8. In the first row of the table, insert the ▦ symbol (character code 191) from the **Webdings** font. Adjust the font size of the symbol to **20**. Add a space after the symbol.

9. Insert the **Register** building block. Add a space. **Copy** the monitor symbol, and then at the end of the row, paste using **Keep Source Formatting**.

10. In the first blank cell in the table's *Total* column, insert a formula that adds *INT01, CLD01, WP01,* and *WP02* together. Apply the **0** number format. Repeat for rows four and five.

11. Insert a formula in the last cell that sums the *Total* column. Apply the **0** number format.

12. In the first cell below *INT01*, select *1*. Replace it with 0 Update the appropriate formulas.

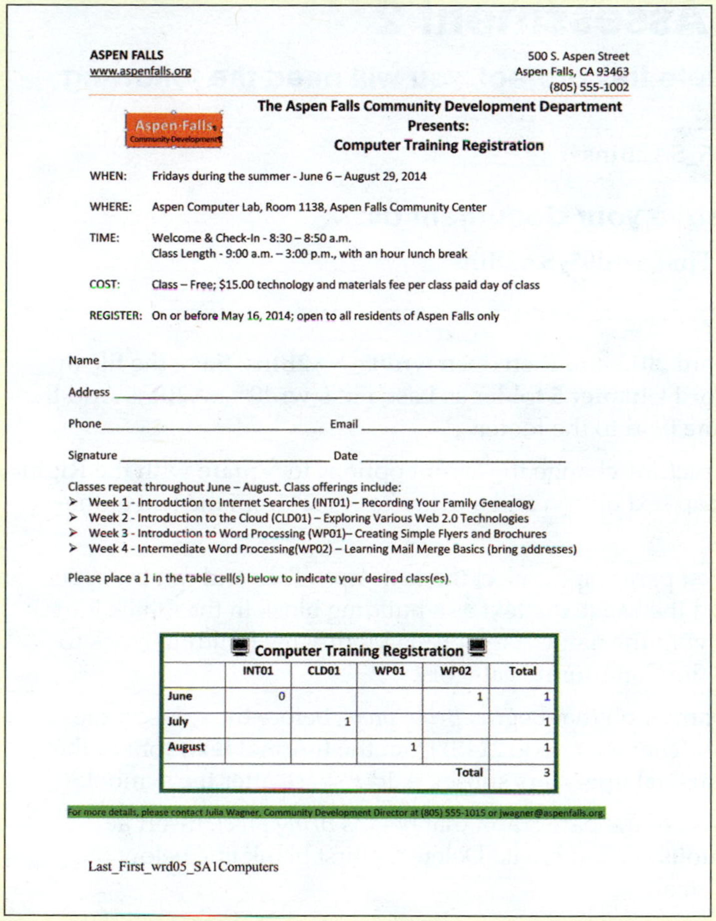

13. For the last paragraph of the document, apply the **Bright Green** Text Highlight Color.

14. For the table border, apply the **Green**—the sixth color under Standard Colors—**Pen Color** with the third **Line Style** from the bottom and a **Line Weight** of **2 ¼ pt**. Compare your screen with **Figure 1**.

15. Delete the *Register* building block.

16. **Save** the document and **Close** Word. Submit your work as directed by your instructor.

✔ **DONE!** You have completed Skills Assessment 1

ASPEN FALLS
www.aspenfalls.org

500 S. Aspen Street
Aspen Falls, CA 93463
(805) 555-1002

The Aspen Falls Community Development Department Presents:
Computer Training Registration

WHEN: Fridays during the summer - June 6 – August 29, 2014

WHERE: Aspen Computer Lab, Room 1138, Aspen Falls Community Center

TIME: Welcome & Check-In - 8:30 – 8:50 a.m.
Class Length - 9:00 a.m. – 3:00 p.m., with an hour lunch break

COST: Class – Free; $15.00 technology and materials fee per class paid day of class

REGISTER: On or before May 16, 2014; open to all residents of Aspen Falls only

Name _____

Address _____

Phone_____ Email _____

Signature _____ Date _____

Classes repeat throughout June – August. Class offerings include:
- Week 1 - Introduction to Internet Searches (INT01) – Recording Your Family Genealogy
- Week 2 - Introduction to the Cloud (CLD01) – Exploring Various Web 2.0 Technologies
- Week 3 - Introduction to Word Processing (WP01)– Creating Simple Flyers and Brochures
- Week 4 - Intermediate Word Processing(WP02) – Learning Mail Merge Basics (bring addresses)

Please place a 1 in the table cell(s) below to indicate your desired class(es).

🖥 Computer Training Registration 🖥				
	INT01	CLD01	WP01	WP02	Total
June	0			1	1
July		1			1
August			1		1
				Total	3

For more details, please contact Julia Wagner, Community Development Director at (805) 555-1015 or jwagner@aspenfalls.org

Last_First_wrd05_SA1Computers

Figure 1

Skills Assessment 2

To complete this project, you will need the following file:

- wrd05_SA2Bins

You will save your document as:

- Last_First_wrd05_SA2Bins

---

1. Start **Word 2013** and then open **wrd05_SA2Bins**. **Save** the file in your **Word Chapter 5** folder as Last_First_wrd05_SA2Bins Add the **FileName** field to the footer.

2. For the picture, change the layout options to **Square** with the **Right only** Wrap text option and a distance of **0.2"** from the text at the right.

3. In the first paragraph, select the text *Aspen Falls* and not the space after, and then save the text as a building block in the Quick Part Gallery with the name Aspen Falls Modify the building block to include the Community category.

4. In the paragraph that begins *Bring proof,* before the *3,* insert the ≈ symbol (character code 2248) from the **(normal text)** font in the **Mathematical operators** subset. Add a space after the symbol.

5. At the end of the paragraph that begins *Bring proof,* insert a **Continuous** section break. Delete the first blank line below the section break.

6. In the lower document section, change the left and right margins to .75"

7. Click before the letter *P* in *Please.* Use Shift + - to create a horizontal line.

8. In the *Phone* and *Signature* lines, move the tab marker at **5 inches** to **3.5 inches**.

9. In the paragraph that begins *How did,* **Copy** the blue box symbol. **Paste** three times using the **Keep Source Formatting** paste option to the left of *Web, Newspaper,* and *Radio.* Be sure there is one blank space between the symbol and the text.

10. Click the beginning of the *Community Center* paragraph, and then insert the **Aspen Falls** building block and add a space. In the same paragraph, select the entire paragraph and change the **Font Size**

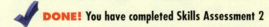

Figure 1

to **12**. In the same paragraph, apply the **Yellow** Text Highlight Color. Compare your screen with **Figure 1**.

11. Delete the *Aspen Falls* building block.

12. **Save** the document and **Close** Word. Submit your work as directed by your instructor.

✔ **DONE! You have completed Skills Assessment 2**

Visual Skills Check

To complete this project, you will start with a:

- New, blank Word document

You will save your document as:

- Last_First_wrd05_VSParty

Use the skills practiced in this chapter to create the holiday party form shown in **Figure 1**. Unless otherwise indicated, use Calibri 11 point font. Use a continuous section break in the blank paragraph before *Employee Contact Information*, and then customize the left and right margins for the bottom form section to **.75"**. In the blank paragraph above the table, draw a horizontal line. Include tabs at **6.5 inches** on the horizontal rule that are used to collect information for *Name, Employee ID, Building, Email,* and *Signature* and at **3.5 inches** for *Department* and *Phone*. Use the **Bright Green Text Highlight Color** to highlight the last paragraph. Insert the check box symbols using the 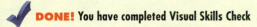 symbol (character code 113) from the Wingdings font. Adjust the font size of the symbol to **12**. Add a space after the symbol. Use formulas to create totals in the *Total* column of the table.

Save the file as Last_First_wrd05_VSParty in your **Word Chapter 5** folder. Add the **FileName** field to the footer. In the *FROM:* line, select *Your Name*, and then type your first and last name. **Close** the Word window, and then submit the file as directed by your instructor.

✔ **DONE!** You have completed Visual Skills Check

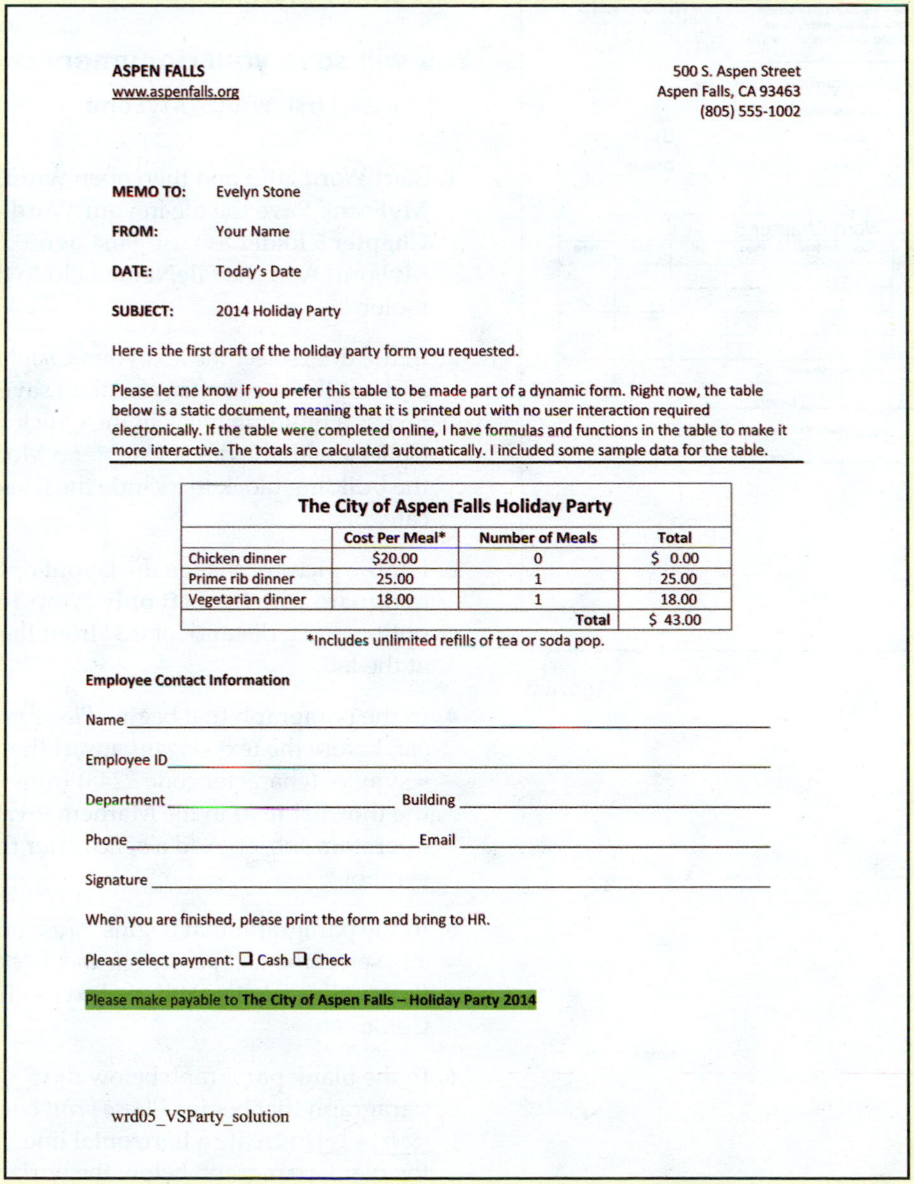

ASPEN FALLS
www.aspenfalls.org

500 S. Aspen Street
Aspen Falls, CA 93463
(805) 555-1002

MEMO TO: Evelyn Stone

FROM: Your Name

DATE: Today's Date

SUBJECT: 2014 Holiday Party

Here is the first draft of the holiday party form you requested.

Please let me know if you prefer this table to be made part of a dynamic form. Right now, the table below is a static document, meaning that it is printed out with no user interaction required electronically. If the table were completed online, I have formulas and functions in the table to make it more interactive. The totals are calculated automatically. I included some sample data for the table.

The City of Aspen Falls Holiday Party

	Cost Per Meal*	Number of Meals	Total
Chicken dinner	$20.00	0	$ 0.00
Prime rib dinner	25.00	1	25.00
Vegetarian dinner	18.00	1	18.00
		Total	$ 43.00

*Includes unlimited refills of tea or soda pop.

Employee Contact Information

Name _____

Employee ID _____

Department _____ Building _____

Phone_____ Email _____

Signature _____

When you are finished, please print the form and bring to HR.

Please select payment: ☐ Cash ☐ Check

Please make payable to **The City of Aspen Falls – Holiday Party 2014**

wrd05_VSParty_solution

Figure 1

Word Chapter 5 - Creating Static Forms

Instructions:
Please print out this document. Please use this form to share your level of understanding with the chapter name provided in the title. Please use the table to identify the ≈ amount of time you spent studying and working on the chapter each day. When you are finished, please sign and date the form, and then return it to your teacher.

Please check the box to indicate if a phone call is required. ☐ Yes ☐ No

Please check the box(es) for the skills where you need additional help.

☐ Skill 1   ☐ Skill 2   ☐ Skill 3   ☐ Skill 4   ☐ Skill 5

☐ Skill 6   ☐ Skill 7   ☐ Skill 8   ☐ Skill 9   ☐ Skill 10

Word Chapter 5

	Sun	Mon	Tues	Wed	Thurs	Fri	Sat	Total
Week 1				1				
Week 2								
Week 3								
Week 4								
Total Hours Studied								

Name _____   Email_____

Please call me at _____   Available times_____

Signature _____   Date_____

Last_First_wrd05_MyForm.docx

Figure 1

My Skills

To complete this project, you will need the following file:

- wrd05_MyForm

You will save your document as:

- Last_First_wrd05_MyForm

1. Start **Word 2013** and then open **wrd05_MyForm**. **Save** the file in your **Word Chapter 5** folder as Last_First_wrd05_MyForm Add the **FileName** field to the footer.

2. In the title, select the text *Word Chapter 5* and not the space after, and then save the text as a building block in the Quick Part Gallery with the name Chapter 5 Modify the building block to include the Class category.

3. For the picture, change the layout options to **Square** with the **Left only** Wrap Text option and a distance of **0.3"** from the text at the left.

4. In the paragraph that begins *Please print out*, before the text *amount*, insert the ≈ symbol (character code 2248) from the **(normal text)** in the **Mathematical operators** subset. Add a space after the symbol.

5. In the paragraph that begins *Please print out*, select the text *please sign and date the form*, and apply the **Yellow** Text Highlight Color.

6. In the blank paragraph below the paragraph that begins *Please print out*, use `Shift` + `-` to create a horizontal line. Delete the blank paragraph below the horizontal line.

7. In the paragraph that begins *Please check the box*, before the text *Yes*, insert the ☐ symbol (character code 113) from the **Wingdings** font. Adjust the font size of the symbol to **12**. Add a space after the symbol. **Copy** the box symbol and the space to the right. **Paste** to the left of the text *No* using the **Keep Source Formatting** paste option.

8. In the paragraph that begins *Skill 1*, **Paste** the box symbol using the **Keep Source Formatting** paste option ten times to the left of the text *Skill 1* through *Skill 10*.

9. In the blank paragraph above the table, insert a **Continuous** section break.

10. In the lower document section, change the left and right margins to .75"

11. In the first row of the table, insert the **Chapter 5** building block.

12. In the *Name*, *Please call me*, and *Signature* lines, move the tab at **4.5 inches** to **4 inches** and the tab at **6.5 inches** to **7 inches**. Compare your screen with **Figure 1**.

13. Delete the *Chapter 5* building block.

14. **Save** the document. **Close** the Word window, and then submit the file as directed by your instructor.

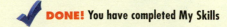 **DONE! You have completed My Skills**

Skills Challenge 1

To complete this project, you will need the following file:

- wrd05_SC1Crafts

You will save your document as:

- Last_First_wrd05_SC1Crafts

In Word 2013, open **wrd05_SC1Crafts**. Add the **FileName** to the footer. Use the skills practiced in this chapter to update the static form. Update the formulas and functions in the table in case someone decides at a later time to make this a dynamic form. Apply the Border Painter to the table using a Line Weight of 2 ¼, a dashed line style, and a Line Color of Green, Accent 6 so the border displays around the entire table. Adjust the tab stops and leader styles so that the form elements are properly spaced and aligned. Be sure the tabbed stops create

lines that are long enough to allow for someone to print out the form and fill in the blanks.

Save the file as Last_First_wrd05_SC1Crafts in your **Word Chapter 5** folder. **Close** the Word window, and then submit the file as directed by your instructor.

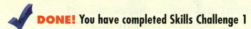 **DONE! You have completed Skills Challenge 1**

Skills Challenge 2

To complete this project, you will start with a:

- New, blank Word document

You will save your document as:

- Last_First_wrd05_SC2FormsResearch

Locate an example of a printed form available at your college that is used by a club, organization, or faculty member. In Word 2013, open a new, blank document, and then use the skills practiced in this chapter to create a static form that is similar to the printed form you located. The static form should collect the same information and include a table and tabs—similar to the static forms practiced in the chapter.

Save the file as Last_First_wrd05_SC2FormsResearch in your **Word Chapter 5** folder. Add the **FileName** field to the footer. **Close** the Word window, and then submit the file as directed by your instructor.

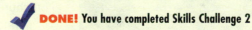 **DONE! You have completed Skills Challenge 2**

CHAPTER 6

Create a Brochure

- ▶ In addition to using the default templates packaged with Word 2013, you can use templates that you or someone else has created.

- ▶ You can apply document formatting to format and enhance your text. You can also change fonts, font colors, and paragraph spacing, and then save the customized settings as a style set or include OpenType features.

- ▶ To enhance your document, you can insert and format shapes and text boxes. You can link text boxes together so the data in one box flows to the other text box. If you decide you no longer want the data in the text box to be linked, you can break the link.

- ▶ To create a document such as a brochure, you can save time by using the collect and paste method to copy items from existing Word documents to the Clipboard and then paste them into any document location.

- ▶ You can insert a Quick Table that includes a preformatted table, calendar, or tabbed list and then customize it with your data.

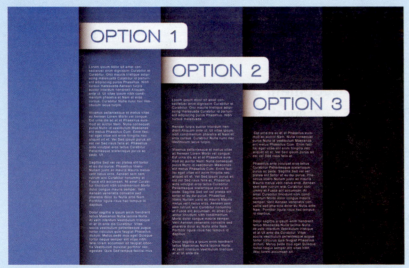

© Petr Vaclavek

Aspen Falls City Hall

In this chapter, you will assist Deborah Davidson, Public Information Specialist, whose job it is to share information about all the City of Aspen Falls has to offer—both to internal employees and to those who live inside or outside of the city. Part of Deborah's job is to determine the best, most cost-effective method to share information with others.

A brochure is one way to display your data in a tri-fold format that you can fold and mail as is, without the added cost of using an envelope. A brochure includes a placeholder where you can type the return and inside addresses. For this project, you will download a two-page, three-column/panel Microsoft Word brochure template. A brochure can be enhanced by adding and formatting shapes and text boxes that can be linked. Brochure text and shapes can be collected, or copied, from another document and then pasted into the brochure using the Windows Clipboard.

In this project, you will use Word to customize a brochure template. Once you have downloaded a template, you will collect pictures and text and paste them in built-in text boxes. You will insert and format shapes, link the text boxes so data flows from one box to the next, change the text direction, and break links between text boxes. You will also insert and customize a Quick Table. You will apply document formatting and OpenType features; change font names, font colors, and paragraph spacing; and save the settings as a style set.

Time to complete all 10 skills – 60 to 90 minutes

Student data files needed for this chapter:

wrd06_ArtAboutUs

wrd06_ArtOfferings

wrd06_ArtPhoto

wrd06_ArtTemplate

You will save your documents as:

Last_First_wrd06_Art

Last_First_wrd06_ArtStyleSet

Outcome

Using the skills in this chapter, you will be able to create brochures such as this:

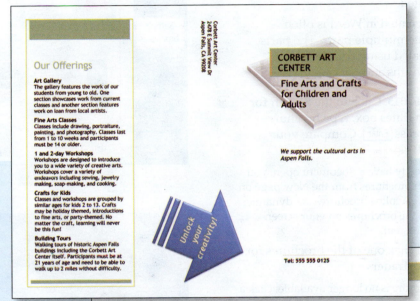

SKILLS

Skills 1-10 Training

At the end of this chapter, you will be able to:

Skill 1 Create Brochures from Templates

Skill 2 Create and Save Style Sets

Skill 3 Work with Shapes and Text Boxes

Skill 4 Insert and Format Text Boxes

Skill 5 Insert and Format Shapes

Skill 6 Collect Objects into the Office Clipboard

Skill 7 Insert Prebuilt Text Boxes

Skill 8 Work with Linked Text Boxes

Skill 9 Insert Quick Tables

Skill 10 Apply OpenType Features

MORE SKILLS

Skill 11 Work with Page Number Building Blocks

Skill 12 Insert Equations

Skill 13 Use Apps for Office

Skill 14 Create Watermark Building Blocks

▶ A **template** is a prebuilt document with placeholders and formatting already in place into which you insert your own text and objects.

▶ A **brochure** is an example of a document often used to promote a business that provides a visual overview using text and objects that can contain one or more columns. The documents may be folded and distributed.

▶ A brochure created in Word is often separated into multiple parts. The parts are often created using columns with adjustable widths and spacing.

1. Start **Word 2013**. Click in the **Search for online templates** box, type brochures and then press Enter. Compare your screen with **Figure 1**.

    If you already have a document open, you can search brochures from the New page on the File tab. Online brochures are dynamic; therefore, the brochures on your screen may be different.

2. Locate and click one of the brochures for **Northwind Traders**.

    If the brochure is no longer available, click a similar brochure.

3. At the bottom of the preview window, to the right of **More Images**, click the **Next arrow**, and then compare your screen with **Figure 2**.

    This is a **tri-fold brochure**, a document that has two pages, with three columns on each page, that contains formatted text, pictures, and text boxes. This file can be opened and used as many times as desired to create any Aspen Falls brochure.

    This brochure positions each column using tables.

■ **Continue to the next page to complete the skill**

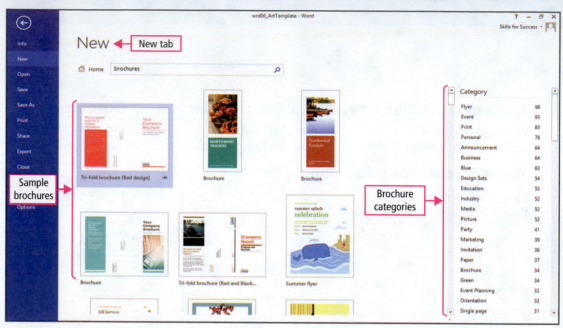

Figure 1

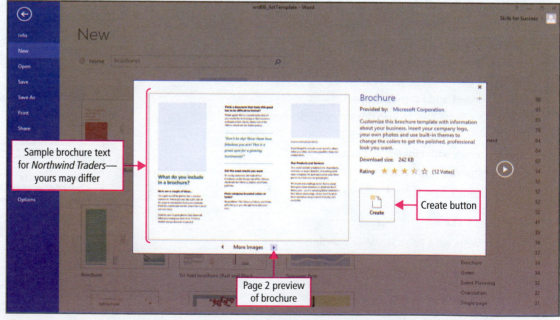

Figure 2

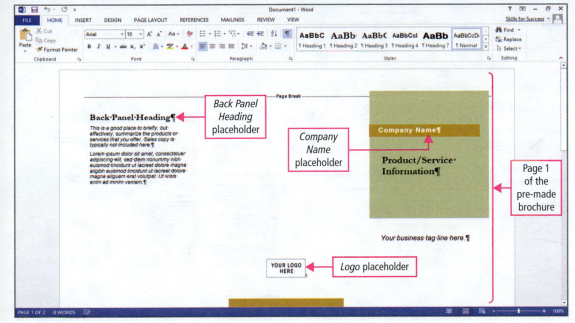

Figure 3

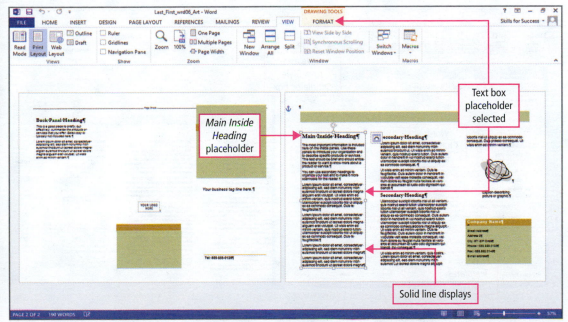

Figure 4

4. Close the brochure preview window. Locate and open **wrd06_ArtTemplate**. Compare your screen with **Figure 3**.

5. Use the **Save As** dialog box to create a **New folder** named Word Chapter 6 Save the document in the new folder as Last_First_wrd06_Art Click the **Save as type arrow**, and then click **Word Document (*.docx)**. Press Enter.

   Template files are often saved as Word documents.

6. On the **View tab**, in the **Zoom group**, click the **Multiple Pages** button.

   The two-page brochure displays with sample text.

7. Click the text *Main Inside Heading*, and then click the border of the text box to select it. Compare your screen with **Figure 4**.

   The template arranges the brochure columns using text boxes that can be modified and deleted.

   Recall that when you insert objects such as pictures and text boxes, they are associated with a paragraph. Here, the text box is associated with the blank paragraph at the top of the page.

8. Save the document.

■ **You have completed Skill 1 of 10**

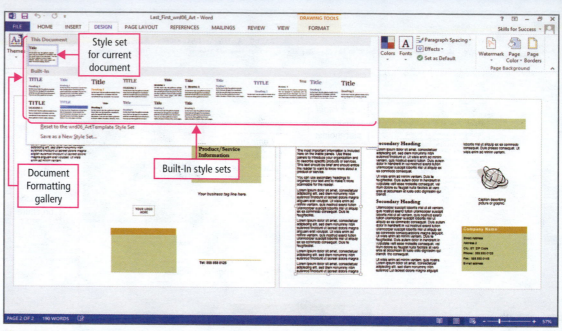

▶ A style is a predefined set of formats that can be applied to parts of a document.

▶ A **style set** is a saved style that can be applied to text and placeholders in other documents. It may include paragraph spacing, font name, font color, font size, and text effects.

1. Verify that your document displays Multiple Pages. Hide the formatting marks.

2. On the **Design tab**, in the **Document Formatting group**, click the **More** button. Compare your screen with **Figure 1**.

3. Under **Built-In**, point to the first style set, **Basic (Elegant)**, and then observe your document. Continue pointing to the various styles in the gallery.

  Live Preview displays what the style set would look like applied to your brochure.

4. Under **Built-In**, click **Minimalist**—the first style in the second row.

5. In the **Document Formatting group**, click the **Fonts** button, scroll down to the bottom of the list, and then click **TrebuchetMS**.

  The TrebuchetMS font is applied to Heading 1 styles.

6. In the **Document Formatting group**, click the **Colors** button, and then click **Paper**.

7. In the **Document Formatting group**, click the **Paragraph Spacing** button, and then click **Tight**.

  The Tight paragraph style includes 0 pt spacing before, 6 pt spacing after, and 1.15 line spacing.

8. In the **Document Formatting group**, click the **More** button, and then click **Save as a New Style Set**. **Save** the style set as Last_First_wrd06_ArtStyleSet in your **Word Chapter 6** folder as shown in **Figure 2**.

■ **Continue to the next page to complete the skill**

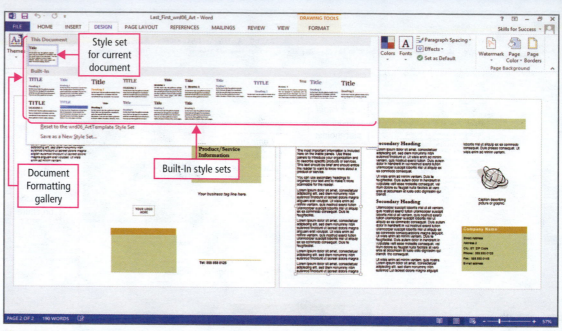

Figure 1

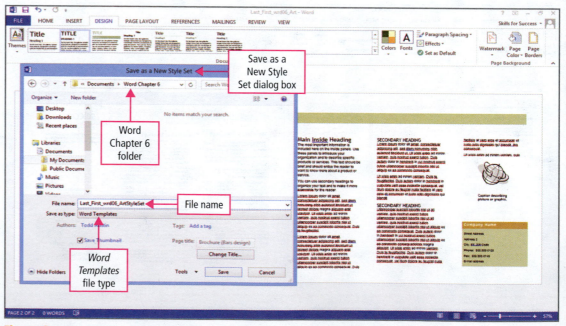

Figure 2

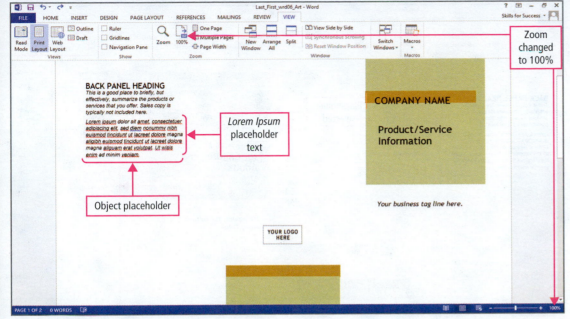

Figure 3

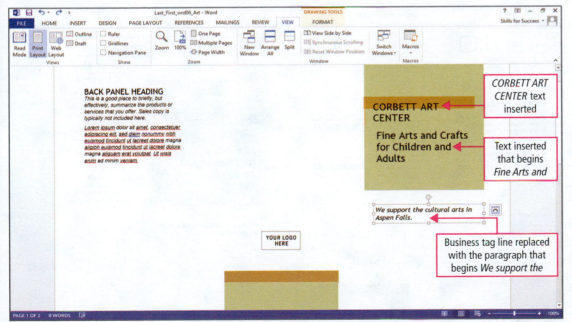

Figure 4

9. On the **View tab**, in the **Zoom group**, click the **100%** button. Press Ctrl + Home, and then compare your screen with **Figure 3**.

   The template includes objects that serve as placeholders into which you can insert your own content. All text boxes will be replaced, and any objects that you do not intend to use can be deleted.

   For example, the object placeholder at the top left displays sample text describing the purpose of the placeholder. It also contains the Latin words that begin **Lorem ipsum**—sample text taken from Cicero that has been changed so that the words no longer have meaning so that you can focus on what the document formatting and effects look like.

10. On Page 1, in the object placeholder at the right, triple-click *COMPANY NAME*, and then type Corbett Art Center

11. In the object placeholder, triple-click *Product/Service Information*, and then type Fine Arts and Crafts for Children and Adults

12. In the object placeholder at the right, triple-click the paragraph that begins *Your business tag*, and then type We support the cultural arts in Aspen Falls. Compare your screen with **Figure 4**.

13. On Page 1, in the bottom right placeholder, replace the telephone number with (805) 555-1699

14. **Save** the document.

■ **You have completed Skill 2 of 10**

▶ You can use shape styles to modify an object. For example, you can fill an object with a picture instead of a fill color. You can also adjust how light or dark the picture display is within the shape.

▶ You can specify the exact location where a text box should display in the document.

1. On Page 1, select the *CORBETT ART CENTER* text box.

2. On the **Format tab**, in the **Arrange group**, click the **Selection Pane** button.

    The *Selection pane* displays a list of shapes, including pictures and text boxes, located on the current page.

3. In the **Selection** pane, click **Rectangle 42** as shown in **Figure 1**.

    In complex documents with multiple items in layers, it is often easier to select the items in the Selection pane instead of clicking them in the document.

4. On the **Format tab**, in the **Size group**, set the **Shape Height** to 0.8" Press [Enter].

5. In the **Shape Styles group**, click the **Shape Fill button arrow**, and then click **Olive Green**, **Accent 1**—the fifth color in the first row.

6. With **Rectangle 42** still selected, in the **Selection** pane, press [Ctrl], and then click **Text Box 43**. In the **Arrange group**, click the **Group** button, and then select **Group**. Compare your screen with **Figure 2**.

    You can *group*—merge separate objects into one object that can be resized as a single object—objects. In this case, a new group, Group 25, is created that includes both the text box and rectangle.

■ **Continue to the next page to complete the skill** ▶

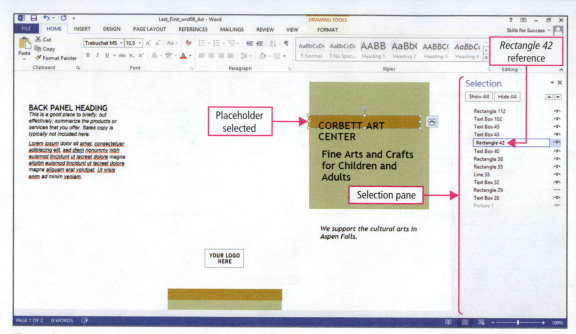

Figure 1

maphotog/Fotolia

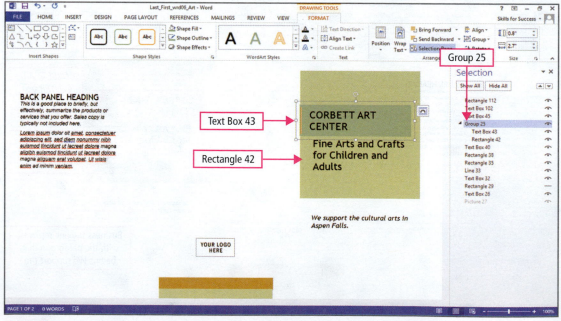

Figure 2

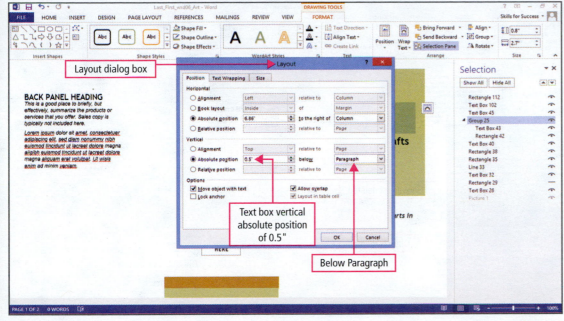

Layout dialog box

Text box vertical absolute position of 0.5"

Below Paragraph

Figure 3

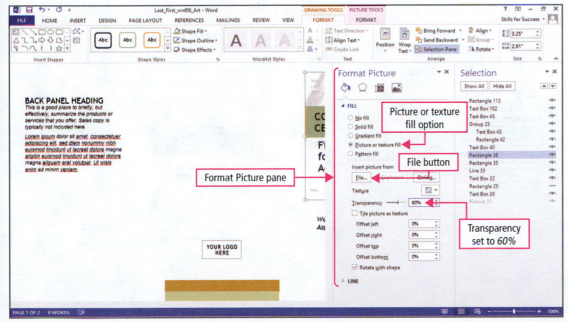

Format Picture pane

Picture or texture fill option

File button

Transparency set to *60%*

Figure 4

7. In the **Arrange group**, click the **Position** button, and then click **More Layout Options**. In the **Layout** dialog box, on the **Position tab**, under **Vertical**, set the **Vertical Absolute position** to 0.5" below **Paragraph** as shown in **Figure 3**. Click **OK**.

> *Absolute positioning* is a layout option that is used to place the object at a fixed position on the page—in this case, at 0.5" on the vertical ruler.

> Absolute positioning is beneficial because Word puts the object in the exact location you desire and you do not have to use the ruler to move the object.

8. In the **Selection** pane, select **Rectangle 38**. On the **Format tab**, click the **Shape Styles Dialog Box Launcher**.

9. In the **Format Shape** pane, if necessary, click the **Fill & Line** button. Click the **Expand Fill** | ▶ FILL | button, and then select the **Picture or texture fill** option button.

10. Under **Insert picture from**, click the **File** button, and then open **wrd06_ArtPhoto**.

11. Set the **Transparency** to 60% and then press | Enter |. Compare your screen with **Figure 4**.

12. Close | × | the **Format Picture** pane. On the **View tab**, in the **Zoom group**, click **One Page**.

13. Save | 🖫 | the document.

■ **You have completed Skill 3 of 10**

▶ WRD 6-4 VIDEO

▶ In a text box, the text can be rotated to face a different direction—sideways or upside down, for example.

▶ Sometimes the direction of the text in a placeholder must be changed to fit the desired area or for ease of reading.

1. Verify that Page 1 displays. In the **Selection** pane, select **Text Box 102** to select the logo object, and then press Delete.

2. Repeat the technique just practiced to Delete the **Rectangle 112** object and the **Rectangle 35** object—the objects in the bottom middle of Page 1. Compare your screen with **Figure 1**.

3. On the **View tab**, in the **Zoom group**, click the **100%** button.

4. On the **Insert tab**, in the **Text group**, click the **Text Box** button, and then click **Simple Text Box**.

   A text box containing sample text displays at the top middle of Page 1.

5. Type Corbett Art Center and then press Enter. Type 2478 E Summit View Dr and then press Enter. Type Aspen Falls, CA 99208

6. Select the text box. On the **Home tab**, in the **Styles group**, click **No Spacing**.

7. On the **Format tab**, in the **Shape Styles group**, click the **Shape Outline button arrow**, and then click **No Outline**. Deselect the object, and then compare your screen with **Figure 2**.

■ **Continue to the next page to complete the skill** ➡

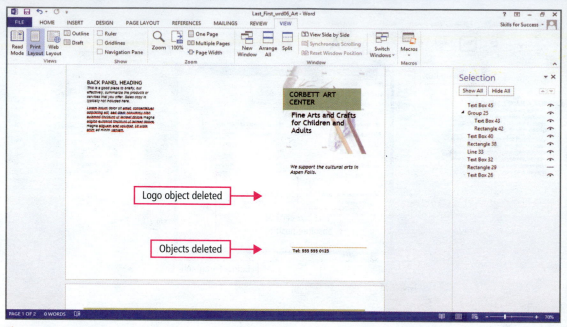

Figure 1

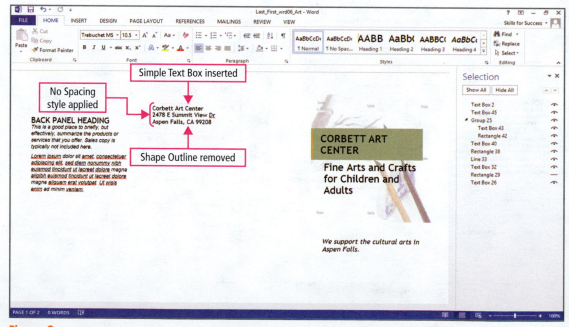

Figure 2

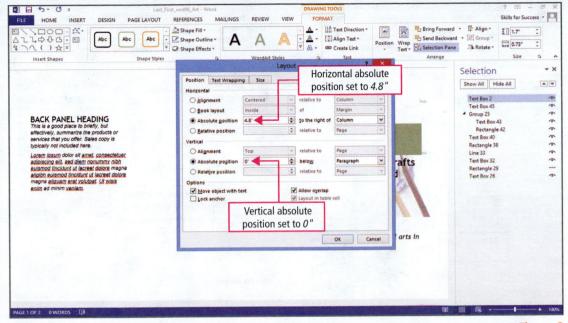

Horizontal absolute position set to 4.8"

Vertical absolute position set to 0"

Figure 3

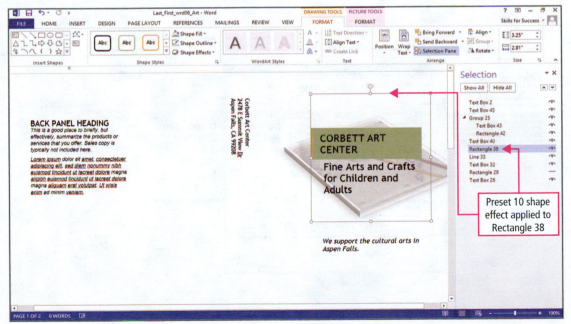

Preset 10 shape effect applied to Rectangle 38

Figure 4

8. Select the text box object you inserted. On the **Format tab**, in the **Text group**, click the **Text Direction** button, and then click **Rotate all text 90°**.

   Text direction button choices include Horizontal, Rotate all text 90°, and Rotate all text 270°.

   The text is rotated because when the brochure is prepared for mailing, this section of the brochure is what is seen when the flyer is folded.

9. In the **Size group**, set the **Shape Height** to 1.7"

10. Click the **Layout Options** button 📄, and then click **See more**. In the **Layout** dialog box, on the **Position tab**, under **Horizontal**, select the **Absolute position** option button, and then set it to 4.8" Under **Vertical**, select the **Absolute position** option button, and then set it to 0" Compare your screen with **Figure 3**, and then click **OK**.

11. In the **Selection** pane, select **Rectangle 38**. On the **Drawing Tools Format tab**, in the **Shape Styles group**, click the **Shape Effects** button, point to **Preset**, and then click **Preset 10**—the second shape effect in the third row. Click **OK**, and then compare your screen with **Figure 4**.

12. **Save** 💾 the document.

■ **You have completed Skill 4 of 10**

▶ **Shapes** are drawing objects, such as stars, rectangles, and arrows, that you insert into a document.

▶ When text is added to a shape, it becomes a text box that can have text box styles applied to it. Sometimes the size and direction of placeholder text must be changed to fit the desired area or for ease of reading.

1. On the **Insert tab**, in the **Illustrations group**, click the **Shapes** button. Under **Stars and Banners**, click **32-Point Star**— the last star in the first row.

2. Click the middle of Page 1. On the **Format tab**, in the **Size group**, set the **Shape Height** to 2.5" Set the **Shape Width** to 2.5" and then press Enter.

3. In the **Arrange group**, click the **Position** button, and then under **With Text Wrapping**, point to the **Position in Bottom Center with Square Text Wrapping** button as shown in **Figure 1**, and then click.

4. In the **Shape Styles group**, click the **More** button ▾, and then click **Intense Effect - Blue-Gray**, **Accent 6**—the last style.

5. Begin typing Unlock your creativity!

   Alternately, right-click the object border, and then click Edit Text.

6. In the star, select the text and the *!*, and then on the **Home tab**, click the **Font Dialog Box Launcher** ⬚. On the **Font tab**, under **Font style**, select **Italic**. Under **Size**, scroll down, and then select **16**.

7. On the **Advanced tab**, under **Character Spacing**, click the **Spacing arrow**, and then click **Expanded**. Click the **Spacing By up spin arrow** three times. Compare your screen with **Figure 2**.

■ **Continue to the next page to complete the skill** ▶

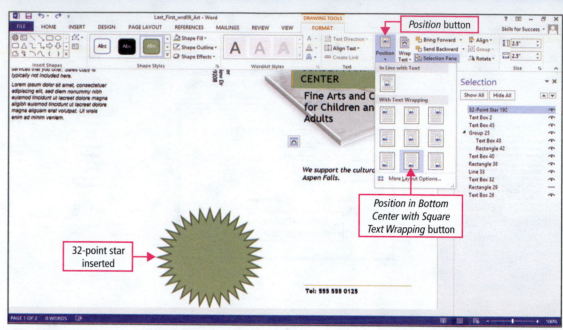

Position button

Position in Bottom Center with Square Text Wrapping button

32-point star inserted

Figure 1

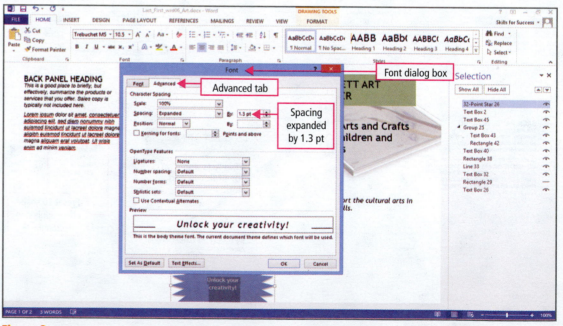

Font dialog box

Advanced tab

Spacing expanded by 1.3 pt

Figure 2

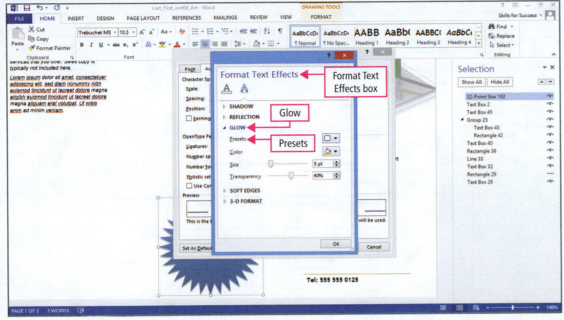

Figure 3

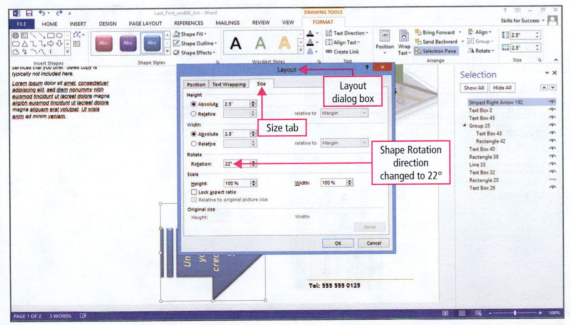

Figure 4

8. At the bottom of the **Advanced tab**, click the **Text Effects** button.

9. In the **Format Text Effects box**, click the **Text Effects** button. **Expand** the **Glow** section, click the **Presets** button, and then click **Orange, 5 pt glow, Accent color 2**—the second choice. Compare your screen with **Figure 3**, and then click **OK** two times.

The text displays on four lines.

10. On the **Format tab**, in the **Insert Shapes group**, click the **Edit Shape** button, click **Change Shape**, and then under **Block Arrows**, select **Striped Right Arrow**—the fifth shape in the second row.

11. Select the arrow placeholder border. In the **Text group**, click the **Text Direction** button, and then click **Rotate all text 270°**.

12. In the **Arrange group**, click the **Rotate** button, and then click **More Rotation Options**.

13. In the **Layout** dialog box, on the **Size tab**, under **Rotate**, set the **Rotation** to **22 degrees** as shown in **Figure 4**, and then click **OK**.

Be careful to rotate the shape, not the text.

14. On the **Format tab**, in the **Size group**, replace the **Shape Height** with 2.8" Close the **Selection** pane.

15. **Save** the document.

■ **You have completed Skill 5 of 10**

▶ To create a document by using text and elements from a variety of different sources, first collect all of the documents and images into the **Office Clipboard**— a temporary storage area maintained by Office that can hold up to 24 items. When you close out of all Office 2013 programs, the Clipboard is cleared.

▶ When you have collected all of the elements of your document, you can paste them into a new document in any order.

1. Click the **File tab**, and then click **Open**. Navigate to the location of your student data files and open **wrd06_ArtOfferings**.

2. On the **Home tab**, click the **Clipboard Pane Launcher** 🔲. In the **Clipboard** pane, if the pane contains any items, click the **Clear All** button. Compare your screen with **Figure 1**.

3. Select the *Art Gallery* heading through the text, *2 miles without difficulty*. In the **Clipboard group**, click the **Copy** button.

   Alternately, press ⎈Ctrl + C to copy the selected text.

4. Under *Photo*, select the picture of the paintbrushes, and then in the **Clipboard group**, click the **Copy** button. Compare your screen with **Figure 2**.

5. Close ☒ the **wrd06_ArtOfferings** document without saving the changes.

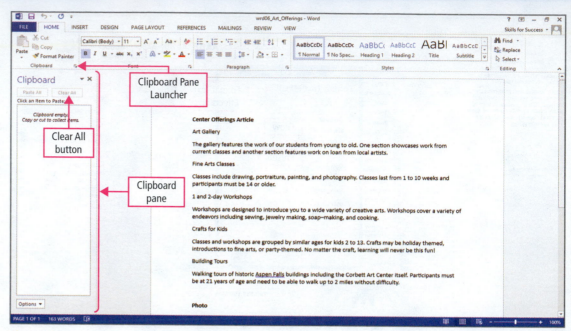

Figure 1

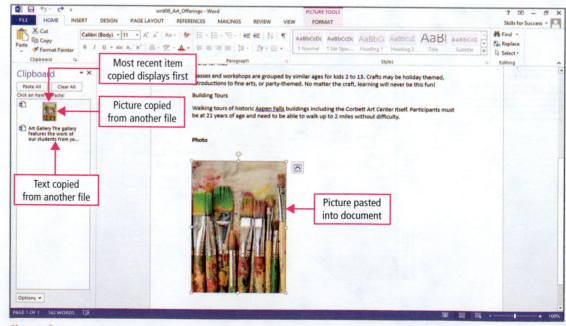

Figure 2

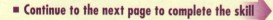
■ **Continue to the next page to complete the skill**

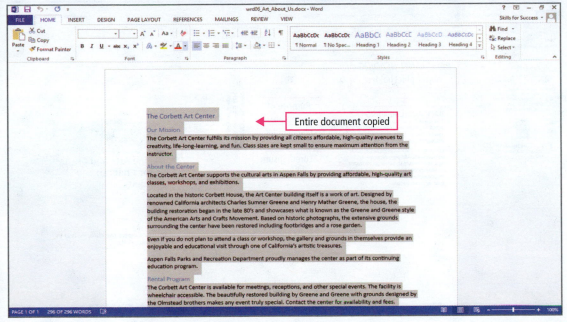

Entire document copied

Figure 3

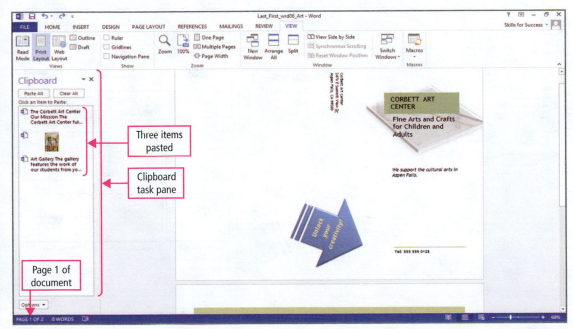

Three items pasted

Clipboard task pane

Page 1 of document

Figure 4

6. Click the **File tab**, and then click **Open**. Navigate to the location of your student data files and then open **wrd06_ArtAboutUs**.

7. On the **Home tab**, in the **Editing group**, click the **Select** button, and then click **Select All**. In the **Clipboard group**, click the **Copy** button. Compare your screen with **Figure 3**.

8. Close ⊠ the **wrd06_ArtAboutUs** document without saving the changes.

9. In **Last_First_wrd06_Art**, on the **Home tab**, select the **Clipboard Pane Launcher**.

10. On the **View tab**, in the **Zoom group**, click the **One Page** button, and then compare your screen with **Figure 4**.

11. Keep the Clipboard pane open. **Save** 🖫 the document.

■ **You have completed Skill 6 of 10**

▶ Word has several built-in text boxes with predefined styles that you can insert without having to draw and format a plain text box.

▶ After inserting a built-in text box, you can replace the text and graphics as needed.

1. On the **View tab**, in the **Zoom group**, click the **100%** button. On Page 1, if necessary, scroll to display the *BACK PANEL HEADING* object. Compare your screen with **Figure 1**.

2. Read the information contained in the text box. Select the placeholder border, and then press ⌈Delete⌋.

3. On the **View tab**, in the **Zoom group**, click the **One Page** button.

4. On the **Insert tab**, in the **Text group**, click the **Text Box** button, and then compare your screen with **Figure 2**. Scroll through the gallery, and then select **Austin Sidebar**—the third text box in the first row.

    The Austin Sidebar displays in the right panel of the brochure.

5. On the **Format tab**, in the **Arrange group**, click the **Selection Pane** button. In the **Selection** pane, click **Group 211**. On the **Format tab**, in the **Size group**, set the **Shape Height** to 7.5" and the **Shape Width** to 3" and then press ⌈Enter⌋.

6. In the **Arrange group**, click the **Position** button. Under **With Text Wrapping**, select the **Position in Top Left with Square Text Wrapping** button 🔲.

7. Click the **Sidebar Title** placeholder, and then type Our Offerings

8. Click the body text placeholder that begins [*Sidebars are great*, and then press ⌈Delete⌋.

■ **Continue to the next page to complete the skill** ➡

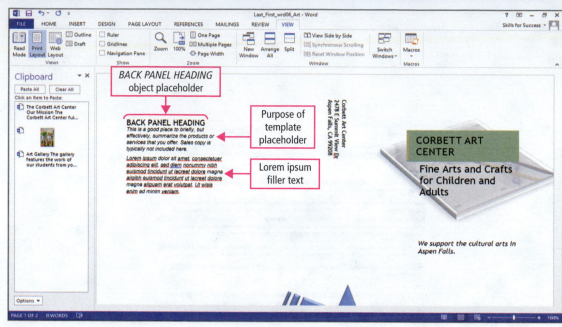

Figure 1

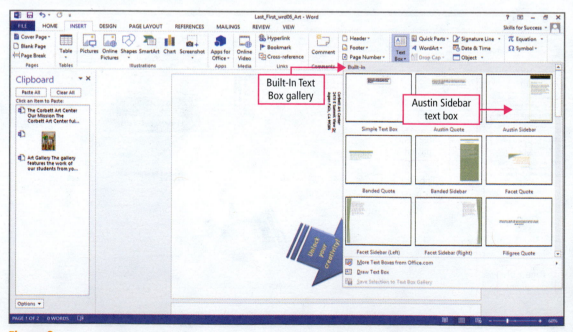

Figure 2

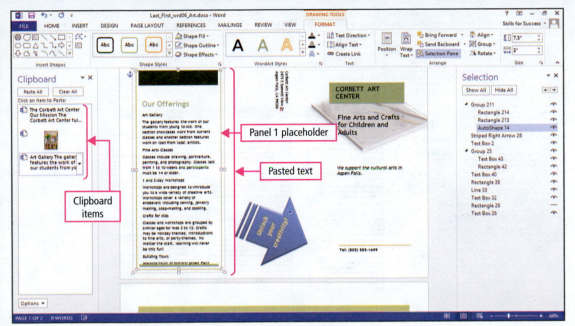

Panel 1 placeholder

Pasted text

Clipboard items

Figure 3

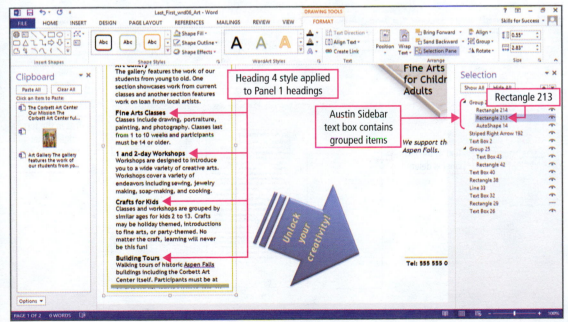

Heading 4 style applied to Panel 1 headings

Austin Sidebar text box contains grouped items

Rectangle 213

Figure 4

9. If necessary, position the insertion point in the placeholder in Panel 1. In the **Clipboard** pane, click the text item that begins *Art Gallery The*. Compare your screen with **Figure 3**.

10. On the **View tab**, in the **Zoom group**, click the **100%** button. On the **Home tab**, in the **Styles group**, apply the **Heading 4** style to the text *Art Gallery*.

11. Select the text, *Art Gallery*, and then on the **Home tab**, in the **Font group**, click **Bold**, deselect **Italics**, and change the **Font Size** to **11**.

12. In the **Styles group**, right-click the **Heading 4 style**, and then click **Update Heading 4 to Match Selection**.

13. Apply the **Heading 4** style to the other four headings: *Fine Arts Classes, 1 and 2-day Workshops, Crafts for Kids,* and *Building Tours*.

14. In the **Selection** pane, under **Group 211**, select **Rectangle 213**, and then compare your screen with **Figure 4**.

    The prebuilt text box is already grouped.

15. On the **Format tab**, in the **Shape Styles group**, click the **Shape Fill** button, and then select **Olive Green, Accent 1**—the fifth color in the first row.

16. On the **Home tab**, in the **Styles group**, right-click **Normal**, and then click **Modify**.

17. In the **Modify Style** dialog box, click the **Format** button, and then click **Paragraph**. In the **Paragraph** dialog box, on the **Indents and Spacing tab**, under **Spacing**, change the **Line spacing** to **Single**, and then click **OK** two times.

18. Save the document.

■ **You have completed Skill 7 of 10**

▶ The contents of two or more text boxes can be linked.

▶ *Linked text boxes* are used so that text automatically flows between one or more text boxes. For example, when there is no longer room to display text in the first text box, the remaining text is automatically placed in the second, linked text box.

1. Click the top of Page 2.

2. In the **Selection** pane, click **Text Box 52**—the left panel. On the **Format tab**, in the **Shape Styles group**, click the **Shape Outline button arrow**, and then click **Black, Text 1**—the second color in the first row.

3. In the **Selection** pane, click **Text Box 54**—the middle panel—and then press F4 to repeat the previous command.

4. In the **Selection** pane, click **Text Box 51**—the top, right panel—and then press F4. Close × the **Selection** pane. Compare your screen with **Figure 1**.

   Temporarily displaying borders around text boxes can help you see them.

5. Under *Main Inside Heading*, read the first two paragraphs. Delete the heading and all of the text in the text box.

6. In the middle panel, select the first two paragraphs that begin *Lorem ipsum*. Watch the text in the right panel move back to the middle panel as you press Delete. Compare your screen with **Figure 2**.

   Because there is more text than will fit in the box, only the text that fits without resizing the box or adjusting the font size will display.

■ **Continue to the next page to complete the skill** ➡

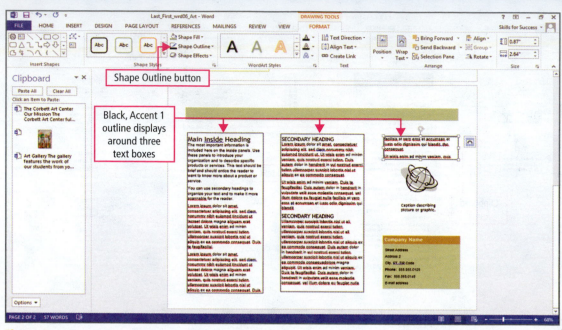

Figure 1

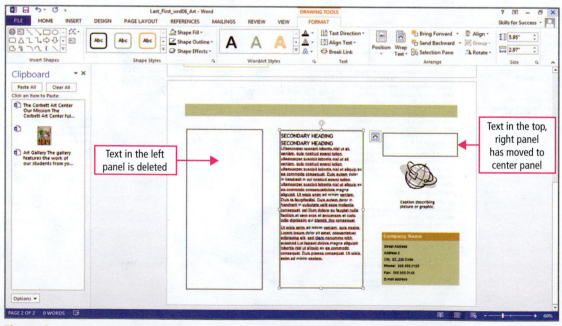

Figure 2

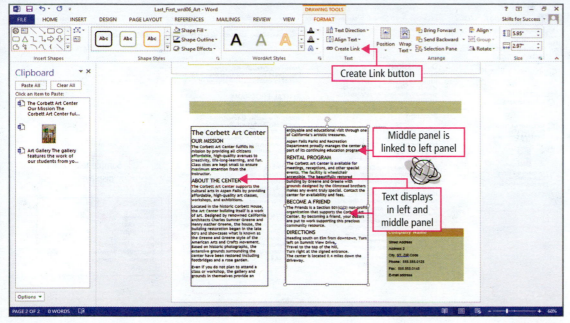

Create Link button

Middle panel is linked to left panel

Text displays in left and middle panel

Figure 3

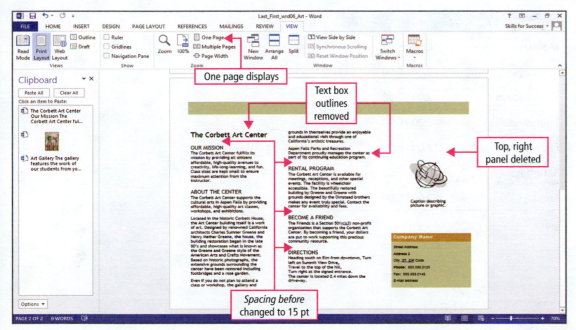

One page displays

Text box outlines removed

Top, right panel deleted

Spacing before changed to 15 pt

Figure 4

Sometimes boxes are linked so that any text that does not fit in one box can display in another box. In this case, the middle and right text boxes are linked. With linked boxes, what does not fit in the middle box can display in the right box.

7. In the middle panel, delete all of the text, including the two headings.

8. With the insertion point in the middle panel, in the **Text group**, click the **Break Link** button.

9. Click the left panel. In the **Clipboard** pane, click the text item that begins *The Corbett Art* to paste it.

10. In the **Text group**, click the **Create Link** button, and then click the middle panel. Compare your screen with **Figure 3**.

11. In the left panel, click the *OUR MISSION* heading, and then on the **Page Layout tab**, in the **Paragraph group**, set the **Spacing Before** to 15 pt.

12. On the **Home tab**, in the **Styles group**, right-click the **Heading 3** style, and then click **Update Heading 3 to Match Selection**.

13. Select the top, right unused panel border, and then press Delete .

14. Select the left panel border. Press Shift , and then select the middle panel border. On the **Format tab**, in the **Shape Styles group**, click the **Shape Outline button arrow**, and then click **No Outline**. Deselect the text boxes.

15. On the **View tab**, in the **Zoom group**, click the **One Page** button, and then compare your screen with **Figure 4**.

16. Save the document.

- **You have completed Skill 8 of 10**

▶ *Quick Tables* are built-in tables that can be used to insert a formatted table into your document.

▶ After a Quick Table is inserted, the data can be replaced with your own.

1. Verify Page 2 displays in **One Page** zoom level.

2. Using either the mouse or **Selection** pane, ⌜Delete⌝ all of the objects in the right panel: *Text Box 47*, *Text Box 106*, *Text Box 70*, *Rectangle 62*, *Text Box 61*, and *Rectangle 60*. If necessary, close the **Selection** pane.

3. On the **Insert tab**, in the **Text group**, click the **Text Box** button, and then click **Simple Text Box**. Press ⌜Delete⌝ to delete the placeholder text.

4. On the **Format tab**, in the **Arrange group**, click the **Position** button, and then click the **Position in Bottom Right with Square Text Wrapping** button ⌷.

5. In the **Size group**, set the **Shape Width** to 3".

6. On the **Insert tab**, in the **Tables group**, click the **Table** button, and then click **Quick Tables**. Scroll down and select **Tabular List**. Compare your screen with **Figure 1**.

7. On the **View tab**, in the **Zoom group**, click the **100%** button.

8. Select row 1 of the table. On the **Layout tab**, in the **Merge group**, click the **Merge Cells** button. Type Hours

9. Type the text as shown in **Figure 2**.

10. In the table, select the row that begins *Scissors*. On the **Layout tab**, in the **Rows & Columns group**, click the **Delete** button, and then click **Delete Rows**.

■ **Continue to the next page to complete the skill** ➤

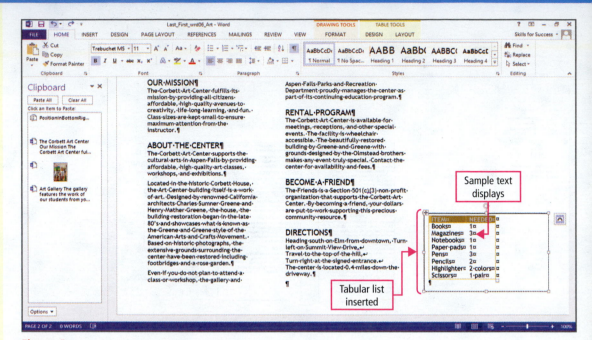

Sample text displays

Tabular list inserted

Figure 1

Hours	
Mondays	Closed
Tuesdays	2:00 - 7:00
Wednesdays	2:00 - 7:00
Thursdays	2:00 - 6:00
Fridays	11:00 - 6:00
Saturdays	9:00 - 5:00
Sundays	2:00 - 5:00

Figure 2

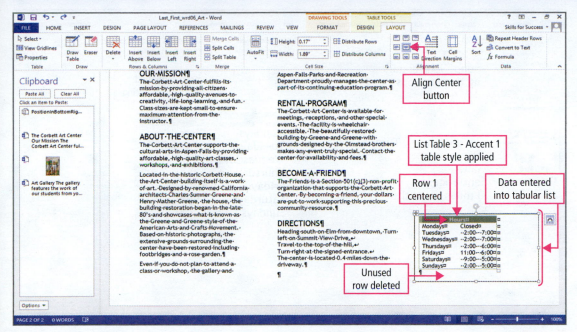

Figure 3

11. With the insertion point in the table, on the **Table Tools Design tab**, in the **Table Styles group**, click the **More** button.

12. Under **List Tables**, click **List Table 3 - Accent 1**—the second style in the third row.

13. Click row 1 of the table. On the **Layout tab**, in the **Alignment group**, click the **Align Center** button. Compare your screen with **Figure 3**.

14. In the **Table group**, click the **Properties** button. In the **Table Properties** dialog box, on the **Table tab**, under **Alignment**, click **Center**, and then click **OK**.

15. With the table selected, on the **Format tab**, in the **Shape Styles group**, click the **Shape Outline button arrow**, and then click **No Outline**. Deselect the table, and then compare your screen with **Figure 4**.

16. **Save** the document.

■ **You have completed Skill 9 of 10**

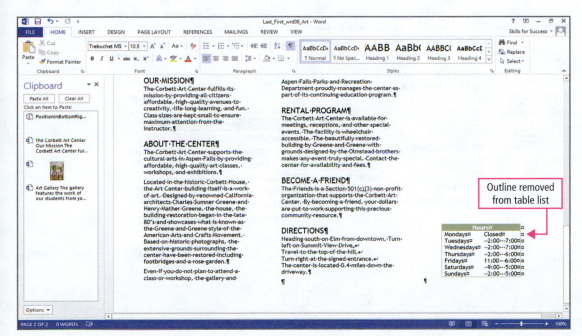

Figure 4

▶ The **OpenType feature** includes fonts that work on multiple platforms, including Macintosh and Microsoft Windows.

▶ An example of an **OpenType font** is the *fi* symbol in the Font list. Two or more symbols or characters are often combined, similar to typesetting.

▶ When preparing documents, OpenType features provide additional character formats and layout options.

1. On the **Status bar**, click **100%**. In the **Zoom** dialog box, select **200%**. Click **OK**.

2. On Page 2, scroll to display the table, and then select the cells that have numbers.

3. On the **Home tab**, click the **Font Dialog Box Launcher** ⊡. In the **Font** dialog box, on the **Advanced tab**, under **OpenType Features**, click the **Number spacing arrow**, and then select **Proportional**. Click **OK**. Compare your screen with **Figure 1**.

   The numbers display with a **proportional typeface**—a font with characters that vary in width. For example, space used for the letter *I* is much narrower than the width used by the letter *M*. Here the proportional widths of the numbers make it difficult to align *11:00* with the other numbers in the table.

4. Click the **Font Box Launcher** ⊡. In the **Font** dialog box, on the **Advanced tab**, under **OpenType Features**, click the **Number spacing arrow**, and then select **Tabular**. Click the **Number forms arrow**, and then select **Old-style**. Click **OK**. Compare your screen with **Figure 2**.

   When working with lists and tables, you can assign the tabular alignment to numbers to make them easier to align.

■ **Continue to the next page to complete the skill** ▶

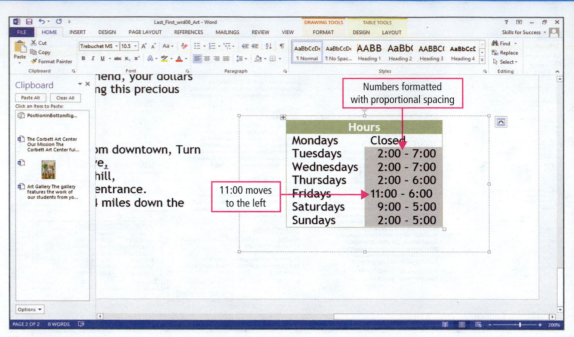

Figure 1

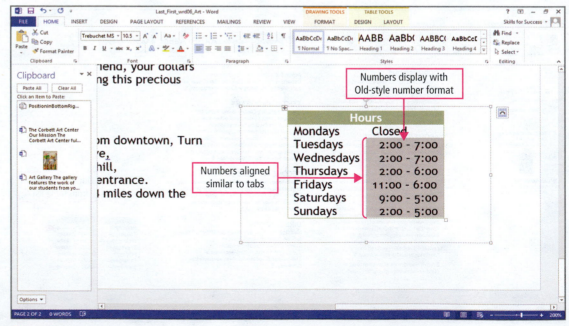

Figure 2

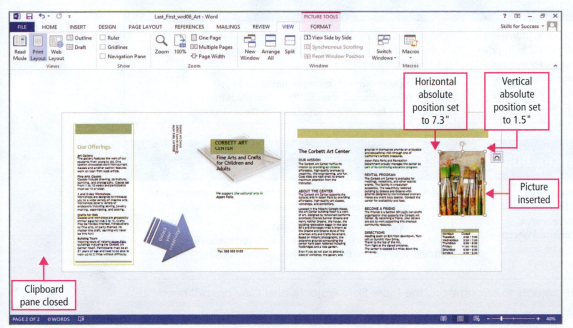

Figure 3

Figure 4

5. On Page 1, in the *Our Offerings* heading, select the letters *ff*.

6. On the **Home tab**, click the **Font Box Launcher**. In the **Font** dialog box, on the **Advanced tab**, under **OpenType Features**, click the **Ligatures arrow**, and then select **Historical and Discretionary** as shown in **Figure 3**. Click **OK**.

   The letters, *ff*, display as *ligatures*—small graphic characters that display when two or more symbols are combined. Here the two letters, *ff*, have been combined into one character. Other examples would be *fi* and *fl*.

7. On the **View tab**, in the **Zoom group**, click the **100%** button.

8. On Page 2, click the blank paragraph at the top of the page. In the **Clipboard** pane, click the picture to paste it in the document.

9. Click the picture. On the **Format tab**, in the **Arrange group**, click the **Wrap Text** button, and then click **Square**.

10. In the **Arrange group**, click the **Position** button, and then click **More Layout Options**. In the **Layout** dialog box, on the **Position tab**, under **Horizontal**, set the **Absolute position** to 7.3" Under **Vertical**, set the **Absolute position** to 1.5" Click **OK**.

11. On the **View tab**, in the **Zoom group**, click the **Multiple Pages** button.

12. In the **Clipboard** pane, click the **Clear All** button, and then click **Close** . Compare your screen with **Figure 4**.

13. **Save** the document. Print or submit the files as directed by your instructor. **Exit** Word.

✔ **DONE!** You have completed Skill 10 of 10, and your document is complete!

More Skills

The following More Skills are located at **www.pearsonhighered.com/skills**

More Skills Work with Page Number Building Blocks

Page numbers can be inserted by selecting a building block from the Page Number gallery. When a page number is selected from the gallery, it is automatically inserted into a header or footer. Page numbers can then be modified. For example, the starting number can be increased and the number format can be changed.

In More Skills 11, you will insert page numbers from the Page Number gallery and then modify the starting number and number format.

To begin, open your web browser, navigate to www.pearsonhighered.com/skills, locate the name of your textbook, and follow the instructions on the website.

More Skills Insert Equations

Word has several built-in equations that can be used to insert common equations into documents. When other types of equations are needed, they can be typed and modified using the Equation Tools tab.

In More Skills 12, you will open a memo and then insert several built-in equations and build your own custom equation.

To begin, open your web browser, navigate to www.pearsonhighered.com/skills, locate the name of your textbook, and follow the instructions on the website.

More Skills Use Apps for Office

Word contains a link to Office applications, known as Office apps, that help you individualize documents, as well as link to Internet sites faster while remaining in Word. You can use a featured Office app or go to the Office Store to purchase additional apps. The apps remain in your Live account, allowing you to use the app in multiple documents and on other computers.

In More Skills 13, you will open a report and then download the dictionary app. You will use the dictionary app to insert a definition into the report.

To begin, open your web browser, navigate to www.pearsonhighered.com/skills, locate the name of your textbook, and follow the instructions on the website.

More Skills Create Watermark Building Blocks

A watermark typically displays in the background of a document. Watermarks can be text or images that are faded and moved to the back of the text. You may have seen a "Confidential" watermark notation on a document. Watermarks can be saved as building blocks so that they can be accessed in the Watermark gallery.

In More Skills 14, you will insert and format a watermark. You will save the watermark as a building block.

To begin, open your web browser, navigate to www.pearsonhighered.com/skills, locate the name of your textbook, and follow the instructions on the website.

Please note that there are no additional projects to accompany the More Skills Projects, and they are not covered in End-of-Chapter projects.

The following table summarizes the **SKILLS AND PROCEDURES** covered in this chapter.

Skills Number	Task	Step	Icon	Keyboard Shortcut
1	Open a local template	File tab → New tab → select desired template		
2	Apply a style set	Design tab → Document Formatting group → More button → select desired format		
2	Change document font	Design tab → Document Formatting group → Fonts button	A	
2	Change document color	Design tab → Document Formatting group → Colors button		
2	Change document paragraph spacing	Design tab → Document Formatting group → Paragraph Spacing button		
2	Save a style set	Design tab → Document Formatting group → More button → Save as a New Style Set	Save as a New Style Set...	
3	Insert shapes	Insert tab → Illustrations group → Shapes button → Select desired shape		
3	Adjust shape or text box position	Select shape or text box → Format tab → Arrange group → Position button		
3	Adjust Fill & Line options	Select shape → Format tab → Arrange group → Selection Pane button → Shape Styles Box Launcher → Fill & Line button		
4	Insert built-in text boxes	Insert tab → Text group → Text Box button		
4	Change text direction	Select the text box border→ Format tab → Text group → Text Direction button → Select desired direction		
5	Modify shapes	Select shape → Format tab → Insert Shapes group → Edit Shape button		
5	Adjust shape or text box text wrapping	Select shape or text box → Format tab → Arrange group → Wrap Text button		
5	Change text effects	Home tab → Font Box Launcher → Advanced tab → Select desired settings		
6	Use collect	Home tab → Clipboard group → Copy button		Ctrl + C
7	Paste from Clipboard	Click in desired location → Home tab → Clipboard Pane Launcher → Clipboard pane → Select item		
8	Link text boxes	Format tab → Text group → Create Link button → Click in desired text box		
8	Break links between text	Select the text box → Format tab → Text group → Break Link button		
9	Insert Quick Tables	Insert tab → Tables group → Quick Tables		
10	Apply OpenType features	Home tab → Font Box Launcher → Advanced tab → Select desired settings		

Key Terms

Online Help Skills

1. Start **Word 2013**, and then in the upper right corner of the start page, click the **Help** button ⸢?⸣.

2. In the **Word Help Search** help box, type online templates and then press ⸢Enter⸣.

3. In the search result list, click **Where do I find templates?**, and then below **What do you want to do?**, click **Find and download a new template**, and then compare your screen with **Figure 1**.

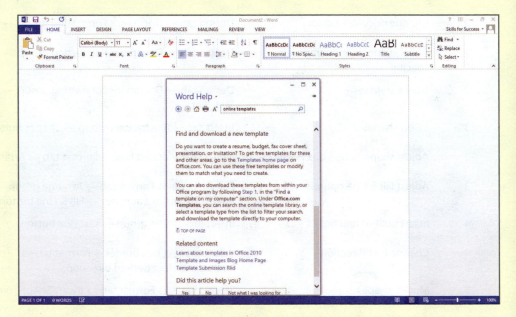

Figure 1

4. Read the article to answer the following question: At office.com in the **Word templates category**, under **Explore new templates**, what is the name of the default tri-fold brochure located at office.com?

Matching

Match each term in the second column with its correct definition in the first column by writing the letter of the term on the blank line in front of the correct definition.

____ **1.** A prebuilt document with placeholders and formatting already in place into which text and objects are inserted.

____ **2.** An example of a document often used to promote a business that provides a visual overview using text and objects that can contain one or more columns.

____ **3.** A section of the Word screen that displays a list of shapes, including pictures and text boxes, located on the current page.

____ **4.** A layout option used to place the object at a fixed position on the page.

____ **5.** A drawing object, such as a rectangle, arrow, or callout, that is inserted into a document.

____ **6.** A temporary storage area maintained by Office that can hold up to 24 items.

____ **7.** A font that works on multiple platforms, including Macintosh and Microsoft Windows.

____ **8.** Two or more symbols or characters that are often combined, similar to typesetting.

____ **9.** A font with characters that vary in width.

____ **10.** A small graphic character that displays when two or more symbols are combined.

A Absolute positioning

B Brochure

C Ligature

D Office Clipboard

E OpenType feature

F OpenType font

G Proportional typeface

H Selection pane

I Shape

J Template

Multiple Choice

Choose the correct answer.

1. When objects such as pictures and text boxes are inserted, they are connected, or associated with this Word part.
   - A. Character
   - B. Paragraph
   - C. Shape

2. The paragraph spacing, font name, font color, font size, and text effects that can be saved and later applied to text and placeholders in the current or other documents.
   - A. Brochure formatting
   - B. Saved document
   - C. Style set

3. A Word feature that includes objects that serve as placeholders into which you can insert your own content.
   - A. Style
   - B. Template
   - C. Zoom

4. Lorem ipsum contains this type of sample text.
   - A. Words that display correct word pronunciations
   - B. Words that display sample formatting and effects
   - C. Words that have no meaning

5. Use this Word feature to merge separate objects into one object that can be resized as a single object.
   - A. Combine
   - B. Group
   - C. Split

6. A built-in feature of Word that includes sidebars and pull quotes in which text can be inserted.
   - A. Merged object
   - B. Text box
   - C. WordArt

7. The text box option used to display text vertically in a text box.
   - A. Horizontal
   - B. Rotate all text 270°
   - C. Vertical

8. The maximum number of items that can be held in the Office Clipboard.
   - A. 24
   - B. 100
   - C. Unlimited

9. The type of text box where the text that does not fit in one text box can be flowed into a second text box.
   - A. Aligned
   - B. Cropped
   - C. Linked

10. The Word feature used to cancel the automatic flow of text in one or more text boxes.
    - A. Break link
    - B. Create link
    - C. Delete link

Topics for Discussion

1. What are some examples of brochures that you have found at your school? What are some examples of brochures that a business might use?

2. What are three Quick Tables that you could use? Why? How would you use them?

Skills Review

The MyITLab logo image is img_2.

To complete this project, you will need the following files:

- wrd06_SRInternTemplate (Word template)
- wrd06_SRInternInserts

You will save your documents as:

- Last_First_wrd06_SRIntern
- Last_First_wrd06_SRInternStyleSet

1. Start **Word 2013**, and then open **wrd06_SRInternInserts**. Select the text *Upon completion of* through *Charles.Gato@aspenfallscc.edu*. On the **Home tab**, click the **Clipboard Pane Launcher**, click the **Clear All** button, and then click **Copy**. Repeat the technique just practiced to select and copy the text below the four yellow and green highlights.

2. Open **wrd06_SRInternTemplate.dotx**. **Save** the file in your **Word Chapter 6** folder as Last_First_wrd06_SRIntern

3. On the **Design tab**, in the **Document Formatting group**, click the **More button arrow**, and then click the **Minimalist** button. Click the **Paragraph Spacing** button, and then click **Tight**.

4. On Page 1, in Panel 1, click before the paragraph mark in the empty box. Open the Clipboard, if necessary. **Paste** the text that begins *Upon completion of*. [Delete] the blank paragraph at the bottom. Repeat the technique just practiced to insert the text that begins *CITY OF ASPEN* in the placeholder at the bottom of Page 1, Panel 3.

5. On the **Insert tab**, in the **Text group**, click the **Text Box** button, and then click **Simple Text Box**. Press [Delete]. On the **Format tab**, in the **Size group**, set the **Shape Height** to 1.7" and the **Shape Width** to 3"

6. To the right of the text box, click the **Layout Options** button, and then click **See more**. In the **Layout** dialog box, on the **Position tab**, set the **Horizontal Absolute position** to 2.6 and the **Vertical Absolute position** to 4.9 Click **OK**.

7. On the **Insert tab**, in the **Tables group**, click the **Table button**, click **Quick Tables**, scroll down, and then click **Tabular List**. Compare with **Figure 1**.

8. In the **Quick Table**, select row 1. Right-click, and then select **Merge Cells**. Type the text in **Figure 2**.

9. Select the last two rows of the table that begin *Highlighter*. Right-click, and then click **Delete Cells**. Select **Delete entire row**. Click **OK**. On the **Layout tab**, in the **Table group**, click **Select**, and then click **Select Table**. In the **Alignment group**, click **Align Center**.

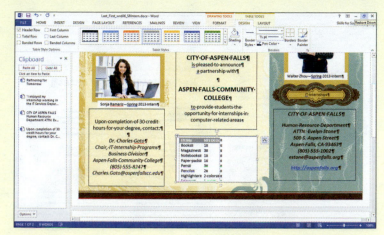

Figure 1

Sergey Nivens/Fotolia; Wong Yu Liang/Fotolia

# of Interns Accepted Each Spring	
Assistant Analysts	2
Computer Teachers	10
Database Designers	3
Help Desk Technicians	5
Office Assistants	4
Presentation Designers	2

Figure 2

■ **Continue to the next page to complete this Skills Review** ➤

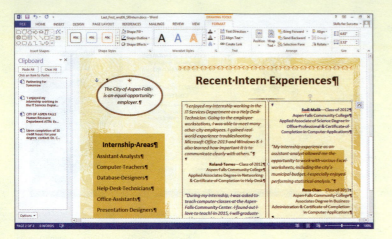

Figure 3

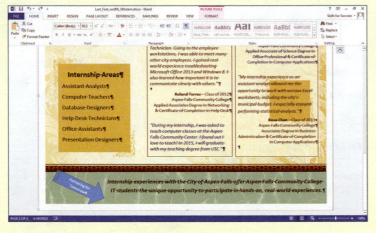
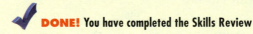

Figure 4

10. On Page 2, click before the paragraph mark in the empty box in Panel 2. In the **Clipboard**, click "*I enjoyed my*. On the **Format tab**, in the **Text group**, click the **Create Link** button. Click the text box in Panel 3 as shown in **Figure 3**.

11. On the **Insert tab**, in the **Illustrations group**, click the **Shapes** button, and then click **Striped Right Arrow**. At the bottom of Page 2, click left of the text box that begins *Internship experiences*. In the **Clipboard**, click the text *Partnering for*. In the **Arrange group**, click the **Rotate** button, and then click **More Rotation Options**. In the **Layout** dialog box, on the **Position tab**, change the **Horizontal Absolute position** to 0.71" and **to the right of** the **Column**, and change the **Vertical Absolute position** to 6.17" and **below** the **Paragraph**. On the **Size tab**, change **Shape Height** to 0.9", **Shape Width** to 2", and **Rotation** to 25° Click **OK**.

12. On Page 2, in the bottom panel, in the word *offer*, select the letters *ff*. On the **Home tab**, click the **Font Box Launcher**. In the **Font** dialog box, on the **Advanced tab**, click the **Ligatures arrow**, select **Historical and Discretionary**, and then click **OK**. For the ligature, change the **Font Name** to **Times New Roman**. Select the text box, and then change the **Font Size** to **16**. Compare your screen with **Figure 4**.

13. Close the **Clipboard**. On Page 2, select the first text box border in Panel 2, press and hold [Shift], and then select the second text box border in Panel 3. On the **Format tab**, in the **Shape Styles group**, click the **Shape Outline arrow**, and then click **No Outline**. On Page 1, repeat the technique just practiced to remove the outline from the Quick Table in Panel 2 and the text box in Panel 3.

14. On Page 1, Panel 3, select the paragraph that begins *CITY OF ASPEN*. On the **Design tab**, in the **Document Formatting group**, click the **More button arrow**, and then click **Save as a New Style Set**. **Save** as Last_First_wrd06_ SRInternStyleSet in your **Word Chapter 6** folder.

15. **Save** the document. **Close** the Word window. Submit the files as directed by your instructor.

DONE! You have completed the Skills Review

Skills Assessment 1  MyITLab® Grader

To complete this project, you will need the following files:

- wrd06_SA1HousingTemplate (Word template)
- wrd06_SA1HousingInserts

You will save your documents as:

- Last_First_wrd06_SA1Housing
- Last_First_wrd06_SA1HousingStyleSet

1. Start **Word 2013**, and then open **wrd06_SA1HousingInserts**. Select the text that begins *Housing Affordability* through the end of the paragraph that begins *In the past*. Open and Clear the **Clipboard**, and then click **Copy**. Repeat the technique just practiced to select and copy the text below the four remaining yellow and green highlights.

2. Open **wrd06_SA1HousingTemplate**. **Save** the file in your **Word Chapter 6** folder as Last_First_wrd06_SA1Housing

3. Apply the **Minimalist Document Formatting** with **Tight Paragraph Spacing**.

4. On Page 1, in Panel 2, click before the paragraph mark. **Paste** the text that begins *Housing Affordability*. Create a link to the text box placeholders on Page 2, Panel 1.

5. Select the *Housing Affordability* heading. Change the **Font Size** to **16 pt** and the **Case** to **Uppercase**. **Save** as a **New Style Set** with the name Last_First_wrd06_SA1HousingStyleSet in your **Word Chapter 6** folder.

6. On Page 1, insert the **Simple Text Box**. Set the **Shape Height** to **2"** and the **Shape Width** to **2.5"** Set the **Horizontal Absolute position** to **0.7"** to the right of the **Page** and the **Vertical Absolute position** to **6.1"** below the **Page**. Select the text. **Paste** the text that begins *ASPEN FALLS WELCOMES*. Delete the last blank paragraph. Set the **Shape Fill** to **None**.

7. On Page 1, at the top of Panel 3, **Paste** the text that begins *ASPEN FALLS Touching*. Delete the blank paragraph.

8. On Page 2, at the top of Panel 2, click before the last paragraph symbol, and then insert a **Tabular List Quick Table** with the text found in **wrd06_SA1HousingInserts**. Delete the last three rows. Select the Quick Table, and then change the **Font Size** to **14** and then **Center**.

9. On Page 2, in the bottom of Panel 3, insert the **Snip and Round Single Corner Rectangle shape** with a **Shape Height of 2"**, a **Shape Width**

John Takai/Fotolia

Figure 1

Alx/Fotolia

Figure 2

of **2.5"**, a **Horizontal Absolute position** of **6.66" to the right of** the **Column**, a **Vertical Absolute position** of **3.86" below** the **Paragraph**. **Paste** the text that begins *Population ~*. Delete the blank paragraph. Select the text and change the **Font Size** to **28**. Change the **Rotation to Flip Horizontal**. If necessary, center the shape.

10. On Page 1, in Panel 2, in the word *affordable*, select the letters *ff*, and then change the **Ligatures** to **Historical and Discretionary**. Change the **Font Name** to **Times New Roman**.

11. Close the **Clipboard**. On Page 1, remove the outlines from the text boxes at the bottom of Panel 1 and Panel 2. Repeat the technique on Page 2, in the bottom of Panel 1. Compare your screen with **Figures 1** and **2**.

12. **Save** the document. **Close** the Word window, and then submit the files as directed by your instructor.

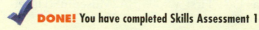 **DONE!** You have completed Skills Assessment 1

Skills Assessment 2

To complete this project, you will need the following files:

- wrd06_SA2MuseumTemplate (Word template)
- wrd06_SA2MuseumExhibits

You will save your documents as:

- Last_First_wrd06_SA2Museum
- Last_First_wrd06_SA2MuseumStyleSet

1. Start **Word 2013**, and then open **wrd06_SA2MuseumExhibits**. Select the text that begins *Museum History* through the end of the paragraph that begins *Personal artifacts*. Open and Clear the **Clipboard**, and then click **Copy**. Repeat the technique just practiced to select and copy each of the five other sections below the yellow and green highlighted text.

2. Open **wrd06_SA2MuseumTemplate**. **Save** the file in your **Word Chapter 6** folder as Last_First_wrd06_SA2Museum

3. If necessary, open the Clipboard. On Page 1, in Panel 1, click before the paragraph mark, and then **Paste** the text that begins *Museum History*.

4. On Page 1, insert the **Simple Text Box**. Change the **Shape Height** to 1.5" the **Shape Width** to 2.4" the **Horizontal Absolute position** to 3" and the **Vertical Absolute position** to 4.3" Select the text, and then **Paste** the text that begins *It's amazing*. Select the text, and then change the font size to **12 pt**.

5. On Page 1, at the top of Panel 2, **Paste** the text that begins *Durango County*. Select the placeholder border, and then **Center**. Change the **Font Size** to **16** and the **Font Color** to **White**.

6. On Page 1, at the top of Panel 3, below *Attendance*, insert a **Tabular List Quick Table** with the text found in **wrd06_SA2MuseumExhibits**. Delete the last four rows. Select the **Quick Table**, change the **Font Size** to **14**, and then **Center**.

7. On Page 2, in Panel 1, click before the paragraph mark, and then **Paste** the text that begins *General Store Situated*. Create a link to the text box placeholders in Panels 2 and 3.

8. On Page 2, select the border of the bottom placeholder, and then **Save as a New Style Set** as Last_First_wrd06_SA2MuseumStyleSet in your **Word Chapter 6** folder.

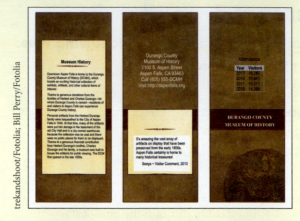

Figure 1

Figure 2

trekandshoot/Fotolia; Bill Perry/Fotolia

9. On Page 2, at the top of Panel 2, insert the **Teardrop** shape with a **Shape Height** of 1" and a **Shape Width** of 2.3" **Paste** the text that begins *Visit the new*. Select the text, and then change the **Font Name** to **Arial Narrow**, **Font Size** to **14**, and **Font Color** to **White**. Change the **Rotation to Flip Horizontal**. Set the **Horizontal Absolute position** to 2.94" and the **Vertical Absolute position** to 0.15"

10. On Page 2, in Panel 3, in the word *first,* select the letters *fi,* and then change the **Ligatures** to **Historical and Discretionary**.

11. Close the **Clipboard**. On Page 2, remove the outlines from the three text boxes. Repeat the technique on Page 1, in the bottom of Panel 2. Compare your screen with **Figures 1** and **2**.

12. **Save** the document. **Close** the Word window, and then submit the files as directed by your instructor.

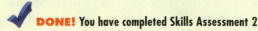

DONE! You have completed Skills Assessment 2

Visual Skills Check

To complete this project, you will need the following files:

- wrd06_VSParksTemplate (Word template)
- wrd06_VSParks

You will save your document as:

- Last_First_wrd06_VSParks

In Word 2013, open **wrd06_VSParksTemplate**. Use the skills practiced in this chapter to create the two-page brochure shown in **Figures 1** and **2**. Open **wrd06_VSParks**. Open the Clipboard. On Page 1 of **wrd06_VSParks**, copy the heading that begins *PARKS AND RECREATION* through the last paragraph under the *Mystic Family Park* heading that ends *Town Centre District* to the Clipboard. On Page 2, copy the picture to the Clipboard. On Page 2, copy the heading that begins *2014 PARK EVENTS* through the last paragraph on Page 3 under the heading *Pumpkin Carving* that ends *and lighted pumpkins*. Close **wrd06_VSParks**. At the top of Page 1, type the title CITY OF ASPEN FALLS PARKS & RECREATION DEPARTMENT In the first panel, paste the text that begins *Aspen Falls City*. In the second panel, create a link to the second box. Apply the **Minimalist Document**

Formatting and **Tw Cen MT Font** to the entire document. Change the **Paragraph Spacing** to **Tight**. On Page 1, paste the picture from the Clipboard. Apply **Square Text Wrapping** and use the **Absolute Horizontal position** of 6.7" and the **Absolute Vertical position** of 1.44" so the picture displays above the contact information. At the top of Page 2, type the heading Park Offerings In the first panel, paste the text that begins *2014 PARK EVENTS*. In the second panel, create a link to the second and third boxes.

Save the file as Last_First_wrd06_VSParks in your **Word Chapter 6** folder. **Close** the Word window, and then submit the file as directed by your instructor.

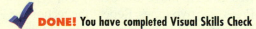 **DONE! You have completed Visual Skills Check**

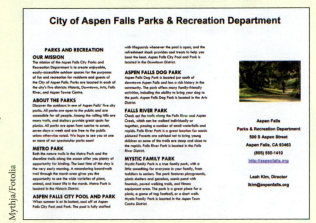

Mythja/Fotolia

Figure 1

Figure 2

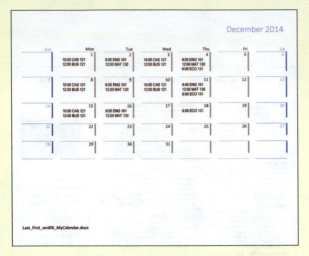

December 2014

Last_First_wrd06_MyCalendar.docx

Figure 1

My Skills

To complete this project, you will need the following file:

- wrd06_MyCalendar

You will save your document as:

- Last_First_wrd06_MyCalendar

1. Start **Word 2013**, and then open **wrd06_MyCalendar**. **Save** the file in your **Word Chapter 6** folder as Last_First_wrd06_MyCalendar Add the **FileName** field to the footer.

2. At the beginning of the document, insert the **Calendar 3 Quick Table**.

3. Click in any table cell. On the **Layout tab**, in the **Cell Size group**, click the **AutoFit** button, and then click **AutoFit Window**.

4. In the top, right corner, select the month, and then, if necessary, replace the text with the current month Press the spacebar, and then type the current year

5. If necessary, click the cell for the first day of the month, and then type 1 Press Tab two times to move to the next cell. Type 2 Press Tab two times. Repeat the technique just practiced to insert the number of days for the desired month.

   When you need to type dates for Sundays, you will need to click the cell for Sunday and then repeat the technique practiced.

6. If necessary, click the number in the cell for any extra day, and then press Delete. Repeat the technique as needed.

7. Select the first date your first college class meets, and then click in the cell to the right of the number. For example, if your class meets for the first time on a Monday, position the insertion point to the right of the number and before the end-of-cell marker in that cell. Press Enter.

8. On the **Home tab**, in the **Paragraph group**, click the **Align Left** button, type the start time of your first class and then press SpaceBar. Type the course section ID and the course number

   For example: 10:00 CAS 121

9. If necessary, press Enter and add the times and class information for the rest of your class schedule on that day.

10. Select the class information for the first day, and then change the entries to **Arial Narrow** with a **Font Size** of **10**.

11. Repeat the technique just practiced to add the rest of your class schedule to the calendar for the current month and to change the font name and font size.

12. If the last row of the table contains no dates, delete the entire row. Compare your screen with the example in **Figure 1**.

13. **Save** the document. **Close** the Word window, and then submit the file as directed by your instructor.

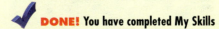

DONE! You have completed My Skills

Skills Challenge 1

To complete this project, you will need the following files:

- wrd06_SC1FoodTemplate (Word template)
- wrd06_SC1FoodInserts

You will save your document as:

- Last_First_wrd06_SC1Food

In Word 2013, open **wrd06_SC1FoodTemplate**. **Save** the file as Last_First_wrd06_SC1Food in your **Word Chapter 6** folder. Add the **FileName** to the footer. Select the text boxes and select an outline color so they are visible as you work with them. Delete the existing text and logos. Open **wrd06_SC1FoodInserts**. Use the skills practiced in this chapter to collect the text and pictures in the Clipboard. In the **Last_First_wrd06_SC1Food** file, insert the text in the text boxes in the appropriate panel as described in the **wrd06_SC1FoodInserts** file. When needed, insert text boxes for the linked data that are the same size as the text box to the left. Close **wrd06_SC1FoodInserts**. Apply the **Casual Document Formatting** with **Calibri-Cambria Font**, and **Tight** Paragraph Spacing. On Page 1, in the text boxes in Panels 1 and 2, change the

font size of the title to **12** pt, all paragraph text to **10** pt, and the headings to **10.5** pt. If necessary, change the spacing after to **6** pt for all paragraphs. On Page 2, at the bottom of Panel 2, insert the **Up Ribbon** shape with a **Shape Height** of 1.7" and a **Shape Width** of 3" Insert the shape text centered with a **Font Size** of 16, **Font Color** of White, and then change the shape **Fill Color** to Purple, Accent 4, Darker 25% and the **Shape Outline** to Purple, Accent 4. If you added any outlines to text boxes, remove them.

Close the Word window, and then submit the file as directed by your instructor.

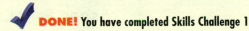 **DONE!** You have completed Skills Challenge 1

Skills Challenge 2

To complete this project, you will need the following files:

- wrd06_SC2NewsletterInserts
- **New document using a two-page, tri-fold brochure template**

You will save your document as:

- Last_First_wrd06_SC2Newsletter

Open **wrd06_SC2NewsletterInserts**, and then use the skills practiced in this chapter to collect the text. In Word 2013, open a new document that uses a two-page, tri-fold brochure online template that you select. Delete the existing pictures, text, logos, etc., and then determine the placeholders to paste the text and pictures from the Clipboard. Insert, resize, and reposition text boxes and Quick Tables, as necessary. Link at least one text box. Apply a document format, and then change the font name and paragraph spacing. Adjust line spacing,

paragraph spacing before and after, font size, etc., to make the document look better. If you added any outlines to text boxes, remove them.

Save the file as **Last_First_wrd06_SC2Newsletter** in your **Word Chapter 6** folder. Insert the **FileName** field into the footer. **Close** the Word window, and then submit the file as directed by your instructor.

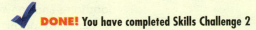 **DONE!** You have completed Skills Challenge 2

CHAPTER 7

Prepare a Document with References

- ▶ Long Word documents should include references—a cover page, a table of contents, a table of figures, and an index, for example—to help the reader locate information. Long documents can also include citations, charts, footnotes or endnotes, and odd and/or even page numbers.

- ▶ The cover page, table of contents, and table of figures go at the beginning of a long document, while words and cross-references marked in the document display in an index at the end of the document.

- ▶ In the table of figures, images and objects that contain captions are referenced by the page on which they display.

- ▶ You can format your document to have different header or footer text for the odd and even pages.

- ▶ When you change a referenced item, you can update that reference in the table of contents, table of figures, and index.

© Bloomua/Fotolia

Aspen Falls City Hall

In this chapter, you will assist Todd Austin, Tourism Director for the City of Aspen Falls, in reviewing and preparing a long document, or report. Todd approves all promotional materials related to Aspen Falls tourism. You will download a multipage report created in Word and prepare it for Mr. Austin who will then present the report to the City of Aspen Falls Planning Commission for approval.

A formal report provides an overview, problem statement, statement of purpose, research question, general research method, findings, and recommendations. The report may also include document references, known as front matter, such as a cover page, a table of contents, and a table of figures. Within the document, there may be charts, citations, and/or footnotes. At the end of the report are an index, a bibliography, and endnotes. The body of the report is typed with either single- or double-spacing—depending on space and printing needs—headings to identify sections of the report, page numbers, specific margins, and citations.

In this project, you will use Word to add document references to a report according to *The Gregg Reference Manual* (Sabin) report style guidelines. When determining required content and its format, follow the style guidelines provided by the organization requesting the report. Once you open the report, you will insert various references to polish the document so that it is presentable to the city council for their review. You will also mark items to go in an index, create cross-references, and insert and modify the index. You will also insert a chart, format a chart, and add a caption to the chart so that it can be included in a table of figures that you will insert. You will use the references currently included as footnotes and convert them to endnotes. You will add page numbers that are formatted to display with specific text for even pages and different text for odd pages.

Time to complete all 10
skills – 60 to 90 minutes

Student data file needed for this chapter:

wrd07_Tourism

You will create and save your document as:

Last_First_wrd07_Tourism

Outcome

Using the skills in this chapter, you will be able to
create long document parts such as this:

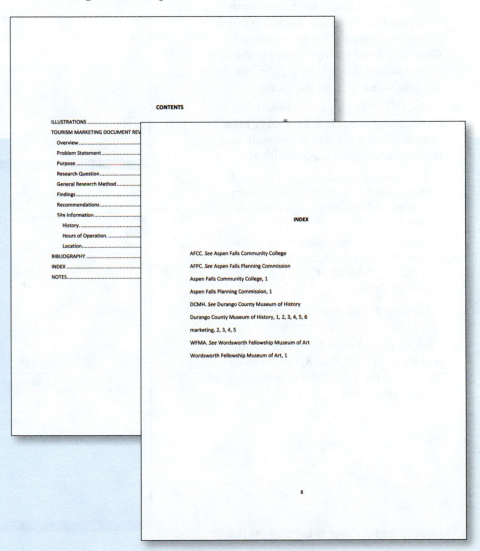

SKILLS

Skills 1-10 Training

At the end of this chapter, you will be able to:

Skill 1   Insert Cover Pages

Skill 2   Add Captions and a Table of Figures

Skill 3   Insert Charts

Skill 4   Format Charts and Update a Table of Figures

Skill 5   Insert Custom Page Numbers

Skill 6   Modify Footnote and Endnote Options

Skill 7   Mark Items for Indexes

Skill 8   Create Cross-references

Skill 9   Insert and Modify Indexes

Skill 10 Create a Table of Contents

MORE SKILLS

Skill 11 Link to Excel Worksheet Data and Charts

Skill 12 Work with Master and Subdocuments

Skill 13 Create a Table of Authorities

Skill 14 Create Bookmarks

▶ A *cover page*, also called a *title page*, is usually the first page of a formal report. It displays information such as the title and subtitle, the date, the author's name, and the company name.

▶ Word provides several built-in cover pages with fields into which you can insert your own information.

1. Start **Word 2013**, and then open **wrd07_Tourism**. Use the **Save As** dialog box to create a **New folder** named Word Chapter 7 **Save** the document in the new folder as Last_First_wrd07_Tourism Add the **FileName** field to the footer.

2. Press Ctrl + Home. On the **Insert tab**, in the **Pages group**, click the **Cover Page** button. Click the **Facet** thumbnail, and then compare your screen with **Figure 1**.

   A page break is automatically inserted along with the cover page. The cover page displays fields where you can type your own information.

3. Scroll down, if necessary, click in the *[Document title]* field, and then type TOURISM MARKETING DOCUMENT REVIEW FOR:

   The default format of the Document Title field text displays in all uppercase letters.

4. Click in the *[Document subtitle]* field, and then type DURANGO COUNTY MUSEUM OF HISTORY Compare your screen with **Figure 2**.

■ Continue to the next page to complete the skill ➤

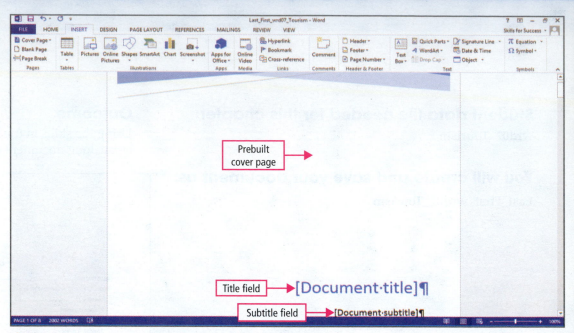

Figure 1

Figure 2

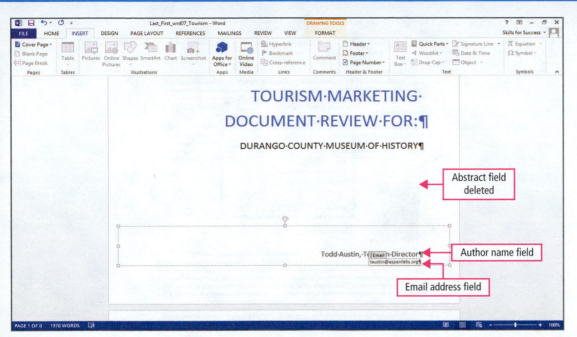

Figure 3

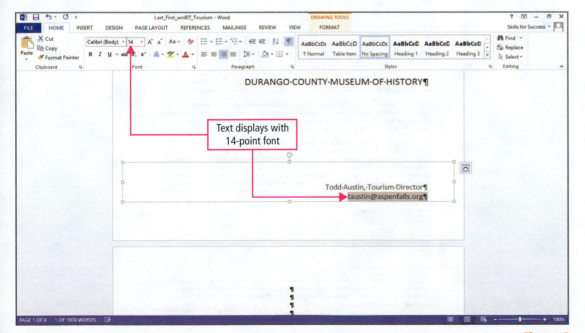

Figure 4

5. Click the border of the *Abstract* placeholder, and then press Delete .

6. Click the *[Author name]* field, and then type Todd Austin, Tourism Director

7. Click the *[Email address]* field, and then type taustin@aspenfalls.org Compare your screen with **Figure 3**.

8. At the bottom of Page 1, select the text *taustin@aspenfalls.org*, and then change the **Font Size** to **14**. Compare your screen with **Figure 4**.

9. At the top of Page 2, select the paragraph that includes *Your Name*, and then type your first and last name.

When creating a cover or title page, you should ask if the organization or instructor you are submitting the report to has a formal style guide that you should follow. That guide will specify the content, formatting, and layout that you will need to follow. Word's prebuilt cover pages may not be accepted.

10. Save 💾 the document.

■ **You have completed Skill 1 of 10**

▶ A *table of figures* contains references to figures, equations, and tables in a document. It usually includes the caption text and page number of each figure, equation, and table.

▶ In a report, the table of figures usually follows the table of contents.

1. On Page 6, select the museum door picture. On the **References tab**, in the **Captions group**, click the **Insert Caption** button. In the **Caption** dialog box, with the insertion point in the **Caption** box, add a space after *Figure 1*, and then type Museum Entrance as shown in **Figure 1**. Verify that Position displays Below selected item and the Exclude label from caption box is deselected. Click **OK**.

2. On Page 7, select the picture of the building, and then in the **Captions group**, click the **Insert Caption** button.

3. In the **Caption** dialog box, with the insertion point after the text *Figure 2*, add a space. Type Restored Building at DCMH and then press Enter. Compare your screen with **Figure 2**.

4. On Page 7, repeat the previous technique to add a caption to the picture of the stagecoach with the text DCMH Pioneer Wagon.

5. Move to the top of Page 2. Click before the first paragraph mark, and then press Enter six times. Type ILLUSTRATIONS

6. Press Enter two times, and then press Ctrl + Enter. On Page 2, apply the **Heading 1** style to the title.

   According to *The Gregg Reference Manual*, ILLUSTRATIONS is the preferred page title text.

■ **Continue to the next page to complete the skill** ➡

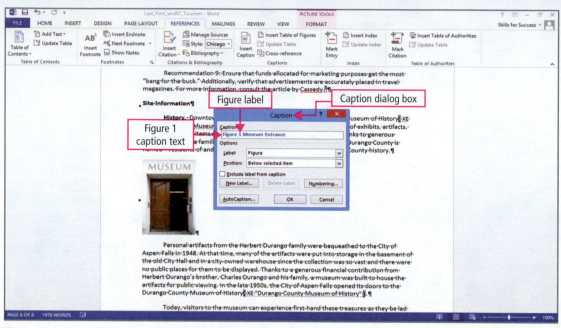

Figure 1

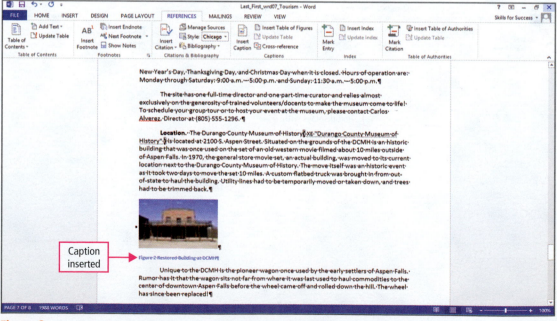

Figure 2

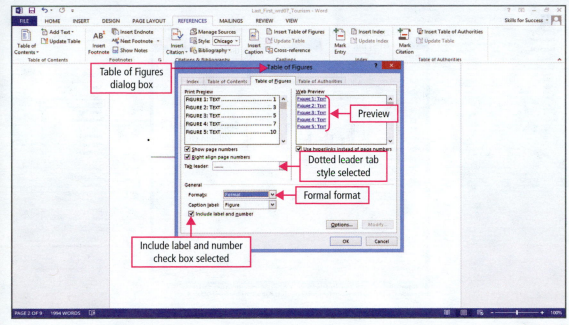

Figure 3

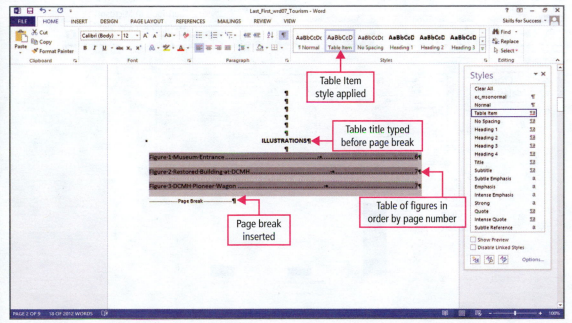

Figure 4

7. On Page 2, click the beginning of the paragraph that has the *Page Break* notation. On the **References tab**, in the **Captions group**, click the **Insert Table of Figures** button.

8. In the **Table of Figures** dialog box, click the **Tab leader arrow**, and then, if necessary, click the second item in the listing, the dotted leader style.

   According to *The Gregg Reference Manual*, the ILLUSTRATIONS page is formatted with right-aligned page numbers with dotted leaders and double-spacing.

9. Under **General**, click the **Formats arrow**, and then click the fifth item in the listing—**Formal**. Compare your screen with **Figure 3**.

10. In the **Table of Figures** dialog box, verify that the **Include label and number** check box is selected, and then click **OK**.

11. Select the paragraphs that begin *FIGURE 1* through *FIGURE 3*.

12. Click the **Home tab**, and then in the **Styles group**, click **Table Item**. Compare your screen with **Figure 4**.

    In formal reports, tables and lists are typically double-spaced.

13. On Page 7, in the **Styles group**, click the **Styles Pane Launcher**, and then apply the **Table Item** style to the *Figure 1* paragraph.

14. On Page 8, apply the **Table Item** style to the *Figure 2* and *Figure 3* paragraphs.

15. At the bottom of Page 9, delete the blank paragraph and the paragraph that contains the Page Break.

16. Save the document.

■ **You have completed Skill 2 of 10**

▶ A *chart* is a graphic representation of data in a worksheet or table. A chart can be created in Excel and then inserted into a Word document. You can create it in Word using the Chart in Microsoft Word window.

1. On Page 6, click the blank paragraph above *Recommendations*.

2. On the **Insert tab**, in the **Illustrations group**, click the **Chart** button.

3. In the **Insert Chart** dialog box, under **All Charts**, verify that **Column** is selected. Verify that the first button—**Clustered Column**—is selected as shown in **Figure 1**, and then click **OK**.

When you insert a chart, a new window, Chart in Microsoft Word window, displays above the Word document. The Word document window displays the chart, and the Chart in Microsoft Word window displays the underlying data used in the chart. The chart datasheet is edited to create a chart with your labels and data.

4. In the **Chart in Microsoft Word window**, click cell **A2**—the cell in the intersection of column A and row 2—and then type Incorrect references Press Enter, and then in cell **A3**, type Inaccurate information Press Enter, and then in cell **A4**, type Broken links

As you type, the chart is updated in Word.

5. Click cell **B1**, type Issues and then press Enter. In cell **B2**, type 24 and then press Enter. In cell **B3**, type 3 and then in cell **B4**, type 4

6. Point to the lower right corner of the blue box surrounding the data in the bottom of cell D5. With the pointer, drag to the left so that the blue box surrounds the range B2 to B4. Compare with **Figure 2**.

■ **Continue to the next page to complete the skill** ➤

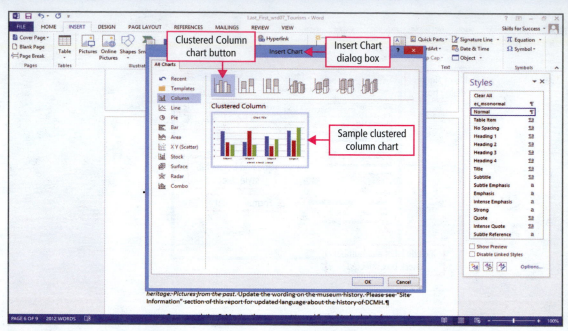

Figure 1

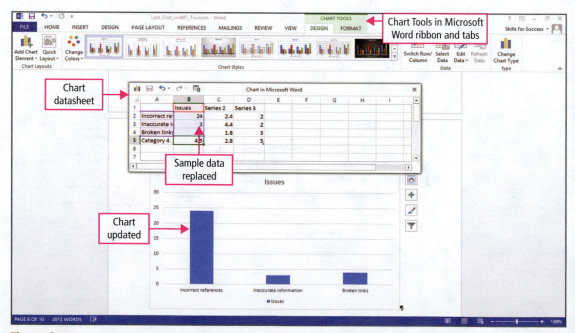

Figure 2

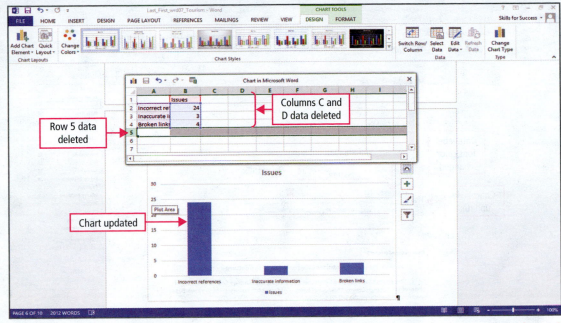

Row 5 data deleted

Columns C and D data deleted

Chart updated

Figure 3

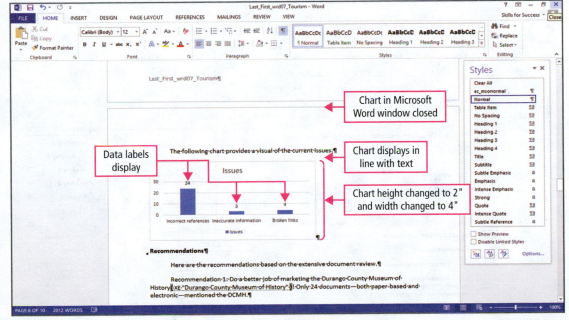

Chart in Microsoft Word window closed

Data labels display

Chart displays in line with text

Chart height changed to 2" and width changed to 4"

Figure 4

7. Position the ⬇ pointer over the column letter C. Drag to the right to select the columns C and D. Right-click one of the column headers, and then click **Delete**.

   In the Chart in Microsoft Word window, each of the three cells within the blue border are data points. A ***data point*** is a value that originates in a datasheet cell. Data points that are related to one another form a ***data series***.

8. Position the pointer over the row number 5. With the ➡ pointer, right-click, and then click **Delete**. Compare your screen with **Figure 3**.

9. **Close** ☒ the **Chart in Microsoft Word window** to return to the Word document.

   The chart includes data from the selected range in the Chart in Microsoft Word window.

10. Click the chart border, if necessary. On the **Format tab**, in the **Size group**, change the **Height** to 2" and the **Width** to 4"

11. To the right of the chart object, click the **Chart Elements** button ➕, and then select the **Data Labels** check box. Click the document, and then compare your screen with **Figure 4**.

12. **Save** 🖫 the document.

- **You have completed Skill 3 of 10**

► A table of figures displays the page reference of figures and their captions. If you change your document and insert a new picture and/or caption and place it in the document before an existing figure, the captions automatically get renumbered in the correct order in the document. However, the captions in the table of figures will not update automatically.

► If you insert, delete, or move captions and/or figures after a table of figures has been inserted into the document, you need to update the table of figures to reflect the new page location.

1. On Page 6, select the border of the chart. On the **Chart Tools Design tab**, in the **Chart Styles group**, click the fourth style in the gallery—**Style 4**.

2. In the chart, select the data label—the number *24*—that displays in the first blue data series. On the **Home tab**, in the **Font group**, click the **Font Color arrow**, and then select **Automatic**. Compare your screen with **Figure 1**.

3. If necessary, select the chart border. On the **References tab**, in the **Captions group**, click the **Insert Caption** button. In the displayed **Caption** dialog box, with the insertion point in the **Caption** box, add a space after *Figure 1*, type Documentation Issues and then click **OK**.

    Because the chart displays before the other figures in the report, the figure caption for the chart will display as Figure 1. The other figures will automatically renumber in sequence.

4. Apply the **Table Item** style to the *Figure 1* caption, and then compare your screen with **Figure 2**.

■ Continue to the next page to complete the skill ➤

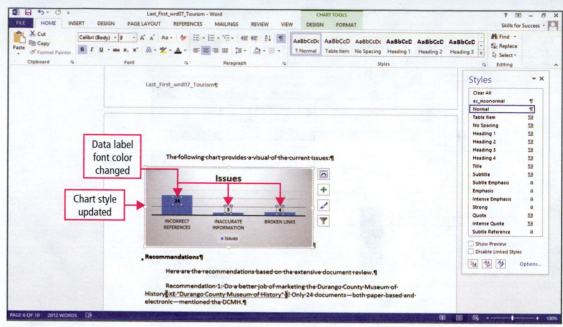

Figure 1

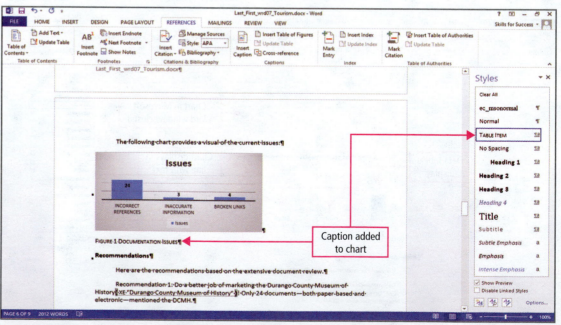

Figure 2

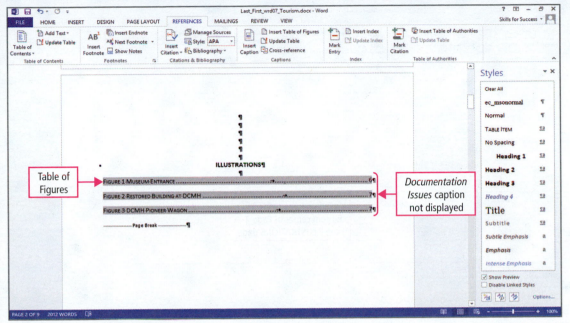

Figure 3

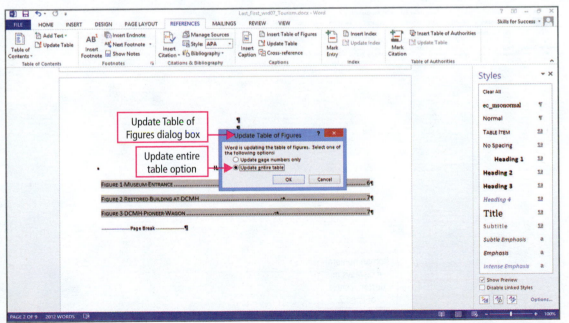

Figure 4

5. On Page 2, click the paragraph that begins *Figure 1* to select the Illustrations/Table of Figures, and then compare your screen with **Figure 3**.

> The changes made previously are not yet reflected in the table.

6. On the **References tab**, in the **Captions group**, click the **Update Table** button.

7. In the **Update Table of Figures** dialog box, select the **Update entire table** option button as shown in **Figure 4**, and then click **OK**.

> In the Update Table of Figures dialog box, the first option updates the page number reference for each figure. The second option—Update entire table—updates the captions and sorts the table by page number.

> The table is sorted by page number order.

8. Select the paragraph that begins *Figure 1* through the paragraph that ends *Figure 4*, and then apply the **Table Item** style.

9. **Close** ✕ the **Styles** pane.

10. **Save** 🖫 the document.

■ **You have completed Skill 4 of 10**

▶ Word contains several built-in page number styles.

▶ According to *The Gregg Reference Manual*, Roman numeral page numbers should display in the bottom center of preliminary pages such as CONTENTS and ILLUSTRATIONS. Arabic numbers should display at the bottom of all report text pages.

1. Press Ctrl + Home. On the **Insert tab**, in the **Header & Footer group**, click the **Page Number** button, click **Bottom of Page**, and then select **Plain Number 2**.

2. Scroll to the bottom of Page 2, and then compare your screen with **Figure 1**. **Close** the **Header & Footer tab**.

   The Table of Figures/Illustrations page currently displays as 1, and the cover page is not counted.

3. In the middle of the ILLUSTRATIONS page, click the beginning of the *Page Break* notation. On the **Page Layout tab**, in the **Page Setup group**, click the **Breaks** button, and then click **Next Page**.

4. On the blank page after the ILLUSTRATIONS table, press Delete two times to remove the *Page Break* notation and the extra paragraph.

5. At the bottom of Page 2, the ILLUSTRATIONS page, double-click the page number to open the **Header & Footer Tools Design tab**. In the **Header & Footer group**, click the **Page Number** button, and then click **Format Page Numbers**.

6. In the **Page Number Format dialog box**, click the **Number format arrow**, select **i, ii, iii**, select the **Continue from previous section** option button, and then click **OK**. Scroll to the bottom of Page 2, and then compare your screen with **Figure 2**.

■ **Continue to the next page to complete the skill** ➤

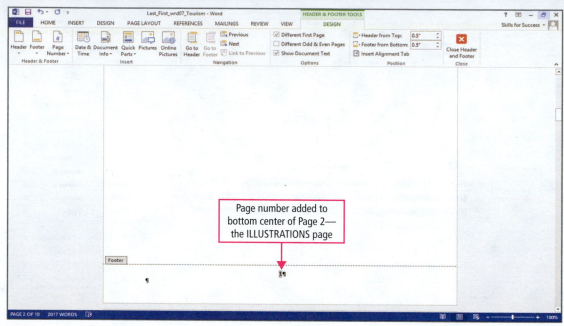

Page number added to bottom center of Page 2— the ILLUSTRATIONS page

Figure 1

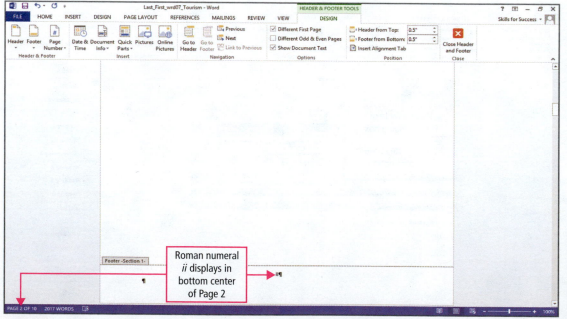

Roman numeral *ii* displays in bottom center of Page 2

Figure 2

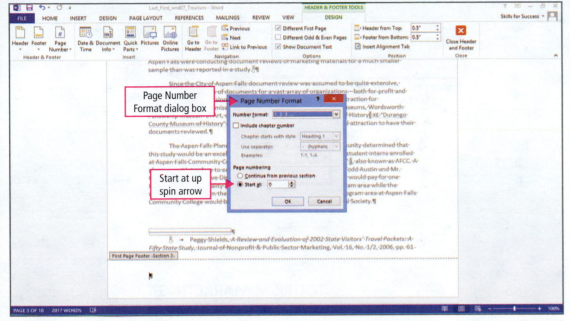

Figure 3

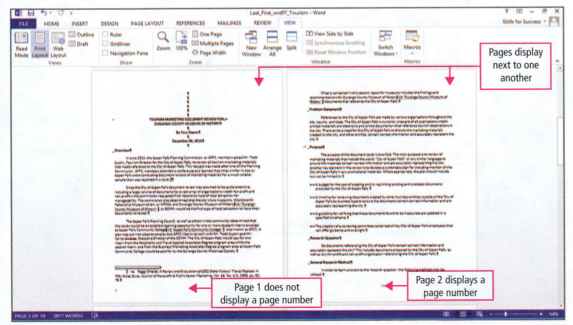

Figure 4

7. Scroll to the bottom of Page 3, and notice a page number does not display.

Page numbers must be set for each section in the document. While you have set page numbers for the first section, you have not done so in the next section.

8. On Page 3, double-click in the Footer area. On the **Header & Footer Tools Design tab**, in the **Navigation group**, click the **Link to Previous** button to turn the feature off.

When using the Link to Previous option, page numbers continue with the next page number.

9. On the **Header & Footer Tools tab**, in the **Header & Footer group**, click the **Page Number** button, and then click **Format Page Numbers**. Compare your screen with **Figure 3**.

10. In the **Page Number Format** dialog box, under **Page numbering**, click the **Start at up spin arrow** one time, and then click **OK**. In the **Close group**, click the **Close Header and Footer** button.

11. On the **View tab**, in the **Zoom group**, click the **Multiple Pages** button, and then scroll to display Pages 1 and 2. Compare your screen with **Figure 4**.

12. In the **Zoom group**, click the **100%** button.

13. On the ILLUSTRATIONS page, select Figure 1. On the **References tab**, in the **Captions group**, click the **Update Table** button. In the **Update Table of Figures** dialog box, click **OK** to update the page numbers.

14. Save 🖫 the document.

■ **You have completed Skill 5 of 10**

▶ Recall that footnotes display at the bottom of the page on which the reference occurs.

▶ *Endnotes* display these references toward the end of the document.

1. Scroll through the report to view the footnotes.

2. On the **References tab**, in the **Footnotes group**, click the **Footnote & Endnote Dialog Box Launcher** ▣. In the **Footnote and Endnote** dialog box, under **Location**, click **Convert**. Compare your screen with **Figure 1**.

   The Convert Notes dialog box converts existing footnotes to endnotes or existing endnotes to footnotes. Here, the option to convert endnotes to footnotes is dimmed because the report currently has no endnotes.

3. In the **Convert Notes** dialog box, verify that the **Convert all footnotes to endnotes** option button is selected, and then click **OK**.

4. In the **Footnote and Endnote** dialog box, click **Close**.

5. Press Ctrl + End, and then compare your screen with **Figure 2**.

   The three footnotes display as endnotes below a solid line after the Bibliography in the report. The endnotes line cannot be removed from the document.

6. Right-click one of the endnote reference numbers, and then click **Note Options**.

7. In the **Footnote and Endnote** dialog box, under **Format**, click the **Number format arrow**, and then select **1, 2, 3**. Click **Apply**.

■ **Continue to the next page to complete the skill** ➡

Figure 1

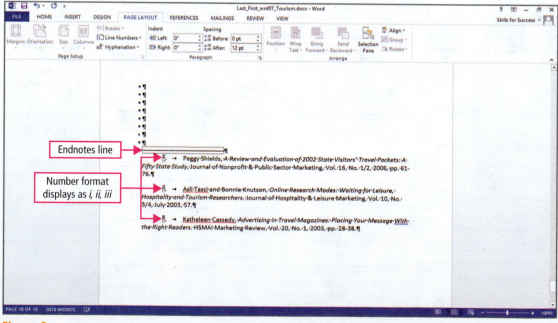

Figure 2

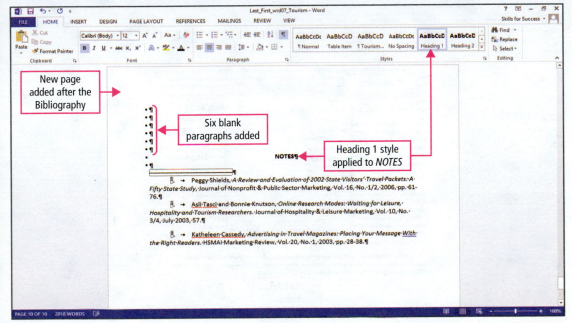

Figure 3

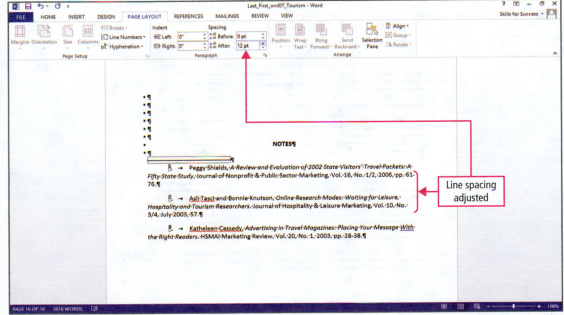

Figure 4

8. On Page 9, point to the left of the first blank paragraph above the endnotes line. Place the insertion point to the left of the paragraph.

9. Press `Ctrl` + `Enter`. Press `Enter` six times, type NOTES and then press `Enter`. Apply the **Heading 1** style to the *NOTES* heading, and then compare your screen with **Figure 3**.

10. Select the endnote that begins *Peggy Shields*, and then on the **Page Layout tab**, in the **Paragraph group**, click the **Spacing After up spin arrow** two times to display **12 pt**. Compare your screen with **Figure 4**.

    According to *The Gregg Reference Manual*, Notes pages are formatted with a double space between endnotes. A period and a tab separate the endnote number from the endnote reference.

11. **Save** the document.

■ **You have completed Skill 6 of 10**

▶ An *index* displays a list of important words and phrases found in a document along with their corresponding page numbers.

▶ An *index entry field* identifies important words, phrases, or cross-references that will be placed in the index. By marking index entries with index entry fields, you provide the information needed for Word to build the index.

1. On Page 3, in the paragraph that begins *In June 2014,* select the first occurrence of the word *marketing*.

2. On the **References tab**, in the **Index group**, click the **Mark Entry** button.

3. In the **Mark Index Entry** dialog box, verify that the **Main entry** box displays *marketing* as shown in **Figure 1**.

   Selected text automatically displays in the Main entry box when you open the Mark Index Entry dialog box.

4. In the **Mark Index Entry** dialog box, click **Mark All**.

   In the document, the marked entry field displays as { XE "marketing" }.

   All occurrences of the word *marketing* on each page are marked in the document. Index entries display in an index located at the back of formal reports. In this case, the word *marketing* would display in the index along with its corresponding page number(s) where it is located in the document. The page number is referenced only once if multiple index entries occur on the same page.

5. Click the document as shown in **Figure 2**. In the same paragraph, select the first occurrence of *Aspen Falls Planning Commission,* and then click the **Mark Index Entry** dialog box.

■ **Continue to the next page to complete the skill** ➤

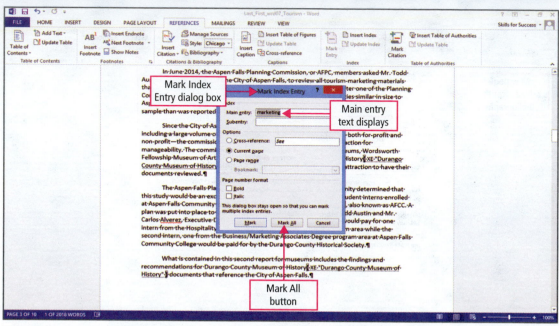

Figure 1

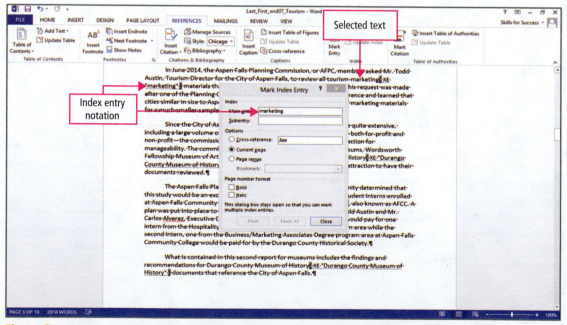

Figure 2

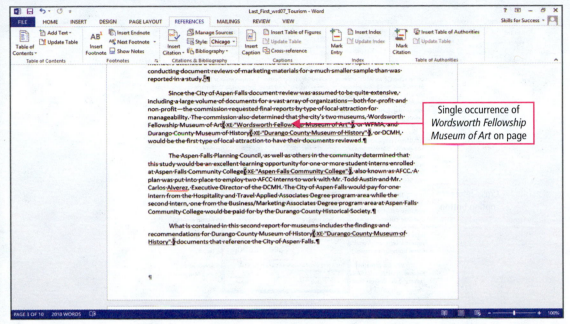

Single occurrence of *Wordsworth Fellowship Museum of Art* on page

Figure 3

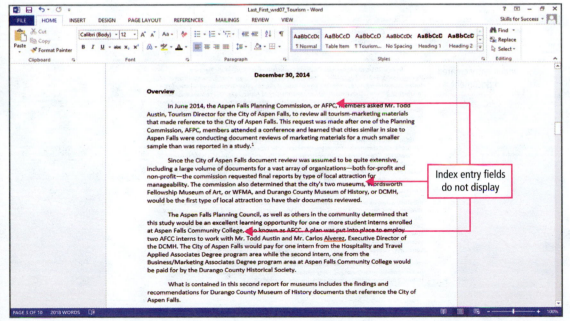

Index entry fields do not display

Figure 4

6. Verify that the **Main entry** box displays *Aspen Falls Planning Commission*, and then click **Mark All**.

> The dialog box can remain open so you can move between the document and the dialog box. When you select text in the document to mark as an index entry and then click in the dialog box, the text display updates in the dialog box.

> If the dialog box covers any document text, point to the dialog box title and drag the box out of the way.

7. Click the document. On Page 3, locate the paragraph that begins *Since the City*. Select the text *Wordsworth Fellowship Museum of Art*.

8. Click the **Mark Index Entry** dialog box. Verify the selected text displays in the **Main entry** box, click **Mark**, and then click **Close**. Compare your screen with **Figure 3**.

9. On the **Home tab**, in the **Editing group**, click the **Find** button to open the **Navigation** pane. In the **Navigation** pane, type marketing to highlight each occurrence of the word in the document.

> The word *marketing* displays in the Navigation pane and displays with a yellow highlight throughout the document.

> *Marketing* is not marked in headings or citations.

10. Click the **Next Search Results** button to continue verifying throughout the document that the Mark All command performed correctly. **Close** ⊠ the Navigation pane.

11. On Page 3, **Hide** ¶ the formatting marks, and then compare your screen with **Figure 4**.

> Index entries are no longer visible because they are nonprinting characters.

12. **Save** 🖫 the document.

■ **You have completed Skill 7 of 10**

► A **cross-reference** is an index entry associated with a different word or phrase that is similar in context to the original index entry.

► A cross-reference is included in the index to help you locate the original index entry.

1. **Show** ¶ the formatting marks. On Page 3, locate the paragraph that begins *In June 2014*, and then select the first occurrence of *AFPC*.

2. On the **References tab**, in the **Index group**, click the **Mark Entry** button.

3. In the **Mark Index Entry** dialog box, in the **Main entry** box, verify that *AFPC* displays.

4. In the **Mark Index Entry** dialog box under **Options**, select the **Cross-reference** option button.

5. Verify that the insertion point displays to the right of *See*, and then type Aspen Falls Planning Commission Compare your screen with **Figure 1**.

   In the index, a cross-reference to *Aspen Falls Planning Commission* will be created for the *AFPC* index entry.

6. Click **Mark**, and then close the **Mark Index Entry** dialog box. Compare your screen with **Figure 2**.

7. On Page 3, in the paragraph that begins *Since the City*, select the text *WFMA*. In the **Index group**, click the **Mark Entry** button.

■ Continue to the next page to complete the skill

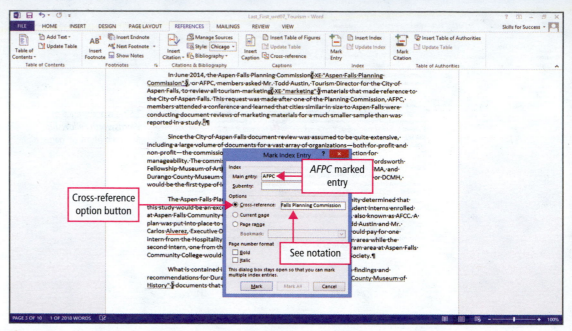

Figure 1

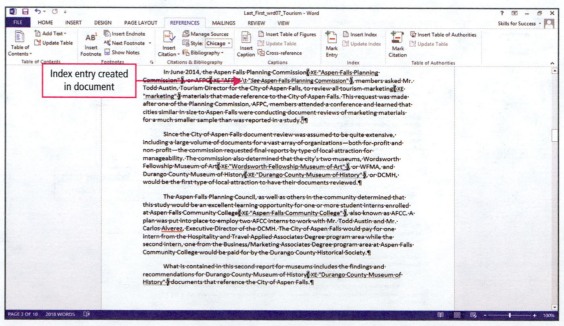

Figure 2

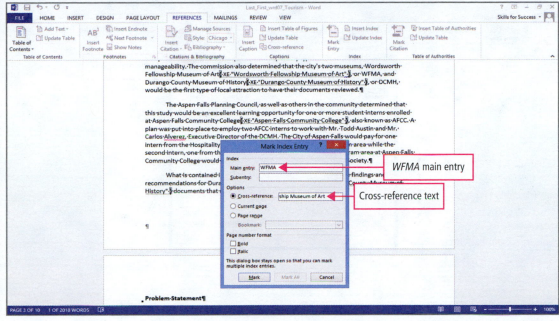

WFMA main entry

Cross-reference text

Figure 3

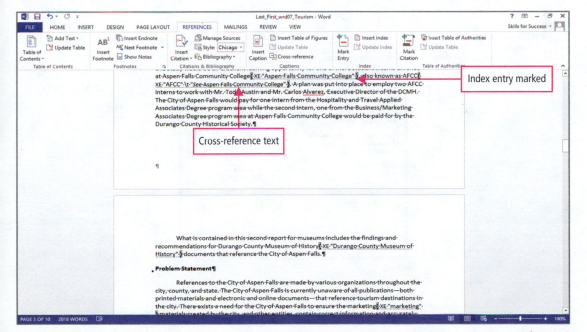

Index entry marked

Cross-reference text

Figure 4

8. In the **Mark Index Entry** dialog box, in the **Main entry** box, verify that *WFMA* displays. Under **Options**, select the **Cross-reference** option button. Verify that the insertion point displays to the right of *See*, and then type Wordsworth Fellowship Museum of Art as shown in **Figure 3**, and then click **Mark**.

9. Click the document. On Page 3, in the same paragraph, select *DCMH*, and then click in the **Mark Index Entry** dialog box.

10. In the **Mark Index Entry** dialog box, verify that *DCMH* displays in the **Main entry** box. Under **Options**, select the **Cross-reference** option button. Verify that the insertion point displays to the right of *See*, type Durango County Museum of History and then click **Mark**.

11. Click the document. On Page 3, in the paragraph that begins *The Aspen Falls*, select *AFCC*, and then click in the **Mark Index Entry** dialog box.

12. In the displayed **Mark Index Entry** dialog box, verify that *AFCC* displays in the **Main entry** box. Under **Options**, select the **Cross-reference** option button. Verify that the insertion point displays to the right of *See*, type Aspen Falls Community College and then click **Mark**.

13. **Close** the **Mark Index Entry** dialog box, and then compare your screen with **Figure 4**.

14. On Page 9, position the insertion point before the Page Break notation, and then press Ctrl + Enter to insert a page break.

   A new page is created between the Bibliography and the Notes pages.

15. **Save** 💾 the document.

■ **You have completed Skill 8 of 10**

**WRD 7-9
VIDEO**

▶ After you mark each index entry in the document, you use the Index dialog box to create and format the index.

▶ An index uses fields to display each entry and page number. If a document is changed after the index is created, the field(s) must be updated so that the correct entries and page numbers display.

1. On Page 10, press [Enter] six times. Type INDEX and then press [Enter] three times. Click in the *INDEX* heading, and then apply the **Heading 1** style.

2. On Page 10, select all the paragraphs, and then apply single-spacing and remove the spacing after the paragraphs.

3. On Page 10, position the insertion point before the Page Break notation, and then click.

4. Click the **References tab**. In the **Index group**, click the **Insert Index** button to display the **Index** dialog box, and then compare your screen with **Figure 1**.

    There are two types of indexes: ***indented***, which places marked entries and subentries on separate lines with spacing before each indexed item, and ***run-in***, which places as many marked entries and subentries for the indexed item on one line as possible.

5. In the **Index** dialog box, click the **Formats arrow**, and then select **From template**. Select the **Run-in Type** option. Click the **Columns down spin arrow** one time. Compare your screen with **Figure 2**, and then click **OK**.

    In the new index, the word *marketing* displays on pages 1, 2, 3, 4, and 5.

■ **Continue to the next page to complete the skill**

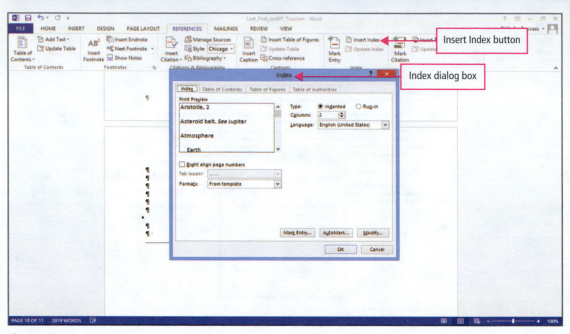

Figure 1

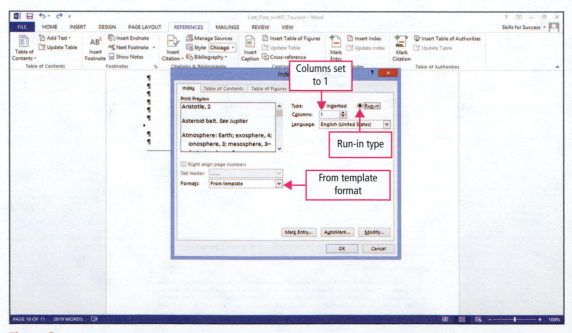

Figure 2

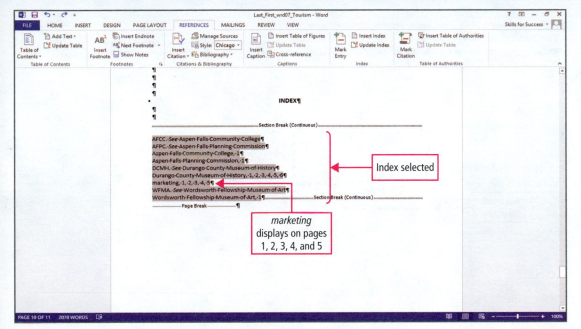

Figure 3

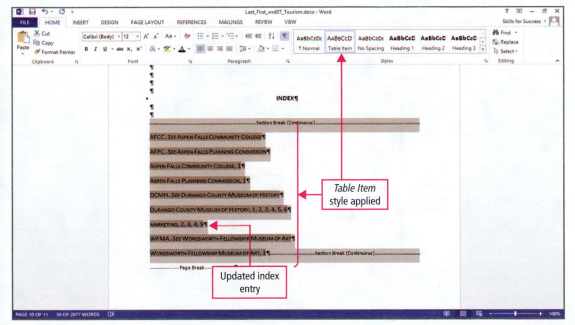

Figure 4

6. On Page 3, in the paragraph that begins *In June 2014,* Delete the index entry field { XE "marketing" }.

7. On Page 10, notice that the *marketing* index entry still displays on Pages 1, 2, 3, 4, and 5 of the report.

8. On Page 10, click the word *marketing* to select the entire index, and then compare your screen with **Figure 3**.

9. On the **References tab**, in the **Index group**, click the **Update Index** button.

> The *marketing* index entry no longer displays a reference to Page 1. Each time an item is added or removed from the index or content is added to or deleted from the document, you need to update the index to reflect current page numbers.

10. In the index, select the paragraph that begins *AFCC* through the paragraph that begins *Wordsworth,* and then apply the **Table Item** style. Compare your completed index with **Figure 4**.

11. Save 🔲 the document.

■ **You have completed Skill 9 of 10**

▶ A *table of contents* displays entries and page numbers for a document's headings and *subheadings*—entries that are part of a broader entry.

▶ To include an item in the table of contents, assign the Heading 1 style to your main headings, the Heading 2 style to your subheadings, and so on.

▶ If the document is changed after the table of contents was created, you need to update the table of contents.

1. At the top of Page 2, type CONTENTS and then press Ctrl + Enter.

2. At the top of Page 2, click before the word *CONTENTS*, press Enter six times, and then press End.

3. Press Enter two times as shown in **Figure 1**.

4. On the **References tab**, in the **Table of Contents group**, click the **Table of Contents** button. Click **Custom Table of Contents**. Compare your screen with **Figure 2**.

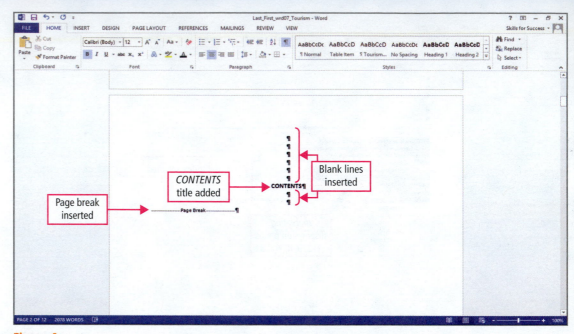

Figure 1

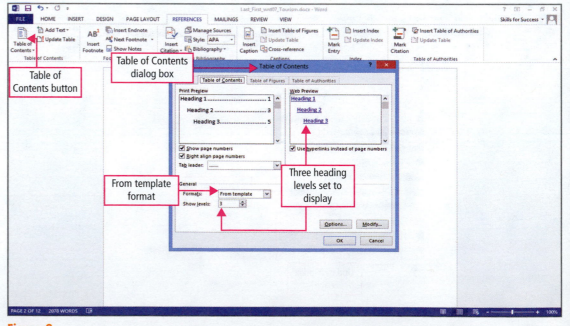

Figure 2

■ **Continue to the next page to complete the skill** ➡

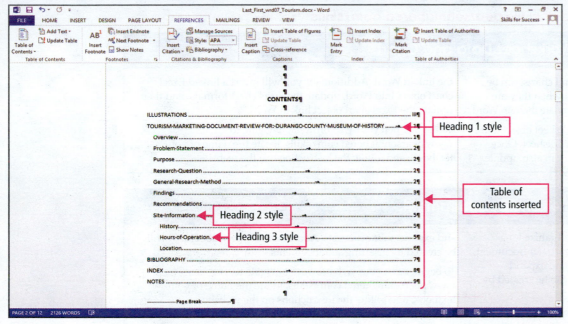

Figure 3

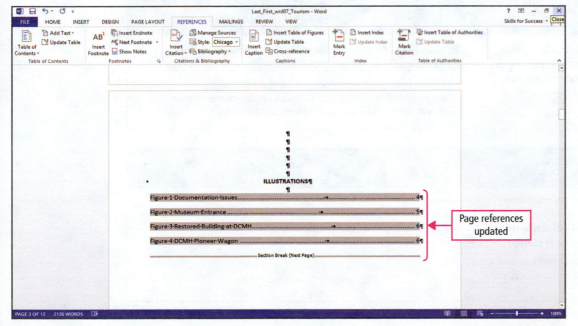

Figure 4

5. In the **Table of Contents** dialog box, review the settings, and then click **OK**. Compare your screen with **Figure 3**.

> The table of contents lists all of the text assigned the Heading 1, Heading 2, and Heading 3 styles with the page numbers where the text is located. In this report, five headings have been assigned the Heading 1 style.

> The indented entries indicate they are subheadings—Heading 2 and Heading 3.

> According to *The Gregg Reference Manual* report guidelines, *CONTENTS* should be formatted with double-spacing and a combination of capital letters and lowercase letters.

6. On Page 3, right-click *Figure 1*, and then click **Update Field**. In the message box, click **OK**. Compare your screen with **Figure 4**.

7. On the **File tab**, in the **Info tab**, click the **Properties** button, and then click **Advanced Properties**.

8. In the **Properties** dialog box, on the **Summary tab**, in the **Author** box, type Todd Austin and then press Enter.

9. In the upper left corner, click the arrow to return to the document. On Page 1, verify that *Todd Austin* displays above the e-mail address.

10. **Save** the document.

11. **Close** ☒ the **Word** window. Submit the file as directed by your instructor.

✔ **DONE!** You have completed Skill 10 of 10, and your document is complete!

More Skills

The following More Skills are located at **www.pearsonhighered.com/skills**

More Skills Link to Excel Worksheet Data and Charts

Objects created in Excel, such as worksheets and charts, can be linked and added to a Word document so that when they are updated in Excel, you also have the option to update them in Word.

In More Skills 11, you will insert an Excel worksheet object that contains a link in Word to the original Excel worksheet. Once you update the linked Excel worksheet object, you can also update the link in Word. Additionally, you will insert a linked Excel chart object into Word, update the Excel chart formats, and then update the Excel chart object link in Word.

To begin, open your web browser, navigate to www.pearsonhighered.com/skills, locate the name of your textbook, and follow the instructions on the website.

More Skills Work with Master and Subdocuments

Word's Outline view can be used to view and organize long documents. In Outline view, you can show the master document, create and insert subdocuments, and collapse and expand subdocuments. Additionally, new documents can be created by inserting subdocuments into a document.

In More Skills 12, you will use the Outline view to show the master document, create and insert subdocuments, and collapse and expand subdocuments. Additionally, a new document will be created by inserting subdocuments.

To begin, open your web browser, navigate to www.pearsonhighered.com/skills, locate the name of your textbook, and follow the instructions on the website.

More Skills Create a Table of Authorities

A table of authorities lists legal cases, statutes and laws, and other authorities that are referenced in a document's citations. Before building a table of authorities, you need to mark the citations that will be used to create the table's entries.

In More Skills 13, you will insert legal citations, mark the citations, and then create a table of authorities.

To begin, open your web browser, navigate to www.pearsonhighered.com/skills, locate the name of your textbook, and follow the instructions on the website.

More Skills Create Bookmarks

A bookmark is a special nonprinting character inserted into a document so that you can quickly navigate to that point in the document. Bookmark names should briefly describe their destination and should not include spaces between words.

In More Skills 14, you will create bookmarks to headings and a picture. You will also change the sort order of bookmark names in the Bookmark dialog box.

To begin, open your web browser, navigate to www.pearsonhighered.com/skills, locate the name of your textbook, and follow the instructions on the website.

Please note that there are no additional projects to accompany the More Skills Projects, and they are not covered in End-of-Chapter projects.

The following table summarizes the **SKILLS AND PROCEDURES** covered in this chapter.

Skills Number	Task	Step	Icon	Keyboard Shortcut
1	Insert cover pages	Insert tab → Pages group → Cover Page button	Cover Page	
2	Insert captions	References tab → Captions group → Insert Caption button		
2	Insert a table of figures	References tab → Captions group → Insert Table of Figures button	Insert Table of Figures	
3	Insert charts	Insert tab → Illustrations group → Chart button → Select desired chart type		
4	Format charts	Select chart border → Chart Tools Design tab → Select desired formats		
4	Update a table of figures	References tab → Captions group → Update Table button	Update Table	
5	Create page numbers at bottom center of page	Insert tab → Header & Footer group → Page Number button → Bottom of Page → Select page format		
6	Convert footnotes and endnotes	References tab → Footnotes group → Footnote & Endnote Dialog Box Launcher → Convert → Convert all footnotes to endnotes option button		
7	Mark index entries	References tab → Index group → Mark Entry button → Mark		Alt + Shift + X
7	Mark all index entries	References tab → Index group → Mark Entry button → Mark All		
8	Create cross-references	References tab → Index group → Mark Entry button → Select Cross-reference option button → Mark		
9	Insert indexes	References tab → Index group → Insert Index button	Insert Index	
9	Update indexes	References tab → Index group → Update Index button	Update Index	
10	Create a table of contents	References tab → Table of Contents group → Table of Contents button → Built-In gallery → Select desired table of contents style		

Key Terms

Online Help Skills

1. Start **Word 2013**, and then in the upper right corner of the start page, click the **Help** button ?.

2. In the **Word Help Search online help** box, click and then type apa Press Enter.

3. In the search result list, click **APA, MLA, Chicago: Automatically format bibliographies**, scroll down, and then compare your screen with **Figure 1**.

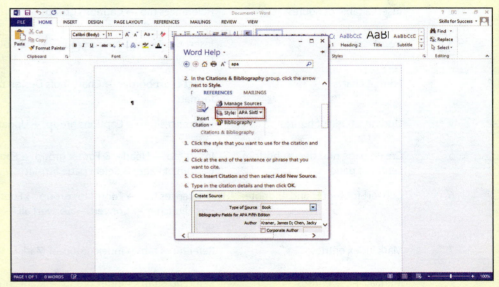

Figure 1

4. Read the article to answer the following question: How can you use Word 2013 to update an APA citation that has no title in the citation?

Matching

Match each term in the second column with its correct definition in the first column by writing the letter of the term on the blank line in front of the correct definition.

___ **1.** Also called a *title page*, this is usually the first page of a report that displays document information such as the title and subtitle, the date, the document author's name, and the company name.

___ **2.** A part of a formal report that contains references to figures, equations, and tables in the document and usually includes the caption text and page number of each figure, equation, and table.

___ **3.** A graphic representation of the data in a worksheet or table.

___ **4.** A part of a formal report that displays references toward the end of the document.

___ **5.** Important words, phrases, or cross-references that will go in the index.

___ **6.** An index entry associated with a different word or phrase that is similar in context to the original index entry.

___ **7.** A list of words and phrases found in a document along with their corresponding page numbers.

___ **8.** An index that places marked entries and subentries on separate lines with spacing before each indexed item.

___ **9.** A part of a formal report that displays entries and page numbers for a document's headings and subheadings.

___ **10.** An entry in a table of contents that is part of a broader entry.

A Chart

B Cross-reference

C Cover page

D Endnote

E Indented index

F Index

G Index entry field

H Subheading

I Table of contents

J Table of figures

Multiple Choice

Choose the correct answer.

1. The location on a built-in cover page where the author, title, and subtitle entries, for example, are entered.
   A. Database
   B. Field
   C. Report Heading

2. The page numbering option used to display the next page number in sequence when using multiple section breaks.
   A. Continue from previous section
   B. Different First Page
   C. Next number

3. The button used to change a label for a selected figure or table.
   A. Insert Caption
   B. Insert Label
   C. Picture

4. The name of the window that displays above the Word document when creating a chart in Word.
   A. Chart in Microsoft Word
   B. Excel
   C. Insert Chart

5. The Word feature used to move a reference from one of the last pages of the document to the bottom of the page where the citation is made.
   A. Convert all footnotes to endnotes
   B. Convert all endnotes to footnotes
   C. Swap footnotes and endnotes

6. The button in the Mark Index Entry dialog box used to identify every occurrence of a word in the document.
   A. Identify
   B. Mark
   C. Mark All

7. The word in the Mark Index Entry dialog box that displays before a cross-reference.
   A. Cross-reference
   B. Mark
   C. See

8. The Word feature used to display cross-references at the end of a document.
   A. Footnote
   B. Index
   C. Table of contents

9. A type of index that places as many marked entries and subentries for the indexed item on one line as possible.
   A. Indented
   B. Run-in
   C. Subheaded

10. The option in the Update Table of Contents dialog box used to change all items that have been modified in the table of contents.
    A. Update All
    B. Update Entire Table
    C. Update Page Numbers Only

Topics for Discussion

1. What are three advantages of preparing a formal report within Word? Why?

2. According to *The Gregg Reference Manual*, what are the parts of a formal report? How can you use Word to prepare them?

Skills Review

To complete this project, you will need the following file:

- wrd07_SRHighland

You will save your document as:

- Last_First_wrd07_SRHighland

1. Start **Word 2013**. Open **wrd07_SRHighland**. **Save** the file in your **Word Chapter 7** folder as Last_First_wrd07_SRHighland On Page 3, replace *Your Name* with your name.

2. On the **Insert tab**, in the **Pages group**, click **Cover Page**, and then select **Grid**. Click the *[Document Title]* field placeholder. Type HIGHLAND LAKE PROPOSAL Delete the **Abstract** text box as shown in **Figure 1**.

3. On Page 3, click the second blank paragraph below *ILLUSTRATIONS*. On the **References tab**, in the **Captions group**, click the **Insert Table of Figures** button. In the **Table of Figures** dialog box, select the **Formal Format**, and then click **OK**. Compare your screen with **Figure 2**.

4. On the **Insert tab**, in the **Header & Footer group**, click the **Page Number** button, click **Bottom of Page**, and then click **Plain Number 2**.

5. On Page 5, double-click the page number. Right-click the page number, and then click **Format Page Numbers**. Change the **Number format** to **1, 2, 3**, click **OK**, and then change the **Start at value** to **1**. Click **OK**. On the **Header & Footer Tools Design tab**, in the **Navigation group**, click the **Link to Previous** button. **Close** the **Footer**.

6. On Page 7, click the first blank paragraph. On the **Insert tab**, in the **Illustrations group**, click the **Chart** button. In the **Insert Chart** dialog box, click **Pie**, and then click **OK**.

7. In cell **B1**, type Use Press Enter. Type 70% Press Enter. Type 30% Press Enter.

8. In cell **A2**, type Human Press Enter. Type Wildlife/Preservation Press Enter.

9. Delete rows 4 and 5. Close the **Chart in Microsoft Word** window. Select the chart border. On the **Format tab**, change the **Shape Height** to 1.5" Change the **Shape Width** to 3"

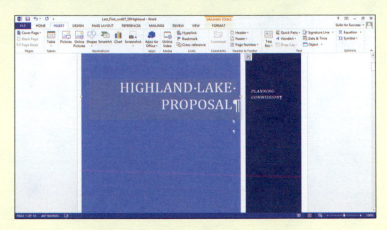

Figure 1

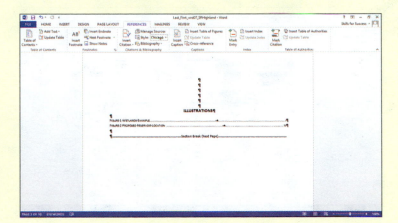

Figure 2

➤ Continue to the next page to complete this Skills Review

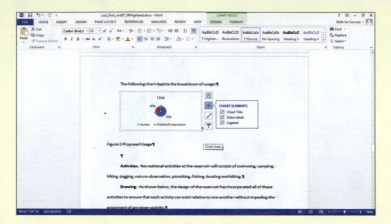

Figure 3

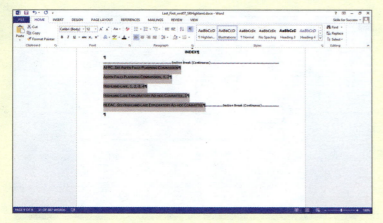

Figure 4

10. With the chart selected, on the **References tab**, in the **Captions group**, click the **Insert Caption** button. In the **Caption** dialog box, add a space, type Proposed Usage The **Exclude label from caption** should be deselected, and the **Position** should be set to **Below** selected item. Click **OK**. Apply the **HighlandCaption** style to the *Figure 2* paragraph.

11. In the pie chart, click the *Human* slice—blue. Click the **Chart Elements** button. Select the **Data Labels** box. Compare your screen with **Figure 3**.

12. On Page 3, right-click the text *Figure 1*, and then click **Update Field**. In the **Update Table of Figures** dialog box, select **Update entire table**, and then click **OK**. Apply the **Illustrations** style to the captions *Figure 1* through *Figure 3*.

13. On Page 4, in the paragraph that begins *In February*, select **Aspen Falls Planning Commission**. On the **References tab**, in the **Index group**, click the **Mark Entry** button. In the **Mark Index Entry** dialog box, click **Mark All**.

14. In the same paragraph, select **AFPC**. In the **Mark Index Entry** dialog box, select the **Cross-reference** option button, type Aspen Falls Planning Commission click **Mark**, and then click **Close**.

15. On Page 9, click the second blank paragraph below *INDEX*. In the **Index group**, click the **Insert Index** button. In the **Index** dialog box, select the **Run-in type** option button. Verify the **Columns** are set to **1**, and then click **OK**.

16. On the **References tab**, click the **Footnotes Box Launcher**, and then click **Convert**. Click **OK**, and then click **Close**. On Page 10, Delete the *Page Break* notation through the end of the document. On Page 7, at the end of the *Specifications* paragraph, Delete the *Page Break* notation.

17. On Page 2, position the insertion point in the second blank paragraph below *CONTENTS*. On the **References tab**, in the **Table of Contents group**, click the **Table of Contents** button, click **Custom Table of Contents**, and then click **OK**.

18. On Page 3, right-click the text *Figure 1*, click **Update Field**, and then click **OK**.

19. On Page 9, right-click the text *AFPC*, and then click **Update Field**. Select the *Index* entries, and then apply the **Illustrations** style to the paragraphs *AFPC* through *HLEAC*. Compare your screen with **Figure 4**.

20. **Save** the document. **Close** the Word window. Submit the file as directed by your instructor.

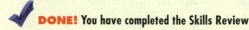

DONE! You have completed the Skills Review

Skills Assessment 1

To complete this project, you will need the following file:

- wrd07_SA1Expansion

You will save your document as:

- Last_First_wrd07_SA1Expansion

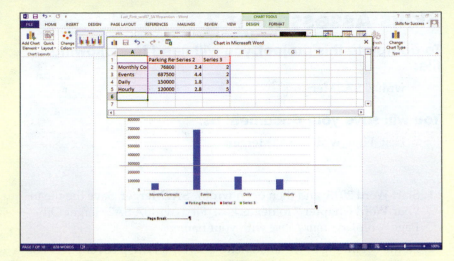

Figure 1

1. Start **Word 2013**, and then open **wrd07_SA1Expansion**. **Save** the file in your **Word Chapter 7** folder as Last_First_wrd07_SA1Expansion On Page 3, replace *Your Name* with your name.

2. At the beginning of the document, insert the **Whisp** cover page. For the *document title*, type PARKING LOT EXPANSION For the *date*, select **May 21**, **2014**. For the *author* field, replace *Skills for Success* with Your Name

3. Insert the **Plain Number 2** page number style into the bottom of the page. In Section 1, format the page numbers to display as **i**, **ii**, **iii** and to start at **ii**. Verify the Section 2 page numbers display as **1**, **2**, **3**. In Section 2, do not display the page number on Page 1, and ensure that Page 1 displays instead of Page 4. Deselect the **Link to Previous**.

4. On Page 3, in the second blank paragraph below *ILLUSTRATIONS*, insert a **Table of Figures** with the **Simple** format and the **dotted line** tab leader.

5. On Page 7, in the blank paragraph above the *Page Break* notation, insert the default **Clustered Column** chart. Type the data in columns A and B as shown in **Figure 1**. In the chart datasheet, delete columns C and D. **Close** the Chart in Microsoft Word window. Adjust the chart height to 3" and the chart width to 4"

6. On Page 7, select the chart and insert the caption 2012 Parking Lot Revenue - Convention Center and then apply the **ExpansionCaption** style.

7. On Page 3, in the table of figures, update the entire table. Apply the **Illustrations** style to the paragraphs *Figure 1*, *Figure 2*, and *Figure 3*.

8. On Page 4, in the paragraph that begins *In June 2012*, select the first occurrence of *convention center* and mark all index entries.

9. On Page 9, in the second blank paragraph below *INDEX*, create an index that has the **From template format**, **Run-in type**, and **1 column**.

10. On Page 4, in the paragraph that begins *The Aspen Falls*, select the first occurrence of *LID* and create a cross-reference to low impact design On Page 9, update the *INDEX*. Apply the **Illustrations** style to the paragraph that begins *AFPC* through the paragraph that begins *low impact*.

11. Convert the endnotes to footnotes. On Page 9, at the end of the page, Delete the *Page Break* notation and the remaining paragraphs.

12. On Page 2, in the paragraph above the *Page Break* notation, create a **Custom** table of contents.

13. **Save** the document. **Close** the Word window. Submit the file as directed by your instructor.

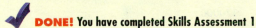

DONE! You have completed Skills Assessment 1

Skills Assessment 2

To complete this project, you will need the following file:

- wrd07_SA2Merger

You will save your document as:

- Last_First_wrd07_SA2Merger

---

1. Start **Word 2013**, and then open **wrd07_SA2Merger**. Save the file in your **Word Chapter 7** folder as Last_First_wrd07_SA2Merger On Page 3, replace *Your Name* with your name.

2. At the beginning of the document, insert the **Whisp** cover page. For the *Document title*, type MERGER OF COMMUNITY OFFICES For the *date*, select **July 16, 2014**. For the *author*—where the text *Skills for Success* displays—type Your Name

3. Insert the **Plain Number 2** page number style into the bottom of the page. In Section 1, format the page numbers to display as **i, ii, iii**. Verify the Section 2 page numbers display as **1, 2, 3**. In Section 2, do not display the page number on Page 1 and ensure that *Page 2* displays instead of *Page 4*. Deselect the **Link to Previous**.

4. On Page 3, in the second blank paragraph below *ILLUSTRATIONS*, insert a **Table of Figures** with the **From template** format and the **dotted line** tab leader.

5. On Page 6, in the blank paragraph below the paragraph beginning *The following*, insert the default **Clustered Column** chart. Type the data in columns A and B as shown here:

	A	B
1		Savings
2	Salaries/Benefits	249000
3	Fixed Costs	82000
4	Variable Costs	170000

6. In the chart datasheet, delete columns *C* and *D*. Delete row *5*. **Close** the Chart in Microsoft Word window. Adjust the chart height to 1.7" and the chart width to 4"

7. Select the chart and, insert the caption Projected Savings and then apply the **MergerCaption** style.

8. On Page 3, in the Table of Figures, update the entire table. Apply the **Illustrations** style to the paragraphs *Figure 1* and *Figure 2*.

9. On Page 4, in the paragraph that begins *The City of*, select the first occurrence of *merger* and mark all index entries.

10. On Page 9, in the second blank paragraph below *INDEX*, create an index that has the **From template format**, **Run-in type**, and **1** column.

11. On Page 4, in the paragraph that begins *The two offices*, select the text *AFCDSG* and create a cross-reference to Principles of Sound Government On Page 9, update the *INDEX*. Apply the **Illustrations** style to the paragraph that begins *AFCDSG* through the paragraph that begins *merger*.

12. On Page 2, in the paragraph above the *Page Break* notation, create a **Custom** table of contents.

13. **Save** the document. **Close** the Word window. Submit the file as directed by your instructor.

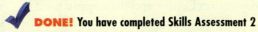 **DONE!** You have completed Skills Assessment 2

Visual Skills Check

To complete this project, you will need the following file:

- wrd07_VSGrant

You will save your document as:

- Last_First_wrd07_VSGrant

Open **wrd07_VSGrant**, and then on Page 3, replace *Your Name* with your name. Use the skills practiced in this chapter to mark the index entries as needed to create the index page that will display on the last page of the report as shown in **Figure 1**. Apply the **Illustrations** style to the index entries and the Table of Figures. At the beginning of the document, insert the **Whisp** cover page that has *Your Name* as the author. Update the Table of Contents, the Table of Figures, and the Index. Insert the Plain 2 page number style in the bottom center of the report. For the *ILLUSTRATIONS* and *CONTENTS* pages, format the page numbers as ii and iii. For the body text pages, format the page numbers as 2, 3, 4, etc. Do not include the page number 1.

Save the file as Last_First_wrd07_VSGrant in your **Word Chapter 7** folder. **Close** the Word window. Submit the file as directed by your instructor.

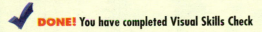 **DONE!** You have completed Visual Skills Check

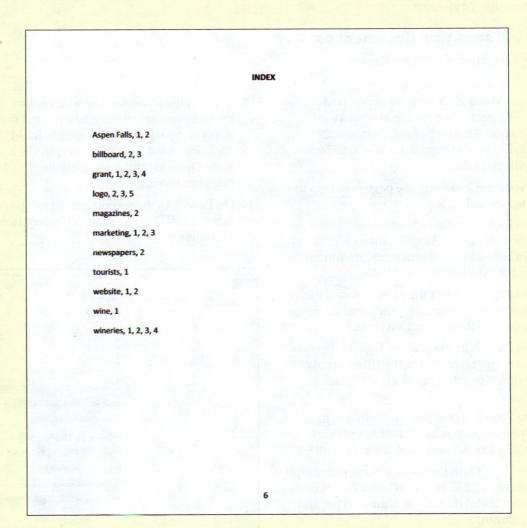

INDEX

Aspen Falls, 1, 2

billboard, 2, 3

grant, 1, 2, 3, 4

logo, 2, 3, 5

magazines, 2

marketing, 1, 2, 3

newspapers, 2

tourists, 1

website, 1, 2

wine, 1

wineries, 1, 2, 3, 4

6

Figure 1

My Skills

To complete this project, you will need the following file:

- wrd07_MyReport

You will save your document as:

- Last_First_wrd07_MyReport

1. Start **Word 2013**, and then open **wrd07_MyReport**. **Save** the file in your **Word Chapter 7** folder as Last_First_wrd07_MyReport On Page 4, replace *Your Name* with your name.

2. In Section 2, modify the page numbers to display as **1**, **2**, **3**.

3. On Page 3, in the second blank paragraph below *ILLUSTRATIONS*, insert a **Table of Figures** with the **From template** format and the **dotted line** tab leader.

4. On Page 11, select the picture, insert the caption Sign language guide and then apply the **ReportCaption** style.

5. On Page 3, in the Table of Figures, update the entire table. Apply the **Illustrations** style to the paragraphs *Figure 1* through *Figure 3*.

6. On Page 5, in the paragraph that begins *Under the new*, select *Americans with Disabilities Act* and mark all index entries.

7. On Page 14, in the second blank paragraph below *INDEX*, create an index that has the **From template format**, **Run-in type**, and **1 column**.

8. On Page 5, in the paragraph that begins *Under the new*, select the text *ADA* and create a cross-reference to Americans with Disabilities Act

9. Convert the footnotes to endnotes. On the last page, select the citations, and then **Remove Space After Paragraph**. Right-click one of the Roman numerals. Click **Note Options**, and then apply the **1**, **2**, **3 Number format**.

10. On Page 2, in the second blank paragraph below *CONTENTS*, create a **Custom** table of contents.

11. Update the page numbers for the *ILLUSTRATIONS*. On Page 13, update the *INDEX*. Apply the **Illustrations** style to the marked entries as shown in **Figure 1**.

12. **Save** the document. **Close** the Word window. Submit the file as directed by your instructor.

DONE! You have completed My Skills

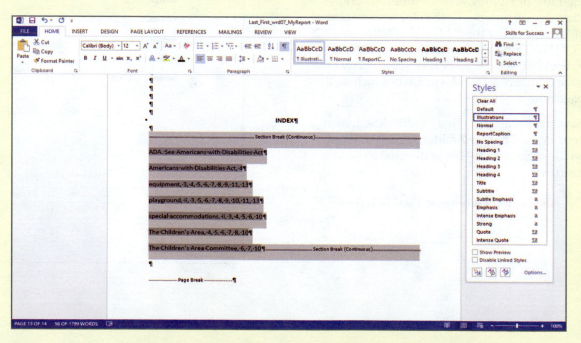

Figure 1

Skills Challenge 1

To complete this project, you will need the following file:

- **wrd07_SC1Building**

You will save your document as:

- **Last_First_wrd07_SC1Building**

In Word 2013, open **wrd07_SC1Building**. Use the skills practiced in this chapter to modify the report according to *The Gregg Reference Manual* (Sabin) guidelines. Insert the **Whisp** cover page that uses a date of June 19, 2014 Include Your Name as the author name and ASPEN FALLS as the company name. If necessary, update the Document Properties to include Your Name and the company name. Prepare a table of contents and the table of figures using the default formats. Create custom page numbers using the **Plain Number 2** style at the bottom of the page. Be sure to format *Section 1* to display Roman numeral page numbers and *Section 2* to display Arabic numbers. The table of contents page should be page *ii*. In Section 2, remove the **Link to Previous**, and be sure that Page 1 starts as Page 1

and does not display on the first page. Insert an Index that uses the Run-in type and has 1 column. Convert the endnotes to footnotes and remove the *ENDNOTES* page from the document. On the first page of the body of the report, update *Your Name* and the *Current Date*. Update the Table of Contents, the Table of Figures, and the Index. Apply the **Illustrations** style to the Table of Figures and to the Index.

Save the file as Last_First_wrd07_SC1Building in your **Word Chapter 7** folder. **Close** the Word window. Submit the file as directed by your instructor.

 DONE! You have completed Skills Challenge 1

Skills Challenge 2

To complete this project, you will start with a:

- **New, blank Word document**

You will save your document as:

- **Last_First_wrd07_SC2Formal**

Select a report that you have written before for this class or another class. If you have not written a report, locate an example of a report at your college that is used by a club, organization, or faculty member. In Word 2013, edit the report so that it includes Heading 1 and Heading 2 styles applied to headings and subheadings in the report, a table of contents, at least two figures, captions for each figure, a table of figures, at least five marked index entries, at least two cross-references, at least three footnotes, a bibliography, and an index. Create

custom page numbers for your report. Use the skills practiced in this chapter to update your report. The report format should follow *The Gregg Reference Manual* (Sabin).

Save the file as Last_First_wrd07_SC2Formal in your **Word Chapter 7** folder. **Close** the Word window. Submit the file as directed by your instructor.

 DONE! You have completed Skills Challenge 2

CHAPTER 8

Collaborate and Share Documents

- ▶ Review tools help you collaborate with others while building documents. Team members can add comments and track their changes so that their input can be used to create the final version of a document.

- ▶ Review tools help you prepare documents. You can count words or estimate the grade level needed to read your document.

- ▶ When you collaborate to create a document, you may be asked to be a reviewer. As a reviewer, you can track changes made in Word.

- ▶ When changes are tracked in Word, the original author can see the changes that a reviewer proposes and then accept or reject each change. The author can then print the changes, and the final document can be marked as final so that no additional changes can be included.

- ▶ When reviewers have made changes in multiple files, the documents can be combined into a single file.

© Kzenon/Fotolia

Aspen Falls City Hall

In this chapter, you will assist Julia Wagner, Community Development Director, and her co-workers with whom she has shared the RFP, request for proposal, used to seek bids for website updates. Julia must work with several people/departments at the City to prepare the RFP guidelines that others, who are not employed by the city, will follow.

When the cost of a project exceeds a certain dollar value, businesses often seek multiple quotes, or bids. Some businesses seek the lowest bid, whereas others look for excellent service for the best value. For this scenario, the City has a large project that includes updating the website for the best design service for the best price. You will work with Julia to create an RFP to be shared with the public so that all interested bidders can explain their plan and how they will provide services.

Julia and other city employees will exchange the RFP electronically and track suggestions. You will assist in the review by tracking changes; changing tracking options; inserting, modifying, and deleting comments; restricting who can edit the RFP; and verifying the intended audience will be able to read and understand the document(s). You will also change document permissions, combine multiple RFPs into one document, and accept or reject tracked changes. You will create one document and mark the document as final so that it can be shared with others without them being able to make changes to it. You will use Word to collaborate with others and prepare a document that will be shared electronically that incorporates the best comments and revisions included in the RFPs by all reviewers.

Time to complete all 10 skills – 60 to 90 minutes

Student data files needed for this chapter:

wrd08_Request
wrd08_Request2

You will save your documents as:

Last_First_wrd08_Request
Last_First_wrd08_RequestDraft
Last_First_wrd08_RequestFinal

Outcome

Using the skills in this chapter, you will be able to make changes to documents such as this:

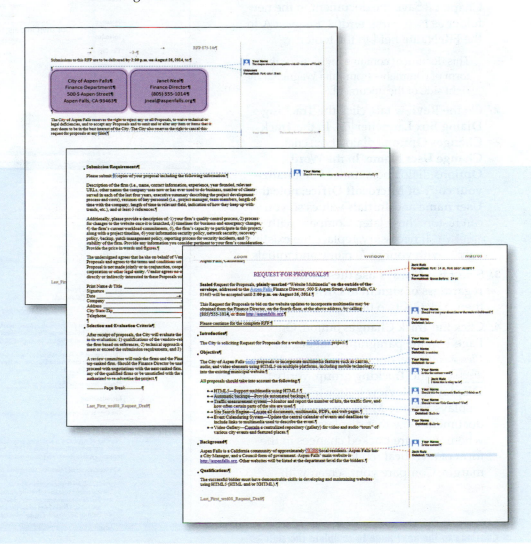

SKILLS

MyITLab®
Skills 1-10 Training

At the end of this chapter, you will be able to:

Skill 1 Track Changes and Insert Comments
Skill 2 Check Document Statistics and Compatibility
Skill 3 Modify and Delete Comments
Skill 4 Change Tracking Options
Skill 5 Restrict Editing Options
Skill 6 Review Documents
Skill 7 Change Document Permissions
Skill 8 Compare and Combine Documents
Skill 9 Accept or Reject Tracked Changes
Skill 10 Mark Documents as Final

MORE SKILLS

Skill 11 Use Outlook Contacts to Merge to E-mail
Skill 12 Share Documents Online
Skill 13 Create Blog Posts
Skill 14 Manage Versions

▶ Review tools can be used to mark each change you make in a document so that others can see your revisions, or changes.

▶ A **comment** is a message inserted by a person reviewing a document.

1. Start **Word 2013**, and then open **wrd08_Request**. Use the **Save As** dialog box to create a **New folder** named Word Chapter 8 Save the document in the new folder as Last_First_wrd08_Request Add the **FileName** field to the footer.

   This document contains revisions in the form of comments from Julia Wagner at the right side of the document.

2. On the **Review tab**, click the **Tracking Dialog Box Launcher** [⬚]. In the **Track Changes Options** dialog box, click **Change User Name**. In the **Word Options** dialog box, under **Personalize your copy of Microsoft Office**, note the **User name** and **Initials** values so you can restore these later. Compare with **Figure 1**. If necessary, replace the existing values with your own name and initials.

3. Select the **Always use these values regardless of sign in to Office**. box, and then click **OK** two times.

4. Click the **Track Changes** button. On Page 1, in the paragraph that begins *Please continue*, double-click *below*. Press [Delete]. In the **Tracking group**, verify the **Display for Review** button [Simple Markup ▾] displays **Simple Markup**—a cleaned-up document view that displays indicators where there are tracked changes in the form of a vertical red line in the left margin. Compare your screen with **Figure 2**.

■ **Continue to the next page to complete the skill**

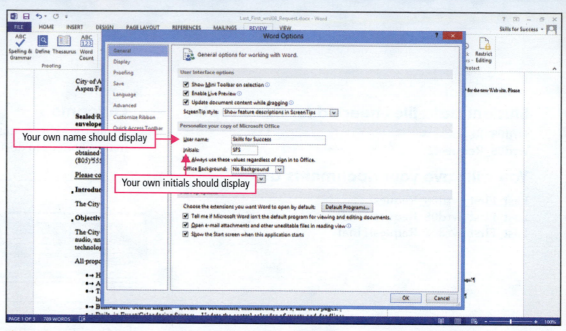

Figure 1

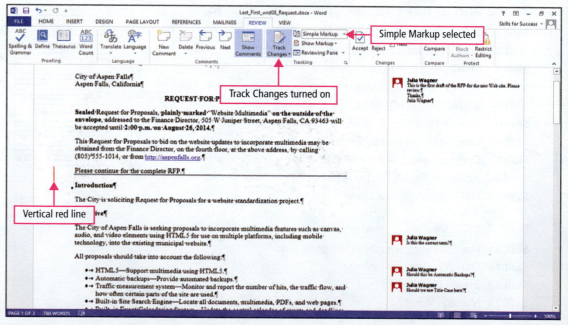

Figure 2

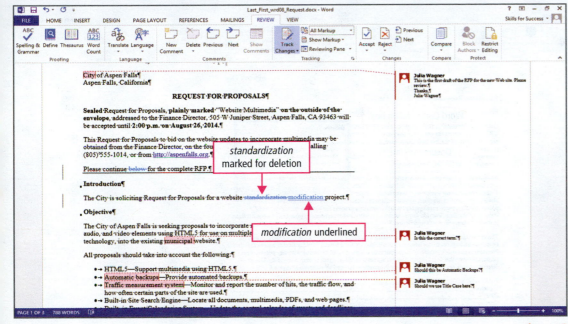

standardization marked for deletion

modification underlined

Figure 3

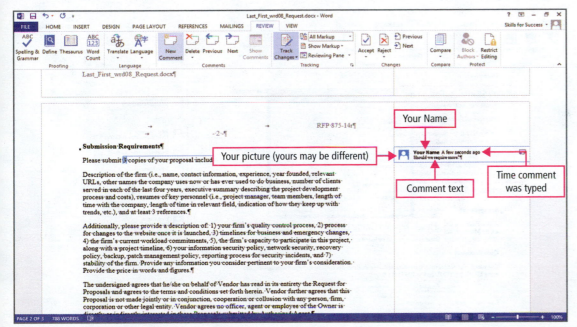

Your Name

Your picture (yours may be different)

Comment text

Time comment was typed

Figure 4

5. In the **Tracking group**, click the **Display for Review** button [Simple Markup ▾], and then click **All Markup**.

In the ***All Markup*** mode, a document view that displays the revised text in the document, the deleted word displays in a new color and has a line through it indicating that the word has been marked for deletion. In All Markup mode, a gray line displays in the left margin.

Alternately, in the paragraph that begins *Please continue*, click the vertical line in the left margin.

6. In the paragraph that begins *The City is*, double-click *standardization*. Type *modification* as shown in **Figure 3**.

The inserted word displays in a new color and is underlined. Changes are tracked.

7. On Page 1, select *(805) 555-1014*. In the **Comments group**, click the **New Comment** button.

A comment balloon displays with your picture, or the figure shape in a predefined color, *Your Name*, and the time.

8. In the comment balloon, type Should we use your direct line?

9. On Page 1, in the fourth bulleted entry, select *Built-in*, and then in the **Comments group**, click the **New Comment** button. In the comment, type Is this necessary?

10. In the comment *Should we use*, click the **Reply to Comment** button 🔲, and then type Or, the main switchboard?

11. Select *75,000*, and then insert the comment Is this current?

12. On Page 2, in the second paragraph, select *3*, and then insert the comment Should we require more? as shown in **Figure 4**.

13. **Save** 🔲 the document.

- **You have completed Skill 1 of 10**

▶ **Document statistics** are data that summarize document features such as the number of pages, words, characters without spaces, characters including spaces, paragraphs, and lines.

▶ **Readability statistics** measure the reading level for a document based on certain document statistics such as the length of words, the number of syllables in words, and the length of sentences and paragraphs.

1. On the **Review tab**, in the **Proofing group**, click the **Word Count** button. Compare your screen with **Figure 1**.

2. **Close** the **Word Count** dialog box.

3. On the **File tab**, click **Options**, and then click the **Proofing tab**.

4. Under **When correcting spelling and grammar in Word**, verify the **Mark grammar errors as you type** check box is selected, and then select the **Show readability statistics** check box. Click **OK**.

5. On the **Review tab**, in the **Proofing group**, click the **Spelling & Grammar** button. Notice the Grammar pane displays with the word *contain* selected. Click the **Ignore** button.

   In this document, ignoring rules is acceptable.

6. In the Microsoft Word window, click **OK**.

7. Take a moment to review the **Readability Statistics** shown in **Figure 2**.

   The **Flesch Reading Ease** is a 100-point scale that measures readability. A score of 100 indicates an easy-to-understand document. The **Flesch-Kincaid Grade Level** estimates the U.S. grade level needed to understand a document.

■ **Continue to the next page to complete the skill** ▶

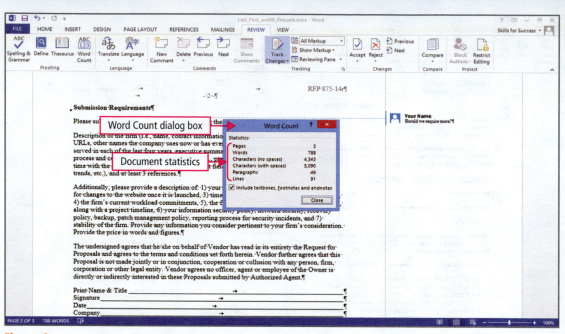

Figure 1

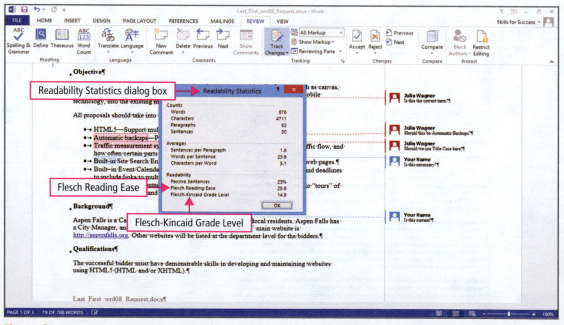

Figure 2

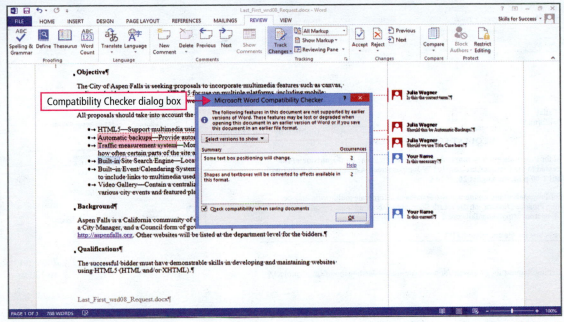

Figure 3

8. Record the **Flesch-Kincaid Grade Level** value on a piece of paper to refer to in the next skill, and then click **OK**.

9. On the **File tab**, click **Options**, and then click the **Proofing tab**.

10. Under **When correcting spelling and grammar in Word**, clear the **Show readability statistics** check box, and then click **OK**.

11. On the **File tab**, click the **Check for Issues** button, and then click **Check Compatibility**. Compare your screen with **Figure 3**.

The **Compatibility Checker** locates features in a Word 2013 document that are not supported in earlier versions of Word. Individuals using earlier versions of Word may not be able to see these features correctly.

Here, the text box locations would change if the document were opened in an earlier version of Word. Features supported in Word 2013 that are not supported in earlier versions are summarized in the table shown in **Figure 4**.

12. In the displayed dialog box, click **OK**, and then **Save** the document.

■ **You have completed Skill 2 of 10**

Word 2013 Features Incompatible with Word 2010 and Earlier	
Apps for Office	Web video

Word 2013 Features Incompatible with Word 2007 and Earlier	
Alternative text on tables	New shapes and text boxes
Blocking authors	New WordArt effects
New content controls	OpenType features
New numbering formats	Text effects

Word 2013 Features Incompatible with Word 97-2003	
Bibliographies and citations	Margin tabs
Building blocks	Open XML embedded objects
Charts and diagrams	Relative positioning text boxes
Content controls	SmartArt graphics
Custom XML	Themes
Equations	Tracked moves
Major/minor fonts	

Figure 4

▶ Comments inserted into a document can be edited or deleted in their comment balloons or in the Reviewing pane.

▶ When a comment is deleted, the remaining comments are automatically renumbered.

1. Press `Ctrl` + `Home`. On the **View tab**, in the **Zoom group**, click the **Zoom** button.

   Zoom is the magnification level of the document as displayed on the screen. Increasing the zoom percentage increases the size of the text and comments, but does not increase the actual font size.

2. In the **Zoom** dialog box, in the **Percent** box, select the current setting. Type 130 Click **OK**.

3. Scroll to the right to view the first comment. Compare with **Figure 1**.

   Comments are easier to work with when the zoom percentage is higher than 100%.

4. On the **Review tab**, in the **Comments group**, click the **Next** button to move to the comment that begins *This is the*. Read the comment. In the **Comments group**, click the **Delete** button. In the **Comments group**, click the **Next** button. Compare with **Figure 2**.

   Your date may differ.

5. In the **Comments group**, click the **Next** button two times. With the comment from Julia active, click the **Reply to Comment** button 🗨, and then type Yes

6. In the bottom right corner of the status bar, click the **Zoom Out** button `-` three times to set the zoom to **100%**.

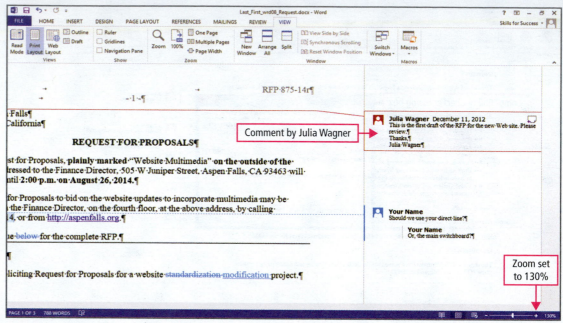

Figure 1

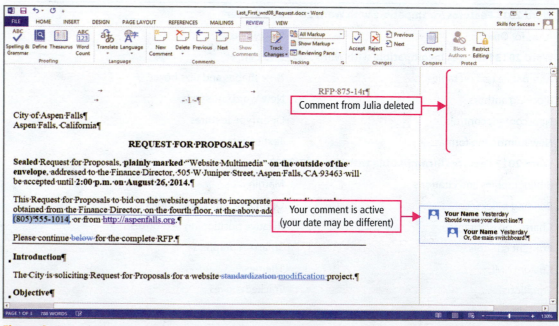

Figure 2

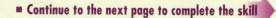
■ **Continue to the next page to complete the skill**

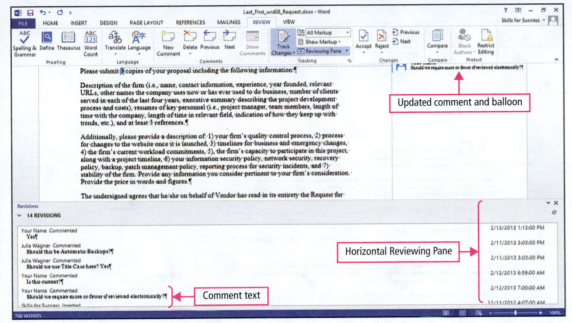

Updated comment and balloon

Horizontal Reviewing Pane

Comment text

Figure 3

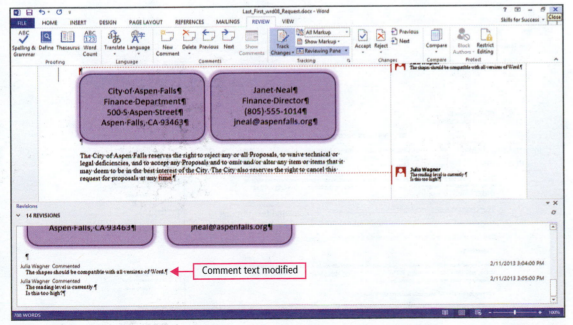

Comment text modified

Figure 4

7. On the **Review tab**, in the **Tracking group**, click the **Reviewing Pane arrow**, and then click **Reviewing Pane Horizontal**.

> The ***Reviewing pane*** displays at the left (vertically) or at the bottom (horizontally) of the screen and lists all comments and tracked changes, along with the date and time they were made.

8. In the **Comments group**, click the **Next** button. In the **Reviewing pane**, click the end of the comment that begins *Should we use*. Add a space, and then type Yes

> When a comment is edited in the Reviewing Pane, the comment balloon also changes.

9. Click the comment that begins *Is this necessary?*, and then in the **Comments group**, click the **Delete** button.

10. Locate the comment that begins *Should we require*, and then click to the left of the question mark (*?*). Add a space, and then type or fewer if reviewed electronically as shown in **Figure 3**.

11. In the comment that begins *The Shapes*, click before the *a* in *are*, type should be and then delete the word *are* as shown in **Figure 4**.

12. Locate the last comment, click the end of the line that begins *The reading level*, and then type the **Flesch-Kincaid Grade Level** value recorded in the previous skill. Add a period.

13. Right-click the last comment. In the shortcut menu, select **Mark Comment Done**.

> The ***Mark Comment Done*** feature identifies a comment as completed so you know what other comments you still need to finalize.

14. **Close** ✕ the **Reviewing pane**, and then **Save** 🖫 the document.

■ **You have completed Skill 3 of 10**

▶ When tracking changes, you can alter how revisions display.

▶ Proposed revisions can be placed in balloons or displayed in the document in final form with the changes made.

1. On the **Review tab**, in the **Tracking group**, verify the Track Changes button is selected.

2. On Page 1, in the paragraph that begins *Sealed Request for,* click before *Finance,* type Aspen Falls and then add a space.

3. In the **Tracking group**, verify the **Display for Review** button [Simple Markup] displays **All Markup**. Compare your screen with **Figure 1**.

4. In the **Tracking group**, click the **Show Markup** button, point to **Balloons**, and then click **Show Revisions in Balloons**. Compare your screen with **Figure 2**.

   Here, inserted words display in the document and deleted words display in balloons.

5. On Page 1, in the paragraph under *Objective,* select *is seeking,* and then type seeks

6. On Page 1, in the same paragraph, select *for use,* and then press [Delete].

■ **Continue to the next page to complete the skill** ▶

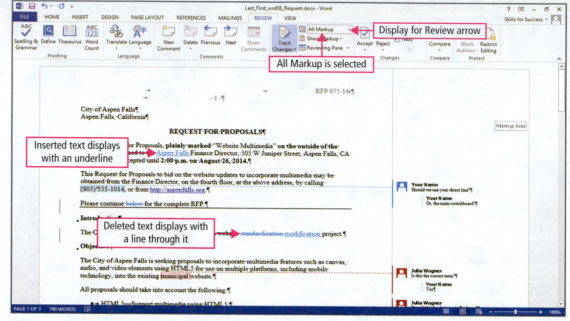

Figure 1

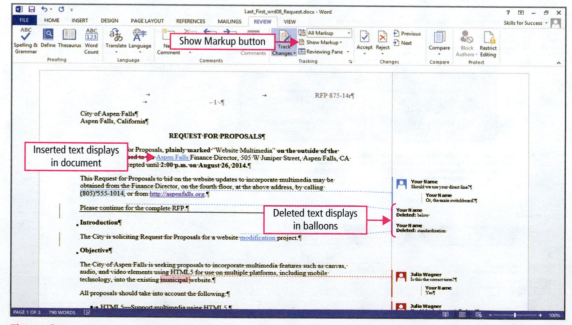

Figure 2

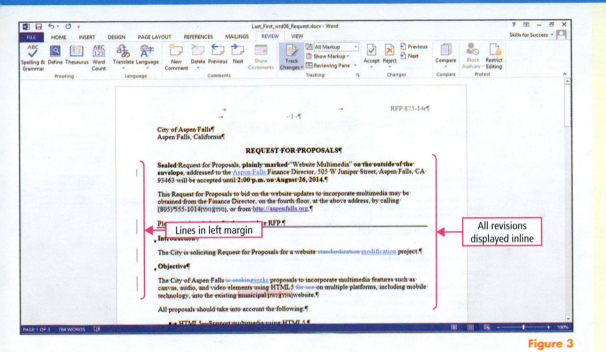

Lines in left margin

All revisions displayed inline

Figure 3

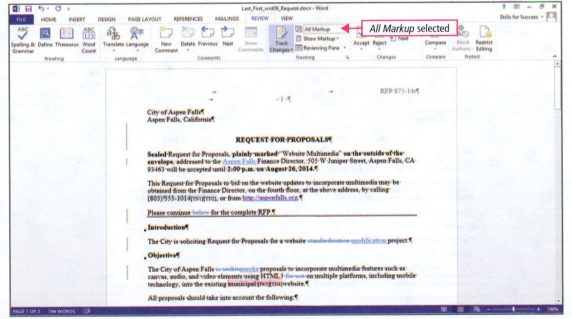

All Markup selected

Figure 4

7. On Page 1, in the bulleted list, select the first occurrence of *Built-in*, and then press Delete . Delete the second occurrence of *Built-in*.

8. Press Ctrl + Home . In the **Tracking group**, click the **Show Markup** button, point to **Balloons**, and then click **Show All Revisions Inline**. Compare your screen with **Figure 3**.

> *Inline Revisions* display all changes within the text instead of within revision balloons. Comments display with [YN], or your initials, and a number that represents the initials of the author of the comment, and the number of comments by that author. If you move the mouse and hover over a comment notation, the comment will display.

9. In the **Tracking group**, click the **Display for Review** button Simple Markup ⌄ , and then click **No Markup**.

> *No Markup* is a document view that displays how the document will look if all changes are accepted.

10. On Page 1, click anywhere in the title *REQUEST FOR PROPOSALS*, and then click the **Page Layout tab**. In the **Paragraph group**, click the **Spacing Before up spin arrow** two times to change the value to **24**.

11. On the **Review tab**, in the **Tracking group**, click the **Display for Review** button Simple Markup ⌄ , and then click **All Markup**. Compare your screen with **Figure 4**.

12. Save 💾 the document.

■ **You have completed Skill 4 of 10**

▶ When sharing a Word document for review, you may need to restrict what options are available to the reviewer during the reviewing process.

▶ Editing options include tracked changes, comments, filling in forms, and no changes.

1. On the **Review tab**, in the **Protect group**, click the **Restrict Editing** button.

2. In the **Restrict Editing** pane, under **Editing Restrictions**, select the **Allow only this type of editing in the document** check box.

3. Click the **No changes (Read only) arrow**, and then click **Tracked changes**.

   When editing restrictions are enforced, the only changes that can be made to the document are the ones that are tracked.

4. Under **Start enforcement**, click **Yes, Start Enforcing Protection**, and then compare your screen with **Figure 1**.

   The Start Enforcing Protection dialog box is used to enter an optional password.

5. In the **Start Enforcing Protection** dialog box, type Success! Press ⎡Tab⎤, type Success! to confirm, and then click **OK**. Compare your screen with **Figure 2**.

   When protection is enforced, the options in the Restrict Editing task pane do not display. At the bottom of the pane, the Stop Protection button displays.

■ **Continue to the next page to complete the skill** ➤

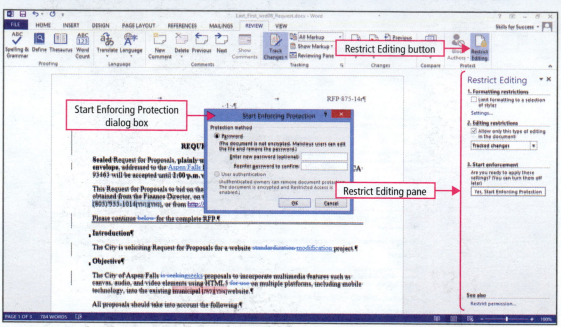

Figure 1

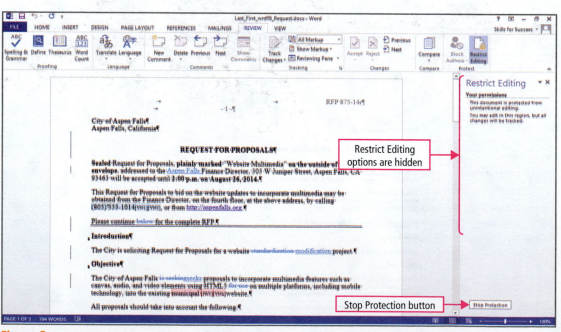

Figure 2

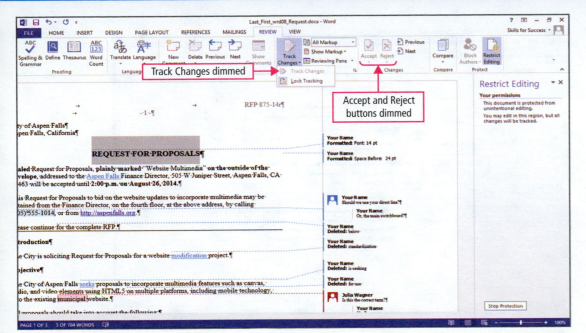

Track Changes dimmed

Accept and Reject buttons dimmed

Figure 3

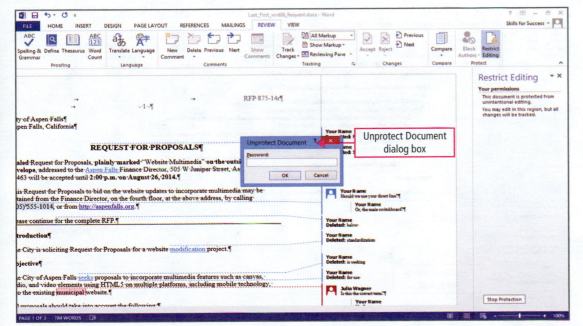

Unprotect Document dialog box

Figure 4

6. In the **Tracking group**, click the **Show Markup** button, point to **Balloons**, and then click **Show Revisions in Balloons**.

7. Select the title that begins *REQUEST FOR*, and then on the **Home tab**, in the **Font group**, change the **Font Size** to **14**. Scroll to the right, and notice that the balloon displays the tracked change.

8. On the **Review tab**, in the **Tracking group**, click the **Track Changes arrow**, and then compare your screen with **Figure 3**.

   The Track Changes command is dimmed, and in the Changes group, the Accept and Reject buttons are also dimmed. With the current editing restrictions, all changes will be tracked.

9. Click the document. In the **Restrict Editing** pane, click the **Stop Protection** button.

10. Notice that the Unprotect Document dialog box prompts you for a password, as shown in **Figure 4**.

    Only individuals with the password will be able to stop enforcing the protection. In this manner, only those who are authorized can make untracked changes.

11. Click **Cancel** to leave protection in place. **Close** ✖ the **Restrict Editing** pane. **Save** 🖫 the document.

■ **You have completed Skill 5 of 10**

► In a collaborative project, documents are often revised by multiple reviewers.

► Different colors are assigned to each reviewer's balloons and inline revisions to help distinguish each team member's proposed changes and comments.

1. On the **Review tab**, in the **Tracking group**, click the **Show Markup** button, point to **Balloons**, and then click **Show All Revisions Inline**.

2. In the **Tracking group**, click the **Tracking Dialog Box Launcher**, and then in the **Track Change Options** dialog box, click **Change User Name**.

3. In the **Word Options** dialog box, on the **General tab**, under **Personalize your copy of Microsoft Office**, in the **User name** box, type Jack Ruiz and then change the initials to JR Verify the Always use these values regardless of sign in to Office box is selected. Compare your screen with **Figure 1**.

Word relies on the user name value to track which reviewer is working with the document. Here, Jack Ruiz is now reviewing the document. In this case, the user name overrides the Windows account name.

4. Click **OK** two times to close the dialog boxes.

5. On the **Review tab**, in the **Tracking group**, click the **Reviewing Pane** button.

6. In the **Reviewing pane**, click the end of the third comment that begins *Is this the*.

7. In the **Comments group**, click the **New Comment** button. Type I think this is okay. Compare your screen with **Figure 2**.

■ **Continue to the next page to complete the skill** ➡

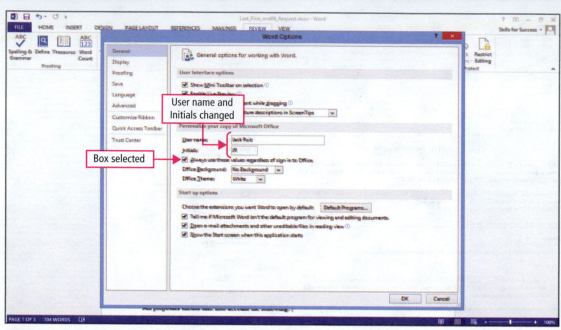

Figure 1

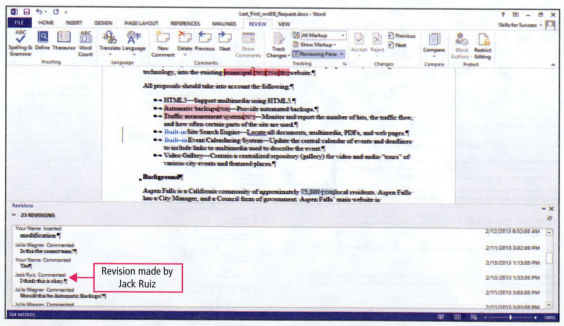

Figure 2

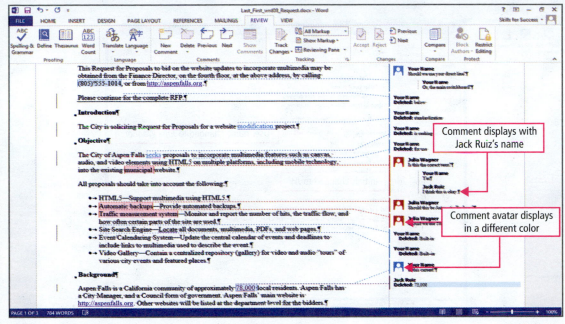

Comment displays with Jack Ruiz's name

Comment avatar displays in a different color

Figure 3

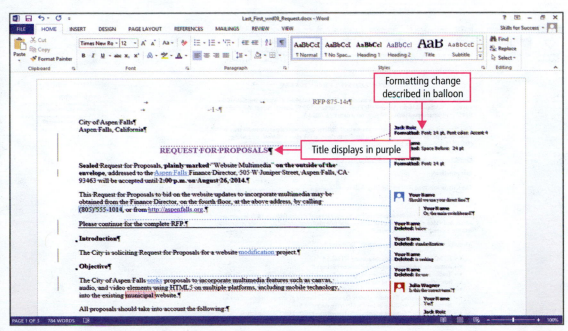

Formatting change described in balloon

Title displays in purple

Figure 4

8. At the bottom of Page 1, in the paragraph that begins *Aspen Falls is*, select *75,000*, and then type *78,000*

9. In the **Tracking group**, click the **Show Markup** button, point to **Balloons**, and then click **Show Revisions in Balloons**.

   Comments by each reviewer are assigned a unique avatar color and identified by the author's name, here *Jack Ruiz*.

10. In the **Tracking group**, click the **Reviewing Pane** button to close it. Compare your screen with **Figure 3**.

11. On Page 1, select the title that begins *REQUEST FOR PROPOSALS*. On the **Home tab**, in the **Font group**, click the **Font Color arrow** [A ▾], and then click the eighth color in the first row—**Purple, Accent 4**. Click below the title to deselect the text. Compare your screen with **Figure 4**.

12. On the **Review tab**, in the **Tracking group**, click the **Display for Review** button [Simple Markup ▾], and then click **No Markup**.

13. Save [💾] the document.

■ **You have completed Skill 6 of 10**

▶ A ***split window*** is a window separated into two parts to allow scrolling through each window independently to view different areas of the document at the same time.

▶ When printing, you can choose to include the ***markups***—the balloons and inline revisions in a reviewed document.

1. On the **File tab**, click **Save As**. Save the file in your **Word Chapter 8** folder with the name Last_First_wrd08_RequestDraft Open the footer, and then select the **FileName** field. Press F9 to update the FileName field in the footer, and then **Close** the Header and Footer area.

   The original file will retain all the tracked changes and comments you and Jack made.

2. On the **Review tab**, in the **Tracking group**, click the **Tracking Dialog Box Launcher** , and then in the **Track Change Options** dialog box, click **Change User Name**.

3. In the **Word Options** dialog box, change the **User name** to Julia Wagner Change the **Initials** to JW Compare your screen with **Figure 1**, and then click **OK** two times.

   Julia Wagner, the original author of the document, is now the current reviewer.

4. On the **Review tab**, in the **Protect group**, click the **Restrict Editing** button.

5. In the **Restrict Editing** pane, click **Stop Protection**, and then compare your screen with **Figure 2**.

6. In the **Unprotect Document** dialog box, type Success! and then click **OK**. **Close** ☒ the **Restrict Editing** pane.

■ **Continue to the next page to complete the skill**

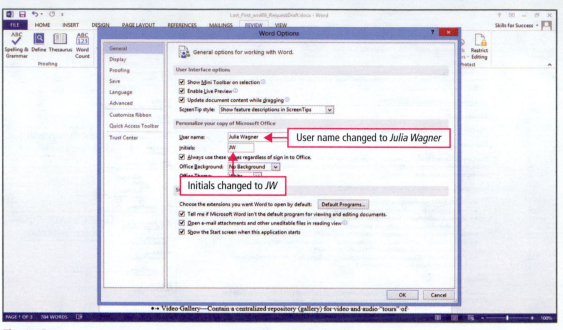

Figure 1

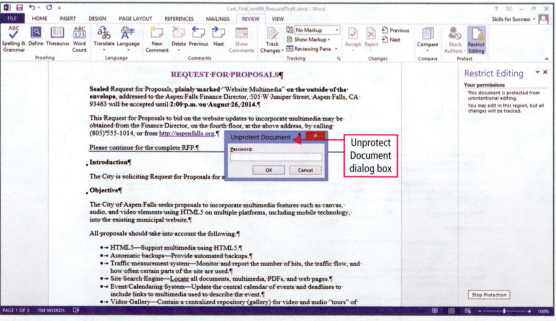

Figure 2

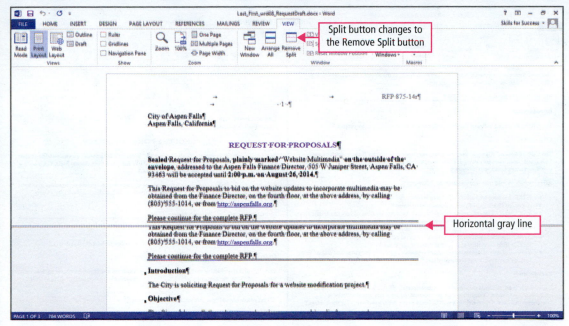

Figure 3

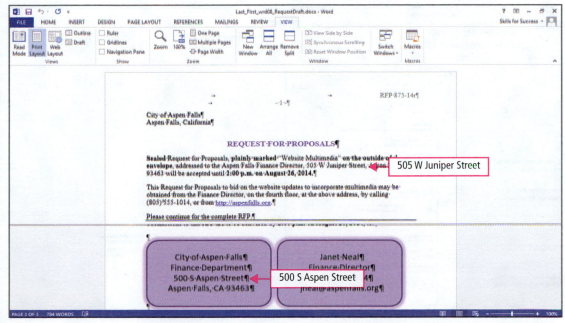

Figure 4

7. Press Ctrl + Home to move to the beginning of the document.

8. On the **View tab**, in the **Window group**, click the **Split** button. With the ÷ pointer displayed, drag the horizontal gray line above the paragraph that begins *Introduction*. Compare your screen with **Figure 3**.

The position of the horizontal gray line above the paragraph determines the placement of the line in the window.

9. In the lower window, scroll to Page 3, and then display the address in the text box. Notice that the address in the upper window does not match the address in the lower window, as shown in **Figure 4**.

10. In the upper window, select *505 W Juniper*, and then type 500 S Aspen

11. In the **Window group**, click the **Remove Split** button.

Alternately, double-click the Resize bar located above the horizontal ruler in the lower window.

12. On the **Review tab**, in the **Tracking group**, click the **Display for Review button** Simple Markup ▾, and then click **Simple Markup**.

13. On the **View tab**, in the **Zoom group**, click **Multiple Pages**.

14. On the **File tab**, click **Print**. Under **Settings**, click **Print All Pages**, and then, if necessary, click Print Markup. If you are printing your work for this chapter, click **Print**.

15. Click the **Back** button ⊙. On the **View tab**, in the **Zoom group**, click the **100%** button.

16. Save 🖫 the document.

■ **You have completed Skill 7 of 10**

▶ When copies of a document are tracked in separate files, the changes may need to be compared or combined into a single file.

▶ To compare two documents at the same time, you can use **Side by Side view**—a view that displays two different documents in vertical windows so that they can be compared.

1. If necessary, open **Last_First_wrd08_RequestDraft.**

2. On the **Review tab**, in the **Tracking group**, click the **Display for Review** button Simple Markup ▾, and then click **All Markup.**

3. On the **File tab**, click **Open.** Open the student data file **wrd08_Request2.**

4. In the taskbar, click the Word icon , and then click **Last_First_wrd08_RequestDraft** to make it the active window.

5. On the **View tab**, in the **Window group**, click the **View Side by Side** button, and then compare your screen with **Figure 1**.

   The two documents display in their own window so that both can be viewed at the same time. If more than two documents are open, the names of all open windows would display in a dialog box. You would click one of the Request files.

6. In **Last_First_wrd08_RequestDraft**, scroll up and to the right to display the balloons. Compare your screen with **Figure 2**.

   In Side by Side view, **synchronous scrolling** scrolls both windows when you scroll either the vertical or horizontal scroll bar in either window.

■ **Continue to the next page to complete the skill** ➡

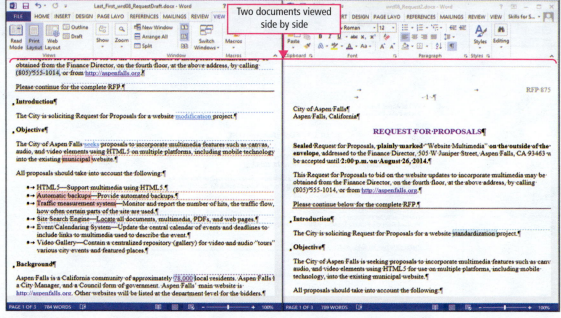

Figure 1

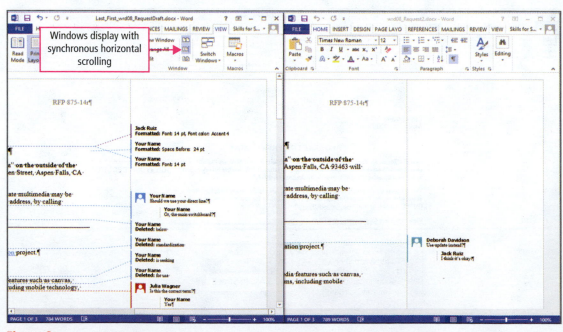

Figure 2

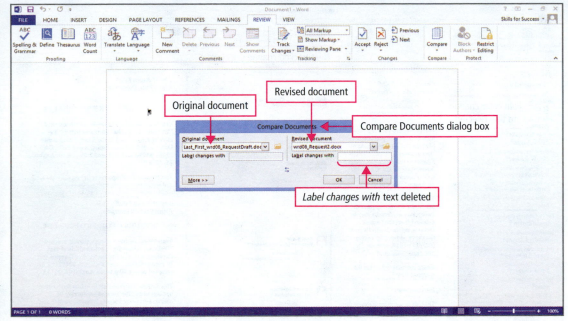

Original document

Revised document

Compare Documents dialog box

Label changes with text deleted

Figure 3

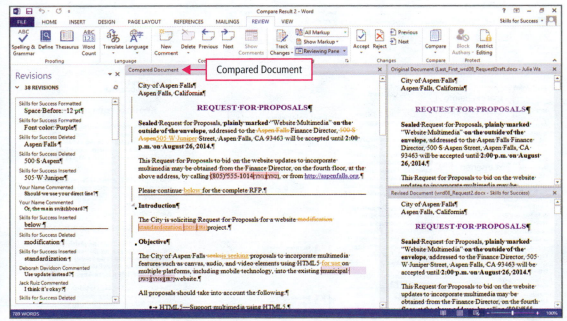

Compared Document

Figure 4

7. **Save** ⊟ **Last_First_wrd08_ RequestDraft**. **Close** ✖ both documents. If necessary, start Word, and then display a new, blank document.

8. On the **Review tab**, in the **Compare group**, click the **Compare** button, and then click **Compare**.

   When you compare or combine, a new document is opened. Revisions from the source document and another copy of the compared document are merged into one main document for reviewing. In a compared document, the Reviewing pane displays comments. In a combined document, the Reviewing pane displays both comments and revisions.

9. In the **Compare Documents** dialog box, click **Open** 📂. In the **Open** dialog box, navigate to where you are saving your files, click **Last_First_ wrd08RequestDraft**. Click **Open**.

10. To the right of the **Revised document** box, click **Open** 📂. Navigate to the student data files, click **wrd08_Request2**, and then click **Open**.

11. Under **Revised document**, delete the text in the **Label changes with** box, as shown in **Figure 3**.

    When comparing documents, the **revised document** is the document that has changes that you want to merge with the original document.

12. Click **OK**. Read the displayed message. Click **Yes**. Compare with **Figure 4**.

    When documents are compared, the tracked changes are moved into a single, new compared document.

13. View the displayed changes to the compared document, and then click **Save** ⊟. Save the document in your **Word Chapter 8** folder as **Last_First_wrd08_RequestFinal**

■ **You have completed Skill 8 of 10**

▶ After a document has completed the review process, the original author can accept or reject each change.

▶ Content can be revised based on the comments, and the comments can then be deleted.

1. Verify that the insertion point is at the beginning of the **Compared Document** of the **Last_First_wrd08_RequestFinal** window. On the **Review tab**, in the **Tracking group**, click the **Show Markup** button, point to **Balloons**, and then click **Show Revisions in Balloons**.

2. In the **Changes group**, click the **Next** button.

   The title that includes formatting changes is selected.

3. In the **Changes group**, click the **Reject** button, and then compare your screen with **Figure 1**.

   The formatting change is rejected—made final—and the title color is not changed to purple.

4. In the balloon, read the proposed change, and then in the **Changes group**, click the **Reject** button one time to reject the change.

   The title spacing before changes from the first proposed change, 12 point, to 24 point.

5. Review the comment, and then click **Reject** to insert the text *Aspen Falls*.

6. Read the proposed address change, and then in the **Changes group**, click the **Reject** button two times. Compare your screen with **Figure 2**.

   When evaluating text that has been replaced, two changes have been made. Different text has been inserted, and text has been deleted.

■ **Continue to the next page to complete the skill**

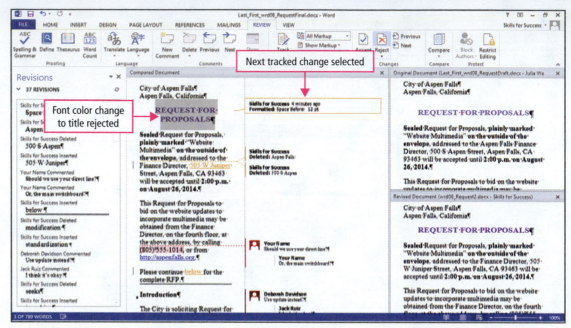

Figure 1

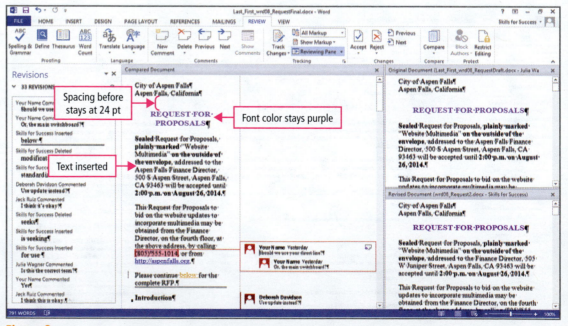

Figure 2

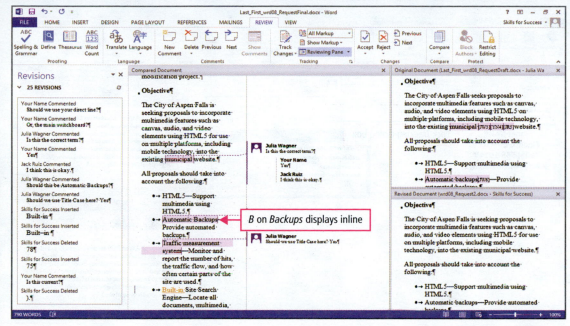

Figure 3

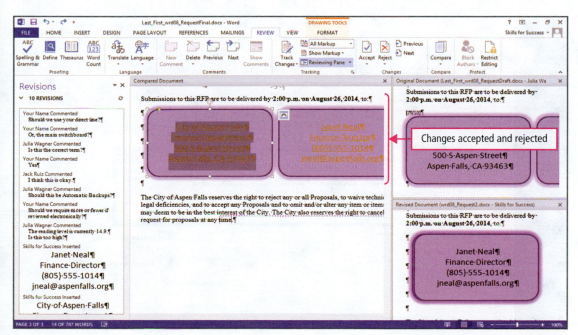

Figure 4

7. In the **Changes group**, click **Next** two times to select the word *below*. **Reject** the next three changes. **Accept** the next six changes to select *Automatic backups*.

8. In the paragraph that begins *Automatic backups*, select the *b*, and then type B Compare your screen with **Figure 3**.

9. In the next paragraph, repeat the technique to replace the M on *measurement* and the S on *system*.

10. In the **Changes group**, click **Reject** seven times to select *3*.

11. In the **Changes group**, click **Accept** five times to select the text in the second text box.

12. In the **Changes group**, click **Next** one time, and then compare your screen with **Figure 4**. Click **Accept** one time.

13. In the **Compared Document** window, select the first comment, and then on the **Review tab**, in the **Comments group**, click **Delete**.

14. In the **Comments group**, click **Next**, and then click **Delete**. Repeat the technique just practiced to delete all comments with the exception of the comment related to the reading level.

15. On the **File tab**, click **Options**, and then on the **General tab**, replace the values in the **User name** and **Initial** boxes with the information you recorded on paper in Skill 1, Step 2. Clear the **Always use these values regardless of sign in to Office**. box. Click **OK**.

16. Add the **FileName** field to the footer, close the Header & Footer area, and then **Save** 🖫 the document.

■ **You have completed Skill 9 of 10**

▶ When a document is *marked as final*, it is locked—no one can type, edit, or use the proofing tools to make additional changes.

▶ Documents can be marked as final to prevent those reading the document from making changes to it.

1. In **Last_First_wrd08_RequestFinal**, on the **Review tab**, in the **Tracking group**, verify that the Track Changes button is not selected.

2. In the **Tracking group**, click the bottom of the **Track Changes** button, and then click **Lock Tracking**. Compare your screen with **Figure 1**.

    No further changes can be made to the document.

3. In the **Lock Tracking** dialog box, type Complete! and then press [Tab]. Type Complete! and then click **OK**.

4. On the **File tab**, under **Protect Document**, click the **Protect Document** button, and then click **Mark as Final**.

5. Read the displayed dialog box, and then click **OK** to mark the document as final and save.

6. Read the displayed dialog box shown in **Figure 2**, and then click **OK**.

    The displayed message indicates the document has been marked as final, all edits have been made, and the final version of the document has been created.

    When no one can type, edit, or use the proofing tools within the document, it is considered to be *marked as final*.

■ **Continue to the next page to complete the skill** ▶

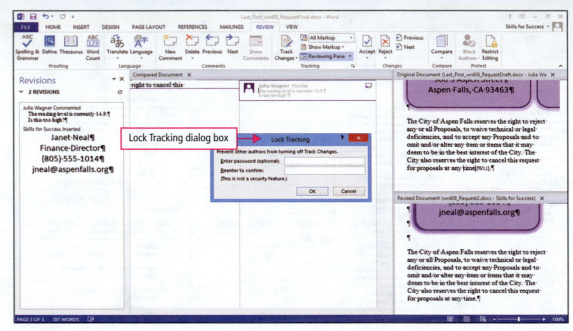

Figure 1

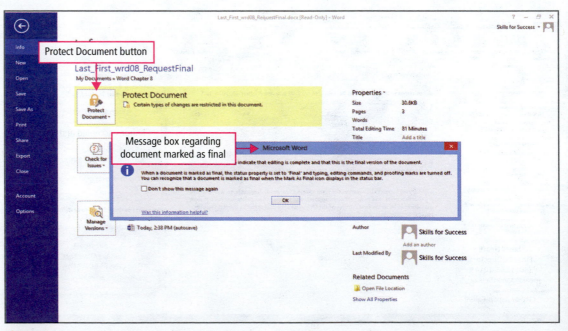

Figure 2

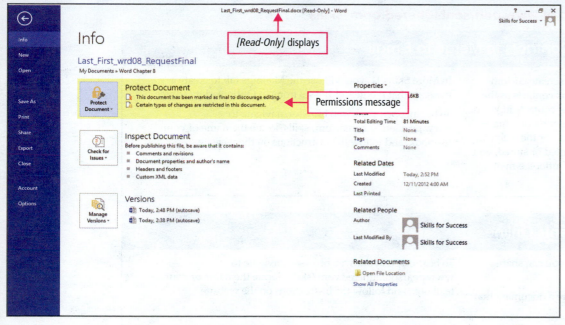

Figure 3

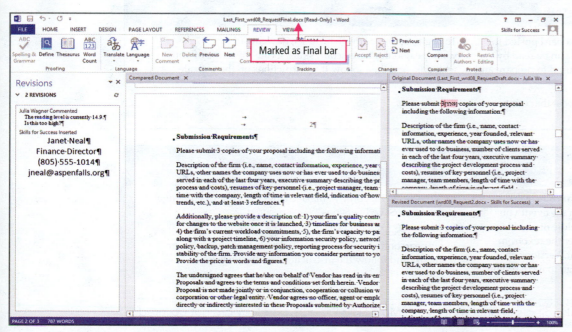

Figure 4

7. Observe that *[Read-Only]* displays in the title bar after the file name to indicate that you can only read the document and not make any changes to it.

8. On the **File tab**, observe the message under Protect Document. Compare your screen with **Figure 3**.

9. Click the **Back** button. On the **Home tab**, observe that the only buttons available are Show/Hide ¶, Find, and Select.

   These three buttons are available because they can be used without making any changes to the current document.

10. In the **Compared Document** window, scroll to the left and up to display the top of Page 2. Click before the *Submission* heading, and type Proposal

    You cannot type in the document because it is marked as final.

11. Click the **Insert tab**, click the **Page layout tab**, and then click the **Review tab**.

    Some buttons on the Ribbon are no longer available because changes cannot be made.

12. With **Last_First_wrd08_RequestFinal** the active window, compare your screen with **Figure 4**.

13. **Close** the Word window.

    ✔ **DONE! You have completed Skill 10 of 10, and your document is complete!**

The following More Skills are located at **www.pearsonhighered.com/skills**

More Skills Use Outlook Contacts to Merge to E-mail

You can use the mail merge feature in Word to create custom e-mail messages that use your existing Outlook contacts as the data source instead of creating your own list of contacts in Word. All mail merge document types—letters, envelopes, or e-mail—can use your Outlook Contacts as a data source for the recipient list. Instead of creating a document that is printed or stored, you can also send, or merge, the message into an Outlook e-mail message.

In More Skills 11, you will use the Mailings tab to create a message that merges addresses from an Outlook data source.

To begin, open your web browser, navigate to www.pearsonhighered.com/skills, locate the name of your textbook, and follow the instructions on the website.

More Skills Share Documents Online

When you save your documents to SkyDrive, you can share them with others.

In More Skills 12, you will invite others to share a document that is stored in your SkyDrive account.

To begin, open your web browser, navigate to www.pearsonhighered.com/skills, locate the name of your textbook, and follow the instructions on the website.

More Skills Create Blog Posts

A blog, also known as a weblog, is a message board posted to the web that is used to share information that can be read by others. Word includes a template that can be used to prepare and publish a blog.

In More Skills 13, you will create a new blog post that can be published to the web.

To begin, open your web browser, navigate to www.pearsonhighered.com/skills, locate the name of your textbook, and then follow the instructions on the website.

More Skills Manage Versions

By default, your documents are saved automatically every 10 minutes. You can change this time interval. In the event your machine shuts down while you are in the middle of working on your document, you may be able to recover the text from the last time Word AutoSaved your document. Versions enable you to select how far back you would like to go to recover your AutoSaved data.

In More Skills 14, you will make changes to your document and review AutoSaved versions.

To begin, open your web browser, navigate to www.pearsonhighered.com/skills, locate the name of your textbook, and follow the instructions on the website.

Please note that there are no additional projects to accompany the More Skills Projects, and they are not covered in End-of-Chapter projects.

The following table summarizes the **SKILLS AND PROCEDURES** covered in this chapter.

Skills Number	Task	Step	Icon	Keyboard Shortcut
1	Change user name	Review tab → Tracking Dialog Box Launcher → Change User Name button → Type User name and Initials		
1	Track changes	Review tab → Tracking group → Track Changes button		Ctrl + Shift + E
1	Insert comments	Review tab → Comments group → New Comment button		
1	Change display options	Review tab → Tracking group → Display for Review button	Simple Markup	
2	Check document statistics	Review tab → Proofing group → Word Count button	ABC 123	
2	Check document compatibility	File tab → Info tab → Inspect Document → Check for Issues button → Check Compatibility		
3	Show Reviewing pane	Review tab → Tracking group → Reviewing Pane button		
3	Delete comments	Review tab → Comments group → Delete button		
3	Mark comment as done	Right-click comment → Click Mark Comment Done		
4	Change markup options	Review tab → Tracking group → Show Markup button		
5	Restrict editing options	Review tab → Protect group → Restrict Editing Or File tab → Info group → Protect Document button → Restrict Editing		
7	Split windows	View tab → Window group → Split button		
7	Print markups	File tab → Print tab → Print All Pages → Print Markup		
7	Change document permissions	Review tab → Tracking group → Tracking Dialog Box Launcher → Track Change Options dialog box → Change User Name		
8	View documents side by side	View tab → Window group → View Side by Side		
8	Compare documents	Review tab → Compare group → Compare button → Compare		
8	Combine documents	Review tab → Compare group → Compare button → Combine		
9	Accept tracked changes	Review tab → Changes group → Accept button		
9	Reject tracked changes	Review tab → Changes group → Reject button		
10	Mark documents as final	File tab → Info tab → Protect Document button → Mark as Final		

Key Terms

Online Help Skills

1. Start **Word 2013**, and then in the upper right corner of the start page, click the **Help** button ⟦?⟧.

2. In the **Word Help** window **Search online help** box, type permissions and then press ⟦Enter⟧.

3. In the search result list, click **Protect your document, workbook, or presentation with passwords, permission, and other restrictions**, and then below **Add a Digital Signature**, click **Digital signatures and certificates**. Compare your screen with **Figure 1**.

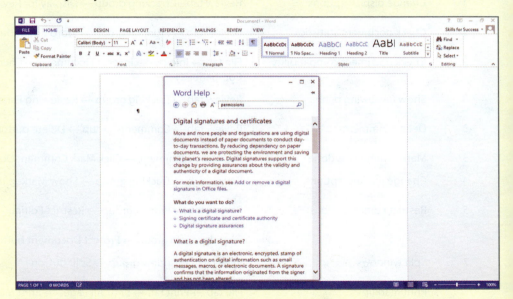

Figure 1

4. Read the article to answer the following question: When you sign a document with your digital signature, what else gets attached to the document for your signature?

Matching

Match each term in the second column with its correct definition in the first column by writing the letter of the term on the blank line in front of the correct definition.

___ **1.** A message that is inserted by a person reviewing a document.

___ **2.** A document view that displays the suggested insertions and deletions in the document.

___ **3.** Data that summarizes document features such as the number of pages, words, characters without spaces, characters including spaces, paragraphs, and lines.

___ **4.** Feature listing the items in your document that may not be compatible with earlier versions of Word.

___ **5.** The feature used to view your Word document in various magnifications.

___ **6.** Displays on the screen and lists all comments and tracked changes.

___ **7.** A notation that displays all changes within the text instead of within revision balloons.

___ **8.** A window that separates a single document into two parts.

___ **9.** A view that displays two different documents in two synchronized windows.

___ **10.** A way to move windows when you scroll either the vertical or horizontal scroll bar in either window.

A All Markup

B Comment

C Compatibility Checker

D Document statistics

E Inline Revision

F Reviewing pane

G Side by Side view

H Split window

I Synchronous scrolling

J Zoom

Multiple Choice

Choose the correct answer.

1. The button used when typing another reviewer's name and initials.
   A. Change User Name
   B. Track Changes
   C. User comment

2. In addition to the number, the other item often included with a comment when inline revisions are displayed.
   A. Document name
   B. User initials
   C. User name

3. The location where the reading level needed to understand text as determined by the length of words, the number of syllables in words, and the length of sentences and paragraphs can be found.
   A. Compatibility Checker
   B. Readability Statistics
   C. Word Count

4. The number of points possible on the Flesch Reading Ease that measures how simple a Word document is to comprehend.
   A. 50
   B. 75
   C. 100

5. The Word feature used to increase the size of the text and comments as displayed on the screen without increasing the actual font size.
   A. 100%
   B. Two Pages
   C. Zoom

6. The pane where comments can be viewed when not in a balloon.
   A. Clipboard
   B. Restrict Editing
   C. Reviewing

7. A document view that displays the revised text in the document and the deleted text in a new color with a line through it.
   A. All Markup
   B. Original
   C. Simple Markup

8. A window separated into two parts so that you can scroll through each window independently to view different areas of the document at the same time.
   A. Side by Side
   B. Split Window
   C. Synchronous Scrolling

9. The button used to move both windows at the same time when the vertical scroll bar or horizontal scroll bar is used.
   A. Side by Side
   B. Split Window
   C. Synchronous Scrolling

10. When comparing documents, the document that you want to merge with the original document.
    A. Compared document
    B. Original document
    C. Revised document

Topics for Discussion

1. What are two advantages of combining two documents? Why?

2. Restricting areas that users can edit helps prevent unnecessary changes to documents that are being used or tracked by others. How could a business use Restrict Editing with their documents? What are some examples of the documents and the data that might be restricted?

Skills Review

To complete this project, you will need the following files:

- wrd08_SRRemodel
- wrd08_SRRemodel2

You will save your documents as:

- Last_First_wrd08_SRRemodel
- Last_First_wrd08_SRRemodelFinal

1. Start **Word 2013**, and then open **wrd08_SRRemodel**. **Save** the file in your **Word Chapter 8** folder as Last_First_wrd08_SRRemodel Add the **FileName** field to the footer.

2. On the **Review tab**, in the **Tracking group**, click the **Tracking Dialog Box Launcher**, and then click **Change User Name**. Under **Personalize your copy of Microsoft Office**, note the values in the **User name** and **Initials** boxes so you can restore these values later. If necessary, replace the existing values with your own name and initials. Select the **Always use these values regardless of sign in to Office**. box.

3. In the **Word Options** dialog box, click the **Proofing tab**. Select the **Show readability statistics** check box. Click **OK** two times.

4. On the **File tab**, click **Check for Issues**, and then click **Check Compatibility**. Read the message, and then click **OK**.

5. On the **Review tab**, in the **Tracking group**, click the **Track Changes** button.

6. In the **Comments group**, click the **Next** button. In the *Donald, is it* comment, click the **Reply to Comment** button, and then type Donald said it is okay.

7. In the **Comments group**, click the **Next** button, read the *Is there a* comment, and then click the **Delete** button.

8. On Page 2, click the end of the paragraph that begins *The successful bidder*. In the **Comments group**, click the **New Comment** button, and then type Should we include a LEED website? as shown in **Figure 1**.

9. In the **Protect group**, click the **Restrict Editing** button. In the **Restrict Editing** pane, under **Editing restrictions**, select the **Allow only this type of editing in the document** check box. Click the **No changes (Read only) arrow**, and then click **Tracked changes**.

10. Under **Start enforcement**, click **Yes, Start Enforcing Protection**. Type Success! for both passwords. Click **OK**. Compare your screen with **Figure 2**.

- Continue to the next page to complete this Skills Review

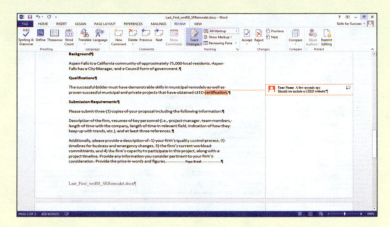

Figure 1

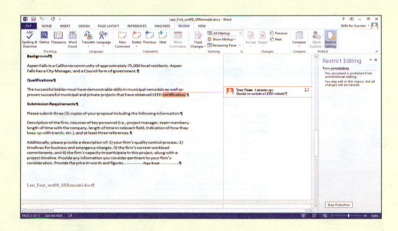

Figure 2

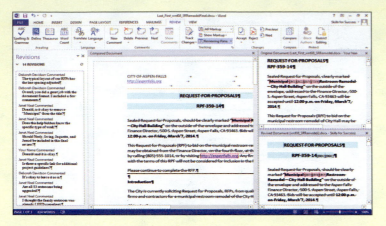

Figure 3

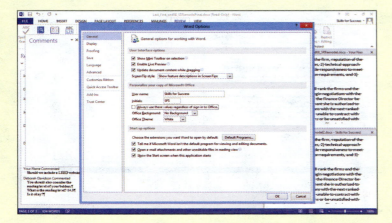

Figure 4

11. On Page 2, in the bullet that begins *Low-flush or,* delete the text *high flush.*

12. In the **Restrict Editing** pane, click **Stop Protection**. Type Success! Click **OK**. **Close** the **Restrict Editing** pane.

13. **Save** and **Close** the document. **Open** a new, blank document.

14. On the **Review tab**, in the **Compare group**, click the **Compare** button, and then click **Compare**. Under **Original document**, click the arrow, and then click **Last_First_wrd08_SRRemodel**. Under **Revised document**, click the **Open** button and open **wrd08_SRRemodel2**.

15. Delete the text in the **Label changes with** box, and then click **OK**. Click **Yes**. **Save** the compared document as Last_First_wrd08_SRRemodelFinal Add the **FileName** field to the footer.

16. Click the **Compared Document** window. On the **Review tab**, in the **Tracking group**, click the **Show Markup** button, click **Balloons**, and then, if necessary, click **Show Revisions in Balloons**.

17. In the **Changes group**, click the **Accept arrow**, and then click **Accept All Changes**. Compare your screen with **Figure 3**.

18. In the **Proofing group**, click the **Spelling & Grammar** button. Click **Ignore All** once. Click **OK**. Record the **Flesch-Kincaid Grade Level** on a piece of paper, and then click **OK**. Edit the last comment in the document to include this number. Right-click the comment, and then click **Mark Comment Done**.

19. On the **File tab**, click **Print**. Click the **Print All Pages** button, and then, if necessary, click to select **Print Markup**. If you are printing your work for this chapter, click **Print**. **Save** the document.

20. On the **File tab**, click **Info**. Click the **Protect Document** button, and then click **Mark as Final**. Click **OK** two times.

21. On the **File tab**, click **Options**. In the **Word Options** dialog box, on the **General tab**, return the **User name** and **Initials** boxes to their original values. If necessary, clear the **Always use the values regardless of sign in to Office**. box as shown in **Figure 4**. On the **Proofing tab**, clear the **Show readability statistics** check box. Click **OK**.

22. **Close** Word. Submit your work as directed by your instructor.

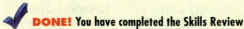

DONE! You have completed the Skills Review

Skills Assessment 1

To complete this project, you will need the following file:

- wrd08_SA1Run

You will save your documents as:

- Last_First_wrd08_SA1Run
- Last_First_wrd08_SA1RunCompare

1. Start **Word 2013**, and then open **wrd08_SA1Run**. **Save** the file in your **Word Chapter 8** folder as Last_First_wrd08_SA1Run Add the **FileName** field to the footer.

2. Change the User name and Initials to your own. Note the values to restore later. Verify the Always use these values regardless of sign in to Office. box. Turn on the **Track Changes** feature. Set the **Display for Review** to **All Markup**.

3. In the paragraph that begins *Aspen Falls, California,* replace *7:00* with 6:30 Replace the text *will be run* with occurs

4. In the comment that begins *Are you sure,* reply with Yes! We can start one half-hour earlier! and then mark the comment as done. Delete the last comment from Deborah.

5. Run the **Compatibility Checker**. Read the displayed dialog box. Select the entire table that begins *WAVE.* Add the comment ___ compatibility issues if using another version. (# of issues found in the **Compatibility Checker** dialog box).

6. Use **Word Options** to change the **Proofing** settings to include **Show readability statistics**. Check **Spelling & Grammar**. If necessary, ignore any issues that are found. On paper, record the **Flesch-Kincaid Grade Level**. Reply to your last comment with The reading level is ___. (the level).

7. **Print** the document showing markups. Use the **Accept arrow** to **Accept All Changes** in the document, and then turn off **Track Changes**. **Save** the document.

8. **Restrict Editing** to **allow only Tracked changes editing in the document**. **Start Enforcing Protection**, and use Success! as the password. Protect the document. Mark the document as final.

9. On the **Home tab**, at the top of the document, select the **Edit Anyway** button, **Stop Protection**, type the password. **Close** the **Restrict Editing** pane.

10. If necessary, in Word Options, restore the User name and Initials, clear the Always use these values regardless of sign in to Office box, and then under Proofing, clear the Show readability statistics box.

11. **Save** and **Close** the document. In a new, blank Word document, **Compare** the original document, **wrd08_SA1Run**, and the revised document, **Last_First_wrd08_SA1Run**. Remove all labels. Click **Yes**.

12. **Save** the compared document as Last_First_wrd08_SA1RunCompare Update the footer, **Save**, and then **Close** Word. Submit your work as directed by your instructor. Compare your completed document with **Figure 1**.

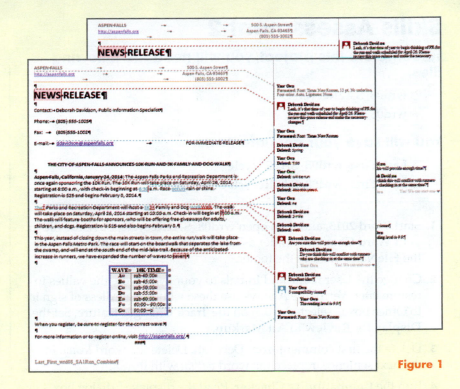

Figure 1

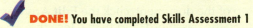 **DONE! You have completed Skills Assessment 1**

Skills Assessment 2

To complete this project, you will need the following files:

- wrd08_SA2Recycle
- wrd08_SA2Recycle2

You will save your documents as:

- Last_First_wrd08_SA2Recycle
- Last_First_wrd08_SA2RecycleCompare

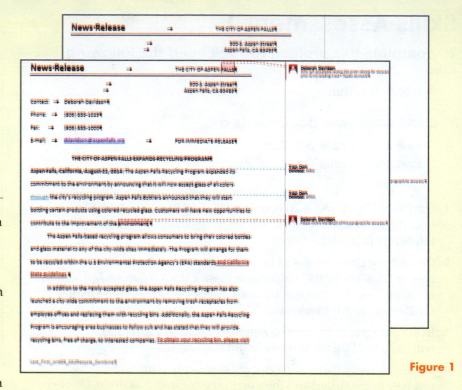

1. Start **Word 2013**, and then open **wrd08_SA2Recycle**. **Save** the file in your **Word Chapter 8** folder as Last_First_wrd08_SA2Recycle Add the **FileName** field to the footer.

2. Change the User name and Initials to your own. Note the values to restore later. Verify the Always use these values regardless of sign in to Office box is selected. Turn on the **Track Changes** feature. Set the **Display for Review** to **All Markup**.

3. Delete the first comment from Deborah. Delete the word *today*. In the next sentence, replace the word *within* with through

4. Run the **Compatibility Checker**. Read the displayed dialog box. On Page 2, modify the last comment to include the number of issues found in the **Compatibility Checker** dialog box. Click the comment after the words *There are*, add a space, and then type the #.

5. Use **Word Options** to change the **Proofing** settings to include **Show readability statistics**. Check **Spelling & Grammar**. Ignore any issues that are found. Record the **Flesch-Kincaid Grade Level**. On Page 2, update the second to last comment from Deborah with the grade level. Mark the comment as done.

6. **Print** the document showing markups. Use the **Accept arrow** to **Accept All Changes in Document**. Turn off **Track Changes**. **Save** the document.

7. **Restrict Editing** to allow only Tracked changes editing in the document. **Start Enforcing Protection**. Use the password, Success! Protect the document. Mark the document as final.

8. On the **Home tab**, at the top of the document, click the **Edit Anyway** button, **Stop Protection**, type the password, and then **Close** the **Restrict Editing** pane.

Figure 1

9. **Save**, and then **Close** the file. **Compare** the original document, **wrd08_SA2Recycle2**, and the revised document, **Last_First_wrd08_SA2Recycle**. Remove all labels. Click **Yes**.

10. If necessary, in Word Options, restore the User name and Initials, clear the Always use these values regardless of sign in to Office box, and under Proofing, clear the Show readability statistics box.

11. **Save** the compared document as Last_First_wrd08_SA2RecycleCompare Update the footer, **Save**, and then **Close** Word. Compare your compared document with **Figure 1**.

12. Submit your work as directed by your instructor.

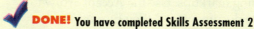

DONE! You have completed Skills Assessment 2

Visual Skills Check

To complete this project, you will need the following file:

- wrd08_VSWellness

You will save your document as:

- Last_First_wrd08_VSWellness

Start **Word 2013**, and then open the student data file **wrd08_VSWellness**. In **Word Options**, use the skills practiced in this chapter to change the **User name** to **Leah Kim** and the **Initials** to **LK**. Verify the **Always use these values regardless of sign in to Office** box is selected. Turn on **Track Changes**, and then insert the comments and changes to the flyer as shown in **Figure 1**. Turn off Track Changes. Restore the User name and Initials, and clear the **Always use these values regardless of sign in to Office** box.

Save the file as Last_First_wrd08_VSWellness in your **Word Chapter 8** folder. Add the **FileName** field to the footer. **Close** the Word window, and then submit the file as directed by your instructor.

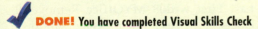 **DONE! You have completed Visual Skills Check**

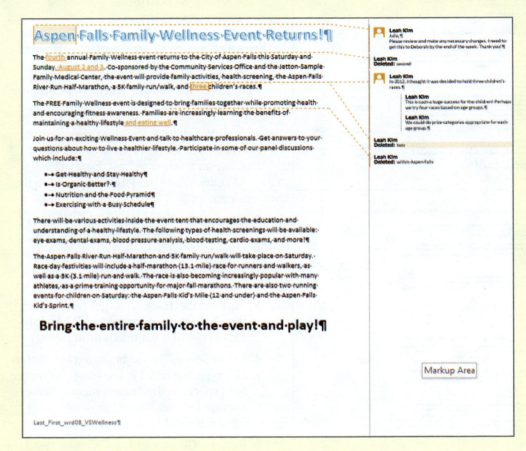

Figure 1

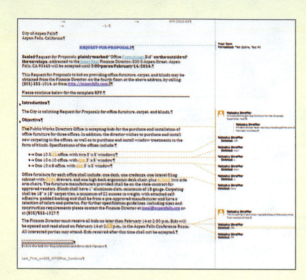

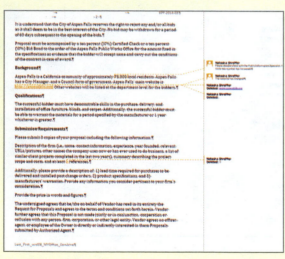

Figure 1

My Skills

To complete this project, you will need the following files:

- wrd08_MYOffice
- wrd08_MYOffice2

You will save your documents as:

- Last_First_wrd08_MYOffice
- Last_First_wrd08_MYOfficeCompare

1. Start **Word 2013**, and then open **wrd08_MYOffice**. **Save** the file in your **Word Chapter 8** folder as Last_First_wrd08_MYOffice Add the **FileName** field to the footer.

2. Change the **User name** and **Initials** to your own. Note the values to restore later. Verify the Always use these values regardless of sign in to Office. box is selected.

3. Turn on the **Track Changes** feature. Set the **Display for Review** to **All Markup**. Delete the first comment from Janet.

4. In the *Sealed Request for* paragraph, before *Bid*, type the word Furnishings followed by a space. In the same sentence, before *Finance Director,* insert the words Janet Neal followed by a space.

5. Run the **Compatibility Checker**. Read the displayed dialog box. Press `Ctrl` + `End`. Insert the comment I ran the compatibility check and found that Include the # and types of issue(s).

6. Use **Word Options** to change the **Proofing** settings to include **Show readability statistics**. Record the **Flesch-Kincaid Grade Level**. Reply to the last comment from Janet with the grade level. Mark the comment as done.

7. **Accept All Changes in Document**. Turn off **Track Changes**. **Print** the document showing markups. **Save** the document.

8. **Restrict Editing** to **allow only Tracked changes editing in the document**. **Start Enforcing Protection**. Use the password Success! Protect the document. Mark the document as final.

9. On the **Home tab**, select the **Edit Anyway** button, **Stop Protection**, type the password, and then **Close** the **Restrict Editing** pane.

10. **Compare** the original document, **wrd08_MYOffice2**, and the revised document, **Last_First_wrd08_MYOffice**. Remove all labels. Click **Yes** in the message window.

11. If necessary, in **Word Options**, restore the **User name** and **Initials**, clear the **Always use these values regardless of sign in to Office** box, and then under **Proofing**, clear the **Show readability statistics** box.

12. **Save** the compared document as Last_First_wrd08_MYOfficeCompare Update the footer, **Save**, and then **Close** Word. Submit your work as directed by your instructor. Compare your completed document with **Figure 1**.

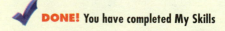 **DONE! You have completed My Skills**

Skills Challenge 1

To complete this project, you will need the following file:

- wrd08_SC1Screening

You will save your document as:

- Last_First_wrd08_SC1Screening

In Word 2013, open **wrd08_SC1Screening**. Add the **FileName** field to the footer. In **Word Options**, use the skills practiced in this chapter to change the **User name** and the **Initials** to **Leah Kim** and **LK**. Verify the **Always use these values regardless of sign in to Office** box is selected. Turn on **Track Changes**. In the subtitle, replace *Information* with Request In the paragraph that begins *The fourth annual*, before the word *Saturday*, type on and add a space, change the word *three* to four In the last sentence of the same paragraph, change the word *event* to screenings and the start time from *7:00* to 9:00 In the paragraph that begins *This event is*, delete the entire second sentence. At the end of the *Staff Phone* paragraph, position the pointer before the paragraph symbol and then press Enter. Insert

the text Screening Provided and then press Tab. Reword the document so that the document is at the eighth grade reading level. Review the document and add at least three additional comments and tracked changes. Turn off Track Changes. Restore the User name and Initials and clear the **Always use these values regardless of sign in to Office** check box.

Save the file as Last_First_wrd08_SC1Screening in your **Word Chapter 8** folder. **Close** the Word window, and then submit the file as directed by your instructor.

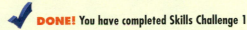 **DONE!** You have completed Skills Challenge 1

Skills Challenge 2

To complete this project, you will start with a:

- **Word document you have prepared for this or another class**

You will save your document as:

- Last_First_wrd08_SC2ReportChanges

Open a document you have prepared for this class or another class in Word 2013. In **Word Options**, use the skills practiced in this chapter to change the **User name** and the **Initials** to your name. Verify the **Always use these values regardless of sign in to Office** box is selected. Turn on **Track Changes**, and then review the paper or report. Edit the document for spelling and grammar. Run the Compatibility Checker and record the results in a comment at the end of the document. Check the Readability Statistics, and record the Flesch-Kincaid Grade Level in a comment at the end of the document. Record the word count in a separate comment. Insert at least 10 comments, delete at least five words or phrases, and insert at

least five words or phrases. If necessary, adjust the line spacing, font name and font size, margins, etc. Turn off Track Changes. Reword the document so that the document is at the fifth grade reading level. Restore the User name and Initials and clear the **Always use these values regardless of sign in to Office** check box.

Save the file as Last_First_wrd08_SC2ReportChanges in your **Word Chapter 8** folder. **Close** the Word window, and then submit the file as directed by your instructor.

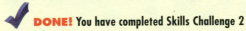 **DONE!** You have completed Skills Challenge 2

CHAPTER 9

Work with Styles and Hyperlinks

- ▶ You can use styles to apply large sets of formatting choices with a single click.

- ▶ In addition to the prebuilt styles that come with Word 2013, you can create and modify your own styles and then apply them to characters, paragraphs, lists, and tables.

- ▶ You can use linked styles to apply either character or paragraph styles, based on what you have selected in the document.

- ▶ You can create hyperlinks to bookmarks within a document, from pictures, and to e-mail addresses.

- ▶ To ensure consistent formatting, you can copy the styles that you have modified or created in one document to another document.

© Maxim_Kazmin/Fotolia

Aspen Falls City Hall

In this chapter, you will assist Julia Wagner, Community Development Director, whose job is to promote the city both in Aspen Falls and around the country. You will update an existing promotional document and add various Word styles to enhance the document so that each similar document created in the department has a consistent look.

The promotional document is a way for businesses to display two columns of information that have styles applied to the characters, paragraphs, lists, and tables. Using the same style across multiple documents provides consistency and a common look. Adding a hyperlink to a picture allows you to work in an online document and move from the document to a corresponding website.

In this project, you will use Word to enhance the existing document by creating and applying character, list, table, and linked styles. You will set styles to update automatically, work with paragraph spacing styles, add hyperlinks to pictures, and link hyperlinks to websites, bookmarks, and e-mail addresses. Finally, you will change the Styles pane options and use the Organizer to copy styles from one document to another.

Time to complete all 10 skills – 60 to 90 minutes

Student data files needed for this chapter:

wrd09_Housing   wrd09_Housing2

You will save your document as:

Last_First_wrd09_Housing

Outcome

Using the skills in this chapter, you will be able to create documents such as this:

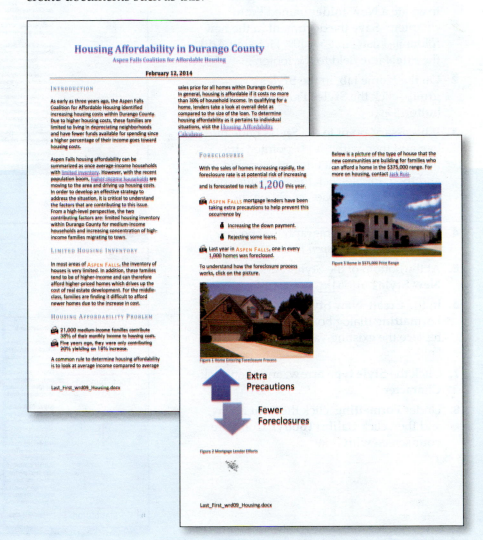

SKILLS

Skills 1-10 Training

At the end of this chapter, you will be able to:

WRD 9-1 VIDEO

▶ Recall that Word 2013 has several built-in styles that display in the Quick Styles gallery and Styles pane.

▶ A ***character style*** is a style type that formats selected letters, numbers, and symbols.

1. Start **Word 2013**, and then open **wrd09_Housing**. Use the **Save As** dialog box to create a **New folder** named Word Chapter 9 **Save** the document in the new folder as Last_First_wrd09_Housing Add the **FileName** field to the footer.

2. On the **Home tab**, in the **Styles group**, click the **Styles Pane Launcher** button.

3. If necessary, point to the Styles pane title bar, and then with the ⊕ pointer, drag the pane to the right edge of the window, and then double-click the pane title so the pane fills the space, as shown in **Figure 1**.

4. In the first body paragraph that begins *As early as*, select *Aspen Falls*.

5. At the bottom of the **Styles** pane, click the **New Style** button.

6. In the **Create New Style from Formatting** dialog box, in the **Name** box, replace the existing value with Aspen Falls

7. Click the **Style type arrow**, and then click **Character**.

8. Under **Formatting**, click the **Font arrow**, and then click **Calibri (Body)**. Compare your screen with **Figure 2**.

■ **Continue to the next page to complete the skill** ➤

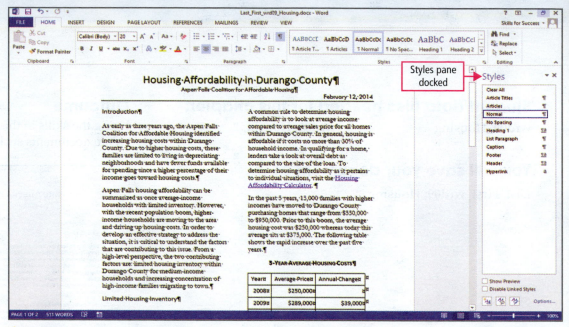

Figure 1

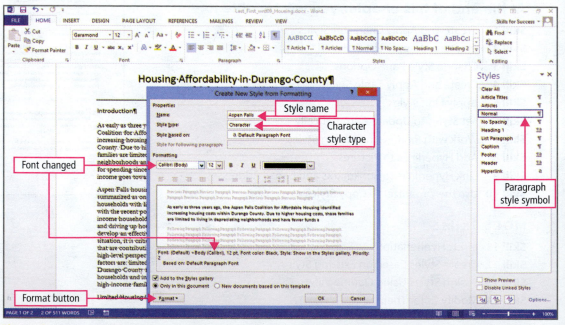

Figure 2

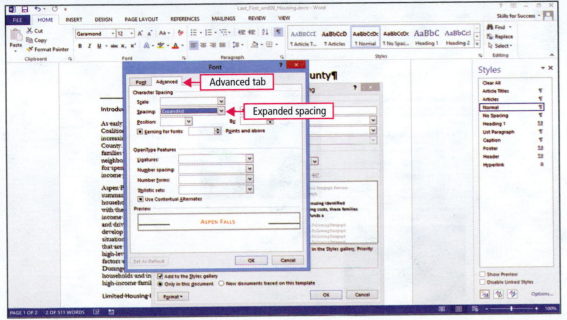

Figure 3

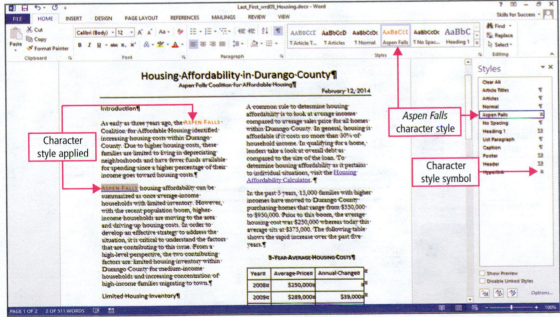

Figure 4

9. Click the **Format** button, and then from the list, click **Font**.

10. In the **Font** dialog box, click the **Font color arrow**, and then select the last color in the fifth row—**Orange, Accent 6, Darker 25%**. Select the **Small caps** check box.

11. In the dialog box, click the **Advanced tab**, click the **Spacing arrow**, and then click **Expanded**. Compare your screen with **Figure 3**.

12. Click **OK** two times.

   The formatting is applied to the selected text, and the character style name—*Aspen Falls*—displays in the Quick Styles gallery and Styles pane. The letter **a** symbol labels each character style—here, the *Aspen Falls* character style. In the Styles pane, the ¶ symbol labels each ***paragraph style***—a style type that formats an entire paragraph.

13. In the second body paragraph that begins *Aspen Falls housing*, select the text *Aspen Falls*, and then in the **Styles** pane, click **Aspen Falls** to apply the character style. Compare your screen with **Figure 4**.

   Recall that to apply a paragraph style, you may position the insertion point anywhere in the paragraph. To apply a character style, you must first select the text.

14. Repeat the technique just practiced to locate the three remaining occurrences of *Aspen Falls*, and then apply the **Aspen Falls** character style to each. Do not apply the style to the newsletter subtitle.

15. **Save** 🖫 the document.

■ **You have completed Skill 1 of 10**

► A *list style* is a style type that formats bullets, numbers, and indent settings.

1. On Page 2, select the four paragraphs that begin *Aspen Falls mortgage* through *Last year in.*

2. In the **Styles** pane, notice that the **List Paragraph** style has been applied, as shown in **Figure 1**.

    List Paragraph is the default paragraph style applied to bulleted lists.

3. At the bottom of the **Styles** pane, click the **New Style** button.

4. In the **Create New Style from Formatting** dialog box, in the **Name** box, replace the existing value with Aspen List

5. Click the **Style type arrow**, and then click **List**. Compare your screen with **Figure 2**.

    When a List style type is selected, the dialog box displays options for formatting lists. A preview pane displays the formatting for the list levels.

6. In the box with the text *Bullet: •*, click the **arrow**, scroll to the bottom of the list, and then click **New Bullet**.

7. In the **Symbol** dialog box, click the **Font arrow**, scroll down, and then select **Webdings**. In the **Character code** box, replace the number with 72 to select the house, and then click **OK**. Click the **Font Size arrow**, and then click **14**. Click the **Decrease Indent** button one time.

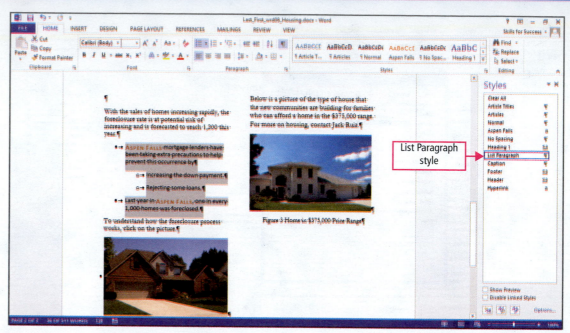

Figure 1

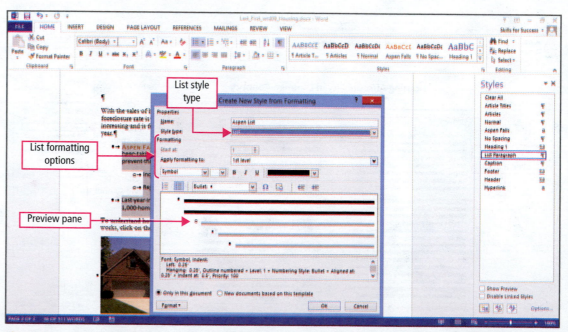

Figure 2

■ **Continue to the next page to complete the skill**

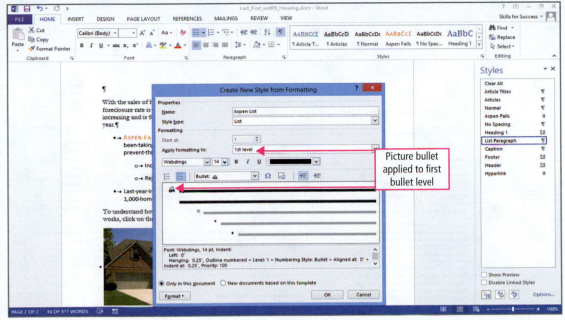

Picture bullet applied to first bullet level

Figure 3

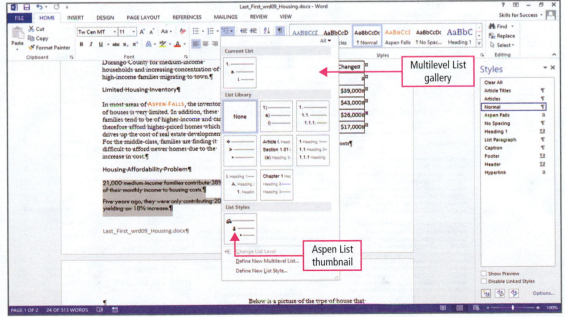

Multilevel List gallery

Aspen List thumbnail

Figure 4

8. In the preview, notice that the picture bullet is applied to the first level, as shown in **Figure 3**.

9. Click the **Apply formatting to arrow**, and then click **2nd level**.

10. Click the **Bullet arrow**, select **New Bullet**, and then repeat the technique just practiced to select the **Webdings Font**, **Character code** 145—the money bag—and then click **OK**. Click the **Font Size arrow**, and then click **14**. Click the **Decrease Indent** button one time. Click **OK** to close the dialog box.

> By default, list styles do not display in the Quick Styles gallery or the Styles pane.

11. Scroll to Page 1, and at the bottom of column 1, select the two paragraphs that begin *21,000 medium-income* and *Five years ago*. On the **Home tab**, in the **Paragraph group**, click the **Multilevel List** button. Compare your screen with **Figure 4**.

> The list styles you created can be found at the bottom of the Multilevel List gallery.

12. In the **Multilevel List gallery**, under **List Styles**, point to the first thumbnail, and then click the **Aspen List** thumbnail to apply the list style to the selected paragraphs.

> The type of bullet applied is determined by the indent level assigned to the bullet.

13. Press Ctrl + Home, and then **Save** the document.

■ **You have completed Skill 2 of 10**

▶ WRD 9-3
VIDEO

- ▶ The Style Pane Options dialog box is used to change how styles display in the Styles pane.

- ▶ The **Normal template** is a Word template that stores the default styles that are applied when a new document is created.

1. At the bottom of the **Styles** pane, click **Options**.

2. In the **Style Pane Options** dialog box, click the **Select styles to show arrow**, and then click **All styles**. Click **OK**, and then compare your screen with **Figure 1**.

   With the All styles option selected, the Styles pane displays all of the styles stored in the Normal template. Depending on the Style Pane Options you have selected, your results may differ.

3. In the **Styles** pane, click **Options**. In the **Style Pane Options** dialog box, click the **Select styles to show arrow**, and then click **In current document**.

4. Click the **Select how list is sorted arrow**, and then click **By type**.

5. Select the **Bullet and numbering formatting** check box, and then click **OK**.

6. In the **Styles** pane, select the **Show Preview** check box, and then compare your screen with **Figure 2**.

   The document's character styles are listed first, followed by the paragraph styles.

■ **Continue to the next page to complete the skill**

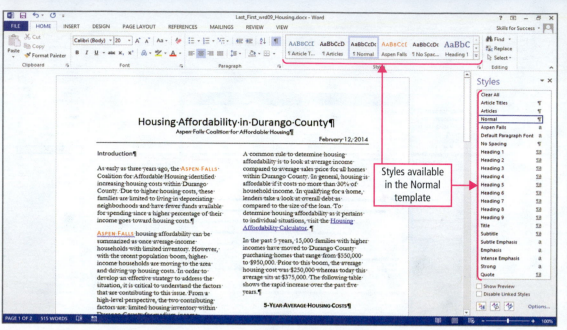

Styles available in the Normal template

Figure 1

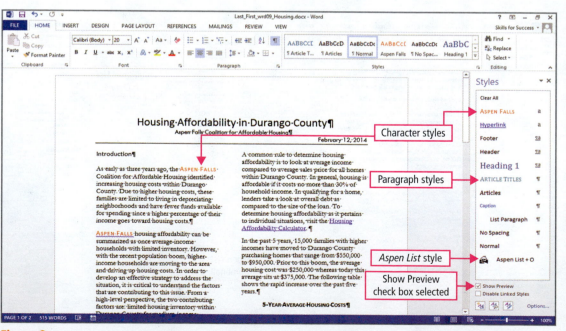

Character styles

Paragraph styles

Aspen List style

Show Preview check box selected

Figure 2

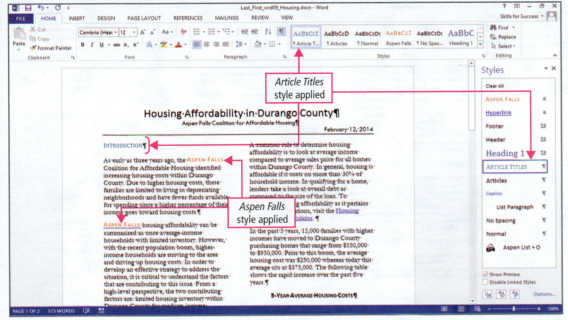

Article Titles style applied

Aspen Falls style applied

Figure 3

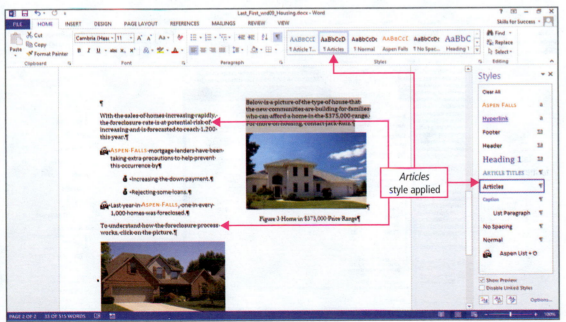

Articles style applied

Figure 4

7. At the top of Page 1, click the first article title, *Introduction*, and then in the **Styles** pane, click **Article Titles** to apply the paragraph style. Compare your screen with **Figure 3**.

   The Article Titles style is a paragraph style created for this skill and previously saved with the file. It is not one of the default styles.

8. Repeat the technique just practiced to apply the **Article Titles** style to the article titles *Limited Housing Inventory* and *Housing Affordability Problem*.

9. Below the *INTRODUCTION* heading, select the paragraphs that begin *As early as* and *Aspen Falls housing,* and then in the **Styles** pane, click **Articles**.

   The Articles style is a paragraph style previously created and saved for this skill.

   When a paragraph style is applied, any character styles in the paragraph retain their formatting. Previously formatted character styles remain unchanged.

10. Repeat the technique just practiced to apply the **Articles** style to paragraphs that begin as follows: *In most areas of Aspen Falls, A common rule to determine, In the past 5 years, With the sales of homes, To understand,* and *Below is a picture.* Compare your screen with **Figure 4**.

11. **Save** the document.

■ **You have completed Skill 3 of 10**

▶ A *table style* is a style type that formats table rows, columns, and cells.

▶ Table style options include separate formatting settings for row and column headers, alternate rows or columns, and summary rows or columns.

1. At the bottom of Page 1, in column 2, click any cell in the first row of the table. On the **Table Tools Layout tab**, in the **Table group**, click the **Select** button, and then click **Select Row**.

   Alternately, point to the row with the 🔼 pointer and click.

2. In the **Styles** pane, notice that the **Normal** style has been applied to the selected row, as shown in **Figure 1**.

3. In the **Styles** pane, click the **New Style** button 🗟, and then in the **Create New Style from Formatting** dialog box, replace the **Name** box value with Table Heading Format

4. Click the **Style type arrow**, click **Table**, and then compare your screen with **Figure 2**.

   When the Table style type is selected, the Create New Style from Formatting dialog box displays style options for formatting tables.

5. Under **Formatting**, click the **Apply formatting to arrow**, and then click **Header row**.

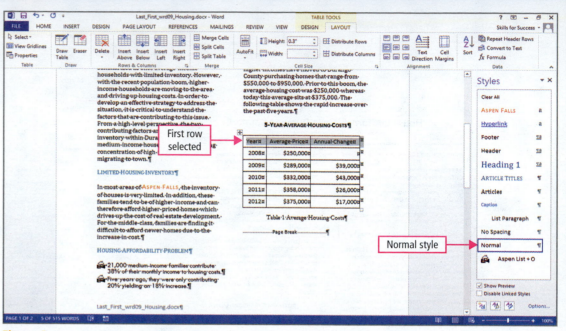

Figure 1

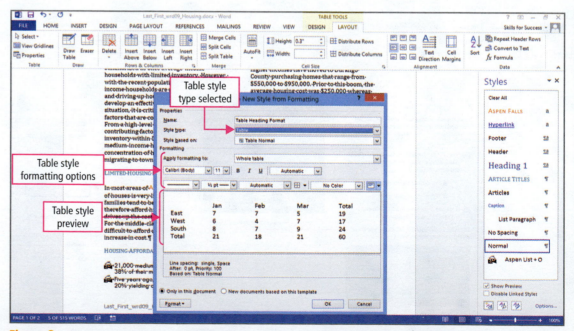

Figure 2

■ **Continue to the next page to complete the skill** ➤

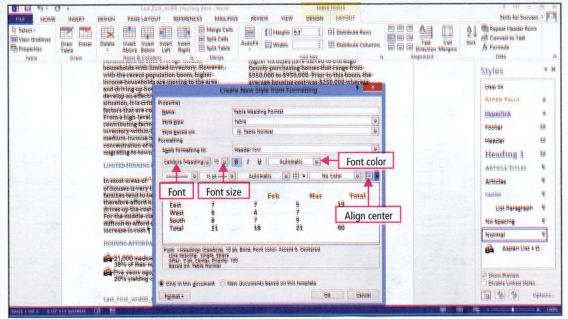

Figure 3

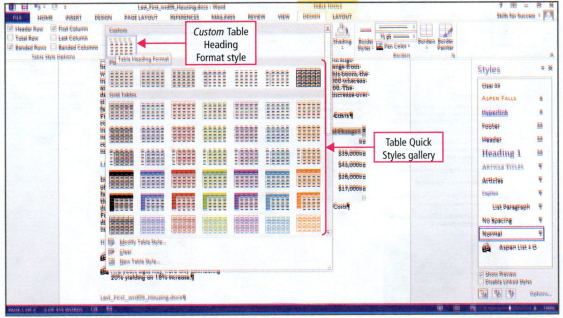

Figure 4

6. Click the **Font arrow** —the first empty box—and then click **Cambria (Headings)**. Click the **Font Size arrow**—the second box—and then click **10**.

7. Click the **Bold** button.

8. To the right of the **Underline** button, click the **Font Color arrow**, and then click the last color in the sixth row—**Orange, Accent 6, Darker 50%**.

9. Click the **Align arrow**, and then click the second style in the second row—**Align Center**. Compare your screen with **Figure 3**.

10. Verify that the **Only in this document** option button is selected, and then click **OK**.

11. On the **Table Tools Design tab**, in the **Table Styles group**, click the **More** button, and then in the displayed gallery, under **Custom**, point to the **Table Heading Format** thumbnail, as shown in **Figure 4**.

    Table styles you create display in the Table Quick Styles gallery.

12. **Save** the document.

■ **You have completed Skill 4 of 10**

▶ A *linked style* is a style type that can be applied as a character style in one place and as a paragraph style in another. The Heading 1 style is an example of a linked style.

▶ When a linked style is applied to a word or a phrase, only the text level formatting is applied. When a linked style is applied to an entire paragraph, both the text level and paragraph formatting are applied.

1. At the top of Page 2, in column 1, click the blank paragraph, and then type **Foreclosures**

   The *Foreclosures* style has been assigned the Normal style, as displayed on the Home tab.

2. In the **Styles** pane, click **Heading 1**, and then compare your screen with **Figure 1**.

   In the Styles pane, the Heading 1 style has both a paragraph and a character symbol next to it, indicating that it is a linked style that can be applied to just the selected characters or to an entire paragraph.

3. At the bottom of the **Styles** pane, click the **Style Inspector** button. Point to the **Style Inspector** title bar. If necessary, with the pointer, drag the pane to the right edge of the window, and then double-click the Style Inspector title bar to dock it. Compare your screen with **Figure 2**.

   The *Style Inspector* pane displays information about the paragraph and character styles for the style applied to the active paragraph or selection.

■ **Continue to the next page to complete the skill** ➤

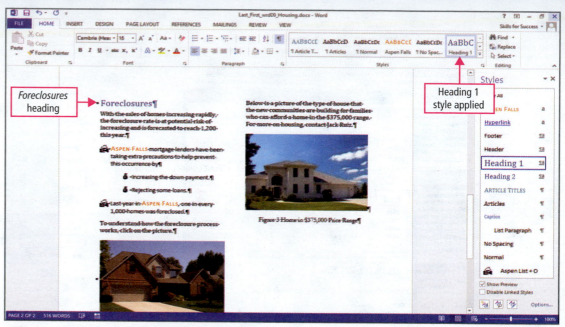

Figure 1

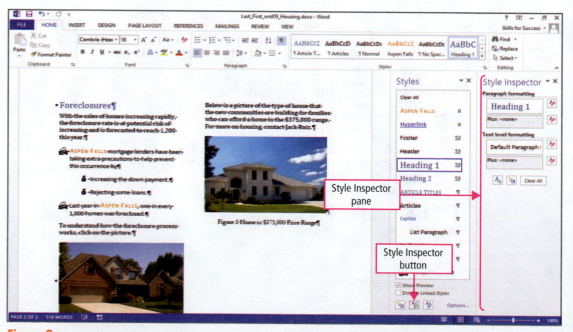

Figure 2

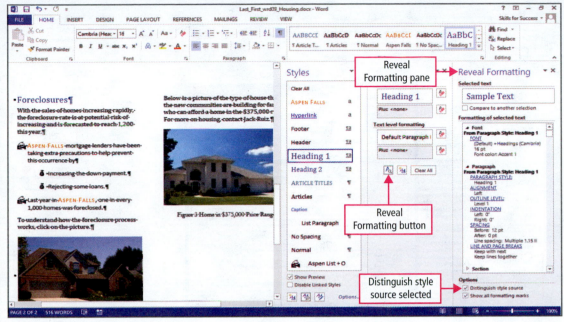

Figure 3

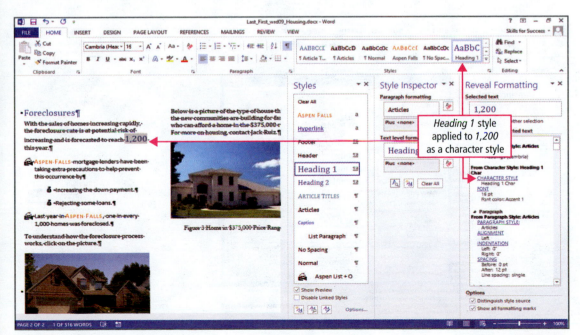

Figure 4

4. In the **Style Inspector** pane, click the **Reveal Formatting** button to open and then dock the **Reveal Formatting** pane to the right edge of your screen.

The *Reveal Formatting* pane displays the selected text and the font, paragraph, and section formatting currently in use.

5. In the **Reveal Formatting** pane, below **Options**, select the **Distinguish style source** check box. Compare your screen with **Figure 3**.

The Distinguish style source option displays the paragraph style used in the selection.

6. In the paragraph that begins *With the sales*, select *1,200*.

In the Style Inspector pane and the Reveal Formatting pane, observe that the Articles paragraph style is in use.

7. In the **Styles** pane, click **Heading 1**, and then compare your screen with **Figure 4**.

Heading 1 is applied as a character style because only selected text, or characters, in the paragraph was selected.

8. **Close** the **Reveal Formatting** pane, and then **Close** the **Style Inspector** pane.

9. **Save** the document.

■ **You have completed Skill 5 of 10**

▶ When a style is set to update automatically, you can modify the style by formatting the text directly instead of using the Modify style dialog box to apply the formatting.

▶ When a style is updated automatically, all occurrences of text assigned that style are changed when formatting changes are made to a single occurrence.

1. Press Ctrl + Home to move to the top of the document.

2. Click the first article title, *INTRODUCTION*.

   Recall that the Article Titles style has been applied to all of the newsletter titles.

3. In the **Styles** pane, point to **Article Titles**, click the arrow that displays, and then click **Modify**.

4. In the **Modify Style** dialog box, select the **Automatically update** check box as shown in **Figure 1**, and then click **OK**.

5. Select the text *INTRODUCTION*, and then on the **Home tab**, click the **Font Dialog Box Launcher**.

6. In the **Font** dialog box, on the **Advanced tab**, click the **Spacing arrow**, and then click **Expanded**.

7. Change the **Spacing By** value to **1.5 pt**. Compare your screen with **Figure 2**, and then click **OK**.

   The Article Titles style updated automatically, and all of the article titles assigned that style are now formatted with expanded character spacing.

■ **Continue to the next page to complete the skill**

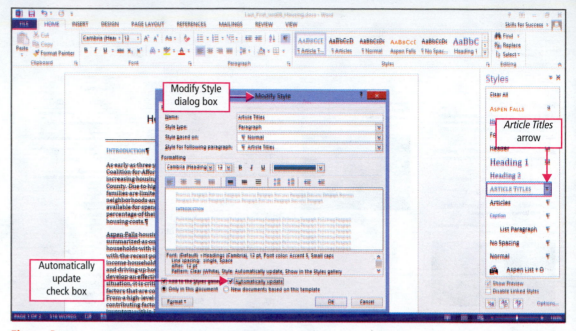

Figure 1

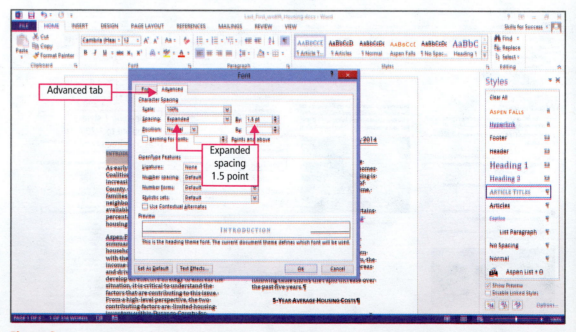

Figure 2

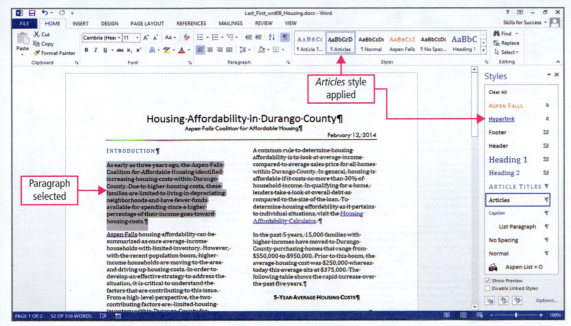

Figure 3

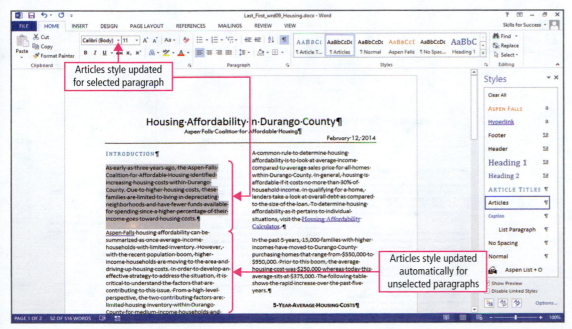

Figure 4

8. Select the paragraph that begins *As early as three years*, as shown in **Figure 3**.

9. In the **Styles** pane, display and click the **Articles arrow**, and then click **Modify**.

10. In the **Modify Style** dialog box, select the **Automatically update** check box, and then click **OK**.

11. In the **Font group**, click the **Font arrow**, and then click **Calibri (Body)**. Compare your screen with **Figure 4**.

 The style is updated automatically, and all paragraphs assigned the Articles style— whether selected or not—are updated.

12. In the **Styles** pane, clear the **Show Preview** check box, and then click **Options**.

13. In the **Style Pane Options** dialog box, click the **Select how list is sorted arrow**, click **As Recommended**, clear the **Bullet and numbering formatting** check box, and then click **OK**.

14. At the bottom of Page 1, in column 2, select the caption *Table 1 Average Housing Costs*. In the **Styles** pane, display and click the **Caption arrow**, and then click **Modify**.

15. In the **Modify Style** dialog box, select the **Automatically update** check box, and then click **OK**.

16. On the **Home tab**, in the **Font group**, click the **Font arrow**, and then click **Calibri (Body)**.

17. **Save** 🖫 the document.

■ **You have completed Skill 6 of 10**

▶ Word has six built-in Paragraph Spacing styles that you can use to assign paragraph spacing. You can also create your own custom paragraph spacing style.

▶ The default Paragraph Spacing style is the Open Built-In style.

1. Press [Ctrl] + [Home] to move to the top of the document.

2. Click the **Design tab**, and then in the **Document Formatting group**, click the **More** button ⮟.

3. Under **Built-In**, point to the eighth thumbnail—**Centered**. Compare your screen with **Figure 1**, and then click the thumbnail.

4. In the **Document Formatting group**, click the **Paragraph Spacing** button. Under **Built-In**, point to **Double**. Compare your screen with **Figure 2**, and then click **Double**.

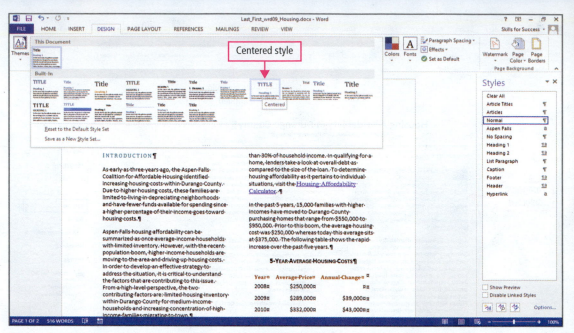

Figure 1

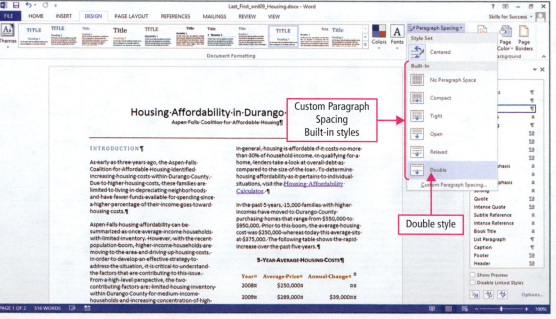

Figure 2

■ **Continue to the next page to complete the skill** ➡

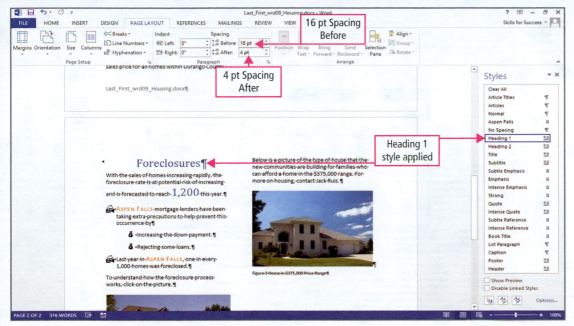

Figure 3

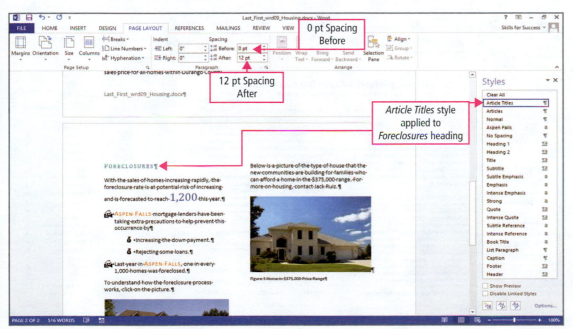

Figure 4

5. On Page 2, click anywhere in the heading *Foreclosures*. Click the **Page Layout tab**, and then observe the **Paragraph Spacing** settings. Compare your screen with **Figure 3**.

   The *Foreclosures* heading displays the Centered document formatting.

6. In the **Styles** pane, click the **Article Titles** style. In the **Paragraph group**, verify the **Spacing Before** displays **0 pt** and the **Spacing After** displays **12 pt**. Compare your screen with **Figure 4**.

7. **Save** 🖫 the document.

▪ **You have completed Skill 7 of 10**

▶ WRD 9-8
VIDEO

▶ **Hyperlinks** help the online reader move quickly to predefined areas within a document or to external documents.

▶ Hyperlinks can be inserted into objects and pictures so that when the reader clicks the object, they can navigate to the specified location within the document or outside of the document.

▶ Hyperlinks for text are formatted so that you can visually recognize them. You can view a hyperlink for an object or picture by pointing to the object in the document. For example, a different color is assigned to hyperlinks that you have already clicked.

1. On Page 1, in the paragraph that begins *Aspen Falls,* select the text *higher-income households* without selecting the space after *households*.

2. Click the **Insert tab**, and then in the **Links group**, click the **Hyperlink** button.

3. If necessary, in the Insert Hyperlink dialog box, under Link to, click the Existing File or Web Page button.

4. In the **Address** box, type http://www. census.gov/housing Compare your screen with **Figure 1**.

5. Click **OK** to insert the hyperlink. Point to the hyperlink just inserted—*higher-income households*—and then press and hold Ctrl. Compare your screen with **Figure 2**.

   To use a hyperlink in Word, press the Ctrl key while clicking the hyperlink.

6. While pressing Ctrl, click the hyperlink *higher-income households* to follow the link. Wait for the U.S. Census Bureau Housing web page to display in your browser. If you see an error message, right-click the hyperlink, click Edit Hyperlink, and then carefully check your typing.

■ **Continue to the next page to complete the skill** ➤

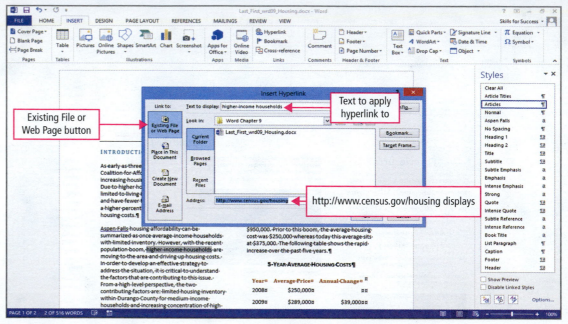

Existing File or Web Page button

Text to apply hyperlink to

http://www.census.gov/housing displays

Figure 1

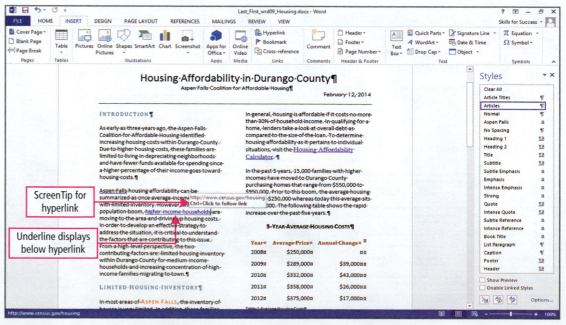

ScreenTip for hyperlink

Underline displays below hyperlink

Figure 2

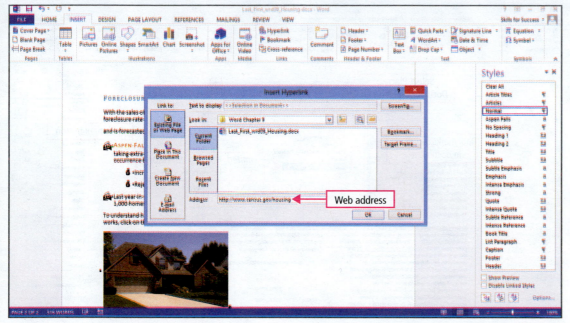

Figure 3

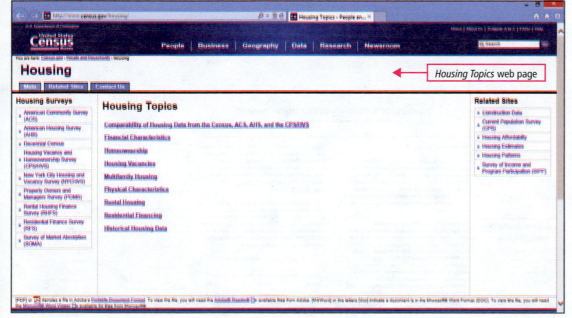

Figure 4

7. **Close** the browser window. On Page 2, right-click the second picture, which has the caption that begins *Figure 3*, and then from the shortcut menu, click **Hyperlink**.

   The hyperlink *higher-income households* displays in magenta to indicate that it has been followed. The *Housing Affordability Calculator* hyperlink displays in blue to indicate that you have not yet clicked the link.

8. If necessary, in the Insert Hyperlink dialog box, under Link to, click the Existing File or Web Page button.

9. In the **Address** box, begin to type http://www.census.gov/housing Compare your screen with **Figure 3**, and then click **OK**.

   As you begin to type the URL in the Address box, the URL you previously typed begins to display to help you save time.

10. Click anywhere in the document so that the picture is no longer selected. While pressing Ctrl, click the picture with the *Figure 3* caption to open the page in your web browser. Compare your screen with **Figure 4**. If you see an error message, right-click the picture, click Edit Hyperlink, and then carefully check your typing.

11. **Close** the browser window. Click in the Word window, and then press Ctrl + Home.

12. **Save** the document.

■ **You have completed Skill 8 of 10**

▶ A **bookmark** is a special nonprinting character inserted into a document so that you can quickly navigate to that point in the document.

▶ You can create a hyperlink that links to a bookmark that has been placed in a document or to an e-mail address.

1. On Page 1, in the paragraph that begins, *Aspen Falls,* in the first sentence, select the text *limited inventory.* On the **Insert tab**, in the **Links group**, click the **Hyperlink** button.

   The followed hyperlink text displays with a purple font color.

2. In the **Insert Hyperlink** dialog box, under **Link to**, verify **Existing File or Web Page** is selected, and then click the **Bookmark** button.

3. In the **Select Place in Document** dialog box, if necessary, expand the Bookmarks list by clicking the Expand button ⊞, click *Limited_Housing_Inventory,* as shown in **Figure 1**, and then click **OK**.

4. In the **Insert Hyperlink** dialog box, verify the **Address** displays **#Limited_ Housing_Inventory**, and then click **OK**. Compare your screen with **Figure 2**.

   The *limited inventory* text displays with an underline to indicate it is a hyperlink to a bookmark that has not been followed.

5. In the paragraph that begins *Aspen Falls,* while pressing ⌃Ctrl, click the *limited inventory* hyperlink to follow the hyperlink.

   The insertion point moves from the text *limited inventory* to the beginning of the *LIMITED HOUSING INVENTORY* heading.

6. On Page 2, in column 2, select the text *Jack Ruiz.* In the **Links group**, click the **Hyperlink** button.

■ **Continue to the next page to complete the skill**

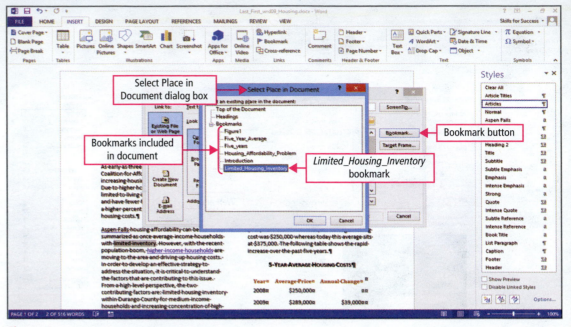

Figure 1

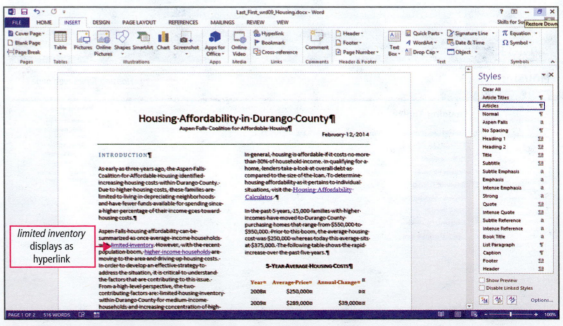

Figure 2

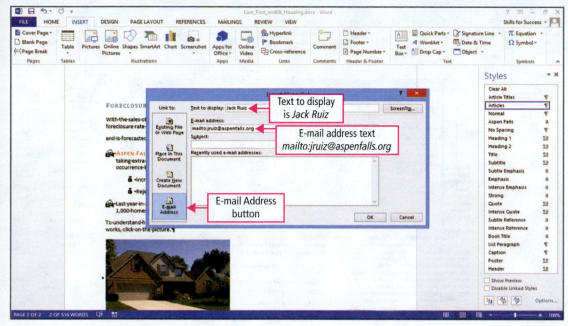

Figure 3

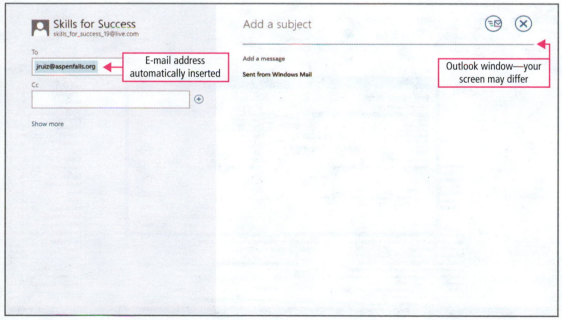

Figure 4

7. In the **Insert Hyperlink** dialog box, under **Link to**, click the **E-mail Address** button. In the **Text to display** box, verify *Jack Ruiz* displays.

The hyperlink text to display identifies the text that will display in the document with the underline.

8. Click the **E-mail address** box, and then type jruiz@aspenfalls.org

When you type the first letter in the E-mail address box, the text *mailto:* automatically displays. The ***mailto*** protocol designates what protocol should be used when the link is clicked, in this case, the mailto: protocol. The hyperlink will open in your computer's default e-mail program. The e-mail address typed into the Insert Hyperlink dialog box will display automatically in the TO: box.

9. Compare your screen with **Figure 3**, and then click **OK**.

10. While pressing Ctrl, point to and then click on *Jack Ruiz*. Compare your screen with **Figure 4**, and then click anywhere in your document.

In Word, when you point to the e-mail address hyperlink and press Ctrl, a box may display with choices for different e-mail programs on your computer. The three choices are your default e-mail application, Microsoft Outlook on the desktop, or an e-mail app available from the Office Store—you will need to select a choice. Your screen may also display a new Outlook message. If you are working on your home or business computer, or if you are using Office 365, your computer may automatically open Microsoft Outlook.

11. If necessary, Close your e-mail application without sending the e-mail. **Save** 🖫 the document.

■ **You have completed Skill 9 of 10**

▶ The Organizer is a dialog box that can be used to manage styles in documents and the Normal template.

▶ You can use the Organizer to copy styles from one document to another.

1. Open **wrd09_Housing2**. If necessary, display the Styles pane. Click anywhere in the document title, which begins *Housing Affordability*.

   The Aspen Title style is applied.

2. Click anywhere in the document subtitle, *Aspen Falls Growth,* and then observe the Aspen Subtitle style.

3. Click anywhere in the date, and then observe the Aspen Date style.

4. **Close** ✖ the file.

5. In the **Styles** pane, click the **Manage Styles** button 🖉, and then click the **Import/Export** button to open the **Organizer** dialog box. Compare your screen with **Figure 1**.

   The Organizer displays the styles in the open document on one side of the dialog box and the styles in the Normal template—*normal.dotm*—on the other side.

6. On the right side of the **Organizer** dialog box, click the **Close File** button.

7. On the right side of the **Organizer** dialog box, click the **Open File** button.

8. In the bottom right corner of the **Open** dialog box, click **All Word Templates**, and then from the list, click **All Files**. Navigate to your student data files, and then double-click **wrd09_Housing2** to display the styles in the original newsletter, as shown in **Figure 2**.

■ Continue to the next page to complete the skill ➤

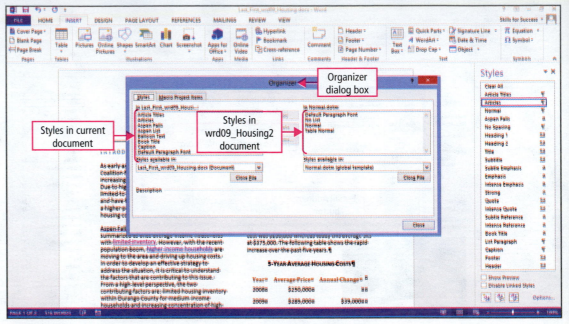

Figure 1

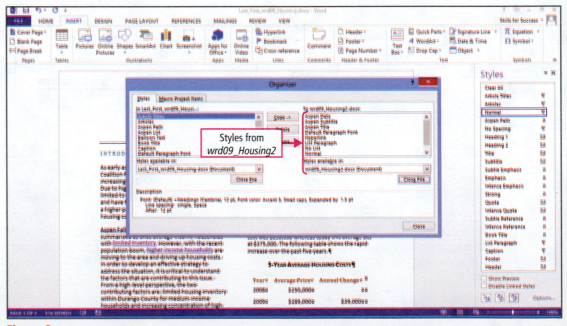

Figure 2

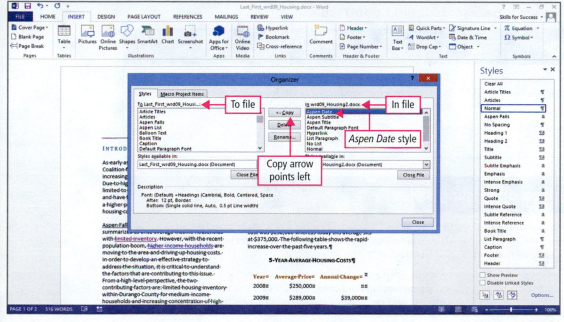

Figure 3

Figure 4

9. Under **To wrd09_Housing2**, click **Aspen Date**, and then compare your screen with **Figure 3**. Click the **Copy** button.

    The In file and To file switch places, and the Copy arrow changes direction.

10. Repeat this technique to copy the **Aspen Subtitle** and **Aspen Title** styles.

    In this manner, you can copy styles into the current, open document, where they can be saved with the document for future use.

11. **Close** ✕ the **Organizer** dialog box. Using the techniques practiced in this chapter, apply the **Aspen Title** style to the title that begins *Housing Affordability*.

12. Apply the **Aspen Subtitle** style to the subtitle that begins *Aspen Falls Coalition*.

13. Apply the **Aspen Date** style to the date, *February 12, 2014*. Compare your screen with **Figure 4**.

14. **Close** ✕ the **Styles** pane.

15. **Save** 🖫 the document. Print or submit the file as directed by your instructor. **Close** ✕ Word.

 DONE! You have completed Skill 10 of 10, and your document is complete!

More Skills

The following More Skills are located at **www.pearsonhighered.com/skills**

More Skills Insert Hyphenation

Many publications divide words between two lines by placing a hyphen between the syllables in a word. You can use Word 2010 to hyphenate words in a document.

In More Skills 11, you will use the Hyphenation tool to hyphenate a document.

To begin, open your web browser, navigate to www.pearsonhighered.com/skills, locate the name of your textbook, and then follow the instructions on the website.

More Skills Create Styles Based on Existing Styles

New styles can be based on an existing style. When changes are made to the base style, both the base style and the new style are updated. Several styles can be based on a single style so that you can change many styles at once.

In More Skills 12, you will create a new style based on an existing style. You will then modify the base style to change both the new and base styles.

To begin, open your web browser, navigate to www.pearsonhighered.com/skills, locate the name of your textbook, and then follow the instructions on the website.

More Skills Assign Styles Using Outline View

When documents are organized in Outline view, styles are automatically assigned to each level in the outline. For example, Level 1 text is assigned the Heading 1 style. When you return to Print Layout view, all of the document headings will be assigned an appropriate style.

In More Skills 13, you will use Outline View to organize and apply heading styles to the document.

To begin, open your web browser, navigate to www.pearsonhighered.com/skills, locate the name of your textbook, and then follow the instructions on the website.

More Skills Modify Color Themes

You can modify prebuilt themes, and you can also create new theme colors, fonts, and effects. You can then apply the new theme to your documents.

In More Skills 14, you will apply a theme and then customize the theme colors, fonts, and effects. You will then create a new theme color.

To begin, open your web browser, navigate to www.pearsonhighered.com/skills, locate the name of your textbook, and then follow the instructions on the website.

Please note that there are no additional projects to accompany the More Skills Projects, and they are not covered in End-of-Chapter projects.

The following table summarizes the **SKILLS AND PROCEDURES** covered in this chapter.

Skill	Task	Step	Icon	Keyboard Shortcut
1	Open Styles pane	Home tab → Styles Pane Launcher button		Alt + Ctrl + Shift + S
1	Create character styles	Home tab → Styles Pane Launcher button → New Style → Style type → Character		
2	Create list styles	Home tab → Styles Pane Launcher button → New Style → Style type → List		
3	Change Style Pane options	Home tab → Styles Pane Launcher button → Options		
4	Create table styles	Home tab → Styles Pane Launcher button → New Style → Style type → Table		
5	Apply link styles	Home tab → Styles Pane Launcher button → New Style → Style based on		
6	Set styles to update automatically	Home tab → Styles Pane Launcher button → New Style (or Modify existing style) → Automatically update check box		
7	Work with paragraph spacing styles	Design tab → Document Formatting group → Paragraph Spacing		
8	Add hyperlinks to pictures	Select picture → Insert tab → Links group → Hyperlink	🔗	Ctrl + K
9	Link hyperlinks to bookmarks	Select text or place in document → Insert tab → Links group → Hyperlink → Link to Existing File or Web Page → Bookmark button → Select bookmark		
9	Link hyperlinks to e-mail addresses	Select text → Insert tab → Links group → Hyperlink button → Link to E-mail Address		
10	Open the Organizer dialog box	Home tab → Styles Pane Launcher button → Manage Styles button → Import/Export button		
10	Move styles between documents	Open the Organizer dialog box → Under In Normal.dotm, click Close File button → Click Open File button → Select All Word Templates → Select All Files → Select file that has styles to copy → Click Open → Select style → Click Copy button → Repeat		

Key Terms

Online Help Skills

1. Start **Word 2013**, and then in the upper right corner of the start page, click the **Help** button ⟨?⟩.

2. In the **Word Help** window **Search online help** box, type hyperlink and then press ⟨Enter⟩.

3. In the search results list, click **Create a hyperlink**. Scroll down to find **Turn off Ctrl + Click to follow a link**. Compare your screen with **Figure 1**.

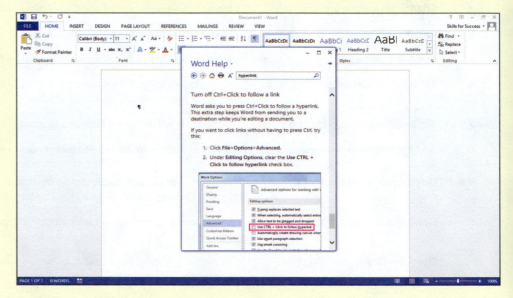

Figure 1

4. Read the article to answer the following question: Where do you turn off CTRL + click to follow the hyperlink?

Matching

Match each term in the second column with its correct definition in the first column by writing the letter of the term on the blank line in front of the correct definition.

____ **1.** The style type applied to selected letters, numbers, and symbols.

____ **2.** The style type used to format spacing, indents, and alignment.

____ **3.** A style type applied to bullets, numbers, and indent settings.

____ **4.** A Word template that stores the default styles that are applied when a new document is created.

____ **5.** A style type applied to rows, columns, and cells.

____ **6.** A style type that can be applied as either a character style or a paragraph style.

____ **7.** A pane that displays information about the paragraph and character styles for the style applied to the active paragraph or selection.

____ **8.** A pane that displays the selected text and the font, paragraph, and section formatting currently in use.

____ **9.** A special nonprinting character inserted into a document so that you can quickly navigate to that point in the document.

____ **10.** A hyperlink designation programmed into a Word document that indicates how the e-mail will be sent and automatically directs the user to select an e-mail application to open.

A Bookmark

B Character style

C Linked style

D List style

E mailto

F Normal

G Paragraph style

H Reveal Formatting

I Style Inspector

J Table style

Multiple Choice

Choose the correct answer.

1. The button clicked to access a stored list style thumbnail.
   A. Bullets
   B. More Styles
   C. Multilevel List

2. The button clicked to display table styles in the Table Quick Styles gallery.
   A. Manage Styles
   B. Styles More
   C. More

3. The dialog box used to update the style's formatting settings.
   A. Manage Styles
   B. Modify Style
   C. Update Style

4. A feature that updates a style as soon as the formatting is changed in the Ribbon.
   A. Add to Quick Style list
   B. Automatically update
   C. List formatting to permitted styles

5. The text color that displays for a hyperlink not yet visited.
   A. Black
   B. Blue
   C. Purple

6. The text color that displays when a hyperlink has been previously visited.
   A. Black
   B. Blue
   C. Purple

7. In the Insert Hyperlink dialog box, select this button under Link to in order to display the Bookmark button.
   A. E-mail Address
   B. Existing File or Web Page
   C. Place in This Document

8. In the Insert Hyperlink dialog box, select this button under Link and start typing to in order to view text that begins mailto.
   A. E-mail Address
   B. Existing File or Web Page
   C. Place in This Document

9. The dialog box used to copy styles from other documents.
   A. Modify Styles
   B. Organizer
   C. Style Pane Options

10. When copying styles, the default template that first displays where styles to be copied from are stored.
    A. Master.dotm
    B. Normal.dotm
    C. Style.dotm

Topics for Discussion

1. What are three advantages of using the Organizer within Word? Why?

2. Character and paragraph styles help ensure accuracy and consistency of documents shared by multiple users. How could a business use character and paragraph styles? What are some examples of the character and paragraph styles that they might use?

Skills Review  MyITLab® Grader

To complete this document, you will need the following files:

- wrd09_SRCenter1
- wrd09_SRCenter2

You will save your document as:

- Last_First_wrd09_SRCenter

1. Start **Word 2013**, and then open **wrd09_SRCenter1**. **Save** the file in your **Word Chapter 9** folder as Last_First_wrd09_SRCenter Add the **FileName** field to the footer.

2. On the **Home tab**, in the **Styles group**, click the **Styles Pane Launcher** button. Select the **Show Preview** check box. Click the **Manage Styles** button, and then click **Import/Export**.

3. On the right side of the **Organizer** dialog box, click the **Close File** button. Click **Open File**, click **All Word Templates**, and then select **All Files**. Open **wrd09_SRCenter2**.

4. At the right, click **Article Titles**, and then hold Ctrl while clicking **Articles** and **Table Heading**. Click **Copy**, and then **Close** the Organizer.

5. On Page 1, in column 1, at the end of the *Aspen Falls' newest* paragraph, select the text *Julia Wagner*. On the **Insert tab**, in the **Links group**, click the **Hyperlink** button. In the **Insert Hyperlink** dialog box, click the **E-mail Address** button. In the **E-mail address** box, type jwagner@aspenfalls.org and then click **OK**.

6. In column 2, select the *Figure 2* picture. In the **Links group**, click the **Hyperlink** button. Click the **Existing File or Web Page** button, click the **Address** box, and then type http://www.ars.usda.gov/recovery/nal.htm as shown in **Figure 1**. Click **OK**.

7. At the bottom of column 2, select the word *Features*, and then in the **Links group**, click **Hyperlink**. Click **Bookmark**, and then under **Headings**, click **Features**. Click **OK** two times.

8. On Page 2, select the *Cost* heading. In the **Styles** pane, display and click the **Article Titles arrow**. Click **Modify**, change the **Font Color** to **Dark Blue, Text 2**—the fourth color in the first row, and then select the **Automatically update** check box, as shown in **Figure 2**. Click **OK**. For the six article titles, such as *Introduction*, apply the **Article Titles** style.

- ■ **Continue to the next page to complete this Skills Review** ▶

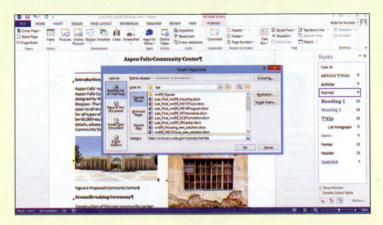

Figure 1

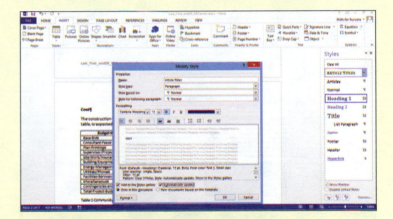

Figure 2

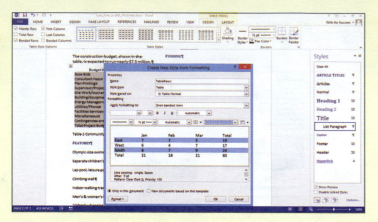

Figure 3

Figure 4

9. On Page 2, select the table's first row. On the **Table Tools Design tab**, in the **Table Styles group**, click the **More** button, and then under **Custom**, click the **Table Heading** style.

10. Select the remaining rows of the table. In the **Styles** pane, click the **New Style** button. Create a table style with the **Name** TableRows and a **Style type** of **Table**. Click the **Apply formatting to arrow**, and then click **Even banded rows**. Click the **Fill Color arrow**, click the fourth color in the third row—**Dark Blue**, **Text 2**, **Lighter 60%**—as shown in **Figure 3**, and then click **OK**.

11. On Page 2, under the *Features* section, select the paragraph that begins *Olympic-size* through the paragraph that begins *Outdoor skate*. Create a list style with the **Name** FeaturesList In the **Numbering Style** box to the right of the **Bullets** button, click the arrow, scroll down, and then click **New Bullet**. In the **Symbol** dialog box, select the **Wingdings 3** font, in the **Character code** box, replace the value with 134 to select ▶, and then click **OK** two times.

12. Click the **New Style** button. Create a character style named Center Apply **Bold**, **Dark Blue**, **Text 2** font color, and **Small caps** format available using the **Format** button. Click **OK** two times, and then apply the **Center** style to each occurrence of *Community Center* and *community center*, except in the title and figure captions.

13. For each body paragraph—but not the bulleted list or captions—apply the **Articles** style.

14. On Page 1, in the paragraph that begins *Construction of*, select *Aspen Falls*. In the **Styles** pane, click **Heading 1** to apply a linked style.

15. In the **Styles** pane, clear the **Show Preview** check box. **Close** the **Styles** pane.

16. At the top of Page 1, click the date. On the **Design tab**, in the **Document Formatting group**, click the **Paragraph Spacing** button, and then click **Relaxed**. Compare your screen with **Figure 4**.

17. Click before the *CONSTRUCTION* heading. On the **Page Layout tab**, in the **Page Setup group**, click the **Breaks** button, and then click **Column**. Repeat the technique just practiced to insert a column break before the *FUNDING* heading.

18. **Save** the document, and then **Close** Word. Submit your work as directed by your instructor.

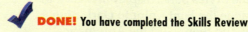 **DONE!** You have completed the Skills Review

Skills Assessment 1

To complete this document, you will need the following files:

- wrd09_SA1Travel1
- wrd09_SA1Travel2

You will save your files as:

- Last_First_wrd09_SA1Travel (Word document)
- Last_First_wrd09_SA1TravelSnip (Image file)

1. Start **Word 2013**, and then open **wrd09_SA1Travel1**. **Save** the file in your **Word Chapter 9** folder as Last_First_wrd09_SA1Travel Add the **FileName** field to the footer.

2. Use **Organizer** to import the *Travel Table Heading* and *Travel Title* styles from the file **wrd09_SA1Travel2**.

3. Display the styles available **In current document** sorted **By type** and with the **Bullet and numbering formatting** displayed. Create a full-screen snip of the **Style Pane Options** dialog box, **Save** the snip in your **Word Chapter 9** folder as Last_First_wrd09_TravelSnip and then close the **Snipping Tool** window. Click **OK**.

4. In the *6:00 a.m.* paragraph, select *Flight*. Create the Travel **character style**. Apply **Bold** and change the **Font Color** to **Blue, Accent 1**. Apply **Small caps**. Apply the **Flight** style to the other two occurrences of *flight*.

5. On Page 1, at the end of the paragraph that begins *The following table*, select *Reimbursement Guidelines*. Create a hyperlink to it.

6. On Page 2, at the end of the paragraph that begins *Please adhere to*, select *Finance Director*. Create a hyperlink to the e-mail address jneal@aspenfalls.org

7. In the same paragraph, select *guidelines*, and then apply the **Heading 1** style as a linked style. Select the picture, and then create a hyperlink to http://aspenfalls.org

8. On Page 2, select the five paragraphs that begin *In-room movies*. Create a new **List** style type named TravelList For the first-level bullet, select **New Bullet**. Use the **Webdings font** and select **Character code** 241—✈.

9. Select all rows in the table beginning with *Air*. Create a new **Table** style named TravelRows Apply the formatting to **Even banded rows**. Change the **Fill Color** to **Blue, Accent 1, Lighter 60%**.

10. Apply the **Travel Title** style to titles that begin *International Conference*, *Reimbursed Expenses*, and *Reimbursement Guidelines*. Set the **Travel Title** style to update automatically.

11. On the **Design tab**, use the **Paragraph Spacing** button to apply the **Relaxed** style.

12. In the **Styles** pane, show the **Recommended** styles available sorted **As Recommended**, and clear the **Bullet and numbering formatting** check box. **Close** the **Styles** pane. Compare your screen with **Figure 1** and **Figure 2**.

13. **Save** the document, and then **Close** Word. Submit your work as directed by your instructor.

✔ **DONE!** You have completed Skills Assessment 1

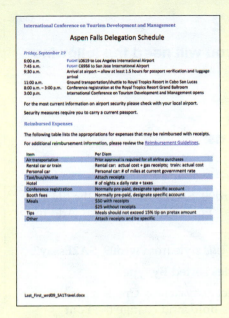

Figure 1

Figure 2

Nmedia/Fotolia

Skills Assessment 2

To complete this document, you will need the following files:

- wrd09_SA2Essay1
- wrd09_SA2Essay2

You will save your document as:

- Last_First_wrd09_SA2Essay

---

1. Start **Word 2013**, and then open **wrd09_SA2Essay1**. **Save** the file in your **Word Chapter 9** folder as Last_First_wrd09_SA2Essay Add the **FileName** field to the footer.

2. Use **Organizer** to import the *Essay Title* style from **wrd09_SA2Essay2**.

3. In the **Styles** pane, display **All styles** sorted **By type**.

4. In the *To encourage* paragraph, select *essay contest*. Create a new **character style** named Essay that is **Bold**, and change the **Font Color** to **Olive Green, Accent 3, Darker 25%**. Apply the **Essay** style to all occurrences of *essay contest* except in headings.

5. On Page 1, at the end of the *To encourage* paragraph, select *prizes*. Create a hyperlink to the bookmark, **Essay_Contest_Prizes**.

6. At the end of the *For examples* paragraph, select *Community Development Director*. Create a hyperlink to the e-mail address jwagner@aspenfalls.org

7. Select the picture, and then create a hyperlink to http://aspenfalls.org

8. On Page 2, select *Citizens for a Greener Falls*. Apply the **Heading 2** style as a linked style.

9. Select all rows in the table beginning with *Brennan*. Create a new **Table** style named EssayRows Apply the formatting to **Even banded rows**. Change the **Fill Color** to **Olive Green, Accent 3, Lighter 60%**.

10. Under the *First Place* heading, select all bullets. Create a new **List** style type named EssayList For the first-level bullet, select **New Bullet**, and then from the **Wingdings 3 font**, select **Character code** 186—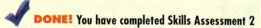. Apply the **Essay List** style to the bullets below *Second Place* and *Third Place*.

11. Apply the **Essay Title** style to the seven document titles that begin *Essay Contest, Topic*, through *Third Place*. Set the **Essay Title** style to update automatically. Change the **Essay Title Font** to **Cambria (Headings)**.

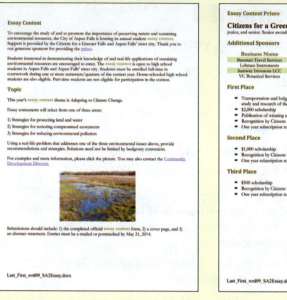

Figure 1

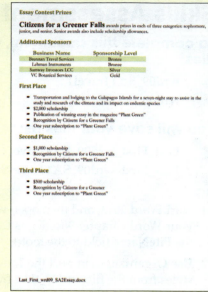

Figure 2

12. On the **Design tab**, use the **Paragraph Spacing** button to apply the **Compact** style.

13. In the **Styles** pane, show the **Recommended** styles available sorted **As Recommended**. **Close** the **Styles** pane. Compare your screen with **Figures 1** and **2**.

14. **Save** the document, and then **Close** Word. Submit your work as directed by your instructor.

DONE! You have completed Skills Assessment 2

Visual Skills Check

To complete this document, you will need the following file:

- wrd09_VSWines

You will save your document as:

- Last_First_wrd09_VSWines

Use the skills practiced in this chapter to create the document shown in **Figure 1**. Open **wrd09_VSWines**. The text *Aspen Falls* (not including the table) has been assigned a character style named Aspen Falls that contains the following formatting: **Bold** with the **Purple, Accent 4** font color. The bullet list has been assigned a list style named WineList that uses character code **150** from the **Wingdings** font. The **Heading 2** style should be applied to the headings and modified to the **Purple** font color and set to update automatically. The table rows have been assigned a table style named TableRows that applies the formatting to the **Even banded rows** with a **Fill Color** of **Purple, Accent 4, Lighter 40%**. The *City of Aspen Falls Tourism Department* hyperlink links to the **e-mail address** taustin@aspenfalls.org The *activities* hyperlink is a link to the **Activities bookmark**. The picture contains a hyperlink to the **Web Page** http://aspenfalls.org The document used the **Relaxed Paragraph Spacing** style.

Save the file as Last_First_wrd09_VSWines in your **Word Chapter 9** folder. Add the **FileName** field to the footer. **Close** the Word window, and then submit the file as directed by your instructor.

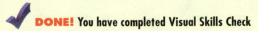

DONE! You have completed Visual Skills Check

Winery Tasting and Tour

Have you considered a wine tour but are unsure of the best place to visit? The Aspen Falls wine region offers a beautiful and peaceful atmosphere that is sure to offer a memorable experience. For more information, please contact the City of Aspen Falls Tourism Department.

There are many activities within the Aspen Falls wineries area in Durango County. You will find breath-taking views in a peaceful and relaxing settings far from the stresses of everyday living. Walk among the vines as you take in the fresh air while sipping on an award-winning wine.

Enjoy delicious dining offered by Aspen Falls' chefs. Relax with a massage from one of the area's specially-trained masseuses. At the end of the day, stay overnight in a romantic bed and breakfast.

Best Time to Go

The best time to plan your trip is in May or during the fall harvest in September and October. The views are spectacular and the crowds are smaller. You can still enjoy all the services offered during peak-season.

WINE TOURS	
Tour Duration	4 hours
Group Size	6-15 people
Destination	Aspen Falls Wine Region
Season	May-October
Price per Person	$100

Activities

If you desire a planned trip, Aspen Falls' wineries offer an array of activities.

- Experience one of our winery tours in the comforts of a limousine.
- Take a winemaking class taught by some of the best wine makers in the region.
- Relax while enjoying the full-service spas around the area.

Last_First_wrd09_VSWines.docx

Figure 1

© mrfoto/Fotolia

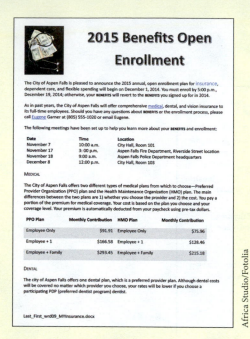

2015 Benefits Open Enrollment

The City of Aspen Falls is pleased to announce the 2015 annual, open enrollment plan for insurance, dependent care, and flexible spending will begin on December 1, 2014. You must enroll by 5:00 p.m., December 19, 2014; otherwise, your BENEFITS will revert to the BENEFITS you signed up for in 2014.

As in past years, the City of Aspen Falls will offer comprehensive medical, dental, and vision insurance to its full-time employees. Should you have any questions about BENEFITS or the enrollment process, please call Eugene Garner at (805) 555-1020 or email Eugene.

The following meetings have been set up to help you learn more about your BENEFITS and enrollment:

Date	Time	Location
November 7	10:00 a.m.	City Hall, Room 101
November 17	3: 00 p.m.	Aspen Falls Fire Department, Riverside Street location
November 18	9:00 a.m.	Aspen Falls Police Department headquarters
December 8	12:00 p.m.	City Hall, Room 103

MEDICAL

The City of Aspen Falls offers two different types of medical plans from which to choose—Preferred Provider Organization (PPO) plan and the Health Maintenance Organization (HMO) plan. The main differences between the two plans are 1) whether you choose the provider and 2) the cost. You pay a portion of the premium for medical coverage. Your cost is based on the plan you choose and your coverage level. Your premium is automatically deducted from your paycheck using pre-tax dollars.

PPO Plan	Monthly Contribution	HMO Plan	Monthly Contribution
Employee Only	$91.91	Employee Only	$75.96
Employee + 1	$166.58	Employee + 1	$128.46
Employee + Family	$293.45	Employee + Family	$215.18

DENTAL

The city of Aspen Falls offers one dental plan, which is a preferred provider plan. Although dental costs will be covered no matter which provider you choose, your rates will be lower if you choose a participating PDP (preferred dentist program) dentist.

Last_First_wrd09_MYInsurance.docx

Plan	Monthly Contribution
Employee Only	$10.71
Employee + 1	$18.26
Employee + Family	$29.45

VISION

The city of Aspen Falls offers one vision plan, which is a preferred provider plan. Although provider and eyewear costs will be covered no matter which provider you choose, your rates will be lower if you choose a participating PVP (preferred vision program) eye doctor.

Plan	Monthly Contribution
Employee Only	$7.96
Employee + 1	$15.03
Employee + Family	$24.13

FLEXIBLE SPENDING ACCOUNTS

Your Flexible Spending Account (FSA), also called a Health Savings Account (HSA), can be used to reimburse for or help pay for eligible medical expenses not covered by your health plan. A list of common eligible expenses includes the following:

➪ Health care plan copays
➪ Dental work and orthodontia
➪ Doctor fees
➪ Eye exams
➪ Hearing aids
➪ Lab fees
➪ Prescriptions
➪ Mental health counseling

DEPENDENT CARE

Your Dependent Care Reimbursement Account can be used to reimburse for eligible daycare expenses for children age 12 and under. You can also use the account for adult daycare expenses for a disabled spouse. The maximum annual deduction has changed to a maximum of $2,500.

Last_First_wrd09_MYInsurance.docx

Africa Studio/Fotolia

Figure 1

My Skills

To complete this document, you will need the following files:

- wrd09_MYInsurance1
- wrd09_MYInsurance2

You will save your file as:

- Last_First_wrd09_MYInsurance

1. Start **Word 2013**, and then open **wrd09_MYInsurance1**. **Save** the file in your **Word Chapter 9** folder as Last_First_wrd09_MYInsurance Add the **FileName** field to the footer.

2. Use the **Organizer** to import the *Ins Title* style from the file **wrd09_MYInsurance2**.

3. In the **Styles** pane, display **All styles** sorted **By type**.

4. Select the picture, and then create a hyperlink to http://aspenfalls.org

5. On Page 1, in the paragraph that begins *The City of*, select *insurance*, and then apply the **Heading 2** style as a linked style.

6. In the paragraph that begins *The City of*, select the word *benefits*. Create a new **character style** named Benefits For the new style, apply **Bold** and **Small Caps**. Apply the **Benefits** style to all occurrences of *benefits* except in the title.

7. In the paragraph that begins *As in past*, select *medical*. Create a hyperlink to the bookmark **Medical**.

8. In the same paragraph, select *Eugene*. Create a hyperlink to the e-mail address egarner@aspenfalls.org

9. Select the four table rows that begin *PPO Plan*. Create a new **Table** style named InsRows Apply the formatting to **Even**

banded rows. Change the **Fill Color** to **Gray-25%**, **Background 2**. On Page 2, apply the **InsRows** style to the *Dental* and *Vision* tables.

10. On Page 2, under the *Flexible Spending* heading, select the paragraphs that begin *Health care* through *Mental health*. Create a new **List** style type named InsList For the first-level bullet, select **New Bullet**, and then from the **Wingdings 3 font**, select **Character code** 91—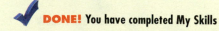.

11. Apply the **Ins Title** style to the five document titles that begin *Medical, Dental,* through *Dependent Care*.

12. Set the **Ins Title** style to update automatically. Change the **Ins Title Spacing Before** to **12 pt**.

13. On Page 1, use the **Design tab** to set the **Paragraph Spacing** to **Tight**.

14. In the **Styles** pane, show the **In use** styles available sorted **As Recommended**. **Close** the **Styles** pane. Compare your screen with **Figure 1**.

15. **Save** the document. **Close** the Word window, and then submit the file as directed by your instructor.

✔ **DONE! You have completed My Skills**

Skills Challenge 1

To complete this document, you will need the following file:

- wrd09_SC1CrimeStoppers

You will save your document as:

- Last_First_wrd09_SC1CrimeStoppers

In Word 2013, open **wrd09_SC1CrimeStoppers**. Use the skills practiced in this chapter to update the promotional document. In the first paragraph, select the first occurrence of *Crime Stoppers* and then create a character style named Crime Stoppers that is **Bold**, with the **Red**, **Accent 2 Font Color**. Apply the **Crime Stoppers** style to the other occurrences of *Crime Stoppers*, not including the document title, headings, or meeting dates. Under the *GOALS* heading, select the three paragraphs, and then create a first-level list style named GoalsList that uses a new bullet with from the **Wingdings** font with the character code 169— . On Page 2, below the *EVENTS* heading, apply the **Heading 2** style to the text *funded entirely by donations*. Modify the Heading 2 style to automatically update. With the text still selected, change the **Font Color** to **Red**, **Accent 2**. Select the entire table that begins *Arrests Made*. Create a table style named TableRows

that applies the formatting to the **Odd banded rows** with a **Fill Color** of **Red**, **Accent 2**, **Lighter 60%**. On Page 1, in column 2, in the second paragraph, select the first occurrence of the word *tips*, and then create a hyperlink to the **SUBMITTING_TIPS bookmark**. On Page 2, at the end of column 2, select the text *Aspen Falls Police Department*, and then create a hyperlink to the e-mail address rmack@aspenfalls.org At the end of the document, select the Crime Stoppers picture, and then create a hyperlink to the Web Page http://aspenfalls.org Apply the **Compact Paragraph Spacing** style.

Save the file as Last_First_wrd09_SC1CrimeStoppers in your **Word Chapter 9** folder. Add the **FileName** field to the footer. **Close** the Word window, and then submit the file as directed by your instructor.

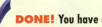 **DONE!** You have completed Skills Challenge 1

Skills Challenge 2

To complete this document, you will start with a:

- New, blank Word document

You will save your document as:

- Last_First_wrd09_SC2Promotion

Locate an example of a printed promotional document that includes a list, picture, and a table that is available at your college and is used by a club, organization, or faculty member. In Word 2013, open a new, blank document, and then use the skills practiced in this chapter to create a document that is similar to the printed document that you located. Create at least one character style, one list style, and one table style. Apply at least one linked style, set one style to update

automatically, and change the paragraph spacing style. Add a hyperlink to a picture, a bookmark, and an e-mail address.

Save the file as Last_First_wrd09_SC2Promotion in your **Word Chapter 9** folder. Add the **FileName** field to the footer. **Close** the Word window, and then submit the file as directed by your instructor.

DONE! You have completed Skills Challenge 2

CHAPTER 10

Create Forms and Macros

► You create interactive forms so that others can enter information by typing text in form field text controls, selecting dates from the calendar, choosing an item from a drop-down list, or selecting desired check boxes.

► You can use the Developer tab in Word to add Legacy tools that insert form field controls and display helpful information about each field.

► Form documents can be locked, or protected, so that only the form fields can be filled in—no other changes to the form can be made.

► You can create and run macros that perform a series of common tasks with a single mouse click or by using a keyboard shortcut.

► When a document contains macros, you can determine the security level settings used by Word to determine whether to open the document.

► You can customize the Ribbon and change buttons on the Quick Access Toolbar for the tasks you use the most. You can also reset the customizations back to the default Word settings.

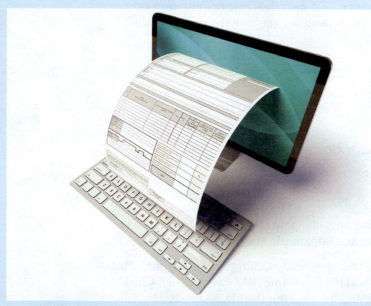

© Leszekglasner/Fotolia

Aspen Falls City Hall

In this chapter, you will assist Deborah Davidson, Public Information Specialist, whose job is to promote the city both in Aspen Falls and around the country. You will update an existing document, add Word form controls and macros to enhance it, and protect it so that the document can be used as an electronic form that prospective student interns can complete.

Having someone complete an electronic form created in Microsoft Word is a way to collect information that can be used in businesses. In this case, the form will be used to electronically obtain schedule preferences of Aspen Falls Community College students who plan to intern with the City of Aspen Falls. Businesses often create electronic forms to automate work flow and to obtain a consistent data collection method. For this assignment, you will enhance a document by turning it into an interactive form document that could be used online. The form will have areas, or fields, for end users to type responses, as well as protected text that cannot be changed.

In this project, you will use the Developer tab in Word to insert text controls, date picker controls, drop-down lists, check boxes, Legacy Tools, and help content. You will create and run a macro, set the macro security level, protect, and make the document available for distribution. Additionally, you will customize the Word Ribbon and change buttons on the Quick Access Toolbar, and then reset the customizations to the Word default settings.

Time to complete all 10 skills – 60 to 90 minutes

Student data file needed for this chapter:

wrd10_Intern

You will save your documents as:

Last_First_wrd10_Intern
Last_First_wrd10_InternLocked
Last_First_wrd10_InternMacro

Outcome

Using the skills in this chapter, you will be able to create an electronic form such as this:

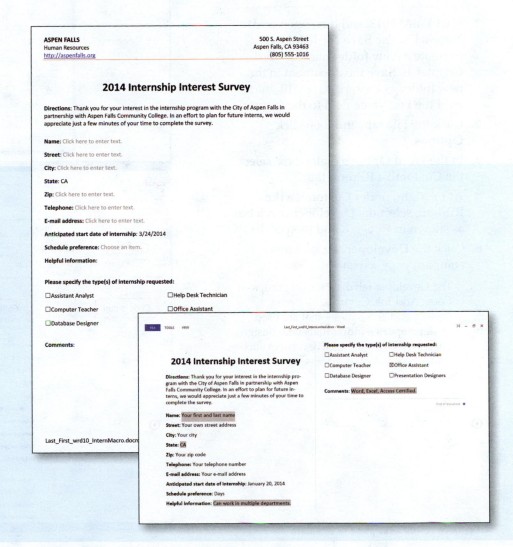

Skills 1-10 Training

SKILLS

At the end of this chapter, you will be able to:

Skill 1   Display the Developer Tab and Insert Text Controls
Skill 2   Insert Date Picker Controls
Skill 3   Insert Drop-Down Lists and Check Boxes
Skill 4   Insert Legacy Tools and Add Help Content to Form Fields
Skill 5   Protect and Distribute Forms
Skill 6   Test Interactive Forms and Remove Protection
Skill 7   Record Macros and Set Macro Security
Skill 8   Customize the Ribbon
Skill 9   Change Buttons on the Quick Access Toolbar
Skill 10 Run Macros and Reset Customizations

MORE SKILLS

Skill 11 Work with Captions
Skill 12 Manage Documents with Multiple Sections
Skill 13 Move and Copy Macros and Building Blocks Between Documents
Skill 14 Create Accessible Documents with Signature Lines

► The Developer tab has tools for working with forms, macros, and XML (eXtensible Markup Language) documents that do not contain macros. The Developer tab does not display until it is selected in the Word Options dialog box.

► To design an interactive form, you insert *controls*—interactive objects such as text boxes, buttons, or list boxes.

1. Start **Word 2013**, and then open **wrd10_ Intern**. Use the **Save As** dialog box to create a **New folder** named Word Chapter 10 **Save** the document in the new folder as Last_First_wrd10_Intern Add the **FileName** field to the footer.

2. Click the **File tab**, and then click **Options**.

3. In the **Word Options** dialog box, select the **Customize Ribbon tab**.

4. At the right, under **Customize the Ribbon**, select the **Developer** check box as shown in **Figure 1**, and then click **OK**.

5. Click the **Developer tab**, and then compare your screen with **Figure 2**.

   The Developer tab displays six groups—Code, Add-Ins, Controls, Mapping, Protect, and Templates—that are used by *developers*—individuals who design documents with interactive content such as content controls and macros.

■ **Continue to the next page to complete the skill**

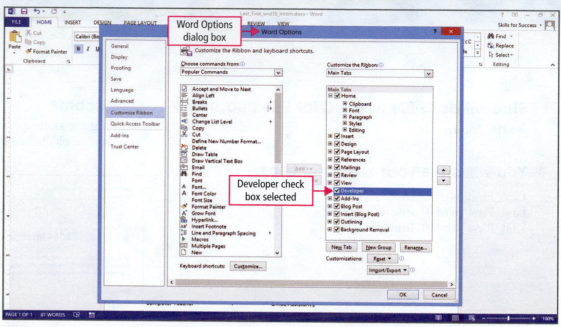

Figure 1

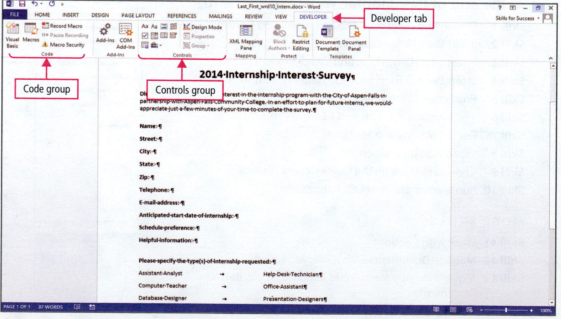

Figure 2

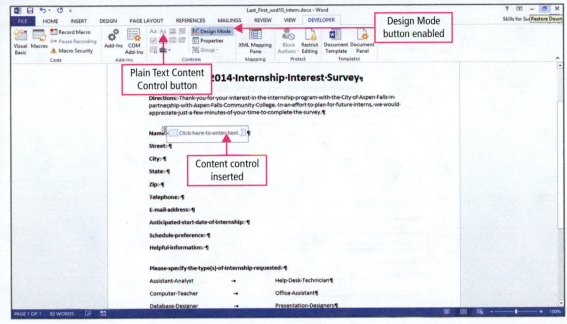

Figure 3

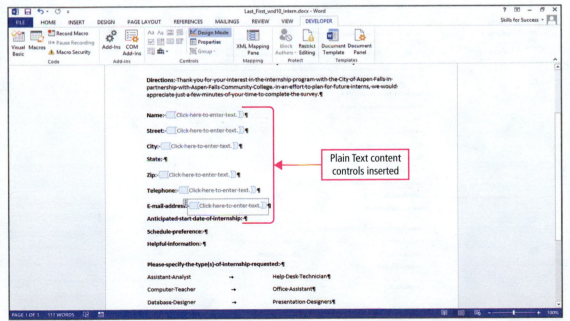

Figure 4

6. In the **Controls group**, click the **Design Mode** button.

   The Design Mode button is a toggle button. **Design mode** is a view that allows you to work as a developer. When Design mode is turned off, you are working as an **end user**—an individual who works with the document the developer designs.

7. Locate the line that begins *Name*. Place the insertion point at the end of the paragraph.

8. In the **Controls group**, click the **Plain Text Content Control** button [Aa] to insert a text control, as shown in **Figure 3**.

   The **Plain Text content control** is inserted into forms so that the end user can type text into a text box. Here, the text control displays **instructional text**—text in a form control that instructs the end user how to enter information.

9. Locate the line that begins *Street*. Place the insertion point at the end of the paragraph. In the **Controls group**, click the **Plain Text Content Control** button [Aa].

10. Repeat the technique just practiced to insert a **Plain Text content control** after *City, Zip, Telephone*, and *E-mail address*. Compare your screen with **Figure 4**.

11. **Save** [disk] the document.

■ **You have completed Skill 1 of 10**

▶ The **Date Picker content control** displays an interactive calendar used to insert a specific date into a document.

▶ When you need to use the form as an end user, you must turn off Design mode.

1. Locate the line that begins *Anticipated start date of internship*, and then place the insertion point at the end of the paragraph.

2. On the **Developer tab**, in the **Controls group**, click the **Date Picker Content Control** button, and then compare your screen with **Figure 1**.

   The Date Picker content control displays the instructional text *Click here to enter a date*. The calendar will not display until the control is clicked.

3. In the **Controls group**, click the **Design Mode** button to turn off Design mode.

4. If necessary, click the Date Picker content control. Click the **Date Picker Content Control arrow** to display the calendar.

5. In the upper right corner of the calendar, click the ▶ button as many times as needed to display *March, 2014*. Click **24** to select and insert the date *3/24/2014*, as shown in **Figure 2**.

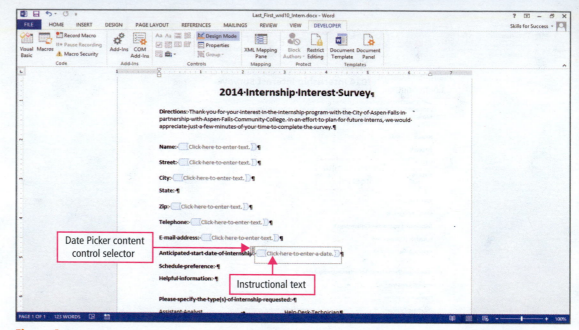

Figure 1

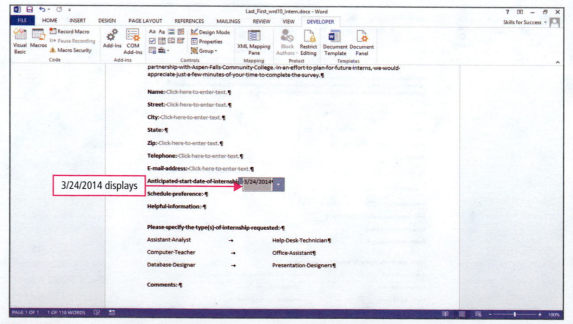

Figure 2

■ **Continue to the next page to complete the skill** ▶

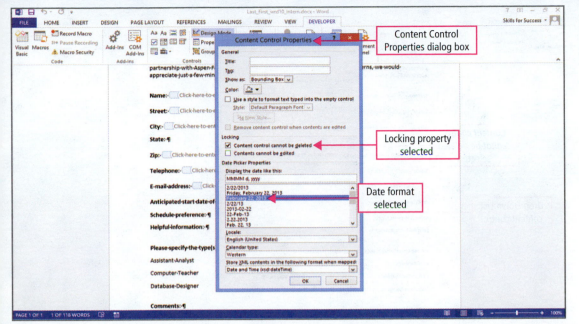

Content Control Properties dialog box

Locking property selected

Date format selected

Figure 3

6. In the **Controls group**, click the **Design Mode** button to turn on Design mode.

7. With the **Date Picker content control** still selected, in the **Controls group**, click the **Properties** button.

8. In the **Content Control Properties** dialog box, under **Locking**, select the **Content control cannot be deleted** check box.

    The Locking properties are used to prevent the end user from deleting form controls.

9. Under **Display the date like this**, notice that the current date displays in different formats. Click the following date format: **March 24, 2014**, or similar date, to display **MMMM d, yyyy**. Compare your screen with **Figure 3**.

10. Click **OK** to close the dialog box, and then notice that the *Anticipated start date of internship* displays in the selected format, as shown in **Figure 4**.

11. **Save** 🖫 the document.

■ **You have completed Skill 2 of 10**

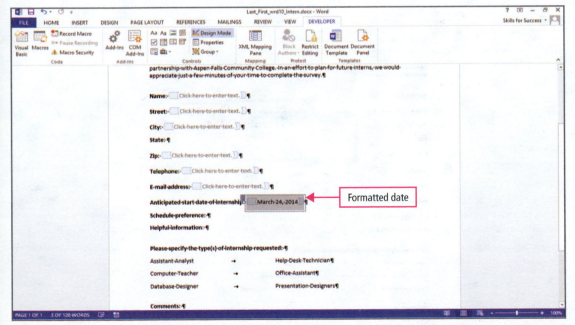

Formatted date

Figure 4

▶ When clicked, a **Drop-Down List content control** displays a list of choices.

▶ A **Check Box Content control** is a form field with a box that can be selected or cleared. In a group of check boxes, multiple choices may be selected.

1. Locate the paragraph that begins *Schedule preference*. Place the insertion point at the end of the paragraph.

2. Click the **Developer tab**, and then in the **Controls group**, click the **Drop-Down List Content Control** button.

3. With the insertion point in the **Drop-Down List content control**, in the **Controls group**, click the **Properties** button.

4. In the **Content Control Properties** dialog box, under **Locking**, select the **Content control cannot be deleted** check box, and then compare your screen with **Figure 1**.

5. In the **Display Name** box, click **Choose an item**, and then click **Remove**.

6. Click **Add**, and then in the **Add Choice** dialog box, type Days as shown in **Figure 2**.

> You use the Add Choice dialog box to add items to drop-down lists. Here, *Days* will be the first item in the Value list box.

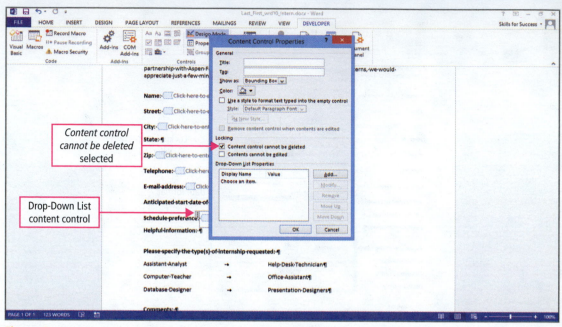

Figure 1

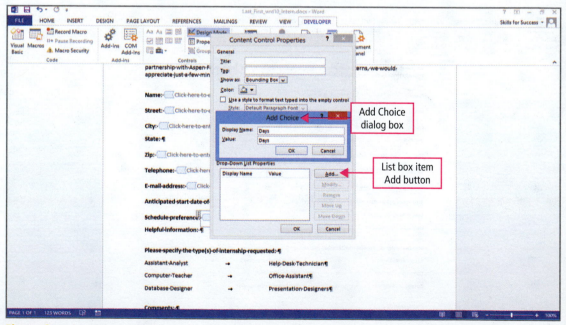

Figure 2

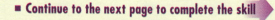
■ Continue to the next page to complete the skill ▶

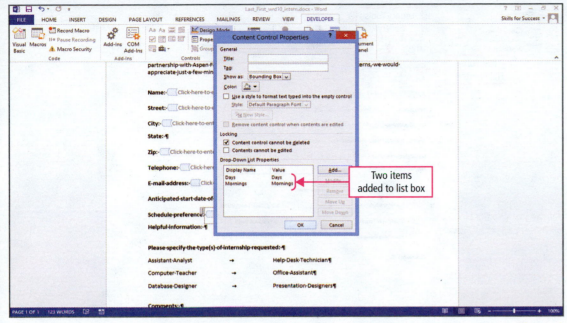

Figure 3

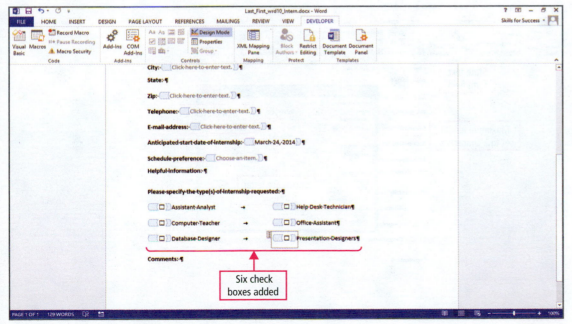

Figure 4

7. Click **OK**. Click **Add**, type Mornings and then click **OK**. Compare your screen with **Figure 3**.

8. Repeat the technique just practiced to add the following list items:

   Afternoons

   Evenings

   Any

9. In the **Content Control Properties** dialog box, under **Display Name Properties**, click *Evenings*. Click the **Move Up** button two times to arrange the list, and then click **OK**.

10. Locate the internship type, *Assistant Analyst*, at the bottom of the form. Place the insertion point just before the text.

11. In the **Controls group**, click the **Check Box Content Control** button ☑.

12. Click left of *Computer Teacher*. In the **Controls group**, click the **Check Box Content Control** button ☑.

13. Repeat the technique just practiced to insert a **Check Box content control** before each of the four remaining internship types. Compare your screen with **Figure 4**.

14. **Save** 🖫 the document.

■ **You have completed Skill 3 of 10**

▶ *Legacy Tools* are a set of controls that work with earlier versions of Word.

▶ Legacy Tools include the following form fields: text, check box, and drop-down box.

1. Locate the paragraph that begins *State*. Place the insertion point at the end of the paragraph.

2. Click the **Developer tab**, and then in the **Controls group**, click the **Legacy Tools** button.

3. In the **Legacy Tools gallery**, under **Legacy Forms**, point to **Text Form Field**, as shown in **Figure 1**. Click **Text Form Field**.

   In the Legacy Tools gallery, the form controls display below Legacy Forms.

   A *text form field* is a legacy tool that creates a placeholder for entering text in an interactive form.

4. Select the *State* **Text form field**, and then in the **Controls group**, click the **Properties** button.

5. In the **Text Form Field Options** dialog box, click the **Default text** box, and then type CA

6. Click the **Maximum length up spin arrow** two times to change the maximum length to 2

7. Click the **Text format arrow**, and then click **Uppercase**. Compare your screen with **Figure 2**, and then click **OK**.

8. Locate the paragraph that begins *Helpful information*. Place the insertion point at the end of the paragraph. In the **Controls group**, click the **Legacy Tools** button.

■ **Continue to the next page to complete the skill** ➤

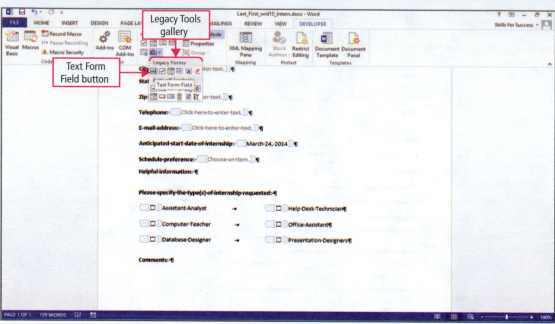

Figure 1

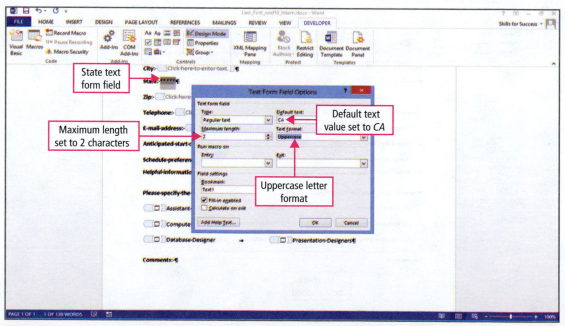

Figure 2

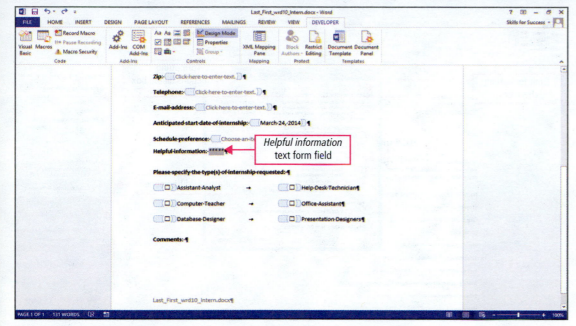

Figure 3

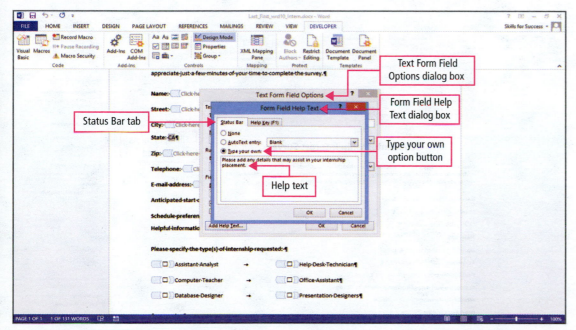

Figure 4

9. In the displayed **Legacy Tools gallery**, under **Legacy Forms**, click **Text Form Field** [abl], and then compare your screen with **Figure 3**.

10. If necessary, select the *Helpful Information* **Text form field**, and then in the **Controls group**, click the **Properties** button.

11. In the **Text Form Field Options** dialog box, click the **Text Format arrow**, and then click **First capital**. Click the **Add Help Text** button.

12. In the **Form Field Help Text** dialog box, on the **Status Bar tab**, select the **Type your own** option button, and then in the box, type Please add any details that may assist in your internship placement. Compare your screen with **Figure 4**, and then click **OK** two times.

13. Repeat the technique just practiced to insert a **Legacy Forms Text form field** after *Comments* with the **Title case** property. Add the **Help Text** Please provide any other information that you feel is necessary. Click **OK** twice.

14. Save [icon] the document.

■ **You have completed Skill 4 of 10**

▶ Before making an interactive form available for use, you should protect it.

▶ When a form is protected, the form fields can be filled in, but the form's design cannot be changed.

1. Press Ctrl + Home.

2. On the **Developer tab**, in the **Controls group**, click the **Design Mode** button to turn off Design mode.

> To enable document protection, the Design Mode must be turned off.

3. In the **Protect group**, click the **Restrict Editing** button.

4. In the **Restrict Editing** pane, under **Formatting restrictions**, select the **Limit formatting to a selection of styles** check box, and then click **Settings**.

5. In the **Formatting Restrictions** dialog box, click the **None** button. Compare your screen with **Figure 1**.

> The Formatting Restrictions dialog box is used to specify which styles can be formatted. When no styles are selected, formatting changes cannot be made.

6. Click **OK**, read the displayed message, and then click **No**.

7. In the **Restrict Editing** pane, under **Editing Restrictions**, select the **Allow only this type of editing in the document** check box.

8. Click the **Editing restrictions arrow**, and then click **Filling in forms**. Compare your screen with **Figure 2**.

■ **Continue to the next page to complete the skill**

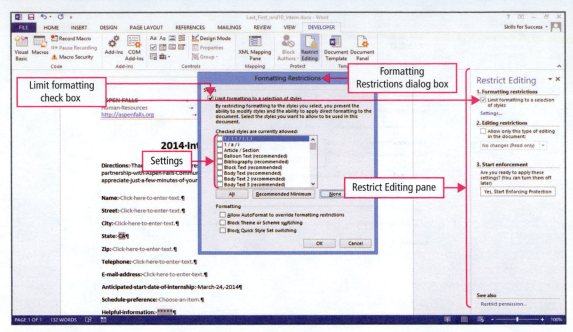

Figure 1

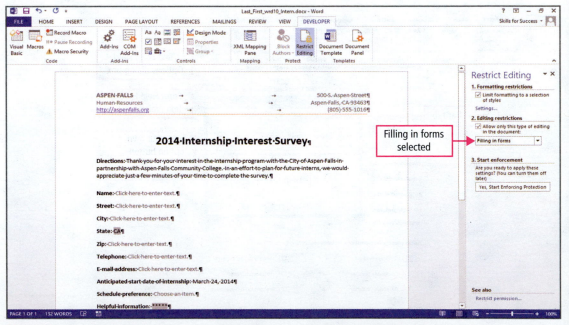

Figure 2

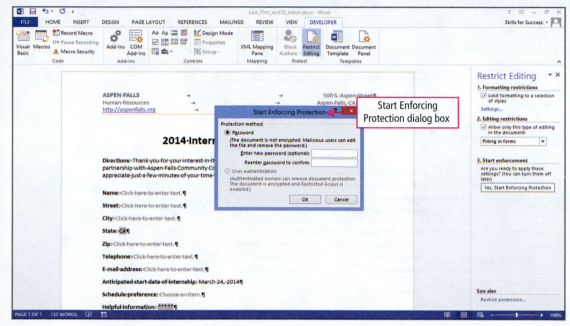

Figure 3

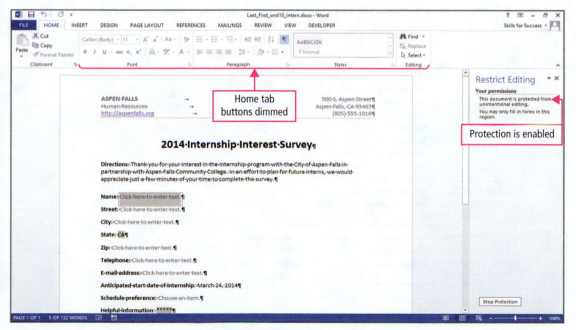

Figure 4

9. Click the **Yes, Start Enforcing Protection** button, and then compare your screen with **Figure 3**.

   When a password is assigned, only those who know the password will be able to make changes to the document. Assigning a password is optional. When the password field is left blank, the end user will be able to remove the protection.

10. In the **Start Enforcing Protection** box, type Success! and then press Tab. Type Success! again, and then click **OK**.

11. Click the **Home tab**, and then compare your screen with **Figure 4**.

    When a document is protected, most of the buttons on the Home tab are dimmed. The Restrict Formatting and Editing pane explains that the document is protected from unintentional editing.

12. **Close** ✕ the **Restrict Editing** pane.

13. Click the form title, *2014 Internship Interest Survey,* and then verify that the insertion point cannot be placed in the paragraph.

14. **Save** 💾 the document.

15. Click the **File tab**, and then click **Save As**. Navigate to your **Word Chapter 10** folder, and then save the file as Last_First_wrd10_InternLocked

    The form is ready to distribute electronically—as an e-mail attachment for example.

▪ **You have completed Skill 5 of 10**

► Once a form is created, the designer should test the form by filling in the fields as the end user will.

► To make changes to the design of the form, protection must first be disabled.

1. In **Last_First_wrd10_InternLocked**, if necessary, click the Name form field, and then type your first and last name.

2. Press Tab, and then in the **Street** form field, type your own street address.

3. Press Tab, and then in the **City** form field, type your city.

4. Click the **State** form field. If you live in California, then press Tab. If your state differs, type your two-letter state abbreviation. Repeat the technique just practiced to insert the Zip code, telephone number, and e-mail address. Compare your screen with **Figure 1**.

   In this manner, the end user will be able to quickly fill out the fields on the form. The size of the text controls will resize to fit the information entered.

5. For the **Anticipated start date of internship**, use the Date Picker to replace the date with *January 20, 2014*.

6. Click the **Schedule preference** drop-down list field, and then click the field's **arrow**. Compare your screen with **Figure 2**.

   The list box displays the items that you added to the control's properties.

7. From the displayed list, click *Days*.

■ **Continue to the next page to complete the skill** ➤

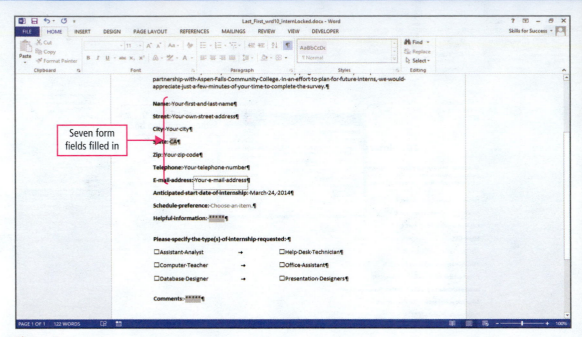

Figure 1

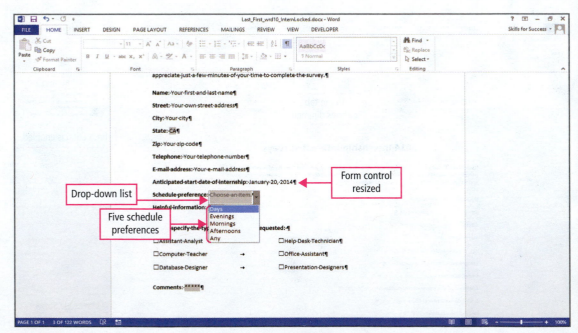

Figure 2

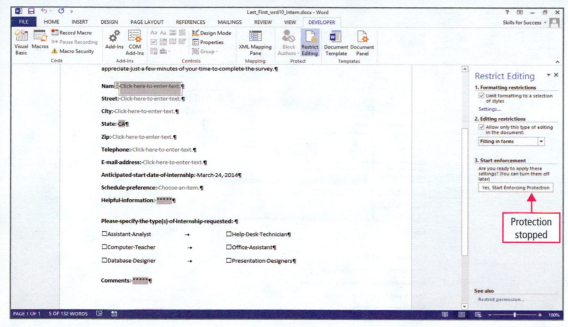

Figure 3

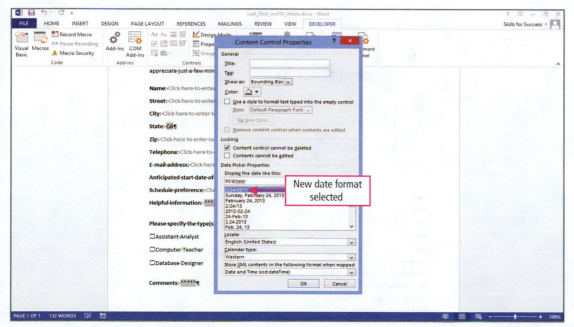

Figure 4

8. Click the **Helpful information** text field, and then type can work in multiple departments. Press Tab.

   The *c* in *can* updates to *C* because the First capital is selected.

9. Select the *Office Assistant* check box.

   A selected check box is the equivalent of *yes*. A cleared check box is the equivalent of *no*.

10. In the **Comments** field, type word, excel, access certified and then press Tab.

11. **Save** , and then **Close** the document. Open **Last_First_wrd10_ Intern**.

12. Click the **View tab**, and then click **Edit Document**.

13. Click the **Developer tab**, and then in the **Protect group**, click the **Restrict Editing** button.

14. In the **Restrict Editing** pane, click the **Stop Protection** button.

15. In the **Unprotect Document** box, type Success! and then click **OK**. Compare your screen with **Figure 3**.

   When the correct password is entered, protection is stopped.

16. **Close** the **Restrict Editing** pane, and then **Save** the document.

17. Locate the paragraph that begins *Anticipated start date*, and then click the **Date Picker** form field. In the **Controls group**, click **Properties**.

18. In the **Content Control Properties** dialog box, select date format **M/d/yyyy**—the first format in the list. Compare your screen with **Figure 4**, and then click **OK**.

19. Press Ctrl + Home.

20. **Save** the document.

■ **You have completed Skill 6 of 10**

▶ A *macro* is a stored set of instructions that automates common tasks.

▶ Create a macro by using the macro recorder to record all of the steps you perform. The recorded steps are then performed whenever the macro is run.

1. Click the **Developer tab**, and then in the **Code group**, click the **Record Macro** button. In the **Macro name** box, type **AddDateTime**

2. Click the **Store macro in arrow**. Click **Last_First_wrd10_Intern (document)**, as shown in **Figure 1**.

   Storing a macro to the Normal template makes the macro available for all files created from the Normal template. Here, the macro is available only in the current document.

3. Under **Assign macro to**, click the **Keyboard** button.

4. In the **Customize Keyboard** dialog box, press and hold [Ctrl], and then press [F].

5. Click the **Assign** button. Compare your screen with **Figure 2**, and then click **Close**.

   Keyboard shortcuts should be assigned before the macro is created. Here, [Ctrl] + [F] will be used to run the macro.

   The pointer displays to indicate that the macro recorder is recording each step.

6. Click the **Insert tab**. In the **Header & Footer group**, click the **Footer** button, and then click **Edit Footer**.

7. Click the **Header & Footer Tools Design tab**, and then in the **Insert group**, click the **Date & Time** button.

8. In the **Date and Time** dialog box, click the format **2/24/2014 2:12:47 PM**—or today's date/time. If necessary, select the Update automatically check box. Click **OK**.

■ Continue to the next page to complete the skill ▶

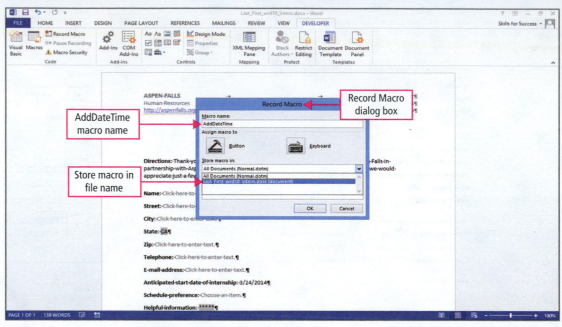

Figure 1

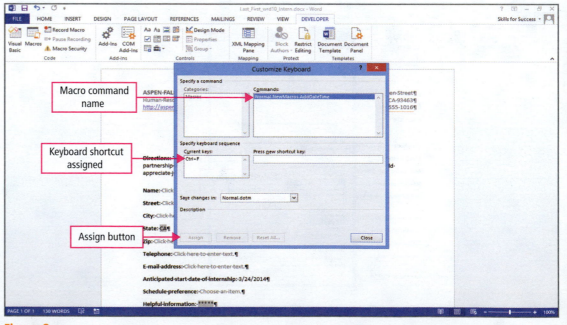

Figure 2

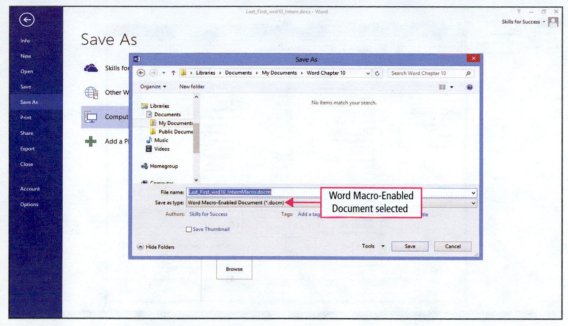

Word Macro-Enabled Document selected

Figure 3

Macro Security Options

Macro Option	Description
Disable all macros without notification	Disables all macros and security alerts.
Disable all macros with notification	Disables all macros and displays security alert from which you can choose to enable the macro.
Disable all macros except digitally signed macros	Enables macros that have a digital signature from a publisher that you have added to your trusted publishers list. Disables unsigned macros and displays security alerts.
Enable all macros	Enables all macros without a security alert.

Figure 4

9. Press the [SpaceBar] one time to insert a space between the Date/Time field and the FileName field.

10. In the **Close group**, click **Close Header and Footer**.

11. Click the **Developer tab**, and then in the **Code group**, click the **Stop Recording** button.

   The macro recorder has recorded each step.

   If you make a mistake while recording a macro, on the Developer tab, in the Code group, click the Macros button. In the Macros dialog box, select the macro, and then click Delete. You can then name and record a new macro.

12. Click the **File tab**, and then click **Save As**. In the **Save As** dialog box, type Last_First_wrd10_InternMacro Click **Save as type**, and then click **Word Macro-Enabled Document**. Compare your screen with **Figure 3**, and then click **Save**.

   Documents that contain macros must be saved in a file format that has the *.docm* file extension.

13. In the **Code group**, click the **Macro Security** button.

14. In the **Trust Center** dialog box, if necessary, select the *Disable all macros with notification* option button, and then click **OK**. Macro security settings are summarized in **Figure 4**.

   With the current security setting, Word will ask your permission before enabling a macro. Macros are sometimes maliciously used to spread viruses. Only enable macros that are from trusted sources.

15. Save [💾] the document.

■ **You have completed Skill 7 of 10**

▶ You can customize the Ribbon by creating your own tabs and groups.

1. Click the **File tab**, and then click **Options**.

2. In the **Word Options** dialog box, select the **Customize Ribbon tab**. Under **Main Tabs**, click **Developer**, and then click the **New Tab** button. Compare your screen with **Figure 1**.

3. Under **Main Tabs**, click **New Tab (Custom)**, and then click **Rename**.

4. In the **Rename** dialog box, type Student and then click **OK**.

5. Under **Main Tabs**, click **New Group (Custom)**, and then click **Rename**.

6. In the **Rename** dialog box, type Print In the **Rename** dialog box, click the picture of the printer 🖨, and then click **OK**.

7. In the list at the left, under the **Choose commands** list, scroll down, click **Print Preview and Print**, and then click **Add**.

8. Verify **Quick Print** is selected, and then click **Add**. Compare your screen with **Figure 2**.

9. Under **Main Tabs**, click **Student (Custom)**, and then click **New Group**.

10. In the list at the left, under **Choose commands from**, click the **Choose commands arrow**, and then click **All Commands**.

11. Scroll down to locate and click **Save**, and then click **Add**.

12. Repeat the technique just learned to add the **Save All**, **Save As**, and **Save As Other Format** commands.

■ **Continue to the next page to complete the skill** ➤

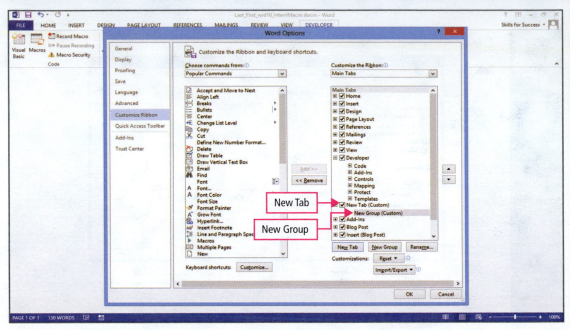

Figure 1

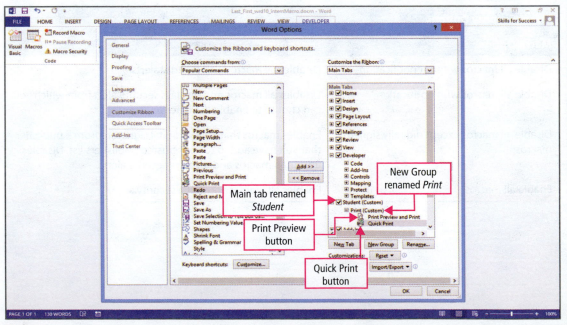

Figure 2

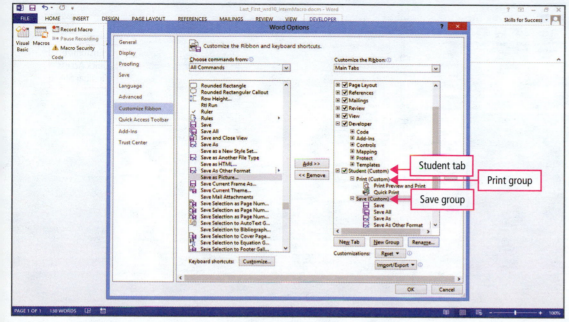

Figure 3

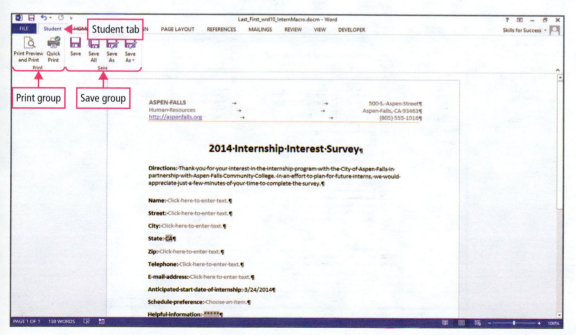

Figure 4

13. Under **Main Tabs**, click **New Group (Custom)**, and then click **Rename**.

14. In the **Rename** dialog box, type Save In the **Rename** dialog box, click the picture of the disk 🖫, and then click **OK**. Compare your screen with **Figure 3**, and then click **OK**.

15. In the Ribbon, click the **Student tab**.

> When you customize the Ribbon in this manner, the tabs and groups are available in any Word document.

16. In the **Save group**, click the **Save** button.

17. Click the **File tab**, and then click **Options**.

18. In the **Word Options** dialog box, select the **Customize Ribbon tab**.

19. Under **Customize the Ribbon**, in the **Main Tabs** list, click **Student (Custom)**, and then click the **Move Up** button 🔼 nine times to display the tab name at the top of the list.

20. Click **OK**. Compare your screen with **Figure 4**.

> The Student tab now displays as the second tab in the ribbon.

21. Save 🖫 the document.

■ **You have completed Skill 8 of 10**

▶ You can add your own buttons to the Quick Access Toolbar, or QAT, to perform common tasks. For example, you can add Ribbon commands, commands not found on the Ribbon, and buttons to run macros.

1. Click the **Quick Access Toolbar arrow** 🔽 , and then click **More Commands**.

2. In the **Word Options** dialog box, click the **Customize Quick Access Toolbar arrow**, and then click **For Last_First_wrd10_ InternMacro**. Compare with **Figure 1**.

    The changes to the Quick Access Toolbar will apply only to the current document.

3. In the list of **Popular Commands**, verify that <Separator> is selected. Click **Add**.

    A *separator* is a vertical line that groups buttons or commands. Here, the separator divides the default QAT buttons and the custom buttons.

4. In the list of **Popular Commands**, click **Insert a Comment**, and then click **Add**.

5. Click the **Choose commands from arrow**, and then click **File Tab**. In the list, scroll down, and then click **Save As**. Click **Add**.

6. Click the **Choose commands from arrow**, and then click **Developer Tab**. In the list, click **Date Picker Content Control**. Click **Add**. Compare your screen with **Figure 2**.

7. Repeat the steps just practiced to add the **Plain Text content control**.

8. Click the **Choose commands arrow**, and then click **Macros**.

9. In the **Macros** list, click **Project. NewMacros.AddDateTime**, and then click **Add**.

10. In the list at the right, click **Project. NewMacros.AddDateTime**, and then click **Modify.**

■ **Continue to the next page to complete the skill** ➤

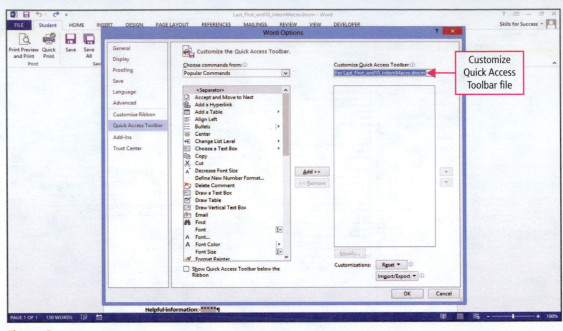

Figure 1

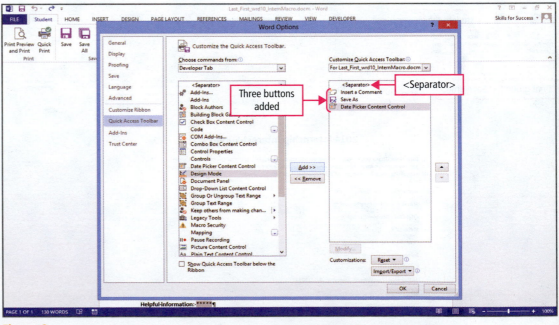

Figure 2

Figure 3

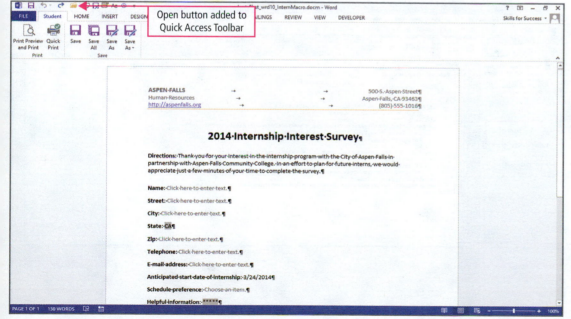

Figure 4

11. In the **Modify Button** dialog box, click the ninth button in the fourth row—. Click **OK** two times. Compare your screen with **Figure 3**.

    The commands display on the QAT. The macro button displays the custom clock.

12. Click the **Quick Access Toolbar arrow**, click **Open**, and then compare your screen with **Figure 4**.

    The Open button displays before the separator. When you add a button to the QAT using this technique, the button is added to all documents.

13. Point to the footer. Double-click to activate the footer area. In the footer, delete the **Date/Time** field.

14. Click to the right of the **FileName** field, and then add a space. On the QAT, click the **Project.NewMacros. AddDateTime** button. If necessary, close the footer area.

15. **Save** and then **Close** the document. Open **Last_First_wrd10_ InternMacro**.

    Recall that macros were disabled in Skill 7. The Microsoft Office Security Options box displays when a document contains macros and provides an option to enable the macros.

16. In the **Security Warning**, click the **Enable Content** button. If the button does not display, perform the following: click the Developer tab, and then in the Code group, click the Macro Security button. In the Trust Center dialog box, click the Trusted Documents tab, and then click the Clear button. In the message box, click Yes, and then click OK. Close and then reopen the file.

    In this manner, macros are enabled, and the document becomes a trusted document.

■ **You have completed Skill 9 of 10**

WRD 10-10
VIDEO

▶ When you run a macro, the macro performs the steps you completed while recording the macro.

▶ When macros do not work as intended, you can perform the macro one step at a time to discover where the error occurs.

1. Press Ctrl + End, and then activate the footer area. In the footer, select the **Date/Time** field, and then press Delete.

2. Press Ctrl + F to run the **AddDateTime** macro.

3. Observe the footer. Repeat the steps above to delete the **Date/Time** field. Click the **Developer tab**, and then in the **Code group**, click the **Macros** button as shown in **Figure 1**.

4. In the **Macros** dialog box, with the **AddDateTime** macro selected, click the **Run** button.

> In this manner, you can run macros from the Macros dialog box.

5. In the **Code group**, click the **Macros** button. With the **AddDateTime** macro selected, in the **Macros** dialog box, click **Step Into**. Compare your screen with **Figure 2**.

> When you record a macro, the macro recorder writes instructions in *Visual Basic for Applications (VBA)*—a programming language that can be used to write and modify macros.

> Here, the Visual Basic Editor displays the VBA code in the AddDateTime macro. The yellow arrow and highlight indicate the current step the macro will perform.

6. From the menu bar, click **Debug**, and then click **Step Into**.

> To *debug* is to check for errors. Here, the next step is highlighted.

■ **Continue to the next page to complete the skill** ▶

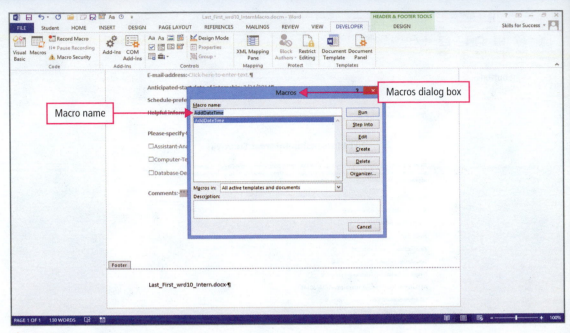

Figure 1

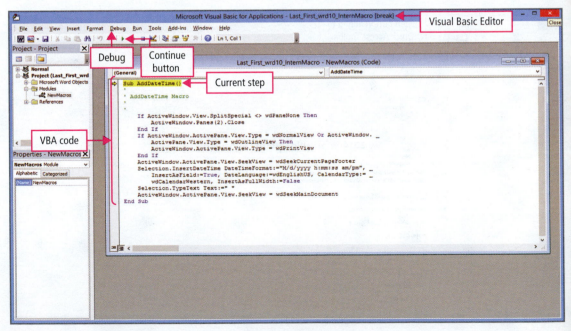

Figure 2

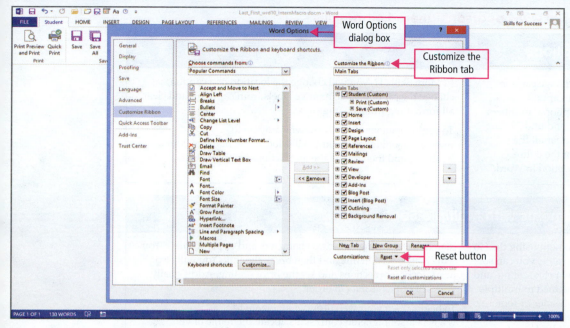

Figure 3

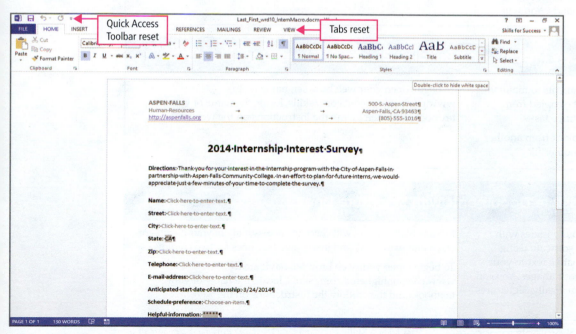

Figure 4

7. On the Standard toolbar, click the **Continue** button ▶.

   The remaining steps in the macro are performed. When the macro finishes, none of the VBA code will be highlighted.

8. From the **File** menu, click **Close and Return to Microsoft Word**.

   Notice that the date/time displays where the insertion point is located.

9. Open the footer area, and then delete all but the first **Date/Time** field. Close the footer area.

   During the Debug phase, the macro is run.

10. Click the **File tab**, and then click **Options**.

11. In the **Word Options** dialog box, select the **Customize the Ribbon tab**, and then compare your screen with **Figure 3**.

12. Under **Customizations**, click **Reset**, and then click **Reset all customizations**. In the message box, click **Yes**, and then click **OK**.

    Ribbon and Quick Access Toolbar customizations are both reset.

13. Verify that the Developer tab no longer displays. Click the **File tab**, and then click **Options**.

14. In the **Word Options** dialog box, select the **Quick Access Toolbar tab**. Click the **Customize Quick Access Toolbar arrow**, and then select **For Last_First_wrd10_InternMacro.docm**.

15. Under **Customizations**, click **Reset**, and then click **Reset only Quick Access Toolbar**. In the message box, click **Yes**, and then click **OK**. Compare your screen with **Figure 4**.

16. **Save** 🖫 the document. Print or submit the files as directed by your instructor, and then **Close** ⊠ Word.

 DONE! You have completed Skill 10 of 10, and your document is complete!

More Skills

The following More Skills are located at **www.pearsonhighered.com/skills**

More Skills Work with Captions

You can determine the location of a caption, change caption labels, and remove labels from captions. If the caption location changes within the document, the caption renumbers accordingly. Instead of removing bold, italics, and underlining from a word or phrase, for example, you can clear all the formatting from a word, phrase, paragraph, or the entire document by using the Clear All Formatting option in Word.

In More Skills 11, you will change the location of a caption, change the caption label, remove labels from captions, and clear all formatting from a paragraph.

To begin, open your web browser, navigate to www.pearsonhighered.com/skills, locate the name of your textbook, and then follow the instructions on the website.

More Skills Manage Documents with Multiple Sections

You can move to specific items in a Word document using the Go To and Find and Replace commands. Within a table, you can sort table data. You can search for text to format, set print scaling, and print document sections. You can link text contained in multiple sections in a document, such as the text in the header or footer, so that it displays in all sections. You can also break the link so that different text displays in the header or footer for each section.

In More Skills 12, you will manage a multisection document using the Go To and Find and Replace commands. You will

search for text using wildcard characters and apply formats. You will create a section link and then break the link. You will also print document sections and set the print scaling. Additionally, you will put table data in order.

To begin, open your web browser, navigate to www.pearsonhighered.com/skills, locate the name of your textbook, and then follow the instructions on the website.

More Skills Move and Copy Macros and Building Blocks Between Documents

Building blocks can be moved between documents to maintain consistency in text and formats. Macros can be copied from document to document to save time on repetitive tasks.

In More Skills 13, you will insert a building block from another document and copy and use a macro from another file.

To begin, open your web browser, navigate to www.pearsonhighered.com/skills, locate the name of your textbook, and then follow the instructions on the website.

More Skills Create Accessible Documents with Signature Lines

You can review your document for compatibility issues with screen readers or other assistive devices and software using the Accessibility Checker. You can add alternative text to your document to provide helpful information about images. You can also add your signature to a document automatically. Signatures can be verified for document integrity.

In More Skills 14, you will check the accessibility of your document, insert alternative text, and insert signature lines for two employees.

To begin, open your web browser, navigate to www.pearsonhighered.com/skills, locate the name of your textbook, and then follow the instructions on the website.

Please note that there are no additional projects to accompany the More Skills Projects, and they are not covered in End-of-Chapter projects.

The following table summarizes the **SKILLS AND PROCEDURES** covered in this chapter.

Skill	Task	Step	Icon
1	Display the Developer tab	File tab → Options tab → Customize Ribbon tab → Click Developer check box	
1	Turn on Design Mode	Developer tab → Controls group → Design Mode	Design Mode
1	Insert Plain Text content controls	Developer tab → Controls group → Plain Text Content Control	Aa
2	Insert Date Picker content controls	Developer tab → Controls group → Date Picker Content Control	
3	Insert Drop-Down List content controls	Developer tab → Controls group → Drop-Down List Content Control	
3	Insert Check Box content controls	Developer tab → Controls group → Check Box Content Control	
4	Insert Legacy Tools	Developer tab → Controls group → Legacy Tools	
4	Add Help content to form fields	Select legacy text form field → Developer tab → Properties button → Add Help Text	Add Help Text...
5	Protect and distribute forms	Developer tab → Protect group → Restrict Editing	
6	Remove protection	Developer tab → Restrict Editing pane → Stop Protection button	Stop Protection
7	Record macros	Developer tab → Code group → Record Macro	
7	Assign macro to keyboard	Developer tab → Code group → Record Macro → Keyboard	
7	Set macro security	Developer tab → Code group → Macro Security	
8	Add new tabs to the Ribbon	File tab → Options tab → Customize Ribbon tab → Click New Tab (Custom) → Click Rename	Rename...
8	Add new groups to the Ribbon	File tab → Options tab → Customize Ribbon tab → Click New Group (Custom) → Click Rename	Rename...
9	Change Quick Access Toolbar buttons	File tab → Options tab → Quick Access Toolbar tab → Select button(s) → Modify	
10	Run macros from the Macro dialog box	Developer tab → Code group → Macros	Run
10	Debug macros in Visual Basic	Developer tab → Code group → Macros → Step Into → Debug	Debug
10	Step into macros in Visual Basic	Developer tab → Code group → Macros → Step Into → Debug → Step Into	Step Into
10	Reset Ribbon customizations	File tab → Options tab → Customize Ribbon tab → Reset	Reset ▼

Key Terms

Online Help Skills

1. Start **Word 2013**, and then in the upper right corner of the start page, click the **Help** button [?].

2. In the **Word Help** window **Search online help** box, type enable macros and then press [Enter].

3. In the search results list, click **Enable or disable macros in Office files**, and then below **In this article**, click **Change macro settings in the Trust Center**. Compare your screen with **Figure 1**.

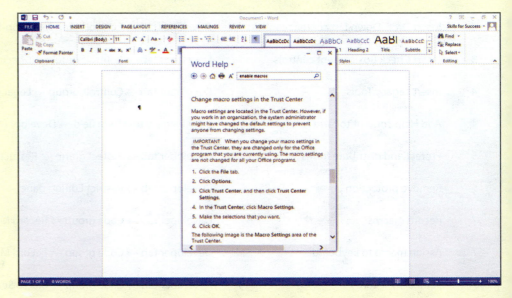

Figure 1

4. Read the article to answer the following questions: Why would the system administrator change the default settings for macros? What is affected when macro settings are changed in the Trust Center?

Matching

Match each term in the second column with its correct definition in the first column by writing the letter of the term on the blank line in front of the correct definition.

___ **1.** An interactive object such as a text box, a button, or a list box.

___ **2.** A person who designs documents with interactive content such as content controls and macros.

___ **3.** Allows you to work as a developer.

___ **4.** An individual who works with the document the developer designs.

___ **5.** A control inserted into forms so that the end user can type text into a text box.

___ **6.** Text in a form control that instructs the end user how to enter information.

___ **7.** A control that displays an interactive calendar used to insert a specific date into a document.

___ **8.** A form field with a box that can be selected or cleared.

___ **9.** A set of controls that works with earlier versions of Word.

___ **10.** A stored set of instructions that automates common tasks.

A Check Box content control

B Control

C Date Picker content control

D Design mode

E Developer

F End user

G Instructional text

H Legacy Tools

I Macro

J Plain Text content control

Multiple Choice

Choose the correct answer.

1. Another name for the document designer.
   A. Developer
   B. End user
   C. VBA

2. Used to make only the document's form fields available.
   A. Debug
   B. Disable
   C. Lock

3. The content control format that displays as *September 19, 2014*.
   A. d-MM-yy
   B. MMMM yy
   C. MMMM d, yyyy

4. The type of control used to select one item from a single box containing several choices.
   A. Check Box
   B. Drop-Down List
   C. Text Form Field

5. The type of control used to select multiple items.
   A. Check Box
   B. Drop-Down List
   C. Text Form Field

6. Button used to cancel the Restrict Editing feature.
   A. Cancel
   B. Disable
   C. Stop Protection

7. By default, macros are stored in this location.
   A. Buttons
   B. Desired files
   C. Normal template

8. The toolbar that contains Save, Undo, and Redo by default.
   A. Mini
   B. Quick Access Toolbar
   C. Ribbon

9. The security option to enable macros to be available when the document is opened.
   A. Allow
   B. Enable Content
   C. Macro

10. A command that helps analyze and test macros.
    A. Edit
    B. Run
    C. Step Into

Topics for Discussion

1. Imagine you are interested in promoting an Art in the Park weekend event. What types of forms might you need? What types of information would you need to collect, and which form controls would work best for collecting that information?

2. Imagine you are preparing a donor form for a nonprofit organization. What buttons might you display in the Quick Access Toolbar?

Skills Review

To complete this project, you will need the following file:

- wrd10_SRCheck

You will save your documents as:

- Last_First_wrd10_SRCheck
- Last_First_wrd10_SRCheckMacro

1. Start **Word 2013**, and then open **wrd10_SRCheck**. **Save** the file in your **Word Chapter 10** folder as Last_First_wrd10_SRCheck Add the **FileName** field to the footer.

2. Click the **File tab**, and then click **Options**. Click the **Customize Ribbon tab**, and then select the **Developer** check box.

3. Click the **New Tab** button, and then click **New Tab (Custom)**. Click **Rename**, type Student and then click **OK**. Click **New Group (Custom)**, click **Rename**, and then type Macros Click the first symbol, and then click **OK**.

4. Click the **Choose commands from arrow**, click **All Commands**, and then select the first **Macros** button—MacroPlay. Click **Add**. Select **Macro Security**, and then click **Add**. Compare your screen with **Figure 1**.

5. Click **OK**. Click the **Developer tab**, and then in the **Controls group**, click **Design Mode** to turn it on.

6. Position the insertion point to the right of the space after *Service Date:*. In the **Controls group**, click the **Date Picker Content Control** button.

7. Click the space after *Officer*. In the **Controls group**, click the **Plain Text Content Control** button.

8. Click the space after *Type*. In the **Controls group**, click the **Drop-Down List Content Control** button. In the **Controls group**, click the **Properties** button. Click **Choose an item**, and then click **Remove**. Click **Add**, click the **Display Name** box, type Car and then click **OK**. Repeat the technique just practiced to add SUV and Truck and Van to the list, and then click **OK** two times.

9. Click the space after *Description*. In the **Controls group**, click the **Legacy Tools** button. Click **Text Form Field**. In the **Controls group**, click **Properties**. Click the **Add Help Text** button, select the **Type your own** option button, and then type Model Click **OK** two times.

10. Click to the left of *Oil*. In the **Controls group**, click the **Check Box Content Control** button. Compare your screen with **Figure 2**.

- **Continue to the next page to complete this Skills Review**

Figure 1

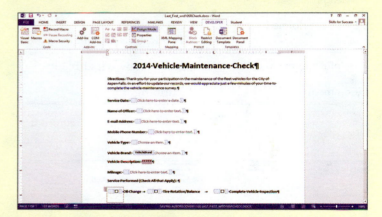

Figure 2

Data for Vehicle Form

Field	Text to Type
Service Date	9/19/2014
Name of Officer	Brian Carnival
E-Mail Address	bcarnival@aspenfalls.org
Mobile Phone Number	(805) 555-2014
Vehicle Type	Truck
Vehicle Brand	Ford
Vehicle Description	F-150
Mileage	49,139
Service Performed	Oil Change Tire Rotation/Balance
Helpful Information	Needs new wiper blades.
Comments	Running fine.

Figure 3

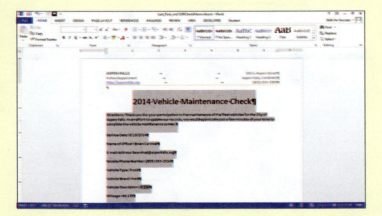

Figure 4

11. Turn off **Design Mode**, and then **Save** the file.

12. In the **Protect group**, click the **Restrict Editing** button. In the **Restrict Editing** pane, select the **Allow only this type of editing in the document** check box. Click the **Editing Restrictions arrow**, and then click **Filling in forms**.

13. Click **Yes, Start Enforcing Protection**. In the **Start Enforcing Protection** box, type Success! in both password boxes. Click **OK**. Fill in the form using the information in **Figure 3**. **Save** the file.

14. In the **Restrict Formatting and Editing** pane, click **Stop Protection**, and then type Success! Click **OK**, and then **Close** the **Restrict Editing** pane.

15. In the **Code group**, click the **Record Macro** button, and then type UnBold. Click the **Store macro in arrow**, and then select **Last_First_wrd10_SRCheck**.

16. Under **Assign macro to**, click **Button**. In the dialog box, click the **Customize Quick Access Toolbar arrow**, and then click **For Last_First_wrd10_SRCheck**. Click **Project.NewMacros.UnBold**, and then click **Add**. At the right, click **Project.NewMacros.Unbold**, and then click **Modify**. In the dialog box, click the first button in the seventh row—**black box with shading**. Click **OK** two times.

17. Click the **Home tab**. In the **Editing group**, click the **Select** button, and then click **Select All**. Click **Bold** to turn it off in this step. Click the **Developer tab**, and then in the **Code group**, click the **Stop Recording** button.

18. **Save** the file in your chapter folder as Last_First_wrd10_SRCheckMacro as a **Word Macro-Enabled Document**. Click **No** to any messages that display. Update the **FileName** field in the footer.

19. Click the **Student tab**. In the **Macros group**, click the **Macros** button, if necessary, click **UnBold**, and then click **Step Into**. On the **Debug** menu, click **Step Into**, and then click **Continue**. Click the **File** menu, and then click **Close and Return to Microsoft Word**.

20. On the **Student tab**, in the **Macros group**, click the **Macro Security** button. If necessary, select the Disable all macros with notification option. Click **OK**, **Save**, and then **Close** the document.

21. Open **Last_First_wrd10_SRCheckMacro**, and then click **Enable Content**.

22. In the **Quick Access Toolbar**, click the **Project.NewMacros.UnBold** button. Compare your screen with **Figure 4**.

23. **Save**, and then **Close** the document. Submit your work as directed by your instructor.

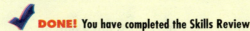

DONE! You have completed the Skills Review

Skills Assessment 1

To complete this project, you will need the following file:

- wrd10_SA1Repairs

You will save your documents as:

- Last_First_wrd10_SA1Repairs
- Last_First_wrd10_SA1RepairsMacro

1. Start **Word 2013**, and then open **wrd10_SA1Repairs**. **Save** the file in your **Word Chapter 10** folder as Last_First_wrd10_SA1Repairs Add the **FileName** field to the footer.

2. Display the **Developer tab**, and then enable **Design Mode**. After *Date of Request:*, insert a **Date Picker** control. Insert a **Drop-Down List** control after *City Neighborhood:* that contains Neighborhood 1 and Neighborhood 2 and Neighborhood 3

3. Insert a **Plain Text** control after *Name of Applicant:*. After *Zip*, insert a **Text Form Field** from the **Legacy Tools**. Add the Help text 5- or 9-digit zip code format Insert a **Check Box** control before *Sidewalk*.

4. Turn off **Design Mode**. Protect the document to allow only filling in forms using the password Success! Fill in the form using the information in **Figure 1**.

5. **Stop Protection**, and close the **Restrict Editing** pane. **Save** the file. **Save** the file as a **Word Macro-Enabled Document** with the name Last_First_wrd10_SA1RepairsMacro In the footer, update the **FileName** field.

6. Record a macro with the name NoBold that is stored in the current document. Assign the macro to a new button on the **Quick Access Toolbar** for the current file only. Modify the button to display with the first button in the sixth row—the green box. The macro should select the entire document and remove bold.

7. **Save**, and then **Close** the document.

8. Open **Last_First_wrd10_SA1RepairsMacro**, and then enable the macro. Select the entire document, and then apply **Bold**. From the **Quick Access Toolbar**, run the **NoBold** macro. Deselect the text, and then compare your screen with **Figure 2**.

Data for Repair Form	
Field	**Text to Type**
Date of Request	12/15/2014
City Neighborhood	Neighborhood 3
Name of Applicant	Emma Grace Samuels
Address	3112 Durkin Drive
Zip	93463
Daytime Phone	(805) 555-1300
Repair or Maintenance	Sidewalk Water Main Break

Figure 1

ASPEN FALLS
Public Works
http://aspenfalls.org

500 S. Aspen Street
Aspen Falls, CA 93463
(805) 555-1023

2014 Repair and Maintenance Request Form

Directions: Thank you for reporting repair and/or maintenance issues throughout the city limits of Aspen Falls. In an effort to update our records, we would appreciate your time to complete the form.

Date of Request: 12/15/2014

City Neighborhood: Neighborhood 3

Name of Applicant: Emma Grace Samuels

Address: 3112 Durkin Drive

Zip: 93463

Daytime Phone: (805) 555-1300

Repair or Maintenance: (Check all that apply)

☒ Sidewalk ☐ Pothole ☐ Street Paved ☐ Downed Power Line ☒ Water Main Break

Figure 2

9. Remove the **Developer tab** from the Ribbon. **Save**, and then **Close** the document. Submit your work as directed by your instructor.

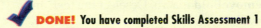 **DONE! You have completed Skills Assessment 1**

Skills Assessment 2

To complete this project, you will need the following file:

- wrd10_SA2Bins

You will save your documents as:

- Last_First_wrd10_SA2Bins
- Last_First_wrd10_SA2BinsMacro

1. Start **Word 2013**, and then open **wrd10_SA2Bins**. **Save** the file in your **Word Chapter 10** folder as Last_First_wrd10_SA2Bins Add the **FileName** field to the footer.

2. Display the **Developer tab**, and then enable **Design Mode**. After *Date of Request:,* insert a **Date Picker** control. Insert a **Drop-Down List** control after *City Neighborhood:* that contains Neighborhood 1 and Neighborhood 2 and Neighborhood 3

3. Insert a **Plain Text** control after *Name of Applicant:.* After *Zip:,* insert a **Text Form Field** from the **Legacy Tools**. Add the **Help text** of 5- or 9-digit zip code format Insert a **Check Box** control before *1 bin:.*

4. Turn off **Design Mode**. Protect the document so forms can be filled in only by using the password Success! Fill in the form using the information in **Figure 1**.

5. **Stop Protection**, and close the **Restrict Editing** pane. **Save** the file. **Save** the file as a **Word Macro-Enabled Document**, Last_First_wrd10_SA2BinsMacro In the footer, update the **FileName** field.

6. Record a macro with the name RemoveBold that is stored in the current document. The macro should select the entire document and remove bold. Assign the macro to a new button on the **Quick Access Toolbar** in the current file only. Modify the button to display with the last button in the fifth row—the blue box.

7. If necessary, change the Macro Security to Disable all macros with notification. **Save**, and then **Close** the file.

8. Open **Last_First_wrd10_BinsMacro**, and then enable the macro. Select the entire document, and then apply **Bold**. From the **Quick Access Toolbar**, run the **RemoveBold** macro. Deselect the text, and then compare your screen with **Figure 2**.

Data for Recycling Bin Request Form	
Field	**Text to Type**
Date of Request	8/28/2014
City Neighborhood	Neighborhood 2
Name of Applicant	Abby Nathaniel
Address	1517 Hazelwood
Zip	93463
Daytime Phone	(805) 555-7709
Recycling Bin Request Type	1 bin with wheels and rope I have not requested… I have valid identification…

Figure 1

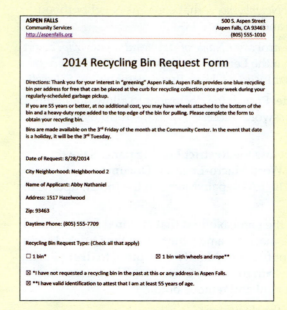

Figure 2

9. Remove the **Developer tab** from the Ribbon. **Save**, and then **Close** the document. Submit your work as directed by your instructor.

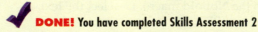 **DONE! You have completed Skills Assessment 2**

Visual Skills Check

To complete this project, you will need the following file:

- wrd10_VSReservation

You will save your document as:

- Last_First_wrd10_VSReservation

In Word 2013, open **wrd10_VSReservation**. Use the skills practiced in this chapter to add controls to create the form shown in **Figure 1**. Insert **Plain Text content controls** after *Name of Applicant, Name of Organization, Address, City, Zip, Daytime Phone, Fax Number, E-mail Address, No. of Occupants,* and *No. of Rental Hours Requested.* After *State,* insert a **Text Form Field Legacy Tool** with CA as its default text. Set the State control's maximum length to **2**, change the text format to uppercase, and include the Help text Please use a 2-letter abbreviation. To the left of the space before *Wedding,* insert a **Check Box content control.** Insert another **Check Box content control** before *Reception.* Insert the **Date Picker content control** next to *Date of Event.*

For *Location Requested,* insert a **Drop-Down List content control.** Include these items in the drop-down list in alphabetical order:

Sandy Beach

Presidents Pavilion

Honeywell Shelter

Vista Pines Shelter

Cobblestone Pavilion

Save the document as Last_First_wrd10_VSReservation in your **Word Chapter 10** folder. Add the **FileName** field to the footer. **Save**, and then **Close** the document. Submit your work as directed by your instructor.

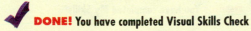

DONE! You have completed Visual Skills Check

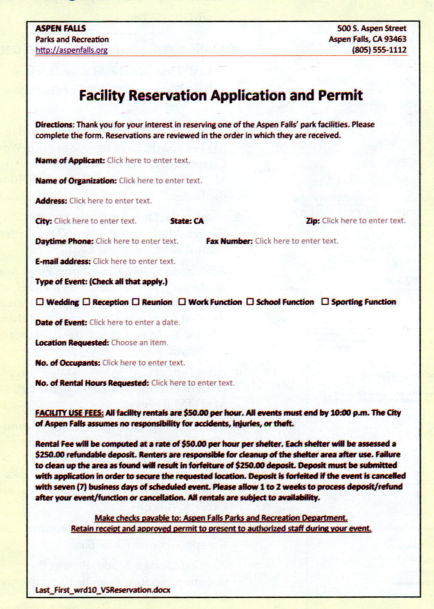

Figure 1

Data for Customer Satisfaction Survey

Field	Text to Type
Name	Dr. Tsong Oh
Street	4167 Lincoln Avenue
City	Aspen Falls
State	CA
Zip	93463
Telephone	(805) 555-4943
E-mail address	dr_oh@goaspenfalls.com
Date of visit	6/19/2014
Department visited	City Clerk
Nature of visit	Met with City Clerk to appeal the property tax increase for my doctor's office.
Planning Commission member to call	Hisako Lavoy Jung Ortolano
Comments	None

Figure 1

ASPEN FALLS
City Hall
http://aspenfalls.org

500 S. Aspen Street
Aspen Falls, CA 93463
(805) 555-1000

2014 Customer Satisfaction Survey

Directions: Thank you for your recent visit to the Aspen Falls City Hall. In an effort to improve our customer service to the Aspen Falls residents, we would appreciate just a few minutes of your time to complete the survey.

Name: Dr. Tsong Oh

Street: 4167 Lincoln Avenue

City: Aspen Falls

State: CA

Zip: 93463

Telephone: (805) 555-4943

E-mail address: dr_oh@goaspenfalls.com

Date of visit: June 19, 2014

Department visited: City Clerk

Nature of visit: Met with City Clerk to appeal the property tax increase for my doctor's office.

Please request the Planning Commission member(s) you wish to call you:

☐ Richie Bona ☒ Jung Ortolano
☒ Hisako Lavoy ☐ Jerrold Calhaun
☐ Octavio Coogan ☐ Gwyneth Rondeau
☐ Barton Bierschbach ☐ Tammi Markewich

Comments: None

Figure 2

My Skills

To complete this project, you will need the following file:

- wrd10_MYFeedback

You will save your documents as:

- Last_First_wrd10_MYFeedback
- Last_First_wrd10_MYFeedbackMacro

1. Start **Word 2013**, and then open **wrd10_MYFeedback**. **Save** the file in your **Word Chapter 10** folder as Last_First_wrd10_MYFeedback Add the **FileName** field to the footer.

2. Display the **Developer tab**, and then enable **Design Mode**. Insert a **Plain Text content control** after *Name* and *E-mail address*.

3. After *State*, insert a **Text Form Field** from the **Legacy Tools**. Use CA as the **Default text**. Set the **Maximum length** to **2**, change the **Text format** to **Uppercase**, and then add the **Help text** Please use a 2-letter abbreviation.

4. After *Date of visit*, insert a **Date Picker content control** that displays the dates as **MMMM d**, yyyy.

5. Insert a **Drop-Down List content control** after *Department visited* that contains City Clerk, City Hall, Community Services, Fire, Human Resources, Library, Parks and Recreation, Police, Public Works and Other in this order.

6. Insert a **Check Box content control** before the space before *Richie Bona*.

7. Turn off **Design Mode**. Protect the document so forms can be filled in only by using the password Success!

8. Fill in the form using the information in **Figure 1**.

9. **Stop Protection**, close the **Restrict Editing** pane, and then **Save** the file.

10. **Save** the file as a **Word Macro-Enabled Document** with the name Last_First_wrd10_MYFeedbackMacro In the footer, update the **FileName** field.

11. Record a macro with the name UndoBold that is stored in the current document.

12. Assign the macro to a new button on the **Quick Access Toolbar** in the current file only. Modify the button to display with the third button in the sixth row—the coral box. The macro should select the entire document and remove bold.

13. If necessary, change the Macro Security to Disable all macros with notification. **Save**, and then **Close** the file.

14. Open Last_First_wrd10_MYFeedbackMacro, and then enable the macro. Select the entire document, and then apply **Bold**. From the **Quick Access Toolbar**, run the **UndoBold** macro. Deselect the text, and then compare your screen with **Figure 2**.

15. Remove the **Developer tab** from the Ribbon.

16. **Save**, and then **Close** the document. Submit your work as directed by your instructor.

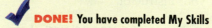 **DONE! You have completed My Skills**

Skills Challenge 1

To complete this project, you will start with a:

- New, blank Word document

You will save your document as:

- Last_First_wrd10_SC1Sports

In Word 2013, open a new, blank document. Use the skills practiced in the chapter to prepare a one-page Word survey form for the Aspen Falls Parks and Recreation Department that could be accessed by the parents of children participating in the summer sports programs in Aspen Falls. Use the Developer tab and include **Plain Text Form Field controls**, a **Date Picker content control**, and **Legacy Tools Text Form Fields** with **Help Text** appropriate for application date, parent/guardian name, child's name and birthdate, home phone, mobile phone, street, city, and Zip code. Include **Check Box content controls** for the following sports: T-Ball,

Coach-Pitch Baseball, Softball, Soccer, Swimming, and Tennis Additionally, include a **Drop-Down List content control** for the following age groups: 4 to 5, 6 to 7, 8 to 9, 10 to 11, 12 to 13, 14 to 15, and 16 to 18 in this order. Protect the form, and then test the form by filling it in with information of your choosing.

Save the file as Last_First_wrd10_SC1Sports in your **Word Chapter 10** folder. Add the **FileName** field to the footer. **Save** and **Close** the document, and then submit the file as directed by your instructor.

 DONE! You have completed Skills Challenge 1

Skills Challenge 2

To complete this project, you will start with a:

- New, blank Word document

You will save your document as:

- Last_First_wrd10_SC2Survey

Locate an example of a printed or an electronic form available at your college that is used by a club, organization, or faculty member. Use the skills practiced in this chapter to create a one-page Word survey form that could be accessed electronically that is similar to the form you located. Use the Developer tab and include at least five **Plain Text Form Field controls**, one **Date Picker content control**, at least two **Legacy Tools Text Form Fields** with **Help Text**, at least four **Check Box content controls**, and at least one **Drop-Down List content control**.

Protect the form, and then test the form by filling it in with information of your choosing.

Save the file as Last_First_wrd10_SC2Survey in your **Word Chapter 10** folder. Add the **FileName** field to the footer. **Save** and **Close** the document, and then submit the file as directed by your instructor.

 DONE! You have completed Skills Challenge 2

Student data file needed for this project:

wrd_CPBenefits

You will save your documents as:

Last_First_wrd_CPBenefits   Last_First_wrd_CPBenefits_Snip

1. Start **Word 2013**, and then open **wrd_CPBenefits**. **Save** the file in your **Word Capstone** folder as Last_First_wrd_CPBenefits On Page 1, replace *Ms. Evelyn Stone* with your first and last name.

2. On Page 1, open and save the header as a building block with the name Letterhead to the Quick Parts Gallery using the new category Aspen Falls Create a full-screen snip that shows the Create New Building Block dialog box and save it as Last_First_wrd_CPBenefitsSnip

3. On Page 1, select the text *Mr. Eugene Garner* and create a hyperlink to the e-mail address egarner@aspenfalls.org

4. On Page 2, insert the **Slice (Light)** cover page. For the *DOCUMENT TITLE*, type INSURANCE AND RELATED BENEFITS REPORT For the *Document subtitle*, type Prepared for the Aspen Falls City Council Delete the text box at the bottom of the page.

5. On Page 2, insert the **Plain Number 2** page number style into the footer. In Section 1, format the page numbers to display as **i, ii, iii** and to start at **ii**. Format the Section 2 page numbers to display as **1, 2, 3**, and to start at **1**.

6. On Page 4, in the second blank paragraph below *ILLUSTRATIONS*, insert a **Table of Figures** with the **Simple** format and the **dotted line** tab leader. Deselect the **Use hyperlinks instead of page numbers** check box.

7. On Page 7, select the chart border and insert the caption Proposed Increase so that the caption displays below the selected item as *Figure 2 Proposed Increase*—you need to deselect the **Exclude label from caption** check box. Compare your screen with **Figure 1**.

8. On Page 4, update the entire table of figures. Modify the **Illustrations** paragraph style that changes the **Font Size** to **12** point, removes **Bold**, applies **Single** line spacing, and sets the paragraph spacing before and after to 12 Apply the **Illustrations** style to the paragraphs *Figure 1, Figure 2*, and *Figure 3*.

9. On Page 5, in the *In August 2014* paragraph, select the first occurrence of *Human Resources*. **Mark All** index entries. In the same paragraph, select *HR* and create a cross-reference to Human Resources

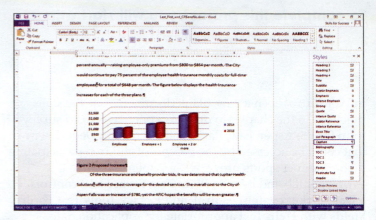

Figure 1

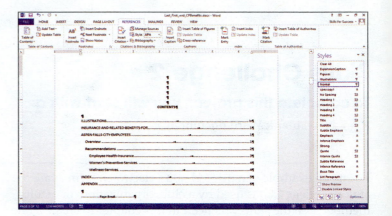

Figure 2

10. On Page 3, in the paragraph above the *Page Break* notation, create a **Custom** table of contents **From template**. Deselect the **Use hyperlinks instead of page numbers** check box. Compare with **Figure 2**.

■ **Continue to the next page to complete the skill**

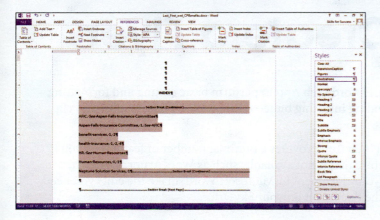

Figure 3

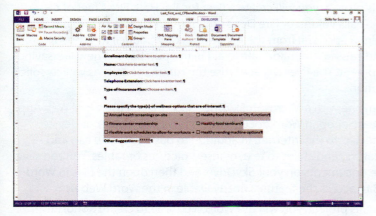

Figure 4

11. Convert the endnotes to footnotes. On Page 11, at the end of the page, Delete the Page Break notation and the remaining paragraphs of the *NOTES* page.

12. On Page 10, in the second blank paragraph below *INDEX*, create an index that has the **From template format**, **Run-in** type, and **1** column. Apply the **Illustrations** style to the index entries that begin *AFIC* through the paragraph that begins *Neptune*. Compare your screen with **Figure 3**, and then close the **Styles** pane.

13. On Page 8, select the table. Use the Border Painter to apply the line weight of **1 ½ pt** and the Pen Color **Blue**, **Accent 1** to the four outside borders.

14. On Page 11, turn on the **Developer tab**. Insert the **Letterhead** building block in the header area. In the paragraph that begins *Enrollment*, click after the *:*, and then insert the **Date Picker** content control.

15. In the paragraph that begins *Name,* click after the *:*, and then insert the **Plain Text** content control.

16. In the paragraph that begins *Type of,* click after the *:*, and then insert the **Drop-Down List** content control that includes the four plans in this order:

Employee

Employee+1

Employee+2_or_more

HSA

17. In the paragraph that begins *Annual,* click before the space at the beginning of the paragraph, and then insert the **Check Box** content control.

18. In the paragraph that begins *Other,* click after the *:*, and then insert the **Legacy Text Form Field** control with the **Uppercase** Text format.

19. Select the three paragraphs that contain the check box data, and then using the ruler, modify the tab settings from **3"** to 3.5" Compare your screen with **Figure 4**.

20. Turn off the **Developer tab**. Delete the **Letterhead** building block that you created.

21. **Save** the document. Mark the document as final. **Close** the Word window. Submit the file as directed by your instructor.

DONE! You have completed Word Capstone Project

Use Word Web App to Create a Flyer

▶ Recall that **Word Web App** is a cloud-based application used to create, edit, and format basic documents using a web browser.

▶ The SkyDrive, a free cloud-based service from Microsoft, allows you to save your work to the cloud from one Internet-enabled computer, and then work on the file from any other computer that is connected to the Internet.

▶ You can use Word Web App to perform basic editing and formatting tasks including inserting bulleted lists, tables, photographs, and clip art images.

▶ The Word Web App provides a minimal number of features. If you need a feature that is not available, such as WordArt or SmartArt, you can open your document in Microsoft Word, make the edits you need, and save the document on your SkyDrive.

© Silverpics/Fotolia

Aspen Falls Volunteer Fire Department

In this project, you will create a flyer for Jim Holt, Fire Chief of the Aspen Falls Volunteer Fire Department (AFVFD). The AFVFD has obtained approval from the Aspen Falls City Council to sponsor a fund-raising rummage sale to aid in the purchase of new life-saving equipment. The flyer will advertise the rummage sale, as well as solicit donations.

Anyone with a Microsoft SkyDrive account can use Word Web App to create or open Word documents from any computer or device connected to the Internet. In addition to basic text, you can add formatting and styles to text, or insert pictures or tables. You can save these documents on your SkyDrive, and then open the files in Word 2013 to access the features not available in the Word Web App.

In this project, you will use Word Web App to create a short flyer with formatted and styled text, a bulleted list, a table, and two images. You will resize and reposition the images. You will open the document in Word 2013 to format the table, add a WordArt title, and save the file back to your SkyDrive.

Time to complete this
project – 30 to 60 minutes

Student data files needed for this project:

New Word Web App document
wrd_WAFirefighter
wrd_WARummageSale

You will save your file as:

Last_First_wrd_WARummageFlyer

SKILLS MyITLab®

At the end of this project you will be able to use Word Web App to:

▶ Create a new Word document
▶ Type text in Editing view
▶ Apply styles
▶ Format text
▶ Change text alignment
▶ Insert pictures from files
▶ Create a table
▶ Switch to Word 2013 to complete editing
▶ Apply text effects
▶ Format a table
▶ Save document to SkyDrive
▶ View documents in Reading view

Outcome

Using the skills in this project, you will be able to create and edit a Word Web App document like this:

Aspen Falls Volunteer Fire Department

1st Annual Fund-Raising Rummage Sale

Help Save Lives in Our Community

Proceeds will aid in the purchase of:

- Jaws of Life
- Hydraulic Cutters

See You There!	
Location:	Aspen Falls Fair Grounds
Date:	Saturday, June 25, 2016
Time:	8:00 a.m. - 6:00 p.m.

Donations Appreciated

(Drop off at Central Station by June 21, 2016)

1. Start Internet Explorer, navigate to skydrive.com and then log on to your Microsoft account. If you do not have an account, follow the links and directions on the page to create one.

2. Navigate as needed to display the **SkyDrive** page. Compare with **Figure 1**.

   The formatting and layout of some pages in SkyDrive may appear different from the figures in this book.

3. On the toolbar, click **Create**, and then click **Word document**. In the **New Microsoft Word document** dialog box, name the file Last_First_wrd_WARummageFlyer and then press Enter to save the document and start Word Web App.

4. On the **Home tab**, in the **Styles group**, click the **Heading 4** style, and then type Aspen Falls Volunteer Fire Department Select the text you just typed, and then in the **Font group**, click the **Bold** button B. Position the insertion point at the end of the text, and then press Enter.

5. In the **Styles group**, click the **Heading 1** style, and then type 1st Annual Fund-Raising Rummage Sale

6. Select the first two lines, and then in the **Paragraph group**, click **Center** ≡.

7. Select the first line of text, and then change the font size to 18 Select the second line of text, and then change the font size to 24

8. Select both lines of text. In the **Font group**, click the **Font Color arrow** A ·, and then click **Orange, Accent 2**.

9. Above the **File tab**, click the **Save** button 🖫. Compare with **Figure 2**.

■ **Continue to the next page to complete the skill**

Figure 1

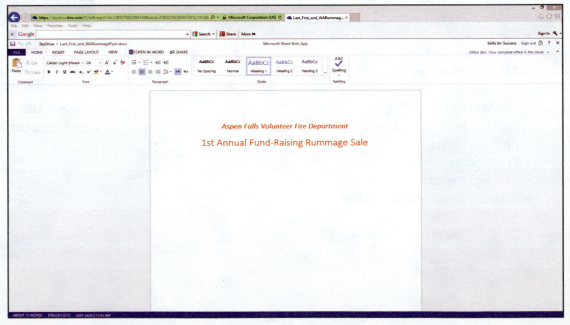

Figure 2

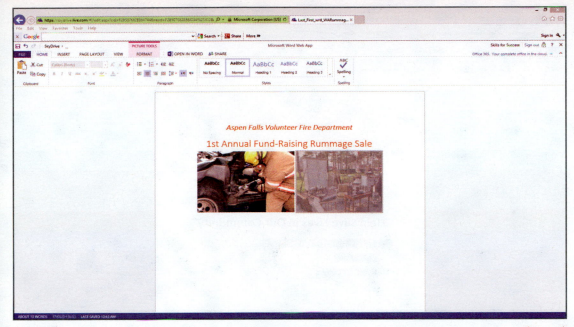

Figure 3

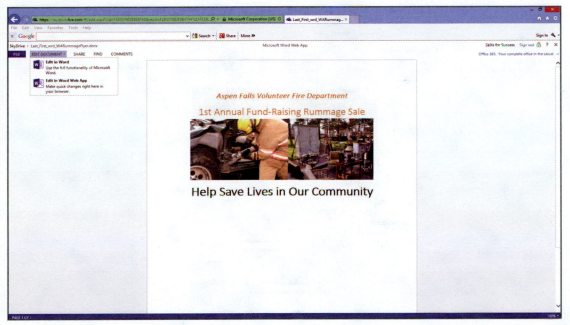

Figure 4

10. Position the insertion point to the right of *Sale*, and then press `Enter` twice. Click the **Insert tab**. In the **Pictures group**, click the **Picture** button. In the **Choose File to Upload** window, navigate to your student data files, select **wrd_WAFirefighter**, and then click **Open**.

11. With the picture selected, click the **Picture Tools Format tab**. In the **Image Size group**, change the **Scale** to 56% On the **Home tab**, **Center** the picture.

12. Click the white area to the right of the photograph. On the **Insert tab**, in the **Pictures group**, click the **Picture** button. In the **Choose File to Upload** window, open **wrd_WARummageSale**.

13. With the picture selected, click the **Picture Tools Format tab**. In the **Image Size group**, change the **Scale** to 50% Compare with **Figure 3**.

14. Click in the white area at the right of the photograph and verify that the insertion point is at the bottom right side of the photograph. Press `Enter` twice. Type Help Save Lives in Our Community

15. Select the text you just typed. On the **Home tab**, in the **Styles group**, click the **Styles arrow**, and then click **Title**. In the **Paragraph group**, click the **Center** button ☰. In the **Font group**, click the **Bold** button ☐. Click **Font Size** and then type 30 Press `Enter`.

16. **Save** ☐ the document. Click the **View tab**. In the **Document Views group**, click the **Reading View** button.

17. Click **Edit Document**. Compare with **Figure 4**, and then click **Edit in Word Web App**.

■ **Continue to the next page to complete the skill** ➡

18. Press `Ctrl` + `End`, and then press `Enter` twice. Type Proceeds will aid in the purchase of: Press `Enter`.

19. On the **Home tab**, in the **Paragraph group**, click the **Bullets button arrow** ▤▾, and then click **Square Bullet**. Type Jaws of Life and then press `Enter`. Type Hydraulic Cutters and then press `Enter`. Click the **Bullets** button ▤▾ to turn off the bullets format.

20. Select the last three lines of text you typed, and then change the font size to 20 Compare your screen with **Figure 5**.

21. Press `Ctrl` + `End`, and then press `Enter`.

22. Click the **Insert tab**, and then in the **Tables group**, click the **Table** button. In the fourth row, click the second square to create a **2x4** table.

23. In the first table cell, type See You There! and then press `Tab` twice.

24. Type Location: and press `Tab`. Type Aspen Falls Fair Grounds and press `Tab`.

25. Type Date: and press `Tab`. Type Saturday, June 25, 2016 and press `Tab`.

26. Type Time: and press `Tab`. Type 8:00 a.m. – 6:00 p.m.

27. Click below the last table row. Press `Enter` twice. Type Donations Appreciated and then press `Enter`. Type (Drop off at Central Station by June 21, 2016) Select the last two rows of text, and then **Center** ☰ the text. Compare with **Figure 6**.

28. **Save** 🖫 the document. To the right of the **View tab**, click **OPEN IN WORD**. Read all messages that display, and then click **Allow** or **Yes** as needed to open the document in Word 2013.

■ **Continue to the next page to complete the skill** ▶

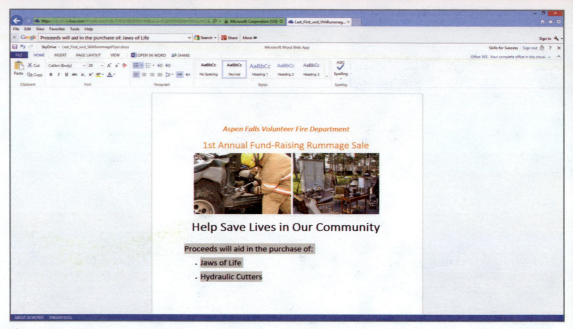

Figure 5

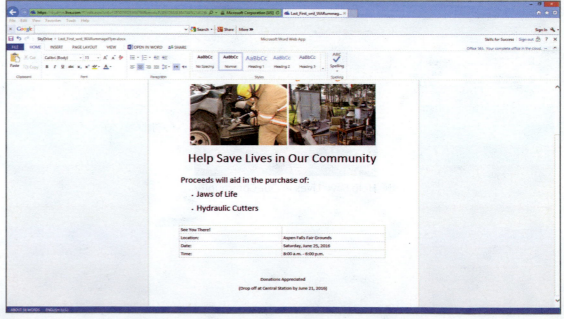

Figure 6

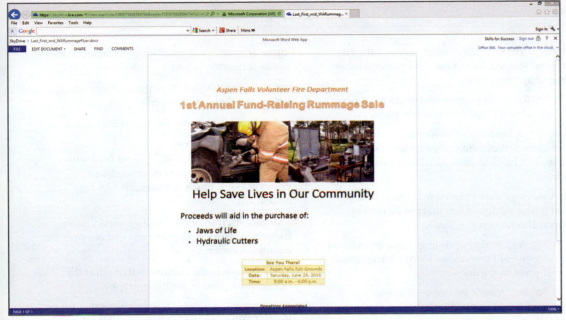

Figure 7

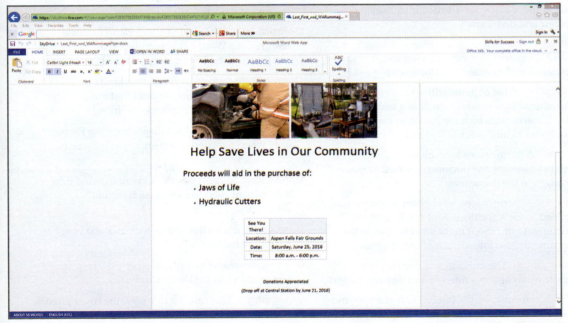

Figure 8

29. Select the paragraph beginning *1st Annual.* On the **Home tab**, in the **Font group**, click the **Text Effects and Typography** button [A]. Click **Fill – Orange, Accent 2, Outline – Accent 2**. Press Enter.

30. In the **Font group**, change the **Font** to **Arial Rounded MT Bold**.

31. Select the top two table cells. On the **Table Tools Layout tab**, in the **Merge group**, click the **Merge Cells** button. In the **Align group**, click **Align Center**.

32. Click the **Table Tools Design tab**. Click **More** [▾], and then under **Grid Tables**, click the fifth style in the sixth row—**Grid Table 6 Colorful - Accent 4**.

33. Select the table. On the **Table Tools Layout tab**, in the **Cell Size group**, click **AutoFit**, and then click **AutoFit Contents**. On the **Home tab**, in the **Paragraph group**, click **Center**. In the **Font group**, click **Increase Font size**.

34. **Save** the document, and then **Close** [✗] Word 2013.

35. On SkyDrive, open the **Last_First_wrd_WARummageFlyer** document to open the document in the Word Web App Reading view. Compare with **Figure 7**.

36. Click **Edit Document**, and then click **Edit in Word Web App**. Scroll to the bottom of the page. Compare with **Figure 8**.

> Features not supported by Word Web App will not be available in Edit view. These features, however, do display in Reading view and when opened in Word 2013.

37. Click the **View tab**, and then click **Reading View**. Submit the document as directed by your instructor.

38. In Internet Explorer, click your name, and then **Close** [✗] the browser window.

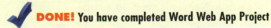

✔ **DONE! You have completed Word Web App Project**

Glossary

.docx extension The file extension typically assigned to Word documents.

.pdf extension The file extension assigned to PDF documents.

Absolute positioning A layout option used to place the object at a fixed position on the page.

Accessibility Working with technologies that adapt the display for nonvisual users.

Accessibility Checker A Word tool used to review your document for compatibility issues with screen readers or other assistive devices and software.

Alignment Guide A line that displays when an object is aligned with a document object such as a margin or heading.

All Markup A document view that displays the revised text in the document. The deleted word displays in a new color and has a line through it indicating that the word has been marked for deletion. In All Markup mode, a gray line displays in the left margin.

Alternative text Provides helpful information about images and objects, including tables, pictures, or charts, for people using a screen reader. As you move over an image or object or its placeholder, the alt text displays in most browsers even when the table, picture, or chart does not. Also known as *alt text* or *Alt Text*.

Anchor A symbol that displays to the left of a paragraph to indicate which paragraph an object is associated with.

Ascending order A way of sorting text or numbers in a series. Also known as *alphabetical* or *A-Z order*.

Author-date citation A short citation format that contains the author's last name, the publication year, and the page number if one is available.

AutoCorrect A feature that corrects common spelling errors as you type.

AutoRecover The feature in Word that automatically saves the document being worked on. The default for AutoRecover is every 10 minutes.

Backstage view A collection of pages on the File tab used to open, save, print, and perform other file management tasks.

Bibliography A compilation of sources referenced in a report and listed on a separate page.

Block style A business letter format that begins all lines at the left margin except for letterheads, tables, and block quotes. Also known as *full-block style*.

Blog A message board posted to the web that is used to share information that can be read by others; also known as a *weblog*.

Bookmark A special nonprinting character inserted into a document that allows for quick navigation to that point in the document.

Border Painter A table feature used to apply formatted borders to table cells with a single click.

Brochure An example of a document, often used to promote a business, that provides a visual overview using text and objects that can contain one or more columns. The documents may be folded and distributed.

Building block Any object or group of objects in a Word document that can be saved and that can be retrieved and inserted into documents quickly.

Bulleted list A list of items with each item introduced by a symbol—such as a small circle or check mark—in which the list items can be presented in any order.

Can edit A permissions level given so the person invited can view the document as well as make changes to the document.

Can view A permissions level given so the person invited to view the document can look at the document but cannot make any changes to the document. Also known as *read-only access*.

Caption label The uniform text that displays before each caption's number and descriptive text.

Cell A box formed by the intersection of a row and column into which text, objects, and data can be inserted.

Character graphic A small graphic character that can be formatted as text.

Character style A style type that formats selected letters, numbers, and symbols.

Chart A graphic representation of the data in a worksheet or table.

Check Box content control A form field with a box that can be selected or cleared. In a group of check boxes, multiple choices may be selected.

The Cloud An Internet technology used to store files and to work with programs that are stored in a central location.

Citation A note in the document that refers the reader to a source in the bibliography.

Column break A nonprinting character that forces the text following the break to flow into the next column.

Comment A message inserted by a person reviewing a document.

Compatibility Checker A check done to locate features in a Word 2013 document that are not supported in earlier versions of Word.

Compatibility mode A mode that limits formatting and features to ones that are supported in earlier versions of Office.

Contextual tab A tab that displays on the Ribbon only when a related object such as a graphic or chart is selected.

Continuous section break A break inserted into a document used to format each section differently.

Control An interactive object such as a text box, button, or list box.

Copy A command that places a copy of the selected text or object in the Office Clipboard.

Cover page Also called a *title page,* the cover page is usually the first page of a formal report that displays document information such as the title and subtitle, the date, the document author's name, and the company name.

Cross-reference An index entry associated with a different word or phrase that is similar in context to the original index entry.

Cut A command that deletes the selected text or object and places a copy in the Office clipboard.

Data point A value that originates in a datasheet cell.

Data series A series formed by data points that are related to one another.

Data source The file that contains the information—such as names and addresses—that changes with each letter or label in the main mail merge document.

Date Picker content control A control that displays an interactive calendar used to insert a specific date into a document.

Debug The process of reviewing Visual Basic for Applications code that checks for errors.

Default printer The printer that is automatically selected when you do not choose a different printer.

Design mode A mode that allows you to work as a developer.

Developer An individual who designs documents with interactive content such as content controls and macros.

Document properties Information about a document that can help you identify or organize your files, such as the name of the document author, the file name, and key words.

Document statistics Data that summarizes document features such as the number of pages, words, characters without spaces, characters including spaces, paragraphs, and lines.

Dot leader A series of evenly spaced dots that precedes a tab stop.

Double-click To click the left mouse button two times quickly without moving the mouse.

Double-spacing The equivalent of a blank line of text displays between each line of text.

Double-tap To tap the screen in the same place two times quickly.

Drag To press and hold the left mouse button while moving the mouse.

Drop cap The first letter (or letters) of a paragraph, enlarged and either embedded in the text or placed in the left margin.

Drop-Down List content control A control that displays a list of choices when clicked.

E-mail attachment A file that is sent with an e-mail message so that the recipient can open and view the file.

Edit To insert, delete, or replace text in an Office document, workbook, or presentation.

Editing View A view in Word Web App in which you can edit documents.

Em dash A long dash based on the width of the capital letter M in the current font and font size. It marks a break in thought, similar to a comma but stronger.

End user An individual who works with the document the developer designs.

Endnote A note or comment placed at the end of a section or a document, as in a formal report.

Fax service provider A company that receives faxes sent to them from the Internet and then relays the fax to the recipient using phone lines. Fax service providers typically charge fees for their service.

Field A category of data—such as a file name, a page number, or the current date—that can be inserted into a document.

First line indent The location of the beginning of the first line of a paragraph in relation to the left edge of the remainder of the paragraph.

Flagged error A wavy line indicating a possible spelling, grammar, or style error.

Flesch-Kincaid Grade Level An estimate of the U.S. grade level needed to understand a document.

Flesch Reading Ease A 100-point scale that measures readability. A score of 100 indicates an easy-to-understand document.

Floating object An object that you can move independently of the surrounding text.

Font A set of characters with the same design and shape.

Footer A reserved area for text, graphics, and fields that displays at the bottom of each page in a document.

Footnote A note or comment placed at the bottom of the page.

Form A database object that is used to find, update, and add table records.

Format To change the appearance of the text—for example, changing the text color to red.

Formatting mark A character that displays in your document to represent a nonprinting character such as a paragraph, space, or tab.

Full-block style A business letter format that begins all lines at the left margin except for letterheads, tables, and block quotes. Also known as *block style*.

Gallery A visual display of selections from which you can choose.

Group A Word feature used to merge separate objects into one object that can be resized as a single object.

Hanging indent An indent where the first line extends to the left of the rest of the paragraph.

Header A reserved area for text, graphics, and fields that displays at the top of each page in a document.

Horizontal line A line that separates document text so that it is easier to read.

Hyperlink Text or other objects that display another document, location, or window when they are clicked and that lead to more information.

Hyphen A character that divides a word between the end of one line and the beginning of the next.

Indent The position of paragraph lines in relation to the page margins.

Indented index An index that places marked entries and subentries on separate lines with spacing before each indexed item.

Index A list of important words and phrases found in a document along with their corresponding page numbers.

Index entry field Includes words, phrases, or cross-references that will go in the index.

Inline Revision A notation that displays all changes within the text instead of within revision balloons.

Insertion point A flashing vertical line that indicates where text will be inserted when you start typing.

Instructional text Text in a form control that instructs the end user how to enter information.

Justified text A paragraph alignment that aligns the text with both the left and right margins.

Keep Source Formatting A paste option used to paste text with the formatting from the original location.

Keep Text Only A paste option used to paste text with all formatting removed.

Keyboard shortcut A combination of keys that performs a command.

Leader A series of characters that forms a solid, dashed, or dotted line to fill the space preceding a tab stop.

Leader character The symbol used to fill the space in a leader.

Legacy Tools A set of controls that works with earlier versions of Word that includes the following form fields: text, check box, and drop-down box.

Ligature A small graphic character that displays when two or more symbols are combined.

Line spacing The vertical distance between lines of text in a paragraph; can be adjusted for each paragraph.

Linked object An object that is updated whenever the original source file is modified.

Linked style A style type that can be applied as a character style in one place and as a paragraph style in another.

Linked text box Two or more text boxes used so that text automatically flows from one text box to the next.

List style A style type that formats bullets, numbers, and indent settings.

Live Preview A feature that displays what the results of a formatting change will be if you select it.

Lorem ipsum A sample of text taken from Cicero that has been changed so that the words no longer have meaning so that you can focus on what the document formatting and effects look like.

Macro A stored set of instructions that automates common tasks.

Mail merge A Word feature used to customize letters or labels by combining a main document with a data source.

mailto A protocol that designates what protocol should be used when the link is clicked. The protocol designation is programmed into a Word document and indicates how the e-mail will be sent and automatically directs the user to select an e-mail application to open. Once the e-mail application opens, the e-mail address should display in the TO: box.

Main document The mail merge document that contains the text that remains constant.

Manage Versions The feature that allows the recovery of AutoSaved data.

Manual page break A document feature that forces a page to end at a location you specify.

Margins The spaces between the text and the top, bottom, left, and right edges of the paper.

Mark Comment Done A reviewing feature that identifies a comment as completed so you know what other comments you still need to finalize.

Marked as final A document state in which no one can type, edit, or use the proofing tools to make additional changes.

Markup The balloons and inline revisions in a reviewed document.

Merge field A field that merges and displays data from a specific column in the data source.

Merge Formatting A paste option used to paste text that applies the formatting in use in the new location.

Metadata Information and personal data that is stored with your document.

Mini toolbar A toolbar with common formatting commands that displays near selected text.

No Markup A document view that displays how the document will look if all changes are accepted.

Normal template A Word template that stores the default styles that are applied when a new document is created.

Nudge To move an object in small increments by pressing one of the arrow keys.

Numbered list A list of items with each item introduced by a consecutive number or letter to indicate definite steps, a sequence of actions, or chronological order.

Object Text, a chart, SmartArt, or a picture that can be added to an Office document.

Office 2013 RT A version of Office optimized for working on portable devices with touch screens such as Windows phones and tablets.

Office applications Help you individualize your Word documents and gain access to the Internet faster while remaining in Word. Also known as *Office apps.*

Office Clipboard A temporary storage area maintained by Office that can hold up to 24 items. When you close out of all Office 2013 programs, the Clipboard is cleared.

Office Store privacy statement Similar to a contract. It explains the license terms and what you can and cannot do once you download the app.

Online image A graphic, drawing, or photograph accessed from Bing Image Search, SkyDrive, or other online providers.

Online video A video stored on the web typically through a service such as YouTube or Bing video.

OpenType feature A font that works on multiple platforms, including Macintosh and Microsoft Windows.

OpenType font Two or more symbols or characters that are often combined, similar to typesetting. An example is the *fi* symbol.

Orphan The first line of a paragraph that displays as the last line of a page.

Outline View A view where each document heading is indented according to its level in the document's structure.

Outlook Data File A file that stores e-mail messages, contacts, tasks, and other elements so that they can be moved between different computers. It has the .pst file extension.

Paragraph spacing The vertical distance above and below each paragraph; can be adjusted for each paragraph.

Paragraph style A style type that formats an entire paragraph.

Paste A command that inserts a copy of the text or object from the Office Clipboard.

Paste Options Provide formatting choices when pasting text or objects.

PDF document An image of a document that can be viewed using a PDF reader such as Adobe Acrobat Reader instead of the application that created the original document.

Pinch Slide two fingers closer together to shrink or zoom out.

Placeholder A reserved, formatted space into which you enter your own text or object. If no text is entered, the placeholder text will not print.

Plain Text content control A control that is inserted into forms so that the end user can type text into a text box.

Point A unit of measure with 72 points per inch typically used for font sizes and character spacing.

Poster The URL and thumbnail saved when an online video is inserted into a Word document.

Proportional typeface A font with characters that vary in width. For example, space used for the letter *I* is much narrower than the width used by the letter *M*.

Protected View A view applied to documents downloaded from the Internet that allows you to decide if the content is safe before working with the document.

Query A database object that displays a subset of data in response to a question.

Quick Style A style that can be accessed from a Ribbon gallery of thumbnails.

Quick Table A built-in table that can be used to insert a formatted table into a document.

RAM The computer's temporary memory.

Read Mode A view that is used when you need to read, but not edit, electronic documents.

Read-only access A permissions level given so that when a file is opened, the user can look at the document but cannot make any changes to the document.

Readability statistics A check that measures the reading level for a document based on certain document statistics such as the length of words, the number of syllables in words, and the length of sentences and paragraphs.

Reading View A view in Word Web App in which you can view the document as it will print.

Report A database object that presents tables or query results in a way that is optimized for onscreen viewing or printing.

Requirements section Part of an Office app that explains what software can be used with the app and the purpose of the app.

Reveal Formatting A pane that displays the selected text and the font, paragraph, and section formatting currently in use.

Reviewing pane A pane that displays either at the left (vertically) or at the bottom (horizontally) of the screen and lists all comments and tracked changes.

Revised document The document that has changes that you want to merge with the original document.

Run-in index An index that places as many marked entries and subentries for the indexed item on one line as possible.

Sans serif font A font where the letters do not have serifs.

Screenshot A picture of your computer screen, a window, or a selected region that can be saved as a file or printed electronically.

Section A portion of a document that can be formatted differently from the rest of the document.

Section break A nonprinting character that marks the end of one section and the beginning of another section.

Selection pane A section of the Word screen that displays a list of shapes, including pictures and text boxes, located on the current page.

Separator A vertical line that groups buttons or commands.

Separator character A character such as a tab or comma designated as the character to separate columns of unformatted text.

Serif An extra detail or hook at the end of a character stroke.

Serif font A font where the letters have serifs or extra details or hooks at the end of each stroke.

Shape A drawing object, such as a star, rectangle, or arrow, that can be inserted into a document.

Side by Side view A view that displays two different documents in vertical windows so that they can be compared.

Simple Markup A cleaned-up document view that displays indicators where there are tracked changes in the form of a vertical red line in the left margin.

Sizing handle A small square or circle on an object's border that is used to resize the object by dragging.

SkyDrive Cloud storage that can be used to save and open your files from any computer connected to the Internet.

Slide (PowerPoint) An individual page in a presentation that can contain text, pictures, or other objects.

Slide (touch screen) Touch an object and then move the finger across the screen.

Small caps A font effect that displays all characters in uppercase while making any character originally typed as an uppercase letter taller than the ones typed as lowercase characters.

SmartArt graphic A prebuilt visual representation of information.

Source The reference used to find information or data.

Split bar A bar that splits a document into two windows.

Split window A window separated into two parts to allow scrolling through each window independently to view different areas of the document at the same time.

SQL Select Query A command that selects data from a data source based on the criteria you specify.

Stretch Slide two fingers apart to enlarge or zoom in.

Style A prebuilt collection of formatting settings that can be assigned to text.

Style Inspector A pane that displays information about the paragraph and character styles for the style applied to the active paragraph or selection.

Style set A saved style that can be applied to text and placeholders in other documents. It may include paragraph spacing, font name, font color, font size, and text effects.

Subheading An entry in a table of contents that is part of a broader entry.

Superscript Text that is positioned higher and smaller than the other text.

Swipe To slide in from a screen edge to display app commands, charms, or other temporary areas.

Symbol A character such as the copyright symbol © or a bullet character that is not found on common keyboards.

Synchronous scrolling A way to move both windows when scrolling either the vertical or horizontal scroll bar in either window.

Tab stop A specific location on a line of text marked on the Word ruler to which you can move the insertion point by pressing the Tab key.

Table A database object that stores the database data so that records are in rows and fields are in columns.

Table of authorities Displays cases, statutes, and other authorities marked in the document.

Table of authorities entry field Identifies words, phrases, or cross-references that will go in the table of authorities.

Table of contents A part of a formal report that displays entries and page numbers for a document's headings and subheadings.

Table of figures A part of a formal report that contains references to figures, equations, and tables in the document and usually includes the caption text and page number of each figure, equation, and table.

Table style A style type that formats table rows, columns, and cells.

Tag The product category for an app.

Tap To touch one time with the finger.

Template A prebuilt document with placeholders and formatting already in place into which text and objects can be inserted.

Terms and conditions A file that explains what you can and cannot do with the app once you download it.

Text box A movable, resizable container for text or graphics.

Text effects A prebuilt set of decorative formats, such as outlines, shadows, text glow, and colors, that make text stand out in a document.

Text form field A legacy tool that creates a placeholder for entering text in an interactive form.

Theme A coordinated set of font choices, color schemes, and graphic effects.

Thesaurus A reference that lists words that have the same or similar meaning to the word you are looking up.

Toggle button A button used to turn a feature both on and off.

Tri-fold brochure A document that has two pages, with three columns on each page, that contains formatted text, pictures, and text boxes.

Vertical alignment The space above and below a text or object in relation to the top and bottom of a table cell or top and bottom margins.

Visual Basic for Applications (VBA) A high-level programming language that can be used to write and modify macros.

Watermark A semitransparent image often used for letters and business cards.

Widow The last line of a paragraph that displays as the first line of a page.

Wildcard A special character, such as the question mark (?) symbol that represents one character or the asterisk (*) symbol that represents multiple characters. These substitute characters can be used when Word searches for any combination of letters of characters in a document.

Windows account logon A unique e-mail address that you use to access your Microsoft account.

Word Web App A cloud-based application used to complete basic document editing and formatting tasks using a web browser.

Word wrap Words at the right margin automatically move to the next line if they do not fit.

WordArt A set of graphic text styles that can be used to make text look like a graphic.

XML Paper Specification A file format that preserves formatting and embeds its fonts in such a way that it can be shared on many different devices and programs.

XPS An acronym for XML Paper Specification.

Zoom The magnification level of the document as displayed on the screen. Increasing the zoom percentage increases the size of the text and comments as displayed on the screen, but it does not increase the actual font size.

Index

 The internet icon represents Index entries found within More Skills on the Companion Website: www.pearsonhighered.com/skills